CompTIA©

Security+

Get Certified Get Ahead

SY0-701 Study Guide

Darril Gibson and Joe Shelley

Certification Experts, LLC
joe@certificationexperts.net

Technical editor: Shahla Pirnia

ISBN: 979-8-9889848-0-1 (print)
979-8-9889848-2-5 (hardcover)
979-8-9889848-1-8 (ebook)

LCCN: 2023915429

For Darril Gibson

In loving memory

Dear Reader,

I am thrilled to write this foreword for Joe Shelley, who purchased my brother's business in 2022. Since Darril Gibson's passing, I have had the opportunity to get to know Joe well, and I am truly impressed. I eagerly await seeing where Joe takes the Security+ books!

Many of you are already aware of Darril's exceptional intellect in the field of security, as evidenced by his publication of over 60 books internationally and his active blogging. Yet, Darril was much more than his books. He embraced life with enthusiasm, seeking joy in every moment. His greatest pleasure came from helping others, particularly in the realm of security and certification. He delighted in sharing stories of individuals who successfully passed their exams, fully understanding the challenges they faced, especially those of us who balanced work and certification pursuits.

Darril's unwavering dedication to ensuring the long-lasting impact of the Security+ books exemplified his passion for sharing knowledge and supporting others in the security field. It brings me great comfort to know that Joe has wholeheartedly embraced the torch, devoting himself to expanding and refining these books for the benefit of us all.

Darril held the belief that these books must continue to exist, and I have no doubt that Joe will nurture and enhance them for our collective benefit. Under Joe's stewardship, I am confident that the Security+ books will not only thrive but also preserve the spirit and expertise that Darril poured into them. Joe, I extend my heartfelt gratitude for our enlightening conversations and for providing me with this space to honor my brother. And to you reader, I sincerely thank you for taking the time to delve into this foreword.

Please feel free to share your success stories proudly on LinkedIn, tagging both Joe Shelley and me, so we can celebrate your achievements alongside you.

With profound gratitude,

Dawn Grzena
Life is meant to be fun, fulfilling, and filled with fabulous fortunes.

Contents

Introduction

Congratulations on purchasing the CompTIA Security+: Get Certified Get Ahead Study Guide. You are one step closer to becoming CompTIA Security+ certified. This certification has helped many individuals get ahead in their jobs and careers, and it can help you get ahead as well.

Security+ is a popular certification within the IT field. One IT hiring manager told me that if a résumé doesn't include the Security+ certification or higher-level security certification, he simply sets it aside. He won't even talk to applicants who aren't certified. That's not the same with all IT hiring managers, but it does help illustrate how important certification is within the IT field.

Who This Book Is For

If you're studying for the CompTIA Security+ exam and want to pass it on your first attempt, this book is for you. It covers 100 percent of the objectives identified by CompTIA for the Security+ exam.

The first target audience for this book is students in CompTIA Security+ classes. My goal is to give students a book they can use to study the relevant and important details of CompTIA Security+ in enough depth for the challenging topics but without the minutiae in topics that are clear for most IT professionals. I regularly hear from instructors who use versions of the book to help students master the topics and pass the Security+ exam the first time they take it.

Second, this book is for those people who like to study on their own. If you're one of the people who can read a book and learn the material without sitting in a class, this book has what you need to take and pass the exam.

Additionally, you can keep this book on your shelf (or in your Kindle) to remind yourself of important, relevant concepts. These concepts are important for security professionals and IT professionals in the real world.

Based on many conversations with students and readers of the previous versions of this book, I know that many people use the Security+ certification as the first step in achieving other security certifications. For example, you may follow Security+ with one of these cybersecurity certifications:

- (ISC)2 Systems Security Certified Practitioner (SSCP)
- (ISC)2 Certified Information Systems Security Professional (CISSP)
- CompTIA Advanced Security Practitioner (CASP+)
- CompTIA Cybersecurity Analyst (CySA+)

If you plan to pursue any of these advanced security certifications, you'll find this book will help you lay a solid foundation of security knowledge. Learn this material, and you'll be a step ahead on the other exams.

Appendices

In past versions of this book, some readers have expressed interest in learning more about certain core IT concepts. Even though this information may not appear directly on the exam, this background knowledge provides important context that may be especially helpful for those new to IT. I've created some free downloadable appendices to fill in the gaps for anyone who needs them. The following appendices are all available online:

- **Appendix A—Command Line Basics.** If you're unfamiliar with how to launch the Windows command line or the Linux terminal, this appendix will help you. It also includes some basics related to switches and the use of upper- and lowercase letters.
- **Appendix B—Log Basics.** Administrators look at logs almost daily, so they dissect log entries from multiple sources regularly. Even when looking at a new source's log entry (such as from a new firewall), they can identify common elements and determine the log entry's meaning. This appendix outlines some basics about logs and how to look for common elements.
- **Appendix C—Well-Known Ports.** This describes how logical ports are mapped to protocols and how computers use these ports. You sometimes need to know well-known ports when setting up firewalls, and this appendix includes a couple of tables of ports mapped to protocols.
- **Appendix D—The OSI Model.** Security and networking professionals use the Open Systems Interconnection (OSI) model to describe how networks function. Most people have heard about this and maybe even learned in depth while studying for another certification. However, you don't need to know the OSI model in depth for the Security+ exam. This appendix will give you an overview of the model that you'll find useful on the job.
- **Appendix E—Glossary.** The glossary provides you with an alphabetized list of key terms related to the exam.

How to Use This Book

Over the years, I've taught Security+ courses many times. During this process, I learned the best way to present the material so that students understand and retain the most knowledge. The book is laid out the same way.

For most people, the easiest way to use the book is by starting with the pre-assessment exam (after the intro) to gauge your initial understanding of the topics. Then, go through each chapter sequentially, including the end-of-chapter practice test questions. By doing so, you'll build a solid foundation of knowledge. This helps make the more advanced topics in later chapters easier to understand.

If you have a high level of IT security knowledge and only want to study the topics that are unclear to you on this exam, you can review the objective map listed at the end of this Introduction. The objective map lists all the objectives and identifies the chapter where they are covered. Additionally, you can look at the index to locate the exact page for these topics. If you have the Kindle edition, it includes an excellent search feature to find specific topics. When practicing for any certification exam, the following steps are a good recipe for success:

- **Review the objectives.** The objectives for the SY0-701 exam are listed in the "Exam Objectives to Chapter Map" section in this Introduction.
- **Learn the material related to the objectives.** This book covers all the objectives, and the Introduction includes a map showing which chapter (or chapters) covers each objective. Along those lines, my goal when writing the book was to cover the objectives in enough depth to help you pass the exam. However, these topics all have a lot more depth. When I study for a certification exam, I typically dig in much deeper than necessary, often because the topics interest me. You can, too, if you want, but don't lose sight of the exam objectives.
- **Take practice questions.** When preparing for any certification exam, a key step is to make sure you can answer the exam questions. Yes, you need the knowledge, but you also must be able to read a question and select the correct answer. This simply takes practice. When using practice test questions, ensure they have explanations. Questions without explanations often encourage rote memorization without understanding the content. Worse, they sometimes even give you the wrong answers.
- **Achieve high scores on practice exams.** I typically tell people that they should get scores of at least 90 percent on practice tests for the CompTIA Security+ exam. However, don't focus on only your scores. Make sure you understand the content, too.
- **Read and understand the explanations.** Ideally, you should be able to look at any practice test question and know why the correct answers are correct and why the incorrect answers are incorrect. Within this book, you'll find this information in the text and the explanations for the questions. When you understand the explanations, you have the best chance of accurately interpreting the questions on the live exam and answering them correctly no matter how CompTIA words or presents them.

This book has over 300 practice test questions that you can use to test your knowledge and your ability to answer them correctly. Every question has a detailed explanation to help you understand why the correct answers are correct and why the incorrect answers are incorrect. You can find the practice questions in the following areas:

- **Pre-assessment exam.** Use these questions at the beginning of the book to get a feel for what you know and what you need to study more.
- **End-of-chapter practice questions.** Each chapter has practice questions to help you test your comprehension of the material in the chapter.
- **Post-assessment exam.** Use this as a practice exam to test your comprehension of the subject matter and readiness to take the actual exam.

It's OK if you do the practice questions in a different order. You may decide to tackle all the chapters in the book and then do the pre-assessment and post-assessment questions. That's fine. However, I strongly suggest you review all the questions in the book. Also, make sure you check out the additional free online resources at: **https://getcertifiedgetahead.com/**.

Remember This

You'll see text boxes throughout the book that highlight important testable information. The surrounding content provides additional information needed to understand these key points fully, and the text boxes summarize the important points. These text boxes look like this:

> ### 📌 *Remember This!*
>
> I strongly encourage you to repeat the information in the text boxes to yourself as often as possible. The more you repeat the information, the more likely you are to remember it when you take the exam.

A tried-and-true method of repeating key information is to take notes when you're first studying the material and then rewrite the notes later. This will expose you to the material a minimum of three times.

Vendor Neutral

CompTIA certifications are vendor-neutral. In other words, certifications are not centered on any single vendor, such as Microsoft, Apple, or Linux distributions. However, you can expect to see questions that are focused on specific vendors or operating systems.

Additional Online Resources

There are many additional free resources available to you at:
https://GetCertifiedGetAhead.com/.

Additional Web Resources

Check out **https://GetCertifiedGetAhead.com** for up-to-date details on the CompTIA Security+ exam. This site includes additional information on the CompTIA Security+ exam and this book.

Although many people have spent a lot of time and energy trying to ensure that there are no errors in this book, errors occasionally slip through. This site includes an errata page listing any errors we've discovered.

If you discover any errors, please let me know through the Contact Us link on the website. I'd also love to hear about your success when you pass the exam. I'm constantly getting good news from readers and students successfully earning their certifications.

Assumptions

The CompTIA Security+ exam assumes you have the equivalent of two years of experience working in a security or systems administrator job role. However, I'm aware that two years of experience in an IT role could mean many different things. Your two years of experience may expose you to different technologies than someone else's two years of experience. When it's critical that you understand an underlying concept to master the relevant exam material, I often include some background information to make it easier to understand.

Set a Goal

Look at a calendar right now and determine the date 45 days from today. This will be your target date to take this exam. Set this as your goal to complete studying the materials and to take the exam.

This target allows you to master about one and a half chapters per week. It may be that some of the chapters take you less time, and some of the chapters take you more time. No problem. If you want to modify your target date later, do so. However, a recipe for success in almost any endeavor includes setting a goal.

When I teach CompTIA Security+ at a local university, I often help the students register for the exam on the first night. They pick a date close to the end of the course and register. I've found that when we do this, about 90 percent of the students take and pass the exam within one week after completing the course. On the other hand, when I didn't help the students register on the first night, more than half of them did not complete the exam in the same time frame. Setting a goal helps.

About the Exam

CompTIA first released the Security+ exam in 2002, which has quickly grown in popularity. They revised the exam objectives in 2008, 2011, 2014, 2017, 2020, and again in 2023. The 2023 version of the exam is labeled SY0-701. Here's a summary of the exam details:

- **Number of questions:** Maximum of 90 questions
- **Length of test:** 90 minutes
- **Passing score:** 750
- **Grading criteria:** Scale of 100 to 900 (about 83 percent)
- **Question types:** Multiple choice and performance-based
- **Exam format:** Traditional—can move back and forth to view previous questions
- **Exam test provider:** Pearson VUE (*https://home.pearsonvue.com/*)
- **Exam prerequisites:** None required but CompTIA lists the following recommendations:
  - At least 2 years of work experience in IT systems administration with a focus on security
  - Hands-on technical information security experience
  - Broad knowledge of security concepts

Passing Score

A score of 750 is required to pass. This is on a scale of 100 to 900. If you take the exam but don't get a single question correct, you get a score of 100. If you get every question correct, you get a score of 900. However, you'll most likely receive a score somewhere in between.

It's tempting to try to figure out how many questions you need to answer correctly to pass the Security+ exam, but you just can't do that. CompTIA does not publish the formula they use to compute the exam scores and it's not a simple percentage. Different questions have different weights and CompTIA scales the scores so that everyone taking different versions of the exam receives a score that can be compared to every other version of the exam.

Exam Prerequisites

There are no enforced prerequisites for the Security+ exam. However, to successfully pass the exam, you're expected to have "A minimum of 2 years of experience in IT administration with a focus on security, hands-on experience with technical information security, and broad knowledge of security concepts." If you have more than that, the exam materials will likely come easier to you. If you have less, the exam may be more difficult.

Beta Questions

Your exam will have some beta questions. They aren't graded but instead are used to test the validity of the questions. If everyone gets a beta question correct, it's probably too easy. If everyone gets it incorrect, there's probably something wrong with the question. After enough people have tested a beta question, CompTIA personnel analyze it and decide if they want to add it to the test bank. They may also rewrite it and test it again as a new beta question. The good news is that CompTIA doesn't grade the beta questions. However, you don't know which questions are ungraded beta questions and which questions are live questions. You need to treat every question as if it was graded.

Exam Format

The exam uses a traditional format. You start at question 1 and go to the last question. You can skip questions and mark any questions you want to review as you're going through the exam. When you finish, you can go back to all your marked questions. Additionally, you can view previous questions if desired. For example, if you get to question 10 and then remember something that helps you answer question 5, you can go back and redo question 5.

Question Types

You will see two primary question types on the exam: multiple-choice and performance-based. Each type is described in the following sections.

Multiple Choice

Most questions are multiple-choice types where you select one answer or multiple answers. When you need to select multiple answers, the question will include a phrase such as "Select TWO" or "Select THREE."

You may also see questions that use phrases such as "BEST choice," "BEST description," or "MOST secure." In these examples, don't be surprised if you see two answers that could answer the question, while only one is the best choice. As an example, consider this simple question:

Which one of the following numbers is between 1 and 10 and is the HIGHEST?

> A. 2
> B. 8
> C. 14
> D. 23

Clearly, 2 and 8 are between 1 and 10, but 14 and 23 are not. However, only 8 is both between 1 and 10 and the highest.

Performance-Based Questions

You can expect several performance-based questions. These include simulations, matching, drag and drop, and data entry questions. CompTIA refers to these as performance-based questions, and instead of picking from a multiple-choice answer, you're often required to perform a task. Comp-TIA's goal is to provide more accurate testing to verify people have a full understanding of a topic.

People often ask if they get partial credit. CompTIA has said that you may get partial credit on some questions, but other questions may not give you partial credit. However, you'll never know which questions give you partial credit and which questions don't give you partial credit. It's best to do the best you can with each question. The following sections cover the different types of performance-based questions you can expect.

Matching

In a matching performance-based question, you will see two lists, and you need to match them. As an example, one list might include control types such as technical, managerial, and physical. The second list might include specific controls such as risk assessments, security guards, and encryption. You would match technical with encryption, managerial with risk assessments, and physical with security guards. If you understand the common security control types, this becomes trivial. Then again, if you don't understand the control types, this can be quite difficult.

Drag and Drop

You might need to drag items from one location on the screen to another location to answer some questions. You can think of these as multiple-choice questions with multiple answers that are correct. However, instead of selecting the checkboxes to indicate a correct answer, you drag it to somewhere else on the screen. As an example, consider this question:

Arrange the following list in order from most volatile to least volatile:

- Paging file
- File on local drive
- Archive media
- RAM
- Cache

You would drag and drop the items until they were in the following order:

- Cache
- RAM
- Paging file
- Files on local drive
- Archive media

Performance-Based Questions Strategy

You'll see the performance-based questions first, and they take much longer than typical multiple-choice questions. If the answer is clear, then take the time to answer it. However, if the question isn't clear, mark the question and skip it. You can come back to it later. The question may be a poorly worded beta question that doesn't even count. However, if you spend 45 minutes on it, you might run out of time before finishing the multiple-choice questions.

Performance-based questions have occasionally caused problems for the test systems. A common problem is that instead of displaying the question, the screen is mostly blank. If this happens, you can often just use the reset button for the question. This allows you to move past the problem and continue with the test. However, resetting the question erases any answer you've entered for that particular question, so you'll have to come back to it after you finish other questions.

Some readers reported that they skipped all of the performance-based questions and still passed. This was usually because the performance-based questions weren't working correctly, or they simply weren't clear. After finishing the multiple-choice questions, they ran out of time but still passed.

It's common for people to be nervous when thinking about these performance-based test questions. However, most people who take the test say that they usually aren't that difficult. If you understand the concepts from the exam objectives, you won't have any problems.

Question Complexity

In the past, the Security+ test questions were relatively straightforward. For example, a question may have been like this "What is 5 × 5?" Either you know the answer is 25, or you don't. In other words, the exam simply required you to remember and recall facts and basic concepts.

However, the questions have been getting progressively more complex. Instead of just remembering facts, you're expected to understand concepts and apply your knowledge in different situations. Some advanced questions require you to analyze a scenario, evaluate various indicators, and select the best possible answer.

Many of the objectives start with the phrase "given a scenario," indicating you can expect advanced questions related to these objectives. Performance-based questions are often used to test these types of objectives. However, it's also possible to use complex multiple-choice questions to test the same objectives. Consider this example:

You are driving a bus from Springfield to Shelbyville at 55 mph with 22 passengers. The bus is painted blue. At the same time, a train is traveling from Shelbyville to Springfield at 40 mph. The train has a yellow caboose. What color are the bus driver's eyes?

Notice that the question adds a lot of superfluous information. The actual question is in the last sentence, and only one comment is directly related to this question. The question starts by saying,

"You are driving a bus..." and then ends by asking, "What color are the bus driver's eyes?" You're required to put the two together and weed through the irrelevant information to come to the correct answer.

Some people memorize practice test questions and answers. However, this is not a successful path to success because CompTIA often modifies the questions. Ideally, you should know why the correct answers are correct and why the incorrect answers are incorrect. This will give you a much better chance of interpreting the questions and answering them correctly. Consider this question:

Your organization hires temporary help and contractor personnel on a seasonal basis. These personnel need access to network resources, but only during working hours. Management has stressed that it is critically important to safeguard trade secrets and other confidential information. Which of the following account management concepts would be MOST important to meet these goals?

> A. Account expiration
> B. Account lockout
> C. Password history
> D. Password recovery
> E. Time-of-day restrictions

The key phrase is here is "only during working hours." Time-of-day restrictions can be applied to ensure these seasonal personnel cannot access network resources during off-hours or the weekend. If someone merely memorizes a few keywords to the previous question along with the answer, they will likely have problems if CompTIA modifies the question. Compare it with this question:

Your organization hires temporary help and contractor personnel on a seasonal basis. These personnel need access to network resources, but only during their employment period. Management has stressed that it is critically important to safeguard trade secrets and other confidential information. Which of the following account management concepts would be MOST important to meet these goals?

> A. Account expiration
> B. Account lockout
> C. Password history
> D. Password recovery
> E. Time-of-day restrictions

The key phrase here is "only during their employment period." Setting account expiration will ensure the accounts are disabled when the employment period ends. Notice that only a few words in the questions are different. The first question emphasizes working hours, while the second one emphasizes the employment period. However, if someone memorized questions and answers, they might jump on time-of-day restrictions for the second question without reading the full question.

Practice Test Questions Strategy

Some people want more and more practice test questions, but the quantity of practice test questions you use isn't as important as their quality. And how you use them. At the core, you want to ensure you understand the underlying concept.

Imagine you're being tested on addition. You could have 10,000 questions asking you to add 1+1, 1+2, 1+3, and so on up to 1+100, along with 2+1, 3+1, and so on, up to 100+100. That kind of repetition just isn't needed. However, if you can add 28+17 correctly, you probably understand the concept.

When going through practice test questions, it's important to remind yourself why the incorrect answers are incorrect. This effectively gives you four questions for every single question you take. Imagine this question:

What two numbers added together will give you a sum of 45?

> A. 19 + 24
> B. 21 + 26
> C. 28 + 17
> D. 14 + 33

By reminding yourself why each of the incorrect answers is incorrect (19+24=43, 21+26=47, 28+17=45, 14+33=47), it essentially gives you four questions from just one. Additionally, many people report that this strategy allows them to eliminate obvious incorrect answers and arrive at the correct answer, which wasn't obvious at first.

Exam Test Provider

You can take the exam at a Pearson VUE testing site or at your home or office using Pearson's remote proctoring service. Some testing sites provide testing and nothing else. However, most testing sites are part of another organization, such as a training company, college, or university. You can take an exam at the training company's testing site even if you haven't taken a course with them.

The Pearson VUE website includes search tools you can use to find a testing site close to you. Check them out at **https://home.pearsonvue.com/**.

Voucher Code for 10 Percent Off

The cost of the CompTIA Security+ exam voucher is $392 in the United States if you purchase it at full price, though CompTIA may raise the price in the future. However, you can get a **10 percent discount using the discount code CERT10** in the CompTIA store. This code sometimes changes, so if you have any difficulty using it, visit **https://getcertifiedgetahead.com/** to check for an updated code. That site also includes instructions on how to use the voucher.

When you purchase a voucher, you'll get a voucher number that you can use to register at a testing site. A word of caution: some fraudsters sell bogus vouchers on Internet sites such as eBay. You won't know you've been ripped off until you try to use it, and by that time, the person who sold you the code will probably have disappeared. In contrast, if you use my discount code, you buy the voucher directly from CompTIA and can be confident that it is legitimate and that you are receiving the best possible authorized price for your exam.

Exam Domains

The exam objectives are divided into the following domains, or general topic areas. Additionally, CompTIA publishes the percentage of questions you can anticipate in any of the domains:

- **1.0 General Security Concepts.** 12 percent of examination content
- **2.0 Threats, Vulnerabilities, and Mitigations.** 22 percent of examination content
- **3.0 Security Architecture.** 18 percent of examination content
- **4.0 Security Operations.** 28 percent of examination content
- **5.0 Security Program Management and Oversight.** 20 percent of examination content

CompTIA publishes a listing of the objectives on its website. They also include these comments:

"The lists of examples provided in bulleted format are not exhaustive lists. Other examples of technologies, processes, or tasks pertaining to each objective may also be included on the exam, although not listed or covered in this objectives document. CompTIA is constantly reviewing the content of our exams and updating test questions to be sure our exams are current, and the security of the questions is protected. When necessary, we will publish updated exams based on existing exam objectives. Please know that all related exam preparation materials will still be valid."

This indicates that you may see something that isn't on the objectives list. I've done my best to predict how test item writers will interpret these objectives when writing test questions. You can check this book's companion site at **https://GetCertifiedGetAhead.com** for up-to-date information on the exam.

Exam Objectives to Chapter Map

The following list shows the SYO-701 exam objectives published by CompTIA. The chapter or chapters where the objective is covered is listed next to each objective.

1.0 General Security Concepts

1.1 Compare and contrast various types of security controls. Chapter 1

- Categories Chapter 1
  - Technical Chapter 1
  - Managerial Chapter 1
  - Operational Chapter 1
  - Physical Chapter 1
- Control Types Chapter 1
  - Preventive Chapter 1
  - Deterrent Chapter 1
  - Detective Chapter 1
  - Corrective Chapter 1
  - Compensating Chapter 1
  - Directive Chapter 1

1.2 Summarize fundamental security concepts. Chapters 1, 2, 3, 4, 8, 9, 10

- Confidentiality, integrity, and availability (CIA) Chapter 1
- Non-repudiation Chapter 10
- Authentication, authorization, and accounting (AAA) Chapter 2
  - Authenticating people Chapter 2
  - Authenticating systems Chapter 2
  - Authorization models Chapter 2
- Gap analysis Chapter 8
- Zero trust Chapter 3
  - Control plane Chapter 3
    - Adaptive identity Chapter 3
    - Threat scope reduction Chapter 3
    - Policy-driven access control Chapter 3
    - Policy Administrator Chapter 3
    - Policy Engine Chapter 3
  - Data Plane Chapter 3
    - Implicit trust zones Chapter 3

- Subject/System Chapter 3
- Policy Enforcement Point Chapter 3
- Physical Security Chapter 9
  - Bollards Chapter 9
  - Access control vestibule Chapter 9
  - Fencing Chapter 9
  - Video surveillance Chapter 9
  - Security guard Chapter 9
  - Access badge Chapter 9
  - Lighting Chapter 9
  - Sensors Chapter 9
    - Infrared Chapter 9
    - Pressure Chapter 9
    - Microwave Chapter 9
    - Ultrasonic Chapter 9
- Deception and disruption technology Chapter 4
  - Honeypot Chapter 4
  - Honeynet Chapter 4
  - Honeyfile Chapter 4
  - Honeytoken Chapter 4

1.3 Explain the importance of change management processes and the impact to security. Chapter 11

- Business processes impacting security operation Chapter 11
  - Approval process Chapter 11
  - Ownership Chapter 11
  - Stakeholders Chapter 11
  - Impact analysis Chapter 11
  - Test results Chapter 11
  - Backout plan Chapter 11
  - Maintenance window Chapter 11
  - Standard operating procedure Chapter 11

- Technical implications Chapter 11
  - Allow lists/deny lists Chapter 11
  - Restricted activities Chapter 11
  - Downtime Chapter 11
  - Service restart Chapter 11
  - Application restart Chapter 11
  - Legacy applications Chapter 11
  - Dependencies Chapter 11
- Documentation Chapter 11
  - Updating diagrams Chapter 11
  - Updating policies / procedures Chapter 11
- Version control Chapter 11

1.4 Explain the importance of using appropriate cryptographic solutions. Chapters 5, 10

- Public key infrastructure (PKI) Chapter 10
  - Public key Chapter 10
  - Private key Chapter 10
  - Key escrow Chapter 10
- Encryption Chapters 5, 10
  - Level Chapter 5
    - Full-disk Chapter 5
    - Partition Chapter 5
    - File Chapter 5
    - Volume Chapter 5
    - Database Chapter 5
    - Record Chapter 5
  - Transport/communication Chapter 10
  - Asymmetric Chapter 10
  - Symmetric Chapter 10
  - Key exchange Chapter 10

- Algorithms Chapter 10
- Key length Chapter 10
- Tools Chapter 5, 10
  - Trusted Platform Module (TPM) Chapter 5
  - Hardware Security Module (HSM) Chapter 5
  - Key management system Chapter 10
  - Secure enclave Chapter 5
- Obfuscation Chapter 10
  - Steganography Chapter 10
  - Tokenization Chapter 10
  - Data masking Chapter 10
- Hashing Chapter 10
- Salting Chapter 10
- Digital signatures Chapter 10
- Key stretching Chapter 10
- Blockchain Chapter 10
- Open public ledger Chapter 10
- Certificates Chapter 10
  - Certificate authorities Chapter 10
  - Certificate revocation lists (CRLs) Chapter 10
  - Online certificate status protocol (OCSP) Chapter 10
  - Self-signed Chapter 10
  - Third-party Chapter 10
  - Root of trust Chapter 10
  - Certificate signing request (CSR) generation Chapter 10
  - Wildcard Chapter 10

2.0 Threats, Vulnerabilities, and Mitigations

2.1 Compare and contrast common threat actors and motivations. Chapter 6

- Threat actors Chapter 6
  - Nation-state Chapter 6
  - Unskilled attacker Chapter 6
  - Hacktivist Chapter 6
  - Insider threat Chapter 6
  - Organized crime Chapter 6

- Shadow IT Chapter 6
- Attributes of actors Chapter 6
  - Internal/external Chapter 6
  - Resources/funding Chapter 6
  - Level of sophistication/capability Chapter 6
- Motivations Chapter 6
  - Data exfiltration Chapter 6

- Espionage Chapter 6
- Service disruption Chapter 6
- Blackmail Chapter 6
- Financial gain Chapter 6
- Philosophical/political beliefs Chapter 6
- Ethical Chapter 6
- Revenge Chapter 6
- Disruption/chaos Chapter 6
- War Chapter 6

2.2 Explain common threat vectors and attack surfaces. Chapter 6

- Message-based Chapter 6
  - Email Chapter 6
  - Short Message Service (SMS) Chapter 6
  - Instant messaging (IM) Chapter 6
- Image-based Chapter 6
- File-based Chapter 6
- Voice call Chapter 6
- Removable device Chapter 6
- Vulnerable software Chapter 6
  - Client-based vs. agentless Chapter 6
- Unsupported systems and applications Chapter 6
- Unsecure networks Chapter 6
  - Wireless Chapter 6
  - Wired Chapter 6
  - Bluetooth Chapter 6
- Open service ports Chapter 6
- Default credentials Chapter 6
- Supply chain Chapter 6
  - Managed service providers (MSPs) Chapter 6
  - Vendors Chapter 6
  - Suppliers Chapter 6
- Human vectors/social engineering Chapter 6
  - Phishing Chapter 6
  - Vishing Chapter 6
  - Smishing Chapter 6
  - Misinformation/disinformation Chapter 6
  - Impersonation Chapter 6
  - Business email compromise Chapter 6
  - Pretexting Chapter 6
- Watering hole Chapter 6
- Brand impersonation Chapter 6
- Typosquatting Chapter 6

2.3 Explain various types of vulnerabilities. Chapters 4, 5, 7, 8, 10

- Application Chapter 7
  - Memory injection Chapter 7
  - Buffer overflow Chapter 7
  - Race conditions Chapter 7
    - Time-of-check (TOC) Chapter 7
    - Time-of-use (TOU) Chapter 7
  - Malicious update
- Operating systems (OS)-based Chapter 5
- Web-based Chapter 7
  - Structured Query Language injection (SQLi) Chapter 7
  - Cross-site scripting (XSS) Chapter 7
- Hardware Chapter 5
  - Firmware Chapter 5
  - End-of-life Chapter 5
  - Legacy Chapter 5
- Virtualization Chapter 5
  - Virtual machine (VM) escape Chapter 5
  - Resource reuse Chapter 5
- Cloud-specific Chapter 5
- Supply chain Chapter 8
  - Service provider Chapter 8
  - Hardware provider Chapter 8
  - Software provider Chapter 8
- Cryptographic Chapter 10
- Misconfiguration Chapter 5
- Mobile Device Chapter 5
  - Side loading Chapter 5
  - Jailbreaking Chapter 5
- Zero-day Chapter 4

2.4 Given a scenario, analyze indicators of malicious activity. Chapters 2, 4, 8, 6, 7, 9, 10

- Malware attacks Chapter 6
  - Ransomware Chapter 6
  - Trojan Chapter 6

- Worm Chapter 6
- Spyware Chapter 6
- Bloatware Chapter 6
- Virus Chapter 6
- Keylogger Chapter 6
- Logic bomb Chapter 6
- Rootkit Chapter 6
- Physical attacks Chapters 4, 9
  - Brute force Chapter 9
  - Radio frequency identification (RFID) cloning Chapter 4
  - Environmental Chapter 9
- Network attacks Chapters 4, 6, 7
  - Distributed denial-of-service (DDoS) Chapter 7
    - Amplified Chapter 7
    - Reflected Chapter 7
  - Domain Name System (DNS) attacks Chapter 7
  - Wireless Chapter 4
  - On-path Chapter 7
  - Credential replay Chapter 7
  - Malicious code Chapter 6, 7
- Application attacks Chapters 7, 8
  - Injection Chapter 7
  - Buffer overflow Chapter 7
  - Replay Chapter 7
  - Privilege escalation Chapter 8
  - Forgery Chapter 7
  - Directory traversal Chapter 7
- Cryptographic attacks Chapter 10
  - Downgrade Chapter 10
  - Collision Chapter 10
  - Birthday Chapter 10
- Password attacks Chapter 10
  - Spraying Chapter 10
  - Brute force Chapter 10

- Indicators Chapter 2
  - Account lockout Chapter 2
  - Concurrent session usage Chapter 2
  - Blocked content Chapter 2
  - Impossible travel Chapter 2
  - Resource consumption Chapter 2
  - Resource inaccessibility Chapter 2
  - Out-of-cycle logging Chapter 2
  - Published/documented Chapter 2
  - Missing logs Chapter 2

2.5 Explain the purpose of mitigation techniques used to secure the enterprise. Chapters 1, 2, 3, 5

- Segmentation Chapter 5
- Access control Chapter 2
  - Access control list (ACL) Chapter 2
  - Permissions Chapter 2
- Application allow list Chapter 5
- Isolation Chapter 3
- Patching Chapter 5
- Encryption Chapter 5
- Monitoring Chapter 1
- Least privilege Chapter 1
- Configuration enforcement Chapter 5
- Decommissioning Chapter 5
- Hardening techniques Chapters 3, 5
  - Encryption Chapter 5
  - Installation of endpoint protection Chapter 5
  - Host-based firewall Chapter 3
  - Host-based intrusion prevention system (HIPS) Chapter 5
  - Disabling ports/protocols Chapter 5
  - Default password changes Chapter 5
  - Removal of unnecessary software Chapter 5

3.0 Security Architecture

3.1 Compare and contrast security implications of different architecture models. Chapters 3, 5, 9

- Architecture and infrastructure concepts Chapter 5
  - Cloud Chapter 5
    - Responsibility matrix Chapter 5
    - Hybrid considerations Chapter 5
    - Third-party vendors Chapter 5
  - Infrastructure as code (IaC) Chapter 5
  - Serverless Chapter 5
  - Microservices Chapter 5
  - Network infrastructure Chapters 3, 5
    - Physical isolation Chapter 3
    - Air-gapped Chapter 3
    - Logical segmentation Chapter 3
    - Software-defined networking (SDN) Chapter 5
  - On-premises Chapter 5
  - Centralized vs. decentralized Chapter 5
  - Containerization Chapter 5
  - Virtualization Chapter 5
  - IoT Chapter 5
  - Industrial control systems (ICS)/supervisory control and data acquisition (SCADA) Chapter 5
  - Real-time operating system (RTOS) Chapter 5
  - Embedded systems Chapter 5
  - High availability Chapter 9
  - Considerations Chapter 5
    - Availability Chapter 5
    - Resilience Chapter 5
    - Cost Chapter 5
    - Responsiveness Chapter 5
    - Scalability Chapter 5
    - Ease of deployment Chapter 5
    - Risk transference Chapter 5
    - Ease of recovery Chapter 5
    - Patch availability Chapter 5
    - Inability to patch Chapter 5
    - Power Chapter 5
    - Compute Chapter 5

3.2 Given a scenario, apply security principles to secure enterprise infrastructure. Chapters 1, 3, 4, 5

- Infrastructure considerations Chapters 3, 4
  - Device placement Chapter 3
  - Security zones Chapter 3
  - Attack surface Chapter 3
  - Connectivity Chapter 3
  - Failure modes Chapter 3
    - Fall-open Chapter 3
    - Fall-closed Chapter 3
  - Device Attribute Chapter 4
    - Active vs. passive Chapter 4
    - Inline vs. tap/monitor Chapter 4
  - Network appliances Chapter 3, 4
    - Jump server Chapter 3
    - Proxy server Chapter 3
    - Intrusion prevention system (IPS)/intrusion detection system (IDS) Chapter 4
    - Load balancer Chapter 3
    - Sensors Chapter 4
  - Port security Chapter 4
    - 802.1X Chapter 4
    - Extensible Authentication Protocol (EAP) Chapter 4
  - Firewall types Chapter 3
    - Web application firewall (WAF) Chapter 3
    - Unified threat management (UTM) Chapter 3
    - Next-generation firewall (NGFW) Chapter 3
    - Layer 4/Layer 7 Chapter 3
- Secure communication/access Chapter 3, 4, 5
  - Virtual private network (VPN) Chapter 4
  - Remote access Chapter 4
  - Tunneling Chapter 4
    - Transport Layer Security (TLS) Chapter 3

- Internet protocol security (IP-Sec) Chapter 4
  - Software-defined wide area network (SD-WAN) Chapter 5
  - Secure access service edge (SASE) Chapter 3
- Selection of effective controls Chapter 1

3.3 Compare and contrast concepts and strategies to protect data. Chapters 3, 5, 9, 10, 11

- Data types Chapter 11
  - Regulated Chapter 11
  - Trade secret Chapter 11
  - Intellectual property Chapter 11
  - Legal information Chapter 11
  - Financial information Chapter 11
  - Human- and non-human-readable Chapter 11
- Data classifications Chapter 11
  - Sensitive Chapter 11
  - Confidential Chapter 11
  - Public Chapter 11
  - Restricted Chapter 11
  - Private Chapter 11
  - Critical Chapter 11
- General data considerations Chapters 5, 9, 10
  - Data states Chapter 10
    - Data at rest Chapter 10
    - Data in transit Chapter 10
    - Data in use Chapter 10
  - Data sovereignty Chapter 9
  - Geolocation Chapter 5
- Methods to secure data Chapters 3, 10, 11
  - Geographic restrictions Chapter 11
  - Encryption Chapter 10
  - Hashing Chapter 10
  - Masking Chapter 10
  - Tokenization Chapter 10
  - Obfuscation Chapter 10

- Segmentation Chapter 3
- Permission restrictions Chapter 11

3.4 Explain the importance of resilience and recovery in security architecture. Chapters 5, 9

- High availability Chapter 9
  - Load balancing vs. clustering Chapter 9
- Site considerations Chapter 9
  - Hot Chapter 9
  - Cold Chapter 9
  - Warm Chapter 9
  - Geographic dispersion Chapter 9
- Platform diversity Chapter 9
- Multi-cloud systems Chapter 5
- Continuity of operations Chapter 9
- Capacity planning Chapter 9
  - People Chapter 9
  - Technology Chapter 9
  - Infrastructure Chapter 9
- Testing Chapter 9
  - Tabletop exercises Chapter 9
  - Fail over Chapter 9
  - Simulation Chapter 9
  - Parallel processing Chapter 9
- Backups Chapter 9
  - Onsite/offsite Chapter 9
  - Frequency Chapter 9
  - Encryption Chapter 9
  - Snapshots Chapter 9
  - Recovery Chapter 9
  - Replication Chapter 9
  - Journaling Chapter 9
- Power Chapter 9
  - Generators Chapter 9
  - Uninterruptible power supply (UPS) Chapter 9

4.0 Security Operations

4.1 Given a scenario, apply common security techniques to computing resources. Chapters 1, 3, 4, 5, 7

- Secure baselines Chapter 5
  - Establish Chapter 5
  - Deploy Chapter 5
  - Maintain Chapter 5
- Hardening targets Chapter 3, 5
  - Mobile devices Chapter 5
  - Workstations Chapter 5
  - Switches Chapter 3
  - Routers Chapter 3
  - Cloud Infrastructure Chapter 5
  - Servers Chapter 5
  - ICS/SCADA Chapter 5
  - Embedded systems Chapter 5
  - RTOS Chapter 5
  - IoT devices Chapter 5
- Wireless devices Chapter 4
  - Installation considerations Chapter 4
    - Site surveys Chapter 4
    - Heat maps Chapter 4
- Mobile solutions Chapter 5
  - Mobile device management (MDM) Chapter 5
  - Deployment models Chapter 5
    - Bring your own device (BYOD) Chapter 5
    - Corporate-owned, personally enabled (COPE) Chapter 5
    - Choose your own device (CYOD) Chapter 5
  - Connection methods Chapter 5
    - Cellular Chapter 5
    - Wi-Fi Chapter 5
    - Bluetooth Chapter 5
- Wireless security settings Chapter 4
  - Wi-Fi protected Access 3 (WPA3) Chapter 4

- AAA/Remote Authentication Dial-In User Service (RADIUS) Chapter 4
- Cryptographic protocols Chapter 4
- Authentication protocols Chapter 4
- Application security Chapter 7
  - Input validation Chapter 7
  - Secure cookies Chapter 7
  - Static code analysis Chapter 7
  - Code signing Chapter 7
- Sandboxing Chapter 7
- Monitoring Chapter 1

4.2 Explain the security implications of proper hardware, software, and data asset management. Chapters 9, 11

- Acquisition/procurement process Chapter 9
- Assignment/accounting Chapter 9
  - Ownership Chapter 9
  - Classification Chapter 9
- Monitoring/asset tracking Chapter 9
  - Inventory Chapter 9
  - Enumeration Chapter 9
- Disposal/decommissioning Chapter 11
  - Sanitization Chapter 11
  - Destruction Chapter 11
  - Certification Chapter 11
  - Data retention Chapter 11

4.3 Explain various activities associated with vulnerability management. Chapters 6, 8, 11

- Identification methods Chapters 6, 8, 11
  - Vulnerability scan Chapter 8
  - Application security Chapter 11
    - Static analysis Chapter 11
    - Dynamic analysis Chapter 11
    - Package monitoring Chapter 11
  - Threat feed Chapter 6
    - Open-source intelligence (OSINT) Chapter 6

- Operating system security Chapters 2, 3
    - Group policy Chapter 3
    - SELinux Chapter 2
- Implementation of secure protocols Chapter 3
    - Protocol selection Chapter 3
    - Port selection Chapter 3
    - Transport method Chapter 3
- DNS filtering Chapter 7
- Email security Chapter 3
    - Domain-based Message Authentication Reporting and Conformance (DMARC) Chapter 3
    - DomainKeys Identified Mail (DKIM) Chapter 3
    - Sender Policy Framework (SPF) Chapter 3
    - Gateway Chapter 3
- File integrity monitoring Chapter 6
- DLP Chapter 5
- Network access control (NAC) Chapter 4
- Endpoint detection and response (EDR)/ extended detection and response (XDR) Chapter 5
- User behavior analytics Chapter 1

4.6 Given a scenario, implement and maintain identity and access management. Chapters 2, 3

- Provisioning/de-provisioning user accounts Chapter 2
- Permission assignments and implications Chapter 2
- Identity proofing Chapter 2
- Federation Chapter 2
- Single sign-on (SSO) Chapters 2, 3
    - Lightweight Directory Access Protocol (LDAP) Chapter 3
    - Open authorization (OAuth) Chapter 2
    - Security Assertions Markup Language (SAML) Chapter 2
- Interoperability Chapter 2
- Attestation Chapter 2
- Access controls Chapter 2

- Mandatory Chapter 2
- Discretionary Chapter 2
- Role-based Chapter 2
- Rule-based Chapter 2
- Attribute-based Chapter 2
- Time-of-day restrictions Chapter 2
- Least privilege Chapter 2
- Multifactor authentication Chapter 2
    - Implementations Chapter 2
        - Biometrics Chapter 2
        - Hard/soft authentication tokens Chapter 2
        - Security keys Chapter 2
    - Factors
        - Something you know Chapter 2
        - Something you have Chapter 2
        - Something you are Chapter 2
        - Somewhere you are Chapter 2
- Password concepts Chapter 2
    - Password best practices Chapter 2
        - Length Chapter 2
        - Complexity Chapter 2
        - Reuse Chapter 2
        - Expiration Chapter 2
        - Age Chapter 2
    - Password managers Chapter 2
    - Passwordless Chapter 2
- Privileged access management tools Chapter 2
    - Just-in-time permissions Chapter 2
    - Password vaulting Chapter 2
    - Ephemeral credentials Chapter 2

4.7 Explain the importance of automation and orchestration related to secure operations. Chapter 7

- Use cases of automation and scripting Chapter 7
    - User provisioning Chapter 7
    - Resource provisioning Chapter 7
    - Guard rails Chapter 7
    - Security groups Chapter 7

- Ticket creation Chapter 7
- Escalation Chapter 7
- Enabling/disabling services and access Chapter 7
- Continuous integration and testing Chapter 7
- Integrations and application programming interfaces (APIs) Chapter 7
  - Benefits Chapter 7
    - Efficiency/time saving Chapter 7
    - Enforcing baselines Chapter 7
    - Standard infrastructure configurations Chapter 7
    - Scaling in a secure manner Chapter 7
    - Employee retention Chapter 7
    - Reaction time Chapter 7
    - Workforce multiplier Chapter 7
  - Other considerations Chapter 7
    - Complexity Chapter 7
    - Cost Chapter 7
    - Single point of failure Chapter 7
    - Technical debt Chapter 7
    - Ongoing supportability Chapter 7

4.8 Explain appropriate incident response activities. Chapter 9, 11

- Process Chapter 11
  - Preparation Chapter 11
  - Detection Chapter 11
  - Analysis Chapter 11
  - Containment Chapter 11
  - Eradication Chapter 11

- Recovery Chapter 11
- Lessons learned Chapter 11
- Training Chapter 11
- Testing Chapter 11
  - Tabletop exercise Chapter 11
  - Simulation Chapter 11
- Root cause analysis Chapter 11
- Threat hunting Chapter 11
- Digital forensics Chapter 11
  - Legal hold Chapter 11
  - Chain of custody Chapter 11
  - Acquisition Chapter 11
  - Reporting Chapter 11
  - Preservation Chapter 11
  - E-discovery Chapter 11

4.9 Given a scenario, use data sources to support an investigation. Chapters 1, 8

- Log data Chapter 1
  - Firewall logs Chapter 1
  - Application logs Chapter 1
  - Endpoint logs Chapter 1
  - OS-specific security logs Chapter 1
  - IPS/IDS logs Chapter 1
  - Network logs Chapter 1
  - Metadata Chapter 1
- Data sources Chapters 1, 8
  - Vulnerability scans Chapter 8
  - Automated reports Chapter 1
  - Dashboards Chapter 1
  - Packet captures Chapter 1

5.0 Security Program Management and Oversight

5.1 Summarize elements of effective security governance. Chapter 11

- Guidelines Chapter 11
- Policies Chapter 11
  - Acceptable use policy (AUP) Chapter 11
  - Information security policies Chapter 11
  - Business continuity Chapter 11
  - Disaster recovery Chapter 11
  - Incident response Chapter 11

- Software development lifecycle (SDLC) Chapter 11
- Change management Chapter 11
- Standards Chapter 11
  - Password Chapter 11
  - Access control Chapter 11
  - Physical security Chapter 11
  - Encryption Chapter 11
- Procedures Chapter 11

5.2 Explain elements of the risk management process. Chapters 8, 9

5.3 Explain the processes associated with third-party risk assessment and management. Chapter 11

- Memorandum of understanding (MOU) Chapter 11
- Master service agreement (MSA) Chapter 11
- Work order (WO)/Statement of work (SOW) Chapter 11
- Non-disclosure agreement (NDA) Chapter 11
- Business partners agreement (BPA) Chapter 11
- Vendor monitoring Chapter 11
- Questionnaires Chapter 11
- Rules of engagement Chapter 11

5.4 Summarize elements of effective security compliance. Chapter 11

- Compliance reporting Chapter 11
  - Internal Chapter 11
  - External Chapter 11
- Consequences of non-compliance Chapter 11
  - Fines Chapter 11
  - Sanctions Chapter 11
  - Reputational damage Chapter 11
  - Loss of license Chapter 11
  - Contractual impacts Chapter 11
- Compliance monitoring Chapter 11
  - Due diligence/care Chapter 11
  - Attestation and acknowledgement Chapter 11
  - Internal and external Chapter 11
  - Automation Chapter 11
- Privacy Chapter 11
  - Legal implications Chapter 11
    - Local/regional Chapter 11
    - National Chapter 11
    - Global Chapter 11
  - Data subject Chapter 11
  - Controller vs. processor Chapter 11
  - Ownership Chapter 11
  - Data inventory and retention Chapter 11
  - Right to be forgotten Chapter 11

5.5 Explain types and purposes of audits and assessments. Chapter 8, 11

- Attestation Chapter 8
- Internal Chapter 8
  - Compliance Chapter 8
  - Audit committee Chapter 8
  - Self-assessments Chapter 8
- External Chapter 8
  - Regulatory Chapter 8
  - Examinations Chapter 8
  - Assessment Chapter 8
  - Independent third-party audit Chapter 8
- Penetration testing Chapter 8
  - Physical Chapter 8
  - Offensive Chapter 8
  - Defensive Chapter 8
  - Integrated Chapter 8
  - Known environment Chapter 8
  - Partially known environment Chapter 8
  - Unknown environment Chapter 8
  - Reconnaissance Chapter 8
    - Passive Chapter 8
    - Active Chapter 8

5.6 Given a scenario, implement security awareness practices. Chapter 11

- Phishing Chapter 11
  - Campaigns Chapter 11
  - Recognizing a phishing attempt Chapter 11
  - Responding to reported suspicious messages Chapter 11
- Anomalous behavior recognition Chapter 11
  - Risky Chapter 11
  - Unexpected Chapter 11
  - Unintentional Chapter 11
- User guidance and training Chapter 11
  - Policy/handbooks Chapter 11
  - Situational awareness Chapter 11
  - Insider threat Chapter 11
  - Password management Chapter 11
  - Removable media and cables Chapter 11
  - Social engineering Chapter 11

- Operational security Chapter 11
- Hybrid/remote work environments Chapter 11
- Reporting and monitoring Chapter 11f
  - Initial Chapter 11

- Recurring Chapter 11
- Development Chapter 11
- Execution Chapter 11

Recertification Requirements

The CompTIA Security+ certification was previously a lifetime certification. You passed the exam once, and you were certified for life. However, if you take it now, the certification expires after three years unless you renew it. You can renew the certification by either taking the next version of the exam or by enrolling in CompTIA's Continuing Education (CE) program. You will be required to pay an annual fee and complete Continuing Education Units (CEUs). You can earn CEUs through a variety of activities. Some examples include presenting or teaching topics to others, attending training sessions, participating in industry events or seminars, or writing relevant articles, white papers, blogs, or books.

701 Pre-Assessment Questions

Use this pre-assessment exam to test your knowledge of the topics before you start reading the book, and again before you take the live exam. An answer key with explanations immediately follows the pre-assessment. You'll also find a post-assessment exam at the end of the book. Test your knowledge again after studying this material.

1. Your organization is planning to expand the data center to support more systems. Management wants the plan to focus on resiliency and uptime. Which of the following methods would BEST support these goals? (Select TWO.)

    A. UPS
    B. Cold site
    C. NIC teaming
    D. Off-site backups

2. You are tasked with improving the overall security of several servers in your data center. Which of the following are preventive controls that will assist with this goal? (Choose TWO.)

    A. Disabling unnecessary services
    B. Adding cable locks
    C. Monitoring logs on SIEM systems
    D. Implementing a backup plan
    E. Closing unneeded ports

3. Your organization houses a server room, and management wants to increase the server room security. You are tasked with identifying some deterrent controls that can be implemented to protect it. Which of the following choices would BEST meet this objective?

    A. Signs warning intruders of monitoring
    B. Data encryption
    C. A vulnerability assessment
    D. Backups

4. You are comparing different types of authentication. Of the following choices, which one uses multifactor authentication?

   A. A system that requires users to enter a username and password
   B. A system that checks an employee's fingerprint and does a vein scan
   C. A cipher door lock that requires employees to enter a code to open the door
   D. A system that requires users to have a smart card and a PIN

5. The chief information officer (CIO) at your organization suspects someone is entering the data center after normal working hours and stealing sensitive data. Which of the following actions can prevent this?

   A. Upgrade the CCTV system.
   B. Require that visitors sign a log book.
   C. Implement time-based logins.
   D. Enable advanced auditing.

6. You suspect that attackers have been performing a password spraying attack against a Linux server. Which of the following would be the BEST method of confirming your suspicions?

   A. Use the cat command to view the *auth.log* file.
   B. Implement an account lockout policy.
   C. Salt passwords to prevent the success of the spraying attack.
   D. Use the logger command to view unsuccessful logins.

7. Your network includes dozens of servers. Administrators in your organization are having problems aggregating and correlating the logs from these servers. Which of the following provides the BEST solution for these problems?

   A. SIEM
   B. Syslog
   C. NetFlow
   D. sFlow

8. A SQL database server was recently attacked. Cybersecurity investigators discovered the attack was self-propagating through the network. When it found the database server, it used well-known credentials to access the database. Which of the following would be the BEST action to prevent this from occurring again?

   A. Change the default application password.
   B. Remove the worm.
   C. Implement 2FA.
   D. Conduct a code review.

9. You are reviewing security controls and their usefulness. You notice that account lockout policies are in place. Which of the following attacks will these policies thwart?

   A. Brute force
   B. DNS poisoning
   C. Replay
   D. Buffer overflow

10. After a recent attack, security investigators discovered that attackers logged on with an administrator account. They recommend implementing a solution that will thwart this type of attack in the future. The solution must support the following requirements:

    ▪ Allow authorized users to access the administrator account without knowing the password.
    ▪ Allow authorized users to check out the credentials when needed.
    ▪ Log each time the credentials are used.
    ▪ Automatically change the password.

    Which of the following answers would meet these requirements?

    A. Privileged access management
    B. OpenID Connect
    C. MAC scheme
    D. MFA

11. Lisa wants to implement a secure authentication system on a website. However, instead of collecting and storing user passwords, she wants to use a third-party system. Which of the following is the BEST choice to meet this goal?

    A. SAML
    B. Kerberos
    C. SSH
    D. OAuth

12. Your organization is implementing an SDN. Management wants to use an access control scheme that controls access based on attributes. Which of the following is the BEST solution?

    A. DAC
    B. MAC
    C. Role-BAC
    D. ABAC

13. Your organization plans to deploy a server in the screened subnet that will perform the following functions:

    ■ Identify mail servers
    ■ Provide data integrity
    ■ Prevent poisoning attacks
    ■ Respond to requests for A and AAAA records

    Which of the following will BEST meet these requirements?

    A. DNS
    B. DNSSEC
    C. TLS
    D. ESP

14. Your organization has added a hot site as shown in the following graphic.

    All firewalls should enforce the following requirements:

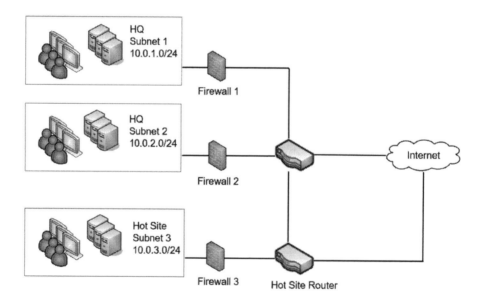

    ■ Use only secure protocols for remote management
    ■ Block cleartext web traffic

    Users in the hot site are unable to access websites in the Internet. The following table shows the current rules configured in Firewall 3.

Rule	Destination	Source	Protocol	Action
HTTPS Outbound	Any	10.0.3.0/24	HTTPS	Allow
HTTP Outbound	Any	10.0.3.0/24	HTTP	Block
DNS	Any	10.0.1.0/24	DNS	Allow
HTTPS Inbound	10.0.3.0/24	Any	HTTPS	Allow
HTTP Inbound	10.0.3.0/24	Any	HTTP	Block
Telnet	10.0.3.0/24	Any	Telnet	Block
SSH	10.0.3.0/24	Any	SSH	Allow

You're asked to verify the rules are configured correctly. Which rule, if any, should be changed in Firewall 3?

A. HTTPS Outbound

B. HTTP Outbound

C. DNS

D. Telnet

E. SSH

F. None. All rules are correct.

15. Maggie is a sales representative for a software company. While in a coffee shop, she uses her laptop to connect to the public Wi-Fi, check her work emails, and upload details of a recent sale. Which of the following would she use to prevent other devices on the public network from accessing her laptop? (Choose the BEST two choices.)

A. TPM

B. HSM

C. Firewall

D. DLP

E. VPN

16. Your organization wants to combine some of the security controls used to control incoming and outgoing network traffic. At a minimum, the solution should include stateless inspection, malware inspection, and a content filter. Which of the following BEST meets this goal?

A. VLAN

B. NAT

C. UTM

D. DNSSEC

E. WAF

17. Administrators are deploying a new Linux server in the screened subnet. After it is installed, they want to manage it from their desktop computers located within the organization's private network. Which of the following would be the BEST choice to meet this need?

    A. Forward proxy server
    B. Reverse proxy server
    C. Web application firewall
    D. Jump server

18. Attackers have recently launched several attacks against servers in your organization's screened subnet. You are tasked with identifying a solution that will have the best chance at preventing these attacks in the future. Which of the following is the BEST choice?

    A. An anomaly-based IDS
    B. An inline IPS
    C. A passive IDS
    D. A signature-based IDS

19. Administrators are designing a site-to-site VPN between offices in two different cities. Management mandated the use of certificates for mutual authentication. Additionally, they want to ensure that internal IP addresses are not revealed. Which of the following is the BEST choice to meet these requirements?

    A. IPsec VPN using Tunnel mode
    B. IPsec VPN using Transport mode
    C. L2TP VPN
    D. VLAN VPN

20. Network administrators are considering adding an HSM to a server in your network. What functions will this add to the server?

    A. Provide full drive encryption
    B. Reduce the risk of employees emailing confidential information outside the organization
    C. Provide webmail to clients
    D. Generate and store keys used with servers

21. Bart needs to send an email to his supervisor with an attachment that includes sensitive information. He wants to maintain the confidentiality of this information. Which of the following choices is the BEST choice to meet his needs?

    A. Digital signature
    B. Encryption
    C. Data masking
    D. Hashing

22. Your organization is planning to implement a CYOD deployment model. You're asked to provide input for the new policy. Which of the following concepts are appropriate for this policy?

    A. SCADA access
    B. Storage segmentation
    C. Database security
    D. Embedded RTOS

23. During a vulnerability scan, you discover some new systems on the network. After investigating this, you verify that these systems aren't authorized because someone installed them without going through a standard approval process. What does this describe?

    A. Hacktivist
    B. Unskilled attacker
    C. Shadow IT
    D. Authorized hacker

24. Homer recently received a phishing email with a malicious attachment. He was curious so he opened it to see what it was. It installed malware on his system, and quickly spread to other systems on the network. Security investigators discovered that the malware exploited a vulnerability that wasn't previously known by any trusted sources. Which of the following BEST describes this attack?

    A. Open-source intelligence
    B. Zero-day
    C. Hoax
    D. DDoS

25. Lisa completed an antivirus scan on a server and detected a Trojan. She removed the Trojan but was concerned that unauthorized personnel might still be able to access data on the server and decided to check the server further. Of the following choices, what is she MOST likely looking for on this server?

    A. Backdoor
    B. Logic bomb
    C. Rootkit
    D. Botnet

26. Employees at the Marvin Monroe Memorial Hospital are unable to access any computer data. Instead, they occasionally see a message indicating that attackers encrypted all the data and it would remain encrypted until the attackers received a hefty sum as payment. Which of the following BEST describes this attack?

    A. Criminal syndicate
    B. Ransomware
    C. Fileless virus
    D. Rootkit

27. You're reviewing the logs for a web server and see several suspicious entries. You suspect that an attacker is attempting to write more data into a web application's memory than it can handle. What does this describe?

    A. Pointer/object dereference
    B. Race condition exploit
    C. DLL injection attack
    D. Buffer overflow attack

28. An attacker has launched several successful XSS attacks on a web application hosted by your organization. Which of the following are the BEST choices to protect the web application and prevent this attack? (Select TWO.)

    A. Dynamic code analysis
    B. Input validation
    C. Code obfuscation
    D. WAF
    E. Normalization

29. Hacker Harry has an account on a website that he uses when posting comments. When he visits, he enters his username and password to log on, and the site displays his username with any comments he makes. Today, he noticed that he could enter JavaScript code as part of his username. After entering the code, other users experienced unexpected results when hovering over his username. What does this describe?

    A. Cross-site scripting
    B. Input validation
    C. Privilege escalation
    D. Directory traversal

30. Which of the following BEST describes the purpose of a risk register?

    A. It shows risks on a plot or graph.
    B. It provides a listing of risks, the risk owner, and the mitigation measures.
    C. It shows risks on a color-coded graph.
    D. It evaluates the supply chain.

31. Maggie is performing a risk assessment for an organization. She estimates the loss for the coming year due to a specific risk will be $5,000. What does this represent?

    A. SLE
    B. ARO
    C. MTBF
    D. ALE

32. Ziffcorp is developing a new technology that they expect to become a huge success when it's released. The CIO is concerned about someone stealing their company secrets related to this technology. Which of the following will help the CIO identify potential dangers related to the loss of this technology?

    A. Threat hunting
    B. Vulnerability scan
    C. SOAR
    D. SIEM

33. Your organization hired a cybersecurity expert to perform a security assessment. After running a vulnerability scan, she sees the following error on a web server:

    `- Host IP 192.168.1.10 OS Apache httpd 2.433 Vulnerable to mod_auth exploit`

    However, she verified that the mod_auth module has not been installed or enabled on the server. Which of the following BEST explains this scenario?

    A. A false negative
    B. A false positive
    C. The result of a credentialed scan
    D. The result of a non-credentialed scan

34. You are reviewing a report created after a recent vulnerability scan. However, it isn't clear if the scan was run as a credentialed scan or a non-credentialed scan. Which of the following would give you the BEST indication that the scan was a credentialed scan?

    A. The report shows software versions of installed applications.
    B. The report shows a large number of false positives.
    C. The report shows a listing of IP addresses it discovered.
    D. The report shows a listing of open ports.

35. You suspect servers in your screened subnet are being attacked by an Internet-based attacker. You want to view IPv4 packet data reaching these servers from the Internet. Which of the following would be the BEST choice to meet this need?

    A. Protocol analyzer
    B. IP scanner
    C. Vulnerability scanner
    D. Proxy server
    E. Heuristic-based IDS

36. Administrators at your organization want to increase cybersecurity resilience of key servers by adding fault tolerance capabilities. However, they have a limited budget. Which of the following is the BEST choice to meet these needs?

    A. Alternate processing site
    B. RAID
    C. Backups
    D. Faraday cage

37. Your organization's backup policy for a file server dictates that the amount of time needed to restore backups should be minimized. Which of the following backup plans would BEST meet this need?

    A. Full backups on Sunday and incremental backups on the other six days of the week
    B. Full backups on Sunday and differential backups on the other six days of the week
    C. Incremental backups on Sunday and differential backups on the other six days of the week
    D. Differential backups on Sunday and incremental backups on the other six days of the week

38. A security analyst recently completed a BIA and defined the maximum acceptable outage time for a critical system. What does this identify?

    A. RTO
    B. RPO
    C. MTTR
    D. MTBF

39. The new chief technology officer (CTO) at your organization wants to ensure that critical business systems are protected from isolated outages. Which of the following would let her know how often these systems will experience outages?

    A. MTTR
    B. MTBF
    C. RTO
    D. RPO

40. The Ninth National Bank of Springfield is considering an alternate location as part of its continuity of operations plan. It wants to identify a site resiliency solution that provides the shortest recovery time. Which of the following is the BEST choice?

    A. Cold site
    B. Warm site
    C. Hot site
    D. Snapshot

41. Cybersecurity experts in your organization are creating a detailed plan identifying how to recover critical systems if these systems suffer a complete loss. What type of plan are they MOST likely creating?

    A. Backup plan
    B. Incident response plan
    C. Communications plan
    D. Disaster recovery plan

42. As a security administrator, you receive an antivirus alert from a server in your network indicating one of the files has a hash of known malware. The file was pushed to the server from the organization's patch management system and is scheduled to be applied to the server early the next morning. The antivirus software indicates that the file and hash of the malware are:

   - File: gcga_upgrade.exe
   - Hash: 518b571e26035d95e5e9232b4affbd84

   Checking the logs of the patch management system, you see the following information:

Status	Update Name	Hash
Pushed	gcga_upgrade.exe	518b571e26035d95e5e9232b4affbd84

   Which of the following indicates what MOST likely occurred?

   A. The file was infected after it was pushed out to the server.
   B. The file was embedded with crypto-malware before it was pushed to the server.
   C. The file was listed in the patch management system's deny list.
   D. The file was infected when the patch management system downloaded it.

43. An organization requested bids for a contract and asked companies to submit their bids via email. After winning the bid, BizzFad realized it couldn't meet the requirements of the contract. BizzFad instead stated that it never submitted the bid. Which of the following would provide proof to the organization that BizzFad did submit the bid, if it was used?

   A. Digital signature
   B. Integrity
   C. Repudiation
   D. Encryption

44. An application requires users to log on with passwords. The application developers want to store the passwords in such a way that it will thwart rainbow table attacks. Which of the following is the BEST solution?

   A. Implement salting.
   B. Implement hashing.
   C. Implement homomorphic encryption.
   D. Implement perfect forward secrecy.

45. Lisa and Bart need to exchange emails over the Internet using an unsecured channel. These emails need to provide non-repudiation. They decide to use certificates on each of their computers. What would they use to sign their certificates?

    A. CRL
    B. OCSP
    C. CSR
    D. CA
    E. DSA

46. Your organization is negotiating with an outside vendor to host cloud-based resources. Management wants to ensure the vendor commits to returning the systems to full operation after an outage within a certain time frame. Which of the following is the organization MOST likely negotiating?

    A. MTTR
    B. NDA
    C. SLA
    D. DLP

47. Security administrators have been responding to an increasing number of incident alerts, making it harder for them to respond to each promptly. Management wants to implement a solution that will automate the response of some of these incidents without requiring real-time involvement by security administrators. Which of the following will BEST meet this need?

    A. SOAR
    B. DLP
    C. STIX
    D. TAXII

48. Security administrators have isolated a Linux server after a successful attack. A forensic analyst is tasked with creating an image of the hard drive of this system for analysis. Which of the following will the analyst MOST likely use to create the image?

    A. tcpreplay
    B. chmod
    C. dd
    D. Cuckoo

49. Your company hosts an e-commerce site that sells renewable subscriptions for services. Customers can choose to renew their subscription monthly or annually automatically. However, management doesn't want to store customer credit card information in any database or system managed by the company. Which of the following can be used instead?

    A. Pseudo-anonymization
    B. Tokenization
    C. Data minimization
    D. Anonymization

50. Which one of the following is NOT a common use case for automation in relation to security operations?

    A. User provisioning
    B. Resource provisioning
    C. Policy writing
    D. Ticket creation

Pre-Assessment Answers

1. **A** and **C** are correct. An uninterruptible power supply (UPS) and network interface card (NIC) teaming support resiliency and uptime goals. The UPS ensures the system stays up if power is lost. NIC teaming automatically recovers if one of the NICs or NIC inputs fail. Resiliency methods help systems heal themselves and recover from faults automatically. A cold site cannot take over automatically and is not quick. Off-site backups would need to be retrieved and applied by a person, so they aren't automatic. This question comes from exam objective 3.1, "Compare and contrast security implications of different architecture models" and is covered in Chapter 1.

2. **A** and **E** are correct. Disabling unnecessary services and closing unneeded ports are steps you can take to harden a server. They are preventive controls because they help prevent an incident. Cable locks are a type of physical control and are typically used on laptops, not on servers. Monitoring logs on security information and event management (SIEM) systems is a detective control. A backup plan is a corrective control. This question comes from exam objective 2.5, "Explain the purpose of mitigation techniques used to secure the enterprise" and is covered in Chapter 1.

3. **A** is correct. Signs are deterrent controls because they would deter someone from entering or accessing the servers. They do not actually prevent anyone from doing anything. They are also examples of physical controls. None of the other answers increase the security of the server room. Data encryption is a technical control designed to protect data on the servers. A vulnerability assessment is a managerial control designed to discover vulnerabilities. Backups are corrective controls designed to reverse the impact of data loss or corruption. This question comes from exam objective 1.1, "Compare and contrast various types of security controls" and is covered in Chapter 1.

4. **D** is correct. A system that requires users to have a smart card and a personal identification number (PIN) uses multifactor authentication or two-factor authentication. The card is in the something you have factor, and the PIN is in the something you know factor. A

username provides identification, and a password is in the something you know factor, providing single-factor authentication. Fingerprints and vein scans are both in the something you are factor, providing single-factor authentication. A code for a cipher door lock is in the something you know factor, providing single-factor authentication. This question comes from exam objective 4.6 "Given a scenario, implement and maintain identity and access management" and is covered in Chapter 2.

5. **C** is correct. Time-based logins (sometimes called time-of-day restrictions) would prevent this. They would prevent anyone from logging in after normal working hours and accessing sensitive data. All of the other answers can detect suspicious behavior, but they wouldn't prevent the users from logging in after normal working hours and stealing the data. This question comes from exam objective 4.6 "Given a scenario, implement and maintain identity and access management" and is covered in Chapter 2.

6. **A** is correct. The cat command (short for concatenate) displays the entire contents of a file and the auth.log file shows all unsuccessful (and successful) logins, and this is the only choice of the available answers that confirms past activity. An account lockout policy locks an account after too many incorrect passwords within a certain time frame, but a spraying attack uses a time lapse between each password attempt to bypass an account lockout policy. Salting passwords is often used to prevent rainbow table-based attacks, but salts aren't effective against spraying attacks. The logger command is used to add log entries into the syslog file but doesn't examine log entries. This question comes from exam objective 4.9, "Given a scenario, use data sources to support an investigation" and is covered in Chapter 1.

7. **A** is correct. A security information and event management (SIEM) system collects, aggregates, and correlates logs from multiple sources. Syslog is a protocol that specifies log entry formats that many SIEMs use. It is also the name of a log on Linux systems. NetFlow is a network protocol (developed by Cisco) used to collect and monitor network traffic. The sFlow (short for sampled flow) protocol is used to collect a sampling of network traffic for monitoring. This question comes from exam objective 4.4 "Explain security alerting and monitoring concepts and tools" and is covered in Chapter 1.

8. **A** is correct. The default application password for the SQL server should be changed. Some SQL Server software implementations can have a default blank password for the SA account (the System Administrator account), and these default credentials are well-known. While the scenario describes a worm because it is self-propagating, the question is asking for the best preventive action to take. Using two-factor authentication (2FA) is a good practice for users, but it isn't always feasible for application passwords. A code

review can detect flaws and vulnerabilities in internally developed applications, but SQL Server is Microsoft software. This question comes from exam objective 2.2 "Explain common threat vectors and attack surfaces" and is covered in Chapter 2.

9. **A** is correct. Brute force attacks attempt to guess passwords, but an account lockout control locks an account after the wrong password is guessed too many times. The other attacks are not password attacks, so they aren't mitigated using account lockout controls. Domain Name System (DNS) poisoning attempts to redirect web browsers to malicious URLs. Replay attacks attempt to capture packets to impersonate one of the parties in an online session. Buffer overflow attacks attempt to overwhelm online applications with unexpected code or data. This question comes from exam objective 2.4 "Given a scenario, analyze indicators of malicious activity" and is covered in Chapters 2 and 10.

10. **A** is correct. A privileged access management system protects and limits access to privileged accounts such as administrator accounts. OpenID Connect is used for authentication on the Internet, not internal networks. A mandatory access control (MAC) scheme uses labels to control access, but it isn't used to control access to administrator accounts. Multifactor authentication (MFA) uses more than one factor of authentication, but it doesn't meet any of the requirements of this scenario. This question comes from exam objective 4.6 "Given a scenario, implement and maintain identity and access management" and is covered in Chapter 2.

11. **A** is correct. Security Assertion Markup Language (SAML) is a single sign-on SSO solution that can use third-party websites, and it provides authentication. Kerberos is an SSO solution used on internal networks such as in Microsoft Active Directory domains. Secure Shell (SSH) is used for remote administration. OAuth (think of this as Open Authorization) is used for authorization, but the scenario wants a solution for authentication. This question comes from exam objective 4.6 "Given a scenario, implement and maintain identity and access management" and is covered in Chapter 2.

12. **D** is correct. A software-defined network (SDN) typically uses an attribute-based access control (ABAC) scheme. The ABAC scheme is based on attributes that identify subjects and objects within a policy. A discretionary access control (DAC) scheme has an owner, and the owner establishes access for the objects. A mandatory access control (MAC) scheme uses labels assigned to subjects and objects. A role-based access control scheme uses roles or groups to assign rights and permissions. This question comes from exam objective 4.6 "Given a scenario, implement and maintain identity and access management" and is covered in Chapter 2.

13. **B** is correct. Domain Name System Security Extensions (DNSSEC) add security to DNS systems and can prevent DNS poisoning attacks by adding data integrity to DNS records. The functions on the list indicate that the server in the screened subnet (sometimes called a demilitarized zone or DMZ) is a DNS server but for the DNS server to provide data integrity and prevent DNS poisoning, it needs DNSSEC. DNSSEC uses a Resource Record Signature (RRSIG), commonly referred to as a digital signature, to provide data integrity and authentication for DNS replies. RRSIG can use Transport Layer Security (TLS) to create the signature, but TLS by itself doesn't provide the required protection. Internet Protocol security (IPsec) uses Encapsulating Security Payload (ESP) to encrypt data. This question comes from exam objective 2.5 "Explain the purpose of mitigation techniques used to secure the enterprise" and is covered in Chapter 3.

14. **C** is correct. The Domain Name System (DNS) rule should be changed because the source IP address is incorrect. It should be 10.0.3.0/24 instead of 10.0.1.0/24. All other rules are configured correctly. This question comes from exam objective 4.5 "Given a scenario, modify enterprise capabilities to enhance security" and is covered in Chapter 3.

15. **C** and **E** are correct. A firewall and a virtual private network (VPN) would prevent other devices from accessing her laptop. A host-based firewall provides primary protection. The VPN encrypts all of her Internet-based traffic going over the public Wi-Fi. A Trusted Platform Module (TPM) provides full drive encryption and would protect the data if someone accessed the laptop, but it doesn't prevent access. A hardware security module (HSM) is a removable device that can generate and store RSA keys used with servers. A data loss prevention (DLP) device helps prevent unauthorized data from leaving a network, but it doesn't prevent access. This question comes from exam objective 3.2 "Given a scenario, apply security principles to secure enterprise infrastructure" and is covered in Chapter 4.

16. **C** is correct. A unified threat management (UTM) device is an advanced firewall and combines multiple security controls into a single device such as stateless inspection, malware inspection, and a content filter. None of the other answers include these components. You can configure a virtual local area network (VLAN) on a switch to provide network segmentation. Network Address Translation (NAT) translates public IP addresses to private IP addresses and private addresses back to public IP addresses. Domain Name System Security Extensions (DNSSEC) is a suite of extensions for DNS that provides validation for DNS responses. A web application firewall (WAF) protects a web server from Internet-based attacks. This question comes from exam objective 3.2 "Given a scenario, apply security principles to secure enterprise infrastructure" and is covered in Chapter 3.

17. **D** is correct. A jump server is a server placed between different security zones, such as an internal network and a screened subnet (sometimes called a demilitarized zone or DMZ) and is used to manage devices in the other security zone. In this scenario, administrators could connect to the jump server with Secure Shell (SSH) and then connect to the Linux server using SSH forwarding on the jump server. A forward proxy server (often called a proxy server) is used by internal clients to access Internet resources, not resources in the screened subnet. Reverse proxy servers accept traffic from the Internet, not the internal network, and forward the traffic to one or more internal web servers. A web application firewall (WAF) protects a web server from Internet-based attacks but isn't used to control traffic between an internal network and the screened subnet. This question comes from exam objective 3.2 "Given a scenario, apply security principles to secure enterprise infrastructure" and is covered in Chapter 3.

18. **B** is correct. The best solution of the given choices is an inline intrusion prevention system (IPS). Traffic goes through the IPS, and the IPS can prevent attacks from reaching internal systems. An intrusion detection system (IDS) is passive and not inline, so it can only detect and react to the attacks, not block them. A signature-based IDS can detect known attacks based on the attack's signature, but there isn't any indication that the past attacks were known. This question comes from exam objective 3.2 "Given a scenario, apply security principles to secure enterprise infrastructure" and is covered in Chapter 4.

19. **A** is correct. Internet Protocol security (IPsec) using Tunnel mode is the best choice of the available answers. IPsec provides mutual authentication, and Tunnel mode will encrypt both the payload and the packet headers, hiding the internal IP addresses. Transport mode will encrypt the payload only, leaving the internal IP addresses exposed. A VPN using Layer 2 Tunneling Protocol (L2TP) only doesn't provide any encryption. Virtual local area networks (VLANs) provide network segmentation but can't be used as a VPN. This question comes from exam objective 3.2 "Given a scenario, apply security principles to secure enterprise infrastructure" and is covered in Chapter 4.

20. **D** is correct. A hardware security module (HSM) is a removable device that can generate and store RSA keys used with servers. The keys can be used to encrypt data sent to and from the server, but they wouldn't be used for full drive encryption. A Trusted Platform Module (TPM) provides full drive encryption and is included in most laptops. A data loss prevention (DLP) device is a device that can reduce the risk of employees emailing confidential information outside the organization. Software as a Service (SaaS) provides software or applications, such as webmail, via the cloud. This question comes from exam objective 1.4 "Explain the importance of using appropriate cryptographic solutions" and is covered in Chapter 5.

21. **B** is correct. Encryption is the best choice to provide confidentiality of any type of information, including sensitive information. A digital signature provides integrity, non-repudiation, and authentication. Data masking modifies the original data, replacing the original characters with placeholder values. Hashing provides integrity. This question comes from exam objective 2.5 "Explain the purpose of mitigation techniques used to secure the enterprise" and is covered in Chapter 5.

22. **B** is correct. Storage segmentation creates separate storage areas in mobile devices and can be used with a choose your own device (CYOD) mobile device deployment model where users own their devices. None of the other answers are directly related to mobile devices. A supervisory control and data acquisition (SCADA) system controls industrial control systems (ICSs), such as those used in nuclear power plants or water treatment facilities, and SCADA systems should be isolated. Database security includes the use of permissions and encryption to protect data in a database but is unrelated to mobile device deployment. Some embedded systems use a real-time operating system (RTOS) when the system must react within a specific time. This question comes from exam objective 4.1 "Given a scenario, apply common security techniques to computing resources" and is covered in Chapter 5.

23. **C** is correct. Shadow IT refers to any systems or applications installed on a network without authorization or approval. Employees often add them to bypass security controls. A hacktivist launches attacks as part of an activist movement or to further a cause. An unskilled attacker is an attacker who uses existing computer scripts or code to launch attacks and typically has limited technical skills. An authorized hacker (sometimes referred to as a white hat attacker) is a security professional working within the law to protect an organization from attackers. This question comes from exam objective 2.1 "Compare and contrast common threat actors and motivations" and is covered in Chapter 6.

24. **B** is correct. A zero-day exploit is one that isn't known by trusted sources such as antivirus vendors or operating system vendors. Attackers use open-source intelligence to identify a target. Some typical sources are social media sites and news outlets. A hoax is not a specific attack. It is a message, often circulated through email that tells of impending doom from a virus or other security threat that simply doesn't exist. A distributed denial-of-service (DDoS) attack comes from multiple sources, not as a single phishing email. This question comes from exam objective 2.3 "Explain various types of vulnerabilities" and is covered in Chapter 6.

25. **A** is correct. She is most likely looking for a backdoor because Trojans commonly create backdoors, and a backdoor allows unauthorized personnel to access data on the system. Logic bombs and rootkits can create backdoor accounts, but Trojans don't create logic

bombs and would rarely install a rootkit. The computer might be joined to a botnet, but a botnet is a group of computers. This question comes from exam objective 2.4 "Given a scenario, analyze indicators of malicious activity" and is covered in Chapter 6.

26. **B** is correct. The scenario describes ransomware, where attackers typically encrypt data and demand payment to release the data. Although the attack might have been launched by a criminal syndicate because their motivation is primarily money, the question is asking about the attack, not the attacker. A fileless virus injects code into existing scripts and may install ransomware, but a fileless virus is not ransomware. A rootkit is a program or a group of programs that provides root-level access to a system but hides itself to evade detection. This question comes from exam objective 2.4 "Given a scenario, analyze indicators of malicious activity" and is covered in Chapter 6.

27. **D** is correct. A buffer overflow attack attempts to write more data into an application's memory than it can handle. A pointer or object dereference is a programming error that can corrupt memory, but programmers, not attackers, cause it. A race condition is a programming conflict when two or more applications or application models attempt to access or modify a resource at the same time. A dynamic link library (DLL) injection attack injects a DLL into memory and causes it to run. This question comes from exam objective 2.4 "Given a scenario, analyze indicators of malicious activity" and is covered in Chapter 7.

28. **B** and **D** are correct. Input validation and a web application firewall (WAF) are the best choices of the available answers. Both protect against cross-site scripting (XSS) attacks. Input validation validates data before using it to help prevent XSS attacks. A WAF acts as an additional firewall that monitors, filters, and/or blocks HTTP traffic to a web server. None of the other answers will directly prevent XSS attacks. Dynamic code analysis (such as fuzzing) can test code. Code obfuscation makes the code more difficult to read. Normalization refers to organizing tables and columns in a database to reduce redundant data and improve overall database performance. This question comes from exam objective 4.1 "Given a scenario, apply common security techniques to computing resources" and is covered in Chapter 3 and 7.

29. **A** is correct. This is an example of a cross-site scripting (XSS) attack. It can be prevented by using proper input validation techniques to prevent users from entering malicious code into a site's text box. Privilege escalation techniques attempt to give an attacker more rights and permissions. In a directory traversal attack, the attacker can navigate a system's directory structure and read files. This question comes from exam objective 2.3 "Explain various types of vulnerabilities" and is covered in Chapter 7.

30. **B** is correct. A risk register lists risks and often includes the name of the risk, the risk owner, mitigation measures, and a risk score. A risk matrix plots risks onto a graph or chart, and a heat map plots risks onto a color-coded graph or chart. While a risk register may evaluate supply chain risks, it does much more. This question comes from exam objective 5.2 "Explain elements of the risk management process" and is covered in Chapter 8.

31. **D** is correct. The annual loss expectancy (ALE) identifies the expected loss for a given year based on a specific risk and existing security controls. The single loss expectancy (SLE) identifies the cost of any single loss. The annual rate of occurrence (ARO) identifies how many times a loss is expected to occur in a year. Multiplying SLE × ARO identifies the ALE. Note that the scenario refers to a specific risk, but it doesn't indicate how many times the loss occurred. This could have been five incidents (ARO of 5) incurring losses of $1,000 for each incident (SLE), resulting in an ALE of $5,000. The mean time between failures (MTBF) provides a measure of a system's reliability and is usually represented in hours. This question comes from exam objective 5.2 "Explain elements of the risk management process" and is covered in Chapter 8.

32. **A** is correct. Threat hunting is the process of actively looking for threats within a network before an automated tool detects and reports on the threat. It typically includes several elements. A vulnerability scan evaluates vulnerabilities (or weaknesses) with a network or a specific system, but it doesn't look for threats. A Security Orchestration, Automation, and Response (SOAR) platform can be configured to automatically respond to low-level incidents, but this scenario indicates that they need to look for more than just low-level threats. A security information and event management (SIEM) is used to collect and aggregate logs and can assist with threat hunting, but threat hunting is much broader. This question comes from exam objective 4.8 "Explain appropriate incident response activities" and is covered in Chapter 11.

33. **B** is correct. This is an example of a false positive. The vulnerability scanner is indicating a vulnerability exists with the mod_auth module. However, the mod_auth module is not installed or enabled on the server, so it cannot represent a vulnerability on the server. A false negative occurs when a vulnerability exists, but the scanner doesn't report it. The scenario doesn't give enough information to determine if this is a credentialed or a non-credentialed scan. However, a credentialed scan would allow a vulnerability scanner to have more visibility over the systems it scans, allowing it to get a more accurate view of the systems. This question comes from exam objective 4.3 "Explain various activities associated with vulnerability management" and is covered in Chapter 8.

34. **A** is correct. A credentialed scan will show software versions of installed applications. A credentialed scan will show fewer false positives, not more. Any scan should list IP addresses it discovered along with open ports on these hosts. This question comes from exam objective 4.3 "Explain various activities associated with vulnerability management" and is covered in Chapter 8.

35. **A** is correct. A protocol analyzer can capture and analyze packets on a network. An IP scanner (sometimes called a network scanner) identifies hosts within a network by identifying active IP addresses and additional information about each active host. Vulnerability scanners scan hosts within a network looking for vulnerabilities. Proxy servers (also known as forward proxy servers) forward requests for services from a client. Heuristic-based (sometimes called behavior-based) intrusion detection systems (IDSs) detect intrusions by identifying anomalies. This question comes from exam objective 4.9 "Given a scenario, use data sources to support an investigation" and is covered in Chapter 8.

36. **B** is correct. A redundant array of inexpensive disks subsystem provides fault tolerance for disks and increases cybersecurity resilience. In this context, cybersecurity resilience refers to a system's ability to continue to operate even after an adverse event. An alternate processing site can provide cybersecurity resilience for an entire site, but it is expensive and does much more than provide fault tolerance for some servers. Backups contribute to cybersecurity resilience, but they do not help with fault tolerance. A Faraday cage is a room or enclosure that prevents signals from emanating beyond the room or enclosure. This question comes from exam objective 3.4 "Explain the importance of resilience and recovery in security architecture" and is covered in Chapter 9.

37. **B** is correct. A full/differential backup strategy is best with one full backup on one day and differential backups on the other days. A restore would require only two backups, making it quicker than the other options. A full/ incremental backup would typically require you to restore more than two backups. For example, data loss on Friday would require you to restore the full backup, plus four incremental backups. Backups must start with a full backup, so neither an incremental/differential nor a differential/incremental backup strategy is possible. This question comes from exam objective 3.4 "Explain the importance of resilience and recovery in security architecture" and is covered in Chapter 9.

38. **A** is correct. A recovery time objective (RTO) identifies the maximum amount of time it can take to restore a system after an outage. It is directly related to the maximum acceptable outage time defined in a business impact analysis (BIA). None of the other answers are related to the maximum acceptable outage time. A recovery point objective (RPO)

identifies a point in time where data loss is acceptable, and refers to databases. The mean time between failures (MTBF) provides a measure of a system's reliability and is usually represented in hours. The mean time to repair (MTTR) identifies the average (the arithmetic mean) time it takes to restore a failed system. This question comes from exam objective 5.2 "Explain elements of the risk management process" and is covered in Chapter 9.

39. **B** is correct. The mean time between failures (MTBF) provides a measure of a system's reliability and would provide an estimate of how often the systems will experience outages. The mean time to repair (MTTR) refers to the time it takes to restore a system, not the time between failures. The recovery time objective (RTO) identifies the maximum amount of time it can take to restore a system after an outage. The recovery point objective (RPO) identifies a point in time where data loss is acceptable. This question comes from exam objective 5.2 "Explain elements of the risk management process" and is covered in Chapter 9.

40. **C** is correct. Hot sites have the shortest recovery time, but they are also the most expensive. Cold sites have the longest recovery time and are the least expensive. Warm sites have a shorter recovery time than cold sites but a longer recovery time than hot sites. A snapshot backup provides a backup of a disk at a moment in time and is sometimes used in digital forensics. This question comes from exam objective 3.4 "Explain the importance of resilience and recovery in security architecture" and is covered in Chapter 9.

41. **D** is correct. A disaster recovery plan (DRP) identifies how to recover critical systems after a disaster. Backup plans are typically focused on backing up and restoring data, not systems. An incident response plan is implemented after a security incident, but all security incidents do not result in a complete loss of systems. A communications plan is part of an incident response plan and provides direction on how to communicate issues related to an incident. This question comes from exam objective 5.1 "Summarize elements of effective security governance" and is covered in Chapter 9.

42. **D** is correct. Of the given choices, the file was most likely infected when the patch management system downloaded it. This is because the name and hash of the file is the same on the server as it is on the patch management system. If it were infected after it was pushed out to the server, it would have a different hash. The scenario doesn't indicate what type of infection the malware has, so it isn't possible to tell if it is crypto-malware or another type of malware. A deny list blocks files so if the file were listed in the patch management system's deny list, the patch management system wouldn't push it out to systems. This question comes from exam objective 2.5 "Explain the purpose of mitigation techniques used to secure the enterprise" and is covered in Chapter 10.

43. **A** is correct. If BizzFad submitted the bid via email using a digital signature, it would provide proof that BizzFad submitted the bid. Digital signatures provide verification of who sent a message, non-repudiation preventing them from denying it, and integrity verifying the message wasn't modified. Integrity verifies the message wasn't modified. Repudiation isn't a goal of security mechanisms. Encryption protects the confidentiality of data, but it doesn't verify who sent it or provide non-repudiation. This question comes from exam objective 1.4 "Explain the importance of using appropriate cryptographic solutions" and is covered in Chapter 10.

44. **A** is correct. Salting passwords is a common method of preventing rainbow table attacks. Salting adds additional data to the password before hashing it. Rainbow table attacks use precomputed hashes to discover passwords so hashing the passwords won't thwart rainbow table attacks. Homomorphic encryption can be used to process data using cloud computing services and it allows data to remain encrypted while it is being processed. Perfect forward secrecy is related to encryption and indicates that a cryptographic system generates random keys for each session. This question comes from exam objective 1.4 "Explain the importance of using appropriate cryptographic solutions" and is covered in Chapter 10.

45. **D** is correct. A certificate authority (CA) manages certificates and would sign certificates issued to users. Note that non-repudiation would be provided with digital signatures and each user would need a certificate assigned to them that they would use to create the digital signatures. A certificate revocation list (CRL) is a list of revoked certificates. Online Certificate Status Protocol (OCSP) is an alternative to a CRL and provides a real-time response indicating the validity of a certificate. The certificate signing request (CSR) is used to request a certificate. A Digital Signature Algorithm (DSA) is used to create a digital signature. They would use digital signatures to sign their emails, and they need a certificate to create a digital signature, but they can't sign their certificates with a digital signature. This question comes from exam objective 1.4 "Explain the importance of using appropriate cryptographic solutions" and is covered in Chapter 10.

46. **C** is correct. A service level agreement (SLA) is an agreement between a company and a vendor that stipulates performance expectations, including returning a system to full operation within a specific timeframe. The mean time to repair (MTTR) identifies the average (the arithmetic mean) time it takes to restore a failed system, but it does not provide a guarantee that the vendor will restore the system within the MTTR every time. A non-disclosure agreement (NDA) ensures that individuals do not share proprietary data with others. Data loss prevention (DLP) technologies typically monitor outgoing traffic to prevent confidential information from getting outside the organization. This question comes from exam objective 5.3 "Explain the processes associated with third-party risk assessment and management" and is covered in Chapter 11.

47. **A** is correct. A Security Orchestration, Automation, and Response (SOAR) solution can be configured with SOAR runbooks to automate the response of these incidents and is the best choice of the available answers. Data loss prevention (DLP) technologies typically monitor outgoing traffic to prevent confidential information from getting outside the organization. While a SOAR runbook may include DLP action, a SOAR runbook can do much more. Structured Threat Information eXpression (STIX) defines a standardized language used to share cyber threat information. TAXII (Trusted Automated eXchange of Intelligence Information) defines a set of services and message exchanges that can be used to share information. STIX identifies what to share and TAXII identifies how to share it. This question comes from exam objective 4.4 "Explain security alerting and monitoring concepts and tools" and is covered in Chapter 11.

48. **C** is correct. The **dd** command is available on Linux systems, and it is used to copy disks and files for analysis. As an example, the **dd if=/dev/sda2 of=sd2disk.img** command creates an image of a disk without modifying the original disk. None of the other choices creates an image of a drive. Tcpreplay is a suite of utilities used to edit packet captures and resend them, and it includes the **tcpreplay** command. The **chmod** (short for change mode) command is used to change permissions on Linux systems. Cuckoo is an open source malware analysis system. It analyzes malware within a sandbox environment. This question comes from exam objective 4.8 "Explain appropriate incident response activities" and is covered in Chapter 11.

49. **B** is correct. Tokenization is the best choice. It stores a token created by the credit card processor instead of the credit card number, and this token can be used to make charges. Pseudo-anonymization replaces data with artificial identifiers, but the process can be reversed. Data anonymization modifies data to protect the privacy of individuals by either removing all Personally Identifiable Information or encrypting it. Data minimization is a principle requiring organizations to limit the data they collect and use. This question comes from exam objective 1.4 "Explain the importance of using appropriate cryptographic solutions" and is covered in Chapter 10.

50. **C** is correct. The common use cases for automation include user and resource provisioning, guard rails, security groups, ticket creation and escalation, enabling/disabling services and access, continuous integration and testing, and integrations and APIs. Automation is not commonly used to write policies, as this is a human-focused task. This question comes from exam objective 4.7 "Explain the importance of automation and orchestration related to secure operations" and is covered in Chapter 7.

Chapter 1

Mastering Security Basics

CompTIA Security+ objectives covered in this chapter:

1.1 Compare and contrast various types of security controls.

- Categories (Technical, Managerial, Operational, Physical)
- Control types (Preventive, Deterrent, Detective, Corrective, Compensating, Directive)

1.2 Summarize fundamental security concepts.

- Confidentiality, Integrity, and Availability (CIA)

2.5 Explain the purpose of mitigation techniques used to secure the enterprise.

- Monitoring
- Least privilege

3.2 Given a scenario, apply security principles to secure enterprise infrastructure.

- Selection of effective controls

4.1 Given a scenario, apply common security techniques to computing resources.

- Monitoring

4.4 Explain security alerting and monitoring concepts and tools.

- Monitoring computing resources (Systems, Applications, Infrastructure)
- Activities (Log aggregation, Alerting, Scanning, Reporting, Archiving, Alert response and remediation/validation, Alert tuning)
- Tools (Security information and event management (SIEM))

4.5 Given a scenario, modify enterprise capabilities to enhance security.

- User behavior analytics

4.9 Given a scenario, use data sources to support an investigation.

- Log data (Firewall logs, Application logs, Endpoint logs, OS-specific security logs, IPS/IDS logs, Network logs, Metadata)
- Data sources (Automated reports, Dashboards, Packet captures)

Before you dig into some of the details related to IT security, you should have a solid understanding of core security goals. This chapter introduces many of these core goals to provide a big picture and presents basic risk concepts. Security controls reduce risks; you'll learn about different security control categories in this chapter. Finally, you'll learn about the importance of security monitoring programs.

Understanding Core Security Goals

Security starts with several principles that organizations include as core security goals. These principles drive many security-related decisions at multiple levels. Understanding these basic concepts will help you create a solid foundation in security. Cybersecurity has three core goals: confidentiality, integrity, and availability. These three goals form the CIA security triad, shown in Figure 1.1. The triad is a model used to guide an organization's security principles. Each element is essential to address in any security program.

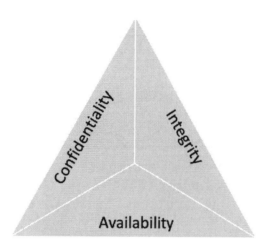

Figure 1.1: CIA Triad

- Confidentiality prevents the unauthorized disclosure of information. It keeps secret information secret.
- Integrity prevents the unauthorized alteration of information or systems. It keeps our information safe from intentional or accidental changes.
- Availability ensures authorized users are able to access information and systems when they need them.

★ Remember This!

The CIA Triad is the foundation of everything we do in cybersecurity. It's one of the essential concepts listed in the Security+ exam objectives, and you should be very familiar with it when you take the exam. As you learn about different security threats and controls throughout this book, try to relate each of them to one or more of the three goals of confidentiality, integrity, and availability.

Security Scenarios

CompTIA uses the phrase "given a scenario" throughout the Security+ exam objectives. You'll need to get comfortable with security scenarios because they often appear on exam questions. All this means is that the question writers will tell you a story about a business or security situation and then ask you how you might react in that situation. The scenario will often describe a goal that an organization wants to achieve.

When you see an exam question telling you a story, you've encountered a scenario-based question. You want to read that scenario carefully because it will contain clues to the correct answer. One of the most important things you can do is figure out which of the three primary security goals is driving the scenario – is it a story about an organization trying to address confidentiality, integrity, or availability issues? That frame of mind will help you figure out the correct answer to the question.

The following sections discuss some common security scenarios related to confidentiality, integrity, and availability.

Ensure Confidentiality

Confidentiality prevents the unauthorized disclosure of information. Only authorized personnel may access confidential. You can ensure confidentiality using several different methods discussed in the following sections.

Encryption

Encryption scrambles data to make it unreadable by unauthorized personnel. Authorized personnel can decrypt the data to access it, but encryption techniques make it extremely difficult for unauthorized personnel to access encrypted data. Chapter 10, "Understanding Cryptography and PKI," covers encryption in much more depth, including commonly used encryption algorithms like the Advanced Encryption Standard (AES).

For example, imagine you need to transmit Personally Identifiable Information (PII), such as medical information or credit card data, via email. You wouldn't want any unauthorized personnel to access this data, but once you click Send, you can no longer control the data. However, if you encrypt the email before you send it, you protect the data's confidentiality as it travels over the network.

Access Controls

Identification, authentication, and authorization are the three core identity and access management activities that help ensure that only authorized personnel can access data. Imagine that you want to grant Maggie access to some data but don't want Homer to access the same data. You use access controls to grant and restrict access. The following list introduces key elements of access controls:

- **Identification.** Users claim an identity with a unique username. For example, both Maggie and Homer have separate user accounts identified with unique usernames. When Maggie uses her account, she is claiming the identity of her account.
- **Authentication.** Users prove their identity with authentication, such as with a password. For example, Maggie knows her password, but no one else should know it. When she logs on to her account with her username and password, she claims her account's identity and proves her identity with the password.
- **Authorization.** Next, you can grant or restrict access to resources using an authorization method, such as permissions. For example, you can grant Maggie's account full access to some files and folders. Similarly, you can ensure that Homer doesn't have any permissions to access the data.

★ *Remember This!*

Confidentiality ensures that data is only viewable by authorized users. The best way to protect the confidentiality of data is by encrypting it. This includes any type of data, such as PII, data in databases, and data on mobile devices. Access controls help protect confidentiality by restricting access.

Provide Integrity

Integrity ensures that data has not changed. This includes ensuring that the data has not been modified, tampered with, or corrupted. Ideally, only authorized users can modify data. However, there are times when unauthorized or unintended changes occur. This can be from unauthorized users, from malicious software (malware), and through system and human errors. When this happens, the data has lost integrity.

You can use hashing techniques to enforce integrity. Chapter 10 discusses the relevant hashing algorithms, such as the various versions of the Secure Hash Algorithm (SHA). Briefly, a hash is simply an alphanumeric string created by executing a hashing algorithm against data, such as a file or message. A hashing algorithm creates a fixed-length, irreversible output. If the data never changes, the resulting hash will always be the same. By comparing hashes created at two different times, you can determine if the original data is still the same. If the hashes are the same, the data is the same. If the hashes are different, the data has changed.

For example, imagine Homer is sending a message to Marge and they both want assurances that the message retains integrity. Homer's message is, "The price is $19.99." He creates a hash of this message. For simplicity's sake, imagine the hash is 123. He then sends both the message and the hash to Marge.

Marge receives both the message and the hash. She (or software on her computer) can calculate the hash on the received message and compare her hash with the hash that Homer sent. If the hash of the received message is 123 (the same as the hash of the sent message), she knows the message hasn't lost data integrity. However, if the hash of the received message is something different, such as 456, she knows that the message she received is not the same as Homer's message. Data integrity is lost.

A variation in the hashes doesn't tell you what modified the message. It only tells you that the message has been modified. This lets you know that you shouldn't trust the integrity of the message.

You can use hashes with messages, such as emails, and any other type of data files. However, when you look at a fixed-length hash, you can't tell if it was created from a message, a file, or another data source.

Hashing techniques can also verify that integrity is maintained when files are downloaded or transferred. Some programs can automatically check hashes and determine if a file loses even a single bit during the download process. The program performing the download will detect it by comparing the source hash with the destination hash. If a program detects that the hashes are different, it knows that integrity has been lost and reports the problem to the user.

As another example, a website administrator can calculate and post the hash of a file on a website. Users can manually calculate the hash of the file after downloading it and compare the hash with the posted hash. If a virus infects a file on the web server, the hash of the infected file would be different from the hash of the original file (and the hash posted on the website). You can use freeware such as **md5sum.exe** to calculate MD5 hashes. If you want to see this in action, check out the Creating and Comparing Hashes Lab in the online exercises for this book at `https://getcertifiedgetahead.com/`.

> ### 📌 *Remember This!*
>
> Integrity verifies that data has not been modified. Loss of integrity can occur through unauthorized or unintended changes. Hashing algorithms, such as SHA, calculate hashes to verify integrity. A hash is simply an alphanumeric string created by applying a hashing algorithm to a file or message. You can then later run the same algorithm on the data and you should get the same hash value. By comparing the hashes, you can verify that there haven't been any changes (authorized or unauthorized) to the data. If the hashes are the same, the data is unchanged. If the hash has changed, the data has changed.

Increase Availability

Availability ensures that data and services are available when needed. For some organizations, this simply means that the data and services must be available between 8:00 a.m. and 5:00 p.m.,

Monday through Friday. For other organizations, this means they are expected to be available 24 hours a day, 7 days a week, 365 days a year.

Organizations commonly implement redundancy and fault-tolerant methods to ensure high levels of availability for key systems. Additionally, organizations ensure systems stay up to date with current patches to ensure that software bugs don't affect their availability.

★ Remember This!

Availability ensures that systems are up and operational when needed and often addresses single points of failure. You can increase availability by adding fault tolerance and redundancies, such as RAID, failover clusters, backups, and generators.

Redundancy and Fault Tolerance

Redundancy adds duplication to critical systems and provides **fault tolerance**. If a critical component has a fault, the redundancy's duplication allows the service to continue without interruption. In other words, a system with fault tolerance can suffer a fault, but it can tolerate it and continue to operate.

A common goal of fault tolerance and redundancy techniques is to remove each **single point of failure (SPOF)**. If a SPOF fails, the entire system can fail. For example, if a server has a single drive, the drive is a SPOF because its failure takes down the server.

Chapter 9, "Implementing Controls to Protect Assets," covers many fault tolerance and redundancy techniques in more depth. As an introduction, here are some common examples:

- **Disk redundancies.** Fault-tolerant disks, such as RAID-1 (mirroring), RAID-5 (striping with parity), and RAID-10 (striping with a mirror), allow a system to continue to operate even if a disk fails.
- **Server redundancies.** Failover clusters include redundant servers and ensure a service will continue to operate, even if a server fails. In a failover cluster, the service switches from the failed server in a cluster to a redundant or standby server in the same cluster.
- **Network redundancies.** Load balancing uses multiple servers to support a single service, such as a high-volume website. Network interface card (NIC) teaming can provide both redundancy support and increased bandwidth by putting two or more network cards in a single server.
- **Power redundancies.** Uninterruptible power supplies (UPSs) and power generators can provide power to key systems even if commercial power fails.

Scalability and Elasticity

Both scalability and elasticity contribute to high availability. ***Scalability*** means that you are able to increase the capacity of a system or service to meet new demand. For example, if you have a website that uses three web servers to run, one type of scalability would be adding additional servers to handle the work. Adding additional servers is also called ***horizontal scaling***.

Vertical scaling doesn't add more servers, but instead adds resources, such as memory or processing power, to individual servers. For example, a server may have 16 GB of random-access memory (RAM) installed. Administrators can scale the system up by manually adding an additional 16 GB of RAM, giving it 32 GB. However, there is typically a limit to scalability based on the system. For example, a server may only support 32 GB of RAM. Once it has 32 GB of RAM, you can no longer scale up the RAM.

Elasticity automates scalability by having the system add and remove resources as needed. For example, that web server may need three servers to operate right now, but might need four or five servers during periods of high demand. If that website is built with elasticity in mind, it would automatically add servers when they are needed and then remove those servers when they are no longer necessary. Think of a rubber band. Pull it, and it automatically stretches, but let it go, and it returns to its original size.

> ### 📌 *Remember This!*
>
> Redundancy and fault tolerance methods increase the availability of systems and data. Scalability refers to manually adding servers to a service or resources to a system to meet new demand. Elasticity refers to automatically adding or removing resources as needed.

Cloud resources typically have elasticity capabilities allowing them to automatically adapt to this increased and decreased demand. To consumers, the elasticity of cloud resources often appears to be unlimited.

Patching

Another method of ensuring systems stay available is by keeping them up-to-date with patches. Software bugs cause a wide range of problems, including security issues and random crashes. When software vendors discover the bugs, they develop and release code that patches or resolves these problems. Organizations commonly implement patch management programs to ensure that systems stay up-to-date with current patches. Chapter 5, "Securing Hosts and Data," covers patching and patch management in greater depth.

Understanding Resiliency

A current trend is to increase the resiliency of systems rather than seek the highest possible availability. This ensures that systems are reliable but without the high cost associated with highly available systems. As an example, it's possible to achieve 99.999 percent uptime (five nines) with systems. However, this requires eliminating every possible SPOF and adding multiple redundancies. These steps raise the total cost of ownership (TCO) significantly.

Resiliency methods help systems heal themselves or recover from faults with minimal downtime. They often use similar techniques that a highly available system uses. As an example, a system using resiliency methods may regularly perform and test full backups, have backup power sources (such as an uninterruptible power supply or generators), network interface card (NIC) teaming, or redundant disks. If power fails, or one of the NICs stops receiving traffic, or one of the disk drives fails, the system can quickly recover.

Also, resiliency methods expect components to retry failed processes. If it fails at first, it tries again. For example, imagine a web server is slower than expected for some reason or returns error messages. You may not know why it slowed down or replied with the error message. However, the system will take steps to recover, and if the web browser requests the page again, it will succeed. Some web browsers do this automatically. For example, if you lose Internet access and visit *google.com* with the Chrome browser, it fails. However, when you restore your Internet access, Chrome automatically recovers and shows the Google home page.

Network protocols have implemented this concept for a long time. When using Transmission Control Protocol (TCP), packets may fail to reach the destination. If that happens, TCP processes simply ask the source to resend it. We'll discuss TCP more in Chapter 3, "Exploring Network Technologies and Tools".

Resource Availability Versus Security Constraints

Organizations frequently need to balance resource availability with security constraints. Consider using encryption to maintain the confidentiality of data. If encryption makes data more secure, why wouldn't you just encrypt every piece of data you can find? The reason is that encryption consumes resources.

As an example, the above paragraph is about 265 characters. Here's what that same paragraph looks like when it is encrypted using the Advanced Encryption Standard (AES):

```
+JLHsaXgsGg3p0nh+NiqnAqsteINHI503/eE43LBfC7mMeXtePI1K5n+XfCL3p
D5dVSTdZtM64PgC9cot0DsllJzHqYsE0lCZp2i4eLplFr1Zk2Av7pi0Oc/yo7nQ
WialYV4LcRMA5eBXVHJbZgMgrJB5I9Z+uiM8zYIkmYLGPv4YRIAIt9BfPXvy8
L3iKtrIXZ0qhJM/Lx4T9sDBL8f2GEb0YilF4t+ex+FoP/ry0OrUgTeCGRoAyxbM
e+gxANRbPzBsSwlm83rTomUGcWZ40CPn+HTVMWxXWkJFNXZEBinElpuy06R
```

```
4jY8Dmq1KZv2VgMkQjgUTv5YIghU7IZggQz7QMfqcWi5/Kps6mEQZuNMnq8l3
316hxwUCBWAAm7gLiFqPNjm509mGYj4lb8xl3z9SdZOxOrL86Zgj7JaVzg=
```

When we encrypt the text, it goes from 265 characters to 430 characters. That's an increase of about 60 percent, which is typical with many encryption methods. If a company decides to encrypt all data, it will need approximately 60 percent more disk space to store it. Additionally, the act of encrypting and decrypting the data requires memory and processing power, slowing down applications.

Security experts might say the cost for additional resources is worth it, but executives looking to increase the company's value might not feel the same way. Executives have a responsibility to minimize costs without sacrificing security. They do this by looking for the best balance between resource costs and security needs.

Introducing Basic Risk Concepts

One of the basic goals of implementing IT security is to reduce risk. Because risk is so important and so many chapters refer to elements of risk, it's worth providing a short introduction here.

Risk is the possibility or likelihood of a threat exploiting a vulnerability resulting in a loss. A **threat** is any circumstance or event that has the potential to compromise confidentiality, integrity, or availability. A **vulnerability** is a weakness. It can be a weakness in the hardware, the software, the configuration, or even the users operating the system.

If a threat (such as an attacker) exploits a vulnerability, it can result in a security incident. A **security incident** is an adverse event or series of events that can negatively affect the confidentiality, integrity, or availability of an organization's information technology (IT) systems and data. This includes intentional attacks, malicious software (malware) infections, accidental data loss, and much more.

Threats can come from inside an organization, such as from a disgruntled employee (also known as a malicious insider). They can come from outside the organization, such as from an attacker anywhere in the world. Threats can be natural, such as hurricanes, tsunamis, or tornadoes, or human-made, such as malware written by a criminal. Threats can be intentional, such as from attackers, or accidental, such as from employee mistakes or system errors.

Reducing risk is also known as risk mitigation. **Risk mitigation** reduces the chances that a threat will exploit a vulnerability or the impact that the risk will have on the organization if it does occur. You reduce risks by implementing controls (also called countermeasures and safeguards), and many of the actions described throughout this book are different types of controls. You can't prevent most threats. For example, you can't stop a tornado or prevent a criminal from writing malware. However, you can reduce risk by reducing vulnerabilities to the threat or reducing the threat's impact.

For example, access controls ensure that only authorized personnel can access specific areas, systems, or data. If employees become disgruntled and want to cause harm, access controls reduce the amount of potential damage by reducing what they can access. If a natural disaster hits, business continuity and disaster recovery plans help reduce the impact. Similarly, antivirus software tries to intercept and block malware before it causes any harm.

> ### ✦ Remember This!
>
> Risk is the likelihood that a threat will exploit a vulnerability. Risk mitigation reduces the chances that a threat will exploit a vulnerability or reduces the risk's impact by implementing security controls.

Selecting Effective Security Controls

There are hundreds, perhaps thousands, of security controls that organizations can implement to reduce risk. The good news is that you don't need to be an expert on all the possible security controls to pass the CompTIA Security+ exam. However, you do need to have a basic understanding of control categories and control types.

Control categories describe how a control works. CompTIA lists the following control categories in the objectives:

- **Technical controls** use technology such as hardware, software, and firmware to reduce risk.
- **Managerial controls** are primarily administrative in function. They are typically documented in an organization's security policy and focus on managing risk.
- **Operational controls** help ensure that the day-to-day operations of an organization comply with the security policy. People implement them.
- **Physical controls** impact the physical world, such as locks on doors, fences, security guards, and other objects that you can physically touch.

Control types describe the goal that the control is trying to achieve. CompTIA lists the following control types in the objectives:

- **Preventive controls** attempt to prevent an incident from occurring.
- **Detective controls** attempt to detect incidents after they have occurred.
- **Corrective controls** attempt to restore normal operations after an incident occurs.
- **Deterrent controls** attempt to discourage individuals from causing an incident.
- **Compensating controls** are alternative controls used when a primary control is not feasible.
- **Directive controls** provide instruction to individuals on how they should handle security-related situations that arise.

> ### ✦ *Remember This!*
>
> You may find all this talk of categories and types a little confusing. Remember that every control you encounter will belong to at least one category and at least one type. For example, a firewall is a technical control because it uses technology to achieve its goals. It is also a preventive control because its goal is to stop unwanted traffic from entering the network, preventing an incident from occurring.

Control Categories

The control categories (technical, managerial, operational, and physical) describe how the control works. Technical controls use technology to achieve their goals. Managerial controls use administrative functions. Operational controls are implemented by operational staff. Physical controls use physical safeguards. Let's look at each of these categories.

Technical Controls

Technical controls use technology such as hardware, software, and firmware to reduce vulnerabilities. An administrator installs and configures a technical control, and the technical control then provides protection automatically. Throughout this book, you'll come across several examples of technical controls. The following list provides a few examples:

- **Encryption.** Encryption is a strong technical control used to protect the confidentiality of data. This includes data transferred over a network as well as data stored on devices like servers, desktop computers, and mobile devices.
- **Antivirus software.** Once installed, the antivirus software provides protection against malware infection. Chapter 6, "Comparing Threats, Vulnerabilities, and Common Attacks," covers malware and antivirus software in depth.
- **Intrusion detection systems (IDSs)** and **intrusion prevention systems (IPSs)**. IDSs and IPSs can monitor a network or host for intrusions and provide ongoing protection against various threats. Chapter 4, "Securing Your Network," covers different types of IDSs and IPSs.
- **Firewalls**. Network firewalls restrict network traffic going in and out of a network. Chapter 3, "Exploring Network Technologies and Tools," covers firewalls in depth.
- **Least privilege**. The least privilege principle specifies that individuals or processes are granted only the privileges they need to perform their assigned tasks or functions, but no more. Privileges are a combination of rights and permissions.

Managerial Controls

Managerial controls are primarily administrative in function and are typically documented in an organization's written security policy. These controls use planning and assessment methods to review the organization's ability to reduce and manage risk. Chapter 8, "Using Risk Management Tools," covers vulnerability assessments and penetration tests, which fall into this category. For example, two common managerial controls are:

- **Risk assessments**. These help organizations quantify and qualify risks within an organization so that team members can focus on the serious risks. For example, a quantitative risk assessment uses cost and asset values to quantify risks based on monetary values. A qualitative risk assessment uses judgments to categorize risks based on probability and impact.
- **Vulnerability assessments**. A vulnerability assessment attempts to discover current vulnerabilities. When necessary, additional controls are implemented to reduce the risk from these vulnerabilities.

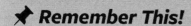

✦ Remember This!

Managerial controls are administrative in function and documented in security policies. Operational controls are implemented by people who perform the day-to-day operations to comply with an organization's overall security plan.

Operational Controls

Operational controls help ensure that the day-to-day operations of an organization comply with their overall security plan. These are controls that are primarily implemented and executed by people instead of systems. Operational controls include the following families:

- **Awareness and training**. The importance of training to reduce risks cannot be overstated. Training helps users maintain password security, follow a clean desk policy, understand threats such as phishing and malware, and much more.
- **Configuration management**. Configuration management often uses baselines to ensure that systems start in a secure, hardened state. Change management helps ensure that changes don't result in unintended configuration errors. Chapter 5 covers change and configuration management in more detail.
- **Media protection**. Media includes physical media such as USB flash drives, external and internal drives, and backup tapes. That media may contain sensitive information and must be protected against loss or theft. Media protection policies describe how you use backups and encryption to protect media containing sensitive information. These concepts are covered in more detail in Chapter 9.

NIST and SP 800 Documents

The National Institute of Standards and Technology (NIST) is a part of the U.S. Department of Commerce. They publish Special Publications (SPs) in the 800 series, which are important references for the security community.

Many IT security professionals use these documents to design secure systems and networks better. Additionally, many security-related certifications (beyond the CompTIA Security+ certification) also reference the SP 800 documents both directly and indirectly.

SP 800-53 "Security and Privacy Controls for Information Systems and Organizations," includes a wealth of information on security controls. It includes three chapters that discuss security controls, followed by three appendices. Appendix C is a security control catalog that provides details on hundreds of individual security controls divided into 20 different families.

It's worth noting that earlier versions of SP 800-53 attempted to identify every control as managerial, operational, or technical. However, many controls included characteristics from more than just one of these classifications and things got confusing. To simplify things, NIST removed these references.

If you're interested in pursuing other security-related certifications or making IT security a career, the SP 800 documents are well worth your time. You can download SP 800-53 and other NIST security standards at **https://csrc.nist.gov/publications/sp800**.

Physical Controls

Physical controls are any controls that you can physically touch. Some examples include bollards and other barricades, access control vestibules (sometimes called mantraps), lighting, signs, fences, sensors, and more. It's important to realize that you can identify physical controls as other control types. For example, physical controls such as locks are both preventive and deterrent controls. A locked door prevents personnel from entering a secure area and deters individuals from even trying if they know the door is locked.

You'll need to understand a variety of physical security controls for the Security+ exam. You'll find them covered in Chapter 9.

Remember This!

Security controls are categorized as managerial (documented in written policies), operational (performed in day-to-day operations), technical (implemented with technology), or physical (impacting the physical world).

 Remember This!

Technical controls use technology to reduce vulnerabilities. Some examples include encryption, antivirus software, IDSs, IPSs, firewalls, and the least privilege principle. Physical security and environmental controls include motion detectors and fire suppression systems.

Control Types

The control types (preventive, deterrent, detective, corrective, compensating, and directive) describe the goal the control hopes to achieve. For example, preventive controls try to prevent a security incident from occurring in the first place. Detective controls try to identify security incidents that have occurred, and corrective controls try to clean up the effects of an incident.

Preventive Controls

Ideally, an organization won't have any security incidents, which is the primary goal of preventive controls— to prevent security incidents. You may see preventive controls referred to as preventative controls, but both terms mean the same thing. Some examples include:

- **Hardening**. Hardening is the practice of making a system or application more secure than its default configuration. This uses a defense-in-depth strategy with layered security. It includes disabling unnecessary ports and services, implementing secure protocols, keeping a system patched, using strong passwords along with a robust password policy, and disabling default and unnecessary accounts. Chapter 5 covers these topics in more depth.
- **Training**. Ensuring that users are aware of security vulnerabilities and threats helps prevent incidents. Users who understand how social engineers operate are less likely to be tricked. For example, uneducated users might be tricked into giving a social engineer their passwords, but educated users will see through the tactics and keep their passwords secure.
- **Security guards**. Guards prevent and deter many attacks. For example, guards can prevent unauthorized access into secure areas of a building by first verifying user identities. Although a social engineer might attempt to fool a receptionist into letting him into a secure area, the presence of a guard will deter many social engineers from even trying these tactics.

- **Account disablement process**. An account disablement process ensures that user accounts are disabled when an employee leaves the organization. This prevents anyone, including ex-employees, from continuing to use these accounts. Chapter 2 covers account disablement in more depth.
- **Intrusion prevention system (IPS)**. An IPS can block malicious traffic before it reaches a network. This prevents security incidents. Chapter 4 covers IPSs in more depth.

★ Remember This!

Preventive controls attempt to prevent security incidents. Hardening systems modifies the basic configuration to increase security. Security guards can prevent unauthorized personnel from entering a secure area. Change management processes help prevent outages from configuration changes. An account disablement process ensures that accounts are disabled when a user leaves the organization.

Deterrent Controls

Deterrent controls attempt to discourage a threat. Some deterrent controls attempt to discourage potential attackers from attacking, and others attempt to discourage employees from violating a security policy.

You can often describe many deterrent controls as preventive controls. For example, imagine an organization hires a security guard to control access to a building's restricted area. This guard will deter most people from trying to sneak in simply by discouraging them from even trying. This deterrence prevents security incidents related to unauthorized access. The following list identifies some physical security controls used to deter threats:

- **Warning signs**. Signs around the outside of a facility may warn potential intruders that the facility is monitored. The only purpose of these signs is to deter an intruder from even trying to break into the facility.
- **Login banners**. Login banners on computer systems are the digital version of warning signs. Before a user enters a username and password, they see a message warning them that attempting to access the system without permission is a crime.

Detective Controls

Although preventive and deterrent controls attempt to prevent security incidents, some incidents will still occur. Detective controls attempt to detect when vulnerabilities have been exploited, resulting in a security incident. The important point is that detective controls discover the event after it has occurred. Some examples of detective controls are:

- **Log monitoring.** Several different logs record details of activity on systems and networks. For example, firewall logs record details of all traffic that the firewall blocked. By monitoring these logs, it's possible to detect incidents. Some automated methods of log monitoring automatically detect potential incidents and report them right after they've occurred.
- **Security information and event management (SIEM) systems.** In addition to monitoring logs to detect any single incident, you can also use SIEMs to detect trends and raise alerts in real time. By analyzing past alerts, you can identify trends, such as an increase of attacks on a specific system.
- **Security audit.** Security audits can examine the security posture of an organization. For example, an account audit can determine if personnel and technical policies are implementing account policies correctly.
- **Video surveillance.** A closed-circuit television (CCTV) system can record activity and detect events that have occurred. It's worth noting that video surveillance can also be used as a deterrent control.
- **Motion detection.** Many alarm systems can detect motion from potential intruders and raise alarms.
- **Intrusion detection system (IDS).** An IDS can detect malicious traffic after it enters a network. It typically raises an alarm to notify IT personnel of a potential attack.

Corrective Controls

Corrective controls attempt to reverse the impact of an incident or problem after it has occurred. Their purpose is to get things back to normal as quickly as possible after an incident takes place. They restore the confidentiality, integrity, and/or availability that was affected by the incident.

Some examples of corrective controls are:

- **Backups and system recovery.** Backups ensure that personnel can recover data if it is lost or corrupted. Similarly, system recovery procedures ensure administrators can recover a system after a failure. Chapter 9 covers backups and disaster recovery plans in more depth.
- **Incident handling processes.** Incident handling processes define steps to take in response to security incidents. This typically starts with an incident response policy and an incident response plan. Chapter 11, "Implementing Policies to Mitigate Risks," covers incident handling in more depth.

Compensating Controls

Compensating controls are alternative controls used instead of a primary control. For example, an organization might require employees to use smart cards when authenticating to a system. However, it might take time for new employees to receive their smart card. To allow new employees to access the network and still maintain a high level of security, the organization might choose to implement a Time-based One-Time Password (TOTP) as a compensating control. The compensating control still provides a strong authentication solution.

Directive Controls

Directive controls are designed to provide instruction to individuals on how they should handle security-related situations that arise. These are generally written documents that provide instructions rather than technical mechanisms that enforce a goal.

- **Policies, standards, procedures, and guidelines**. Security professionals use many different types of documents to direct actions. Policies provide high-level goal statements for the organization. Standards describe how to configure systems, applications, and security controls properly. Procedures offer step-by-step guidance on achieving a goal. Guidelines offer advice on achieving goals. All these topics are discussed in Chapter 11.

- **Change management**. Change management ensures that changes don't result in unintended outages. In other words, instead of administrators making changes whenever they'd like, they submit the change to a change management process. Notice that change management is an operational control which attempts to prevent incidents. In other words, it's both an operational and directive control.

Combining Control Categories and Types

It's important to realize that the control categories and control types are not mutually exclusive. In other words, you can describe most controls using more than one category and more than one type.

As an example, encryption is a preventive technical control. It helps prevent the loss of data confidentiality, so it is a preventive control. You implement it with technology, so it is a technical control. If you understand control categories, you shouldn't have any problems picking out the correct answers on the exam, even if CompTIA combines them in a question, such as a preventive technical control.

Similarly, a fire suppression system is a physical technical control. It is a physical security control because you can touch it. However, it's also a technical control because it uses technology to detect, suppress, or extinguish fires.

Logging and Monitoring

The CompTIA Security+ exam expects test takers to look at and interpret log entries. For administrators who work with logs every day, this becomes second nature. However, some test takers don't look at logs every day. For them, log entries can sometimes look like a foreign language. If you're the latter, please check out the Appendix, "Log Basics," to help you gain some insight into common elements in log entries and how to interpret them. The appendices for this book are available at **https://getcertifiedgetahead.com/**.

Log entries help administrators and security investigators determine what happened, when, where, and who or what did it. When examining entries from multiple logs, personnel create an audit trail that identifies all the events preceding a security incident. Logging is an important part of an organization's security monitoring strategy. The following sections discuss many log concepts that you should understand before test day.

Operating System/Endpoint Logs

Every operating system provides the ability to generate and store log entries. As you prepare for the Security+ exam, you should be familiar with the logging capabilities of Windows and Linux systems. These logs provide important information about events that occur on endpoint systems.

Windows Logs

Windows systems have several common logs that record what happened on a Windows computer system. These logs are viewable using the Windows Event Viewer. The primary Windows logs are:

- **Security log.** The Security log functions as a security log, an audit log, and an access log. It records auditable events such as successes or failures. A success indicates an audited event completed successfully, such as a user logging on or successfully deleting a file. A failure means that a user tried to perform an action but failed, such as failing to log on or attempting to delete a file but receiving a permission error instead. Windows enables some auditing by default, but administrators can add additional auditing.
- **System log.** The operating system uses the System log to record events related to the functioning of the operating system. This can include when the system starts up and shuts down, information on services starting and stopping, drivers loading or failing, or any other system component event deemed important by the system developers.
- **Application log.** The Application log records events sent to it by applications or programs running on the system. Any application has the capability of writing events in the Application log. This includes warnings, errors, and routine messages.

Figure 1.2 shows an example of Event Viewer in action. Notice that the Windows Logs folder on the left side of the figure shows the Application, Security, and System logs. In this figure, Event Viewer is displaying records from the Security log.

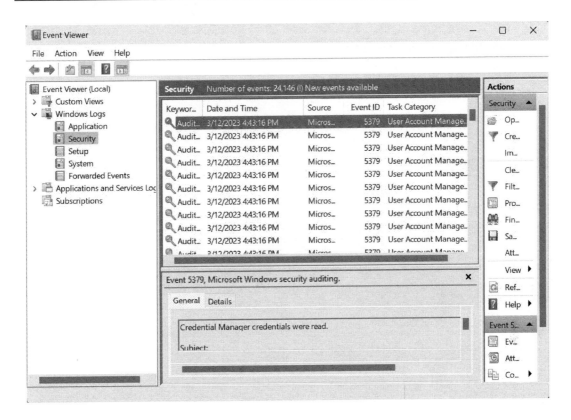

Figure 1.2: Windows Event Viewer

If a system is attacked, you may be able to learn details of the attack by reviewing the operating system logs. Depending on the attack type, any operating system logs may be useful.

Linux Logs

Linux systems are commonly used in modern organizations and you should also be familiar with their logging abilities. Linux systems store logs in the /var/log/ directory. You can view logs using the system log viewer on Linux systems or by using the **cat** command from the terminal. As an example, you can view the authentication log (*auth.log*) with the following command:

```
cat /var/log/auth.log
```

Some common Linux logs are shown in the following list:

- ***/var/log/syslog*** and/or ***/var/log/messages*** vary somewhat between different versions of the Linux operating system. They contain a wide variety of general system messages. This includes messages logged during startup, messages related to mail, the kernel, and other system activities.
- ***/var/log/secure*** This log contains information related to the authentication and authorization of user sessions. Figure 1.3 shows an example of the text-based /var/log/secure file.

The entries in the figure are from invalid users attempting (and failing) to connect to a server using an SSH connection.

```
Mar 12 04:56:01 ip-172-30-0-80 sshd[10289]: Invalid user kingbase from 100.25.138.37 port 37540
Mar 12 04:56:01 ip-172-30-0-80 sshd[10289]: input_userauth_request: invalid user kingbase [preauth]
Mar 12 04:56:01 ip-172-30-0-80 sshd[10289]: Connection closed by 100.25.138.37 port 37540 [preauth]
Mar 12 04:56:01 ip-172-30-0-80 sshd[10306]: Invalid user ftpuser from 100.25.138.37 port 37234
Mar 12 04:56:01 ip-172-30-0-80 sshd[10306]: input_userauth_request: invalid user ftpuser [preauth]
Mar 12 04:56:01 ip-172-30-0-80 sshd[10306]: Connection closed by 100.25.138.37 port 37234 [preauth]
Mar 12 04:56:01 ip-172-30-0-80 sshd[10292]: Invalid user ubuntu from 100.25.138.37 port 37522
Mar 12 04:56:01 ip-172-30-0-80 sshd[10292]: input_userauth_request: invalid user ubuntu [preauth]
Mar 12 04:56:01 ip-172-30-0-80 sshd[10299]: Invalid user odoo from 100.25.138.37 port 37476
Mar 12 04:56:01 ip-172-30-0-80 sshd[10292]: Connection closed by 100.25.138.37 port 37522 [preauth]
Mar 12 04:56:01 ip-172-30-0-80 sshd[10302]: Invalid user abc from 100.25.138.37 port 37382
Mar 12 04:56:01 ip-172-30-0-80 sshd[10299]: input_userauth_request: invalid user odoo [preauth]
Mar 12 04:56:01 ip-172-30-0-80 sshd[10308]: Invalid user linaro from 100.25.138.37 port 37538
Mar 12 04:56:01 ip-172-30-0-80 sshd[10302]: input_userauth_request: invalid user abc [preauth]
Mar 12 04:56:01 ip-172-30-0-80 sshd[10302]: Connection closed by 100.25.138.37 port 37382 [preauth]
Mar 12 04:56:01 ip-172-30-0-80 sshd[10308]: input_userauth_request: invalid user linaro [preauth]
Mar 12 04:56:01 ip-172-30-0-80 sshd[10303]: Connection closed by 100.25.138.37 port 37410 [preauth]
```

Figure 1.3: Example of entries from /var/log/secure

Network Logs

Network logs record traffic on the network. These logs are on a variety of devices such as routers, firewalls, web servers, and network intrusion detection/prevention systems. You can typically manipulate these devices to log specific information, such as logging all traffic that the device passes, all traffic that the device blocks, or both. These logs are useful when troubleshooting connectivity issues and when identifying potential intrusions or attacks.

Firewall Logs

Firewalls serve as the border guards of the network. They decide what traffic is allowed to enter and leave the network and what traffic will be blocked. You'll learn more about how firewalls work in Chapter 3. Firewalls are also an excellent source of log information because they can track every attempt to access the network and create detailed logs recording that information.

IDS/IPS Logs

Intrusion detection systems (IDS) and intrusion prevention systems (IPS) monitor networks for malicious activity. IDS simply alert administrators to possible intrusions while IPS go further and try to block suspicious content. Because of the important security roles that they play, IDS and IPS systems are also excellent sources of security log data.

Packet Captures

Protocol analyzers (sometimes called sniffers) capture network traffic allowing administrators to view and analyze individual packets. Investigators looking into an active security incident may use a packet capture tool like Wireshark to capture network traffic related to the incident that they can later examine in careful detail to reconstruct what happened.

Application Logs

While some applications store log information in system logs, such as the Windows Application log, many applications also manage their own log files.

For example, web servers typically log requests to the web server for pages. These often follow the Common Log format standardized by the World Wide Web Consortium (W3C). A typical entry includes the following data:

- **host:** The IP address or hostname of the client requesting the page.
- **user-identifier:** The name of the user requesting the page (if known)
- **authuser:** The user's logon name requested in the page, if the user logged on.
- **date:** The date and time of the request.
- **request:** The actual request line sent by the client.
- **status:** The HTTP status code returned to the client
- **bytes:** The byte length of the reply.

Metadata

Metadata is data that provides information about other data. Many applications store metadata about files and messages that can be very helpful to security investigators. For example, Figure 1.4 shows a portion of the metadata from an email message. Every email message contains this detailed information about how the email was routed, but it is normally hidden from the user's view.

```
Delivered-To: joe@certificationexperts.net
Received: by 2002:ab3:e7cf:0:b0:4d2:f705:d4f7 with SMTP id f15csp587565qnq;
        Wed, 8 Mar 2023 13:57:25 -0800 (PST)
Return-Path: <docusign@esign.docusign.com>
Received: from mail07.esign.docusign.com (mail07.esign.docusign.com.
[209.17.50.1])
        by mx.google.com with ESMTPS id k30-
20020a0cb25e000000b0056eb35b2b4csi12430053qve.151.2023.03.08.13.57.25
        for <joe@certificationexperts.net>
        (version=TLS1_3 cipher=TLS_AES_256_GCM_SHA384 bits=256/256);
        Wed, 08 Mar 2023 13:57:25 -0800 (PST)
Received: from P01SNJ114 (10.32.140.5) by mail07.esign.docusign.com id
h142c832bv07 for <joe@certificationexperts.net>; Wed, 8 Mar 2023 16:57:24 -0500
(envelope-from <docusign@esign.docusign.com>)
Message-ID: <b0d0ff4493f847a5b1abb5c4df2df276@566810826>
From: DocuSign <docusign@docusign.com>
Reply-To: DocuSign <emailreply@docusign.com>
To: joe@certificationexperts.net
Subject: Wondering where to begin, Joe? We have a few ideas
Date: Wed, 08 Mar 2023 16:57:24 -0500
MIME-Version: 1.0
Content-Type: multipart/alternative; boundary="=-CkgvAWisDAdhsfQ931gZOA=="
```

Figure 1.4: Metadata from an email message

Similarly, image files contain metadata that provides information about the camera that took the photo, the geographic location, date, time, and other details. Figure 1.5 shows an example of the metadata from a photograph.

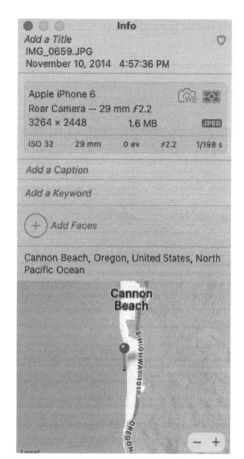

Figure 1.5: Metadata from a photograph

Centralized Logging and Monitoring

It can be quite challenging to routinely check the logs on all the systems, applications, and infrastructure devices within a network. A standard solution is to use a centralized system to collect log entries. Let's examine the technologies and procedures that support this work.

SIEM Systems

A **security information and event management (SIEM)** system provides a centralized solution for collecting, analyzing, and managing data from systems, applications, and infrastructure devices. It combines the services of security event management (SEM) and security information management (SIM) solutions. A SEM provides real-time monitoring, analysis, and notification of security events, such as suspected security incidents. A SIM provides long-term storage of data, along with methods of analyzing the data looking for trends or creating reports needed to verify compliance with laws or regulations.

SIEM systems are very useful in large enterprises that have massive amounts of data and activity to monitor. Consider an organization with over 1,000 servers. When an incident occurs on just one of those servers, administrators need to know about it as quickly as possible. A benefit is that SIEM systems use scripts to automate the monitoring and reporting.

Vendors sell SIEMs as applications that can be installed on centralized systems and as dedicated hardware appliances. However, no matter how a vendor bundles it, it will typically have common capabilities. The following list outlines some additional capabilities shared by most SIEMs:

- **Log collectors.** The SIEM collects log data from devices throughout the network and stores these logs in a searchable database.
- **Data inputs.** Log entries come from various sources, such as firewalls, routers, network intrusion detection, and prevention systems. They can also come from any system or application an organization wants to monitor, such as web servers, proxy servers, and database servers.

- **Log aggregation.** Aggregation refers to combining several dissimilar items into a single similar format. The SIEM system collects data from multiple systems, and these systems typically format log entries differently. However, the SIEM system can aggregate the data and store it so it is easy to analyze and search.

- **Correlation engine.** A correlation engine is a software component used to collect and analyze event log data from various systems within the network. It typically aggregates the data looking for common attributes. It then uses advanced analytic tools to detect patterns of potential security events and raises alerts. System administrators can then investigate the alert.

- **Automated reports.** Most SIEM systems include multiple built-in reports. These are typically grouped in different categories, such as network traffic event monitoring, device events (such as events on border firewalls), threat events, logon/logoff events, compliance with specific laws, and more. Additionally, security professionals can create their own reports by specifying filters.

- **User behavior analysis.** User behavior analysis (UBA) focuses on what users are doing, such as application and network activity. Some UBA processes watch critical files looking for who accessed them, what they did, and how frequently they access these files. UBA typically looks for abnormal patterns of activity that may indicate malicious intent.

- **Security alerts.** A SIEM typically comes with predefined alerts, which can provide continuous monitoring of systems and provide notifications of suspicious events. For example, if it detects a port scan on a server, it might send an email to an administrator group or display the alert on a heads-up display. SIEMs also include the ability to create new alerts.

- **Automated triggers.** Triggers cause an action in response to a predefined number of repeated events. As an example, imagine a trigger for failed logins is set at five. If an attacker repeatedly tries to log on to a server using Secure Shell (SSH), the server's log will show the failed login attempts. When the SIEM detects more than five failed SSH logins, it can change the environment and stop the attack. It might modify a firewall to block these SSH login attempts or send a script to the server to temporarily disable SSH. A SIEM includes the ability to modify predefined triggers and create new ones.

- **Time synchronization.** All servers sending data to the SIEM should be synchronized with the same time. This becomes especially important when investigating an incident so that security investigators know when events occurred. Additionally, large organizations can have locations in different time zones. Each of these locations might have servers sending data to a single centralized SIEM. If the server logs use their local time, the SIEM needs to ensure that it compensates for the time offset. The Network Time Protocol (NTP) provides a way to keep the system clocks of all devices in an organization synchronized.

- **Archiving.** SIEMs handle massive amounts of information and can't keep it all on active storage. That would be too expensive. Instead, they provide the ability to move older logs offline to cheaper storage where they are not immediately accessible but can be restored if needed later.

> ### ★ Alert Tuning
>
> A challenge with triggers and alerts is tuning the sensitivity levels to limit false positives while avoiding false negatives. As an example, imagine Homer enters an incorrect password when logging on. This isn't an attack but an honest error. If the SIEM system raises an alert, it would be a false positive. Alternatively, imagine a system is under attack and logs 100 failed login tries in about five minutes. If the SIEM system doesn't raise an alert, it is a false negative. When tuning the sensitivity level for failed logins, administrators choose a number between 1 and 100.

SIEM Dashboards

Dashboards in automobiles provide drivers with a view of what they need to know while driving. Similarly, a **SIEM dashboard** gives administrators views of meaningful activity. These views vary from system to system and are usually customizable. They provide continuous monitoring and real-time reporting. In a large network operations center (NOC), the SIEM might display alerts on a large heads-up display. In a smaller network, a single computer may show the dashboard. Some common elements of a SIEM dashboard are listed below:

- **Sensors**. Many SIEM systems use agents placed on systems throughout a network. These collect logs from devices and send these logs to the SIEM system. Dashboards can display data received from these agents.
- **Alerts**. After setting triggers in a SIEM system, it sends out alerts when the event occurs. These alerts may trigger specific responses (such as sending an email to a group), but they are also displayed in the dashboard.
- **Correlation**. As log entries arrive at the SIEM system, it correlates and analyzes the data. Administrators can configure the dashboard to display this data in multiple ways depending on their needs.
- **Trends**. As the SIEM system is analyzing the data, it can identify trends. For example, if there is suddenly a high rate of failed logins, it can identify the trend and raise an alert. Many SIEM systems display trends in graphs allowing users to digest a lot of information in a single picture.

Syslog

The **syslog** protocol specifies a general log entry format and the details on how to transport log entries. You can deploy a centralized syslog server to collect syslog entries from a variety of devices in the network. In fact, most SIEM systems use the syslog format and contain syslog servers that collect log entries from other devices on the network.

Any systems sending syslog messages are ***originators***. They send syslog log entries to a ***collector*** (a syslog server). The collector can receive messages from external devices or services and applications on the same system.

It's important to note that the syslog protocol only defines how to format the syslog messages and send them to a collector. It doesn't define how the syslog server handles these log entries.

Chapter 1 Exam Topic Review

When preparing for the exam, make sure you understand these key concepts covered in this chapter.

Understanding Core Security Goals

- Confidentiality ensures that data is only viewable by authorized users. Encryption is the best choice to provide confidentiality. Access controls also protect the confidentiality of data.
- Integrity provides assurances that data has not been modified, tampered with, or corrupted through unauthorized or unintended changes. Data can be a message, a file, or data within a database. Hashing is a common method of ensuring integrity.
- Availability ensures that data and services are available when needed. A common goal is to remove single points of failure. Fault tolerance methods and redundancies are commonly added to support high availability.
- Systems scale up by adding additional hardware resources such as memory, processing power, bandwidth capability, and/or drive space. Systems scale out by adding additional nodes or servers. They can scale down or scale in by removing these resources.
- Scalability is the ability of a system to handle increased workload either by scaling up or by scaling out. This is done manually by administrators.
- Elasticity is the ability of a system to handle the increased workload by dynamically adding or removing resources as the need arises. Cloud resources typically have elasticity capabilities allowing them to adapt to this increased and decreased demand automatically.
- Resiliency methods help systems heal themselves or recover from faults with minimal downtime.
- Organizations balance resource availability with security constraints. Security professionals may want to apply security controls everywhere without considering the cost. However, executives have a responsibility to minimize costs without sacrificing security.

Introducing Basic Risk Concepts

- Risk is the possibility of a threat exploiting a vulnerability and resulting in a loss.
- A threat is any circumstance or event that has the potential to compromise confidentiality, integrity, or availability.

- A vulnerability is a weakness. It can be a weakness in the hardware, software, configuration, or users operating the system.

- Risk mitigation reduces risk by reducing the chances that a threat will exploit a vulnerability or reduce the risk's impact.

- Security controls reduce risks. For example, antivirus software is a security control that reduces the risk of virus infection. One of the core jobs of security professionals is selecting an effective set of security controls to manage different types of risk.

Understanding Security Controls

- The four security control categories are managerial, operational, technical, and physical.

- Managerial controls are primarily administrative and include items such as risk and vulnerability assessments.

- Operational controls are focused on the day-to-day operations of an organization. They help ensure an organization is complying with its overall security plan. Some examples include security awareness and training, configuration management, and change management.

- Technical controls use technology to reduce vulnerabilities. Encryption, antivirus software, IDSs, firewalls, and the principle of least privilege are technical controls.

- Physical controls are any controls that you can physically touch. Some examples are bollards and other barricades, access control vestibules (sometimes called mantraps), lighting, fences, and signs.

- The six control types are preventive, deterrent, detective, corrective, compensating, and directive.

- Preventive controls attempt to prevent security incidents. Examples include system hardening, user training, guards, change management, and account disablement processes.

- Detective controls attempt to detect when a vulnerability has been exploited. Examples include log monitoring, security information and event management (SIEM) systems, trend analysis, video surveillance systems, and motion detection systems.

- Deterrent controls attempt to prevent incidents by discouraging threats. Examples include locks and guards. Note that these can also be described as preventive controls. The primary difference is that they try to discourage people from trying to exploit a weakness.

- Corrective controls attempt to reverse the impact of an incident or problem after it has occurred. Examples include backups, system recovery plans, and incident handling processes.

- Compensating controls are alternative controls used when it isn't feasible or possible to use the primary control.

- Directive controls provide instruction to individuals on how they should handle security-related situations that arise.

Understanding Logs

- Windows includes several logs that you can view with the Windows Event Viewer. The Security log functions as a security log, an audit log, and an access log. Windows records events related to the operating system in the System log. Some applications record events in the Application log.
- Linux systems store log information in text files contained in the **/var/log** directory. The **/var/log/syslog** and/or **/var/log/messages** files contain general system messages. The **/var/log/secure** file records authentication and authorization events.
- Network logs are important sources of information about network activity. Common sources of network logs include firewalls, intrusion detection systems (IDS), intrusion prevention systems (IPS), and packet captures.
- Many applications store log records in operating system log files, while others maintain their own logs. Web servers commonly store records of every request that they receive and process.
- Some applications track and store metadata about the data that they process. Common examples of metadata include email headers and image metadata.
- Security information and event management (SIEM) systems provide a centralized solution for collecting, analyzing, and managing data from multiple sources.
- The syslog protocol specifies a log entry format and the details on how to transport log entries. You can deploy a centralized syslog server to collect syslog entries from a variety of devices in the network.

Chapter 1 Practice Questions

1. Management within your organization has defined a use case to support the confidentiality of data stored in a database. Which of the following solutions will BEST meet this need?

   A. Hashing
   B. Disk redundancies
   C. Encryption
   D. Patching

2. Moe manages network devices in his store and maintains copies of the configuration files for all the managed routers and switches. On a weekly basis, he creates hashes for these files and compares them with hashes he created on the same files the previous week. Which of the following use cases is he MOST likely supporting?

   A. Supporting confidentiality
   B. Supporting integrity
   C. Supporting encryption
   D. Supporting availability

3. Which of the following is a cryptographic algorithm that will create a fixed-length output from a data file but cannot be used to re-create the original data file?

    A. MD5
    B. AES
    C. IDS
    D. SIEM

4. Your organization hosts an e-commerce web server selling digital products. The server randomly experiences a high volume of sales and usage, which causes spikes in resource usage. These spikes occasionally take the server down. Which of the following would be the BEST way to prevent these outages?

    A. Elasticity
    B. Scalability
    C. Normalization
    D. Stored procedures

5. An administrator recently installed an IDS to help reduce the impact of security incidents. Which of the following BEST identifies the control type of an IDS?

    A. Preventive
    B. Physical
    C. Deterrent
    D. Detective

6. Maggie works in the security section of the IT department. Her primary responsibilities are to monitor security logs, analyze trends reported by the SIEM, and validate alerts. Which of the following choices BEST identifies the primary security control she's implementing?

    A. Compensating control
    B. Preventive control
    C. Detective control
    D. Corrective control

7. A server in your network's DMZ was recently attacked. The firewall logs show that the server was attacked from many different external IP addresses. It received an overwhelming number of requests from those addresses that caused the website hosted on the server to fail. What security goal was most directly affected by this attack?

    A. Integrity
    B. Non-repudiation
    C. Confidentiality
    D. Availability

8. You are in the process of logging into a service hosted by your organization. You entered your username and now you are being asked to complete a fingerprint scan. What element of access control is taking place when you scan your fingerprint?

    A. Authentication
    B. Authorization
    C. Availability
    D. Identification

9. Which one of the following technologies is generally NOT considered a fault tolerance or redundancy control?

    A. UPS
    B. SIEM
    C. RAID
    D. NIC teaming

10. Kate's manager asked her to organize a new process for conducting periodic vulnerability assessments of her organization's infrastructure. She is working to create a standard operating procedure for this scanning. What category BEST describes the control is she creating?

    A. Technical
    B. Detective
    C. Physical
    D. Managerial

11. Lisa is logging into a system and, before typing in her username and password, sees the message below:

    This is a U.S. Government computer system, which may be accessed and used only for authorized Government business by authorized personnel. Unauthorized access or use of this computer system may subject violators to criminal, civil, and/or administrative action.

    What type of control is Lisa experiencing?

    A. Detective
    B. Compensating
    C. Deterrent
    D. Corrective

12. You are investigating an active security incident and you want to view the contents of network traffic that passed between two systems. What data source would BEST provide this information?

    A. Operating system log
    B. Application log
    C. Firewall log
    D. Packet capture

13. Moe is overwhelmed by the number of log records generated by the many different security systems in his organization and would like to use a technology that aggregates those records in a single location and correlates them. What technology would best meet his needs?

    A. Syslog
    B. SIEM
    C. IPS
    D. Firewall

14. Maggie is reviewing log entries from many different systems and notices that the clocks on those systems are not synchronized, making it difficult to correlate the log entries. What protocol can she use to synchronize the system clocks?

    A. NTP
    B. FTP
    C. SFTP
    D. HTTPS

15. Which of the following describes the proper format of log entries for Linux systems?

    A. Event Viewer
    B. logger
    C. SIEM
    D. Syslog

Chapter 1

Practice Question Answers

1. **C** is correct. Encryption is the best choice to provide confidentiality of any type of information, including data stored in a database. Hashing supports a use case of supporting integrity. Disk redundancies provide resilience and increase availability. Patching systems increases availability and reliability.

2. **B** is correct. He is most likely using a use case of supporting integrity. By verifying that the hashes are the same on the configuration files, he is verifying that the files have not changed. Confidentiality is enforced with encryption, access controls, and steganography. Encryption is a method of enforcing confidentiality, and it doesn't use hashes. Availability ensures systems are up and operational when needed.

3. **A** is correct. Message Digest 5 (MD5) is a hashing algorithm that creates a fixed-length, irreversible output. Hashing algorithms cannot re-create the original data file from just the hash. Advanced Encryption Standard (AES) is an encryption algorithm, and you can re-create the original data file by decrypting it. An intrusion detection system (IDS) is not a cryptographic algorithm but is a detective control. A security information and event management (SIEM) system provides centralized logging.

4. **A** is correct. Elasticity is the best choice because it allows the server to dynamically scale as needed in response to changes in demand. Scalability isn't the best answer because it is done manually; in this case, the high resource usage is random and manually adding resources can't respond to the random spikes quickly enough. Normalization refers to organizing tables and columns in a database to reduce redundant data and improve overall database performance. Stored procedures are a group of SQL statements that execute as a whole and help prevent SQL injection attacks.

5. **D** is correct. An intrusion detection system (IDS) is a detective control. It can detect malicious traffic after it enters a network. A preventive control, such as an intrusion prevention system (IPS), tries to prevent malicious traffic from entering the network. An IDS uses technology and is not a physical control. Deterrent controls attempt to

discourage a threat, but attackers wouldn't know if a system had an IDS, so the IDS can't deter attacks.

6.   **C** is correct. Monitoring security logs, analyzing trend reports from a security information and event management (SIEM), and validating alerts from a SIEM are detective controls. Detective controls try to detect security incidents after they happened. A compensating control is an alternative control used when a primary security control is not feasible or is not yet deployed. Preventive controls attempt to prevent incidents, but the scenario doesn't specifically describe any preventive controls. A corrective control attempts to reverse the impact of a security incident after it has happened.

7.   **D** is correct. This attack disrupted the ability of legitimate users to access the website hosted on the server, which is an attack against the availability of that website. The goal of confidentiality is to prevent unauthorized access to information. The goal of integrity is to prevent unauthorized changes. The goal of non-repudiation (which you will learn about in Chapter 10) is to prevent someone from denying that they were the source of a message. The goals of confidentiality, integrity, and non-repudiation were not affected by this attack.

8.   **A** is correct. The three steps of the access control process are identification, authentication, and authorization. You already completed the identification step when you entered your username. You are scanning your fingerprint to prove your claim of identity, which is the authentication step. Authorization occurs when the system decides what you are allowed to access after completing the authentication process.

9.   **B** is correct. A security information and event management (SIEM) system is designed to improve the organization's ability to monitor and manage security issues. It does not generally provide redundancy or fault tolerance. Uninterruptible power supplies (UPS) provide backup power when commercial power briefly fails, offering fault tolerance for power. Redundant arrays of inexpensive disks (RAID) allow a single disk to fail without losing data, offering redundancy and fault tolerance for storage. NIC teaming allows the use of multiple network interface cards (NICs) so that a server may remain connected to the network even if one of those cards fails, providing network redundancy.

10. **D** is correct. This question is a little tricky because there are several possible correct answers. You are being asked to choose the BEST answer. Pay careful attention when you see a word like "best" in a question because it is a clue that you need to think very carefully about each answer choice. Vulnerability assessments are an assessment method used to reduce risk and are an example of a managerial control. You could also argue that since they use vulnerability scanners, they are also an example of a technical control. The clues that managerial is the correct answer here are that there

is no mention of the technology being used to complete the assessments and there is a focus on policy and procedure. Also, you should note that a vulnerability assessment is detective, but detective is a control *type* and the question is asking about the control *category*.

11. **C** is correct. The purpose of a warning banner such as the one shown in this question is to make an intruder less likely to attempt an attack. That is the goal of a deterrent control. Detective controls are designed to identify attacks and a warning banner does not do that. Corrective controls attempt to reverse the impact of an incident or problem after it has occurred. A warning banner does not correct an incident. Compensating controls are alternative controls used instead of a primary control. There is no indication in this question that the warning banner is being used in place of some other control.

12. **D** is correct. Investigators looking into an active security incident may use a packet capture tool like Wireshark to capture network traffic related to the incident that they can later examine in careful detail to reconstruct what happened. Firewall logs may contain records of the systems that communicated with each other, but they would not normally contain the content of that communication. Operating system and application logs are not an ideal source of this type of information because they only pertain to one computer or application and would not have access to all contents of network traffic.

13. **B** is correct. A security information and event management (SIEM) solution is designed to aggregate and correlate log entries. Syslog servers also perform aggregation of log entries because they are a centralized collection point for logs, but they do not also perform the correlation that is typical of a SIEM. Intrusion prevention systems (IPS) and firewalls are sources of log entries rather than aggregators of those entries.

14. **A** is correct. The Network Time Protocol (NTP) is used to synchronize system clocks with a centralized time source. The File Transfer Protocol (FTP) and Secure File Transfer Protocol (SFTP) are used to transfer files and not to synchronize clocks. The Hypertext Transfer Protocol Secure (HTTPS) is used to transfer web pages and not to synchronize system clocks.

15. **D** is correct. The syslog protocol (defined in RFC 5424) identifies the format of Linux log entries and describes how to transport these log entries. Note that syslog is also the name of a log on Linux systems. The logger command is used to add entries into the syslog file but it doesn't describe the format. A security information and event management (SIEM) system collects, aggregates, and correlates logs from multiple sources. Event Viewer is a log viewing utility on Windows systems.

Chapter 2

Understanding Identity and Access Management

CompTIA Security+ objectives covered in this chapter:

1.2 Summarize fundamental security concepts.

- Authentication, authorization, and accounting (AAA) (Authenticating people, Authenticating systems, Authorization models)

2.4 Given a scenario, analyze indicators of malicious activity.

- Indicators (Account lockout, Concurrent session usage, Blocked content, Impossible travel, Resource consumption, Resource inaccessibility, Out-of-cycle logging, Published/documented, Missing logs)

2.5 Explain the purpose of mitigation techniques used to secure the enterprise.

- Access control (Access control list (ACL), Permissions)

4.5 Given a scenario, modify enterprise capabilities to enhance security.

- Operating system security (SELinux)

4.6 Given a scenario, implement and maintain identity and access management.

- Provisioning/de-provisioning user accounts
- Permission assignments and implications
- Identity proofing
- Federation
- Single sign-on (SSO) (Open authorization (OAuth), Security Assertions Markup Language (SAML))
- Interoperability
- Attestation
- Access controls (Mandatory, Discretionary, Role-based, Rule-based, Attribute-based, Time-of-day restrictions, Least privilege)

- Multifactor authentication (Implementations, Biometrics, Hard/soft authentication tokens, Security keys, Factors, Something you know, Something you have, Something you are, Somewhere you are)
- Password concepts (Password best practices, Length, Complexity, Reuse, Expiration, Age, Password Managers, Passwordless)
- Privileged access management tools (Just-in-time permissions, Password vaulting, Temporal accounts)

Identity and access management includes many important concepts that are tested on the CompTIA Security+ exam. Users claim an identity with a username and prove their identity by authenticating (such as with a password). They are then granted access to resources based on their proven identity. In this chapter, you'll learn about various authentication concepts and methods, along with some basic security principles used to manage accounts. This chapter closes with a comparison of some access control schemes.

Exploring Authentication Management

Authentication proves an identity with some type of credentials, such as a username and password. For example, *identification* occurs when users make a claim about their identity with unique identifiers such as usernames or email addresses. Users then prove their identity with authentication, such as with a password. In this context, a user's credentials refer to both a claimed identity and an authentication mechanism.

Think about how this process might work in the physical world. I might walk up to a bank teller and say, "Hello, my name is Darril Gibson, and I would like to withdraw $1,000 from my account." No bank teller in their right mind is going to just say "OK" and hand over the money. I've claimed that I'm Darril Gibson (identification), but I haven't proven that claim (authentication). The bank teller would probably ask me to show my driver's license to authenticate me before handing over the cash.

In the digital world, users go through this same identification and authentication process. They just use different means to authenticate. You're already familiar with using passwords to prove a claim of identity. Later in this chapter, we'll look at other authentication techniques that are based on something you know, something you have, something you are, and somewhere you are.

Authentication is not limited to people. Services, processes, workstations, servers, and network devices all use authentication to prove their identities. For example, a web server might offer site visitors a copy of its digital certificate as proof of the server's identity. When the visitor's web browser verifies the digital certificate, that is an example of authentication. The browser verifies the web server's claim of identity.

Comparing Identification and AAA

Authentication, authorization, and accounting (AAA) work together with identification to provide a comprehensive access management system. If you understand identification (claiming an identity, such as with a username) and authentication (proving the identity, such as with a password), it's easier to add in the other two elements of AAA—authorization and accounting.

If users can prove their identity, that doesn't mean they are automatically granted access to all resources within a system. Instead, users are granted **authorization** to access resources based on their proven identity. This can be as simple as granting a user permission to read data in a shared folder. Access control systems include multiple security controls to ensure that users can access resources they're authorized to use, but no more.

Accounting methods track user activity and record the activity in logs. For example, audit logs track activity, and administrators use these to create an **audit trail**. An audit trail allows security professionals to re-create the events that preceded a security incident.

Effective access control starts with strong authentication mechanisms, such as robust passwords, smart cards, digital certificates, or biometrics. If attackers can bypass the authentication process, the authorization and accounting processes are ineffective.

> ### 📌 *Remember This!*
>
> Identification occurs when a user claims an identity, such as with a username or email address. Authentication occurs when the user proves the claimed identity (such as with a password) and the credentials are verified (such as with a password). Access control systems provide authorization by granting access to resources based on permissions granted to the proven identity. Logging provides accounting.

Comparing Authentication Factors

There are many different ways that users and systems can perform authentication. We group them into categories known as authentication factors to better describe how they work. Some factors provide stronger assurances of a user's identity than others, and many highly secure systems require the use of more than one factor to complete the authentication process.

The four authentication factors described by CompTIA are:

- Something you know, such as a password or personal identification number (PIN)
- Something you have, such as a smart card, a phone, or a USB token
- Something you are, such as a fingerprint or other biometric identification
- Somewhere you are, such as your home or office

Three or Four Factors?

Most cybersecurity professionals recognize three types of strong authentication factors: something you know, something you have, and something you are. These are all categories that can be used on their own to prove someone's claim of identity.

Notice that the fourth factor listed above, somewhere you are, isn't on that list. The reason is that location is not really a strong authentication factor by itself. For example, would you trust the fact that someone is located in your home as proof that they are you? Of course not! Location-based authentication is not normally used by itself and is instead treated as an added assurance when combined with one or more of the other three factors.

Something You Know

The **something you know** authentication factor typically refers to a shared secret, such as a password or a PIN. This factor is the least secure form of authentication because knowledge can be stolen. If I can find out someone's password, I can use it to impersonate them.

Best practice recommendations related to passwords have changed over the years. NIST SP 800-63B, "Digital Identity Guidelines," recommends users create easy-to-remember and hard-to-guess passwords. Microsoft and the U.S. Department of Homeland Security (DHS) have adopted several of the same recommendations. As you read through the explanations in the following sections, consider some of NIST, Microsoft, and the U.S. DHS' current password recommendations:

- Hash all passwords.
- Require multi-factor authentication.
- Don't require mandatory password resets.
- Require passwords to be at least eight characters.
- Check for common passwords and prevent their use.
- Tell users not to use the same password on more than one site.
- Allow all special characters, including spaces, but don't require them.

In the next few sections, we're going to look at some of the types of password policies that organizations put in place. You'll see that some of these policies don't necessarily meet these best practices, but you do need to know them for the exam because they are still used in many organizations.

Chapter 10, "Understanding Cryptography and PKI," covers hashing, salting, and key stretching to protect stored passwords. These techniques make it much harder for attackers to discover stored passwords.

Password Length and Complexity

One of the most common requirements for passwords is to set a minimum **password length**. The longer a password is, the harder it is to guess. For example, imagine that a password consisted of only one character, and that character was always a lowercase letter. There would only be 26 possible passwords! If you used two lowercase letters, that increases the number of possible passwords from 26 to 26 * 26 = 676. The longer the password gets, the more possible combinations there will be. An eight-character password consisting only of lowercase letters has more than 200 *billion* possible values!

Passwords can also be made stronger by requiring that they include different character types. This increases the number of possible values for each character of the password. Password complexity policies require that passwords contain several different types of characters. The four common character types included in passwords are:

- Uppercase characters (26 letters A–Z)
- Lowercase characters (26 letters a–z)
- Numbers (10 numbers 0–9)
- Special characters (such as !, $, and *)

Another component of password complexity is ensuring that the password isn't a simple word or name that might be easily guessed. For example, if I made my password "DarrilGibson!", that would meet the rules of having eight or more characters and using three different character types, but it is not a great choice for a password!

Password Expiration/Age

A **password expiration** setting identifies when users must change their password. As an example, a password expiration of 60 days means that users must change their password every two months. If they don't change their password ahead of time, they will be forced to change it the next time they log in after it expires.

These days, the best practice for password security is <u>not</u> to have password expiration policies and allow users to keep their passwords as long as they would like. This is based upon the idea that users are more likely to use strong, secure passwords if they don't need to keep changing them all the time. This advice is only true if the organization is using multifactor authentication.

> ### ★ *Remember This!*
>
> Complex passwords use a mix of character types. Strong passwords use a mix of character types and have a minimum password length of at least eight characters. A password expiration identifies when a password must be changed.

Password History and Password Reuse

Many users would prefer to use the same password forever simply because it's easier to remember. Even when technical password policies force users to change their passwords, many users simply change them back to the original password. This defeats the purpose of a password expiration policy!

A **password history** system remembers past passwords and prevents users from reusing them. It's common for password policy settings to remember the last 24 passwords and prevent users from reusing them until they've used 24 new passwords.

When using password history, it's common to also use the minimum password age setting. Imagine this is set to 1 day, and the password history is set to 24. After users change their password, they can't change it again until a day has passed. It'll take them 24 days of changing their password every day before they can reuse the original password. Otherwise, a crafty user who was determined to keep the same password could just immediately change their password 24 times and then return it to the original password once that password is cleared out of the history!

Password Managers

A password manager (or password vault) is a single source designed to keep most of your passwords. Instead of requiring you to memorize many different passwords, you only need to remember the password to open the vault. It keeps these passwords in an encrypted format, preventing unauthorized users from seeing them.

For example, Google Chrome includes a password manager built into the browser. Once you log in to Google and enter a username and password at another site, Chrome will ask if you want to save it. Click Save, and Chrome will store your credentials for you. The next time you go to the same site, Chrome will automatically fill in the credentials. Chrome allows you to sync your passwords across multiple devices, too. When you enable this option, your passwords are stored with your Google account. After launching Chrome and logging onto Google, you'll have access to all your passwords stored with your account.

Some password vaults are individual applications stored on a single computer. Once you open the vault with a password, you can store your credentials in it, and the app automatically fills in credentials when needed. Of course, this places all of your passwords on a single device and you'll lose access to them if that device is lost, stolen, or damaged. Make sure you keep a backup of the password vault in a secure location!

Password vaults use strong encryption to protect their contents, preventing anyone who steals the computer from accessing the passwords in the vault.

Knowledge-Based Authentication

Some organizations use **knowledge-based authentication (KBA)** to verify the identity of individuals. There are two types: static KBA and dynamic KBA.

Static KBA is typically used to verify your identity when you've forgotten your password. After creating your account (or when you create your account), you're prompted to answer questions about yourself, such as your first dog's name or your mother's maiden name. Later, when you try to retrieve a forgotten password, you're first prompted to answer the same questions.

Dynamic KBA identifies individuals without an account. Organizations use this for high-risk transactions, such as with a financial institution or a healthcare company. The site queries public and private data sources like credit reports, vehicle registrations, and property records. It then crafts multiple-choice questions that only the user would know and often includes an answer similar to "none of these apply." Some examples are:

- At which of the following addresses have you lived?
- Which of the following amounts is closest to your mortgage payment?
- When was your home built?

Users typically have a limited amount of time to answer these questions. This limits the amount of time an attacker can do searches on the Internet to identify accurate answers.

Knowledge-based authentication may also be used to help confirm a new user's identity when they are creating an account for the first time. This process is known as **identity proofing**. Identity proofing is an important step in the **provisioning** process that creates accounts for new users as they join the organization.

Implementing Account Lockout Policies

Accounts will typically have lockout policies preventing users from guessing the password. If a user enters the wrong password too many times (such as three or five times), the system locks the user's account. Two key phrases associated with account lockout policies on Microsoft systems are:

- **Account lockout threshold.** This is the maximum number of times a user can enter the wrong password. When the user exceeds the threshold, the system locks the account.

- **Account lockout duration.** This indicates how long an account remains locked. It could be set to 30, indicating that the system will lock the account for 30 minutes. After 30 minutes, the system automatically unlocks the account. If the duration is set to 0, the account remains locked until an administrator unlocks it.

Account lockout policies thwart some password attacks, such as brute force attacks and dictionary attacks. Chapter 10 covers common password attacks.

> ## ✦ Remember This!
>
> Account lockout policies thwart some password attacks, such as brute force and dictionary attacks. Many applications and devices have default passwords. These should be changed before putting the application or device into service.

Changing Default Passwords

Some systems and devices come with default passwords. A basic security practice is to change these defaults before connecting the system to the network. As an example, many wireless routers have default accounts named "admin" or "administrator" with a default password of "admin." If you don't change the password, anyone who knows the defaults can log on and take control of the router. In that case, the attacker can even go as far as locking you out of your own network.

Changing defaults also includes changing the default name of the Administrator account, if possible. In many systems, the Administrator account can't be locked out through regular lockout policies, so an attacker can continue to try to guess the administrator's password without risking being locked out. Changing the name of the Administrator account to something else, such as Not4U2Know, reduces the chances of success for the attacker. The attacker needs to know the administrator account's new name before he can try to guess the password.

Training Users About Password Behaviors

Some users don't understand the value of their password or the potential damage if they give it out. Organizations need to provide adequate training to users on password security if they use passwords within the organization. This includes creating strong passwords, not using the same password with other systems, and never giving their password to someone else.

For example, the password "123456" frequently appears on lists as the most common password in use. The users who are creating this password probably don't know that it's almost like using no password at all. Also, they probably don't realize they can significantly increase the password strength by using a simple passphrase such as "ICanCountTo6." A little training can go a long way.

Something You Have

The **something you have** authentication factor refers to something you can physically hold. This section covers many of the common items in this factor, including smart cards, security keys, software tokens, and hardware tokens. It also covers two open-source protocols used with both hardware and software tokens.

Smart Card Authentication

Smart cards are credit card-sized cards that have an embedded microchip and a certificate. Users insert the **smart card** into a smart card reader, similar to how someone would insert a credit card into a credit card reader. The smart card reader reads the card's information, including the details from the embedded digital certificate, which provides certificate-based authentication.

Chapter 10 covers certificates in more detail, but as an introduction, they are digital files that support cryptography for increased security. The embedded certificate allows the use of a complex encryption key and provides much more secure authentication than is possible with a simple password. Additionally, the certificate can be used with digital signatures and data encryption. The smart card provides confidentiality, integrity, authentication, and non-repudiation.

Requirements for a smart card are:

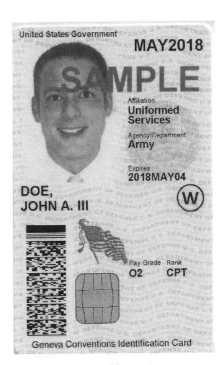

- **Embedded certificate.** The embedded certificate holds a user's private key (which is only accessible to the user) and is matched with a public key (that is publicly available to others). The private key is used each time the user logs on to a network.
- **Public Key Infrastructure (PKI).** Chapter 10 covers PKI in more depth, but in short, the PKI supports issuing and managing certificates.

Figure 2.1 shows an example of the Common Access Card (CAC), a smart card authentication technology used by the U.S. military. Notice that the card contains a chip that is used to interface with the card reader.

Smart cards are often used with another factor of authentication. For example, a user may also enter a PIN or password and use the smart card. Because the smart card is in the something you have factor and the PIN is in the something you know factor, this combination provides two-factor authentication.

Figure 2.1: U.S. Military Common Access Card (Source: U.S. Department of Defense)

Security Keys

A **security key** is an electronic device about the size of a remote key for a car. You can easily carry one in your pocket or purse or connect it to your key chain. The security key is used to authenticate to systems.

The security key contains cryptographic information that completes the authentication process. In this case, the token has a USB connector or wireless interface to connect to your computer or phone. Figure 2.2 shows an example of a security key that is attached to a user's keychain.

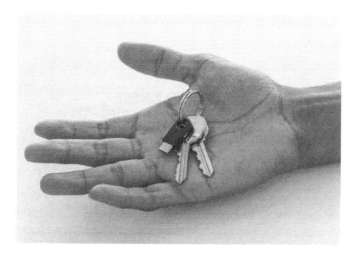

Figure 2.2: Security key attached to a keychain (Source: Yubico)

Hard Tokens

A **hard token** (or hardware token) is an electronic device about the size of a remote key for a car. You can easily carry one in your pocket or purse or connect it to your key chain. The token is used to authenticate to systems. The token includes a liquid crystal display (LCD) that displays a number on the screen, such as the one shown in Figure 2.3. This number is known as a **one-time password (OTP)** and the user provides it to the authentication server to prove that they currently have possession of the token.

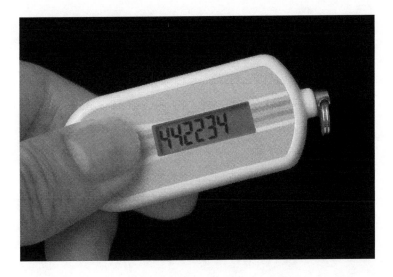

Figure 2.3: Hardware token displaying a one-time password

Soft Tokens

A ***soft token*** (or software token) is an application that runs on a user's smartphone and generates one-time passwords in the same way that hardware tokens display them on their LCD screen. Figure 2.4 shows an example of the Google Authenticator app displaying a one-time password.

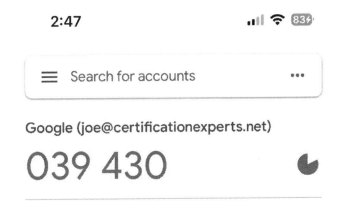

Figure 2.4: Software token displaying a one-time password

HOTP and TOTP

At this point, you might be wondering how a hard or soft token knows what numbers to display and how the remote authentication server knows what numbers are displaying on the token. Especially because the token doesn't have to be connected to a network and doesn't communicate with the authentication server!

There are actually two different ways that tokens remain in sync with authentication servers:

Tokens using the **HMAC-based One-Time Password (HOTP)** algorithm change their code based upon a moving counter. Each time the code is used, both the authentication server and the token use the algorithm with a shared secret key to generate the next code. Since they have the same shared secret, they both generate the same code. You can often identify HOTP tokens by the fact that the user presses a button to generate the next password.

Tokens using the **Time-based One-Time Password (TOTP)** algorithm change their code based upon the current time. You can recognize TOTP tokens by the fact that their code changes automatically, often every 30-60 seconds.

★ Remember This!

HOTP and TOTP are open-source standards used to create one-time-use passwords. HOTP creates a one-time-use password that does not expire until it is used, and TOTP creates a one-time password that expires after 30-60 seconds. Both can be used as software tokens for authentication.

SMS/Push Notifications

Some authentication systems use **Short Message Service (SMS)** to send one-time passwords to user's phones. As an example, after you enter your credentials, the system may challenge you by sending a code to your phone and asking you to enter the code on the system. This proves that you have access to the phone.

Be careful, though! NIST SP-800-63B (mentioned earlier) points out several vulnerabilities with SMS for two-step authentication and discourages its use. Normally, mobile devices display SMS text on the screen when it arrives. If someone stole the mobile device, they would see the PIN without logging on to the mobile device. Also, it may be possible for an attacker to hijack your phone number and reroute the text message to their own device.

Push notifications send messages to users on another device but instead of including a code, they ask the user to acknowledge the request on their phone. Imagine Lisa registered her smartphone with a website. Later, when she accesses the website and enters her username, the site sends a push notification to her phone. She can then approve or decline the access by pressing a button on her smartphone.

Something You Are

The **something you are** authentication factor uses biometrics for authentication. **Biometrics** measure some physical characteristic of the user to confirm their identity. In most cases, biometrics are the strongest form of authentication because they are the most difficult for an attacker to falsify. While you might be able to easily steal someone's password, it's much harder to steal their retina!

Biometric Methods

Biometrics uses a physical characteristic, such as a fingerprint, for authentication. Most biometric systems use a two-step process. In the first step, users register or enroll with the authentication system. For example, an authentication system first captures a user's fingerprint and then associates it with the user's identity. Later, when users want to access the system, they use their fingerprints to prove their identity. There are multiple types of biometrics, including:

- **Fingerprints.** Many laptop computers include **fingerprint scanners** or fingerprint readers, and they are also common on tablet devices and smartphones. Similarly, some USB flash drives include a fingerprint scanner. They can store multiple fingerprints to share access to the same USB device. Law enforcement agencies have used fingerprints for decades, but they use them for identification, not biometric authentication.
- **Vein matching** systems identify individuals using near-infrared light to view their vein patterns Most vein recognition systems measure the veins in an individual's palm because there are more veins in the palm than a finger. Many hospitals and health care systems use palm scanners as a quick and easy way to identify patients and prevent patient misidentification.
- **Retina imaging** systems scan the retina of one or both eyes and use the pattern of blood vessels at the back of the eye for recognition. Some people object to the use of these scanners for authentication because retinal scans may identify certain medical issues, and you typically need to make physical contact with the scanner.
- **Iris scanners** use infrared camera technology to capture the unique patterns of the iris around the pupil for recognition. They are used in many passport-free border crossings around the world. They can take pictures from about 3 to 10 inches away, avoiding physical contact.
- **Facial recognition** systems identify people based on facial features. This includes the size, shape, and position of their eyes, nose, mouth, cheekbones, and jaw. As an example,

iPhones use the Face ID facial recognition system. After setting it up, you can unlock your iPhone simply by glancing at it.

- **Voice recognition** methods identify who is speaking using speech recognition. One person's voice varies from another person's voice due to differences in their mouth and throat, and behavioral patterns that affect their speaking style. As an example, Apple's Siri supports voice recognition.

- **Gait analysis** identifies individuals based on the way they walk or run. It measures how someone's feet hit and leave the ground while walking. Some methods focus primarily on the feet, knees, and hips. Other methods have expanded this to examine silhouette sequences of individuals for identification. However, an individual can purposely change their gait, doing something as simple as adding a limp. In contrast, individuals can't change their fingerprints or the appearance of their iris at will.

★ Remember This!

The third factor of authentication (something you are, defined with biometrics) is the strongest individual authentication factor. Biometric methods include fingerprint recognition, vein pattern matching, retinal and iris scans, facial recognition, voice recognition, and gait analysis.

It's worth noting that a formal enrollment process isn't always necessary, especially if the goal is identification instead of authentication. Many Las Vegas casinos have sophisticated systems that capture people's faces as they enter and roam around the casino. Casino personnel can match these faces to people recorded in massive databases. Similarly, imagine Marge is crossing a border between two countries. As she presents her passport, a passive biometric system can capture her face. Gait analysis can also be passive by just observing and recording the gait patterns of individuals. Combining facial recognition with gait analysis increases identification accuracy and can help prevent someone from using a fraudulent passport.

★ Remember This!

Iris and retina scans are the strongest biometric methods mentioned in this section. Iris scans are commonly preferred over retinal scans because retinal scans are intrusive and may reveal private medical concerns. Facial recognition and gait analysis can bypass the enrollment process when used for identification instead of authorization.

Biometric Efficacy Rates

The biometric **efficacy rate** refers to the performance of the system under ideal conditions. If the system is implemented correctly, it can be very exact. However, if it isn't implemented correctly, its real-world effectiveness may not match the efficacy rate.

The following bullets describe the four possibilities when a biometric system tries to authenticate a user. Refer to Figure 2.5 as you're reading them:

- **False acceptance.** This is when a biometric system incorrectly identifies an unknown user as a registered user. The **false acceptance rate** (FAR) identifies the percentage of times false acceptance occurs.
- **False rejection.** This is when a biometric system incorrectly rejects a registered user. The **false rejection rate** (FRR) identifies the percentage of times false rejections occur.
- **True acceptance.** This indicates that the biometric system correctly identified a registered user.
- **True rejection.** This indicates that the biometric system correctly rejected an unknown user.

	Biometric System Not Accurate	Biometric System Accurate
Registered User	**False Acceptance**	True Acceptance
Unknown User	**False Rejection**	True Rejection

Figure 2.5: Acceptance and rejection matrix

Biometric systems allow you to adjust the sensitivity or threshold level where errors occur. Increasing sensitivity decreases the number of false matches and increases the number of false rejections. In contrast, reducing sensitivity increases false matches and decreases false rejections. By plotting the FAR and FRR using different sensitivities, you can determine a biometric system's efficacy.

Figure 2.6 shows the crossover error rate (CER) for two biometric systems (one using solid lines and the second using dotted lines). The CER is the point where the FAR crosses over with the FRR. A lower CER indicates that the biometric system is more accurate. The system represented with the solid lines is more accurate than the system represented by the dashed lines.

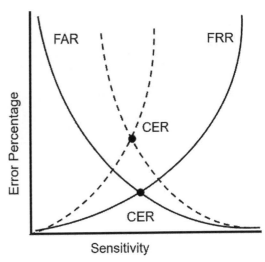

Figure 2.6: Crossover error rate for two different systems

Somewhere You Are

The **somewhere you are** authentication attribute identifies a user's location. Geolocation is a group of technologies used to identify a user's location and is the most common method used in this factor. Many authentication systems use the Internet Protocol (IP) address for geolocation. The IP address provides information on the country, region, state, city, and sometimes even the zip code.

As an example, I once hired a virtual assistant in India to do some data entry for me. I created an account for the assistant in an online application called Hootsuite and sent him the logon information. However, Hootsuite recognized that his IP was in India when he attempted to log on. This looked suspicious, so Hootsuite blocked his access and then sent me an email saying that someone from India was trying to log on. They also provided me directions on how to grant him access if he was a legitimate user, but it was comforting to know they detected and blocked this access automatically.

The somewhere you are authentication attribute can also be used to identify **impossible travel time** or risky login situations. As an example, imagine Lisa logs in to her account from her home in Springfield, and then a moment later, someone else logs in to her account from the country of Certaheadistan. Unless Lisa has a teleportation machine, she can't log in from both places simultaneously.

It's worth noting that using an IP address for geolocation isn't foolproof. There are many virtual private network (VPN) IP address changers available online. For example, a user in Russia can use one of these services in the United States to access a website. The website will recognize the VPN service's IP address but won't see the Russian IP address.

Within an organization, it's possible to use the computer name or the media access control (MAC) address of a system for the somewhere you are factor. For example, in a Microsoft Active Directory domain, you can configure accounts so that users can only log on to the network through one specific computer. If they aren't at that computer, the system blocks them from logging on at all.

Two-Factor and Multifactor Authentication

Two-factor authentication (sometimes called dual-factor authentication) uses two different authentication factors: something you have and something you know, or something you know and something you are. Some examples of two-factor authentication include:

- A soft token (something you have) and a password (something you know)
- A fingerprint scan (something you are) and a PIN (something you know)
- A security key (something you have) and a retinal scan (something you are)

It's worth noting that using two methods of authentication in the same factor is not two-factor authentication. For example, requiring users to enter a password and a reusable PIN (both in the something you know factor) is single-factor authentication, not two-factor authentication. In this case, the reusable PIN isn't sent to users via a smartphone. Instead, the user enters a PIN value known only to them, just as if it was a password. Similarly, using a thumbprint and a retina scan is not two-factor authentication because both methods are in the **something you are** factor.

 Remember This!

Using two or more methods in the same factor of authentication (such as a PIN and a password) is single-factor authentication. Two-factor authentication uses two different authentication factors, such as using a hardware token and a PIN. Multifactor authentication uses two or more factors.

Passwordless Authentication

Users dislike passwords, and passwords are one of the least secure ways to authenticate, so many organizations are trying to get rid of them entirely. **Passwordless authentication** approaches eliminate passwords and replace them with other authentication factors, such as something you have or something you are.

 Remember This!

Passwordless authentication is not necessarily multifactor authentication. You can use a single something you have or something you are factor to use passwordless authentication.

Authentication Log Files

Authentication log files can track both successful and unsuccessful login attempts. It's most important to monitor login activity for any privileged accounts, such as administrators. Chapter 1 discusses security information and event management (SIEM) systems. It's common to send entries from authentication logs to a SIEM system for analysis and notification of suspicious events.

As mentioned in Chapter 1, log entries help administrators determine what happened, when it happened, where it happened, and who or what did it. For authentication log entries:

- What happened is either a login success or failure
- When it happened is determined by the time and date stamps

- Where it happened is typically an IP address or computer name
- Who or what did it refers to the user account

Managing Accounts

Account management is concerned with creating, managing, disabling, and terminating accounts. When the account is active, access control methods are used to control what the user can do. Additionally, administrators use access controls to control when, where, and how users can log on. The following sections cover common account management practices and some basic principles used with account management.

An important concept to remember when creating accounts is to give users only the account permissions they need to perform their job, and no more. Chapter 11, "Implementing Policies to Mitigate Risks," covers the principle of least privilege, emphasizing this in more depth.

Credential Policies and Account Types

Credential policies define login policies for different personnel, devices, and accounts. This includes items in the something you know factor (such as passwords) or any other factor or combination of factors. It's common for an organization to apply credential policies differently to different types of accounts. The following list identifies different account types and credential policies associated with each:

- **Personnel or end-user accounts.** Most accounts are for regular users or the personnel working in the organizations. Administrators create these accounts and then assign appropriate privileges based on the user's job responsibilities. It's common to assign a basic credential policy that applies to all personnel. This could be a password policy defining things like the minimum password length, password history, and account lockout policies, as defined earlier in this chapter.
- **Administrator and root accounts.** Administrator and root accounts are privileged accounts that have additional rights and privileges beyond what a regular user has. As an example, someone with administrator privileges on a Windows computer has full control over the Windows computer. Linux systems have a root account, which grants additional privileges, similar to an administrator account on Windows systems. Credential policies require stronger authentication methods for these privileged accounts, such as multifactor authentication. Additionally, privileged access management techniques (described in the next section) apply additional controls to protect these accounts.
- **Service accounts.** Some applications and services need to run under the context of an account, and a service account fills this need. As an example, SQL Server is a database application that runs on a server, and it needs access to resources on the server and the network. Administrators create a regular user account, name it something like sqlservice,

assign it appropriate privileges, and configure SQL Server to use this account. Note that this is like a regular end-user account. The only difference is that it's used by the service or application, not an end user. Credential policies may require long, complex passwords for these accounts, but they should not expire. If the password expires, the account can no longer log on, and the service or application will stop.

- **Device accounts.** Computers and other devices also have accounts though it isn't always apparent. As an example, Microsoft Active Directory only allows users to log on to computers joined to the domain. These computers have computer accounts and Active Directory manages their passwords.

- **Third-party accounts.** Third-party accounts are accounts from external entities that have access to a network. As an example, many organizations use security applications that have administrative access to a network. These should have strong credential policies in place with strong password policies enforced at a minimum.

- **Guest accounts.** Windows operating systems include a Guest account. These are useful if you want to grant someone limited access to a computer or network without creating a new account. For example, imagine an organization contracts with a temp agency to have someone do data entry. The agency may send a different person every day. Enabling the Guest account for this person would be simpler than creating a new account every day. Administrators commonly disable the Guest account and only enable it in special situations.

- **Shared and generic account/credentials.** An organization can create a regular user account that temporary workers will share. Shared accounts are discouraged for normal work. However, if a temp agency is sending someone different every day, a shared account may provide a better solution than a guest account because access can be tailored for the shared account. Basic credential policies apply to shared and generic accounts.

Privileged Access Management

Privileged access management (PAM) allows an organization to apply more stringent security controls over accounts with elevated privileges, such as administrator or root-level accounts. PAM implements the concept of ***just-in-time permissions***. In other words, administrators don't have administrative privileges until they need them. When they need them, their account sends a request for the elevated privileges. The underlying PAM system grants the request, typically by adding the account to a group with elevated privileges. After a pre-set time (such as 15 minutes), their account is automatically removed from the group, revoking the elevated privileges.

> ★ **Remember This!**
>
> Privileged access management (PAM) systems implement stringent security controls over accounts with elevated privileges such as administrator or root-level accounts. Some capabilities include allowing authorized users to access the administrator account without knowing the password, logging all elevated privilege usage, and automatically changing the administrator account password.

PAM systems also safeguard administrative accounts by storing their passwords in a password vault. In many cases, they are set up so that no human ever sees or accesses the password for an administrative account. Instead, the PAM system uses that password on their behalf.

In addition to just-in-time permissions that provide administrative permissions to a user account when they are needed, PAM systems are also capable of creating **temporal accounts**. These are temporary accounts with administrative privileges that are issued for a limited period of time (such as few hours) and then are destroyed when the user is finished with their work.

Some capabilities of PAM are:

- Allow users to access the privileged account without knowing the password
- Automatically change privileged account passwords periodically
- Limit the time users can use the privileged account
- Allow users to check out credentials
- Log all access of credentials

If an attacker can log on as an administrator, there's almost no limit to what they can do. Ideally, that isn't possible, but there are many different attack methods where an attacker can get an administrator password no matter how long or complex it is. PAM is the protection against these types of attacks. It reduces the opportunities for attackers to use administrative privileges. PAM systems use logging and monitoring to show when these accounts are used and what users did with them.

Requiring Administrators to Use Two Accounts

It's common to require administrators to have two accounts. They use one for regular day-to-day work. It has the same limited privileges as a regular end user. The other account has elevated privileges required to perform administrative work, and they use this only when performing administrative work. The benefit of this practice is that it reduces the exposure of the administrative account to an attack.

For example, when malware infects a system, it often attempts to gain additional rights and permissions using privilege escalation techniques. It may exploit a bug or flaw in an application or operating system. Or, it may simply assume the rights and permissions of the logged-on user. If an administrator logs on with an administrative account, the malware can assume these elevated privileges. In contrast, if the administrator is logged on with a regular standard user account, the malware must take additional steps to escalate its privileges.

This also reduces the risk to the administrative account for day-to-day work. Imagine Homer is an administrator, and he's called away to a crisis. He may walk away without locking his computer. If he was logged on with his administrator account, an attacker walking by could access the system and have administrative privileges. Although systems often have password-protected screen savers, these usually don't start until about 10 minutes or longer after a user walks away.

Prohibiting Shared and Generic Accounts

Account management policies often dictate that personnel should not use shared or generic accounts. Instead, each user has at least one account, which is only accessible to that user. If multiple users share a single account, you cannot implement basic authorization controls. As a reminder, four key concepts are:

- **Identification**. Users claim an identity with an identifier such as a username.
- **Authentication**. Users prove their identity using an authentication method such as a password.
- **Authorization**. Users are authorized access to resources, based on their proven identity.
- **Accounting**. Logs record activity using the users' claimed identity.

Imagine that Bart, Maggie, and Lisa all used the Guest account. If you wanted to give Lisa access to certain files, you would grant access to the Guest account, but Bart and Maggie would have the same access. If Bart deleted the files, logs would indicate the Guest account deleted the files, but you wouldn't know who actually deleted them. In contrast, if users have unique user accounts, you can give them access to resources individually. Additionally, logs would indicate who took an action.

Note that having a single, temporary user log on with the Guest account does support identification, authentication, authorization, and accounting. It is only when multiple users are sharing the same account that you lose these controls. Still, some organizations prohibit the use of the Guest account for any purposes.

> ★ *Remember This!*
>
> Requiring administrators to use two accounts, one with administrator privileges and another with regular user privileges, helps prevent privilege escalation attacks. Users should not use shared accounts.

Deprovisioning

Deprovisioning is the process used to disable a user's account when they leave the organization. Most organizations require administrators to disable user accounts as soon as possible when employees leave the organization. This process is often automated, disabling a user's account as soon as they are inactivated in the human resources system.

Disabling is preferred over deleting the account, at least initially. If administrators delete the account, they also delete any encryption and security keys associated with the account. However, these keys are retained when the account is disabled. As an example, imagine that an employee encrypted files with his account. The operating system uses cryptography keys to encrypt and decrypt these files. If administrators deleted this account, these files may remain encrypted forever unless the organization has a key escrow or recovery agent that can access the files.

Some contents of an account disablement policy include:

- **Terminated employee.** An account disablement policy specifies that accounts for ex-employees are disabled as soon as possible. This ensures a terminated employee doesn't become a disgruntled ex-employee who wreaks havoc on the network. Note that "terminated" refers to both employees who resign and employees who are fired.
- **Leave of absence.** If an employee will be absent for an extended period, the account should be disabled while the employee is away. Organizations define extended periods differently, with some organizations defining it as only two weeks, whereas other organizations extending it out to as long as two months.
- **Account deletion.** When the organization determines the account is no longer needed, administrators delete it. For example, the policy may direct administrators to delete accounts that have been inactive for 60 or 90 days.

★ *Remember This!*

An account disablement policy identifies what to do with accounts for employees who leave permanently or are on a leave of absence. Most policies require administrators to disable the account as soon as possible so that ex-employees cannot use the account. Disabling the account ensures that data associated with it remains available. Security keys associated with an account remain available when the account is disabled, but the security keys (and data they encrypted) are no longer accessible if it is deleted.

Time-Based Logins

Time-based logins (sometimes referred to as time-of-day restrictions) ensure that users can only log on to computers during specific times. If a user tries to log on to a system outside the restricted time, the system denies access to the user.

As an example, imagine a company operates between 8:00 a.m. and 5:00 p.m. on a daily basis. Managers decide they don't want regular users logging on to the network except between 6:00 a.m. and 8:00 p.m., Monday through Friday. You could set time-of-day restrictions for user accounts to enforce this. If a user tries to log on outside the restricted time (such as during the weekend), the system prevents the user from logging on.

If users are working overtime on a project, the system doesn't log them off when the restricted time arrives. For example, if Maggie is working late on a Wednesday night, the system doesn't log her off at 8:00 p.m. However, the system will prevent her from creating any new network connections.

Account Audits

An **account audit** looks at the rights and permissions assigned to users and helps enforce the least privilege principle. The audit identifies the privileges (rights and permissions) granted to users and compares them against what the users need. It can detect **privilege creep**, a common problem that violates the principle of least privilege. Privilege creep (or permission bloat) occurs when a user is granted more and more privileges due to changing job requirements, but unneeded privileges are never removed. For example, imagine Lisa is working in the Human Resources (HR) department, so she has access to HR data. Later, she transfers to the Sales department, and administrators grant her access to sales data. However, no one removes her access to HR data even though she doesn't need it to perform her sales department job.

Organizations commonly use a role-based access control model with group-based privileges, as described later in this chapter. For example, while Lisa is working in the HR department, her account would be in one or more HR department security groups to grant her appropriate HR job privileges. When she transfers to the Sales department, administrators would add her to the appropriate Sales department groups, granting her new job privileges. An organization should also have account management controls in place to ensure that administrators remove her account from the HR department security groups. The permission auditing review verifies that these account management practices are followed.

Most organizations ensure that permission auditing reviews are performed at least once a year, and some organizations perform them more often. The goal is to do them often enough to catch potential problems and prevent security incidents. However, unless they can be automated, they become an unnecessary burden if security administrators are required to do them too often, such as daily or even once a week.

Attestation is a formal process for reviewing user permissions. In an attestation process, managers formally review each user's permissions and certify that those permissions are necessary to carry out the user's job responsibilities.

 Remember This!

Usage auditing records user activity in logs. A usage auditing review looks at the logs to see what users are doing and it can be used to re-create an audit trail. Permission auditing reviews help ensure that users have only the access they need and no more and can detect privilege creep issues.

Comparing Authentication Services

Several other authentication services are available that fall outside the scope of the previously described factors of authentication. A common goal they have is to ensure that unencrypted credentials are not sent across a network. In other words, they ensure that credentials are not sent in cleartext. If credentials are sent in cleartext, attackers can use tools such as a protocol analyzer to capture and view them. The following sections describe many of these services.

Single Sign-On

Single sign-on (SSO) refers to a user's ability to log on once and access multiple systems without logging on again. SSO increases security because the user only needs to remember one set of credentials and is less likely to write them down. It's also much more convenient for users to access network resources if they only have to log on one time.

As an example, consider a user who needs to access multiple servers within a network to perform routine work. Without SSO, the user needs to know one set of credentials to log on locally and an additional set of credentials for each of the servers. Many users would write these credentials down to remember them.

Alternatively, in a network with SSO capabilities, the user only needs to log on to the network once. The SSO system typically creates some type of SSO secure token used during the entire login session. Each time the user accesses a network resource, the SSO system uses this secure token for authentication.

SSO requires strong authentication to be effective. If users create weak passwords, attackers might guess them, giving them access to multiple systems. Some people debate that SSO adds in risks because if an attacker can gain the user's credentials, it provides the attacker access to multiple systems.

The power of SSO systems lies in their ***interoperability*** with the many operating systems, devices, applications, and services used in an organization. These services may all be configured to rely upon the SSO system for user identification, authentication, authorization, and accounting.

LDAP

The ***Lightweight Directory Access Protocol (LDAP)*** is a core component of many single-sign-on systems. LDAP allows users and applications to retrieve information about users from the organization's directory – a centralized repository of information about user accounts, devices, and other objects. Windows domains use LDAP to handle queries for information from Active Directory. You'll learn more about LDAP in Chapter 3, "Exploring Network Technologies and Tools."

SSO and a Federation

Some SSO systems can connect authentication mechanisms from different environments, such as different operating systems or different networks. One common method is with a federated identity management system, often integrated as a federated database. This federated database provides central authentication in a non-homogeneous environment.

As an example, imagine that the Springfield Nuclear Power Plant established a relationship with the Springfield school system, allowing the power plant employees to access school resources. It's not feasible or desirable to join these two networks into one. However, you can create a federation of the two networks. Once the federation is established, the power plant employees will log on using their power plant account and then access the shared school resources without logging on again.

A ***federation*** requires a federated identity management system that all members of the federation use. In the previous example, the members of the federation are the power plant and the school system. Members of the federation agree on a standard for federated identities and then exchange the information based on the standard. A federated identity links a user's credentials from different networks or operating systems, but the federation treats it as one identity.

SAML

Security Assertion Markup Language (SAML) is an ***Extensible Markup Language (XML)***–based data format used for SSO on web browsers. Imagine two websites hosted by two different organizations. Normally, a user would have to provide different credentials to access either website. However, if the organizations trust each other, they can use SAML as a federated identity management system. Users authenticate with one website and are not required to authenticate again when accessing the second website.

Many web-based portals use SAML for SSO. The user logs on to the portal once, and the portal then passes proof of the user's authentication to back-end systems. As long as one organization has authenticated users, they are not required to authenticate again to access other sites within the portal.

SAML defines three roles. While reading through these roles, think of Homer, who logs on at work (the nuclear power plant) and then accesses continuing education courses at the Springfield school system's website:

- **Principal**. This is typically a user, such as Homer. The user logs on once. If necessary, the principal requests an identity from the identity provider.
- **Identity provider**. An identity provider (IdP) creates, maintains, and manages identity information, authentication, and authorization for principals. In the scenario, the IdP could be the nuclear power plant, the Springfield school system, or a third party.

★ Remember This!

SAML is an XML-based standard used to exchange authentication and authorization information between different parties. SAML provides SSO for web-based applications.

- **Service provider.** A service provider is an entity that provides services to principals. In this example, the Springfield school system is the service provider for Homer. It hosts one or more websites accessible through a web-based portal. When Homer accesses a school system website, the service provider queries the IdP to verify that he has valid credentials before granting access.

This process sends several XML-based messages between the systems. However, it is usually transparent to the user.

SAML and Authorization

It's important to realize that the primary purpose of SSO is for the identification and authentication of users. Users claim an identity and prove that identity with credentials. SSO does not provide authorization. For example, suppose the power plant and the school system create a federation using SAML. This doesn't automatically grant everyone in the school system full access to the nuclear power plant resources. Authorization is completely separate.

However, many federation SSO systems, including SAML, include the ability to transfer authorization data between their systems. In other words, it's possible to use SAML for single sign-on authentication and for authorization.

OAuth

OAuth is an open standard for authorization that many companies use to provide secure access to protected resources. It allows users to grant one service access to information in another service without disclosing their login credentials.

For example, Google services support OAuth. Imagine that you are signing up for a new scheduling service called Doodle and you would like to allow that service to view and edit entries on your Google Calendar. You don't want to give Doodle the password to your Google account because that would allow them to access your email and anything else. Instead, Doodle asks for authorization to access information in your Google account using the OAuth popup shown in Figure 2.7.

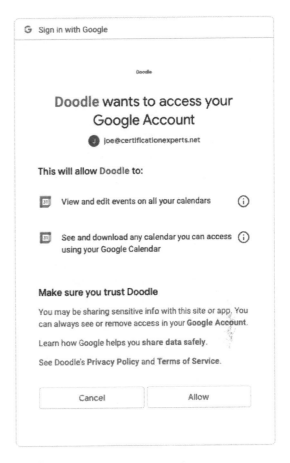

Figure 2.7: OAuth pop-up authorizing access to Google

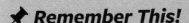 **Remember This!**

It's easy to get confused about what OAuth does because the name is ambiguous! Remember that the "Auth" in OAuth stands for *authorization*, not authentication!

Authorization Models

Access control ensures that only authenticated and authorized entities can access resources. For example, it ensures that only authenticated users who have been granted appropriate permissions can access files on a server. This starts by ensuring that users are accurately identified and authenticated. Then, you grant access using one of several different schemes. The authorization models covered in this section are:

- Role-based access control
- Rule-based access control
- Discretionary access control (DAC)
- Mandatory access control (MAC)
- Attribute-based access control (ABAC)

Each of these authorization models makes it easier to apply access policies to users within a network. By understanding a little more of the underlying design principles, you'll understand why some of the rules are important, and you'll be better prepared to ensure that security principles are followed.

Often, when using any of the models, you'll run across the following terms:

- **Subjects.** Subjects are typically users or groups that access an object. Occasionally, the subject may be a service that is using a service account to access an object.
- **Objects.** Objects are items such as files, folders, shares, and printers that subjects access. The access control helps determine how a system grants authorization to objects. Or, said another way, the access control scheme determines how a system grants users access to files and other resources.

Role-Based Access Control

Role-based access control (role-BAC) uses roles to manage rights and permissions for users. This is useful for users within a specific department who perform the same job functions. An administrator creates the roles and then assigns specific rights and permissions to the roles (instead of to the users). When an administrator adds a user to a role, the user has all the rights and permissions of that role.

Using Roles Based on Jobs and Functions

Imagine your organization has several departments, such as Accounting, Sales, and IT, and each department has a separate server hosting its files. You can create Accounting, Sales, and IT roles and assign these roles to users based on the department where they work. Next, you'd grant these roles access to the appropriate server. For example, you'd grant the accounting role to the accounting server, grant the Sales role to the Sales server, and so on.

Another example of the role-BAC scheme is Microsoft Project Server. The Project Server can host multiple projects managed by different project managers. It includes the following roles:

- **Administrators.** Administrators have complete access and control over everything on the server, including all of the projects managed on the server.

- **Executives.** Executives can access data from any project held on the server but do not have access to modify server settings.
- **Project Managers.** Project managers have full control over their own projects but do not control projects owned by other project managers.
- **Team Members.** Team members can typically report on work that project managers assign to them, but they have little access outside the scope of their assignments.

Microsoft Project Server includes more roles, but you can see the point with these four. Each of these roles has rights and permissions assigned to it, and to give someone the associated privileges, you'd simply add the user's account to the role.

Documenting Roles with a Matrix

Think about the developers of Microsoft Project Server. They didn't just start creating roles. Instead, they did some planning and identified the roles they envisioned in the application. Next, they identified the privileges each of these roles required. It's common to document role-based permissions with a matrix listing all of the job titles and each role's privileges, as shown in Table 2.1.

Role	Server Privileges	Project Privileges
Administrators	All	All
Executives	None	All
Project Managers	None	All on assigned projects No access on unassigned projects
Team Members	None	Access for assigned tasks Limited views within scope of their assigned tasks No views outside the scope of their assigned tasks

Table 2.1: Role-BAC matrix for Project Server

Role-BAC is also called hierarchy-based or job-based:

- **Hierarchy-based.** In the Project Server example, you can see how top-level roles, such as the Administrators role, have significantly more permissions than lower-level roles, such as the Team Members role. Roles may mimic the hierarchy of an organization.
- **Job-, task-, or function-based.** The Project Server example also shows how the roles are centered on jobs or functions that users need to perform.

> ★ *Remember This!*
>
> A role-based access control scheme uses roles based on jobs and functions. A roles and permissions matrix is a planning document that matches the roles with the required privileges.

Establishing Access with Group-Based Privileges

Administrators commonly grant access in the role-BAC scheme using roles, and they often implement roles as groups. Windows systems refer to these as security groups. They assign rights and permissions (privileges) to groups and then add user accounts to the appropriate group. This type of group-based access control based on roles or groups simplifies user administration.

One implementation of the role-BAC scheme is the Microsoft built-in security groups and specially designed security groups that administrators create on workstations, servers, and domains. The Administrators group is an example of a built-in security group. For example, the Administrators group on a local computer includes all the rights and permissions on that computer. If you want to grant Marge full control to a computer, you could add Marge's user account to the Administrators group on that computer. Once Marge is a member of the Administrators group, she has all the group's rights and permissions.

Similarly, you can grant other users the ability to back up and restore data by adding their user accounts to the Backup Operators group. Although the built-in groups are very useful, they don't meet all the requirements in most organizations. For example, if your organization wants to separate backup and restore responsibilities, you can create one group that can only back up data and another group that can only restore data.

In Windows domains, administrators often create groups that correspond to the departments of an organization. For example, imagine that Homer, Marge, and Bart work in the Sales department and need to access data stored in a shared folder named Sales on a network server. An administrator would simplify administration with the following steps, as shown in Figure 2.8:

1. Create a Sales group and add each of the user accounts to the Sales group.
2. Add the Sales group to the Sales folder.
3. Assign appropriate permissions to the Sales group for the Sales folder.

When the company adds new salespeople, the administrator creates accounts for them and places their accounts into the Sales group. These new salespeople now have access to everything assigned to this group. If any users change job roles within the company and leave the Sales department, the administrator removes them from the Sales group. This automatically prevents users from accessing any resources granted to the Sales group. This example shows how to use a group for the Sales department, but you can apply the same steps to any department or group of users.

Groups provide another security benefit. Imagine that a user is promoted out of the Sales department and now works in Marketing. If you have a Marketing group, you can place this user account into the Marketing group and remove the user account from the Sales group. Removing the user from the Sales group removes all the user rights and permissions applied from that group. However, if you're not using groups and assign permissions to users directly, you probably won't remember which resources were assigned to the user as a Sales department employee.

★ Remember This!

Group-based privileges reduce the administrative workload of access management. Administrators put user accounts into security groups and assign privileges to the groups. Users within a group automatically inherit the privileges assigned to the group.

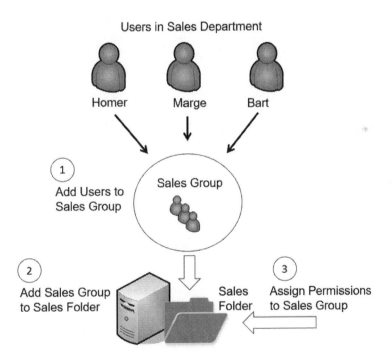

Figure 2.8: Establishing access with groups as roles

Rule-Based Access Control

Rule-based access control (rule-BAC) uses rules. The most common example is with rules in routers and firewalls. However, more advanced implementations cause rules to trigger within applications, too.

Routers and firewalls use rules within access control lists (ACLs). These rules define the traffic that the devices allow into the network, such as allowing Hypertext Transfer Protocol (HTTP) traffic for web browsers. These rules are typically static. In other words, administrators create the rules, and the rules stay the same unless an administrator changes them again.

However, some rules are dynamic. For example, intrusion prevention systems can detect attacks and then modify rules to block traffic from attackers. In this case, the attack triggers a change in the rules.

It's possible to configure user applications with rules. For example, imagine you want to give Homer additional permissions to a database if Marge is absent. You can configure a database rule to trigger a change to these permissions when the system recognizes that Marge is absent.

> ★ **Remember This!**
>
> Rule-based access control is based on a set of approved instructions, such as an access control list. Some rule-BAC systems use rules that trigger in response to an event, such as modifying ACLs after detecting an attack or granting additional permissions to a user in certain situations.

Discretionary Access Control

In the **discretionary access control (DAC)** scheme, objects (such as files and folders) have an owner, and the owner establishes access for the objects. Many operating systems, such as Windows and most Unix-based systems, use the DAC scheme.

A common example of the DAC scheme is the New Technology File System (NTFS) used in Windows. NTFS provides security by allowing users and administrators to restrict access to files and folders with permissions. The following section explains how NTFS uses the DAC scheme.

Filesystem Permissions

Microsoft systems use filesystem permissions with NTFS to describe the actions that users are permitted to take on files and folders. The following list describes basic NTFS permissions:

- **Write**. Users can change the contents of a file, such as changing words in a text file. This doesn't give them the ability to delete a file, but they can delete the contents.
- **Read**. Read permission allows a user to open and view the contents of a file.
- **Read & execute**. This gives a user permission to run any executable files, including scripts.
- **Modify**. Modify allows users to view and change files, including deleting files and folders or adding files to a folder.
- **Full control**. Users can do anything with a file or folder and modify its permissions.

It's possible to assign either Allow or Deny access to any file or folder. However, the filesystem uses a deny by default policy. If allow access is not granted, the system denies access by default. Firewalls often refer to this as implicit deny.

SIDs and DACLs

Microsoft systems identify users with security identifiers (SIDs), though you will rarely see a SID. A SID is a long string of numbers beginning with the letter S and separated by a series of dashes. For example, a SID might look like this: S-1-5-21-3991871189-223218. Instead of the system displaying the SID, it looks up the name associated with the SID and displays that name. Similarly, Microsoft systems identify groups with a SID.

Every object (such as a file or folder) includes a discretionary access control list (DACL) that identifies who can access it in a system using the DAC scheme. The DACL is a list of Access Control Entries (ACEs). Each ACE is composed of a SID and the permission(s) granted to the SID. As an example, a folder named Study Notes might have the following permissions assigned:

- Lisa: Full Control
- Bart: Read
- Maggie: Modify

Each of these entries is an ACE, and combined, all of the entries are a DACL. You can view the DACL for a folder by using The Viewing a DACL Lab in the online exercises for this chapter.

> ★ *Remember This!*
>
> The DAC scheme specifies that every object has an owner, and the owner has full, explicit control of the object. Microsoft NTFS uses the DAC scheme.

If users create a file, they are designated as the owner and have explicit control over the file. As the owner, users can modify the permissions on the object by adding user or group accounts to the DACL and assigning the desired permissions.

The DAC scheme is significantly more flexible than the MAC scheme described in the next section. MAC has predefined access privileges, and the administrator is required to make the changes. With DAC, if you want to grant another user access to a file you own, you simply make the change, and that user has access.

Mandatory Access Control

The **mandatory access control (MAC)** scheme uses labels (sometimes referred to as sensitivity labels or security labels) to determine access. Security administrators assign labels to both subjects (users) and objects (files or folders). When the labels match, the system can grant a subject access to an object. When the labels don't match, the access scheme blocks access.

Military units make wide use of this scheme to protect data. You might have seen movies where they show a folder with a big red and black cover page labeled "Top Secret." The cover page identifies the sensitivity label for the data contained within the folder. Users with a Top Secret label (a Top Secret clearance) and a need to know can access the Top Secret folder's data.

Need to know is an important concept to understand. Just because individuals have a Top Secret clearance doesn't mean they should automatically have access to all Top Secret data. Instead, access is restricted based on a need to know.

Security-enhanced Linux (SELinux) is one of the few operating systems using the mandatory access control scheme. It was created to demonstrate how the MAC scheme can be added to an operating system. In contrast, Windows operating systems use the discretionary access control scheme.

An SELinux policy is a set of rules that override standard Linux permissions. However, even if an SELinux policy is in place, it isn't necessarily enforced. SELinux has three modes:

- Enforcing mode will enforce the SELinux policy and ignore permissions. In other words, even if the permissions allow access to a file or directory, users will be denied access unless they meet the relevant SELinux policy rules.
- Permissive mode does not enforce the SELinux policy but instead uses the permissions. However, the system logs any access that would normally be blocked. This is useful when testing a policy.
- Disabled mode does not enforce the SELinux policy and does not log anything related to the policy.

Acronyms

Don't you just love these acronyms? There are actually three different meanings of MAC within the context of CompTIA Security+:

- Media access control (MAC) addresses are the physical addresses assigned to network interface cards (NICs).

- The mandatory access control (MAC) scheme is one of several access control schemes discussed later in this chapter.

- Message authentication code (MAC) provides integrity similar to how a hash is used.

If you're having trouble keeping them all straight, don't feel alone. The Glossary for this book spells out—and lists brief descriptions—for relevant acronyms. When taking practice test questions, I encourage you to think of the words instead of the acronyms. Knowing what it represents will make the question much easier when you see the acronym on the live test.

Labels and Lattice

The MAC scheme uses different levels of security to classify both the users and the data. These levels are contained in a lattice, which defines the levels of security that are possible for an object and the security levels that a user is cleared to access. Users are only allowed to access an object if their security clearance is equal to or higher than the level of the object.

Figure 2.9 shows how the MAC scheme uses a lattice to divide access into separate compartments based on a need to know. The lattice starts by defining different levels of Top Secret, Secret, Confidential, and For Official Use. Each of these labels defines specific security boundaries. Within these levels, the lattice defines specific compartments. For example, the Top Secret level includes compartments labeled Nuclear Power Plant, 007, and Forbidden Donut.

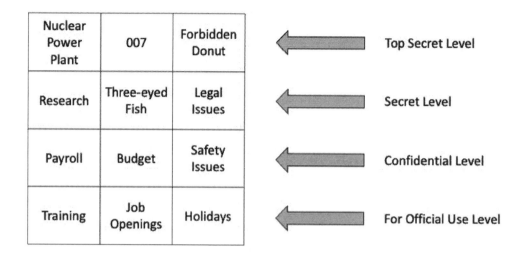

Figure 2.9: MAC scheme lattice

Imagine that Homer has a Top Secret clearance with a Nuclear Power Plant label. This gives him access to data within the Nuclear Power Plant compartment. However, he does not have access to data in the 007 or Forbidden Donut compartment unless he also has those clearances (and associated labels).

Higher-level clearances include lower-level clearances. For example, because Homer has a Top Secret clearance, he can be granted access to Secret and lower-level data. Again, though, he will only be able to access data on these lower levels based on his need to know.

As another example, imagine that Lisa has a Secret level clearance. Administrators can grant her access to data on the Secret level and lower levels based on her need to know. For example, they might grant her access to the Research data by assigning the Research label to her, but not necessarily grant her access to Three-eyed Fish or Legal Issues data. Additionally, they cannot grant her access to any data on the Top Secret level.

Establishing Access

An administrator is responsible for establishing access, but only someone at a higher authority can define the access for subjects and objects. Typically, a security professional identifies the specific access individuals are authorized to access. This person can also upgrade or downgrade the individuals' access when necessary. Note that the security professional does all this via paperwork and does not assign the rights and permissions on computer systems. Instead, the administrator assigns the rights and permissions based on the direction of the security professional.

> 📌 ***Remember This!***
>
> The MAC scheme uses sensitivity labels for users and data. It is commonly used when access needs to be restricted based on a need to know. Sensitivity labels often reflect classification levels of data and clearances granted to individuals.

Multiple approval levels are usually involved in the decision-making process to determine what a user can access. For example, in the military, an officer working in the security professional role would coordinate with higher-level government entities to upgrade or downgrade clearances. These higher-level entities approve or disapprove clearance requests.

Once an individual is formally granted access, a network administrator would be responsible for establishing access based on the clearances identified by the security professional. From the IT administrator's point of view, all the permissions and access privileges are predefined.

If someone needed different access, the administrator would forward the request to the security professional, who may approve or disapprove the request. On the other hand, the security professional may forward the request to higher entities based on established procedures. This process takes time and results in limited flexibility.

Attribute-Based Access Control

An ***attribute-based access control (ABAC)*** system evaluates attributes and grants access based on the value of these attributes. Attributes can be almost any characteristic of a user, the environment, or the resource. ABAC uses policies to evaluate attributes and grant access when the system detects a match in the policy.

As a simple example, Homer is a Nuclear Safety Inspector at the Springfield Nuclear Power Plant. His user account may be defined with the following attributes: employee, inspector, and nuclear aware. A file server at the plant includes a share called Inspector, and it holds documents commonly used by nuclear safety inspectors. An ABAC policy for the share might grant access to the share for any subjects that have the attributes of employee, inspector, and nuclear aware.

Many software-defined networks (SDNs) use ABAC schemes. Instead of rules on physical routers, policies in the ABAC system control the traffic. These policies typically use plain language statements. For example, an ABAC policy rule for a company that employs researchers might be: "Allow logged-on researchers to access research sites via the main network." Policy statements typically include four elements:

- **Subject.** This is typically a user. You can use any user property as an attribute such as employment status, group memberships, job roles, logged-on status, and more. In the example, the subject is identified as being logged on and a member of the researchers group.
- **Object.** This is the resource (such as a file, database, or application) that the user is trying to access. In the example, the object is research sites. The research sites object would include Internet access via a proxy server along with a specific list of URLs of research sites.
- **Action.** The action is what the user is attempting to do, such as reading or modifying a file, accessing specific websites, and accessing website applications. The example allows access to specific websites.
- **Environment.** The environment includes everything outside of the subject and object attributes. This is often referred to as the context of the access request. It can include the time, location, protocols, encryption, devices, and communication method. In the example, it specifies the main network as an environmental attribute.

> ★ *Remember This!*
>
> The ABAC scheme uses attributes defined in policies to grant access to resources. It's commonly used in software-defined networks (SDNs).

An ABAC system has a lot of flexibility and can enforce both a DAC and a MAC scheme. There are also many similarities between the ABAC scheme and the DAC and MAC schemes. In the DAC scheme, owners have control over the access, and in an ABAC scheme, owners can create policies to grant access. The MAC scheme uses labels assigned to both subjects and objects and grants access when the labels match. The ABAC scheme uses attributes that identify both subjects and objects, and grants access when a policy identifies a match.

If you want to dig into the ABAC scheme a little more, check out NIST SP 800-162, "Guide to Attribute Based Access Control (ABAC) Definition and Considerations."

Analyzing Authentication Indicators

Authentication systems provide a rich source of information for cybersecurity analysts looking for signs of potentially malicious activity. Sometimes the signs of this activity are buried in otherwise innocent-looking log entries. Some of the key things that you should look out for when reviewing authentication logs include:

Account lockouts. Watch for user accounts that have been locked out due to repeated failed login attempts, as those failed logins may be a sign of malicious activity.

Concurrent session usage. If the same user is logged in to the same (or different systems) from different locations at the same time, that may indicate that more than one person is using the account.

Impossible travel time. If a user completes a login from one location and then logs in from another geographic location without having spent enough time to travel between those locations, that may also indicate two users sharing the same account.

Blocked content. If content filters are screening out unusual levels of malicious code, that's worthy of further investigation.

Resource consumption. If processor time, memory, storage, or other resources are being used excessively without explanation, that may indicate that malicious code is running on the system.

Resource inaccessibility. If services suddenly become unavailable, malicious activity may be interfering with them. For example, a website may go down because of malicious code running on the web server.

Log anomalies. If logging levels are out-of-cycle, meaning that many log entries are appearing at unusual times or log files have gone missing, that may be an indicator of malicious activity.

These are just some examples of the types of indicators that may exist when malicious activity occurs on a system. You should also keep abreast of cybersecurity news sources and watch for published/documented indicators that reflect new types of malicious activity.

Chapter 2 Exam Topic Review

When preparing for the exam, make sure you understand these key concepts covered in this chapter.

Exploring Authentication Management

- Authentication allows entities to prove their identity by using credentials known to another entity.
- Identification occurs when a user claims or professes an identity, such as with a username, an email address, or biometrics.
- Authentication occurs when an entity provides proof of a claimed identity (such as with a password). A second entity is an authenticator, and it verifies the authentication.
- Authorization provides access to resources based on a proven identity.
- Accounting methods track user activity and record the activity in logs.

- Four factors of authentication are:
- Something you know, such as a username and password
- Something you have, such as a smart card or token
- Something you are, using biometrics, such as fingerprints, vein scans, facial scans, and gait analysis
- Somewhere you are, such as your home or office
- Password managers store and simplify the use of credentials for users. When users access websites needing credentials, the system automatically retrieves the stored credentials and submits them to the website.
- Push notifications are often used for 2FA. Users find them user-friendly and non-disruptive because they can verify their authentication by pressing a screen button.
- Account lockout policies lock out an account after a user enters an incorrect password too many times. This helps prevent brute force and dictionary attacks.
- Default passwords should be changed on any applications or devices before putting them into service.
- The false acceptance rate (FAR) identifies the percentage of times false acceptance occurs. The false rejection rate (FRR) identifies the percentage of times false rejections occur. The crossover error rate (CER) indicates the biometric system's quality or the system's efficacy rate. Lower CERs are better.
- HOTP and TOTP are open-source standards used to generate one-time-use passwords. HOTP generates one-time-use passwords that do not expire until they are used, and TOTP generates one-time passwords that expire after a specified period of time (typically 30-240 seconds).
- Single-factor authentication includes one or more authentication methods that use the same factor, such as a PIN and a password (both something you know). Dual-factor (or two-factor) authentication uses two factors of authentication, such as a token key (something you have) and a PIN (something you know). Multifactor authentication uses two or more factors and is stronger than any form of single-factor authentication.

Managing Accounts

- Users should not share accounts, and most organizations ensure the Guest account is disabled. Shared accounts prevent effective identification, authentication, authorization, and accounting.
- Privileged access management (PAM) implements stringent security controls over accounts with elevated privileges, such as administrator or root accounts. This includes allowing authorized users to access the administrator account without knowing the password, limiting the time users access the elevated privileges, and logging all related activity.
- Account policies often require administrators to have two accounts (an administrator account and a standard user account) to prevent privilege escalation and other attacks.

- An account disablement policy ensures that inactive accounts are disabled. Accounts for employees who either resign or are terminated should be disabled as soon as possible.
- Time-based logins (or time-based restrictions) prevent users from logging on or accessing network resources during specific hours. Location-based policies prevent users from logging on from certain locations.
- An account audit looks at the rights and permissions assigned to users and helps enforce the least privilege principle.

Comparing Authentication Services

- Single sign-on (SSO) allows users to authenticate with a single user account and access multiple resources on a network without authenticating again.
- SSO can be used to provide central authentication on the Internet with a federated database. A federated identity links a user's credentials from different networks or operating systems, but the federation treats it as one identity.
- SAML is an XML-based standard used to exchange authentication and authorization information between different parties. SAML is used with web-based applications.
- OAuth is an open standard for authorization. It allows users to log on with another account such as Google, Facebook, PayPal, Microsoft, or Twitter. It uses API calls to exchange information and a token to show that access is authorized.

Comparing Access Control Schemes

- The role-based access control (role-BAC) scheme uses roles to grant access by placing users into roles based on their assigned jobs, functions, or tasks. A roles and permissions matrix matching job titles with required privileges is useful as a planning document when using role-BAC.
- Group-based privileges are a form of role-BAC. Administrators create groups, add users to the groups, and then assign permissions to the groups. This simplifies administration because administrators do not have to assign permissions to users individually.
- The rule-based access control (rule-BAC) scheme is based on a set of approved instructions, such as ACL rules in a firewall. Some rule-BAC implementations use rules that trigger in response to an event, such as modifying ACLs after detecting an attack.
- In the discretionary access control (DAC) scheme, every object has an owner. The owner has explicit access and establishes access for any other user. Microsoft NTFS uses the DAC scheme, with every object having a discretionary access control list (DACL). The DACL identifies who has access and what access they are granted.
- Mandatory access control (MAC) uses security or sensitivity labels to identify objects (what you'll secure) and subjects (users). It is often used when access needs to be restricted based on a need to know. The administrator establishes access based on predefined

security labels. These labels are often defined with a lattice to specify the upper and lower security boundaries.

- An attribute-based access control (ABAC) evaluates attributes and grants access based on these attributes' values. It is used in many software-defined networks (SDNs).

📌 **Online References**

Have you looked at the online content recently? You can view labs and additional sample questions at **https://getcertifiedgetahead.com**.

Chapter 2 Practice Questions

1. Your organization wants to identify biometric methods used for identification. The requirements are:

   - Collect the data passively.
   - Bypass a formal enrollment process.
   - Avoid obvious methods that let the subject know data is being collected.

   Which of the following biometric methods BEST meet these requirements? (Select TWO.)

   A. Fingerprint
   B. Retina
   C. Iris
   D. Facial
   E. Palm vein
   F. Gait analysis

2. Your organization recently updated an online application employees use to log on when working from home. Employees enter their username and password into the application from their smartphone and the application logs their location using GPS. Which type of authentication is being used?

   A. One-factor
   B. Dual-factor
   C. Something you are
   D. Something you have

3. Management within your organization wants to add 2FA security for users working from home. Additionally, management wants to ensure that 2FA passwords expire after 30 seconds. Which of the following choices BEST meets this requirement?

   A. HOTP
   B. TOTP
   C. SMS
   D. Kerberos

4. Management within your organization has decided to implement a biometric solution for authentication into the data center. They have stated that the biometric system needs to be highly accurate. Which of the following provides the BEST indication of accuracy with a biometric system?

   A. The lowest possible FRR
   B. The highest possible FAR
   C. The lowest possible CER
   D. The highest possible CER

5. The Marvin Monroe Memorial Hospital was recently sued after removing a kidney from the wrong patient. Hospital executives want to implement a method that will reduce medical errors related to misidentifying patients. They want to ensure medical personnel can identify a patient even if the patient is unconscious. Which of the following would be the BEST solution?

   A. Gait analysis
   B. Vein scans
   C. Retina scan
   D. Voice recognition

6. Users regularly log on with a username and password. However, management wants to add a second authentication factor for any users who launch the gcga application. The method needs to be user-friendly and non-disruptive. Which of the following will BEST meet these requirements?

   A. An authentication application
   B. TPM
   C. HSM
   D. Push notifications

7. Your organization hires students during the summer for temporary help. They need access to network resources, but only during working hours. Management has stressed that it is critically important to safeguard trade secrets and other confidential information. Which of the following account management concepts would be MOST important to meet these goals?

   A. Account expiration
   B. Account lockout
   C. Time-of-day restrictions
   D. Password recovery
   E. Password history

8. You need to provide a junior administrator with appropriate credentials to rebuild a domain controller after it suffers a catastrophic failure. Of the following choices, what type of account would BEST meet this need?

   A. User account
   B. Generic account
   C. Guest account
   D. Service account

9. Lisa is reviewing an organization's account management processes. She wants to ensure that security log entries accurately report the identity of personnel taking specific actions. Which of the following steps would BEST meet this requirement?

   A. Implement generic accounts.
   B. Implement role-based privileges.
   C. Use an SSO solution.
   D. Remove all shared accounts.

10. A recent security audit discovered several apparently dormant user accounts. Although users could log on to the accounts, no one had logged on to them for more than 60 days. You later discovered that these accounts are for contractors who work approximately one week every quarter. Which of the following is the BEST response to this situation?

    A. Remove the account expiration from the accounts.
    B. Delete the accounts.
    C. Reset the accounts.
    D. Disable the accounts

11. A software developer is creating an application that must access files stored in the user's Google Drive. What is the best way for the user to grant the application access to their Google account?

A. OpenID Connect

B. Provide their Google password each time they log into the application

C. OAuth

D. Store their Google password in the application

12. Web developers in your organization are creating a web application that will interact with other applications running on the Internet. They want their application to receive user credentials from an app running on a trusted partner's web domain. Which of the following is the BEST choice to meet this need?

A. SSO

B. SAML

C. Kerberos

D. RADIUS

13. Artie has been working at Ziffcorp as an accountant. However, after a disagreement with his boss, he decides to leave the company and gives a two-week notice. He has a user account allowing him to access network resources. Which of the following is the MOST appropriate step to take?

A. Ensure his account is disabled when he announces that he will be leaving the company.

B. Immediately terminate his employment.

C. Force him to take a mandatory vacation.

D. Ensure his account is disabled during his exit interview.

14. You administer access control for users in your organization. Some departments have a high employee turnover, so you want to simplify account administration. Which of the following is the BEST choice?

A. User-assigned privileges

B. Group-based privileges

C. Domain-assigned privileges

D. Network-assigned privileges

15. An administrator needs to grant users access to different shares on file servers based on their job functions. Which of the following access control schemes would BEST meet this need?

A. Discretionary access control

B. Mandatory access control

C. Role-based access control

D. Rule-based access control

Chapter 2

Practice Question Answers

1. **D** and **F** are correct. It's possible to collect facial scan data and perform gait analysis without an enrollment process. You would use cameras to observe subjects from a distance and collect data passively. You need a formal enrollment process for fingerprints, retinas, irises, and palm vein methods. Retina and iris scans need to be very close to the eye and are very obvious. Palm vein methods require users to place their palm on a scanner. While it's possible to collect fingerprints passively, you still need an enrollment process.

2. **A** is correct. This is using one-factor authentication—something you know. The application uses the username for identification and the password for authentication. Note that even though the application is logging the location using Global Positioning System (GPS), there isn't any indication that it is using this information for authentication. Dual-factor authentication requires another factor of authentication such as something you are or something you have. The something you have factor referes to another source of information in your possession.

3. **B** is correct. A Time-based One-Time Password (TOTP) meets the requirement of two-factor authentication (2FA). A user logs on with regular credentials (such as a username and password), and then must enter an additional one-time password. Some smartphone apps use TOTP and display a refreshed password at set intervals, commonly every 30-240 seconds. An HMAC-based One-Time Password (HOTP) creates passwords that do not expire until they are used. Short message service (SMS) is sometimes used to send users a one-time use password via email or a messaging app, but these passwords typically don't expire until at least 15 minutes later. Kerberos uses tickets instead of passwords.

4. **C** is correct. A lower crossover error rate (CER) indicates a more accurate biometric system. The false acceptance rate (FAR) and the false rejection rate (FRR) vary based on the sensitivity of the biometric system and don't indicate accuracy by themselves. A higher CER indicates a less accurate biometric system.

5. **B** is correct. A vein scan implemented with a palm scanner would be the best solution of the available choices. The patient would place their palm on the scanner for biometric identification, or if the patient is unconscious, medical personnel can place the patient's palm on the scanner. None of the other biometric methods can be easily performed on an unconscious patient. Gait analysis attempts to identify someone based on the way they move. A retina scan scans the retina of an eye, but this will be difficult if someone is unconscious. Voice recognition identifies a person using speech recognition.

6. **D** is correct. Push notifications are user-friendly and non-disruptive. Users receive a notification on a smartphone or tablet and can often acknowledge it by simply pressing a button. An authentication application isn't as user-friendly as a push notification. It requires users to log on to the smartphone, find the app, and enter the code. A Trusted Platform Module (TPM) can provide for the implementation of full disk encryption, which would protect the data if someone accessed the laptop, but it doesn't prevent access. A hardware security module (HSM) is a removable device that can generate and store RSA keys used with servers. Neither a TPM nor an HSM is relevant in this question.

7. **C** is correct. Time-of-day restrictions should be implemented to ensure that temporary workers can only access network resources during work hours. The other answers represent good practices, but don't address the need stated in the question that "personnel need access to network resources, but only during working hours." Account expiration should be implemented if the organization knows the last workday of these workers. Account lockout will lock out an account if the wrong password is entered too many times. Password recovery allows users to recover a forgotten password or change their password if they forgot their password. Password history remembers previously used passwords and helps prevent users from using the same password.

8. **A** is correct. A user account is the best choice of the available answers. More specifically, it would be a user account with administrative privileges (also known as a privileged account) so that the administrator can add the domain controller. A generic account (also known as a shared account) is shared between two or more users and is not recommended. A guest account is disabled by default and it is not appropriate to grant the guest account administrative privileges. A service account is an account created to be used by a service or application, not a person.

9. **D** is correct. Removing all shared accounts is the best answer of the available choices. If two employees are using the same account, and one employee maliciously deletes data in a database, it isn't possible to identify which employee deleted the data. Generic accounts are

the same as shared accounts and shouldn't be   used. Role-based (or group-based) privileges assign the same permissions to all members of a group, which simplifies administration. A single sign-on (SSO) solution allows a user to log on once and access multiple resources.

10. **D** is correct. The best response is to disable the accounts and then enable them when needed by the contractors. Ideally, the accounts would include an expiration date so that they would automatically expire when no longer needed, but the scenario doesn't indicate the accounts have an expiration date. Because the contractors need to access the accounts periodically, it's better to disable them rather than delete them. Resetting the accounts implies you are changing the password, but this isn't needed.

11. **C** is correct. The OAuth authorization protocol is explicitly designed for this type of situation. Users of the application can grant the application limited access to resources in their Google account without disclosing their credentials. This protects the security of their account and limits the access granted to the application. If the user discloses their password to the application, this allows the application full access to their account. OpenID Connect is used to log into one service with credentials from another service and does not provide the type of authorization required in this scenario.

12. **B** is correct. Security Assertion Markup Language (SAML) is a single sign-on (SSO) solution used for web-based applications and would meet this requirement. All SSO solutions are not used on the Internet, so SSO isn't the best answer. Kerberos is an SSO solution used on internal networks such as in Microsoft Active Directory domains and Unix realms. Remote Authentication Dial-In User Service (RADIUS) provides authentication, authorization, and accounting (AAA) services for some remote access, wired, and wireless network solutions.

13. **D** is correct. His account should be disabled during the exit interview. It's appropriate to conduct an exit interview immediately before an employee departs. Employees often give a two-week or longer notice. If their access is revoked immediately, they won't be able to do any more work. While some companies do terminate employment when someone gives notice, from a security perspective, that doesn't address the needed action related to the user account. The purpose of a mandatory vacation is to detect fraud, but if the employee is leaving, any potential fraud will be detected when that employee leaves.

14. **B** is correct. Group-based privileges are a form of role-based access control and they simplify administration. Instead of assigning permissions to new employees individually, you can just add new employee user accounts into the appropriate groups to grant them the rights and permissions they need for the job. User- assigned privileges require you to manage

privileges for each user separately, and they increase the account administration burden. Domain-assigned and network-assigned privileges are not valid administration practices.

15. **C** is correct. The role-based access control (role-BAC) scheme is the best choice for assigning access based on job functions. A discretionary access control (DAC) scheme specifies that every object has an owner and owners have full control over objects, but it isn't related to job functions. A mandatory access control (MAC) scheme uses labels and a lattice to grant access rather than job functions. A rule-based access control (rule-BAC) scheme uses rules that trigger in response to events.

Chapter 3

Exploring Network Technologies and Tools

CompTIA Security+ objectives covered in this chapter:

1.2 Summarize fundamental security concepts.

- Zero trust (Control plane, Adaptive identity, Threat scope reduction, Policy-driven access control, Policy Administrator, Policy Engine, Data plane, Implicit trust zones, Subject/System, Policy Enforcement Point)

2.5 Explain the purpose of mitigation techniques used to secure the enterprise.

- Isolation
- Hardening techniques (Host-based firewall)

3.1 Compare and contrast security implications of different architecture models.

- Architecture and infrastructure concepts (Network infrastructure, Physical isolation, Air-gapped, Logical segmentation)

3.2 Given a scenario, apply security principles to secure enterprise infrastructure.

- Infrastructure considerations (Device placement, Security zones, Attack surface, Connectivity, Failure modes, Fail-open, Fail-closed, Network appliances, Jump server, Proxy server, Load balancer, Firewall types, Web application firewall (WAF), Unified threat management (UTM), Next-generation firewall (NGFW), Layer 4/Layer 7)
- Secure communication/access (Transport Layer Security (TLS), Secure access service edge (SASE))

3.3 Compare and contrast concepts and strategies to protect data.

- Segmentation

4.1 Given a scenario, apply common security techniques to computing resources.

- Hardening targets (Switches, Routers)

4.4 Explain security alerting and monitoring concepts and tools.

- Tools (Simple Network Management Protocol (SNMP) traps)

4.5 Given a scenario, modify enterprise capabilities to enhance security.
- Firewall (Rules, Access lists, Ports/protocols, Screened subnets)
- Web filter (Agent-based, Centralized proxy, Universal Resource Locator (URL) scanning, Content categorization, Block rules, Reputation)
- Operating system security (Group Policy)
- Implementation of secure protocols (Protocol selection, Port selection, Transport method)
- Email security (Domain-based Message Authentication, Reporting, and Conformance (DMARC), DomainKeys Identified Mail (DKIM), Sender Policy Framework (SPF), Gateway)

4.6 Given a scenario, implement and maintain identity and access management.
- Single sign-on (SSO) (Lightweight Directory Access Protocol (LDAP))

CompTIA recommends that you have some networking knowledge before you take the Security+ exam. However, many people tackle the exam without a strong background in networking. For example, you may have spent a lot of time troubleshooting connectivity but rarely manipulated access control lists (ACLs) on a router or modified firewall rules. This chapter reviews some basic networking concepts, devices, and network topologies used within secure networks. When appropriate, it digs into these topics a little deeper with a focus on security.

Reviewing Basic Networking Concepts

Before you can tackle any of the relevant security issues on a network, you'll need a basic understanding of networking. This section includes a very brief review of many of the different protocols and networking concepts that are relevant to security. If any of these concepts are completely unfamiliar to you, you might need to pick up a networking book to review them.

Networks carry data between computer systems. They interconnect desktop computers, servers, mobile devices, infrastructure components and anything else that needs network access. They do this using a series of protocols that describe how to encode the bits and bytes used by computers into the electrical signals, radio waves, and light pulses used by different types of networks.

OSI Model

The *Open Systems Interconnection (OSI) model* is a theoretical way to describe all of the different activities that happen on a network. The model has seven layers ranging from layer 1 (Physical) through layer 7 (Application). The lower the layer number, the closer you are to the actual wires and cabling of the network. The higher the layer number, the closer you are to the end user and the software running on a computer system.

> ### ★ *Remember This!*
>
> You can use a memory trick to remember the order of the OSI layers – make a sentence that has words starting with the seven letters of the model layers in order. My personal favorite is "Please Do Not Throw Sausage Pizza Away!" Other people use "All People Seem To Need Data Processing." You can choose whatever works for you!

Table 3.1 shows the seven layers of the OSI model.

Layer	Name	Mnemonic
1	Physical	Please
2	Data Link	Do
3	Network	Not
4	Transport	Throw
5	Session	Sausage
6	Presentation	Pizza
7	Application	Away

Table 3.1: OSI Model Layers

You don't need to know a tremendous amount about the OSI model to take the Security+ exam. If you tackle some other certifications, you'll need to learn the model in more detail. As you prepare, you should know just the basics of what each layer does:

- **Layer 1: Physical** is all about the basic equipment of networking: copper wires, fiber optic cables, and radio waves.
- **Layer 2: Data Link** is where network switches reside. It formats data into data frames and routes it between systems on the local network using their media access control (MAC) addresses.
- **Layer 3: Network** introduces IP addresses. At this layer, routers use IP addresses to send information between systems that are not located on the same local network. The Internet Protocol (IP) is the primary protocol used at this layer.
- **Layer 4: Transport** provides end-to-end communication services for applications. The Transmission Control Protocol (TCP) and User Datagram Protocol (UDP) exist at this layer.
- **Layer 5: Session** establishes, manages, and terminates sessions between applications running on different devices, allowing them to communicate and exchange data.

- **Layer 6: Presentation** translates data into a standard format that can be understood by the application layer, and provides encryption, compression, and other data transformation services.

- **Layer 7: Application** provides network services to applications, allowing them to communicate with other applications over the network.

You'll often hear these layers used by security and network professionals to help describe where a problem exists. For example, if there's a routing problem, someone might say "That's a Layer 3 problem." Or you might hear of a switching problem described as a Layer 2 issue.

That's all you need to know about the OSI model for the Security+ exam. If you'd like to learn more, check out the online appendix covering the OSI model in more detail. You'll find it at **https:// getcertifiedgetahead.com**.

Basic Networking Protocols

Networking protocols provide the rules needed for computers to communicate with each other on a network. Some Transmission Control Protocol/Internet Protocol (TCP/IP) protocols, such as TCP and IP, provide basic connectivity. Other protocols, such as Hypertext Transfer Protocol (HTTP) and Simple Mail Transfer Protocol (SMTP), support specific traffic types. This section includes information on common protocols that you'll need to understand for the CompTIA Security+ exam.

TCP/IP isn't a single protocol, but instead, it's a full suite of protocols. Obviously, there isn't room in this book to teach the details of all the TCP/IP protocols. Instead, the purpose of this section is to remind you of some of the commonly used protocols. Additionally, many of these protocols meet specific use cases, and this section describes these protocols within the context of use cases.

CompTIA has historically placed a lot of emphasis on well-known ports used by protocols. For example, the default port for HTTP is 80, and CompTIA Security+ test-takers needed to know that. The current objectives have deemphasized the importance of ports. However, you may still need to know them when implementing access control lists (ACLs) in routers and stateless firewalls and disabling unnecessary ports and services. With that in mind, I've included the well-known ports for many of the protocols in this chapter and in Appendix C, "Well-Known Ports."

The following list describes some basic networking protocols:

- ***Transmission Control Protocol (TCP)*** provides connection-oriented traffic (guaranteed delivery). TCP uses a three-way handshake, and Figure 3.1 shows the TCP handshake process. To start a TCP session, the client sends a SYN (synchronize) packet. The server responds with a SYN/ACK (synchronize/acknowledge) packet, and the client completes the third part of the handshake with an ACK packet to establish the connection.

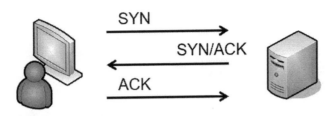

Figure 3.1: TCP handshake process

- **User Datagram Protocol (UDP)** provides connectionless sessions (without a three-way handshake). While TCP traffic provides guaranteed delivery, UDP makes a best effort to deliver data without using extra traffic to ensure delivery. TCP/IP traffic is either connection-oriented TCP traffic or connectionless UDP. Many network-based denial-of-service (DoS) attacks use UDP.

- **The Internet Protocol (IP)** identifies hosts in a TCP/IP network and delivers traffic from one host to another using IP addresses. IPv4 uses 32-bit addresses represented in dotted decimal format, such as 192.168.1.100. IPv6 uses 128-bit addresses using hexadecimal code, such as FE80:0000:0000:0000:20D4:3FF7:003F:DE62.

- **Internet Control Message Protocol (ICMP)** tests basic connectivity and includes tools like ping and tracert. For example, ping can check for basic connectivity between two systems while tracert can trace the network path between two systems. Many denial-of-service (DoS) attacks use ICMP. Because of how often ICMP is used in attacks, it has become common to block ICMP at firewalls and routers, which disables a ping response. Blocking ICMP prevents attackers from discovering devices on a network. For example, a scan can ping every IP address in a subnet. The responses identify what systems are running on that subnet.

- **Address Resolution Protocol (ARP)** resolves IPv4 addresses to MAC addresses. MAC addresses are also called physical addresses or hardware addresses because they are assigned to the device's network interface card (NIC) by the manufacturer. TCP/IP uses the IP address to get a packet to a destination network. It then uses the MAC address to get it to the correct host. In other words, ARP is required once the packet reaches the destination subnet. ARP poisoning attacks (discussed in Chapter 7) use ARP packets to give clients false hardware address updates, and attackers use them to redirect or interrupt network traffic.

Implementing Protocols for Use Cases

Networks don't automatically support all the available protocols. Instead, IT professionals identify a need based on organizational goals and enable the best protocols to meet that need. Many protocols mentioned in the CompTIA Security+ objectives support specific use cases and are discussed in this chapter.

Data in Transit Use Cases

Data in transit is any traffic sent over a network. When data is sent in cleartext, attackers can use a packet capture tool to read it. You can protect the confidentiality of Personally Identifiable Information (PII) and any other sensitive data in transit by encrypting it. Note that you can also encrypt data at rest, which is data stored on any type of medium. Chapter 10, "Understanding Cryptography and PKI," covers several specific encryption algorithms in more depth.

Some common use cases related to transferring files are transmitting data over the network, ensuring confidentiality when transmitting data over a network, and ensuring administrators connect to servers using secure connections. The following list identifies several *insecure* protocols that should *no longer be used* to transfer data over a network:

- **File Transfer Protocol (FTP)** uploads and downloads files to and from an FTP server. By default, FTP transmits data in cleartext, making it easy for an attacker to capture and read FTP data with a protocol analyzer.
- **Trivial File Transfer Protocol (TFTP)** is used to transfer smaller amounts of data, such as when communicating with network devices. Many attacks have used TFTP, but it is not an essential protocol on most networks. Because of this, administrators commonly disable it.
- **Secure Sockets Layer (SSL)** was the primary method used to secure HTTP traffic as Hypertext Transfer Protocol Secure (HTTPS). SSL can also encrypt other types of traffic, such as SMTP and Lightweight Directory Access Protocol (LDAP). However, SSL has been compromised and is not recommended for use.

You should generally not use FTP, TFTP, or SSL on modern networks because they are insecure and lack strong encryption. Fortunately, there are several secure alternatives that you can use. Here are some secure alternatives for protecting data in transit:

- **Transport Layer Security (TLS)** is the designated replacement for SSL and should be used instead of SSL for browsers using HTTPS.
- **Internet Protocol Security (IPsec)** is used to encrypt IP traffic. Chapter 4, "Securing Your Network," covers IPsec in more depth.
- **Secure Shell (SSH)** encrypts traffic in transit and can be used to encrypt other protocols such as FTP. **Secure Copy (SCP)** is based on SSH and is used to copy encrypted files over a network. SSH uses TCP port 22.
- **Secure File Transfer Protocol (SFTP)** is a secure implementation of FTP. It is an extension of Secure Shell (SSH) using SSH to transmit the files in an encrypted format. SFTP transmits data using TCP port 22.

- *File Transfer Protocol Secure (FTPS)* is another secure implementation of FTP. It uses TLS to encrypt FTP traffic.

SSL Versus TLS

SSL has been compromised and is not recommended for use. In September 2014, a team at Google discovered a serious vulnerability with SSL that they nicknamed the POODLE attack. POODLE is short for Padding Oracle On Downgraded Legacy Encryption. The SSL protocol is not maintained or patched, so this vulnerability remains.

This is one of the reasons that the U.S. government and many other organizations prohibit the use of SSL to protect any sensitive data. TLS is the recommended replacement. TLS was designed so that it can be used in almost any implementation that previously used SSL.

✦ Remember This!

Secure Shell (SSH) encrypts traffic over TCP port 22 and is used to transfer encrypted files over a network. Transport Layer Security (TLS) is a replacement for SSL and is used to encrypt many different protocols, including browser-based connections using HTTPS. Secure FTP (SFTP) uses SSH to encrypt traffic. FTP Secure (FTPS) uses TLS to encrypt traffic.

Email and Web Use Cases

Email and web traffic are some of the most common ways that people use the Internet today. These services were originally built without security in mind. Later, secure alternatives were introduced that provide encryption and other security services. Just like TLS replaced SSL with a secure alternative, email and web protocols were also updated to add in security controls. Let's take a look at common email and web protocols and their secure versions.

- *Simple Mail Transfer Protocol (SMTP)* transfers email between clients and SMTP servers. Originally, SMTP used TCP port 25 for unencrypted email. The secure version, **Simple Mail Transfer Protocol Secure (SMTPS)** adds TLS encryption and uses TCP port 587.
- *Post Office Protocol (POP3)* transfers emails from servers to end users. POP3 used TCP port 110 for unencrypted connections. The secure version of POP3 has the same name, but uses TCP port 995 for encrypted connections.
- *Internet Message Access Protocol (IMAP)* is used to store email on a mail server, and it allows users to organize and manage email in folders on the server. IMAP uses TCP port 143 for unencrypted connections and TCP port 993 for encrypted connections.

- **Hypertext Transfer Protocol (HTTP)** transmits web traffic between web servers and browsers. HTTP uses unencrypted connections to transfer data over TCP port 80. **Hypertext Transfer Protocol Secure (HTTPS)** adds TLS encryption to protect that data from prying eyes and uses TCP port 443.

> ### ★ Remember This!
>
> SMTP, POP3, and IMAP4 are primary email protocols. Well-known ports for encrypted and unencrypted traffic (respectively) are: SMTP uses ports 25 and 587, POP3 uses 110 and 995, IMAP4 uses 143 and 993. HTTP and HTTPS use ports 80 and 443, respectively.

Enhancing Email Security

Securing email is a complex task and there are controls other than encryption that you should consider deploying to further protect email, such as preventing forged email messages. SPF, DKIM, and DMARC are all email authentication methods that help prevent email fraud and abuse by verifying the authenticity of the sender's domain and ensuring that the email has not been modified during transit.

- **Sender Policy Framework (SPF)** uses DNS records to define which IP addresses are authorized to send emails on behalf of a domain.
- **DomainKeys Identified Mail (DKIM)** uses public key cryptography to sign and verify an email's domain and content.
- **Domain-based Message Authentication, Reporting, and Conformance (DMARC)** builds on top of SPF and DKIM by allowing domain owners to set policies for how to handle emails that fail authentication checks and providing reporting mechanisms to monitor and improve email authentication performance.

Together, SPF, DKIM, and DMARC provide a robust framework for email authentication and help protect users from spam, phishing, and other types of email-based attacks.

You also may wish to consider the use of **email gateways**. These gateways are network devices or software applications that act as a barrier between an organization's internal email system and the external internet, filtering incoming and outgoing emails for spam, malware, and other types of threats.

Directory Use Cases

Network operating systems commonly use a directory service to streamline management and implement secure authentication. For example, many organizations use Microsoft Active Directory Domain Services (AD DS). AD DS is a database of objects that provides a central access point to manage users, computers, and other directory objects.

The **Lightweight Directory Access Protocol (LDAP)** specifies the formats and methods used to query directories, such as Microsoft AD DS. LDAP uses TCP port 389. **LDAP Secure (LDAPS)** encrypts data with TLS using TCP port 636.

Windows domains use Active Directory, which is based on LDAP. Queries to Active Directory use the LDAP format. Similarly, Unix realms use LDAP to identify objects. LDAP Secure (LDAPS) uses encryption to protect LDAP transmissions. When a client connects with a server using LDAPS, the two systems establish a Transport Layer Security (TLS) session, and TLS encrypts all data sent between the two systems.

📌 *Remember This!*

Directory services, such as Microsoft Active Directory Domain Services (AD DS), provide authentication and authorization services for a network. AD DS uses LDAP, encrypted with TLS when querying the directory.

Voice and Video Use Cases

It's common for an organization to transport voice and video over a network, and some protocols work better with voice and video than others. UDP is commonly used instead of TCP as the underlying protocol with live voice and video streaming.

The **Real-time Transport Protocol (RTP)** delivers audio and video over IP networks. This includes **Voice over Internet Protocol (VoIP)** communications, streaming media, video teleconferencing applications, and devices using web-based push-to-talk features. However, organizations often want to secure these transmissions. The **Secure Real-time Transport Protocol (SRTP)** provides encryption, message authentication, and integrity for RTP.

The **Session Initiation Protocol (SIP)** is used to initiate, maintain, and terminate voice, video, and messaging sessions. SIP uses request and response messages when establishing a session. These messages are text, so it's easy to read them if they are captured. After SIP establishes the session, RTP or SRTP transports the audio or video.

SIP messages don't contain any data, but they do contain metadata about sessions. This includes information on the equipment used, the software used on the equipment, and the private IP. Many VoIP systems support SIP logging and can record these SIP messages. These logs may be useful in detecting SIP-based attacks. They can also be used in forensic investigations when trying to determine who is making certain calls and who they are calling.

Chapter 11, "Implementing Policies to Mitigate Risks," covers incident response and forensics topics. In some cases, both VoIP log files and SIP log files are useful in an investigation. VoIP logs show timestamps, caller phone numbers, recipient phone numbers, extensions (if used), and missed calls. Many third-party VoIP call manager applications support call recording. SIP log files show timestamps, sender IP addresses, and recipient IP addresses, and some third-party applications can also capture SIP messages.

Remote Access Use Case

There are many situations in which personnel need to access systems from remote locations. For example, imagine a server room hosts hundreds of servers, including domain controllers for a Microsoft domain. If administrators need to create a user account or implement a change in a Group Policy Object (GPO), they would rarely go to the server room. Instead, they would access the server remotely and make the change from their desk computer.

Years ago, administrators often used Telnet when remotely administering systems. However, Telnet sends data, including usernames and passwords, over the network in cleartext, and it isn't recommended for use. Today, administrators commonly use SSH (discussed earlier in the "Data in Transit Use Cases" section) instead of Telnet.

Administrators and clients often use **Remote Desktop Protocol (RDP)** to connect to other systems from remote locations. Microsoft uses RDP in different solutions such as Remote Desktop Services and Remote Assistance. RDP uses TCP port 3389. A common reason users cannot connect to systems with RDP is that port 3389 is blocked on a host-based or network firewall.

Another method of supporting remote access use cases is with a virtual private network (VPN). Chapter 4 discusses VPNs in more depth.

> ### ★ *Remember This!*
>
> Administrators connect to servers remotely using protocols such as Secure Shell (SSH) and the Remote Desktop Protocol (RDP). In some cases, administrators use virtual private networks to connect to remote systems.

OpenSSH

OpenSSH is a suite of tools that simplifies the use of SSH to connect to remote servers securely. It also supports the use of SCP and SFTP to transfer files securely. While OpenSSH is open source, many commercial products have integrated it into their applications.

Imagine Maggie wants to connect to a server on the network named gcga from a Linux system. She could use the following command:

```
ssh gcga
```

This initiates an SSH connection to the remote server using the default SSH port of 22 and Maggie's username on the client. It's also possible to initiate the connection with an account on the remote system. For example, the following command initiates an SSH connection using the root account of the remote system.

```
ssh root@gcga
```

The remote server will prompt her to enter a password at this time. However, using a strong, complex password is essential, and it can get old entering these passwords each time. Instead, OpenSSH supports authentication using a passwordless SSH login. You can use OpenSSH to create a public and private key pair. Maggie keeps the private key on her system and copies the public key to the remote server. Later, when she connects to the remote server, it prompts her system to authenticate with the private key.

The following OpenSSH command (ssh-keygen), entered at the client (Maggie's computer), will create the key pair:

```
ssh-keygen -t rsa
```

This creates a matched pair of a public and a private key similar to public/private key pairs used with certificates (described in Chapter 10). The keys are in two separate files. The file holding the public key can be shared, but the private key file must stay private. The names of the two files are:

- **id_rsa.pub.** This is the public key. You copy it to the remote server.
- **id_rsa.** This is the private key. It is stored on the client and must stay private.

The last step is to copy the public key to the remote server with the OpenSSH command ssh-copy-id.

```
ssh-copy-id root@gcga
```

The command knows the public key file's default location and where to copy it to on the remote server. Now, when Maggie connects (using ssh root@gcga), ssh will automatically use the key pair to provide strong authentication without requiring her to enter the password.

> ### ★ *Remember This!*
>
> OpenSSH is a suite of tools that simplifies the use of SSH to connect to remote servers securely. The ssh-keygen command creates a public/private key pair, and the ssh-copy-id command copies the public key to a remote server. The private key must always stay private.

Time Synchronization Use Case

There are many instances when systems need to be using the same time (or at least a reasonably close time). A common use case is to ensure systems have the accurate time. As an example, Kerberos requires all systems to be synchronized and be within five minutes of each other.

Within a Microsoft domain, one domain controller periodically uses the Windows Time service to locate a reliable Internet server running the **Network Time Protocol (NTP)**. NTP is the most commonly used protocol for time synchronization, allowing systems to synchronize their time to within tens of milliseconds. Other domain controllers within the network periodically synchronize their time with the first domain controller. All computers in the domain synchronize their time with one of these domain controllers. This process ensures all the computers have the accurate time.

Network Address Allocation Use Case

Network address allocation refers to allocating IP addresses to hosts within your network. You can do so manually, but most networks use **Dynamic Host Configuration Protocol (DHCP)** to dynamically assign IP addresses to hosts. DHCP also assigns other TCP/IP information, such as subnet masks, default gateways, DNS server addresses, and much more. The following sections provide a review of some basic networking concepts.

IPv4

IPv4 uses 32-bit IP addresses expressed in dotted decimal format. For example, the IPv4 IP address of 192.168.1.5 is four decimals separated by periods or dots. You can also express the address in binary form with 32 bits.

All Internet IP addresses are public IP addresses, and internal networks use private IP addresses. Public IP addresses are tightly controlled. You can't just use any public IP address.

Instead, you must either purchase or rent it. Internet Service Providers (ISPs) purchase entire ranges of IP addresses and issue them to customers. If you access the Internet from home, you are very likely receiving a public IP address from an ISP.

Routers on the Internet include rules to drop any traffic that is coming from or going to a private IP address, so you cannot allocate private IP addresses on the Internet. RFC 1918 specifies the following private address ranges:

- **10.x.y.z.** 10.0.0.0 through 10.255.255.255
- **172.16.y.z–172.31.y.z.** 172.16.0.0 through 172.31.255.255
- **192.168.y.z.** 192.168.0.0 through 192.168.255.255

These are the only three IPv4 address ranges that you may allocate within a private network.

IPv6

Although the number of IP addresses at first seemed inexhaustible, the Internet Assigned Numbers Authority (IANA) assigned the last block of IPv4 addresses in February 2011. The Internet Engineering Task Force (IETF) has since created IPv6, which provides a significantly larger address space than IPv4.

IPv6 uses 128-bit IP addresses expressed in hexadecimal format. For example, the IPv6 IP address of fe80:0000:0000:0000:02d4:3ff7:003f:de62 includes eight groups of four hexadecimal characters, separated by colons. Each hexadecimal character is composed of 4 bits.

Instead of private IP addresses, IPv6 uses unique local addresses. They are only allocated within private networks and not assigned to systems on the Internet. Unique local addresses start with the prefix of fc00.

Domain Name Resolution Use Case

The primary purpose of **Domain Name System (DNS)** is for domain name resolution. DNS resolves hostnames to IP addresses. Systems are constantly querying DNS, though it is usually transparent to users. Imagine that you want to visit **https://getcertifiedgetahead.com/**. You enter the URL into your web browser or click a link on a page, and your system queries a DNS server for the site's IP address. Figure 3.2 shows what is occurring between your system and DNS.

Sometimes, the DNS server you query knows the answer and just gives the response. Other times, it queries one or more other DNS servers to get the answer. When the DNS server queries other DNS servers, it puts the answer in its cache so that it doesn't have to repeat the same query. Similarly, when clients receive answers from DNS servers, they store the answer in their cache so that they don't have to repeat the query.

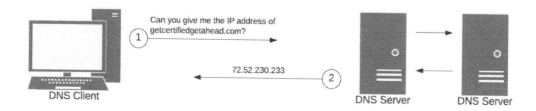

Figure 3.2: A basic DNS query

DNS servers host data in zones, which you can think of as databases. Zone files include multiple records, such as the following types:

- **A**. Also called a host record. This record holds the hostname and IPv4 address and is the most used record in a DNS server. A DNS client queries DNS with the name using a forward lookup request, and DNS responds with the IPv4 address from this record.
- **AAAA**. This record holds the hostname and IPv6 address. It's like an A record except that it is for IPv6.
- **PTR**. Also called a pointer record. It is the opposite of an A record. Instead of a DNS client querying DNS with the name, the DNS client queries DNS with the IP address. When configured to do so, the DNS server responds with the name. PTR records are optional, so these reverse lookups do not always work.
- **MX**. Also called mail exchange or mail exchanger. An MX record identifies a mail server used for email. The MX record is linked to the A record or AAAA record of a mail server. When there is more than one mail server, the one with the lowest preference number in the MX record is the primary mail server.
- **CNAME**. A canonical name, or alias, allows a single system to have multiple names associated with a single IP address. For example, a server named Server1 in the domain **getcertifiedgetahead.com** might have an alias of FileServer1 in the same domain.
- **SOA**. The start of authority (SOA) record includes information about a domain or zone and some of its settings. For example, it includes the TTL (Time to Live) settings for DNS records. DNS clients use the TTL setting to determine how long to cache DNS results. TTL times are in seconds, and lower times cause clients to renew the records more often.

DNSSEC

One risk with DNS is **DNS poisoning**, also known as DNS cache poisoning. When successful, attackers modify the DNS cache with a bogus IP address. For example, imagine an attacker wants to send users to a malicious website each time they want to go to msn.com. One way is to modify the A or AAAA record in the DNS cache for msn.com. Instead of sending users to the IP address used by msn.com, it will send users to the malicious website's IP address.

One of the primary methods of preventing DNS cache poisoning is with **Domain Name System Security Extensions (DNSSEC)**. DNSSEC is a suite of extensions to DNS that provides validation for DNS responses. It adds a Resource Record Signature (RRSIG), commonly referred to as a digital signature, to each record. The RRSIG provides data integrity and authentication for DNS replies. If a DNS server receives a DNSSEC-enabled response with digitally signed records, the DNS server knows that the response is valid.

Understanding Basic Network Infrastructure

Networks connect computing devices together so that users can share resources, such as data, printers, and other devices. Any device with an IP address is a host, but you'll often see them referred to as clients or nodes.

A common use case for a switch is to connect hosts together within a network. A common use case for a router is to connect multiple networks together to create larger and larger networks.

When discussing the different network devices, it's important to remember the primary methods IPv4 uses when addressing TCP/IP traffic:

- **Unicast.** One-to-one traffic. One host sends traffic to another host using a destination IP address. The host with the destination IP address will process the packet. Other hosts on the same network may see the packet, but they will not process it because it isn't addressed to them.
- **Broadcast.** One-to-all traffic. One host sends traffic to all other hosts on the subnet, using a broadcast address such as 255.255.255.255. Every host that receives broadcast traffic will process it. Switches pass broadcast traffic between their ports, but routers do not pass broadcast traffic.

Switches

A **switch** connects computers and other devices to each of its physical ports. It creates internal switched connections when two computers communicate with each other.

Consider Figure 3.3 below. When the switch turns on, it starts out without any knowledge other than knowing it has four physical ports. Imagine that the first traffic is the beginning of a TCP/IP conversation between Lisa's computer and Homer's computer.

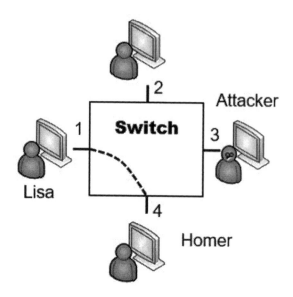

Figure 3.3: Switch

When Lisa's computer sends the first packet, it includes the MAC address of the destination computer. However, because the switch doesn't know which port Homer's computer is connected to, it forwards this first packet to all the ports on the switch.

Included in that first packet is the MAC address of Lisa's computer. The switch logs this information into an internal table. It then directs any future traffic addressed to Lisa's MAC address to port 1, and port 1 only.

When Homer's computer receives the packet, it responds. Embedded in this return packet is the MAC address of Homer's computer. The switch captures Homer's MAC address and logs it with port 4 in the internal table. From here on, any unicast traffic between Lisa's and Homer's computers is internally switched between only ports 1 and 4. Switches will internally switch unicast traffic. However, they pass broadcast traffic to all ports.

Most of the previous discussion is basic networking, but what you really need to know is why it's relevant in security. If an attacker installed a protocol analyzer on a computer attached to another port (such as port 3 in Figure 3.3), the protocol analyzer would not capture unicast traffic going through the switch to other ports. If Lisa and Homer are exchanging data on ports 1 and 4, none of the traffic reaches port 3. The protocol analyzer can't capture traffic that doesn't reach the port.

In contrast, if the computers were connected with a simple hub, the attacker could capture it because unicast traffic goes to all ports on a hub. This is the main security reason why organizations replace hubs with switches. The switch reduces the risk of an attacker capturing data with a protocol analyzer. Of course, switches also increase the efficiency of a network.

Hardening Switches

Security professionals work closely with network professionals to ensure that switches are configured securely. These devices are at the front lines of networking and if they aren't secure they can easily be compromised by an attacker. The process of configuring switches and other devices in a secure manner is known as **hardening** the device.

In the next several sections, we examine common techniques for hardening switches.

Port Security

Port security limits the computers that can connect to physical ports on a switch. At the most basic level, administrators disable unused ports. For example, individual RJ-45 wall jacks in an office lead to specific physical ports on a switch. If the wall jack is not in use, administrators can disable the switch port. This prevents someone from plugging in a laptop or other computer into the wall jack and connecting to the network.

Comparing Ports and Ports

A physical port used by a network device, such as a switch or a router, is entirely different from the logical ports discussed previously. You plug a cable into a physical port. A logical port is a number embedded in a packet and identifies a specific service, service connection endpoint, process or protocol.

MAC filtering is another example of port security. In a simple implementation, the switch remembers the first one or two MAC addresses that connect to a port. It then blocks access to systems using any other MAC addresses. You can also manually configure each port to accept traffic only from a specific MAC address. This limits each port's connectivity to a specific device using this MAC address. This can be very labor-intensive, but it provides a higher level of security.

📌 *Remember This!*

Port security includes disabling unused ports and limiting the number of MAC addresses per port. A more advanced implementation is to restrict each physical port to only a single specific MAC address.

Broadcast Storm and Loop Prevention

In some situations, a network can develop a **switching loop** or bridge loop problem. This floods a network with traffic and can effectively disable a switch. For example, if a user connects two ports of a switch together with a cable, it creates a switching loop where the switch continuously sends and resends unicast transmissions through the switch. In addition to disabling the switch, it also degrades the performance of the overall network.

This is trivial for many network administrators because most current switches have **Spanning Tree Protocol (STP)** or the newer **Rapid STP (RSTP)** installed and enabled. They provide both **broadcast storm prevention** and **loop prevention** for switches. However, if these protocols are disabled, the switch is susceptible to loop problems. The simple solution is to ensure that switches include loop protection such as STP or RSTP.

Spanning Tree Protocol also protects the network against potential attackers. For example, imagine an attacker visits a conference room and has access to RJ-45 wall jacks. If loop protection isn't enabled, he can connect two jacks together with a cable, slowing network performance down to a crawl.

★ *Remember This!*

Broadcast storm and loop prevention such as STP or RSTP is necessary to protect against switching loop problems, such as those caused when two ports of a switch are connected.

Bridge Protocol Data Unit Guard

STP sends **Bridge Protocol Data Unit (BPDU)** messages in a network to detect loops. When the loops are detected, STP shuts down or blocks traffic from switch ports sending redundant traffic. Switches exchange BPDU messages with each other using their non-edge ports.

An edge port is a switch port connected to a device, such as a computer, server, or printer. These devices should not generate BPDU messages. If they do, it indicates a problem, such as a malicious actor sending false BPDU messages.

Many switches support a **BPDU Guard** feature that is enabled on edge ports. It monitors the ports for any unwanted BPDU messages. If it receives any, it disables the port, effectively blocking the BPDU attack.

Routers

A **router** connects multiple network segments into a single network and routes traffic between the segments. Because routers don't pass broadcasts, they effectively reduce traffic on any single segment. Segments separated by routers are sometimes referred to as broadcast domains. If a network has too many computers on a single segment, broadcasts can result in excessive collisions and reduce network performance. Moving computers to a different segment separated by a router can significantly improve overall performance. Similarly, subnetting networks creates separate broadcast domains.

Cisco routers are popular, but many other brands exist. Most routers are physical devices, and physical routers are the most efficient. However, it's also possible to add routing software to computers with more than one NIC. For example, Windows Server products can function as routers by adding additional services to the server.

Hardening Routers

Just as we implement strong security controls to secure network switches, we also want to harden our routers to protect them against attack. Let's look at some of the technologies that we can use to better secure routers.

Router Access Control Lists (ACLs)

Access control lists (ACLs) are rules implemented on routers (and on firewalls) to identify what traffic is allowed and what traffic is denied. Rules within an ACL provide rule-based management for the router and control inbound and outbound traffic.

Router ACLs provide basic packet filtering. They filter packets based on three common characteristics: IP addresses, ports, and protocols:

- **IP addresses and networks.** You can add a rule in the ACL to block access from any single computer based on the IP address. If you want to block traffic from one subnet to another, you can use a rule to block traffic using the subnet IDs. For example, the Sales department may be in the 192.168.1.0/24 network, and the accounting department may be in the 192.168.5.0/24 network. You can prevent these two networks from communicating with each other using a router ACL.
- **Ports.** You can filter traffic based on logical ports. For example, if you want to block HTTPS traffic, you can create a rule to block traffic on TCP port 443. Note that you can choose to block incoming traffic, outgoing traffic, or both. In other words, it's possible to allow outgoing HTTPS traffic while blocking incoming HTTPS traffic.

Implicit Deny

Implicit deny is an important concept to understand, especially in the context of ACLs. It indicates that all traffic that isn't explicitly allowed is implicitly denied. For example, imagine you configure a router to allow Hypertext Transfer Protocol (HTTP) to a web server. The router now has an explicit rule defined to allow this traffic to the server. If you don't define any other rules, the implicit deny rule blocks all other traffic. Firewalls (discussed later in this chapter) also use an implicit deny rule.

The implicit deny rule is the last rule in an ACL. Some devices automatically apply the implicit deny rule as the last rule. Other devices require an administrator to place the rule at the end of the ACL manually. Syntax of an implicit deny rule varies on different systems, but it might be something like DENY ANY ANY, or DENY ALL ALL, where both ANY and ALL refer to any type of traffic.

While implicit deny is a common phrase used with routers and firewalls, it isn't common in everyday language. Simplified, you can think of it as default deny or block by default. In other words, the initial rules in an ACL identify traffic that is allowed. The last rule (implicit deny) denies, or blocks, all other traffic by default.

> ### 📌 *Remember This!*
>
> Routers and stateless firewalls (or packet-filtering firewalls) perform basic filtering with an access control list (ACL). ACLs identify what traffic is allowed and what traffic is blocked. An ACL can control traffic based on networks, subnets, IP addresses, ports, and some protocols. Implicit deny blocks all access that has not been explicitly granted. Routers and firewalls use implicit deny as the last rule in the access control list.

Route Security

The **route** command is used to display or modify a system's routing table on both Windows and Linux systems. Using **route print**, you can see all the paths the system knows to other networks. If the routing table doesn't include an entry to a specific network, the system uses the default gateway. The default gateway is the IP address of a router on a network and typically provides a path to the Internet. If you need to add a path to a different network, you can use the route add command.

You can also use the **route** command to verify route security. For example, the route table should point to a known default gateway. If malicious actors modify routing tables for systems, they can reroute traffic to a different router and use it to capture traffic in an **on-path attack**. You'll learn more about on-path attacks in Chapter 7.

Simple Network Management Protocol

The **Simple Network Management Protocol (SNMP)** monitors and manages network devices, such as routers or switches. This includes using SNMP to modify the devices' configuration or have network devices report status back to a central network management system. SNMP agents installed on devices send information to an SNMP manager via notifications known as **SNMP traps** (sometimes called device traps).

SNMPv1 and v2 both have vulnerabilities, including sending passwords across the network in cleartext, but SNMPv3 encrypts credentials before sending them over the wire. A common use case supported by SNMPv3 is to *provide secure management of network devices*. SNMPv3 uses UDP ports 161 and 162.

> ✦ **Remember This!**
>
> Administrators use SNMPv3 to manage and monitor network devices, and SNMP uses UDP ports 161 and 162. SNMPV3 encrypts credentials before sending them over the network and is more secure than earlier versions.

Firewalls

A **firewall** filters incoming and outgoing traffic for a single host or between networks. In other words, a firewall can ensure only specific types of traffic are allowed into a network or host, and only specific types of traffic are allowed out of a network or host.

The purpose of a firewall in a network is like a firewall in a car. The firewall in a car is located between the engine and passenger compartment. If a fire starts in the engine compartment, the firewall provides a layer of protection for passengers in the passenger compartment. Similarly, a firewall in a network will try to keep the bad traffic (often in the form of attackers) out of the network.

Of course, an engine has a lot of moving parts that can do damage to people if they accidentally reach into it while it's running. The firewall in a car protects passengers from touching any of those moving parts. Similarly, a network can also block users from going to places that an administrator deems dangerous. For example, uneducated users could inadvertently download damaging files, but many firewalls can block potentially malicious downloads.

Firewalls start with a basic routing capability for packet filtering as described in the "Routers and ACLs" section, including the use of an implicit deny rule. More advanced firewalls go beyond simple packet filtering and include advanced content filtering.

Host-Based Firewalls

A **host-based firewall** monitors traffic going in and out of a single host, such as a server or a workstation. It monitors traffic passing through the NIC and can prevent intrusions into the computer via the NIC. Many operating systems include software-based firewalls used as host-based firewalls. For example, Microsoft includes the Microsoft Defender Firewall with Windows operating systems. Additionally, many third-party host-based firewalls are available. Host-based firewalls allow you to configure rules to allow or restrict inbound and outbound traffic.

Host-based firewalls provide valuable protection for systems against unwanted intrusions. Many organizations use host-based firewalls on each system, along with network firewalls, as part of an overall defense-in-depth strategy.

Network-Based Firewalls

While host-based firewalls protect a single system, **network-based firewalls** protect an entire network. A network-based firewall is usually a **network appliance**. That means that it is sold as a hardware unit that already contains all of the software necessary to run as a firewall. Network-based firewalls can also be sold as virtual appliances, ready to run on your organization's virtualization platform.

A network-based firewall has two or more network interface cards (NICs), and all traffic passes through the firewall. The firewall controls traffic going in and out of a network. It does this by filtering traffic based on firewall rules and allows only authorized traffic to pass through it. Most organizations include at least one network-based firewall at the network border between their intranet (or internal network) and the Internet.

> ### ★ Remember This!
>
> Host-based firewalls provide protection for individual hosts, such as servers or workstations. Network-based firewalls run on dedicated hardware and provide protection for an entire network. You should use host-based firewalls and network-firewalls together to achieve a defense-in-depth approach to network security.

Stateless Firewall Rules

Stateless firewalls use rules implemented in ACLs to identify allowed and blocked traffic. They treat each network packet that they see as a new event and don't track any information (or "state") about previous network traffic. This is similar to how a router uses rules within ACLs. In fact, you can think of a router as a stateless firewall.

Firewalls use an implicit deny strategy to block all traffic that is not explicitly allowed. Although rules within ACLs look a little different depending on what hardware you're using, they generally include the following elements:

- **Permission.** You'll typically see this as PERMIT or ALLOW allowing the traffic. Most systems use DENY to block the traffic.

- **Protocol.** Typically, you'll see TCP or UDP here, especially when blocking specific TCP or UDP ports. If you want to block both TCP and UDP traffic using the same port, you can use IP instead. Using ICMP here blocks ICMP traffic, effectively blocking ping and some other diagnostics that use ICMP.

- **Source.** Traffic comes from a source IP address. You identify an IP address to allow or block traffic from a single IP address or from a range of IP addresses, such as from a single subnet. Wildcards such as any or all include all IP addresses.

- **Destination.** Traffic is addressed to a destination IP address. You identify an IP address to allow or block traffic to a single IP address or to a range of IP addresses, such as to an entire subnet. Wildcards such as any or all include all IP addresses.

- **Port or protocol.** Typically, you'll often see a well-known port such as port 443 for HTTPS in a rule. However, some devices support codes such as HTTPS for HTTPS traffic.

📌 *Remember This!*

Firewalls use a deny any any, deny any, or a drop all statement at the end of the ACL to enforce an implicit deny strategy. The statement forces the firewall to block any traffic that wasn't previously allowed in the ACL. The implicit deny strategy provides a secure starting point for a firewall.

Stateful Firewalls

A **stateful firewall** inspects traffic and makes decisions based on the traffic context or state. It keeps track of established sessions, inspects traffic based on its state within a session, and it blocks traffic that isn't part of an established session. As an example, a TCP session starts with a three-way handshake. If a stateful firewall detects TCP traffic without a corresponding three-way handshake, it recognizes this as suspicious traffic and can block it.

Modern network-based firewalls are all stateful firewalls. They operate at the Transport layer of the OSI model, so they are also commonly referred to as **Layer 4 firewalls**.

A common security issue with stateless firewalls is misconfigured ACLs. For example, if the ACL doesn't include an implicit deny rule, it can allow almost all traffic into the network.

Web Application Firewall

A **web application firewall (WAF)** is a firewall specifically designed to protect a web application. A web server hosts the web application, and the WAF is placed between the web server and web server clients. The WAF can be a stand-alone appliance or software added to another device, and it protects the web server from a wide variety of web-based attacks, such as cross-site scripting (XSS) attacks. Chapter 7, "Protecting Against Advanced Attacks," discusses XSS attacks in more depth.

Imagine an organization hosts an e-commerce website to generate revenue. The web server is placed within a screened subnet (discussed later in this chapter), but due to the data that the web server handles, it needs more protection. All traffic destined for the web server goes through the WAF first, and the WAF blocks malicious traffic.

Note that you wouldn't use a WAF in place of a network-based firewall. Instead, it provides an added layer of protection for the web application in addition to a network-based firewall.

> ### ★ Remember This!
>
> A stateless firewall blocks traffic using only an ACL, and a stateful firewalls use ACLs as well but also consider the state of the packet within a session. Web application firewalls provide strong protection for web servers. They protect against several different types of attacks, focusing on web application attacks.

Next-Generation Firewall

A *next-generation firewall (NGFW)* is an advanced firewall that adds capabilities that aren't available in first-generation or second-generation firewalls. The first generation of firewalls were packet-filtering firewalls, using stateless firewall rules, and could only allow or block traffic after evaluating individual packets. The second generation of firewalls added in stateful firewall rules. This allows firewalls to additionally evaluate traffic based on its session state.

Firewalls have steadily improved over the years, and if each improvement was labeled as another generation, we might be on the ninety-ninth generation. Thankfully, we're just using NGFW to indicate that a firewall adds additional capabilities to first- and second-generation firewalls.

An NGFW performs deep-packet inspection, adding application-level inspection as a core feature. The NGFW is aware of common application protocols used on the Internet, such as FTP and HTTP. By using deep-packet inspection, the NGFW can identify application commands and detect potentially malicious traffic. This allows it to apply content filtering and URL filtering.

WAFs and NGFWs both analyze information about all layers of the OSI model, all the way through Layer 7, the Application layer. Therefore, they are often called *Layer 7 firewalls*.

Failure Modes

Security systems that enforce policies sometimes experience failures. Software running on a firewall might crash or a router configuration file might contain errors. The designers of these systems must choose one of two failure modes for their platforms:

- **Fail-open** system allows everything to pass through the system when it fails. In this approach, no security controls are enforced, but there is no disruption to network activity.
- **Fail-closed** system allows nothing to pass through the system when it fails. In this approach, there is a significant disruption to network activity but no security policies are violated.

Generally speaking, security professionals prefer fail-closed systems because they limit risk.

Implementing Network Designs

There are several elements involved in creating a secure network. This includes the use of various topologies and different network appliances. Segmenting network devices and traffic can improve performance and increase security. This section covers physical security and logical security methods used for both segmentation and isolation. It also covers several different network appliances used for segmentation and isolation.

Security Zones

Most networks have Internet connectivity, but it's rare to connect a network directly to the Internet. Instead, it's common to divide the network into different **security zones**, using different topologies. Two terms that are relevant here are:

- **Intranet.** An **intranet** is an internal network. People use the intranet to communicate and share content with each other. While it's common for an intranet to include internal web servers, this isn't a requirement.
- **Extranet.** An **extranet** is part of a network that can be accessed by authorized entities from outside of the network. For example, it's common for organizations to allow limited access to authorized business partners, customers, vendors, suppliers or others.

The network perimeter provides a boundary between the intranet and the Internet. Boundary protection includes multiple methods to protect the network perimeter. The goal of placing systems into different zones is to limit the connectivity they have to each other and reduce the **attack surface** of the organization.

Screened Subnet

A **screened subnet**, also known as a **demilitarized zone (DMZ)**, is a security zone between a private network and the Internet. Attackers seek out servers on the Internet, so any server placed directly on the Internet has the highest amount of risk. However, the screened subnet provides a layer of protection for these Internet-facing servers while also allowing clients to connect to them.

As an example, Figure 3.4 shows a common network configuration with a screened subnet. The screened subnet is the area between the two firewalls (FW1 and FW2) and hosts several Internet-facing servers. Many screened subnets have two firewalls, creating a buffer zone between the Internet and the internal network, as shown in Figure 3.4, though other screened subnet configurations are possible.

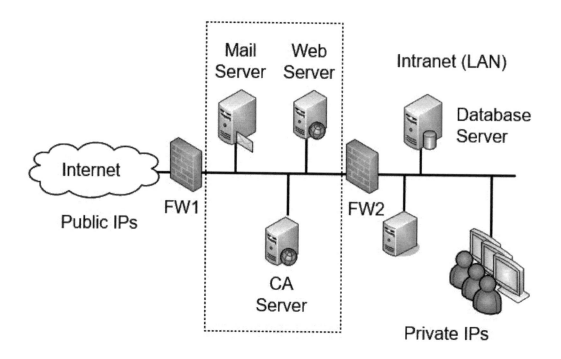

Figure 3.4: Network with screened subnet

In this configuration, one firewall separates the screened subnet from the Internet. The second firewall separates the screened subnet from the internal network. Each firewall includes detailed rules designed to filter traffic and protect both the internal network and public-facing servers. One way of saying this is that the screened subnet provides Internet access to the services hosted in the screened subnet while segmenting access to the internal network.

For example, FW1 can have rules to allow traffic to the servers in the screened subnet but block unsolicited traffic to FW2. The mail server would send and receive email to and from other mail servers on the Internet through port 25 or port 587 of FW1 and send and receive email to internal clients through port 25 or port 587 on FW2. The web server hosts webpages to any Internet users through ports 80 and 443 on FW1, but FW2 blocks incoming traffic using these ports. The certificate authority (CA) server validates certificates for Internet clients by answering through FW1.

Notice in Figure 3.4 that the intranet includes a database server. The web server may use this to create webpages for an e-commerce site. The database server could hold product data, customer data, and much more. FW2 allows traffic between the web server (and only the web server) and the database server on port 1433. FW2 would block all other Internet traffic to the database server.

It's also possible for the web server and the database server to be part of an extranet. For example, imagine that the web server hosts a site that business partners can use to place orders. The web server would first authenticate them before granting them full access. After users log on, the website connects to the back-end database server, allowing them to browse the inventory and place orders. Because this site is only for authorized business partners, it is an extranet.

The screened subnet can host any Internet-facing server, not just those shown in the figure. Other examples include FTP servers used to upload and download files and virtual private network (VPN) servers used for providing remote access.

> ### ★ Remember This!
>
> A screened subnet (sometimes called a DMZ) is a buffer zone between the Internet and an internal network. It allows access to services while segmenting access to the internal network. In other words, Internet clients can access the services hosted on servers in the screened subnet, but the screened subnet provides a layer of protection for the intranet (internal network).

Network Address Translation Gateway

Network Address Translation (NAT) is a protocol that translates public IP addresses to private IP addresses and private IP addresses back to public. A **network address translation gateway** hosts NAT and provides internal clients with private IP addresses a path to the Internet. Instead of using a NAT gateway, it's also possible to enable NAT on an Internet-facing firewall. A commonly used form of NAT is network address and port translation, commonly called Port Address Translation (PAT).

Some of the benefits of these translation technologies include:

- **Public IP addresses don't need to be purchased for all clients**. A home or company network can include multiple computers that can access the Internet through one router running NAT. Larger companies requiring more bandwidth may use more than one public IP address.
- **NAT hides internal computers from the Internet**. Computers with private IP addresses are isolated and hidden from the Internet. NAT provides a layer of protection to these private computers because they aren't as easy to attack and exploit from the Internet.

One of the drawbacks to NAT is that it is not compatible with IPsec. You can use L2TP to create VPN tunnels and use it with IPsec to encrypt VPN traffic. Although there are ways of getting around NAT's incompatibility with IPsec, if your design includes IPsec going through NAT, you'll need to closely examine it. NAT can be either static NAT or dynamic NAT:

- **Static NAT.** Static NAT uses a single public IP address in a one-to-one mapping. It maps a private IP address with a single public IP address.
- **Dynamic NAT.** Dynamic NAT uses multiple public IP addresses in a one-to-many mapping. Dynamic NAT decides which public IP address to use based on load. For example, if several users are connected to the Internet on one public IP address, NAT maps the next request to a less-used public IP address.

> ### ★ *Remember This!*
>
> NAT translates public IP addresses to private IP addresses and private IP addresses back to public. A common form of NAT is Port Address Translation. Dynamic NAT uses multiple public IP addresses, while static NAT uses a single public IP address.

Physical Isolation and Air Gaps

Physical isolation ensures that one network isn't connected to another network. As an example, consider **supervisory control and data acquisition (SCADA)** systems. These are typically industrial control systems within large facilities such as power plants or water treatment facilities. While SCADA systems operate within their own network, it's common to ensure that they are isolated from any other network.

This physical isolation significantly reduces risks to the SCADA system. If an attacker can't reach it from the Internet, it is much more difficult to attack it. However, if the system is connected to the internal network, an attacker can access internal computers and then access any internal network resource.

An **air gap** provides physical isolation, with a gap of air between an isolated system and other systems. When considered literally, an **air-gapped** system is not connected to any other systems. As an example, many government agencies use both classified (red) and unclassified (black) networks. Strict rules ensure that these two systems are not connected to each other. Some rules require physical separation between red network cables and black network cables.

> ### 📌 *Remember This!*
>
> An air gap isolates one network from another by ensuring there is physical space (literally a gap of air) between all systems and cables.

Logical Separation and Segmentation

As mentioned previously in this chapter, routers and firewalls provide a basic level of separation and **segmentation**. Routers segment traffic between networks using rules within ACLs. Administrators use subnetting to divide larger IP address ranges into smaller ranges. They then implement rules within ACLs to allow or block traffic. Firewalls separate network traffic using basic packet-filtering rules and can also use more sophisticated methods to block undesirable traffic.

It's also possible to segment traffic between logical groups of users or computers with a **virtual local area network (VLAN)**. VLANs provide logical separation.

Isolating Traffic with a VLAN

A virtual local area network (VLAN) uses switches to group several computers into a virtual network. You can group the computers based on departments, job functions, or other administrative needs. This provides security because you can isolate the traffic between the computers in the different VLANs.

Normally, a router would group different computers onto different subnets based on physical locations. As an example, computers in a routed segment are typically on the same office or same floor. However, you can use a switch to create multiple VLANs to separate the computers based on logical needs rather than a physical location. Additionally, administrators can easily reconfigure the switch to add or subtract computers from any VLAN if needed.

For example, a group of users who normally work in separate departments may begin work on a project that requires them to be on the same subnet. You can configure a switch to logically group these workers together, even if the computers are physically located in different offices or on different floors of a building. When the project is over, you can simply reconfigure the switch to return the network to its original configuration.

East-West Traffic

Within a network, **east-west** traffic refers to traffic between servers. Imagine looking at a network diagram of servers within a network. These usually show servers configured horizontally (or side-by-side), so traffic between servers travels east and west. In contrast, network diagrams typically show clients above or below the servers, and traffic between clients and servers is north-south.

As another example, VoIP streaming traffic can consume a lot of bandwidth. One way to increase the availability and reliability of systems using this voice traffic is to put them on a dedicated VLAN. Other systems transferring traditional data traffic can be placed on a separate VLAN. This separates the voice and data traffic into their own VLANs.

Similarly, you can use a single switch with multiple VLANs to separate user traffic. For example, if you want to separate the traffic between the HR department and the IT department, you can use a single switch with two VLANs. The VLANs logically separate the computers between the two different departments, even if they are close to each other.

★ Remember This!

Virtual local area networks (VLANs) separate or segment traffic on physical networks, and you can create multiple VLANs with a single switch. A VLAN can logically group several different computers together or logically separate computers without regard to their physical location. VLANs are also used to separate traffic types, such as voice traffic on one VLAN and data traffic on a separate VLAN.

Network Appliances

Network appliances are dedicated systems designed to fulfill a specific need. The intent of the word *appliance* is to evoke a sense of simplicity. For example, you don't have to know the details of how a toaster works to make toast. Similarly, you don't have to know the details of how a computer appliance operates to use it. Vendors handle all of the details under the hood, making it easier for administrators.

Previous sections discussed different types of firewalls, and the following sections discuss proxy servers and jump servers. All of these can be dedicated appliances or services added to another server.

Proxy Servers

Many networks use **proxy servers** (or **forward proxy servers**) to forward requests for services (such as HTTP or HTTPS) from clients. They can improve performance by caching content, and some proxy servers can restrict users' access to inappropriate websites by filtering content. A proxy server is located on the edge of the network bordering the Internet and the intranet, as shown in Figure 3.5.

Administrators configure internal clients to use the proxy server for specific protocols. The proxy server accepts their requests, retrieves the content from the Internet, and then returns the data to the client. Most proxy servers only act as a proxy for HTTP and HTTPS. However, proxy servers can also proxy other Internet protocols, such as FTP.

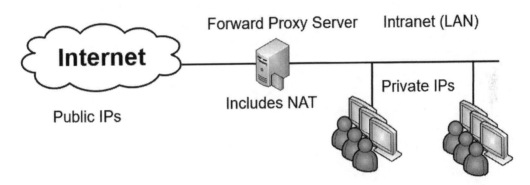

Figure 3.5: Proxy Server

Caching Content for Performance

The proxy server increases the performance of Internet requests by **caching** each result received from the Internet. Any data that is in the proxy server's cache doesn't need to be retrieved from the Internet again to fulfill another client's request. In this context, cache simply means "temporary storage." Cache could be a dedicated area of RAM, or, in some situations, it could also be an area on a high-performance disk subsystem.

As an example, if Lisa retrieves a webpage from **GetCertifiedGetAhead.com**, the proxy server would store the result in the cache. If Homer later requests the same page, the proxy server retrieves the page from the cache and sends it to Homer. This reduces the amount of Internet bandwidth used for web browsing because the page doesn't need to be retrieved again.

Content Filtering

A proxy server can also examine user requests to ensure that they meet the organization's security and content policies before passing the request along to a remote web server. This is known as **content filtering**, and it allows organizations to create **block rules** that restrict web use.

Many third-party companies sell subscription lists for URL filtering. These sites scour the Internet for websites and categorize the sites based on what companies typically want to block. Categories may include sites known to contain malicious code as well as undesirable types of content, such as pornography or gambling. These filters can rely on several different factors when making categorization decisions, including keywords that appear on the site and the site's reputation.

The subscription list can be loaded into the proxy server, and whenever a user attempts to access a site on the URL filter block list, the proxy blocks the request. Often, the proxy server presents users with a warning page when they try to access a restricted page. Many organizations use this page to remind users of the acceptable use policy, and some provide reminders that the proxy server is monitoring their online activity.

Proxy servers include logs that record each site visited by users. These logs can be helpful to identify frequently visited sites and to monitor user web browsing activities.

> ### ✦ *Centralized vs. Agent-Based*
>
> Most organizations use centralized proxy servers that sit on the network in a strategic location where they can intercept and analyze user requests. However, it's also possible to perform content filtering using an agent-based approach where the filter resides on each user's computer. The filter receives a policy from the organization's centralized policy server but then enforces it directly on the user's system.

Reverse Proxy

A *reverse proxy* accepts requests from the Internet, typically for a single web server. It appears to clients as a web server but is forwarding the requests to the web server and serving the pages returned by the web server. Figure 3.6 shows how a reverse proxy server is configured to protect a web server. Note that this configuration allows the web server to be located in the private network behind a second firewall.

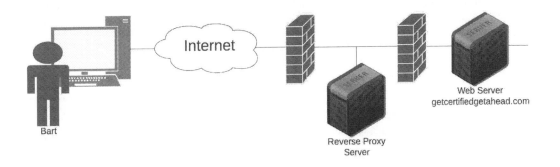

Figure 3.6: Reverse proxy server

Imagine that Bart wants to access **https://GetCertifiedGetAhead.com**. He types the URL into his browser, and it connects to the reverse proxy server. The reverse proxy server connects to the web server and retrieves the webpage. The reverse proxy then sends the webpage to Bart. A reverse proxy server caches the webpages just as a forward proxy server does, so it can improve the overall website performance.

The reverse proxy server can be used for a single web server or a web farm of multiple servers. When used with a web farm, it can act as a **load balancer**. You would place the load balancer in the screened subnet to accept the requests, and it then forwards the requests to different servers in the web farm using a load-balancing algorithm. Chapter 9, "Implementing Controls to Protect Assets," covers load balancing in more depth.

> 📌 *Remember This!*
>
> A proxy server forwards requests for services from a client. It provides caching to improve performance and reduce Internet bandwidth usage. Transparent proxy servers accept and forward requests without modifying them. Non-transparent proxy servers use URL filters to restrict access to certain sites. Both types can log user activity.

Unified Threat Management

Unified threat management (UTM) is a single solution that combines multiple security controls. The overall goal of UTMs is to provide better security while also simplifying management requirements. In many cases, a UTM device will reduce the workload of administrators without sacrificing security.

As IT-based threats first began appearing, security experts created various solutions to deal with each of them. When attackers began releasing malware to infect computers, vendors created antivirus software. Attackers started attacking networks, and in response, security experts developed and steadily improved firewalls. Organizations implemented proxies with URL filters when they recognized a need to control which sites users can visit.

Although these solutions are effective, they are also complex. Administrators often find it challenging to manage each of these solutions separately. Because of this, UTM security appliances have become popular, especially among organizations with smaller networks and smaller budgets. They combine the features of multiple security solutions into a single appliance. For example, a UTM security appliance might include multiple capabilities such as those listed in the following bullets:

- **URL filtering.** URL filters within a UTM security appliance perform the same job as a proxy server. They block access to sites based on the URL. It's common to subscribe to a service and select categories to block access to groups of sites. Administrators can also configure URL filters manually to allow or block access to specific websites.
- **Malware inspection.** Malware often comes into a network via spam or malicious webpages. The malware inspection component of a UTM appliance screens incoming data for known malware and blocks it. Organizations often scan for malware on mail servers and individual systems as part of a layered security or defense-in-depth solution.
- **Content inspection.** Content inspection includes a combination of different content filters. It monitors incoming data streams and attempts to block any malicious content. It can include a spam filter to inspect incoming email and reject spam. It can also block specific types of transmissions, such as streaming audio and video, and specific types of files such as zip files.
- **DDoS mitigator.** A DDoS mitigator attempts to detect DDoS attacks and block them. This is similar to how intrusion prevention systems (IPSs) block attacks. Chapter 4 covers IPSs in more depth.

★ Remember This!

A unified threat management (UTM) appliance combines multiple security controls into a single appliance. It can inspect data streams and often includes URL filtering, malware inspection, and content inspection components. Many UTMs include a DDoS mitigator to block DDoS attacks.

It's common to place UTM appliances at the network border, between the Internet and the intranet (or the private network). This allows it to intercept and analyze all traffic to and from the Internet. However, the placement is dependent on how the UTM appliance is being used. As an example, if it is being used as a proxy server, it can be placed within the screened subnet. Administrators would configure the clients to use the UTM appliance for proxy servers, ensuring that all relevant traffic goes through it.

Jump Server

A jump server (sometimes called a jump box) is a hardened server used to access and manage devices in a different security zone. As an example, if administrators want to administer servers in the screened subnet from the internal network, they could use a jump server. They could connect to the jump server and then access servers in the screened subnet through the jump server.

It's common to connect to a jump server using a passwordless SSH login, described earlier in the "OpenSSH" section, and then connect to the remote server via the jump server. Imagine Maggie has elevated privileges on a jump server (named jump) and on a certificate authority (CA) server in the screened subnet (named ca1). She could use the following command:

```
ssh -J maggie@jump maggie@ca1
```

The -J switch tells ssh to connect to the jump server and then use TCP forwarding to connect to the CA server. While the preceding example used the jump server to connect to a server in the screened subnet, it's also possible to use a jump server to connect to an internal network, such as a SCADA system network isolated with a VLAN.

It's essential to ensure that the jump server is hardened. Ideally, it isn't used for anything else, so it won't have any other services running. Any additional services on the server give attackers another target. Additionally, the target system should restrict connections from systems other than the jump server.

📌 *Remember This!*

A jump server is placed between different security zones and provides secure access from devices in one zone to devices in the other zone. It can provide secure access to devices in a screened subnet from an internal network.

Zero Trust

For many years, the core philosophy around network security was to use firewalls and other security devices to build ***implicit trust zones*** for network devices. Systems belonging to the organization were placed inside of that secured perimeter and protected from systems outside the network. Systems inside the perimeter were trusted because they were considered "ours" while systems on the outside were untrusted because they were considered "not ours."

That philosophy worked well for a long time, but its effectiveness has been fading. While organizations still use firewalls to build secure network perimeters, it's no longer true that everything "ours" will be on the inside of that perimeter. Remote workers, travelers, and the use of cloud services blur the lines between inside and outside.

The new philosophy in network security is known as ***zero trust network access (ZTNA)***. This approach doesn't mean that nothing is trusted, but refers to the idea that we don't make trust decisions based on network location. Instead, we focus on implementing strong authentication systems and then creating policy-driven access controls based upon a user's identity instead of their system's location. The end goal is to achieve threat scope reduction, decreasing the risk to the organization.

Figure 3.7 shows how zero trust approaches function. When a user or system wants to access a resource, the zero-trust environment makes that decision through a system known as the Policy Enforcement Point (PEP).

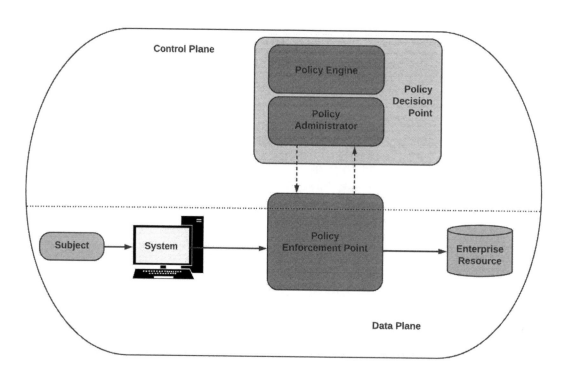

Figure 3.7: Zero Trust Network Access (Source: NIST SP 800-207)

The decision whether to trust an individual may be based upon ***adaptive identity*** authentication. The system changes the way that it asks a user to authenticate based upon the context of the request. For example, a subject on a corporate computer system accessing the network from a corporate office may be only asked to verify their password, while a user in a coffee shop on a personal device may be subjected to multifactor authentication.

Control Plane vs. Data Plane

Zero-trust environments use logical or physical separation to divide two different types of communication. The communications used to control and configure the network take place on a network known as the **control plane**, while the communications used by end users and software to communicate with each other take place on a network called the **data plane**. Separating the control plane from the data plane reduces the likelihood that an attacker will be able to reconfigure the network by accessing the control plane.

Figure 3.8 shows the separation between the control plane and the data plane, as well as the core components that exist in each environment.

The two key components of the control plane are:

- The **Policy Engine (PE)** decides whether to grant access to a resource for a given subject. The PE uses enterprise policy to grant, deny, or revoke access to the resource.
- The **Policy Administrator (PA)** is responsible for communicating the decisions made by the PE to the tools on the network that enforce those decisions, known as the **Policy Enforcement Point (PEP)**.

Together, the PE and the PA are known as the **Policy Decision Point (PDP)**.

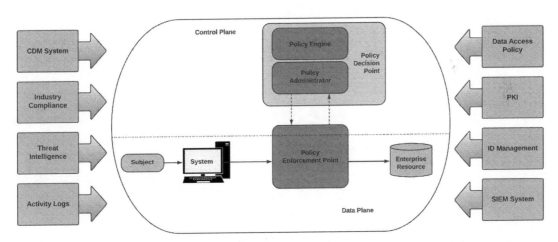

Figure 3.8: Core Zero Trust Components (Source: NIST SP 800-207)

The data plane contains all of the systems that carry out the work of the organization. Core components of the data plane include:

- The **subject** (user) who wishes to access a resource.
- The **system** used by the user to access the resource.
- The **enterprise resource** that the user wishes to access, such as a file, server, or service.

- The Policy Enforcement Point (PEP) that determines whether to allow that access. Notice that the PEP actually crosses between the control plane and the data plane. This is the only system allowed to cross that boundary because it must receive instructions from the Policy Administrator on the control plane and then enforce those instructions on the data plane.

Secure Access Service Edge

Secure access service edge (SASE) is a design philosophy closely related to ZTNA that brings together networking and security functions and delivers them as an integrated cloud service. SASE is a broader philosophy that builds upon zero-trust and adds additional security services, including:

- Firewall services
- Secure web gateway services
- Anti-malware services
- Intrusion prevention services
- Cloud access service broker (CASB) services
- Data loss prevention (DLP) services

Chapter 3 Exam Topic Review

When preparing for the exam, make sure you understand these key concepts covered in this chapter.

Reviewing Basic Networking Concepts

- The OSI model describes network communications using seven layers. Numbered from one through seven, they are: Physical, Data Link, Network, Transport, Session, Presentation, and Application.
- The Transmission Control Protocol (TCP) is a connection-oriented protocol that provides guaranteed delivery while the User Datagram Protocol (UDP) is a connectionless protocol that provides "best effort" delivery.
- File Transfer Protocol (FTP) is used to transfer files over networks, but FTP does not encrypt the transmission. SSH encrypts Secure Copy (SCP) and Secure FTP (SFTP). TLS encrypts FTPS.
- SMTP sends email using either TCP port 25 or port 587, with the latter port being used for email encrypted with TLS. POP3 receives email using TCP port 110 or TCP port 995 for encrypted connections. IMAP4 uses TCP port 143 or port 993 for encrypted connections.
- HTTPS encrypts browser-based traffic with TLS using TCP port 443.
- Directory services use Lightweight Directory Access Protocol (LDAP) over TCP port 389 or LDAP Secure (LDAPS) over TCP port 636.
- Administrators commonly connect to remote systems using SSH instead of Telnet because SSH encrypts the connection. Administrators also use Remote Desktop Protocol (RDP) to connect to remote systems graphically using TCP port 3389.

- The Network Time Protocol (NTP) provides time synchronization services.
- Domain Name System (DNS) provides domain name resolution. DNS zones include A records for IPv4 addresses and AAAA records for IPv6 addresses. MX records identify mail servers, and the MX record with the lowest preference is the primary mail server. DNS uses TCP port 53 for zone transfers and UDP port 53 for DNS client queries.
- Domain Name System Security Extensions (DNSSEC) provides validation for DNS responses by adding a Resource Record Signature (RRSIG). The RRSIG provides data integrity and authentication and helps prevent DNS poisoning attacks.

Understanding Basic Network Devices

- Switches connect computers on a local network. They map media access control (MAC) addresses to physical ports.
- Port security limits access to switch ports. It includes limiting the number of MAC addresses per port and disabling unused ports.
- Routers connect networks to each other and direct traffic based on the destination IP address. Routers (and firewalls) use rules within access control lists (ACLs) to allow or block traffic.
- The route command is used to view and manipulate the routing table.
- Implicit deny indicates that unless something is explicitly allowed, it is denied. It is the last rule in an ACL.
- Host-based firewalls filter traffic in and out of individual hosts
- Network-based firewalls filter traffic in and out of a network. They are placed on the border of a network, such as between the Internet and an internal network.
- A stateless firewall controls traffic between networks using rules within an ACL. The ACL can block traffic based on ports, IP addresses, subnets, and some protocols. Stateful firewalls, additionally, filter traffic based on the state of a packet within a session.
- A web application firewall (WAF) protects a web server against web application attacks. It is typically placed in the screened subnet and will alert administrators of suspicious events.
- Next-generation firewalls (NGFW) perform deep packet inspection, analyzing traffic at the application layer.
- Stateful inspection firewalls are also known as Layer 4 firewalls. NGFWs and WAFs are both examples of Layer 7 firewalls.
- Security devices may be either fail-open, where they allow all traffic to pass when the device fails, or fail-closed, where they allow no traffic to pass when the device fails. Fail-closed devices provide greater security.

Implementing Network Designs

- A screened subnet provides a layer of protection for servers that are accessible from the Internet.
- An intranet is an internal network. People use the intranet to communicate and share content with each other. An extranet is part of a network that can be accessed by authorized entities from outside of the network.

- NAT translates public IP addresses to private IP addresses, private back to public, and hides IP addresses on the internal network from users on the Internet. A NAT gateway is a device that implements NAT.
- Networks use various methods to provide network segregation, segmentation, and isolation.
- An air gap provides physical isolation for systems or networks. Systems or networks are completely isolated from other systems or networks with a gap of air.
- Routers provide logical separation and segmentation using ACLs to control traffic.
- Forward proxy servers forward requests for services from a client. They can cache content and record users' Internet activities.
- Reverse proxy servers accept traffic from the Internet and forward it to one or more internal web servers. The reverse proxy server is placed in the screened subnet and the web servers can be in the internal network.
- A unified threat management (UTM) security appliance includes multiple layers of protection, such as URL filters, content inspection, malware inspection, and a distributed denial-of-service (DDoS) mitigator. UTMs typically raise alerts and send them to administrators to interpret.
- Jump servers are placed between different security zones and provide secure access from devices in one zone to devices in the other zone. They are often used to manage devices in the screened subnet from the internal network.

> ### ★ Online References
>
> Remember, the online content includes some extras, such as labs, performance-based question examples, and more. Check it out at **https://getcertifiedgetahead.com/**.

Chapter 3 Practice Questions

1. An outside consultant performed an audit of the Municipal House of Pancakes network. She identified a legacy protocol being used to access browser-based interfaces on switches and routers within the network. She recommended replacing the legacy protocol with a secure protocol to access these network devices using the same interface. Which of the following protocols should be implemented?

   A. The newest fully supported version of SSL
   B. The newest fully supported version of TLS
   C. The newest fully supported version of LDAPS
   D. The newest fully supported version of SNMP

2. Your organization's security policy requires that confidential data transferred over the internal network must be encrypted. Which of the following protocols would BEST meet this requirement?

    A. FTP
    B. SSH
    C. SNMPv3
    D. SRTP

3. Maggie needs to collect network device configuration information and network statistics from devices on the network. She wants to protect the confidentiality of credentials used to connect to these devices. Which of the following protocols would BEST meet this need?

    A. SSH
    B. FTPS
    C. SNMPv3
    D. TLS

4. Which one of the following components would not be able to communicate on the data plane of a zero trust network?

    A. Subject
    B. Enterprise resource
    C. Policy enforcement point
    D. Policy administrator

5. You are configuring a web server that will contain information about your organization and receive orders from your customers. Which one of the following network locations is the best placement for this server?

    A. Screened subnet
    B. Intranet
    C. Extranet
    D. Internet

6. Maggie is examining traffic on a network searching for signs of insecure protocol use. She sees communications taking place on several different network ports. Which one of these ports most likely contains insecure traffic?

    A. 22
    B. 80
    C. 443
    D. 587

7. You are tasked with enabling NTP on some servers within your organization's screened subnet. Which of the following use cases are you MOST likely supporting with this action?

    A. Encrypting voice and video transmissions
    B. Providing time synchronization
    C. Enabling email usage
    D. Encrypting data in transit

8. Your organization has several switches in use throughout the internal network. Management wants to implement a security control to prevent unauthorized access to these switches within the network. Which of the following choices would BEST meet this need?

    A. Disable unused ports.
    B. Disable STP.
    C. Enable SSH.
    D. Enable DHCP.

9. Network administrators manage network devices remotely. However, a recent security audit discovered they are using a protocol that allows them to send credentials over the network in cleartext. Which of the following is the best method to be adopted to eliminate this vulnerability?

    A. Use SNMPv2c.
    B. Use SSH.
    C. Use SSL.
    D. Use SFTP.

10. Which of the following devices would MOST likely have the following entries used to define its operation?

    - permit IP any any eq 80
    - permit IP any any eq 443
    - deny IP any any

    A. Firewall
    B. Proxy server
    C. Web server
    D. Jump server

11. Your organization's network looks like the following graphic, and you've been asked to verify that Firewall 1 has the correct settings.

All firewalls should enforce the following requirements:

- Use only secure protocols for remote management.
- Block cleartext web traffic.

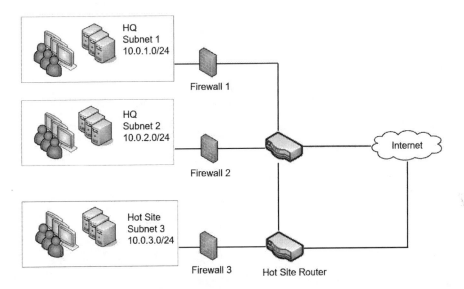

The following table shows the current rules configured in Firewall 1.

Rule	Destination	Source	Protocol	Action
HTTPS Outbound	Any	10.0.1.0/24	HTTPS	Allow
HTTP Outbound	Any	10.0.1.0/24	HTTP	Allow
DNS	Any	10.0.1.0/24	DNS	Allow
HTTPS Inbound	10.0.1.0/24	Any	HTTPS	Allow
HTTP Inbound	10.0.1.0/24	Any	HTTP	Block
Telnet	10.0.3.0/24	Any	Telnet	Allow
SSH	10.0.1.0/24	Any	SSH	Allow

You're asked to verify the rules are configured correctly. Which rule, if any, should be changed to ensure Firewall 1 meets the stated requirements?

A. HTTPS Outbound
B. HTTP Outbound
C. DNS
D. Telnet
E. SSH
F. None. All rules are correct.

12. The Springfield Nuclear Power Plant has several stand-alone computers used for monitoring. Employees log on to these computers using a local account to verify proper operation of various processes. The CIO of the organization has mandated that these computers cannot be connected to the organization's network or have access to the Internet. Which of the following would BEST meet this requirement?

    A. Air gap the computers.
    B. Place the computers in a screened subnet.
    C. Create a separate isolated network for these computers.
    D. Place the computers within a VLAN.

13. You have added another router in your network. This router provides a path to a limited access network that isn't advertised. However, a network administrator needs to access this network regularly. Which of the following could he do to configure his computer to access this limited network?

    A. Implement QoS technologies.
    B. Add a VLAN.
    C. Use the route command.
    D. Open additional ports on the router.

14. Several servers in your organization's screened subnet were recently attacked. After analyzing the logs, you discover that many of these attacks used TCP, but the packets were not part of an established TCP session. Which of the following devices would provide the BEST solution to prevent these attacks in the future?

    A. Stateless firewall
    B. Stateful firewall
    C. Network firewall
    D. Web application firewall

15. Your network currently has a dedicated firewall protecting access to a web server. It is currently configured with only the following two rules in the ACL:

    PERMIT TCP ANY ANY 443
    PERMIT TCP ANY ANY 80

    You have detected DNS requests and DNS zone transfer requests coming through the firewall and you need to block them. Which of the following would meet this goal? (Select TWO. Each answer is a full solution.)

    A. Add the following rule to the firewall: DENY TCP ALL ALL 53.
    B. Add the following rule to the firewall: DENY UDP ALL ALL 53.
    C. Add the following rule to the firewall: DENY TCP ALL ALL 25.
    D. Add the following rule to the firewall: DENY IP ALL ALL 53.
    E. Add an implicit deny rule at the end of the ACL.

Chapter 3

Practice Question Answers

1. **B** is correct. The newest version of Transport Layer Security (TLS) should be implemented to access the network devices. Because the scenario says the same interface is needed, the only possible choices are TLS or Secure Sockets Layer (SSL). However, SSL has been deprecated and should not be used. Lightweight Directory Access Protocol Secure (LDAPS) is used to communicate with directories such as Microsoft Active Directory. Simple Network Management Protocol version 3 (SNMPv3) adds security to SNMP and encrypts the credentials sent to and from the network devices, but it doesn't support access via a browser interface.

2. **B** is correct. You can use Secure Shell (SSH) to encrypt confidential data when transmitting it over the network. Secure File Transfer Protocol (SFTP) uses SSH to encrypt File Transfer Protocol (FTP) traffic, but FTP is unencrypted. Simple Network Management Protocol version 3 (SNMPv3) is used to monitor and manage network devices, not transmit data over a network. Secure Real-Time Transport Protocol (SRTP) provides encryption, message authentication, and integrity for voice and video, but not all data.

3. **C** is correct. Simple Network Management Protocol version 3 (SNMPv3) is a secure protocol that can monitor and collect information from network devices. It includes strong authentication mechanisms to protect the confidentiality of credentials. None of the other protocols listed are used to monitor network devices. Secure Shell (SSH) provides a secure method of connecting to devices but does not monitor them. File Transfer Protocol Secure (FTPS) is useful for encrypting large files in transit, using Transport Layer Security (TLS). TLS is commonly used to secure transmissions but doesn't include methods to monitor devices.

4. **D** is correct. The Policy Administrator (PA) exists entirely on the control plane. It sends decisions to the Policy Enforcement Point (PEP), which is able to communicate on both

the control plane and the data plane. The subject and the enterprise resource that the subject wishes to access communicate only on the data plane and may not access the control plane.

5. **A** is correct. Systems that must be accessed by the general public should always be placed on the screened subnet. This network is designed to house systems that require public access but still must be secured. Organizations should almost never place systems directly on the Internet because they would not be protected by the firewall. The intranet and extranet are private networks with limited access and would not be appropriate locations for a public web server.

6. **B** is correct. Port 80 is used by the unencrypted Hypertext Transfer Protocol (HTTP). Secure web communications should take place using the encrypted HTTP Secure (HTTPS) on port 443. Port 22 is used by Secure Shell (SSH) for encrypted administrative connections and data transfers. Port 587 is used by the Simple Mail Transfer Protocol Secure (SMTPS) to transfer email messages between servers over an encrypted connection.

7. **B** is correct. The Network Time Protocol (NTP) provides time synchronization services, so enabling NTP on servers in the screened subnet (sometimes called a demilitarized zone or DMZ) would meet this use case. The Secure Real-time Transport Protocol (SRTP) provides encryption, message authentication, and integrity for audio and video over IP networks. Protocols such as Simple Mail Transfer Protocol (SMTP), Post Office Protocol v3 (POP3), and Internet Message Access Protocol version 4 (IMAP4) are used for email. Encrypting data isn't relevant to time synchronization services provided by NTP.

8. **A** is correct. You can prevent unauthorized access by disabling unused physical ports on the switches as an overall port security practice. This prevents the connection if someone plugs their computer into an unused disabled ports. Spanning Tree Protocol (STP) prevents switching loop problems and should be enabled. Secure Shell (SSH) encrypts traffic and can be used to connect to network devices for management, but it doesn't directly protect a switch. Dynamic Host Configuration Protocol (DHCP) is used to dynamically issue IP addresses and is unrelated to this scenario.

9. **B** is correct. Secure Shell (SSH) can be used to connect to many network devices and is the best answer of the given choices. It encrypts the entire session, including the credentials. The scenario indicates that administrators are likely using Simple Network Management Protocol v1 (SNMPv1), SNMPv2, or SNMPv2c. These protocols all send a community string over the network in cleartext. SNMPv3 (which isn't available as a possible

answer) encrypts the credentials before sending them over the network. Secure Sockets Layer (SSL) encrypts but has been deprecated and shouldn't be used. Secure File Transfer Protocol (SFTP) is a secure implementation of FTP and is used to transfer files, not manage network devices.

10. **A** is correct. These are rules in an access control list (ACL) within a firewall. The first two rules indicate that traffic from any IP address, to any IP address, using ports 80 or 443 is permitted or allowed. The final rule is also known as an implicit deny rule and is placed last in the ACL. It ensures that all traffic that hasn't been previously allowed is denied. A proxy server would not use an ACL, although it would use ports 80 and 443 for Hypertext Transfer Protocol (HTTP) and HTTP Secure (HTTPS), respectively. A web server wouldn't use an ACL, although it would also use ports 80 and 443. A jump server is a server placed between different security zones (such as an internal network and a screened subnet) and is used to manage devices in the other security zone.

11. **B** is correct. The Hypertext Transfer Protocol (HTTP) rule should be changed from Allow to Block to block cleartext web traffic. The Telnet rule has the incorrect Destination address and the incorrect action. It should be 10.0.1.0/24 and set to Block because it is not a secure protocol for remote management. However, because it has the incorrect address (10.0.3.0/24), it won't have any effect on traffic to Firewall 1.

12. **A** is correct. The best choice of the available answers is to air gap the computers. An air gap provides physical isolation, indicating that there is a gap of air between an isolated system and other systems. A screened subnet (sometimes called a demilitarized zone or DMZ) provides a buffer between the Internet and an internal network and would connect these computers to both the internal network and the Internet. The scenario doesn't indicate the computers need to be connected, so a separate isolated network is not needed. Placing the computers within a virtual local area network (VLAN) would connect the computers to a network.

13. **C** is correct. The **route** command can be used to display and manipulate the routing table on a Linux computer. Using this, you can provide another gateway path through this router to the limited access network. None of the other choices can add routing paths. Quality of Service (QoS) technologies allow administrators to give priority of some network traffic over other network traffic. A virtual local area network (VLAN) is used to segment or isolate a network, so configuring one won't grant access to a network. A router doesn't have ports that can be opened for individual users.

14. **B** is correct. A stateful firewall filters traffic based on the state of the packet within a session. It would filter a packet that isn't part of an established Transmission Control Protocol (TCP) session, which starts with a TCP three-way handshake. A stateless firewall filters traffic based on the IP address, port, or protocol ID. While it's appropriate to place a network firewall in a screened subnet (sometimes called a demilitarized zone or DMZ), a network firewall could be either a stateless firewall or a stateful firewall. A web application firewall (WAF) is specifically designed to protect a web application, commonly hosted on a web server, but the attack was on several servers, not just a web server.

15. **D** and **E** are correct. The easiest way is to add an implicit deny rule at the end of the access control list (ACL) and all firewalls should have this to block all unwanted traffic. You can also deny all IP traffic using port 53 with DENY IP ALL ALL 53. Domain Name System (DNS) requests use UDP port 53, and DNS zone transfers use TCP port 53, so blocking only TCP 53 or UDP 53 does not block all DNS traffic. Port 25 is for Simple Mail Transfer Protocol (SMTP) and unrelated to this question.

Chapter 4

Securing Your Network

CompTIA Security+ objectives covered in this chapter:

1.2 Summarize fundamental security concepts.

- Deception and disruption technology (Honeypot, Honeynet, Honeyfile, Honeytoken)

2.3 Explain various types of vulnerabilities.

- Zero-day

2.4 Given a scenario, analyze indicators of malicious activity.

- Network attacks (Wireless)
- Physical attacks (Radio frequency identification (RFID) cloning)

3.2 Given a scenario, apply security principles to secure enterprise infrastructure.

- Infrastructure considerations (Device attribute, Active vs. passive, In-line vs. tap/monitor, Intrusion prevention system (IPS)/Intrusion detection system (IDS), Sensors, Port security, 802.1X, Extensible Authentication Protocol (EAP))
- Secure communication/access (Virtual private network (VPN), Remote access, Tunneling, Internet protocol security (IPsec))

4.1 Given a scenario, apply common security techniques to computing resources.

- Wireless devices (Installation considerations, Site surveys, Heat maps)
- Wireless security settings (Wi-Fi Protected Access 3 (WPA3), AAA/Remote Authentication Dial-In User Service (RADIUS), Cryptographic protocols, Authentication protocols)

4.4 Explain security alerting and monitoring concepts and tools.

- Activities (Alert response and remediation/validation, Quarantine)
- Tools (Agent/agentless)

4.5 Given a scenario, modify enterprise capabilities to enhance security.

- IDS/IPS (Trends, Signatures)
- Network access control (NAC)

In this chapter, you'll learn about some of the more advanced network security concepts. Topics include intrusion detection systems (IDSs) and intrusion prevention systems (IPSs), methods used to secure wireless networks, common wireless attacks, and virtual private network (VPN) technologies.

Exploring Advanced Security Devices

Chapter 3, "Exploring Network Technologies and Tools," discusses basic network technologies and protocols. This section explores many of the more advanced security devices used to secure networks. We'll discuss the device attributes of different security devices and how to place them on a network.

Understanding IDSs and IPSs

Intrusion detection systems (IDSs) monitor a network and send alerts when they detect suspicious events on a system or network. Intrusion prevention systems (IPSs) react to attacks in progress and prevent them from reaching systems and networks.

Chapter 8, "Using Risk Management Tools," discusses protocol analyzers, or sniffers, in more depth, but as an introduction, administrators use them to capture and analyze network traffic sent between hosts. IDSs and IPSs have the same capability. They capture the traffic and analyze it to detect potential attacks or anomalies.

Both IDSs and IPSs act as detective security controls using similar detection methods. The biggest difference is in their responses to an attack. This section presents IDSs first and then wraps up with some information on IPSs and compares the two. However, as you go through this section, it's worth remembering that IDSs and IPSs can implement the same monitoring and detection methods.

HIDS

A ***host-based intrusion detection system (HIDS)*** is additional software installed on a system such as a workstation or a server. It monitors the individual host, can detect potential attacks, and analyzes critical operating system files. The primary goal of any IDS is to monitor traffic and then alert administrators to suspicious activity. For a HIDS, this traffic passes through the network interface card (NIC).

Many host-based IDSs have expanded to monitor application activity on the system. As one example, you can install a HIDS on different Internet-facing servers, such as web servers, mail servers, and database servers. In addition to monitoring the network traffic reaching the servers, the HIDS can also monitor the server applications.

It's worth stressing that a HIDS can help detect malicious software (malware) that traditional anti-virus software might miss. Because of this, many organizations install a HIDS on every workstation as an extra layer of protection in addition to traditional antivirus software. Just as the HIDS on a server will monitor network traffic, a workstation HIDS will monitor network traffic reaching the workstation. However, a HIDS can also monitor some applications, log files and local resources such as operating system files.

In other organizations, administrators only install a HIDS when there's a perceived need. For example, suppose an administrator is concerned that a specific server with proprietary data is at increased risk of an attack. In that case, the administrator might choose to install a HIDS on this system as an extra layer of protection.

> ### 📌 *Remember This!*
>
> A HIDS can monitor all traffic on a single host system such as a server or a workstation. In some cases, it can detect malicious activity missed by antivirus software.

NIDS

A ***network-based intrusion detection system (NIDS)*** monitors activity on the network. An administrator installs NIDS ***sensors*** or collectors on network devices such as switches, routers, or firewalls. These sensors gather information and report to a central monitoring network appliance hosting a NIDS console.

A NIDS cannot detect anomalies on individual systems or workstations unless the anomaly causes a change in network traffic. Additionally, a NIDS is unable to decrypt encrypted traffic. In other words, it can only monitor and assess threats on the network from traffic sent in plaintext or non-encrypted traffic.

Figure 4.1 shows an example of a NIDS configuration. In the figure, sensors are located before the firewall, after the firewall, and on routers. These sensors collect and monitor network traffic on subnets within the network and report to the NIDS console. The NIDS provides overall monitoring and analysis and can detect attacks on the network.

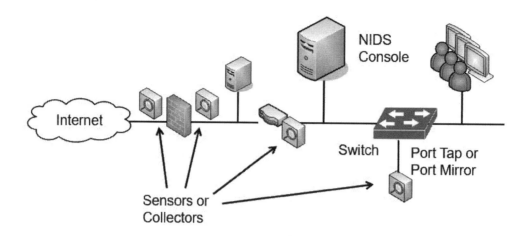

Figure 4.1: NIDS sensors

Figure 4.1 also shows a port tap or port mirror on the internal switch. Most switches support port mirroring (sometimes called port spanning), allowing administrators to configure the switch to send all traffic the switch receives to a single port. After configuring a port mirror, you can use it as a tap to send all switch data to a sensor or collector and forward this to a NIDS console. Similarly, it's possible to configure port taps on routers to capture all traffic sent through the router and send it to the IDS.

Sensor and Collector Placement

The decision on where you want to place the sensors depends on what you want to measure. For example, the sensor on the Internet side of the firewall will see all the traffic. However, the sensor on the firewall's internal side will only see traffic that passes through the firewall. In other words, the firewall will filter some attacks, and the internal sensor won't see them.

If you want to see all attacks on your network, place a sensor on the Internet side. If you only want to see what gets through, place your sensors on the internal network only. If you want to see both, place sensors in both locations.

> ### ★ Remember This!
>
> A NIDS console is installed on a network appliance. Sensors are installed on network devices such as switches, routers, or firewalls to monitor network traffic and detect network-based attacks. You can also use taps or port mirrors to capture traffic. A NIDS cannot monitor encrypted traffic and cannot monitor traffic on individual hosts.

Detection Methods

An IDS can only detect an attack. It cannot prevent attacks. In contrast, an IPS prevents attacks by detecting them and stopping them before they reach the target. In this context, an attack is an attempt to compromise confidentiality, integrity, or availability.

The two primary detection methods are signature-based and heuristic- or behavioral-based (also called anomaly-based). Any IDS can detect attacks based on signatures, anomalies, or both. The HIDS monitors the network traffic reaching its NIC, and the NIDS monitors the network's traffic.

Signature-Based Detection

Signature-based IDSs (sometimes called definition-based) use a database of known vulnerabilities or known attack patterns. For example, tools are available for an attacker to launch a SYN flood attack on a server by simply entering the IP address of the system to attack. The attack tool then floods the target system with synchronize (SYN) packets but never completes the three-way Transmission Control Protocol (TCP) handshake with the final acknowledge (ACK) packet. If the attack isn't blocked, it can consume resources on a system and ultimately cause it to crash.

However, this is a known attack with a specific pattern of successive SYN packets from one IP to another IP. The IDS can detect these patterns when the signature database includes the attack definitions. The process is very similar to what antivirus software uses to detect malware. You need to update both IDS signatures and antivirus definitions from the vendor regularly to protect against current threats.

Trend-Based Detection

Trend-based detection (sometimes called anomaly detection) starts by identifying the network's regular operation or normal behavior. It does this by creating a performance baseline under normal operating conditions.

The IDS continuously monitors network traffic and compares current network behavior against the baseline. When the IDS detects abnormal activity (outside normal boundaries as identified in the baseline), it gives an alert indicating a potential attack.

Trend-based detection is similar to how heuristic-based antivirus software works. Although the internal methods are different, both examine activity and detect abnormal activity that is beyond the capability of signature-based detection.

Trend-based detection can be effective at discovering *zero-day exploits*. A zero-day vulnerability is usually defined as one that is unknown to the vendor, so the vendor has not released a patch. If the vulnerability isn't known and there's no patch for it, there won't be a signature for it either.

SYN Flood Attack

The SYN flood attack is a common denial-of-service (DoS) attack. Chapter 3 describes the three-way handshake to establish a session. As a reminder, one system sends a SYN packet, the second system responds with a SYN/ACK packet, and the first system then completes the handshake with an ACK packet. However, in a SYN flood attack, the attacker sends multiple SYN packets but never completes the third part of the TCP handshake with the last ACK packet.

This is like a friend extending a hand to shake hands with you, you extend your hand in response, and then, at the last instant, the friend pulls his hand away. Although you or I would probably stop extending our hand back to someone doing this, the server doesn't know any better and keeps answering every SYN packet with a SYN/ACK packet.

Each uncompleted session consumes resources on the server, and if the SYN flood attack continues, it can crash the server. Some servers reserve a certain number of resources for connections, and once the attack consumes these resources, the system blocks additional connections. Instead of crashing the server, the attack prevents legitimate users from connecting to the server.

IDSs and IPSs can detect a SYN flood attack, and IPSs can prevent the attack. Additionally, many firewalls include a SYN flood guard that can detect SYN flood attacks and take steps to close the open sessions.

Any time administrators make any significant changes to a system or network that cause the normal behavior to change, they should re-create the baseline. Otherwise, the IDS will constantly alert on what is now normal behavior.

Data Sources and Trends

Any type of IDS will use various raw data sources to collect network activity information. This includes a wide variety of logs, such as firewall logs, system logs, and application logs.

Chapter 1, "Mastering Security Basics," discusses security information and event management (SIEM) systems and how they collect and aggregate information. A SIEM collects data from multiple systems and aggregates the data, making it easier to analyze. Similarly, an IDS includes an **aggregator** to store log entries from dissimilar systems. The IDS can analyze these log entries to provide insight into trends. These trends can detect a pattern of attacks and provide insight into improving a network's protection.

Many IDSs can monitor logs in real-time. Each time a system records a log entry, the IDS examines the log to determine if it is an item of interest or not. Other IDSs will periodically poll relevant logs and scan new entries looking for items of interest.

Reporting Based on Rules

An IDS reports on events of interest based on rules configured within the IDS. All events aren't attacks or actual issues, but instead, they provide a report indicating an event might be an alert or an alarm. Administrators investigate to determine if it is valid. Some systems consider an alarm and an alert as the same thing. Other systems use an alarm for a potentially serious issue and an alert as a relatively minor issue. The goal in these latter systems is to encourage administrators to give higher precedence to alarms than alerts.

★ *Remember This!*

Signature-based detection identifies issues based on known attacks or vulnerabilities. Signature-based detection systems can detect known attack types. Trend-based IDSs (also called anomaly-based) can detect unusual activity. They start with a performance baseline of normal behavior and then compare network traffic against this baseline. When traffic differs significantly from the baseline, the system sends an alert.

The actual reporting mechanism varies from system to system and in different organizations. For example, one IDS might write the event into a log as an alarm or alert, and then send an email to an administrator account. In a large network operations center (NOC), the IDS might send an alert to a monitor easily viewable by all NOC personnel. The point is that administrators configure the rules within the IDS based on the needs of the organization.

Alert Response and Validation

While IDSs use advanced analytics to examine traffic, they sometimes make mistakes. Security professionals need to respond when an alert triggers and validate the situation. They are looking for two types of errors: false positives and false negatives. A false positive is an alert or alarm on an event that is non-threatening, benign, or harmless. A false negative is when an attacker is actually attacking the network, but the system does not detect it. Neither is desirable, but it's impossible to eliminate both. Most IDSs trigger an alert or alarm when an event exceeds a threshold.

The following list describes the four possible responses of an IDS to an attack or perceived attack. Refer to Figure 4.2 as you're reading them:

- **False positive.** A *false positive* occurs when an IDS or IPS sends an alarm or alert when there is no actual attack.
- **False negative.** A *false negative* occurs when an IDS or IPS fails to send an alarm or alert even though an attack exists.
- **True negative.** A *true negative* occurs when an IDS or IPS does not send an alarm or alert, and there is no actual attack.
- **True positive.** A *true positive* occurs when an IDS or IPS sends an alarm or alert after recognizing an attack.

	IDS/IPS Accurate	IDS/IPS Not Accurate
No Attack	**True negative** (No alarm or alert sent)	**False positive** (Alarm or alert sent)
Actual Attack	**True positive** (Alarm or alert sent)	**False negative** (No alarm or alert sent)

Figure 4.2: IDS/IPS false positives and false negatives

Consider the classic SYN flood attack, where the attacker withholds the third part of the TCP handshake. A host will send a SYN packet, and a server will respond with a SYN/ACK packet. However, instead of completing the handshake with an ACK packet, the attacking host never sends the ACK, but continues to send more SYN packets. This leaves the server with open connections that can ultimately disrupt services.

If a system receives 1 SYN packet without the accompanying ACK packet, is it an attack? Probably not. This can happen during normal operations. If a system receives over 1,000 SYN packets from a single IP address in less than 60 seconds without the accompanying ACK packet, is it an attack? Absolutely.

Administrators configure rules within the IDS and set the threshold between 1 and 1,000 to indicate an attack. If administrators set it too low, they will have too many false positives and a high workload as they spend their time chasing ghosts. If they set the threshold too high, actual attacks will get through without administrators knowing about them. Similarly, they can configure many settings based on the analytics and capabilities of the IDS.

Most administrators want to know if their system is under attack. That's the primary purpose of the IDS. However, an IDS that constantly cries "Wolf!" will be ignored when the real wolf attacks. It's important to set the threshold high enough to reduce the number of false positives but low enough to alert on any actual attacks.

There is no perfect number for the threshold. Administrators adjust thresholds in different networks based on the network's activity level and personal preferences.

> ### ★ Remember This!
>
> A false positive incorrectly indicates an attack is occurring when an attack is not active. A high incidence of false positives increases the administrator's workload. A false negative is when an attack occurs, but the system doesn't detect and report it. Administrators often set the IDS threshold high enough to minimize false positives but low enough that it does not allow false negatives.

IPS Versus IDS—In-line Versus Passive

Intrusion prevention systems (IPSs) are an extension of IDSs. Just as you can have both a HIDS and a NIDS, you can also have a HIPS and a NIPS, but a network-based IPS (NIPS) is more common. There are some primary distinctions of an IPS when compared with an IDS:

- An IPS can detect, react to, and prevent attacks.
- In contrast, an IDS monitors and will respond after detecting an attack, but it doesn't prevent attacks.
- An IPS is in-line with the traffic. In other words, all traffic passes through the IPS, and the IPS can block malicious traffic.
- In contrast, an IDS is out-of-band. It monitors the network traffic using a network tap, but the traffic doesn't go through the IDS.
- Because an IPS is in-line with the traffic, it is sometimes referred to as active. In contrast, an IDS is referred to as passive because it is not in-line with the traffic. Instead, it is out-of-band with the network traffic.

> ### ★ Remember This!
>
> An intrusion prevention system (IPS) is a preventive control. It is placed in-line with traffic. An IPS can actively monitor data streams, detect malicious content, and stop attacks in progress. It can also be used internally to protect private networks.

Most IDSs will only respond by raising alerts. For example, an IDS will log the attack and send a notification. The notification can come in many forms, including an email to a group of administrators, a text message, a pop-up window, or a notification on a central monitor.

Some IDSs have additional capabilities allowing them to change the environment in addition to sending a notification. For example, an IDS might be able to modify access control lists (ACLs) on firewalls to block offending traffic, close processes on a system that were caused by the attack, or divert the attack to a safe environment, such as a honeypot or honeynet (discussed later in this chapter).

As a reminder from the introduction of this section, both IDSs and IPSs have protocol analyzer capabilities. This allows them to monitor data streams looking for malicious behavior. An IPS can inspect packets within these data streams and block malicious packets before they enter the network.

In contrast, a NIDS has sensors or data collectors that monitor and report the traffic. An active NIDS can take steps to block an attack, but only after the attack has started. The in-line configuration of the IPS allows an IPS to prevent attacks from reaching the internal network. As an example, Figure 4.3 shows the location of two network-based IPSs (NIPS 1 and NIPS 2). All Internet traffic flows through NIPS 1, giving it an opportunity to inspect incoming traffic. NIPS 1 protects the internal network by detecting malicious traffic and preventing attacks from reaching the internal network.

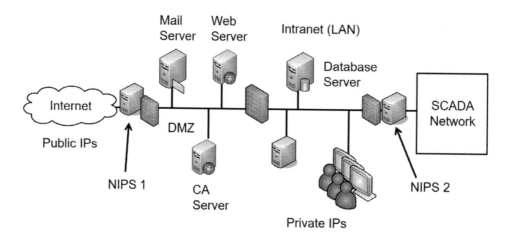

Figure 4.3: NIPS used to detect and prevent attacks

NIPS 2 is protecting an internal private network. As an example, imagine that Homer needs to manage some equipment within a supervisory control and data acquisition (SCADA) network in the nuclear power plant. The SCADA equipment is in the private network. The firewall next to NIPS 2 can have rules that allow traffic from Homer's computer into the network but block all other traffic. NIPS 2 will then inspect all the incoming traffic and block malicious traffic.

This might seem like overkill, but many advanced persistent threats (APTs) have successfully installed remote access Trojans (RATs) onto internal systems through phishing or malware attacks. Once the RAT is installed, attackers can now attack from within. If an attacker began launching attacks on the private network from Homer's system, the firewall wouldn't block it. However, the NIPS will prevent this attack from reaching the private network. Notice that each IPS is placed on the edge of the protected network. NIPS 1 is placed on the edge of the network between the Internet and the screened subnet. NIPS 2 is on the edge of the SCADA network between it and the intranet. This placement ensures that the NIPS can inspect all traffic going into the network.

> ### 📌 *Remember This!*
>
> An IPS is placed in-line with the traffic and can detect, react to, and prevent attacks. An IDS monitors and responds to an attack. It is not in-line but instead collects data passively (also known as out-of-band).

Honeypots

A **honeypot** is a sweet-looking server—at least it's intended to look sweet to the attacker, similar to how honey looks sweet to a bear. It's a server that is left open or appears to have been locked down sloppily, allowing an attacker relatively easy access. The intent is for the server to look like an easy target so that the attacker spends his time in the honeypot instead of on a live network. In short, the honeypot diverts the attacker away from the live network.

For example, a honeypot could be a web server designed to look like a live web server. It would have bogus data, such as files and folders containing fabricated credit card transaction data. If an organization suspects a problem with a malicious insider, it can create an internal honeypot with bogus information on proprietary projects.

Honeypots typically have some protection that an attacker can easily bypass. If administrators don't use any security, the honeypot might look suspicious to experienced attackers, and they might avoid it.

Security personnel often use honeypots to gather intelligence on the attacker. Attackers are constantly modifying their methods to take advantage of different types of attacks. Some sophisticated attackers discover zero-day vulnerabilities before a patch is released. In some cases, security professionals observe attackers launching zero-day vulnerability attacks against a honeypot.

Honeypots never hold any data that is valuable to the organization. The data may appear valuable to an attacker, but its disclosure is harmless. Some goals of honeypots are:

- **Deceive the attackers and divert them from the live network.** If an attacker spends time in the honeypot, they are not attacking live resources.
- **Allow observation of an attacker.** While an attacker is in the honeypot, security professionals can observe the attack and learn from the attacker's methodologies. Honeypots can also help security professionals learn about zero-day exploits or previously unknown attacks.

Honeynets

A **honeynet** is a group of honeypots within a separate network or zone but accessible from an organization's primary network. Security professionals often create honeynets using multiple virtual servers within a single physical server. The servers within this network are honeypots, and the honeynet mimics the functionality of a live network.

For example, you can use a single powerful server with a significant amount of RAM and processing power. This server could host multiple virtual servers, where each virtual server is running an operating system and applications. A physical server hosting six virtual servers will appear as seven systems on a subnet. An attacker looking in will not be able to easily determine if the servers are physical or virtual.

This virtual network aims to deceive the attacker and deflect any attack on the actual network. If the attacker is in the honeynet, he isn't attacking the live network, and administrators can observe the attacker's actions.

Sun Tzu famously wrote in The Art of War, "All warfare is based on deception," and "Know your enemies." Cyberwarfare occurs daily, and security professionals on the front lines of network and system attacks recognize that these attacks mimic warfare in many ways. Honeypots and honeynets provide these professionals with additional tools to use in this war.

Honeyfile

A **honeyfile** is a file designed to attract the attention of an attacker. The primary way a file can attract an attacker is by the name. As an example, a file named password.txt will probably contain passwords.

Experienced administrators won't be so careless with security and name a file with actual credentials password.txt. However, you might be able to deceive some attackers by creating a honeyfile that *looks* like it contains passwords and placing it somewhere that an attacker can find it.

Honeytokens

Data is a valuable asset for many organizations. Your product plans, customer lists, and employee records may be among the most sensitive and important assets that you possess. Attackers know this and may attempt to steal your information. Honeyfiles seek to divert them from finding data with real value, but sometimes they come across it anyway.

Honeytokens have a different purpose. They try to detect cases where an attacker is able to steal data. For example, an organization places fake, but easily detectable, records in their production databases. Then, if they later suspect that data was stolen, they can search for the honeytoken. If they find that fake record in another dataset, they know that it was stolen.

For example, you might create a new email address JamesKate@getcertifiedgetahead.com and insert it into a fake customer record in your database. You then never use that email address anywhere else. If that email ever receives a message, you know that the message came from an attack where the attacker was able to steal your customer database.

📌 *Remember This!*

Honeypots and honeynets attempt to deceive attackers and disrupt attackers. They divert attackers from live networks and allow security personnel to observe current methodologies attackers are using. A honeyfile is a file with a name (such as *password.txt*) that will attract the attacker's attention. A honeytoken is a fake record inserted into a database to detect data theft.

Securing Wireless Networks

Wireless local area networks (WLANs) are an important part of both home and business networks. A wireless network is easy to set up and can quickly connect several computers without running cables, significantly reducing costs.

However, wireless networks have become a popular attack vector, and one of the challenges with wireless networks is security. Wireless security has improved over the years, but wireless networks are still susceptible to vulnerabilities, and many users don't understand how to lock down a wireless network adequately.

Reviewing Wireless Basics

Before digging into wireless security, you must understand some basic concepts related to wireless devices and networks. If you've recently passed the CompTIA Network+ exam, these topics will likely be very familiar to you, but they are still worth looking at to ensure you understand them from the perspective of the CompTIA Security+ exam.

A **wireless access point (AP)** connects wireless clients to a wired network. However, many APs also have routing capabilities. Vendors commonly market APs with routing capabilities as wireless routers, so that's how you'll typically see them advertised. Two distinctions are:

- **All wireless routers are APs.** These are APs with an extra capability—routing.
- **Not all APs are wireless routers.** Many APs do not have any additional capabilities. They provide connectivity for wireless clients to a wired network but do not have routing capabilities.

Figure 4.4 shows a diagram of a wireless router providing connectivity to multiple systems. Notice that the wireless router has both a switch component and a router component, so it serves both wired and wireless clients. The devices connect to the switch component. The router component provides connectivity to the Internet through a broadband modem or similar device depending on the Internet Service Provider (ISP) requirements.

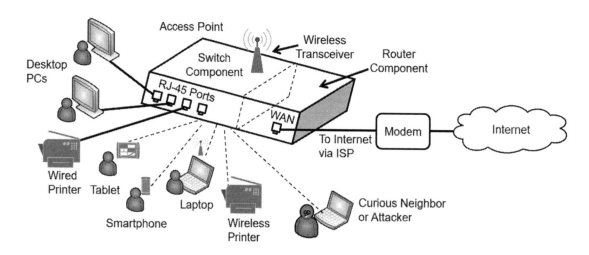

Figure 4.4: Wireless access point with routing capabilities (wireless router)

Most APs include physical ports for wired access (labeled as "RJ-45 Ports" in the diagram) and a wireless transceiver for wireless clients. In other words, some users can connect with regular twisted-pair cable, and other users can connect using wireless transmissions. The wired ports and wireless connections all connect through the switch component of the wireless router. Many vendors label the Internet connection WAN for wide area network, but some vendors label this port as "Internet."

When used as shown in Figure 4.4, the AP also includes extra services and capabilities, such as routing, Network Address Translation (NAT), Port Address Translation (PAT), Dynamic Host Configuration Protocol (DHCP), and more. These extra services reduce the setup time required for the WLAN.

Because wireless networks broadcast on known frequency bands, other wireless users can often see them. This includes authorized users, curious neighbors, and attackers.

Band Selection and Channel Overlaps

Wireless networks use two primary radio bands: 2.4 GHz, and 5 GHz. However, wireless devices don't transmit exactly on 2.4 or 5 GHz. Instead, the two bands have multiple channels starting at about 2.4 GHz and 5 GHz. Wireless signals travel the farthest with the 2.4-GHz frequency range, and you can get the widest bandwidth (transfer the most data) with the 5-GHz frequency. The following list shows some wireless standards along with the radio bands they use:

- 802.11b, 2.4 GHz
- 802.11g, 2.4 GHz
- 802.11n, 2.4 GHz, and 5 GHz
- 802.11ac, 5 GHz
- 802.11ax, 2.4 GHz and 5 GHz

There isn't a single standard that applies to every country, so you'll find that the number of channels within each band varies from country to country. Additionally, some of these channels overlap with others. For example, Figure 4.5 shows channels in the 2.4 GHz range used by 802.11b, 802.11g, and 802.11n.

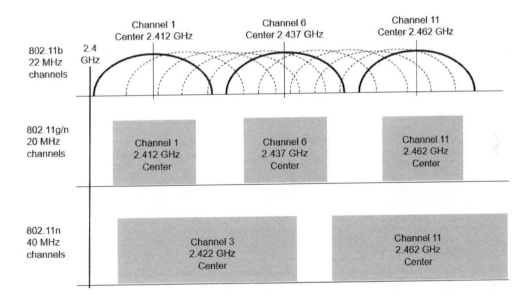

Figure 4.5: Channels and channel overlaps with 802.11 standards

It's easiest to see the channel overlaps in 802.11b. Channels 1, 6, and 11 are solid lines, while the other channels use dotted lines. Channel 1 overlaps with Channels 2 through 5, Channel 6 overlaps with Channels 2 through 10, and Channel 11 overlaps with Channels 7 through 10. Imagine a device is using Channel 6. If another wireless device is using an overlapping channel, it can impact the efficiency of the traffic on Channel 6. The other standards displayed in the figure only show some of the channels, but they also suffer from channel overlap problems.

The frequency band (2.4 GHz or 5 GHz) you select depends on the standard (802.11 b, g, n, ac, or ax) you're using. Most wireless devices will automatically pick the best channel, but some devices allow you to change the channel to improve performance. As an example, if you have a wireless router in an apartment complex, you may find that Channel 6 is noisy because of other wireless routers nearby. By changing your router to Channel 1, you can improve the performance of your wireless network.

Access Point SSID

Wireless networks are identified by a service set identifier (SSID), which is simply the wireless network name. Some APs still come with default SSIDs, though most vendors have moved away from this practice. For example, the default SSID of some older Linksys APs is "Linksys." Some newer APs force you to enter a name for the SSID when you first install it and do not include a default. From a defense-in-depth perspective, it's a good idea to change the SSID name if it comes with a default. This practice gives attackers less information about the AP.

For example, if an attacker sees a wireless network with an SSID of Linksys, the attacker has a good idea that the network uses a Linksys AP. If the attacker knows about specific weaknesses with this AP, he can start exploiting these weaknesses. In contrast, if you gave your AP an SSID of "Success" attackers wouldn't have any clues about your AP.

MAC Filtering

Chapter 3 discusses **media access control (MAC) filtering** in the context of port security for switches. You can also enable MAC filtering on many wireless routers.

The MAC address (also called a physical address or hardware address) is a 48-bit hexadecimal address used to identify network interface cards (NICs). You will usually see the MAC address displayed as six pairs of hexadecimal characters such as 00-16-EA-DD-A6-60. Every NIC, including wireless NICs, has a MAC address. Most wireless routers allow you to specify what MAC addresses to allow, and they will block all others, or you can specify what MAC addresses to block, and they will allow all others.

This might sound secure, but an attacker can easily bypass MAC filtering. Using a wireless sniffer, an attacker can identify MAC addresses allowed in a wireless network. Once he knows what MAC addresses are allowed, he can change his system's MAC address to impersonate one of the allowed MAC addresses.

> ## ★ *Remember This!*
>
> MAC filtering can restrict wireless network access to specific clients. However, an attacker can use a sniffer to discover allowed MAC addresses and circumvent this form of network access control. It's relatively simple for an attacker to spoof a MAC address.

MAC Address Cloning

MAC address cloning refers to changing the MAC address on a PC or other device with the same MAC address as the wide area network (WAN) port on an Internet-facing router. MAC address cloning sometimes resolves connectivity issues on small home or office networks. In a MAC cloning attack (sometimes called a MAC spoofing attack), an attacker changes his computer's MAC address to the MAC address of an authorized system. This will bypass MAC filtering.

Site Surveys and Heat Maps

Administrators often perform a site survey when planning and deploying a wireless network. The **site survey** examines the wireless environment to identify potential issues, such as areas with noise or other devices operating on the same frequency bands. Additionally, administrators and security personnel periodically repeat the site survey to verify that the environment hasn't changed and to detect potential security issues.

One method of performing a site survey is with a **Wi-Fi analyzer**. Wi-Fi analyzers identify and analyze activity on channels within the wireless spectrum. They typically allow you to analyze one frequency range at a time and see each channel's activity level on a graph. Others will give power levels for each channel.

Other site survey tools will create a **heat map**, which gives you a color-coded representation of wireless signals. For example, the color green may show where the wireless signals are the strongest, and the color red may show where they are the weakest. By walking around an organization and recording wireless activity, the heat map will show where the wireless signals are the strongest and where you may have dead spots.

Figure 4.6 shows heat maps for two organizations. Organization 1 has a lot of uncovered areas, while Organization 2 has almost complete coverage of the organization.

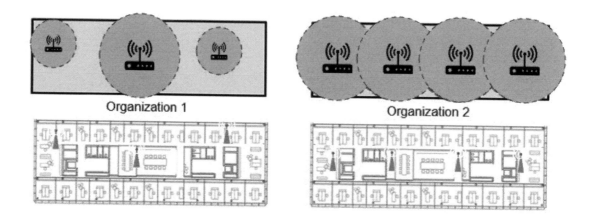

Figure 4.6: Heat map

Wireless **footprinting** creates a detailed diagram of APs and hotspots within an organization. By overlaying the heat map onto a basic architectural drawing of an organization's spaces, it's possible to see the location of the APs along with dead spots and hotspots.

> ★ **Remember This!**
>
> A site survey examines the wireless environment to identify potential problem areas. A heat map shows wireless coverage and dead spots if they exist. Wireless footprinting gives you a detailed diagram of wireless access points, hotspots, and dead spots within an organization.

Access Point Installation Considerations

The most used wireless antenna on both APs and wireless devices is an omnidirectional (or omni) antenna. Omnidirectional antennas transmit and receive signals in all directions at the same time. This allows wireless devices to connect to an AP from any direction. Another type of antenna is a directional antenna. A directional antenna transmits in a single direction and receives signals from the same direction. Because the antenna's power is focused in a single direction, the directional antenna has greater gain than an omni antenna, and it can transmit and receive signals over greater distances.

Data from the site survey can help administrators determine the best place to locate APs. After placing them, administrators commonly do the site survey again to verify that they have the coverage they want.

Wireless Cryptographic Protocols

Because wireless networks broadcast over the air, anyone who has a wireless transceiver can intercept the transmissions. In the early days of wireless networks, security was an afterthought. As a result, early wireless cryptographic protocols such as Wired Equivalent Privacy (WEP) and Wi-Fi Protected Access (WPA) were weak, and attackers quickly found ways to exploit them. WEP and WPA are deprecated and should not be used. The following sections discuss current wireless cryptographic protocols.

WPA2 and CCMP

The Wi-Fi Alliance developed **Wi-Fi Protected Access 2 (WPA2)** to replace earlier cryptographic protocols. WPA2 (also known as IEEE 802.11i) uses strong cryptographic protocols such as Advanced Encryption Standard (AES) and Counter-mode/CBC-MAC Protocol (CCMP).

Although WPA2 provides significant security improvements over previous wireless encryption techniques, some enterprises need stronger security. Another step you can take is to enable authentication with Enterprise mode, described later in this chapter.

Open, PSK, and Enterprise Modes

WPA2 can operate in open, **pre-shared key (PSK),** or **Enterprise** modes. Open mode doesn't use any security. Instead, all data is transferred in cleartext, making it easy for anyone who captured it to read it. Basically, open mode turns off all of the security features of WPA2!

When using PSK mode, users access the wireless network anonymously with a PSK or passphrase. This doesn't provide authentication. As a reminder, authentication proves a user's identity with credentials such as a username and password. Users claim an identity with a username and prove it with a password. Just a passphrase without a username provides authorization without authentication.

Enterprise mode forces users to authenticate with unique credentials before granting access to the wireless network. Enterprise mode uses the 802.1X standard, often implemented with a RADIUS server, which accesses a database of accounts. If users don't have the proper credentials, Enterprise mode (using an 802.1X server) blocks their access. Also, an 802.1X server can provide certificate-based authentication to increase the security of the authentication process. The authentication protocol (discussed later in this chapter) determines if the 802.1X server will use a certificate or not.

When you select Enterprise mode, you'll need to enter three pieces of information:

- **RADIUS server.** You enter the IP address assigned to the 802.1X server, which is often a RADIUS server.

- **RADIUS port.** You enter the port used by the RADIUS server. The official default port for RADIUS is 1812. However, some vendors have used other ports, such as 1645. The key is that you must enter the same port here that the server is using.
- **Shared secret.** The shared secret is similar to a password, and you must enter it here exactly as it is entered on the RADIUS server. This is different than the user's password.

After configuring WPA2 Enterprise on an AP, the AP forwards all connection attempts to the RADIUS authentication server. After users authenticate, the RADIUS server tells the AP to grant the users access.

Wireless authentication systems using an 802.1X server are more advanced than most home networks need, and many larger organizations use them. In other words, most home networks use PSK mode, but organizations that want to increase wireless security may use Enterprise mode. A combination of both a security protocol such as WPA2 and an 802.1X authentication server significantly reduces the chance of a successful access attack against a wireless system.

> ★ **Remember This!**
>
> WPA2-PSK uses a pre-shared key and does not provide individual authentication. Open mode doesn't use security and allows all users to access the AP. Enterprise mode is more secure than Personal mode, providing strong authentication. Enterprise mode uses an 802.1X server (implemented as a RADIUS server) to add authentication.

WPA3 and Simultaneous Authentication of Equals

Wi-Fi Protected Access 3 (WPA3) devices are now widely available on many enterprise wireless networks. This is the newest generation of wireless technology, and it supports three modes of operation:

- **Enhanced open mode** replaces the insecure, unencrypted, open mode of WPA2 with technology that uses strong encryption to protect the communications of unauthenticated users. It allows you to easily run a secure guest network.
- **Simultaneous Authentication of Equals (SAE) mode** replaces the PSK mode of WPA2. SAE uses a passphrase but adds strong security defenses to the technology.
- **Enterprise mode** is also supported in WPA3 using a RADIUS server and individual user authentication.

> 📌 **Remember This!**
>
> WPA2 supports CCMP (based on AES) and replaced earlier wireless cryptographic protocols. WPA3 uses Simultaneous Authentication of Equals (SAE) instead of a pre-shared key (PSK) used with WPA2.

Authentication Protocols

Wireless networks support several different authentication protocols. Many are built on the Extensible Authentication Protocol (EAP), an authentication framework that provides general guidance for authentication methods. IEEE 802.1X servers typically use one of these methods to increase the level of security during the authentication process. Additionally, while they are often used in wireless networks, they can also be used anywhere an 802.1X server is implemented.

A key point to remember for each of these methods is if they support or require certificates. Some methods are:

- **EAP**. EAP provides a method for two systems to create a secure encryption key, also known as a Pairwise Master Key (PMK). Systems then use the Pairwise Transient Key (PTK) to encrypt all data transmitted between the devices. AES-based CCMP uses this key.
- **Protected EAP (PEAP)**. PEAP provides an extra layer of protection for EAP. The EAP designers assumed that EAP would be used with adequate physical security to ensure the communication channel was secure. That wasn't always the case in practice, but PEAP protects the communication channel by encapsulating and encrypting the EAP conversation in a Transport Layer Security (TLS) tunnel. PEAP requires a certificate on the server but not on the clients. A common implementation is with Microsoft Challenge Handshake Authentication Protocol version 2 (MS-CHAPv2).
- **EAP-FAST**. Cisco designed EAP-Flexible Authentication via Secure Tunneling (EAP-FAST) as a secure replacement for Lightweight EAP (LEAP) that Cisco also designed. EAP-FAST supports PAC (Protected Access Credential) instead of certificates.
- **EAP-TLS**. EAP-Transport Layer Security (EAP-TLS) is one of the most secure EAP standards. The primary difference between PEAP and EAP-TLS is that EAP-TLS requires certificates on the 802.1X server and the clients.
- **EAP-TTLS**. EAP-Tunneled TLS (EAP-TTLS) is an extension of EAP-TLS, allowing systems to use some older authentication methods such as Password Authentication Protocol (PAP) within a TLS tunnel. EAP-TTLS requires a certificate on the 802.1X server but not the clients.
- **RADIUS Federation**. Chapter 2, "Understanding Identity and Access Management," covers federations used for single sign-on (SSO). As a reminder, a federation includes two or more entities (such as companies) that share the same identity management system.

Users can log on once, and access shared resources with the other entity without logging on again. Similarly, it's possible to create a federation using 802.1X and RADIUS servers.

Note that EAP-FAST supports PAC (Protected Access Credential) instead of certificates. PEAP and EAP-TTLS require a certificate on the server, but not the clients. EAP-TLS requires certificates on both the server and the clients. Chapter 10, "Understanding Cryptography and PKI," digs into certificates much deeper, but as an introduction, certificates help provide strong authentication and encryption services. A certificate authority (CA) must issue certificates, so an organization must either purchase certificates from a public CA or implement a private CA within the network.

IEEE 802.1X Security

Chapter 3 discusses port security by disabling unused ports or using MAC address filtering. Another method of port security is to use *IEEE 802.1X*, a port-based authentication protocol. It requires users or devices to authenticate when they connect to a specific wireless access point or a specific physical port. Administrators implement it in both wireless and wired networks, and can also use it with virtual private networks (VPNs) described later in this chapter.

802.1X secures the authentication process prior to a client gaining access to a network and blocks network access if the client cannot authenticate. 802.1X can use simple usernames and passwords for authentication, or certificates for certificate-based authentication.

The 802.1X server prevents rogue devices from connecting to a network. Consider open RJ-45 wall jacks. Although disabling them is a good port security practice, you can also configure an 802.1X server to require authentication for these ports. If clients cannot authenticate, the 802.1X server blocks or restricts access to the network.

It's possible to combine an 802.1X server with other network elements such as a virtual local area network (VLAN). For example, imagine you want to provide visitors with Internet access but prevent them from accessing internal network resources. You can configure the 802.1X server to grant full access to authorized clients but redirect unauthorized clients to a guest area of the network via a VLAN.

You can implement 802.1X as a Remote Authentication Dial-In User Service (RADIUS) or Diameter server, as discussed later in this chapter. This helps authenticate virtual private network (VPN) clients before they connect. You can also implement 802.1X in wireless networks to force wireless clients to authenticate before they connect. RFC 3580, "IEEE 802.1X Remote Authentication Dial In User Service (RADIUS) Usage Guidelines," describes IEEE 802.1X in much greater detail in case you want to dig deeper.

> ### ✦ *Remember This!*
>
> Enterprise mode requires an 802.1X server. EAP-FAST supports PACs. PEAP and EAP-TTLS require a certificate on the 802.1X server. EAP-TLS also uses TLS, but it requires certificates on both the 802.1X server and each of the clients. An 802.1X server provides port-based authentication, ensuring that only authorized clients can connect to a device or a network. It prevents rogue devices from connecting.

Controller and Access Point Security

After doing a site survey and determining the best location for APs, it's also important to consider physical security. If attackers can access an AP, they can connect unauthorized devices to collect network traffic. It's also possible for attackers to reset the AP to factory settings, effectively removing access to the network for everyone using the AP. Additionally, it's important to use newer cryptographic protocols such as WPA2 and WPA3. Older deprecated wireless protocols such as WEP and WPA should not be used.

Captive Portals

A captive portal is a technical solution that forces clients using web browsers to complete a specific process before it allows them access to the network. Organizations commonly use it as a hotspot that requires users to log on or agree to specific terms before they can access the Internet. Here are three common examples:

- **Free Internet access.** Many hospitals and other medical facilities provide free Internet access to patients and visitors. The captive portal requires users to acknowledge and agree to abide by an acceptable use policy (AUP). Free captive portals rarely require users to log on but instead, just require them to check a box indicating they agree and then click a button to continue.
- **Paid Internet access.** Many hotels, resorts, cruise ships, and airlines provide Internet access to customers, but on a pay-as-you-go basis. When users attempt to access the Internet, they are redirected to the captive portal. They must successfully log on with a pre-created account or enter credit card information to pay for access.
- **Alternative to IEEE 802.1X.** Adding an 802.1X server can be expensive and is sometimes not a feasible option. Organizations can use captive portals as an alternative. It requires users to authenticate before granting them access.

Understanding Wireless Attacks

There are several known attacks against wireless networks. Most can be avoided by using strong security protocols such as WPA2 with CCMP or WPA3 with SAE. In contrast, WPA is vulnerable to many attacks, especially if it is using TKIP.

Disassociation Attacks

A **disassociation attack** effectively removes a wireless client from a wireless network. It's easier to understand this attack if you understand the normal operation of wireless devices and wireless APs.

After a wireless client authenticates with a wireless AP, the two devices exchange frames, causing the client to be associated with the AP. At any point, a wireless device can send a disassociation frame to the AP to terminate the connection. This frame includes the wireless client's MAC address. When the AP receives the disassociation frame, it deallocates all its memory for the connection.

In a disassociation attack, attackers send a disassociation frame to the AP with a spoofed MAC address of the victim. The AP receives the frame and shuts down the connection. The victim is now disconnected from the AP and must go through the authentication process again to reconnect.

Interestingly, some hotels used this attack to prevent guests from using their own personal wireless networks. For example, if you have an iPhone with cellular access to the Internet, you can enable the Personal Hotspot feature. This lets you share the connection with other devices, such as a laptop. Some hotels looked for these personal wireless networks and launched disassociation attacks against them. Customers were forced to pay for the hotel's wireless services if they needed reliable Internet access.

Wi-Fi Protected Setup

Wi-Fi Protected Setup (WPS) allows users to configure wireless devices without typing in the passphrase. Instead, users can configure devices by pressing buttons or entering a short eight-digit personal identification number (PIN).

For example, a user can configure a new wireless device by pressing a button on the AP and on the wireless device. The AP will automatically configure the device within about 30 seconds, with no other actions needed. These buttons can be physical buttons on the devices or virtual buttons that the user clicks via an application or webpage. When using the PIN method, users first identify the eight-digit PIN on the AP and then enter the PIN on the new wireless device.

Unfortunately, WPS is susceptible to brute-force attacks. A WPS attack keeps trying different PINs until it succeeds. For example, Reaver is an open-source tool that allows attackers to discover the

PIN within about 10 hours and often much quicker. Once it discovers the PIN, it can discover the passphrase in WPA2 wireless networks. However, WPS is safe if it is used with WPA3.

Security experts recommend disabling WPS on all devices. This is typically possible via the AP configuration page. Even if you choose to enable WPS to easily connect some devices, you should immediately turn it off once you're done.

📌 *Remember This!*

A disassociation attack effectively removes a wireless client from a wireless network, forcing it to re-authenticate. WPS allows users to configure a wireless device by entering an eight-digit PIN and/or pressing buttons on the device. A WPS attack guesses all possible PINs until it finds the correct one. It will typically discover the PIN within hours and use it to discover the passphrase.

Rogue Access Point

A *rogue access point (rogue AP)* is an AP placed within a network without official authorization. It might be an employee bypassing security or installed by an attacker. If an employee installs a rogue AP, the chances are higher that this AP will not be adequately managed, increasing vulnerabilities to the network. This is an example of shadow IT described in Chapter 6, "Comparing Threats, Vulnerabilities, and Common Attacks."

Generically, you can think of a rogue as a scoundrel, a crook, or a villain. If a rogue is a crook or villain, then rogue access points are not an administrator's friend. You might also see them called counterfeit access points, which is also a clear indication that they aren't legitimate.

Attackers may connect a rogue access point to network devices in wireless closets that lack adequate physical security. This access point acts as a sniffer to capture traffic passing through the wired network device and then broadcasts the traffic using the AP's wireless capability. The attacker can then capture the exfiltrated data files while sitting in the parking lot. Data exfiltration is the unauthorized transfer of data from an organization to a location controlled by an attacker.

Additionally, attackers may use the rogue access point to connect to the wired network. This works the same way that regular users can connect to a wired network via a wireless network. The difference is that the attacker configures all the security for the counterfeit access point and can use it for malicious purposes.

If you discover an unauthorized AP, disconnect it as quickly as possible. When you discover any attack, the first step is to contain or isolate the threat. By simply unplugging the Ethernet cable, you can stop the unauthorized AP from capturing network traffic.

Evil Twin

An **evil twin** is a rogue access point with the same SSID (or similar) as a legitimate access point. You can think of the SSID of the evil twin as a twin of the legitimate AP's SSID. For example, many public places, such as coffee shops, hotels, and airports, provide free Wi-Fi. An attacker can set up an AP using the same SSID as the public Wi-Fi network, and many unsuspecting users will connect to this evil twin.

Some people have trouble differentiating between rogue access points and evil twins. If you compare them to two twins, it may be clearer. Imagine Sherri and Terri are identical twins. Which of the following MOST accurately describes them? Twins or sisters? The answer is twins because it is the most accurate description. Yes, they are sisters, but not all sisters are twins.

Once a user connects to an evil twin, wireless traffic goes through the evil twin instead of the legitimate AP. Often, the attacker presents bogus login pages to users to capture usernames and passwords. Other times, they simply capture traffic from the connection, such as email or text typed into webpage text boxes, and analyze it to detect sensitive information they can exploit.

Although it might sound complex to set up an evil twin, it's rather easy. Attackers can configure a laptop with a wireless access card as an AP. With it running, the attackers look like any other user in a coffee shop or airport waiting area. They'll have their laptop open and appear to be working, and you'll have no idea they are trying to steal your credentials or other personal data that you send over the Internet via the evil twin. Similarly, attackers can set one up in a parking lot or another location close to an organization and try to trick employees or visitors.

Often, administrators will use wireless scanners to perform site surveys. In addition to detecting noise on frequency bands, they can also detect rogue APs, including evil twins. The site survey can help them identify access points' physical locations because the signal will get stronger as the administrator gets closer.

> ★ **Remember This!**
>
> Rogue access points are often used to capture and exfiltrate data. An evil twin is a rogue access point using the same SSID (or a similar SSID) as a legitimate access point. A secure AP blocks unauthorized users, but a rogue access point provides access to unauthorized users.

Jamming Attacks

Attackers can transmit noise or another radio signal on the same frequency used by a wireless network. This interferes with the wireless transmissions and can seriously degrade performance.

This denial-of-service attack is commonly called **_jamming_**, and it usually prevents all users from connecting to a wireless network. In some cases, users have intermittent connectivity because the interference causes them to lose their association with the AP and forces them to reconnect.

In some cases, you can increase the power levels of the AP to overcome the attack. Another method of overcoming the attack is to use different wireless channels. Each wireless standard has several channels you can use, and if one channel is too noisy, you can use another one. Although this is useful for overcoming interference in home networks, it won't effectively combat an interference attack. If you switch channels, the attacker can also switch channels.

IV Attacks

An initialization vector (IV) is a number used by encryption systems, and a wireless IV attack attempts to discover the pre-shared key after first discovering the IV. Some wireless protocols use an IV by combining it with the pre-shared key to encrypt data in transit. When an encryption system reuses the same IV, an **_IV attack_** can discover the IV easily. As an example, WEP, an early wireless security protocol, uses a relatively small 24-bit number for the IV. This small IV resulted in wireless networks reusing keys, making WEP easy to crack.

In many IV attacks, the attacker uses packet injection techniques to add additional packets into the data stream. The AP responds with more packets, increasing the probability that it will reuse a key. An IV attack using packet injection decreases the time it takes to crack a WEP key. It's worth repeating that WEP has been deprecated and should not be used.

Near Field Communication Attacks

Near field communication (NFC) is a group of standards used on mobile devices that allow them to communicate with other mobile devices when they are close to them. For example, you can share pictures, contacts, and other data with friends. One person shares the data, and after placing the smartphones close to each other, the other person selects it to download.

Many point-of-sale card readers support NFC technologies with credit cards. Instead of swiping your card or inserting it to read the chip data, you wave your card over the reader. It is often advertised as a contactless payment method. Some smartphone applications support payments with NFC-enabled smartphones. Users wave their smartphones over the reader to make a payment.

During a **_near field communication attack_**, an attacker uses an NFC reader to capture data from another NFC device. One method is an eavesdropping attack. The NFC reader uses an antenna to boost its range and intercepts the data transfer between two other devices. For example, imagine Marge is making a purchase at a store, and Bart is behind her with his own NFC reader. If Bart can boost the receiving range of his NFC reader, he can capture Marge's transaction. The primary indication of an NFC attack is unauthorized charges on a credit card statement.

RFID Attacks

Radio-frequency identification (RFID) systems include an RFID reader and RFID tags placed on objects. They are used to track and manage inventory, and any type of valuable assets, including objects and animals.

There's an almost endless assortment of tags available for multiple purposes. This includes tags implanted into animals, packaging for any type of product (such as computers), pharmaceuticals, transportation systems (such as shipping containers, railcars, and busses), and controlled substances (such as pharmaceutical containers). Some tags are only slightly larger than a grain of rice.

Active RFID tags include their own power source, while **passive RFID tags** include electronics that allow them to collect and use power to transmit data stored on the device. This is similar to how a proximity card (described in Chapter 9, "Implementing Controls to Protect Assets") receives a charge from a proximity card reader and then transmits data to the reader. One difference is that RFID transmitters can send to and from tags from a much greater distance than proximity readers. Some of the common RFID attacks are:

- **Sniffing or eavesdropping.** Because RFID transmits data over the air, an attacker can collect it by listening. A key requirement is to know the RFID system's frequency and have a receiver tuned to that frequency. The attacker also needs to know the protocols used by the RFID system to interpret the data.
- **RFID Cloning.** Successful eavesdropping attacks allow the attacker to perform a cloning attack. For example, an attacker can configure a bogus tag to mimic the tag attached to a valuable object. The attacker can then steal the valuable object without the theft being easily detected.
- **A denial-of-service (DoS)** attack attempts to disrupt services. If an attacker knows the RFID system's frequency, it's possible to launch a jamming or interference attack, flooding the frequency with noise. This prevents the RFID system from operating normally.

Bluetooth Attacks

Bluetooth is a short-range wireless system used in personal area networks (PANs) and within networks. A PAN is a network of devices close to a single person. Bluetooth devices include smartphones, headsets, and computer devices.

The Bluetooth range was designed initially for about 10 meters (about 30 feet), but the range is often farther and ultimately extends beyond a person's personal space. Attackers have discovered methods of exploiting these networks. Some common attacks are bluejacking, bluesnarfing, and bluebugging:

- **Bluejacking** is the practice of sending unsolicited messages to nearby Bluetooth devices. Bluejacking messages are typically text but can also be images or sounds. Bluejacking is relatively harmless but does cause some confusion when users start receiving messages.
- **Bluesnarfing** refers to the unauthorized access to, or theft of information from, a Bluetooth device. A bluesnarfing attack can access information, such as email, contact lists, calendars, and text messages.
- **Bluebugging** is like bluesnarfing, but it goes a step further. In addition to gaining full access to the phone, the attacker installs a backdoor. The attacker can have the phone call the attacker at any time, allowing the attacker to listen in on conversations within a room. Attackers can also listen in on phone conversations, enable call forwarding, send messages, and more.

When Bluetooth devices are first configured, they are configured in Discovery mode. Bluetooth devices use MAC addresses, and in Discovery mode, the Bluetooth device broadcasts its MAC address, allowing other devices to see it and connect to it. This is required when pairing Bluetooth devices.

In earlier versions of Bluetooth, this pairing process could happen any time a device is in Discovery mode. However, most software vendors have rewritten their software to prevent this. Today, users typically manually pair the device. If a user doesn't acknowledge an attempted pairing, it fails. As a result, Bluetooth attacks are rare today. However, if a device doesn't require a user to pair a device manually, it is still susceptible to these attacks. Also, by placing devices into conductive metal lockboxes that act as a Faraday cage, it blocks Bluetooth attacks.

> ### ★ Remember This!
>
> Bluejacking is the unauthorized sending of text messages to a nearby Bluetooth device. Bluesnarfing is the unauthorized access to, or theft of information from, a Bluetooth device. Ensuring devices cannot be paired without manual user intervention prevents these attacks and placing them in Faraday cages will prevent pairing.

Wireless Replay Attacks

In a replay attack, an attacker captures data sent between two entities, modifies it, and then attempts to impersonate one of the parties by replaying the data. Chapter 7, "Protecting Against Advanced Attacks," covers replay attacks in a wired network. A wireless replay attack is similar. However, WPA2 and WPA3 are resistant to replay attacks. The best protection is to eliminate the use of deprecated wireless cryptographic protocols.

War Driving and War Flying

War driving is the practice of looking for vulnerable wireless networks. Although war driving is more common in cars, you can just as easily do it by walking around in a large city. Attackers use war driving to discover wireless networks that they can exploit and often use directional antennas to detect wireless networks with weak signals.

Administrators sometimes use war driving as part of a wireless audit. A wireless audit is a detective control and examines the signal footprint, antenna placement, and encryption of wireless traffic. These audits are useful at detecting weaknesses in wireless networks. For example, administrators can sometimes detect the existence of rogue access points and evil twins by war driving and determine when their WAP's footprint extends too far.

War flying is like war driving. However, instead of walking or driving around, people fly around in private planes. In some cases, people have intercepted wireless transmissions at altitudes of 2,500 feet. Most of these transmissions are using 2.4 GHz, which can travel farther than 5-GHz signals. Additionally, there isn't much interference between the access points and the planes. However, planes quickly move out of range of access points because they are flying.

An alternative to a plane is a drone. An aircraft drone's technical definition is any aircraft that can fly on its own without a human in control. However, people commonly think of a drone as any aircraft controlled by remote control instead of an onboard pilot. By adding a little hardware, a drone can look for wireless networks.

It's also possible for attackers to use drones for reconnaissance. Chapter 8 discusses reconnaissance in the context of penetration testing. Pen testers use a variety of methods to collect information on targeted systems. They can also use drones to collect pictures of a target and scan for wireless networks.

> ### ★ *Remember This!*
>
> Administrators use war driving techniques as part of a wireless audit. A wireless audit checks a wireless signal footprint, power levels, antenna placement, and encryption of wireless traffic. Wireless audits using war driving can detect rogue access points and identify unauthorized users. War flying is similar to war driving, but it uses planes or drones instead of cars.

Using VPNs for Remote Access

A *virtual private network (VPN)* is often used for remote access. Remote access VPNs allow users to access private networks via a public network. The public network is most commonly the Internet, but it can also be a semiprivate leased line from a telecommunications company. Because the telecommunications company will often lease access to one physical line to several companies, the leased line is not truly private.

Access over a public network is a core security concern with VPNs. With more people working from home and connecting to company networks via direct access VPNs, these VPNs have become a popular attack vector. Different tunneling protocols encapsulate and encrypt the traffic to protect the data from unauthorized disclosure. The tunnel prevents anyone from reading the data transferred through it.

VPNs and VPN Concentrators

It's possible to create a VPN by enabling services on a server. For example, if you have a Windows server, you can enable the Direct Access VPN role and configure the Routing and Remote Access console. The server may have one or two network interface cards (NICs). In the case where there are two NICs, one NIC is accessible from the Internet, and the second NIC provides access to the private network. If you are only supporting a few VPN clients, this might be the perfect solution.

Larger organizations often use a **VPN concentrator**, which is a dedicated device used for VPNs. A VPN concentrator includes all the services needed to create a VPN, including strong encryption and authentication techniques, and it supports many clients.

> ★ *Remember This!*
>
> A virtual private network (VPN) provides remote access to a private network via a public network. VPN concentrators are dedicated devices used for VPNs. They include all the services needed to create a secure VPN supporting many clients.

When using a VPN concentrator, you would typically place it in the screened subnet. The firewall between the Internet and the screened subnet would forward VPN traffic to the VPN concentrator. The VPN concentrator would route all private VPN traffic to the firewall between the screened subnet and the intranet.

Remote Access VPN

Figure 4.7 shows an example of how users can connect to internal networks from remote locations. You may see this referenced as a remote access VPN or a direct access VPN. The VPN client first connects to the Internet using a broadband connection to an Internet Service Provider (ISP). After connecting to the Internet, the VPN client can then initiate the VPN connection.

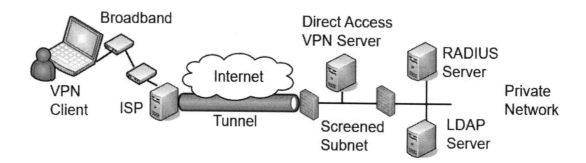

Figure 4.7: Connecting to a VPN server

The VPN server is in the screened subnet and reachable through a public IP address. This makes it accessible from any other host on the Internet. A VPN server needs to authenticate clients, and a common method is to use an internal Remote Authentication Dial-in User Service (RADIUS) server. When a user logs on, the VPN server sends the user's credentials to the RADIUS server.

While the RADIUS server might have a database of users and passwords, it's more common for it to pass the credentials on to another server to validate them. For example, the RADIUS server can pass the credentials on to a Lightweight Directory Access Protocol (LDAP) server during the authentication process. In a Microsoft domain, the LDAP server is a domain controller.

IPsec as a Tunneling Protocol

Chapter 3 introduced Internet Protocol security (IPsec) as a method of encrypting data in transit. IPsec supports both Tunnel mode and Transport mode.

Tunnel mode encrypts the entire IP packet, including both the payload and the packet headers, and VPNs commonly use Tunnel mode. Packet headers include IP addresses and MAC addresses. A benefit of using Tunnel mode is that the IP addressing used within the internal network is encrypted and not visible to anyone who intercepts the traffic. If attackers do intercept the traffic, they can see the source IP address from the client and the destination address to the VPN server, but the internal IP address information remains hidden.

Transport mode only encrypts the payload and is commonly used in private networks, but not with VPNs. If traffic is transmitted and used only within a private network, there isn't any need to hide the IP addresses by encrypting them. IPsec provides security in two ways:

- **Authentication**. IPsec includes an Authentication Header (AH) to allow each of the IPsec conversation hosts to authenticate with each other before exchanging data. AH provides authentication and integrity. AH uses IP protocol number 51.
- **Encryption**. IPsec includes Encapsulating Security Payload (ESP) to encrypt the data and provide confidentiality, authentication, and integrity. ESP uses IP protocol number 50.

The term IP protocol number might look like a typo, but it isn't. AH and ESP are identified with IP protocol numbers, not port numbers. Chapter 3 discusses routers and firewalls. You may remember from Chapter 3 that a basic packet-filtering firewall can filter packets based on IP addresses, ports, and some protocols, such as Internet Control Message Protocol (ICMP) and IPsec. Packet filters use the protocol numbers to identify AH and ESP traffic. IPsec uses Internet Key Exchange (IKE) over port 500 to authenticate clients in the IPsec conversation. IKE creates security associations (SAs) for the VPN and uses these to set up a secure channel between the client and the VPN server.

SSL/TLS as a Tunneling Protocol

Some tunneling protocols use Transport Layer Security (TLS) to secure the VPN channel. As an example, Secure Socket Tunneling Protocol (SSTP) encrypts VPN traffic using TLS over port 443. Using port 443 provides a lot of flexibility for many administrators and rarely requires opening additional firewall ports. It is a useful alternative when the VPN tunnel must go through a device using NAT, and IPsec is not feasible. OpenVPN and OpenConnect are two open-source applications that can use TLS to create a secure channel.

While this can also use Secure Sockets Layer (SSL), SSL has known weaknesses, and TLS is the designated replacement. Even though SSL is rarely, if ever, used today, you'll still see it referenced. For example, SSTP indicates it uses SSL, but it uses TLS.

Split Tunnel Versus Full Tunnel

Imagine that Lisa connects to a company VPN server using IPsec from her home computer. The VPN is using ESP, so all traffic in the tunnel is encrypted. Now, Lisa wants to do an Internet search on saxophones. Will her computer connect directly to the Internet for her search? Or will her computer make a connection through the VPN server first? It depends on the VPN's configuration.

In a ***split tunnel***, a VPN administrator determines what traffic should use the encrypted tunnel. For example, it's possible to configure the tunnel to encrypt only the traffic going to private IP addresses used within the private network. If Lisa did an Internet search with the VPN server configured in a split tunnel configuration, her Internet search traffic would not go through the encrypted tunnel. Instead, her search would go directly to Internet sites via her ISP.

In a **full tunnel**, all traffic goes through the encrypted tunnel while the user is connected to the VPN. If Lisa was connected to the VPN and then tried to connect to a public website, the traffic would first go through the encrypted tunnel and then out to the public website from within the private network. If the private network routed Internet traffic through a unified threat management (UTM) device, Lisa's traffic would go through the organization's UTM device. The website would send webpages back to the UTM device, and the VPN server would encrypt it and send it back to Lisa via the encrypted tunnel.

Chapter 3 discusses UTM devices. A UTM device can perform URL filtering, malware inspection, and content inspection of all traffic sent through it. This is one reason why an organization may choose to use a full tunnel for users connected to a VPN server. A disadvantage is that it can be slow. Not only is the Internet traffic taking an indirect route through the VPN server, but it's also being encrypted and decrypted a couple of times.

> ### ★ Remember This!
>
> IPsec is a secure encryption protocol used with VPNs. Encapsulating Security Payload (ESP) provides confidentiality, integrity, and authentication for VPN traffic. IPsec uses Tunnel mode for VPN traffic and can be identified with protocol ID 50 for ESP. It uses IKE over port 500. A full tunnel encrypts all traffic after a user has connected to a VPN. A split tunnel only encrypts traffic destined for the VPN's private network.

Site-to-Site VPNs

A site-to-site VPN includes two VPN servers that act as gateways for two networks separated geographically. For example, an organization can have two locations. One is its headquarters, and the other is a remote office. It can use two VPN servers to act as gateways to connect the two locations together, as shown in Figure 4.8.

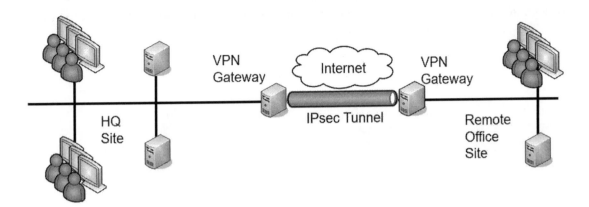

Figure 4.8: Site-to-site VPN

The site-to-site model's benefit is that it connects both networks without requiring additional steps on the part of the user. Users in the remote office can connect to servers in the headquarters location as easily as if the servers were in the remote office. Connecting to the remote server might be slower than connecting to a local server, but otherwise, it's transparent to end users.

In contrast, in a traditional remote access VPN (also called a host-to-gateway model), the end user makes the direct connection to the VPN server and is very much aware of the process.

Always-On VPN

Some VPNs are **always-on VPNs**. They can be used with both site-to-site VPNs and direct access VPNs. When used with a site-to-site VPN, the two VPN gateways maintain the VPN connection. In contrast, some site-to-site VPNs use an on-demand connection. The VPN connection is established when it's needed, such as when a user connects to a remote system.

Several vendors have always-on VPNs for direct access VPNs. They attempt to create a VPN connection as soon as the user's device connects to the Internet. For a home user, this might be right after the user turns on a desktop PC or laptop computer.

When configured on mobile devices, such as cell phones, the device will connect to the always-on VPN anytime the device connects to an Internet connection. For example, if a user visits a coffee shop with free Internet access and the user connects to the network, the device will automatically connect to the always-on VPN.

L2TP as a Tunneling Protocol

Layer 2 Tunneling Protocol (L2TP) is a tunneling protocol that is also used for VPNs. The most recent version is L2TPv3. However, none of the L2TP versions provide any encryption, so it is not used by itself for VPN traffic. Instead, data is encrypted with another protocol, such as IPsec, and then passed to L2TP for transport over the VPN.

HTML5 VPN Portal

Some network devices include the ability to configure an HTML5 VPN portal. An HTML5 VPN allows users to connect to the VPN using their web browser, making it rather simple for the users. It uses TLS to encrypt the session, but it can be very resource intensive. In general, organizations use it to give one or two users access to limited resources. As an example, if a consultant managed a Voice over IP (VoIP) private branch exchange (PBX), an organization could use an HTML5 VPN to give this consultant access to the PBX. However, the other employees would use a traditional VPN for remote access.

Network Access Control

Allowing remote access to your private network can expose your network to many risks from the clients. If a user logs on to a VPN with a malware-infected computer, this computer can then infect other computers on the internal network. **Network access control (NAC)** methods provide continuous security monitoring by inspecting computers and preventing them from accessing the network if they don't pass the inspection.

Most administrators have complete control over computers in their network. For example, they can ensure desktop computers have up-to-date antivirus software installed, operating systems have current patches applied, and their firewalls are enabled. However, administrators don't have complete control of computers that employees use at home or on the road.

NAC provides a measure of control for these other computers. It ensures that clients meet predetermined characteristics before accessing a network. NAC systems often use health as a metaphor, indicating that a client meets these predetermined characteristics. Just as doctors can quarantine patients with certain illnesses, NAC can quarantine or isolate unhealthy clients that don't meet the predefined NAC conditions.

Host Health Checks

Administrators set predefined conditions for healthy clients, and those that meet these preset conditions can access the network. The NAC system isolates computers that don't meet the conditions. Common health conditions checked by a NAC are:

- The client's firewall is enabled.
- The client's operating system is up to date and has all current patches and fixes.
- The client's antivirus software is up to date and has all updated signature definitions.

NAC systems use authentication agents (sometimes called health agents) to inspect NAC clients. These agents are applications or services that check different computer conditions and document the status in a statement of health. When a client connects to a NAC-controlled network, the agent reports the NAC client's health status.

> ### ★ *Remember This!*
>
> Network access control (NAC) includes methods to inspect clients for health, such as having up-to-date antivirus software, and can restrict access of unhealthy clients to a remediation network. You can use NAC for VPN clients and internal clients.

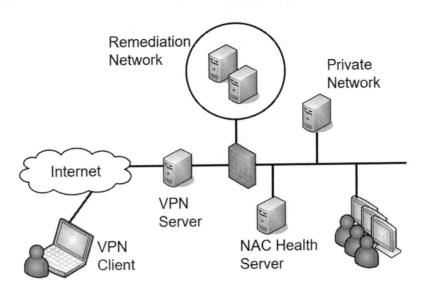

Figure 4.9: Using network access control

Consider Figure 4.9. When a VPN client accesses the network, the VPN server queries the NAC health server to determine required health conditions. The VPN server also queries the client for a statement of the client's health. If the client meets all health requirements, the NAC system allows the client to access the network.

However, if a client doesn't meet the health conditions mandated by the NAC server, the VPN server redirects the client to a remediation network (also called a quarantine network). The remediation network includes resources the client can use to get healthy. For example, it would include currently approved patches, antivirus software, and updated virus signatures. The client can use these resources to improve its health and then try to access the network again.

While NAC can inspect the health of VPN clients, you can also use it to inspect the health of internal clients. For example, internal computers may occasionally miss patches and be vulnerable. NAC will detect the unpatched system and quarantine it. If you use this feature, it's important that the detection is accurate. A false positive by the NAC system can quarantine a healthy client and prevent it from accessing the network.

Similarly, your organization may allow visitors or employees to plug in their mobile computers to live wall jacks for connectivity or connect to a wireless network. NAC inspects the clients, and if they don't meet health conditions, they may be granted Internet access through the network but remain isolated from any other network activity.

Agent Versus Agentless NAC

Agents on clients can be either permanent or dissolvable. A permanent agent (sometimes called a persistent NAC agent) is installed on the client and stays on the client. NAC uses the agent when the client attempts to log on remotely.

A dissolvable agent is downloaded and runs on the client when the client logs on remotely. It collects the information it needs, identifies the client as healthy or not healthy, and reports the status back to the NAC system. Some dissolvable NAC agents remove themselves immediately after they report back to the NAC system. Others remove themselves after the remote session ends. Many NAC vendors refer to dissolvable agents as an agentless capability, though this is somewhat of a misnomer. The NAC is still using an agent to inspect the client, but it is not installing the agent on the client.

An agentless NAC system scans a client remotely without installing code on the client, either permanently or temporarily. This is similar to how vulnerability scanners scan network systems looking for vulnerabilities. Chapter 8 explores vulnerability scanners in more depth.

Authentication and Authorization Methods

An important step when implementing a VPN is to ensure only authorized entities can access it. Authorization begins with authentication, and VPNs support multiple methods of authentication. The following sections describe several remote access authentication methods.

PAP

Password Authentication Protocol (PAP) is used with **Point-to-Point Protocol (PPP)** to authenticate clients. A significant weakness of PAP is that it sends passwords over a network in cleartext, representing a considerable security risk.

PPP was primarily used with dial-up connections. Believe it or not, there was a time when the thought of someone wiretapping a phone was rather remote. Because of this, security was an afterthought with PPP. Today, PPP is only used as a last resort due to passwords being passed in cleartext or used with another protocol that provides encryption.

CHAP

Challenge Handshake Authentication Protocol (CHAP) also uses PPP and authenticates remote users, but it is more secure than PAP. The goal of CHAP is to allow the client to pass credentials over a public network (such as a phone or the Internet) without allowing attackers to intercept the data and later use it in an attack.

The client and server both know a shared secret (like a password) used in the authentication process. However, the client doesn't send the shared secret over the network in plaintext as PAP does. Instead, the client hashes it after combining it with a nonce (number used once) provided by the server. This handshake process is used when the client initially tries to connect to the server and at different times during the connection.

> 📌 **Remember This!**
>
> PAP authentication uses a password. A significant weakness is that PAP sends the information across a network in cleartext, making it susceptible to sniffing attacks. CHAP is more secure than PAP because CHAP doesn't send passwords over the network in cleartext.

RADIUS

Remote Authentication Dial-In User Service (RADIUS) is a centralized authentication service. Instead of each individual VPN server needing a separate database to identify who can authenticate, the VPN servers forward the authentication requests to a central RADIUS server. RADIUS can also be used as an 802.1X server with WPA2 or WPA3 Enterprise mode (described earlier in this chapter).

Imagine your company has locations in Virginia Beach, Atlanta, and Chicago. Each location has a VPN server that users can access. Bart is a traveling salesman, and he can connect to any of these VPN servers. When entering sales data, he connects to the Atlanta VPN. He connects to the Virginia Beach VPN server when using the company-sponsored always-on VPN for his mobile devices. Bart has one account for all company access, and today, he was prompted to change his password.

If each VPN server has a separate database with Bart's username and password, each of these databases must be updated. This can be labor-intensive and result in needless errors.

However, the company could use a centralized RADIUS server, as shown in Figure 4.10, instead. Each VPN server is configured with a shared secret (like a password) and the RADIUS server is configured with a matching shared secret for each of the VPN servers.

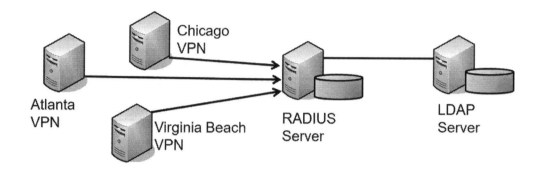

Figure 4.10: RADIUS configuration

This centralized RADIUS server could hold a centralized database of user accounts. However, it is more common for the RADIUS server to access an LDAP server that holds the accounts. For example, in a Microsoft domain, the RADIUS server would pass the credentials to a domain controller. A significant benefit is that there is only one account for the user. If Bart changes his password, the domain controller knows the new password.

RADIUS uses the User Datagram Protocol (UDP), which provides a best-effort delivery mechanism. As a result, RADIUS includes logic to detect communication problems. In contrast, RADIUS alternatives use TCP, which provides guaranteed delivery. These alternatives allow TCP to detect and handle communication issues. Also, RADIUS only encrypts the password by default, while alternatives encrypt the entire authentication process.

Even though RADIUS was created before Extensible Authentication Protocol (EAP) was developed, RADIUS does work with EAP to encrypt entire sessions. RFC 3579 "RADIUS Support for EAP" is an informational RFC and describes how to do so.

TACACS+

Terminal Access Controller Access-Control System Plus (TACACS+) is an alternative to RADIUS, and it provides two essential security benefits over RADIUS. First, it encrypts the entire authentication process, whereas RADIUS encrypts only the password by default. Second, TACACS+ uses multiple challenges and responses between the client and the server.

Although Cisco created TACACS+, it can interact with Kerberos. This allows a Cisco VPN concentrator to interact in a Microsoft Active Directory environment. As a reminder, Microsoft Active Directory uses Kerberos for authentication.

Organizations also use TACACS+ as an authentication service for network devices. In other words, you can use it to authenticate users before they are able to access a configuration page for a router or a switch. The network devices must be TACACS+ enabled, and a TACACS+ server provides the authentication services.

> ### ★ *Remember This!*
>
> RADIUS and TACACS+ provide centralized authentication. RADIUS only encrypts the password by default but can be used with EAP to encrypt entire sessions. TACACS+ encrypts the entire session by default and can be used with Kerberos.

AAA Protocols

AAA protocols provide authentication, authorization, and accounting. Authentication verifies a user's identification, and authorization determines if and to what resources a user should have access. Accounting tracks user access with logs. As an example, RADIUS, TACACS+, and Diameter are considered AAA protocols because they provide all three services of authentication, authorization, and accounting. They authenticate users who attempt remote access, determine if and to what resources the user is authorized for remote access by checking a database, and then record the user's activity. TACACS+ uses multiple challenges and responses during a session. Kerberos is sometimes referred to as an AAA protocol, but it does not provide any accounting services on its own, although it can interface with accounting systems.

Chapter 4 Exam Topic Review

When preparing for the exam, make sure you understand these key concepts covered in this chapter.

Exploring Advanced Security Devices

- Intrusion detection systems (IDSs) and intrusion prevention systems (IPSs) inspect traffic using the same functionality as a protocol analyzer.
- A host-based IDS (HIDS) can detect attacks on local systems such as workstations and servers. The HIDS monitors local resources on the host and can detect some malware that isn't detected by traditional antivirus software. A network-based IDS (NIDS) detects attacks on networks.
- A signature-based IDS or IPS uses signatures to detect known attacks or vulnerabilities.
- Trend-based IDSs (also called anomaly-based IDSs) require a baseline and detect attacks based on anomalies or when traffic is outside expected boundaries.

- A false positive incorrectly raises an alert indicating an attack when an attack is not active. False positives increase the workload of administrators. A false negative is when an attack is active, but not reported.

- An IPS is similar to an active IDS except that it's placed in-line with the traffic (sometimes called in-band) and can stop attacks before they reach the internal network. An IPS can actively monitor data streams, detect malicious content, and prevent it from reaching a network. In contrast, an IDS is out-of-band and passive.

- IDSs and IPSs can also protect internal private networks, such as private supervisory control and data acquisition (SCADA) networks.

- Honeypots and honeynets appear to have valuable data and attempt to divert attackers away from live networks. Security personnel use them to deceive attackers, disrupt attacks, and observe attackers' current attack methodologies. A honeyfile is a file designed to attract the attention of an attacker. Honeytokens are fake records inserted into databases to detect data theft.

Securing Wireless Networks

- Wireless access points (APs) connect wireless clients to a wired network.

- The service set identifier (SSID) is the name of the wireless network. Disabling the SSID broadcast hides a wireless network from casual users.

- You can restrict access to wireless networks with media access control (MAC) filtering. However, attackers can discover authorized MACs and spoof an authorized MAC address.

- A site survey examines the wireless environment to identify potential problem areas. Wireless footprinting uses a heat map to give you a detailed diagram of wireless access points, hotspots, and dead spots within an organization.

- Wi-Fi analyzers show signal levels on individual wireless frequency channels.

- WPA2 uses AES with CCMP and supports open, pre-shared key (PSK), and Enterprise modes.

- Enterprise mode is more secure than Personal mode because it adds authentication. It uses an 802.1X authentication server implemented as a RADIUS server.

- WPA3 uses Simultaneous Authentication of Equals (SAE) instead of the PSK. WPA3 supports Enterprise mode, similar to WPA2 Enterprise mode.

- Open mode doesn't use a PSK or an 802.1X server. Many hotspots use Open mode when providing free wireless access to customers. WPA3 offers a secure open mode that uses encryption, while earlier protocols offer insecure open modes that are subject to eavesdropping.

- 802.1X servers use one of the Extensible Authentication Protocol (EAP) versions, such as Protected EAP (PEAP), EAP-Tunneled TLS (EAP-TTLS), EAP-TLS, or EAP-Flexible Authentication via Secure Tunneling (EAP- FAST).

- The most secure EAP method is EAP-TLS, and it requires a certificate on the server and on each of the clients. PEAP and EAP-TTLS require a certificate on the server, but not the client.
- An 802.1X server provides strong port security using port-based authentication. It prevents rogue devices from connecting to a network by ensuring only authorized clients can connect.
- A captive portal forces wireless clients to complete a process, such as acknowledging a policy or paying for access, before it grants them access to the network.

Understanding Wireless Attacks

- A disassociation attack effectively removes a wireless client from a wireless network, forcing the wireless client to reauthenticate.
- Wi-Fi Protected Setup (WPS) allows users to easily configure a wireless device by pressing a button or entering a short PIN. WPS is not secure with WPA2. A WPS attack can discover the PIN within hours. It then uses the PIN to discover the passphrase. However, WPA3 thwarts WPS attacks.
- A rogue access point (rogue AP) is an AP placed within a network without official authorization. An evil twin is a rogue access point with the same or similar SSID as a legitimate access point.
- A jamming attack floods a wireless frequency with noise, blocking wireless traffic.
- An initialization vector (IV) attack attempts to discover the IV and uses it to discover the passphrase.
- Near field communication (NFC) attacks use an NFC reader to read data from mobile devices.
- Radio-frequency identification (RFID) attacks include eavesdropping, replay, and DoS.
- Bluejacking is the practice of sending unsolicited messages to a phone. Bluesnarfing is the unauthorized access to or theft of information from a Bluetooth device. Placing devices into conductive metal lockboxes that act as a Faraday cage will block Bluetooth attacks.
- In a wireless replay attack, an attacker captures data sent between two entities, modifies it, and then impersonates one of the parties by replaying the data. WPA2 and WPA3 are resistant to wireless replay attacks.

Using VPNs for Remote Access

- A virtual private network (VPN) provides access to private networks via a public network, such as the Internet.
- IPsec is a common tunneling protocol used with VPNs, and it secures traffic within a tunnel. IPsec provides authentication and integrity with an Authentication Header (AH). Encapsulating Security Payload (ESP) encrypts VPN traffic and provides confidentiality, integrity, and authentication.
- IPsec Tunnel mode encrypts the entire IP packet used in the internal network. Ipsec Transport mode only encrypts the payload and is commonly used in private networks, but not with VPNs.

- A full tunnel encrypts all traffic after a user has connected to a VPN. A split tunnel only encrypts traffic destined for the VPN's private network.
- Site-to-site VPNs provide secure access between two networks. These can be on-demand VPNs or always- on VPNs.
- Mobile devices can also use always-on VPNs to protect traffic when users connect to public hotspots.
- Other protocols used with VPNs include TLS, L2TP, and HTML5.
- Network access control (NAC) inspects clients for specific health conditions such as up-to-date antivirus software, and can redirect unhealthy clients to a remediation network.
- A permanent NAC agent (sometimes called a persistent NAC agent) is installed on the client and stays on the client. A dissolvable NAC agent is downloaded and run on the client when the client logs on and is deleted after the session ends.
- An agentless NAC system will scan systems remotely instead of installing an agent on the system.
- Remote access authentication is used when a user accesses a private network from a remote location, such as with a VPN connection.
- Password Authentication Protocol (PAP) uses a password or PIN for authentication. A significant weakness is that PAP sends passwords across a network in cleartext.
- Challenge Handshake Authentication Protocol (CHAP) is more secure than PAP and uses a handshake process when authenticating clients.
- RADIUS provides central authentication for multiple remote access services. RADIUS relies on the use of shared secrets and only encrypts the password during the authentication process, by default. It can be used with EAP to encrypt the entire session.
- Cisco TACACS+ is used as an alternative to RADIUS. TACACS+ uses TCP, encrypts the entire authentication process, and supports multiple challenges and responses.
- RADIUS and TACACS+ are authentication, authorization, and accounting (AAA) protocols.

📌 Online References

More resources to help you prepare for your Security+ exam are available at
https://getcertifiedgetahead.com

Chapter 4 Practice Questions

1. A HIDS reported a vulnerability on a system based on a known attack. After researching the alert from the HIDS, you identify the recommended solution and begin applying it. What type of HIDS is in use?

    A. Network-based
    B. Signature-based
    C. Heuristic-based
    D. Anomaly-based

2. You are preparing to deploy a trend-based detection system to monitor network activity. Which of the   following would you create first?

    A. BPDU guard
    B. Signatures
    C. Baseline
    D. Honeypot

3. Lenny noticed a significant number of logon failures for administrator accounts on the organization's public website. After investigating it further, he notices that most of these attempts are from IP addresses assigned to foreign countries. He wants to implement a solution that will detect and prevent similar attacks. Which of the following is the BEST choice?

    A. Implement a passive NIDS.
    B. Block all traffic from foreign countries.
    C. Implement an in-line NIPS.
    D. Disable the administrator accounts.

4. Lisa created a document called password.txt and put the usernames of two accounts with elevated privileges. She then placed the file on her administrator account desktop on several servers. Which of the following BEST explains her actions?

    A. She can use this file to retrieve the passwords if she forgets them.
    B. This file will divert attackers from the live network.
    C. The document is a honeyfile.
    D. The file is needed by an application to run when the system starts.

5. Your organization is planning to upgrade the wireless network used by employees. It will provide encrypted authentication of wireless users over TLS. Which of the following protocols are they MOST likely implementing?

    A. EAP
    B. PEAP
    C. WPA2
    D. WPA3

6. Lisa is creating a detailed diagram of wireless access points and hotspots within your organization. What is another name for this?

    A. Remote access VPN
    B. Wireless footprinting
    C. Channel overlap map
    D. Architectural diagram

7. You are assisting a small business owner in setting up a public wireless hotspot for her customers. She wants to allow customers to access the hotspot without entering a password. Which of the following is MOST appropriate for this hotspot?

    A. Use Open mode.
    B. Use a PSK.
    C. Use Enterprise mode.
    D. Disable SSID broadcast.

8. A network administrator routinely tests the network looking for vulnerabilities. He recently discovered a new access point set to open. After connecting to it, he found he was able to access network resources. What is the BEST explanation for this device?

    A. Evil twin
    B. A Raspberry Pi device
    C. Rogue AP
    D. APT

9. You are an administrator at a small organization. Homer contacted you today and reported the following:

   - He logged on normally on Monday morning and accessed network shares.
   - Later, when he tried to access the Internet, a pop-up window with the organization's wireless SSID prompted him to log on.
   - After doing so, he could access the Internet but no longer had access to the network shares.
   - Three days later, his bank notified him of suspicious activity on his account.

   Which of the following indicates the MOST likely explanation for this activity?

   A. An evil twin
   B. A rogue access point
   C. A DDoS attack
   D. A captive portal

10. Mobile users in your network report that they frequently lose connectivity with the wireless network on some days, but they don't have any problems on other days. You suspect this is due to an attack. Which of the following attacks is MOST likely to cause these symptoms?

    A. Wireless jamming attack
    B. IV attack
    C. Replay attack
    D. Bluesnarfing attack

11. An attacker can access email contact lists on your smartphone. What type of attack is this?

    A. Bluesnarfing
    B. Bluejacking
    C. Captive portal
    D. WPS

12. Your organization plans to implement a connection between the main site and a remote office giving remote employees on-demand access to resources at headquarters. The chief information officer (CIO) wants to use the Internet for this connection. Which of the following solutions will BEST support this requirement?

    A. Remote access VPN
    B. Site-to-site VPN
    C. Full tunnel VPN
    D. Split tunnel VPN

13. Your organization is allowing more employees to work from home, and they want to up-grade their VPN. Management wants to ensure that after a VPN client connects to the VPN server, all traffic from the VPN client is encrypted. Which of the following would BEST meet this goal?

    A. Split tunnel
    B. Full tunnel
    C. IPsec using Tunnel mode
    D. IPsec using Transport mode

14. An organization is hosting a VPN that employees are using while working from home. Man-agement wants to ensure that all VPN clients are using up-to-date operating systems and antivirus software. Which of the following would BEST meet this need?

    A. NAT
    B. NAC
    C. VLAN
    D. Screened subnet

15. Your organization recently implemented a BYOD policy. However, management wants to ensure that mobile devices meet minimum standards for security before they can access any network resources. Which of the following would the NAC MOST likely use?

    A. Permanent
    B. Health
    C. RADIUS
    D. Agentless

Chapter 4

Practice Question Answers

1. **B** is correct. If the host-based intrusion detection system (HIDS) identified a known issue, it is using signature-based detection (sometimes called definition-based detection). A HIDS is not network-based but a network-based IDS (NIDS) can also use signature-based detection. Trend-based (sometimes called anomaly-based or heuristic-based) detection systems identify issues by comparing current activity against a baseline. They can identify issues that are not previously known.

2. **C** is correct. A trend-based (also called behavior-based or anomaly-based) detection system compares current activity with a previously created baseline to detect any anomalies or changes. Signature-based systems (also called definition-based) use signatures of known attack patterns to detect attacks. A honeypot is a server designed to look valuable to an attacker and can divert attacks. A Bridge Protocol Data Unit (BPDU) guard is used to protect against BPDU-related attacks and is unrelated to this question.

3. **C** is correct. An inline network-based intrusion prevention system (NIPS) can dynamically detect, react to, and prevent attacks. An in-line system is placed inline with the traffic, and in this scenario, it can be configured to detect the logon attempts and block the traffic from the offending IP addresses before it reaches the internal network. A passive network-based intrusion detection system (NIDS) is not placed in-line with the traffic and can only detect the traffic after it has reached the internal network, so it cannot prevent the attack. If you block all traffic from foreign countries, you will likely block legitimate traffic. You should disable administrator accounts if they're not needed. However, if you disable all administrator accounts, administrators won't be able to do required work.

4. **C** is correct. A honeyfile is a file with a deceptive name (such as password.txt) that will deceive an attacker and attract his attention. It is not appropriate to place a file holding credentials on a desktop for any reason. A honeypot or honeynet diverts attackers from

the live network. A file on an administrator's desktop is on the live network. It is unlikely that any application needs a file named password.txt to run. Even if an application needed such a file, the file would be inaccessible if it is placed on an administrator's desktop.

5. **B** is correct. Protected EAP (PEAP) can be used for wireless authentication and it uses Transport Layer Security (TLS) to encapsulate and encrypt the authentication conversation within a TLS tunnel. Extensible Authentication Protocol (EAP) is the basic framework for authentication. By itself, EAP doesn't provide encryption, but it can be combined with other encryption protocols. Neither Wi-Fi Protected Access 2 (WPA2) nor Wi-Fi Protected Access 3 (WPA3) use TLS.

6. **B** is correct. Wireless footprinting creates a detailed diagram of wireless access points and hotspots within an organization. It typically displays a heat map and dead spots if they exist. A remote access virtual private network (VPN) provides access to a private network and is unrelated to this question. Wi-Fi analyzers provide a graph showing channel overlaps but not a diagram of wireless access points. An architectural diagram is typically laid on top of a heat map to create the wireless footprint document, but by itself, it shows the building layout.

7. **A** is correct. Open mode is the best choice of those given for a public wireless hotspot that doesn't require a password. A pre-shared key (PSK) is the same as a password and the scenario says a password isn't desired. Enterprise mode requires each user to authenticate and is typically enabled with a RADIUS server. If you disable service set identifier (SSID) broadcast, it will make it harder for the customers to find the hotspot, but unless Open mode is used, it will still require a password.

8. **C** is correct. This describes a rogue access point (AP). A rogue AP is not authorized (also known as shadow IT) but provides access to an internal network because it has been plugged into the network. In this scenario, the access point has no security, so someone could connect to it from the parking lot and then access the internal network. An evil twin has the same or similar service set identifier (SSID) as a legitimate access point, but the SSID isn't mentioned. A Raspberry Pi device is an embedded system, and it can be configured as a wireless AP, but there isn't any indication of the type of wireless AP in this scenario. An advanced persistent threat (APT) attacks from external locations and is unlikely to connect to a physical wireless AP inside a network.

9. **A** is correct. This describes an evil twin. Normally, a user shouldn't have to log on again to access the Internet. Because he lost access to network resources after logging on, it

indicates he didn't log on to a corporate access point (AP) but instead logged on to an unauthorized AP. Because the service set identifier (SSID) is the same as the corporate SSID, it indicates the AP is an evil twin. An evil twin is a rogue access point with the same or similar SSID as a legitimate AP, so an evil twin is a more accurate description. A distributed denial-of-service (DDoS) attack is an attack against a single computer from multiple attackers and is unrelated to this question. A captive portal forces web browser users to complete a specific process, such as agreeing to an acceptable use policy, before it allows them access to a network.

10. **A** is correct. A wireless jamming attack is a type of denial-of-service (DoS) attack that can cause wireless devices to lose their association with access points and disconnect them from the network. It transmits noise or another radio signal on the same frequency used by the existing wireless network. An initialization vector (IV) attack attempts to discover the passphrase. A replay attack captures traffic intending to replay it later to impersonate one of the parties in the original transmission. Bluesnarfing is a Bluetooth attack that attempts to access information on Bluetooth devices.

11. **A** is correct. A successful bluesnarfing attack allows attackers to access data (including email contact lists) on a smartphone. Bluejacking is the practice of sending unsolicited messages to other Bluetooth devices. A captive portal is not an attack. Instead, it forces users to acknowledge a usage policy or pay for access. A Wi-Fi Protected Setup (WPS) attack attempts to discover an access point WPS PIN by guessing PIN numbers.

12. **B** is correct. A site-to-site virtual private network (VPN) includes two VPN servers that act as gateways for two networks separated geographically, such as a main site network and a remote office network. Individuals use a remote access VPN to connect to the main network, such as employees working from home. A full-tunnel VPN encrypts all traffic to and from the Internet after a user has connected to the VPN. A split tunnel only encrypts traffic destined for the VPN's private network. The scenario didn't provide any directions related to a full-tunnel or a split-tunnel VPN.

13. **B** is correct. A full tunnel encrypts all traffic after a user has connected to a virtual private network (VPN) using a tunnel. A split tunnel only encrypts traffic destined for the VPN's private network. Traffic from the client directly to another Internet site is not encrypted. Internet Protocol security (IPsec) Tunnel mode encrypts the entire IP packet used in the internal network. It encrypts all traffic used within the VPN's private network, but not all traffic from the VPN client. IPsec Transport mode only encrypts the payload and is used within private networks, instead of for VPN traffic.

14. **B** is correct. Network access control (NAC) technologies can inspect virtual private network (VPN) clients for health status, including having up-to-date operating systems and antivirus software. None of the other answers will inspect VPN clients. Network Address Translation (NAT) allows multiple users with private IP addresses to share a single public IP address. A virtual local area network (VLAN) can segment clients, but not inspect them. A screened subnet provides a layer of protection for Internet-facing servers, putting them in a buffer zone between the Internet and an internal network.

15. **D** is correct. An agentless network access control (NAC) system is often used on employee-owned devices and would be appropriate if an organization implemented a bring your own device (BYOD) policy. A permanent network access control (NAC) agent is installed on the device permanently, but this might cause problems for employee-owned devices. Any NAC agent is a health agent. Remote Authentication Dial-In User Service (RADIUS) is used for authentication, authorization, and accounting, not to inspect clients.

Chapter 5

Securing Hosts and Data

CompTIA Security+ objectives covered in this chapter:

1.4 Explain the importance of using appropriate cryptographic solutions.

- Encryption (Level, Full-disk, Partition, File, Volume, Database, Record)
- Tools (Trusted Platform Module (TPM), Hardware security module (HSM), Secure enclave)

2.3 Explain various types of vulnerabilities.

- Operating system (OS)-based
- Hardware (Firmware, End-of-life, Legacy)
- Virtualization (Virtual machine (VM) escape, Resource reuse)
- Cloud-specific
- Misconfiguration
- Mobile device (Side loading, Jailbreaking)

2.5 Explain the purpose of mitigation techniques used to secure the enterprise.

- Segmentation
- Application allow list
- Patching
- Encryption
- Configuration enforcement
- Decommissioning
- Hardening techniques (Encryption, Installation of endpoint protection, Host-based intrusion prevention system (HIPS), Disabling ports/protocols, Default password changes, Removal of unnecessary software)

3.1 Compare and contrast security implications of different architecture models.

- Architecture and infrastructure concepts (Cloud, Responsibility matrix, Hybrid considerations, Third-party vendors, Infrastructure as code (IaC), Serverless, Microservices,

Software-defined networking (SDN), On-premises, Centralized vs. decentralized, Containerization, Virtualization, IoT, Industrial control systems (ICS)/supervisory control and data acquisition (SCADA), Real-time operating system (RTOS), Embedded systems, High availability)

- Considerations (Availability, Resilience, Cost, Responsiveness, Scalability, Ease of deployment, Risk transference, Ease of recovery, Patch availability, Inability to patch, Power, Compute)

3.2 Given a scenario, apply security principles to enterprise infrastructure.

- Secure communication/access (Software-defined wide area network (SD-WAN)

3.3 Compare and contrast concepts and strategies to protect data.

- General data considerations (Geolocation)

3.4 Explain the importance of resilience and recovery in security architecture.

- Multi-cloud systems

4.1 Given a scenario, apply common security techniques to computing resources.

- Secure baselines (Establish, Deploy, Maintain)
- Hardening targets (Mobile devices, Workstations, Cloud infrastructure, Servers, ICS/SCADA, Embedded systems, RTOS, IoT devices)
- Mobile solutions (Mobile device management (MDM), Deployment models, Bring your own device (BYOD), Corporate-owned, personally-enabled (COPE), Choose your own device (CYOD), Connection methods, Cellular, Wi-Fi, Bluetooth)

4.4 Explain security alerting and monitoring concepts and tools.

- Tools (Antivirus, Data loss prevention (DLP))

4.5 Given a scenario, modify enterprise capabilities to enhance security.

- DLP
- Endpoint detection and response (EDR)/extended detection and response (XDR)

In this chapter, you'll learn about different methods used to implement systems securely. This includes hardening endpoints when deploying them and using change management policies to keep them secure.

Most modern organizations run at least some of their systems in the cloud, and this chapter summarizes important cloud concepts. Most employees now also use mobile devices, including personally-owned devices, to access corporate resources. This results in many challenges for an organization, but mobile device management tools help administrators handle these challenges. This chapter also covers the security implications of embedded systems and Internet of Things (IoT) devices.

Virtualization

Virtualization is a popular technology used within data centers. It allows you to host one or more virtual systems, or virtual machines (VMs), on a single physical system. With today's technologies, you can host an entire virtual network within a single physical system, and organizations are increasingly using virtualization to reduce costs. When discussing VMs, you should understand the following terms:

- **Hypervisor.** The hypervisor is specialized software that creates, runs, and manages virtual machines. Several software vendors produce hypervisors, including VMware products, Microsoft Hyper-V products, and Oracle VM VirtualBox.

- **Host.** The physical system hosting the VMs is the host. It requires more resources than a typical system, such as multiple high speed multi-core processors, large amounts of RAM, fast and abundant disk space, and one or more fast network cards. Although these additional resources increase the cost of the host, it is still less expensive than paying for multiple physical systems. It also requires less electricity, less cooling, and less physical space. The host system runs the hypervisor software.

- **Guest.** Operating systems running on the host system are guests or guest machines. Most hypervisors support several different operating systems, including various Microsoft operating systems and various Linux distributions. Additionally, most hypervisors support both 32-bit and 64-bit operating systems.

- **Cloud Scalability.** Scalability refers to the ability to resize the computing capacity of the VM. You do this by assigning it more memory, processors, disk space, or network bandwidth. Scaling is a manual process, and it often requires a reboot. In other words, an administrator would manually change the resources assigned to the VM.

- **Cloud Elasticity.** Elasticity refers to the ability to dynamically change resources assigned to the VM based on the load. As an example, imagine a VM has increased traffic. Monitoring software senses this increased load and automatically increases the VM resources to handle it. This does not require a reboot.

Virtualization typically provides the best return on investment (ROI) when an organization has many underutilized servers. Imagine an organization has nine physical servers, with each using less than 20 percent processing power, memory, and disk space. With virtualization, you could run all of these systems as guest virtual machines on two or three physical servers. They would share resources and you would save money.

Thin Clients and Virtual Desktop Infrastructure

A **thin client** is a computer with enough resources to boot and connect to a server to run specific applications or desktops. When the thin client is a traditional computer, it typically has a keyboard, mouse, and screen and may support other peripherals such as speakers and USB ports. The server is a powerful server located on-site or in the cloud, supporting multiple thin clients.

A ***virtual desktop infrastructure (VDI)*** hosts a user's desktop operating system on a server. While traditional computers typically access VDIs within a network, it's also possible to deploy a VDI that users can access with their mobile device. This allows users to access any applications installed on their desktop. When the organization hosts a remote access solution such as a virtual private network (VPN), users can access the mobile VDI from anywhere if they have Internet access.

Containerization

Containerization is a type of virtualization that runs services or applications within isolated containers or application cells. Figure 5.1 shows an example of containerization. Notice that the containers don't host an entire operating system. Instead, the host's operating system and kernel run the service or app within each of the containers. However, because they are running in separate containers, none of the services or apps can interfere with services and apps in other containers.

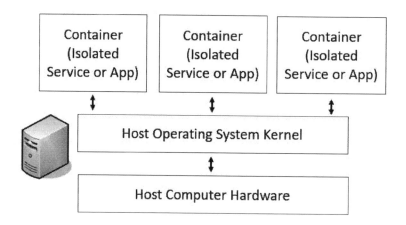

Figure 5.1: Containerization

A benefit of containerization is that it uses fewer resources and can be more efficient than a system using a traditional Type II hypervisor virtualization. Internet Service Providers (ISPs) often use it for customers who need specific applications. One drawback is that containers must use the operating system of the host. As an example, if the host is running Linux, all the containers must run Linux.

VM Escape Protection

VM escape is an attack that allows an attacker to access the host system from within a virtual guest system. As previously mentioned, the host system runs an application or process called a hypervisor to manage the virtual systems. In some situations, the attacker can run code on the virtual system and interact with the hypervisor. This should never be allowed.

Most virtual systems run on a physical server with elevated privileges, similar to administrator privileges. A successful VM escape attack often gives the attacker unlimited control over the host system and each guest virtual machine running on that host.

When vendors discover VM escape vulnerabilities, they write and release patches. Just as with any patches, it is important to test and install these patches as soon as possible. This includes keeping both the physical and the virtual servers patched.

> ### ★ Remember This!
>
> Virtualization allows multiple virtual servers to operate on a single physical server providing increased cybersecurity resilience with lower operating costs. Keeping systems up to date with current patches is the best protection from VM escape attacks.

VM Sprawl Avoidance

VM sprawl occurs when an organization has many VMs that aren't appropriately managed. Most organizations have specific policies in place to ensure physical servers are kept up to date, and personnel only make changes to these servers after going through a change management process. These same policies should also apply to virtual servers.

Consider this scenario. Bart creates a VM running a Microsoft Windows Server version to test a software application. After testing the application, he leaves the VM running. Later, Microsoft releases security patches for the server. The IT department tests these patches and applies them to all the known servers that need them. However, because Bart didn't tell anyone he was creating the VM, it remains unpatched and vulnerable to attack.

Another challenge with VM sprawl is that each VM adds additional load onto a server. If personnel add unauthorized VMs to physical servers, they can consume system resources. The servers might become slower and potentially crash.

Resource Reuse

Resource reuse in the context of cloud computing risks refers to the potential for data or resources to remain on a shared infrastructure even after a customer has finished using them, making them potentially accessible to other users of the cloud service. This can lead to a risk of data leakage or exposure, as well as the potential for malicious actors to gain unauthorized access to sensitive data or systems.

In a cloud environment, customers do not have access to the underlying hardware and it is difficult (or impossible!) for them to perform the same type of secure destruction of data that they would in their own data centers. The best way to protect against this risk is to have contractual requirements with cloud service providers that they securely erase your data when it is no longer needed.

Replication

It's worth pointing out that virtual machines are simply files. These files certainly have some complexity, but still, they are just files. Because the VM is just a group of files, it becomes relatively easy to replicate a VM by copying the files from one physical server to another. If the original VM is damaged, the replicated VM can be used as a backup.

Replication makes it easy to restore a failed virtual server. If you create a backup of the virtual server files and the original server fails, you simply restore the files. You can measure the amount of time it takes to restore a replicated virtual server in minutes. In contrast, rebuilding a physical server can take hours.

Snapshots

A **snapshot** provides you with a copy of a VM at a moment in time, which you can use as a backup. You are still able to use the VM just as you normally would. However, after taking a snapshot, the hypervisor keeps a record of all changes to the VM. If the VM develops a problem, you can revert the VM to the state it was in when you took the snapshot.

Administrators commonly take snapshots of systems prior to performing any risky operation. Risky operations include applying patches or updates, testing security controls, and installing new applications. Ideally, these operations do not cause any problems, but occasionally they do. By creating snapshots before these operations, administrators can easily revert or roll back the system to a known good state with a known good configuration.

Implementing Secure Systems

Secure systems design concepts help ensure that computing systems are deployed and maintained in a secure state. In this context, a system is any host such as a server, workstation, laptop, network device, or mobile device. In an ideal world, systems start in a secure state. Unfortunately, it's not an ideal world, and administrators need to be proactive in securing systems before deployment and keeping them secure after deployment. This section outlines several steps used to secure hosts.

Endpoint Security Software

Endpoints are computing devices such as servers, virtual machines, desktops, laptops, mobile devices, or Internet of Things (IoT) devices. These endpoints often contain sensitive information and provide access to servers and other resources that handle sensitive information. They also travel around the world and connect to many different networks, making them vulnerable to attack. Therefore, it's critical that organizations protect their endpoints against many kinds of attack. Let's discuss four common categories of endpoint security software:

- *Antivirus software* is one of the most basic security controls that should run on every system in an organization. This software scans endpoints for the presence of viruses, worms, Trojan horses, and other malicious code. When an infection is detected, the antivirus software can often step in and resolve the issue automatically. You'll learn more about antivirus software in Chapter 6, "Comparing Threats, Vulnerabilities, and Common Attacks."
- *Endpoint detection and response* (*EDR*) is a security technology that focuses on detecting and responding to threats at the endpoint level, often using advanced behavioral analysis techniques to identify suspicious activity and contain threats before they can cause damage.
- *Extended detection and response* (*XDR*) is a next-generation security technology that goes beyond the endpoint to include other types of devices and systems, such as network devices, cloud infrastructure, and IoT devices, providing a more comprehensive view of the entire IT environment and enabling faster threat detection and response.
- *Host intrusion prevention systems* (*HIPS*) takes the concept of intrusion prevention and applies it to a single host or endpoint, using techniques such as behavior analysis, file integrity monitoring, and application control to prevent unauthorized access, tampering, or other types of attacks.

Hardening Workstations and Servers

Hardening is the practice of making an operating system (OS) or application more secure from its default installation. It helps eliminate vulnerabilities from default configurations, misconfigurations, and weak configurations.

When deploying systems, they should only have the applications, services, and protocols they need to meet their purpose. If a service or protocol is not running on a system, attackers cannot attack it. As a simple example, a system is not vulnerable to any File Transfer Protocol (FTP) attacks if FTP is not running and available on the system. When you disable or close a port on a system, you disable the related protocol or service.

In addition to disabling unnecessary services to reduce vulnerabilities, it's essential to uninstall unneeded software. Software frequently has bugs and vulnerabilities. Although patching software closes these vulnerabilities, you can eliminate these vulnerabilities by simply removing unnecessary applications.

Recently, it's become necessary for administrators to modify the Registry to harden systems. As an example, attackers frequently use PowerShell in attacks. However, the PowerShell scripts that attackers run aren't logged by default. Many administrators modify the Registry as part of the hardening process to ensure that all PowerShell activity is logged.

It has also become more common for organizations to implement disk encryption as part of the hardening process. This chapter covers multiple ways to encrypt disks.

While it's not as common today as it was in the past, systems and software sometimes ship with default passwords set by the manufacturer. These default passwords are commonly published in documentation by the manufacturer and are known in the hacking community and should be removed or changed before a system is connected to a network for the first time.

Chapter 8, "Using Risk Management Tools," discusses the use of vulnerability scanners to discover vulnerabilities in systems. It also includes a list of common vulnerabilities related to weak configurations. By eliminating weak configuration items, it helps administrators harden systems.

Configuration Enforcement

Configuration management practices help organizations deploy systems with secure configurations and enforce requirements that those secure configurations remain in place. Administrators often use baselines and imaging (discussed in the next sections) with configuration management. Change management practices (discussed later in this chapter) complement configuration management practices and help ensure that systems remain secure, even as the configurations change over the lifetime of systems.

Some organizations use diagrams to show configuration management processes. These sometimes use flowcharts to document the decision-making process involved in modifying a configuration.

Large organizations often use standard naming conventions to identify standard configurations. The standard an organization uses isn't as important as identifying a standard and following it consistently. A possible choice is an endpoint device (such as a laptop, desktop, or server), the department or location, and the version. For example, the third major version of an image for a desktop used by employees in the Sales department could be Desktop_Sales_3.0.

Secure Baseline and Integrity Measurements

A baseline is a known starting point, and organizations commonly use secure baselines to provide known starting points for systems. One of the primary benefits of secure baselines is that they improve the overall security posture of systems. Weak security configurations are a common security issue, but secure baselines help eliminate this. The use of baselines works in three steps:

1. **Establish an initial baseline configuration.** Administrators use various tools to deploy systems consistently in a secure state.

2. **Deploy the baseline.** The baseline may be initially deployed on systems during the build process, or it may be pushed out to existing systems through Group Policy or other configuration management tools.

3. **Maintain the baseline.** Organizations change and so does the security landscape. It's natural for system baselines to change over time as well. Security professionals should revise the baseline as needed and push out updates following the organization's configuration and change management policies.

Using Master Images for Baseline Configurations

One of the most common methods of deploying systems is with images starting with a master image. An image is a snapshot of a single system that administrators deploy to multiple other systems. Imaging has become an important practice for many organizations because it streamlines deployments while ensuring they are deployed securely. Figure 5.2 and the following text identify the overall process of capturing and deploying an image:

1. Administrators start with a blank source system. They install and configure the operating system, install, and configure any desired applications, and modify security settings. Administrators perform extensive testing to ensure the system works as desired and that it is secure before going to the next step.

2. Next, administrators capture the image, which becomes their master image. Symantec Ghost is a popular imaging application, and Windows Server versions include free tools many organizations use to capture and deploy images. The captured image is simply a file stored on a server or copied to external media, such as a DVD or external USB drive.

3. In step 3, administrators deploy the image to multiple systems. When used within a network, administrators can deploy the same image to dozens of systems during initial deployment or to just a single system to rebuild it. The image installs the same configuration on the target systems as the original source system created in step 1.

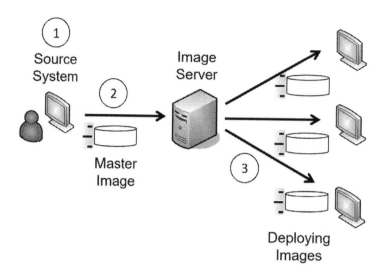

Figure 5.2: Capturing and deploying images

Administrators will often take a significant amount of time to configure and test the source system. They follow the same hardening practices discussed earlier and often use security and configuration baselines. If they're deploying the image to just a few systems, such as in a classroom setting, they may create the image in just a few hours. However, if they're deploying it to thousands of systems within an organization, they may take weeks or months to create and test the image. Once they've created the image, they can deploy it relatively quickly with minimal administrative effort. Imaging provides two important benefits:

- **Secure starting point.** The image includes mandated security configurations for the system. Personnel who deploy the system don't need to remember or follow extensive checklists to ensure that new systems are set up with all the detailed configuration and security settings. The deployed image retains all the settings of the original image. Administrators will still configure some settings, such as the computer name, after deploying the image.
- **Reduced costs.** Deploying imaged systems reduces the overall maintenance costs and improves reliability. Support personnel don't need to learn several different end-user system environments to assist end users. Instead, they learn just one. When troubleshooting, support personnel spend their time helping the end user rather than learning the system configuration. Managers understand this as reducing the total cost of ownership (TCO) for systems.

Imaging isn't limited to only desktop computers. You can image any system, including servers. For example, consider an organization that maintains 50 database servers in a large data center. The organization can use imaging to deploy new servers or as part of its disaster recovery plan to restore failed servers. It is much quicker to deploy an image to rebuild a failed server than rebuild a server from scratch. If administrators keep the images up-to-date, this also helps ensure the re-covered server starts in a secure state.

> ## ★ Remember This!
>
> A master images provides secure starting points for systems. Administrators sometimes cre-ate them with templates or with other tools to create secure baselines. They then use integrity measurements to discover when a system deviates from the baseline.

Patching and Patch Management

Software is not secure. There. I said it. As someone who has written a few programs over the years, that's not easy to say. In a perfect world, extensive testing would discover all the bugs, exploits, and vulnerabilities that cause so many problems.

However, because operating systems, applications, and firmware include millions of lines of code, testing simply doesn't find all the problems. Instead, most companies attempt to create secure and bug-free software as they're developing it and then make a best effort to test the software before releasing it. Later, as problems crop up, companies write and release *patches* or updates that cor-rect those problems. Administrators must apply these patches to keep their systems-up-to-date and protected against known vulnerabilities.

Some smaller organizations enable auto-updates. Systems regularly check for updates, download them when they're available, and automatically apply them.

Patch management ensures that systems and applications stay up-to-date with current patches. This is one of the most efficient ways to reduce operating system and application vulnerabilities because it protects systems from known vulnerabilities. Patch management includes a group of methodologies and consists of identifying, downloading, testing, deploying, and verifying patches.

Administrators often test updates in a sandbox environment such as a virtual machine. A sand-box environment provides an isolated environment. After testing the patches, administrators de-ploy them. They don't typically deploy the patches manually. Instead, they use third-party tools to deploy the patches in a controlled manner. For example, Microsoft Configuration Manager is a systems management tool used for many purposes, including patch management. It examines endpoints to determine if patches are installed.

In addition to deploying patches, systems management tools also include a verification component that verifies patch deployment. They periodically query the systems and retrieve a list of installed patches and updates. They then compare the retrieved list with the list of deployed patches and updates, providing reports for discrepancies. In some networks, administrators combine this with network access control (NAC) technologies and isolate unpatched systems in a quarantine network until they are patched.

Improper or weak patch management results in preventable vulnerabilities that attackers can exploit. This includes vulnerabilities in operating systems, applications, and firmware.

> ### ★ *Remember This!*
>
> Patch management procedures ensure that operating systems, applications, and firmware are up-to-date with current patches. This protects systems against known vulnerabilities. Change management defines the process and accounting structure for handling modifications and upgrades. The goals are to reduce risks related to unintended outages and provide documentation for all changes.

Change Management

The worst enemies of many networks have been unrestrained administrators. A well-meaning administrator can make what appears to be a minor change to fix one problem, only to cause a major problem somewhere else. A misconfiguration can take down a server, disable a network, stop email communications, and even stop all network traffic for an entire enterprise.

For example, I once saw a major outage occur when an administrator was troubleshooting a printer problem. After modifying the printer's IP address, the printer began to work. Sounds like a success, doesn't it? Unfortunately, the new IP address was the same IP address assigned to a Domain Name System (DNS) server, and it created an IP address conflict. The conflict prevented the DNS server from resolving names to IP addresses. This resulted in a major network outage until another administrator discovered and corrected the problem.

These self-inflicted disasters were relatively common in the early days of IT. They still occur today, but organizations with mature change management processes in place have fewer of these problems. ***Change management*** defines the process for any type of system modifications or upgrades, including changes to applications. It provides two key goals:

- To ensure changes to IT systems do not result in unintended outages or security failures.
- To provide an accounting structure or method to document all changes.

When a change management program is in place, administrators are discouraged from making configuration changes without submitting the change for review and approval. In other words, they don't immediately make a change as soon as they identify a potential need for a change. This includes making any type of configuration changes to systems, applications, patches, or any other change. Instead, they follow the change management process before making a change.

Experts from different areas of an organization examine change requests and can either approve or postpone them. The process usually approves simple changes quickly. A formal change review board regularly reviews postponed requests and can approve, modify, or reject the change. This entire process provides documentation for approved changes. For example, some automated change management systems create accounting logs for all change requests. The system tracks the request from its beginning until implementation. Administrators use this documentation for configuration management and disaster recovery. If a modified system fails, change and configuration management documentation identifies how to return the system to its pre-failure state.

Change management isn't only for computing devices. It's important to use these processes for any devices on the network, including firewalls, proxy servers, data loss prevention systems, mobile device management systems, routers, and switches.

Application Allow and Block Lists

Application allow lists (sometimes called whitelists) and **application block lists** (sometimes called application deny lists or blacklists) are two additional methods used as endpoint security solutions. They can help protect hosts, including workstations, servers, and mobile devices.

An application allow list is a list of applications authorized to run on a system. After you identify the allowed list of applications, the system will block all other applications. This is the most restrictive of the two types of lists.

In contrast, an application block list is a list of applications the system blocks. As an example, if you found that users were installing a game called **gcga.exe**, you could create an application block list and add **gcga.exe**. However, all other applications would still be allowed.

Many mobile device management (MDM) applications use application allow lists and block lists to allow or block applications on mobile devices. MDM applications are discussed later in this chapter.

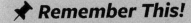 **Remember This!**

An application allow list is a list of authorized software, and it prevents users from installing or running software that isn't on the list. An application block list is a list of unauthorized software and prevents users from installing or running software on the list.

Messages that users see when they can't install an application due to an allow list or block list are sometimes cryptic. When users try to install an application that isn't allowed, the system will often report a permission issue or sometimes just fail with a vague error. However, application logs will typically include details on why the installation failed.

Some systems support quarantining applications that don't comply with allow or block lists. For example, if a user tries to install an application that isn't on an allow list, the system will quarantine the application, placing it in a protected area. A quarantined application won't run on the system but is retained so that administrators can examine it.

Disk Encryption

Full disk encryption (FDE) encrypts an entire disk. This can either be done using technology built-in to major operating systems, such as Windows BitLocker or macOS FileVault, or it may be done using a third-party application. For example, VeraCrypt is an open-source utility that can encrypt partitions or an entire storage device.

Many hardware vendors now manufacture **self-encrypting drives (SEDs)**, also known as hardware-based FDE drives. SEDs include encryption circuitry built into the drive. These typically allow users to enter credentials when they set up the drive. When users power up the system, they enter their credentials to decrypt the drive and boot the system.

> ### ★ Remember This!
>
> Full disk encryption (FDE) protects all of the contents of a disk using encryption. This may be done with specialized software or it may be done using specialized hardware, known as self-encrypting drives (SED).

Boot Integrity

Many organizations implement boot integrity processes. These processes verify the integrity of the operating system and boot loading systems. For example, it can verify that key operating system files haven't been changed.

A **measured boot** goes through enough of the boot process to perform these checks without allowing a user to interact with the system. If it detects that the system has lost integrity and can no longer be trusted, the system won't boot.

Boot Security and UEFI

The Basic Input/Output System (BIOS) includes software that provides a computer with basic instructions on starting. It runs some basic checks, locates the operating system, and boots. The BIOS is a hardware chip that you can physically see and touch, and it includes software that executes code on the computer. Firmware is embedded into hardware.

Newer systems use **Unified Extensible Firmware Interface (UEFI)** instead of BIOS. UEFI performs many of the same functions as BIOS but provides some enhancements. As an example, it can boot from larger disks, and it is designed to be CPU-independent.

Both BIOS and UEFI can be upgraded using a process called flashing. Flashing overwrites the firmware within the chip with newer software.

Trusted Platform Module

A **Trusted Platform Module (TPM)** is a hardware chip on the computer's motherboard that stores cryptographic keys used for encryption. Most desktop and laptop computers include a TPM. Some servers allow for removable and replaceable TPMs. Once enabled, the TPM provides full disk encryption capabilities. It keeps hard drives encrypted and protected until the system completes a system verification and authentication process.

A TPM supports secure **boot attestation** processes. When the TPM is configured, it captures signatures of key files used to boot the computer and stores a report of the signatures securely within the TPM. When the system boots, the **secure boot** process checks the files against the stored signatures to ensure they haven't changed. If it detects that the files have been modified, such as from malware, it blocks the boot process to protect the data on the drive.

A **remote attestation** process works like the secure boot process. However, instead of checking the boot files against the report stored in the TPM, it uses a separate system. Again, when the TPM is configured, it captures the signatures of key files, but sends this report to a remote system. When the system boots, it checks the files and sends a current report to the remote system. The remote system verifies the files are the same and attests, or confirms, that the system is safe.

The TPM ships with a unique encryption key burned into it, which is used for asymmetric encryption and can be used to support authentication. This key provides a **hardware root of trust,** a known secure starting point. The private key remains private and is matched with a public key. Additionally, the TPM can generate, store, and protect other keys used for encrypting and decrypting disks. Chapter 10, "Understanding Cryptography and PKI," discusses asymmetric encryption and public and private keys in more depth.

If the system includes a TPM, you use an application within the operating system to enable it. For example, many Microsoft systems include BitLocker, which you can enable for systems that include the TPM.

BitLocker uses the TPM to detect tampering of any critical operating system files or processes as part of a platform verification process. Additionally, users provide authentication, such as with a smart card, a password, or a personal identification number (PIN). The drive remains encrypted until the platform verification, and user authentication processes are complete.

If a thief steals the system, the drive remains encrypted and protected. An attacker wouldn't have authentication credentials, so he can't access the drive using a normal boot process. If the attacker tries to modify the operating system to bypass security controls, the TPM detects the tampering and keeps the drive encrypted. If a thief moves the drive to another system, the drive remains encrypted because the TPM isn't available.

> ### ✦ *Remember This!*
>
> A Trusted Platform Module (TPM) is a hardware chip included in many desktops and laptops. It provides full disk encryption support and features a secure boot process and remote attestation. The endorsement key is a unique asymmetric key pair burned into the TPM chip that provides a hardware root of trust.

Hardware Security Module

A hardware security module (HSM) is a security device you can add to a system to manage, generate, and securely store cryptographic keys. High-performance HSMs are external network appliances using a TCP/IP network connection. Smaller HSMs come as expansion cards you install within a server or as devices you plug into computer ports.

A *microSD HSM* is a microSD card that includes an HSM. A microSD card is small at 15 mm long x 11 mm wide x 1 mm thick, or .59 inches x .43 inches x .03 inches. You can install a microSD HSM into any device that has a microSD slot. With an adapter, you can install any microSD card into an SD card slot.

HSMs support the security methods of a TPM. They provide a hardware root of trust, secure boot, and can be configured for remote attestation. The cryptographic keys stored within the HSM also support authentication solutions.

One of the noteworthy differences between an HSM and a TPM is that HSMs are removable or external devices. In comparison, the majority of TPMs are embedded into the motherboard, though certain removable TPMs are also on the market. You can easily add an HSM to a system or a network.

If a system didn't ship with a TPM, it may not be feasible to add one later unless if the system has an available TPM header. Both HSMs and TPMs provide secure encryption capabilities by storing and using encryption keys. Many high-performance servers use HSMs to store and protect keys.

> ★ **Remember This!**
>
> A hardware security module (HSM) is a removable or external device that can generate, store, and manage keys used in asymmetric encryption. Many server-based applications use an HSM to protect keys. A microSD HSM is an HSM device installed on a microSD card and can be installed on any device with a microSD or SD slot.

Decommissioning and Disposal

The **decommissioning** of hardware that is no longer needed is a critical aspect of managing the security of an organization's IT infrastructure. Retiring hardware that is no longer in use can help prevent unauthorized access to sensitive data and reduce the risk of attack. However, it is essential to ensure that the decommissioning process is performed securely, following established procedures and guidelines to minimize the risk of data leakage or exposure. This involves wiping all data from the device, including temporary files and backups, and removing all access credentials and software licenses associated with the device. Additionally, the hardware must be physically destroyed or securely disposed of in a manner that prevents it from being reused or repurposed without proper clearance.

Legacy hardware refers to older computer hardware that is no longer being manufactured or widely used in the industry. This can include servers, laptops, desktops, and other types of devices that were once popular but have been superseded by newer, more advanced technology. **End-of-life (EOL) hardware** refers to hardware that has reached the end of its useful life, either because it is no longer supported by the manufacturer or because it is too outdated to meet current technology standards. EOL hardware is typically no longer receiving software updates or security patches, making it more vulnerable to attack. To mitigate these risks, organizations should take three actions:

- Develop a comprehensive plan for managing legacy and EOL hardware, including regular assessments of hardware inventory and a plan for decommissioning devices that are no longer needed.
- Prioritize the security of these devices by implementing security controls such as firewalls, antivirus software, and intrusion detection systems, and monitoring them closely for signs of suspicious activity.

- Consider upgrading to newer hardware and software whenever possible to ensure that IT infrastructure remains secure and up to date.

Protecting Data

Data is one of the most valuable resources any organization manages, second only to its people. You've likely heard about data breaches at organizations around the world. Unfortunately, data breaches are frequent, and they affect millions of people. In the worst-case scenarios, cybercriminals use the stolen data to empty bank accounts, rack up fraudulent charges on credit cards, and steal individuals' identities.

Losing control of data affects the reputation, and often the financial bottom line, of an organization. One of the goals of attackers is often theft of data. If attackers can infiltrate a network, they often try to collect proprietary data and send it out of the network. In other situations, attackers take actions resulting in the loss of availability. For example, ransomware encrypts data so that users can no longer access it unless they pay a ransom.

Chapter 11, "Implementing Policies to Mitigate Risks," covers security policies that an organization can implement to protect data. The security policy helps an organization classify and label its data. This section presents many of the security controls an organization can use to protect data based on the requirements set within a data security policy.

It's also important to use secure coding techniques to prevent data exposure or the loss of confidentiality. Confidentiality is primarily protected through encryption and strong access controls. This chapter discusses software-based and hardware-based encryption methods, and Chapter 10 covers specific encryption algorithms used to protect data. Chapter 6 discusses ransomware in more depth.

Data Loss Prevention

Data exfiltration is the unauthorized transfer of data outside an organization and is a significant concern. In some cases, attackers take control of systems and transfer data outside an organization using malware. It's also possible for malicious insiders to transfer data.

Organizations often use **data loss prevention (DLP)** techniques and technologies to prevent data exfiltration. They can block the use of USB flash drives and control the use of removable media. They can also examine outgoing data and detect many types of unauthorized data transfers.

In network-based DLP, all traffic leaving the network is directed through an appliance that can examine the traffic. Administrators configure the DLP to look for specific words, phrases, or character strings. As an example, imagine an organization is working on a secret project with a code word of "DOH." All documents associated with this project have the keyword within them. The

DLP includes this keyword in its searches, and when it detects the keyword within an email, an attachment, or any other outgoing data, it blocks it. Administrators have the choice of configuring the DLP to notify security personnel, the user who sent it, or both.

Software-based DLP works in a similar manner but is installed on an individual system, identifying data exfiltration attempts and blocking them from succeeding.

DLP systems can scan the text of all emails and the content of any attached files, including documents, spreadsheets, presentations, and databases. Even if a user compresses a file as a zipped file before sending it, the DLP examines the contents by simply unzipping it.

As an example, I know of one organization that routinely scans all outgoing emails looking for Personally Identifiable Information (PII), such as Social Security numbers. The network-based DLP includes a mask to identify Social Security numbers as a string of numbers in the following format: ###-##-####. If an email or an attachment includes this string of numbers, the DLP detects it, blocks the email, and sends an alert to a security administrator.

Many organizations classify and label data using terms such as Confidential, PII, and Proprietary. It is easy to include these search terms in the DLP application, or any other terms considered important by the organization.

Network-based DLP systems are not limited to scanning only email. Many can scan the content of other traffic, such as FTP and HTTP traffic. Sophisticated data exfiltration attacks often encrypt data before sending it out, making it more difficult for a DLP system to inspect the data. However, a DLP system can typically be configured to look for outgoing encrypted data and alert security administrators when it is detected.

> ### ★ Remember This!
>
> Data exfiltration is the unauthorized transfer of data out of a network. Data loss prevention (DLP) techniques and technologies can block the use of USB devices to prevent data loss and monitor outgoing network traffic for unauthorized data transfers.

Removable Media

Removable media refers to any storage system that you can attach to a computer and easily copy data. Common types of removable media include USB flash drives, external hard drives, SD cards, CDs, and DVDs. Users can plug them into a system and easily copy data to and from a system. Additionally, many of today's smartphones include storage capabilities using the same type of memory.

Organizations recognize that removable media can be an attack vector, so it's common for an organization to include security policy statements to prohibit the use of USB flash drives and other removable media. Some technical policies block the use of USB drives completely. A USB data blocker prevents users from writing any data to a USB drive. Some USB data blockers will also prevent systems from reading data from a USB or other removable device. This prevents malware from being delivered via removable media, as discussed in Chapter 9, "Implementing Controls to Protect Assets."

✦ Remember This!

The primary methods of protecting the confidentiality of data is with encryption and strong access controls. Database column encryption protects individual fields within a database.

Protecting Confidentiality with Encryption

As mentioned in Chapter 1, "Mastering Security Basics," one of the primary ways you can prevent the loss of confidentiality is by encrypting data. This includes encrypting data at rest no matter what type of device it is stored on and encrypting data in transit no matter what type of transmission media is used. It is much more difficult for an attacker to view encrypted data than it is to view unencrypted data.

You can use other tools to restrict access to data, but this isn't always effective. For example, consider the Microsoft NTFS, which allows you to configure permissions within access control lists (ACLs). You can use NTFS to set permissions on files and folders to restrict access. However, if a thief steals a laptop with NTFS-protected files, it's a simple matter to access them. The thief simply moves the drive to another system as an extra drive, logs on as the administrator, and takes ownership of the files. Encryption isn't as easy to bypass because the thief would need to have the required decryption key.

Encryption can be applied to data in many ways. Earlier in this chapter, you read how software and self-encrypting drives (SED) can apply encryption to an entire hard disk. Encryption may also be applied to a partition or volume on a drive or to a specific file or directory. You'll need to figure out the appropriate levels of encryption to use in your organization depending upon your security requirements.

Database Security

Another form of software-based encryption is with databases. For example, database management systems such as Oracle Database or Microsoft SQL Server can encrypt data held within the database. Although it's possible to encrypt the entire database, it's more common to encrypt specific database fields (columns) or records (rows) that contain sensitive information.

As an example, imagine a database that includes a table named Customers. Each record within the table has multiple columns, including customer number, last name, first name, credit card number, and security code. Instead of encrypting the entire table, administrators can choose to encrypt only the credit card number and security code fields (columns) within each record. Database field (column) encryption protects the sensitive data but doesn't waste valuable processing power encrypting data that isn't sensitive.

Some customer databases store passwords as hashes or salted hashes. Chapter 10 discusses hashing and salting techniques in more depth, and Chapter 11 discusses tokenization, another database security technique. Tokenization replaces sensitive data elements with substitute values.

Protecting Data in Use

Data-in-use refers to data that is currently being processed or accessed by a system or application. This can include sensitive data such as passwords, encryption keys, and other types of confidential information. Protecting data-in-use is a critical aspect of securing an organization's IT infrastructure, as it is vulnerable to attack during processing and transmission.

Secure enclave, sometimes known as trusted execution environment (TEE), is a type of security technology that provides a secure and isolated area within a system or application for processing sensitive data. Secure enclaves use hardware-based security mechanisms, such as Intel's Software Guard Extensions (SGX), to create a trusted execution environment that is isolated from the rest of the system. This allows sensitive data to be processed and stored securely, even in a potentially insecure computing environment.

Summarizing Cloud Concepts

Cloud computing refers to accessing computing resources via a different location than your local computer. In most scenarios, you're accessing these resources through the Internet.

As an example, if you use web-based email such as Gmail, you're using cloud computing. More specifically, web-based email is a Software as a Service cloud delivery model. You know that you're accessing your email via the Internet, but you don't know the location of the physical server hosting your account. It could be in a data center in the middle of Virginia, tucked away in Utah, or just about anywhere else in the world.

Cloud storage has become very popular for both individuals and organizations. For example, Apple offers iCloud storage, Microsoft offers OneDrive, and Google offers Google Drive. You can typically get some storage for free or pay nominal fees for more storage.

Heavily utilized systems and networks often depend on cloud computing resources to handle increased network traffic. As an example, consider the biggest shopping day in the United States—Black Friday, the day after Thanksgiving, when retailers hope to turn a profit. Several years ago, Amazon.com had so much traffic during the Thanksgiving weekend that its servers could barely handle it. The company learned its lesson, though. The next year, it used cloud computing to rent access to servers specifically for the Thanksgiving weekend, and, despite increased sales, it didn't have any problems.

As many great innovators do, Amazon didn't look at this situation as a problem but as an opportunity. If it needed cloud computing for its heavily utilized system, other companies probably had the same need. Amazon now hosts cloud services to other organizations via its Amazon Elastic Compute Cloud (Amazon EC2) service. Amazon EC2 combines virtualization with cloud computing, and they currently provide a wide variety of services via Amazon EC2.

Cloud Delivery Models

One of the ways that we can classify cloud service offerings is by what type of resources they provide to their customers. These are the **cloud delivery models** and there are three main offerings: software as a service (SaaS), platform as a service (PaaS), and infrastructure as a service (IaaS).

Software as a Service

Software as a Service (SaaS) includes any software or application provided to users over a network such as the Internet. Internet users normally access the SaaS applications with a web browser. It usually doesn't matter which web browser or operating system a SaaS customer uses. They could be using Microsoft Edge, Google Chrome, Mozilla Firefox, or just about any web browser.

As mentioned previously, web-based email is an example of SaaS. This includes Gmail, Yahoo! Mail, and others. The service provides all the components of email to users via a simple web browser.

If you have a Gmail account, you can also use Google Workspace, another example of SaaS. Google Workspace provides access to several SaaS applications, allowing users to open text documents, spreadsheets, presentations, drawings, and PDF files through a web browser.

A talented developer and I teamed up to work on a project a while ago. He's an Apple guy running a macOS while I'm a Microsoft guy running Windows, and we live in different parts of the country. However, we post and share documents through Google Docs, and despite different locations and different applications running on our individual systems, we're able to collaborate easily.

Platform as a Service

Platform as a Service (PaaS) provides customers with a preconfigured computing platform they can use as needed. It provides the customer with an easy-to-configure operating system, combined with appropriate applications and on-demand computing. Many cloud providers refer to this as a managed hardware solution. As an example, I host **https://getcertifiedgetahead.com/** on a virtual server through a hosting provider using one of their offerings.

The cloud hosting provider provides several features, including an installed operating system, a core software package used for web servers, Apache as a web server, antivirus software, spam protection, and more. Additionally, they keep the operating system up to date with relevant updates and patches. I manage the software used for the website, including software changes and updates. However, I don't need to worry about managing the server itself. Often, when the server has developed a problem, the hosting provider fixed it before I was even aware of the problem.

In many cases, users of PaaS services never interact with the actual hardware or operating system. They work through interfaces offered by the service provider. ***Serverless computing*** is a great example of this type of operating environment. In serverless computing environments, such as Amazon's Lambda service, customers provide the software code they want to execute along with execution instructions and the cloud provider handles everything else. There's no need for customers to worry about hardware, virtual machines, operating systems, or any of those details. The serverless computing provider handles all of that work behind the scenes.

Infrastructure as a Service

Infrastructure as a Service (IaaS) allows an organization to outsource its equipment requirements, including the hardware and all support operations. The IaaS service provider owns the equipment, houses it in its data center, and performs all the required hardware maintenance. The customer essentially rents access to the equipment and often pays on a per-use basis.

Many cloud providers refer to this as a self-managed solution. They provide access to a server and may include a default operating system installation, but customers must configure it and install additional software based on their needs. Additionally, customers are responsible for all operating system updates and patches.

IaaS can also be useful if an organization is finding it difficult to manage and maintain servers in its own data center. By outsourcing its requirements, the company limits its hardware footprint. It can do this instead of, or in addition to, virtualizing some of its servers. With IaaS, it needs fewer servers in its data center and fewer resources, such as power and personnel, to manage the servers.

> ### ★ Remember This!
>
> Applications such as web-based email provided over the Internet are Software as a Service (SaaS) cloud-based technologies. Platform as a Service (PaaS) provides customers with a fully managed platform, including hardware, operating systems, and limited applications. The vendor keeps systems up to date with current patches. Infrastructure as a Service (IaaS) provides customers with access to hardware in a self-managed platform.

Cloud Deployment Models

The second way that we can categorize cloud services is by their *cloud deployment model*. This describes where they reside and who may use them. There are four major cloud deployment models: public, private, community, and hybrid.

- *Public cloud* services are available from third-party companies, such as Amazon, Google, Microsoft, and Apple. They provide similar services to anyone willing to pay for them. They're available to the general public, so they're called public cloud.
- *Private cloud* offerings are created for use by a single customer. For example, the Shelbyville Nuclear Power Plant might decide it wants to store data in the cloud but does not want to use a third-party vendor. Instead, the plant chooses to host its own servers and make these servers available to internal employees through the Internet. Organizations may also hire a service provider to create and operate a private cloud environment for their exclusive use.
- *Community cloud* services are shared by a group of customers with shared interests (such as shared goals, security requirements, or compliance considerations). As an example, imagine that the Shelbyville Nuclear Power Plant and several schools within Springfield decided to share educational resources within a cloud. They could each provide resources for the cloud, and only organizations within the community would have access to the resources.
- *Hybrid cloud* environments combine offerings from two or more of the other deployment models. They can be a combination of private, public, or community clouds. These retain separate identities to help protect resources in private clouds. However, they are bridged together, often in such a way that it is transparent to users.

Multi-cloud Systems

Multi-cloud systems combine the resources from two or more cloud service providers. This is a different concept from hybrid cloud, which combines two or more deployment models.

For example, if an organization makes use of IaaS offerings from Amazon Web Services and Microsoft Azure, that is a multi-cloud environment because resources from both Amazon and Microsoft are involved. It is not a hybrid cloud deployment because both of those service providers are public cloud providers.

Some security professionals consider multi-cloud systems a good approach because they increase resiliency and redundancy. If one provider suffers an outage, the other provider will hopefully remain up and running. However, it's important to understand that multi-cloud systems also add complexity to an environment. The organization's IT team must be familiar with and maintain two separate environments. That adds cost and increases the risk of mistakes.

Application Programming Interfaces

An ***application programming interface (API)*** is a software component that gives developers access to features or data within another application, a service, or an operating system. It's common for developers to use APIs with web applications, Internet of Things (IoT) devices, and cloud-based services.

As an example, Amazon.com provides package tracking data by using web service-based APIs provided by different shippers. The input is the tracking ID, and the output is all the tracking data provided by the shipper. Similarly, APIs interact with IoT devices such as wireless thermostats to set and adjust temperatures.

APIs are susceptible to attacks, so developers need to address several API considerations to ensure that APIs aren't vulnerable to common exploits. These include:

- **Authentication.** Strong authentication methods will prevent unauthorized entities from using the APIs. The authentication method used can vary. For example, an API may use passwords with a second authentication factor, such as an authenticator app.

- **Authorization.** Authorization methods secure access to the API. For example, developers may have   one level of access, and web applications may have another level of access. APIs could use cloud-based authorization services, such as OAuth. Chapter 2, "Understanding Identity and Access Management," covers various authentication and authorization methods in more depth.
- **Transport level security.** The API should use strong security, such as TLS when transferring any traffic over the Internet. Early implementations of some wireless thermostats sent data over the Internet leaking information about thermostat owners. TLS encrypts the traffic preventing unauthorized entities from seeing the traffic.

Failure to address these issues increases the chance of successful API attacks. APIs are commonly used to access data. Any data breach is an indicator of a potential attack using an API.

Indicators of potential API attacks vary depending on the API's purpose. If the API is accessing or transmitting data, a primary indicator is data leaked onto the Internet. If the API is interacting with websites, a potential indicator of an attack is hacked websites. API inspection and integration refers to testing the API for security and usability. Effective test processes can discover vulnerabilities before attackers exploit them.

Microservices and APIs

Microservices are code modules designed to do one thing well. They are typically small code modules that receive values, process them, and respond with an output. Think of the Amazon example where the value is the tracking ID, and the output is the tracking data. Amazon must use a different web services-based API for each shipper.

In contrast, a single microservice code module could be used for any shipper. Customers would enter a tracking ID, and the microservice API would determine the shipper. It would then send the tracking ID to the appropriate shipper, receive the tracking data, and send the tracking data to the customer. A web services-based API is tied to a specific business, such as the individual shippers in this example. In contrast, a microservice module isn't tied to any specific business. This allows developers to use it in different applications without modifying it.

Managed Security Service Provider

A managed security service provider (MSSP) is a third-party vendor that provides security services for smaller companies. Many small companies use them to improve their companies' overall security posture without adding an army of security professionals to their staff.

In the early days of the Internet, an Internet Service Provider (ISP) provided basic services to customers. They sometimes sold firewalls to these customers and administered the firewalls remotely. MSSPs have expanded basic firewall service to just about anything a larger organization would have. The following list shows some of the managed services an MSSP may provide:

- Patch management
- Vulnerability scanning
- Spam and virus filtering
- Data loss prevention (DLP)
- Virtual private network connections
- Proxy services for web content filtering
- Intrusion detection and prevention systems
- Unified threat management (UTM) appliances
- Advanced firewalls such as next-generation firewalls (NGFWs)

An MSSP may sell appliances, such as NGFWs and UTMs hosted on the organization's premises and administer them remotely. However, it's also possible to host such devices within the cloud and redirect all organizational traffic through the cloud connection.

> ### 📌 *Remember This!*
>
> A managed security service provider (MSSP) is a third-party vendor that provides security services for an organization. A managed service provider (MSP) provides any IT services needed by an organization, including security services provided by an MSSP.

A managed service provider (MSP) is like an MSSP. However, instead of focusing only on security services, an MSP provides any information technology (IT) services that an organization needs.

Cloud Service Provider Responsibilities

One important consideration with cloud service models is the difference in responsibilities as-signed to a cloud service provider (CSP) and the customer. A CSP is an entity that offers one or more cloud services via one or more cloud deployment models. The responsibility matrix in Figure 5.3 (derived partly from Figure 2 in the US Department of Defense (DoD) "Cloud Computing Security Requirements Guide") shows how responsibilities are divided between the customer and the CSP in the IaaS, PaaS, and SaaS models. This includes both maintenance responsibilities and security responsibilities.

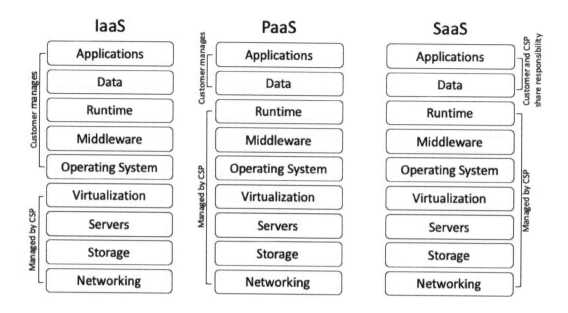

Figure 5.3: Cloud security responsibility matrix

As an example, consider Gmail: a SaaS offering. Google is responsible for maintaining everything to ensure Gmail is available. Additionally, Google has the primary responsibility of ensuring security for Gmail. If you use it, you still have some responsibility, such as ensuring you use a strong password that is different from other online accounts to protect your data.

In the PaaS model, the CSP is responsible for providing a platform and ensuring it remains available. This includes everything except applications and data, which the customer provides. Middleware and runtime components may not be familiar to you.

Middleware is software that is added to an operating system to extend its basic capabilities. As an example, Apache can be added to a Linux operating system to allow the system to function as a web server. Runtime is a hosting environment, such as a container on a server. The CSP typically rents access to any server to multiple users. Each customer has access to core elements of the operating system but runs within a container. The runtime environment isolates each customer's container from other containers on the server.

The customer assumes more responsibility in the IaaS model, taking responsibility for installing and maintaining the operating system and any runtime and middleware components. A CSP will typically rent an entire server to a customer in the IaaS model. This can be either a physical server or a virtual server. CSPs are also responsible for services integration. This ensures that all elements of a cloud solution work together.

Cloud Security Considerations

When picking a CSP, an organization needs to consider various cloud security issues. As you prepare for the Security+ exam, you should be familiar with each of these:

- **Availability**. High availability indicates a system or service remains operational with almost zero downtime. It's typically achieved by using multiple load-balancing nodes, as discussed in Chapter 9. High availability across zones indicates that the nodes are located in different cloud locations, such as separate geographic locations. If one node fails, other nodes can take on its load.

- **Resilience**. Resilience is the ability of a system to maintain its functionality even when faced with adverse conditions or unexpected events, such as natural disasters or cyberattacks. This is achieved by implementing redundancy and failover mechanisms, such as backups and disaster recovery sites, to ensure that the system can continue to operate even in the face of disruptions or failures.

- **Cost**. The cost of a cloud service is an important consideration for any organization. It's important to balance the cost of the service with the organization's budget and requirements, and to ensure that the service is delivering value for money.

- **Responsiveness**. Responsiveness refers to the speed and reliability with which a cloud service can respond to requests and perform tasks. This is typically measured in terms of response time and throughput, and can be optimized through the use of caching, load balancing, and other techniques.

- **Scalability**. Scalability is the ability of a cloud service to handle increasing amounts of data, traffic, and user requests without degradation in performance. This is achieved through the use of elastic computing resources and auto-scaling mechanisms that can dynamically allocate resources as needed to meet demand.

- **Segmentation**. Just as local networks support segmentation with virtual local area networks (VLANs) and screened subnets, cloud-based networks can segment computers or networks. This is important for maintaining security and compliance by isolating sensitive data and applications from other parts of the network.

On-Premises Versus Off-Premises

Organizations can use cloud resources on-premises or off-premises. On-premises indicates that all resources are owned, operated, and maintained within the organization's properties. An on-premises environment is typically used only to support a private cloud deployment. Off-premises equipment, however, can be used to support any of the cloud deployment models. Public clouds are always off-premises.

On-Premises

In an on-premises solution, the organization retains complete control over all the cloud-based resources, including any data stored in the on-premises cloud. This allows the organization to implement multiple security controls to protect the on-premises cloud resources and provide cybersecurity resilience.

The organization can also implement its own authentication and authorization controls. This makes it easier to use single sign-on (SSO) without requiring employees to have separate accounts for cloud-based resources.

However, the organization is responsible for all maintenance of the on-premises resources. Unless the organization already has a large IT department, maintenance of on-premises cloud-based resources may be overwhelming.

When building on-premises deployments, organizations must also choose whether to use a **centralized** approach, in which equipment is located in one or a small number of large data centers, or a **decentralized** approach where equipment is spread across many smaller data centers. The centralized approach tends to reduce costs and simplify management, while the decentralized approach reduces the impact of a single facility failure.

Off-Premises

One of the primary benefits of an off-premises solution is that the CSP performs the maintenance. As discussed previously, the CSP has the most responsibility for maintaining the cloud-based resources in the SaaS model. Even in the IaaS model, the CSP still ensures the hardware is operational.

A drawback with cloud-based resources kept off-premises is that an organization may not know where data is stored. If data is stored in another country, it could result in legal implications requiring the organization to comply with different laws in different countries. However, organizations can contractually require CSPs to store data in a single country only.

Digital forensics (discussed in Chapter 11) can be challenging enough when all the evidence is on-premises. When an organization uses cloud resources, it can add additional risks. Anytime an organization contracts with a cloud provider, the cloud provider becomes a third-party source providing the service. This includes when the cloud provider holds data or provides any type of service.

Hardening Cloud Environments

Cloud security is a critical concern for any organization using cloud-based resources. Let's take a look at different security controls, tools, and techniques that organizations can use to harden their cloud environments and protect their data.

Cloud Access Security Broker

CSPs employ native controls to protect cloud-based resources. This may be enough for some customers, but other customers want more security features and seek third-party solutions, such as a *cloud access security broker* **(CASB)**.

A CASB is a software solution or service deployed between an organization's network and the cloud provider. It provides security by monitoring traffic and enforcing security policies. Anything accessible via the Internet is an attack vector, and that includes cloud-based resources. However, a CASB can help organizations mitigate risks by consistently enforcing security policies across cloud service providers.

Cloud-Based DLP

It's common for personnel within organizations to store data in the cloud. This makes it easier to access the data from any location and from almost any device. Cloud-based DLP solutions allow an organization to implement policies for data stored in the cloud.

As an example, an organization can implement policies to detect Personally Identifiable Information (PII), or Protected Health Information (PHI) stored in the cloud. After detecting the data, a DLP policy can be configured to take one or more actions such as sending an alert to a security administrator, blocking any attempts to save the data in the cloud, and quarantining the data.

> ### ★ Remember This!
>
> A cloud based DLP can enforce security policies for data stored in the cloud, such as ensuring that Personally Identifiable Information (PII) is encrypted.

Next-Generation Secure Web Gateway

A next-generation secure web gateway (SWG) is a combination of a proxy server and a stateless firewall. The SWG is typically a cloud-based service, but it can be an on-site appliance. Clients are configured to access all Internet resources via the SWG, and it filters traffic to prevent threats from infiltrating the network. Some of the services provided by the SWG include:

- URL filtering to prevent users from visiting unauthorized sites
- Packet filtering to detect and block malicious traffic.
- Malware detection and filtering to block malware.
- Network-based data loss protection (DLP)
- Sandboxing to check for threats.

> 📌 ***Remember This!***
>
> A cloud access security broker (CASB) is a software tool or service deployed between an organization's network and the cloud provider. It provides security by monitoring traffic and enforcing security policies. A next-generation secure web gateway (SWG) provides proxy services for traffic from clients to Internet sites, such as filtering URLs and scanning for malware.

Cloud Firewall Considerations

When creating virtual networks in the cloud, there are some additional items to consider. Just as physical networks need firewalls to prevent unauthorized access, virtual networks also need firewalls. Things get a little more complicated in a cloud environment, however.

You can rest assured that cloud service providers have very sophisticated firewalls in place to protect their networks from attack. Those firewalls filter traffic coming to your cloud resources, and you'll need to modify the rules on those firewalls if you want to allow access to your resources. There's a catch, however. The cloud service provider is not about to let you directly modify their firewall rules! You could write all sorts of rules that would affect not only your security but also the security of other customers.

Security groups offer you the ability to write firewall rules that affect only your resources. The cloud service provider uses their firewall to enforce the rules that you create in security groups without letting you directly modify the firewall. These security groups should be carefully managed because, while your mistakes won't affect other customers, those mistakes can definitely undermine the security of your own systems!

Infrastructure as Code

Infrastructure as code (IaC) refers to managing and provisioning data centers with code to define VMs and virtual networks. It reduces the complexity of creating virtual objects by allowing administrators to run a script to create them. System administrators prefer this approach because it creates reusable code and facilitates automation.

Software-Defined Networking

Software-defined networking (SDN) uses virtualization technologies to route traffic instead of using hardware routers and switches. More and more cloud service providers are implanting SDNs as part of an overall IaaS solution.

An SDN separates the data plane and control plane within a network. Another way of thinking of this is that an SDN separates the logic used to forward or block traffic (the data plane) and the logic used to identify the path to take (the control plane).

Hardware routers use rules within an ACL to identify whether a router will forward or block traffic on the data plane. This is always proprietary because it's implemented on specific hardware routers. However, an SDN implements the data plane with software and virtualization technologies, allowing an organization to move away from proprietary hardware.

Routing protocols such as Open Shortest Path First (OSPF) and Border Gateway Protocol (BGP) help routers determine the best path to route traffic on the control plane. Routers use these protocols to share information, creating a map of the known network. An SDN can still use these routing protocols but without the hardware routers. When SDNs work on wide-area networks to connect different sites together, they are known as **software-defined wide area networks (SD-WAN)**.

Edge and Fog Computing

Edge computing is the practice of storing and processing data close to the devices that generate and use the data. Many non-edge solutions store all the data in the cloud, requiring round trips to retrieve and process the data. However, this takes too much time for many situations.

As an example, think of autonomous technologies in automobiles. Imagine the speed limit is 60 miles per hour (MPH), and you set the adaptive cruise control to 60 MPH. If the highway becomes congested, cars ahead of you will start slowing down. However, the adaptive cruise control senses the change and automatically slows down, keeping a specified distance between you and the car in front of you. In some cases, the congestion might appear quickly, requiring quick responses from the adaptive cruise control and a crash avoidance system. If your car is sending sensor data to the cloud for processing, your car may crash before it gets any responses.

However, onboard processors monitor the sensors with edge computing, process the data, and slow your car down almost immediately. This eliminates issues with latency.

Fog computing is almost the same thing as edge computing. The primary difference is that fog computing uses a network close to the device and may have multiple nodes sensing and processing data within the fog network. In contrast, edge computing stores and processes the data on single nodes or appliances.

> ### Cloud Security Alliance
>
> The Cloud Security Alliance (CSA) is a not-for-profit organization that promotes best practices related to the cloud. It's a member-based organization and has several thousand volunteers working on research and other projects. They created the Certificate of Cloud Security Knowledge (CCSK) certification, which focuses on cloud security.
>
> They also created the CSA Cloud Controls Matrix (CCM), a cybersecurity control framework. Version 4.0 of the CCM organizes over 200 security control objectives in 17 domains. Many of the security controls in the CCM are like the security controls in SP-800-53 Revision 5, "Security and Privacy Controls for Information Systems and Organizations." The big difference is that the CCM is focused on security controls related to cloud-based resources. However, SP 800-53 Revision 5 is for all computing systems.

Deploying Mobile Devices Securely

Mobile devices represent significant challenges for organizations today. Organizations need to determine if employees can connect mobile devices to the network. If so, organizations need to identify methods to manage the security related to the devices, monitor the devices, and enforce security policies.

What is a mobile device? Within the context of the CompTIA Security+ exam, you can think of a mobile device as a smartphone or tablet. Further, NIST SP 800-124, "Guidelines for Managing the Security of Mobile Devices in the Enterprise," mentions that mobile devices have additional characteristics, such as at least one wireless network interface, local data storage, an operating system, and the ability to install additional applications.

Mobile devices typically have other optional features. This includes other networking options such as Bluetooth, near field communication (NFC), cellular access for voice communications, and Global Positioning System (GPS) services. They typically include a digital camera, a video recorder, a microphone, and the ability to transfer data to another system such as a traditional computer or to other mobile devices.

NIST SP 800-124 excludes laptop and desktop computers because they don't contain features in many mobile devices, such as a GPS and sensors that monitor the device's movement, such as an accelerometer and a gyroscope. A GPS can pinpoint the location of a device, even if it moves. NIST's definition also excludes basic cell phones, digital cameras, and Internet of Things (IoT) devices. These don't have an operating system or have a limited functioning operating system.

Mobile Device Deployment Models

Any device connected to an organization's network represents a potential risk. As a simple example, if someone connects an infected device to a network, it might be able to infect other devices on the network. To limit this risk, organizations take steps to monitor and manage mobile devices.

If the organization owns all the devices connected to the network, it's a simple matter to monitor and manage them. However, if employees own these devices (such as their own smartphone), monitoring and managing the devices becomes more challenging. As an example, employees want to access the network resources with their own device, but they are sometimes resistant to allowing the organization to monitor and manage their personal devices.

The following list identifies some common deployment models for mobile devices. Notice that in some models, the organization owns the device, but in other models, employees own the device:

- **Corporate-owned**. In this traditional deployment model, the organization purchases devices and issues them to employees.
- **COPE (corporate-owned, personally enabled)**. COPE is similar to the traditional corporate-owned model, but the primary difference is that the employees are free to use the device as if it was their personally owned device. This allows employees to use the devices for personal activities in addition to connecting them to the organization's network. Because the organization owns the devices, it makes it easier to manage them.
- **BYOD (bring your own device)**. Some organizations allow employees to bring their own mobile devices to work and attach them to the network. Employees are responsible for selecting and supporting the device, and they typically must comply with a BYOD policy when connecting their device to the network. While this is simple for the employees, it is sometimes referred to as bring your own disaster among IT professionals. Because employees can have any possible device, the IT department often winds up supporting, monitoring, and managing those devices to some extent.
- **CYOD (choose your own device)**. To avoid some of the challenges related to supporting any possible mobile devices, some organizations create a list of acceptable devices and publish the list in a CYOD policy. Employees can purchase devices on the list and bring them to work. This gives the IT department a specific list of devices to support, monitor, and manage. Some people confuse CYOD with COPE. In the COPE model, the organization purchases the device and may give the employees a choice of different devices. In the CYOD model, the employee purchases the device.

> **📌 Remember This!**
>
> Corporate-owned, personally enabled (COPE) devices are owned by the organization, but employees can use them for personal reasons. A bring your own device (BYOD) policy allows employees to connect their own personal devices to the corporate network. A choose your own device (CYOD) policy includes a list of approved devices that employees can purchase and connect to the network.

Connection Methods and Receivers

There are several methods that mobile devices can use to connect to networks and other devices. They include:

- **Cellular**. Smartphones (and many tablets) include the ability to connect to a cellular network, such as a long-term-evolution (LTE), fourth generation (4G), or 5G network. The type of network you connect with is dependent on your cellular provider, location, and your device. Newer generations typically provide increased speed for digital transfers and improved voice communications.
- **Wi-Fi**. Mobile devices almost always have a wireless network interface that you can configure to connect to a wireless network. Chapter 4 discusses common wireless security methods and wireless protocols.
- **Bluetooth**. Most mobile devices include Bluetooth support. Bluetooth is a wireless protocol commonly used with personal area networks. For example, most smartphones support the use of a Bluetooth headset for hands-free use of the phone. Additionally, some technologies use Bluetooth to connect two smartphones. Chapter 4 discusses some Bluetooth attacks.

Mobile Device Management

Mobile device management (MDM) includes the technologies to manage mobile devices. The goal is to ensure these devices have security controls in place to keep them secure. Some vendors sell *unified endpoint management (UEM)* solutions to manage mobile devices.

> **📌 Remember This!**
>
> Mobile device management (MDM) tools help enforce security policies on mobile devices. This includes the use of storage segmentation, containerization, and full device encryption to protect data. Containerization is useful when using the BYOD model. They also include enforcing strong authentication methods to prevent unauthorized access.

UEM tools ensure systems are kept up to date with current patches, have antivirus software installed with up-to-date definitions, and are secured using standard security practices. While some of these tools initially focused on desktop PCs and laptops, they have expanded to include many mobile devices. As an example, Microsoft Configuration Manager includes support for mobile devices such as Apple iOS-based devices and Android-based devices.

MDM solutions help administrators manage mobile devices. The following bullets describe many of the MDM concepts that apply to mobile devices:

- **Application management.** MDM tools can restrict what applications can run on mobile devices. They often use application allow lists to control the applications and prevent unapproved applications from being installed. Mobile application management (MAM) tools are typically built into MDM tools, but some MAM tools focus only on controlling applications.

- **Full device encryption.** Encryption protects against loss of confidentiality on multiple platforms, including workstations, servers, mobile devices, and data transmissions. Encryption methods such as full device encryption provide device security, application security, and data security. While an organization can ensure corporate-owned devices use full device encryption, this isn't always possible when employees use their own devices.

- **Storage segmentation.** In some mobile devices, it's possible to use storage segmentation to isolate data. For example, users might be required to use external storage for any corporate data to reduce the risk of data loss if the device is lost or stolen. It's also possible to create separate segments within the device. Users would store corporate data within an encrypted segment and personal data elsewhere on the device.

- **Content management.** After creating segmented storage spaces, it's important to ensure that appropriate content is stored there. An MDM system can ensure that all content retrieved from an organization source (such as a server) is stored in an encrypted segment. Also, content management can force the user to authenticate again when accessing data within this encrypted segment.

- **Containerization.** The virtualization section earlier in this chapter discusses the use of container virtualization. Organizations can also implement containerization in mobile devices and encrypt the container to protect it without encrypting the entire device. Running an organization's application in a container isolates and protects the application, including any of its data. This is very useful when an organization allows employees to use their own devices.

- **Passwords and PINs.** Mobile devices commonly support the use of passwords or personal identification numbers (PINs). MDM systems typically support password policies, similar to the password policies used in desktop systems. The only limitation is that some mobile devices only support PINs, while others support either passwords or PINs.

- **Biometrics.** Chapter 2 discusses biometrics as one of the authentication factors (something you are). Many mobile devices now support biometrics for authentication. For example, you can teach the device to recognize your face and then use facial recognition to authenticate instead of entering a password or PIN.

- **Screen locks.** Most devices support the use of a passcode or password to lock the device. This is like a password-protected screen saver on desktop systems that automatically locks the device after a specified number of minutes. It prevents someone from easily accessing the device and the data it contains. This is often combined with an erase function. For example, if someone steals the phone and enters the incorrect passcode 10 times, the smartphone will automatically erase all data on the phone, if the feature is enabled.

- **Remote wipe.** *Remote wipe* capabilities are useful if the phone is lost and remains connected to a Wi-Fi or cellular network. It sends a remote signal to the device to wipe or erase all the data. The owner can send a remote wipe signal to the phone to delete all the data on the phone. This also deletes any cached data, such as cached online banking passwords, and provides a complete sanitization of the device by removing all valuable data.

- **Geolocation**. Mobile devices commonly include GPS capabilities that are used for geolocation. Applications commonly use GPS to identify the location of the device and device movement. GPS can also be used to locate a lost device.

- **Geofencing**. Organizations sometimes use GPS to create a virtual fence or geographic boundary using geofencing technologies. Apps can respond when the device is within the virtual fence. As an example, an organization can configure mobile apps so that they will only run when the device is within the virtual fence. Similarly, an organization can configure a wireless network to only operate for mobile devices within the defined boundary.

- **GPS tagging**. GPS tagging (also called geotagging) adds geographical information to files such as pictures and video, or when posting them to social media websites. For example, when you take a picture with a smartphone with the GPS features enabled, the picture application adds latitude and longitude coordinates to the picture. Thinking of friends and family, this is a neat feature. However, thinking of thieves and criminals, they can exploit this data. For example, if Lisa frequently posts pictures of friends and family at her house, these pictures identify her address. If she later starts posting pictures from a vacation location, thieves can realize she's gone and burglarize her home.

- **Context-aware authentication**. Context-aware authentication uses multiple elements to authenticate a user and a device. It can include the user's identity, geolocation, verification that the device is within a geofence, network, user behavior, time of day, and type of device and operating system. These elements help prevent unauthorized users from accessing apps or data.

- **Push notifications**. Push notification services send messages to mobile devices from apps. As an example, if Lisa installs the Facebook app on her smartphone and enables notifications, the Facebook app will send her notifications. Software developers can configure the notifications to appear even if the device is in screen lock mode and even if the app is not running. MDM apps can send notifications to remind users of security settings or let them know if their device complies with security policy requirements.

> ### ★ Remember This!
>
> Remote wipe sends a signal to a lost or stolen device to erase all data. Geolocation uses Global Positioning System (GPS) and can help locate a lost or stolen device. Geofencing creates a virtual fence or geographic boundary and can be used to detect when a device is within an organization's property. GPS tagging adds geographical data to files such as pictures. Context-aware authentication uses multiple elements to authenticate a user and a mobile device.

Hardening Mobile Devices

MDM tools often manage devices differently depending on who owns them. If the organization owns the device, the MDM tool will typically download and install all required applications and ensure they are kept up to date.

If the device is employee-owned, MDM tools will monitor them for compliance and block access to the network if the device doesn't meet minimum requirements. For example, suppose the device isn't patched or doesn't have up-to-date antivirus software. In that case, the MDM software works with network access control (NAC) technologies to prevent the device from connecting to the network. The following paragraphs identify many common issues that an MDM can monitor and enforce.

Unauthorized Software

Organizations typically want users to only install apps obtained from approved sources. For example, all iPhone and iPad devices would only obtain apps from Apple's App Store. Apple is aggressive in testing these apps for malware, and any developer who attempts to distribute malware through the Apple store is often banned. Similarly, Google maintains the Google Play site for Android devices.

A **third-party app store** is something other than Apple's App Store or Google Play. Apps obtained from these third-party app stores don't undergo the same level of scrutiny as apps on the App Store or Google Play and represent a higher risk. Apple makes it very difficult to obtain apps from a third-party app store, but it is relatively easy to obtain apps from third-party stores for Android devices.

Jailbreaking refers to removing all software restrictions from an Apple device. After jailbreaking a device, users can install software from any third-party source. **Rooting** is the process of modifying an Android device to give the user root-level (or full administrator) access to the device. Rooting and jailbreaking introduce risks and vulnerabilities to the device, so it's common for an MDM to block all access to a network if it detects a device has either been rooted or jailbroken.

Mobile devices typically have the operating system stored in onboard memory, such as flash memory, which retains data even without power. Because the operating system is the software and the memory is hardware, this is commonly called firmware. Updates to the operating system overwrite the firmware using **over-the-air (OTA) updates** techniques. Firmware OTA updates keep the device up to date.

It's also possible to overwrite the firmware with **custom firmware**. Some people do this as another method of rooting Android devices. The process is typically complex and fraught with risks. However, some people find downloadable images and copy them onto their devices to overwrite the firmware.

It's also possible to install applications on Android devices by **sideloading** them. Sideloading is the process of copying an application package in the Application Packet Kit (APK) format to the device and then activating it. The device must be set to allow apps from Unknown Sources, which can significantly weaken security. Sideloading is useful for developers testing apps but considered risky when installing apps from third parties.

Hardware Control

An organization might want to control some of the hardware on mobile devices, and MDM tools can help. Mobile devices commonly include a camera and a recording microphone. These are useful for regular users but can present significant risks for employees within an organization.

As an example, attackers have successfully inserted malicious code into some apps available on some third-party sites. When users install the apps, it allows an attacker to remotely connect to the phone, snap pictures, record audio, and much more.

An organization can configure the MDM software to disable the camera and recording microphone to eliminate the risk. Ideally, the MDM tool will only disable the camera and microphone when it detects the device is within a previously configured geofence. Unfortunately, all MDM tools don't support disabling hardware based on geolocation. If the MDM tool doesn't support this feature, the organization may prohibit the possession of smartphones in certain areas.

Unauthorized Connections

Management within an organization might want to limit a mobile device's connection abilities. For example, if the mobile device can connect to the primary network, management might want to ensure that the mobile device cannot access the Internet using another connection. This section identifies other connections that can be modified and blocked with an MDM tool.

Most smartphones support tethering, which allows you to share one device's Internet connection with other devices. For example, you can connect your smartphone to the Internet and then share this Internet connection with a laptop, a tablet, or any device with a wireless connection. If employees use tethering within the organization, they can bypass security such as firewalls and proxy servers. Imagine Bart wants to visit an unauthorized website with his work laptop. The proxy server blocks his access. However, he can tether his laptop to his smartphone and visit the site. This direct connection will also bypass any content filters in the network and possibly allow malware onto his laptop.

Similarly, many carrier companies sell mobile hotspots. These connect to the Internet and allow multiple systems to access the Internet via the hotspot. If employees bring these to work, they can bypass network controls just as if they were using tethering.

Many mobile devices also support Wi-Fi Direct, a standard that allows devices to connect without a wireless access point or wireless router. This is like a wireless ad hoc network, allowing devices to connect together without a wireless access point or wireless router. The difference is that Wi-Fi Direct uses single radio hop communication. In other words, none of the devices in a Wi-Fi Direct network can share an Internet connection. In contrast, systems in a wireless ad hoc network use multihop wireless communications and can share an Internet connection.

> ### 📌 *Remember This!*
>
> Tethering and mobile hotspots allow devices to access the Internet and bypass network controls. Wi-Fi Direct is a standard that allows devices to connect without a wireless access point or wireless router. MDM tools can block access to devices using tethering, mobile hotspot, or Wi-Fi Direct to access the Internet.

Exploring Embedded Systems

An **embedded system** is any device that has a dedicated function and uses a computer system to perform that function. Desktop PCs, laptops, and servers all use central processing units (CPUs), operating systems, and applications to perform various functions. Similarly, embedded systems use CPUs, operating systems, and one or more applications to perform multiple functions.

As a simple example, a wireless multifunction printer (MFP) typically includes an embedded system. It runs a website that you can access wirelessly to configure the printer. Of course, you can also send print jobs to it, scan documents, and copy documents with the printer. Many include faxing capabilities and can send documents via email.

Understanding Internet of Things

The **Internet of Things (IoT)** refers to a wide assortment of technologies that interact with the physical world. They commonly have embedded systems and typically connect to a central device or app and communicate via the Internet, Bluetooth, or other wireless technologies.

The National Institute of Standards and Technology Internal Report (NISTIR) 8228 "Considerations for Managing Internet of Things (IoT) Cybersecurity and Privacy Risks" states that the full scope of IoT is not precisely defined. This is because the technologies are in a wide assortment of sectors such as health care, transportation, and home security.

Many have sensors used to monitor an environment, such as temperature and humidity. However, they can do much more than control thermostats. Many organizations use IoT devices for facility automation, such as motion-controlled lighting, security cameras and recorders, fire detection and suppression systems, and more.

IoT technologies are also used in many other technologies such as medical systems, vehicles, aircraft, and smart meters. IoT devices can provide remote temperature monitoring for vaccines and capture vital signs for patients. More and more automobiles use both embedded systems and IoT devices to control all facets of the operation of an automobile. As an example, cars regularly update themselves with over-the-air updates. Manufacturers could decide to integrate all the embedded systems in an automobile, making them all accessible via the Internet and accessible by attackers.

Aircraft use IoT technologies to track the maintenance and performance of almost every moving part on the plane. Aircraft and unmanned aerial vehicles (UAVs) include embedded systems. Hobbyists use small UAVs to take pictures remotely. Other organizations such as the military include sophisticated embedded systems for reconnaissance and to deliver weapons.

Smart meters are commonly used on the electrical grid. They remotely monitor and record energy consumption, sending data analytics to centralized servers.

ICS and SCADA Systems

An **industrial control system (ICS)** typically refers to systems within large facilities such as power plants or water treatment facilities. A **supervisory control and data acquisition (SCADA)** system typically controls an ICS by monitoring it and sending it commands. Ideally, these systems are protected within isolated networks that can't access the Internet. From another perspective, attackers on the Internet can't access SCADA systems or an ICS. Common uses of ICS and SCADA systems include:

- **Manufacturing and industrial**. Manufacturing and industrial uses include any plants used to manufacture products. The systems can monitor every processing stage and report anomalies in real time. Many systems can also send signals to adjust processes based on changes in the environment.
- **Facilities**. Facilities uses include monitoring the temperature and humidity and keeping the environment relatively stable. In water treatment facilities, these systems can monitor each phase of the process, report problems, and adjust to changes.
- **Energy**. Energy uses include oil and gas processing, power generation, and more.
- **Logistics**. Logistics uses include monitoring processes within shipping facilities.

★ Remember This!

A supervisory control and data acquisition (SCADA) system has embedded systems that control an industrial control system (ICS), such as one used in a power plant or water treatment facility. Embedded systems are also used for many special purposes, such as medical devices, automotive vehicles, aircraft, and unmanned aerial vehicles (UAVs).

Some SCADA systems and ICSs are connected to the corporate network. However, they are typically placed within an isolated virtual local area network (VLAN), and the VLAN is protected by a network intrusion prevention system (NIPS) to block unwanted traffic. Chapter 3 discusses VLANs, and Chapter 4 discusses NIPS.

Embedded Systems Components

Embedded systems have several components that work together to perform their functions.

One key component of embedded systems is the **system-on-chip (SoC)**. An SoC integrates many components of a computer system onto a single chip, including a processor, memory, input/output interfaces, and other components. This integration enables embedded systems to be compact and power-efficient while still providing the necessary computing power for their specific applications. SoCs are often customized for specific applications, meaning that they are designed and built specifically for a particular embedded system.

Another key component of embedded systems is the **real-time operating system (RTOS)**. An RTOS is a specialized operating system designed for embedded systems that require precise timing and deterministic behavior. RTOSs provide real-time scheduling, which means that they can guarantee that certain tasks will be completed within a specific timeframe. This is critical for many embedded systems, such as medical devices and automotive systems, where timing is crucial for safety and reliability. RTOSs are also designed to be efficient and lightweight, with a small memory footprint and low processing overhead, making them well-suited for embedded systems with limited resources.

 Remember This!

An embedded system is any device that has a dedicated function and uses a computer system to perform that function. It includes any devices in the Internet of Things (IoT) category, such as wearables and home automation systems. Some embedded systems use a system on a chip (SoC).

Hardening Specialized Systems

A challenge with embedded, IoT, and ICS/SCADA systems is keeping them up to date with security fixes. When vendors discover vulnerabilities in computers and applications, they write and release patches. When you apply the patch, the system is no longer vulnerable to the exploit. In contrast, embedded systems vendors are not as aggressive in identifying vulnerabilities and creating patches to fix them.

Also, patch management is a routine function for IT administrators in most organizations. They regularly review patches released by major software and operating system vendors, test them, and apply them when necessary. In contrast, how often do they examine and apply updates for RTOS and similar components?

Segmentation is another effective security control for specialized systems. Since it can be difficult to securely manage these systems, they should be placed on a segmented network where they are tightly locked down and protected from external attack.

Embedded System Constraints

Embedded systems have several constraints that can limit their use. The following list describes these constraints:

- **Compute.** The computing ability of embedded systems is typically limited compared with full computing systems. Because they are small, they don't have full CPUs.
- **Cryptographic limitations.** With limited processing power, embedded systems can't use all cryptographic protocols. If designers sacrifice security by not encrypting data, they may inadvertently create vulnerabilities.
- **Power.** Embedded devices don't have their own power supplies but instead use power from the parent device. In some cases, devices must use batteries that occasionally need

to be replaced. This results in a conflict with the computing capabilities. Stronger computing ability draws more power and requires batteries to be replaced more often.

- **Ease of Deployment.** IoT and ICS/SCADA embedded systems are often deployed in remote and difficult to access locations, making maintenance and updates more challenging. Additionally, real-time operating systems (RTOS) used in many embedded systems require specialized expertise to deploy and maintain, which can increase deployment time and cost.

- **Cost.** The cost of the device can be minimized by sacrificing features such as security. By adding features, it increases the cost. It can sometimes be a challenge between management and designers when balancing the cost against the desired features.

- **Inability to patch/patch availability.** Unlike most endpoint devices such as desktops and mobile devices, it often isn't possible to patch embedded systems. Vendors don't always include methods to patch devices, and even if they do, they don't always write and release patches in a timely manner.

Chapter 5 Exam Topic Review

When preparing for the exam, make sure you understand these key concepts covered in this chapter.

Summarizing Virtualization Concepts

- Virtualization allows multiple servers to operate on a single physical host. It also supports virtual desktops.

- A virtual desktop infrastructure (VDI) hosts a user's desktop operating system on a server. Thin clients, including mobile devices, can connect to a server and access a VDI.

- Container virtualization runs services or applications within isolated containers or application cells. Containers use the kernel of the host.

- VM escape attacks allow an attacker to access the host system from the VM. The primary protection is to keep the host and guests up to date with current patches.

- VM sprawl occurs if personnel within the organization don't manage the VMs.

Implementing Secure Systems

- Endpoints are computing devices such as servers, desktops, laptops, mobile devices, or Internet of Things (IoT) devices. Endpoint detection and response (EDR) provides continuous monitoring of endpoints. Extended detection and response (XDR) includes other types of devices and systems.

- Hardening is the practice of making an operating system or application more secure from its default installation.

- Configuration management practices help organizations deploy systems with secure configurations.

- A master image provides a secure starting point for systems. Master images are typically created with templates or other baselines to provide a secure starting point for systems. Integrity measurement tools detect when a system deviates from the baseline.

- Patch management procedures ensure operating systems, applications, and firmware are kept up to date with current patches. This ensures they are protected against known vulnerabilities.

- Change management policies define the process for making changes and help reduce unintended outages from changes.

- An application allow list identifies authorized software but blocks all other software. An application block list blocks unauthorized software but allows other software to run.

- Full disk encryption (FDE) encrypts an entire disk. A self-encrypting drive (SED) has the encryption circuitry built into the drive.

- A Trusted Platform Module (TPM) is a chip included with many desktops, laptops and some mobile devices, and it supports full disk encryption, a secure boot process, and supports remote attestation. TPMs have an encryption key burned into them and they provide a hardware root of trust.

- A hardware security module (HSM) is a removable or external device used for encryption. An HSM generates and stores RSA encryption keys and can be integrated with servers to provide hardware-based encryption. A microSD HSM is a microSD chip with an HSM device installed on it.

- The primary method of protecting the confidentiality of data is with encryption and strong access controls. File system security includes the use of encryption to encrypt files and folders.

- You can encrypt individual columns in a database (such as credit card numbers), entire databases, individual files, entire disks, and removable media.

- Data loss prevention (DLP) techniques and technologies help prevent data loss. They can block transfer of data to USB devices and analyze outgoing data via email to detect unauthorized transfers.

- Data exfiltration is the unauthorized transfer of data outside an organization.

Summarizing Cloud Concepts

- Cloud computing provides an organization with additional resources. Most cloud services are provided via the Internet or a hosting provider. On-premise clouds are owned and maintained by an organization.

- Software as a Service (SaaS) includes web-based applications such as web-based email.

- Platform as a Service (PaaS) provides an easy-to-configure operating system and on-demand computing for customers. The vendor keeps systems up to date with current patches.

- Infrastructure as a Service (IaaS) provides hardware resources via the cloud. It can help an organization limit the size of its hardware footprint and reduce personnel costs.

- A managed service provider (MSP) is a third-party vendor that provides any IT services needed by an organization, including security services. A managed security service provider (MSSP) focuses on providing security services for an organization.
- A cloud access security broker (CASB) is a software tool or service deployed between an organization's network and the cloud provider. It monitors all network traffic and can enforce security policies.
- Private clouds are designed for use by a single organization.
- Third-party vendors sell access to public cloud services to anyone who wants them.
- Two or more organizations with shared concerns can share a community cloud.
- A hybrid cloud is a combination of two or more cloud deployment models. Multi-cloud systems combine the resources from two or more cloud service providers.
- Cloud-based DLP systems can enforce security policies for any data stored in the cloud.
- A next-generation secure web gateway provides proxy services for traffic from clients to Internet sites. It can filter URLs and scan for malware.
- Common cloud security considerations include availability, resilience, cost, responsiveness, scalability, and segmentation.
- On-premises deployments may be created using a centralized approach, with a small number of physical locations, or a decentralized approach, with many physical locations. Off-premises solutions make use of cloud service providers.
- Infrastructure as code (IaC) refers to managing and provisioning data centers with code to define VMs and virtual networks.
- Software-defined networks (SDN) use virtualization technologies to route traffic instead of using hardware routers and switches.

Deploying Mobile Devices Securely

- Mobile devices include smartphones and tablets and run a mobile operating system.
- Corporate-owned, personally enabled (COPE) mobile devices are owned by the organization, but employees can use them for personal reasons.
- Bring your own device (BYOD) policies allow employees to connect their mobile devices to the organization's network. Choose your own device (CYOD) policies include a list of acceptable devices and allow employees who own one of these devices to connect them to the network.
- A virtual desktop infrastructure (VDI) is a virtual desktop, and these can be created so that users can access them from a mobile device.
- Mobile devices can connect to the Internet, networks, and other devices using cellular, Wi-Fi, and Bluetooth connections.
- Mobile device management (MDM) tools help ensure that devices meet minimum security requirements. They can monitor devices, enforce security policies, and block network access if devices do not meet these requirements.

- MDM tools can restrict applications on devices, segment and encrypt data, enforce strong authentication methods, and implement security methods such as screen locks and remote wipe. Containerization is useful when using the BYOD model.

- A screen lock is like a password-protected screen saver on desktop systems that automatically locks the device after some time. A remote wipe signal removes all the data from a lost phone.

- Geolocation uses Global Positioning System (GPS) to identify a device's location. Geofencing uses GPS to create a virtual fence or geographic boundary. Organizations use geofencing to enable access to services or devices within the boundary and block access outside the boundary.

- Geotagging uses GPS to add geographical information to files (such as pictures) when posting them on social media sites.

- A third-party app store is something other than the primary store for a mobile device. Apple's App Store is the primary store for Apple devices. Google Play is a primary store for Android devices.

- Jailbreaking removes all software restrictions on Apple devices, and rooting provides users with root-level access to an Android device. Custom firmware can also root an Android device. MDM tools block network access for jailbroken or rooted devices.

- Sideloading is the process of copying an application to an Android device instead of installing it from an online store.

- Tethering allows one mobile device to share its Internet connection with other devices. Wi-Fi Direct allows you to connect devices together without a wireless router.

Exploring Embedded Systems

- An embedded system is any device that has a dedicated function and uses a computer system to perform that function. A security challenge with embedded systems is keeping them up to date.

- Internet of Things (IoT) devices interact with the physical world. They commonly have embedded systems and typically communicate via the Internet, Bluetooth, or other wireless technologies.

- A supervisory control and data acquisition (SCADA) system controls an industrial control system (ICS). The ICS is used in large facilities such as power plants or water treatment facilities.

- SCADA and ICS systems are typically in isolated networks without access to the Internet and are often protected by network intrusion prevention systems.

- A system on a chip (SoC) is an integrated circuit that includes a full computing system.

- A real-time operating system (RTOS) is an operating system that reacts to input within a specific time.

- The major constraints associated with embedded systems include computing limitations, cryptographic limitations, power limitations, ease of deployment, cost and the inability to patch/patch availability.

- Embedded systems include smart devices sometimes called the Internet of Things (IoT), such as wearable technology and home automation devices.

📌 *Online References*

Don't forget to check out the online content at **https://getcertifiedgetahead.com/**.

Chapter 5 Practice Questions

1. Attackers recently exploited vulnerabilities in a web server hosted by your organization. Management has tasked administrators with checking the server and eliminating any weak configurations on it. Which of the following will meet this goal?

    A. Installing a NIDS
    B. Disabling unnecessary services
    C. Enabling root accounts
    D. Implementing SSL encryption

2. The BizzFad organization develops and sells software. Occasionally they update the software to fix security vulnerabilities and/or add additional features. However, before releasing these updates to customers, they test them in different environments. Which of the following solutions provides the BEST method to test the updates?

    A. Baseline configuration
    B. BYOD
    C. Sandbox
    D. Change management

3. Network administrators have identified what appears to be malicious traffic coming from an internal computer, but only when no one is logged on to the computer. You suspect the system is infected with malware. It periodically runs an application that attempts to run hping3 via remote websites. After comparing the computer with a list of applications from the master image, they verify this application is likely the problem. What allowed them to make this determination?

   A. Version control
   B. Sandbox
   C. Block list
   D. Integrity measurements

4. While investigating a recent data breach, investigators discovered malware on Bart's computer. Antivirus software didn't detect it. Logs show a user with local administrator privileges installed it. Which of the following answers has the BEST chance of preventing this from happening again in the future?

   A. Enforce an application allow list.
   B. Enforce an application block list.
   C. Implement a BYOD policy.
   D. Implement a DLP system.

5. Salespeople within a company regularly take company-owned laptops with them on the road. The company wants to implement a solution to protect laptop drives against data theft. The solution should operate without user interaction for ease of use. Which of the following is the BEST choice to meet these needs?

   A. DLP
   B. HSM
   C. MDM
   D. SED

6. Managers within your organization want to implement a secure boot process for some key computers. During the boot process, each computer should send data to a remote system to check the computer's configuration. Which of the following will meet this goal?

   A. Trusted Platform Module
   B. Hardware root of trust
   C. Remote attestation
   D. Tokenization

7. Your organization recently updated its security policy to prohibit the use of external storage devices. The goal is to reduce threats from insiders. Which of the following methods would have the BEST chance of reducing the risk of data exfiltration using external storage devices?

    A. Train employees about the policy.
    B. Monitor firewall logs to detect data exfiltration.
    C. Block write capabilities to removable media.
    D. Implement a network-based DLP solution.

8. Maggie, the new CTO at your organization, wants to reduce costs by utilizing more cloud services. She has directed the use of a cloud service instead of purchasing all the hardware and software needed for an upcoming project. She also wants to ensure that the cloud provider maintains all the required hardware and software as a preconfigured environment where you can deploy your own code. Which of the following BEST describes the cloud computing service model that will meet these requirements?

    A. IaaS
    B. PaaS
    C. SaaS
    D. XaaS

9. You are asked to research prices for cloud-based services. The cloud service provider needs to supply servers, storage, and networks, but nothing else. Which of the following will BEST meet your needs?

    A. IaaS
    B. PaaS
    C. SaaS
    D. XaaS

10. Your organization has been using more cloud resources and Lisa, the CIO, is concerned about security. She wants to add a service that is logically placed between the organization's network and the cloud provider. This service will monitor all network traffic and ensure that data sent to the cloud for storage is encrypted. Which of the following will BEST meet these requirements?

    A. CASB
    B. Storage permissions
    C. A storage encryption policy
    D. Firewall

11. Management at your organization wants to add a cloud-based service to filter all traffic going to and from the Internet from internal clients. At a minimum, the solution should include URL filtering, DLP protection, and malware detection and filtering. Which of the following will BEST meets these requirements?

    A. Next-generation SWG
    B. Container security
    C. Cloud-based segmentation
    D. API inspection and integration

12. Your organization is planning to implement a BYOD policy. However, management wants to implement a comprehensive solution to protect the organization's data when the BYOD policy is put into place. Which of the following is the BEST choice to meet these needs?

    A. FDE
    B. SED
    C. MDM
    D. MAM

13. Your organization recently implemented a security policy requiring that all endpoint computing devices have a unique identifier to simplify asset inventories. Administrators implemented this on servers, desktop PCs, and laptops with an RFID system. However, they haven't found a reliable method to tag corporate-owned smartphones and tablet devices. Which of the following choices would be the BEST alternative?

    A. VDI
    B. MDM application
    C. RFID tag
    D. GPS tagging

14. Your organization is switching from a COPE model to a BYOD model due to the cost of replacing lost or damaged mobile devices. Which of the following is the BEST choice to protect the organization's data when using the BYOD model?

    A. Full-disk encryption
    B. Containerization
    C. Remote wipe
    D. Geolocation

15. Bart is showing Wendell a new app that he downloaded from a third party onto his iPhone. Wendell has the same model of smartphone, but when he searches for the app, he is unable to find it. Of the following choices, what is the MOST likely explanation for this?

    A.   Jailbreaking
    B.   Tethering
    C.   Sideloading
    D.   Rooting

Chapter 5
Practice Question Answers

1. **B** is correct. Unnecessary open ports and services are common elements that contribute to weak configurations so it's important to close ports that aren't needed and disable unnecessary services. A network-based intrusion detection system (NIDS) helps protect internal systems, but a NIDS would not be installed on the server and administrators are tasked with checking the server. Unsecured root accounts indicate a weak configuration. If root accounts are disabled, enabling them won't increase security on the server. Secure Sockets Layer (SSL) is a weak encryption protocol and should not be implemented on servers.

2. **C** is correct. A sandbox provides a simple method of testing updates. It provides an isolated environment and is often used for testing. A baseline configuration is a starting point of a computing environment. Bring your own device (BYOD) refers to allowing employee-owned mobile devices in a network and is not related to this question. Change management practices ensure changes are not applied until they are approved and documented.

3. **D** is correct. The master image is the baseline, and the administrators performed integrity measurements to identify baseline deviations. By comparing the list of applications in the baseline with the applications running on the suspect computer, it's possible to identify unauthorized applications. None of the other answers include the troubleshooting steps necessary to discover the problem. Version control tracks software versions as software is updated. A sandbox is an isolated area of a system, typically used to test applications. A block list is a list of prohibited applications.

4. **A** is correct. Enforcing an application allow list (sometimes called an application whitelist) would prevent this. An application allow list identifies the only applications that can be installed on a computer and would not include malware. An application block list identifies applications to block, but malware changes so often, this wouldn't help. A bring your

own device (BYOD) policy identifies mobile devices employees can buy and connect to a network but is unrelated to this question. A data loss prevention (DLP) system typically monitors outgoing traffic and wouldn't stop a user from installing a malicious application.

5. **D** is correct. Self-encrypting drives (SEDs) are the best solution. SEDs have encryption circuitry built into the drive. They encrypt and decrypt data without user interaction, though it's common to require personnel to use credentials to unlock the SED when booted. A data loss prevention (DLP) solution typically monitors outgoing traffic to prevent confidential information from getting outside the organization. A hardware security module (HSM) is used to manage, generate, and store cryptographic keys. It's generally used on a network instead of on laptops. Mobile device management (MDM) refers to technologies used to manage mobile devices.

6. **C** is correct. A remote attestation process checks a computer during the boot cycle and sends a report to a remote system. The remote system attests or confirms that the computer is secure. None of the other answers sends data to a remote system. A Trusted Platform Module (TPM) is a hardware chip on a motherboard and provides a local secure boot process. A TPM includes an encryption key burned into the hardware, which provides a hardware root of trust. Tokenization replaces sensitive data with a token or substitute value, and this token can be used in place of the original data.

7. **C** is correct. Blocking write capabilities to removable media is the best choice. This can be done with a data loss prevention (DLP) solution on all computers. Training employees might help, but it won't stop an insider threat. Monitoring firewall logs might detect data exfiltration out of the network, but it won't monitor the use of external storage devices. A network-based DLP solution might detect and stop data exfiltration out of the network, but it would stop users from copying data to removable media.

8. **B** is correct. Platform as a Service (PaaS) provides customers with a preconfigured computing platform including the hardware and software. The cloud provider maintains the hardware and specified software such as the operating system and key applications such as a web server application. Infrastructure as a Service (IaaS) is a cloud computing option where the vendor provides access to a computer, but customers must install the operating system and maintain the system. Software as a Service (SaaS) provides access to specific applications such as an email application. Anything as a Service (XaaS) refers to cloud services beyond IaaS, PaaS, and SaaS.

9. **A** is correct. An Infrastructure as a Service (IaaS) cloud model provides clients with hard-ware but nothing else. A Platform as a Service (PaaS) model provides customers with a computing platform including operating systems and some applications. A Software as a Service (SaaS) model provides customers with one or more applications. Anything as a Service (XaaS) refers to cloud services beyond IaaS, PaaS, and SaaS, but this scenario clearly describes an IaaS model.

10. **A** is correct. A cloud access security broker (CASB) is placed between a network and a cloud provider and would meet the chief information officer (CIO) requirements. It can monitor traffic and enforce security policies, such as ensuring all data sent to the cloud is encrypted. Permissions should be set on cloud storage locations to ensure only autho-rized personnel can access them, but they don't encrypt the data. A storage encryption policy can be created to require encryption of data stored in the cloud, but the policy wouldn't monitor all traffic to and from the cloud. A firewall can filter traffic, but it doesn't include all the capabilities of a CASB, such as verifying data is encrypted.

11. **A** is correct. A next-generation secure web gateway (SWG) provides proxy services for traffic from clients to Internet sites, such as filtering Uniform Resource Locators (URLs) and scanning for malware. Container security can be applied as a cloud security control to protect data by placing it in different containers with different permissions or encryp-tion controls. Segmentation within a network isolates hosts or networks, and cloud-based segmentation does the same thing, except the isolation occurs within the cloud. Applica-tion programming interface (API) inspection and integration refers to testing an API for usability, but this scenario is much too complex for an API.

12. **C** is correct. A mobile device management (MDM) solution is the best choice because it can manage multiple risks related to mobile devices in a bring your own device (BYOD) scenario. Full disk encryption (FDE) typically isn't feasible in a BYOD scenario because it requires an organization to encrypt devices owned by employees. Some FDE drives use self-encrypting drive (SED) technology, and they aren't feasible for the same reason FDE drives aren't feasible. Mobile application management (MAM) only manages applications on mobile devices, and it isn't a comprehensive solution.

13. **B** is correct. Mobile Device Management (MDM) applications can assign unique digital identifiers to endpoint devices such as smartphones and tablets. It uses this to manage the device remotely, and the identifier can also be used to simplify asset inventories. A virtual desktop infrastructure (VDI) provides a virtual desktop to users (including users with mo-bile devices), allowing them to connect to a server hosting the desktop. Radio-frequency

identification (RFID) tags are being used on other devices, but the scenario states it isn't a reliable method for smartphones and tablet devices. Global Positioning System (GPS) tagging adds geographical data to pictures to indicate where the photo was taken.

14. **B** is correct. Containerization is the best choice. Organizations can ensure that organizational data is encrypted in some containers without encrypting user data. In a bring your own device (BYOD) model, employees own the devices, and an organization typically can't encrypt user data with full-disk encryption. In a corporate-owned, personally enabled (COPE) model, the organization could use full-device encryption. Remote wipe sends a signal to a lost device to erase data, but it won't erase data if the device is damaged, and an attacker may be able to recover data from a damaged device. Geolocation technologies can help locate a lost device, but they won't protect data.

15. **A** is correct. Jailbreaking is the most likely reason for this. It's possible to jailbreak an iPhone to remove all software restrictions, including the ability to install applications from sources other than the Apple App Store. Tethering allows you to share an Internet connection with one mobile device to other mobile devices. Sideloading is the process of installing application packages from an Application Package Kit (APK) but sideloading isn't a relevant term in this context. Rooting is done to Android devices and provides users root-level access to the device.

Chapter 6

Comparing Threats, Vulnerabilities, and Common Attacks

CompTIA Security+ objectives covered in this chapter:

2.1 Compare and contrast common threat actors and motivations.

- Threat actors (Nation-state, Unskilled attacker, Hacktivist, Insider threat, Organized crime, Shadow IT)
- Attributes of attackers (Internal/external, Resources/funding, Level of sophistication/capability)
- Motivations (Data exfiltration, Espionage, Service disruption, Blackmail, Financial gain, Philosophical/political beliefs, Ethical, Revenge, Disruption/chaos, War)

2.2 Explain common threat vectors and attack surfaces.

- Message-based (Email, Short Message Service (SMS), Instant messaging (IM))
- Image-based
- File-based
- Voice call
- Removable device
- Vulnerable software (client-based vs. agentless)
- Unsupported systems and applications
- Unsecure networks (Wireless, Wired, Bluetooth)
- Open service ports
- Default credentials
- Supply chain (Managed service providers (MSPs), Vendors, Suppliers)
- Human vectors/social engineering (Phishing, Vishing, Smishing, Misinformation/disinformation, Impersonation, Business email compromise, Pretexting, Watering hole, Brand impersonation, Typosquatting)

2.4 Given a scenario, analyze indicators of malicious activity.

■   Malware attacks (Ransomware, Trojan, Worm, Spyware, Bloatware, Virus, Keylogger, Logic bomb, Rootkit)

■   Network attacks (Malicious code)

4.3 Explain various activities associated with vulnerability management.

■   Threat feed (Open-source intelligence (OSINT), Proprietary/third-party, Information-sharing organization, Dark web)

4.5 Given a scenario, modify enterprise capabilities to enhance security.

■   File integrity monitoring

Organizations need to understand many different types of threat actors, so it's valuable to know a little about them, their attributes, and the types of attacks they are likely to launch. Malicious software (malware) and social engineering are two common attack categories that any organization will face, but each category has some complexities. Attackers are becoming more and more sophisticated with these attacks, so it's important to know how to reduce attackers' success. This chapter covers these topics along with sources for additional threat intelligence.

Understanding Threat Actors

When considering attacks, it's important to realize that there are several types of threat actors, each with different attributes. Don't let the phrase threat actors confuse you. It's just a fancier name given to attackers—anyone who launches a cyberattack on others. The attackers are the actors, and they represent a threat to organizations and infrastructure.

Threat Actor Types

Some attackers are highly organized and dedicated. **Nation-state attackers** are attackers who are directly employed by or sponsored by a government. Their purpose is to advance that country's interests using hacking tools. These nation-state attackers are an example of an **advanced persistent threat (APT)**. An APT is a group of organized threat actors that engage in targeted attacks against organizations. These APTs typically have both the capability and intent to launch sophisticated and targeted attacks over a long period of time.

While APTs can be any group of highly organized attackers, they are typically sponsored by nation-states or governments. These state actors typically have specific targets, such as a certain company, organization, or government agency. Successful attacks often allow unauthorized access for long periods of time, giving the APTs the ability to exfiltrate a significant amount of data.

The governments that sponsor them provide them with a significant amount of resources and funding. Cybersecurity firms have written about APTs sponsored by several governments, including:

- **China.** Some reported names are PLA Unit 61398, Buckeye, and Double Dragon.
- **Iran.** Some reported names are Elfin Team, Helix Kitten, and Charming Kitten.
- **North Korea.** Some reported names are Ricochet Chollima and Lazarus Group.
- **Russia.** Some reported names are Fancy Bear, Cozy Bear, Voodoo Bear, and Venomous Bear.

These governments deny these reports. With so many governments reportedly sponsoring several APTs, it's clear that this is a threat that organizations need to take seriously.

Organized crime is composed of a group of individuals working together in criminal activities. These groups are typically organized within a hierarchy composed of a leader and workers, like a normal business. Depending on how large the criminal group is, it can have several layers of management. However, unlike a legitimate business, the enterprise is focused on criminal activity. The primary motivation of organized crime is money. Almost all their efforts can be traced back to greed with the goal of getting more money, regardless of how they get it.

For example, Crowdstrike, a cybersecurity technology company, documented a criminal syndicate known as Wizard Spider. Crowdstrike reported this is a Russia-based criminal group. Further, they discovered evidence that this group operated Ryuk, a well-known ransomware that targeted enterprise environments. Ransomware is discussed further later in this chapter.

> ### 📌 *Remember This!*
>
> An advanced persistent threat (APT) refers to an organized and sophisticated group of threat actors. Nation-states (governments) sponsor them and give them specific targets and goals. Organized crime groups are organized individuals involved in crime. Their primary motivation is money.

Years ago, a *hacker* was known as someone proficient with computers who wanted to share knowledge with others. However, the definition has morphed over the years. Today, the media commonly refers to hackers as malicious individuals who use their technical expertise to launch attacks and break into systems or networks for personal gain.

An *unskilled attacker* uses existing computer scripts or code to launch attacks. These unskilled attackers (also known as script kiddies) typically have very little expertise or sophistication and very little funding. Many people joke about the bored teenager as the script kiddie, attacking sites or organizations for fun. However, there isn't any age limit for these attackers. More importantly, they can still obtain powerful scripts and launch dangerous attacks. Their motivations vary, but they are typically launching attacks out of boredom or to see what they can do.

A *hacktivist* launches attacks as part of an activist movement or to further a cause. Hacktivists typically aren't launching these attacks for their benefit but instead to increase awareness about a cause. For example, The Yes Men, an activist group that tries to raise awareness of social and political issues, launches disinformation campaigns against organizations.

In January 2019, The Yes Men created a fake website that looked like BlackRock, a large financial asset manager that owned the largest number of fossil fuel companies at the time. They then released a fake letter from BlackRock's CEO Larry Fink indicating that BlackRock required any company it invests in to align its business model with the Paris Agreement to combat climate change. Many media outlets were fooled and reported the letter as legitimate. While the hoax was quickly revealed, it did raise awareness.

An ***insider threat*** is anyone with legitimate access to an organization's internal resources. Common security issues caused by insider threats include loss of confidentiality, integrity, and availability of the organization's assets. The extent of the threat depends on how much access the insider has. For example, an administrator would have access to many more IT systems than a regular user.

Malicious insiders have a diverse set of motivations. For example, some malicious insiders are driven by greed and simply want to enhance their finances, while others want to exact revenge on the organization. They may steal files that include valuable data, install, or run malicious scripts, or redirect funds to their personal accounts. Chapter 5, "Securing Hosts and Data," covers data loss prevention (DLP) techniques and some DLP solutions that can prevent users from writing data to external media devices.

All insider threats aren't malicious. An uneducated user could open a malicious attachment in an email and unwittingly release malware throughout the organization.

A ***competitor*** is any organization engaged in economic or commercial competition with another organization. Their motivation is typically to gain proprietary information about another company. Although it's legal to gather information using open source intelligence, greed sometimes causes competitors to cross the line into illegal activity. This can be as simple as rummaging through a competitor's trash bin, known as dumpster diving. In some cases, competitors hire employees from other companies and then get these new employees to provide proprietary information about their previous employer.

> ### ✦ Remember This!
>
> An unskilled attacker uses existing computer scripts or code to launch attacks. These unskilled attackers typically have very little expertise, sophistication, and funding. A hacktivist launches attacks as part of an activist movement or to further a cause. An insider is anyone with legitimate access to an organization's internal resources, such as an employee of a company. DLP solutions can prevent users from writing data to external media devices.

Attacker Attributes

In the previous section, you discovered that there are many different kinds of attackers out there. You learned about nation-state attackers, unskilled attackers, hacktivists, organized crime, and the insider threat. We also started to discuss how these attackers differ. Let's look at three major attributes that distinguish different types of attackers:

- **Internal vs. external** – Most of the attackers we think of come from outside of our organizations. Nation-states, hacktivists, organized crime syndicates, and even most unskilled attackers are external forces that threaten to do us harm. The insider threat, however, comes from an internal source and often has privileged access that can make them especially dangerous.

- **Resources/funding** – Different types of attackers have different levels of resources and funding available to them. For example, an unskilled attacker may be a hobbyist who spends some of their free time on hacking but doesn't really dedicate significant time or money to their work. A nation-state attacker, on the other hand, might have large amounts of money and entire teams dedicated to carrying out their work.

- **Level of sophistication/capability** – Along with varying levels of resources, different attackers have different levels of skill and different tools available to them. An unskilled attacker might simply download whatever hacking tools are available on the Internet, while a nation-state might develop extremely sophisticated cyberweapons that aren't available to anyone else.

> **★ Remember This!**
>
> Different types of attackers have different attributes. The major differences are whether an attacker comes from an internal or external source, the resources and funding available to the attacker and the attacker's level of sophistication and capability.

Threat Actor Motivations

Just as threat actors differ in their attributes, they also differ in their motivations – the reasons that they are engaging in their attacks. Let's look at some of the most common threat actor motivations:

- **Data exfiltration** – This is just a fancy term meaning that some attackers are trying to steal information. Exfiltration simply means moving data outside of an area where it is allowed to a place where it is not allowed. Many attackers are motivated to steal sensitive information.

- **Disruption/chaos** – Other attackers want to cause disruption and chaos. They might be trying to make their mark on the world or advance another motivation, but they do this by disrupting the lives and activities of people and businesses.

- **Financial gain** – Many attackers are motivated by the prospect of financial gain. They may engage in activities such as stealing credit card information, committing fraud, or demanding ransom payments in exchange for restoring access to compromised systems or data.

- **Blackmail** – Some attackers aim to acquire sensitive or embarrassing information about individuals or organizations in order to extort money or force them to comply with certain demands. This type of motivation often involves threats of releasing the information to the public if the victim does not comply.

- **Service disruption** – Attackers targeting the availability of systems often try to disrupt the operation of services. For example, a hacktivist trying to stop a political group from spreading their agenda might try to take down that group's website.

- **Philosophical/political beliefs** – Some attackers are driven by their ideological convictions or political beliefs. These individuals or groups may target organizations, governments, or entities that they perceive as opposed to their values, aiming to promote their cause or spread their message.

- **Ethical** – A smaller subset of attackers, known as **ethical hackers** (sometimes called white-hat hackers), engage in hacking activities to identify and report security vulnerabilities. Their motivation is to help improve the security of the systems they test, rather than exploit them for personal gain.

- **Revenge** – In some cases, attackers may seek to exact revenge on an individual, organization, or government that they feel has wronged them. This motivation could involve personal grudges or grievances, leading to targeted cyberattacks to cause harm or damage to the intended victim.

- **Espionage** – Cyber espionage is often carried out by nation-states or other well-funded groups seeking to gain a strategic advantage by stealing sensitive information, intellectual property, or trade secrets from rival organizations or countries.

- **War** – Cyber warfare is a growing concern in the modern world, with nation-states using cyberattacks as a means to disrupt, damage, or destroy critical infrastructure, systems, or networks of their adversaries. These attacks can be considered an extension of traditional warfare, as they serve to advance national objectives or weaken opponents.

📌 *Remember This!*

You need to know the common threat actor motivations when you take the Security+ exam. The motivations listed by CompTIA include data exfiltration, service disruption, blackmail, financial gain, philosophical/political beliefs, ethical hacking, revenge, espionage, and war.

Threat Vectors and Attack Surfaces

Threat vectors are the paths that attackers use to gain access to computers and networks. When successful, these vectors allow attackers to exploit vulnerabilities. Organizations often may think that they aren't a logical attack target. However, it's become increasingly clear that attackers often try to infiltrate lower-level targets to gain access to high-value targets.

Some of the threat vectors discussed in this chapter are:

- **Message-based** – Attackers frequently send out spam with malicious links or attachments. It's estimated that as much as 91 percent of all attacks start with an email. This includes phishing, spear phishing, and whaling attacks, presented later in this chapter.
- **Image-based** – Attackers may use image-based attack vectors by embedding malicious code within image files or using steganography to hide data within an image. When the image is downloaded or viewed, the code is executed, potentially compromising the victim's system.
- **File-based** – File-based attack vectors involve malicious code hidden in seemingly innocuous files, such as documents or spreadsheets. When users open these files, they may inadvertently execute the hidden code, allowing attackers to exploit vulnerabilities or gain unauthorized access.
- **Voice call** – Voice call attack vectors include phone-based social engineering attacks, where attackers impersonate trusted individuals or organizations to manipulate victims into revealing sensitive information or granting access to secure systems.
- **Removable device** – Attackers can exploit removable devices, like USB drives or external hard drives, by loading them with malware. When unsuspecting users plug these devices into their computers, the malware can be automatically executed, compromising the user's system.
- **Software based** – Attackers might target vulnerabilities in software applications, either through client-based attacks (exploiting software installed on users' devices) or agentless attacks (directly targeting web applications or services). Unsupported applications, which no longer receive security updates, are especially vulnerable.
- **System-based** – System-based attack vectors target vulnerabilities in computer systems, such as unsupported operating systems, vulnerable applications, hardware issues, open service ports, or default credentials. These weaknesses can provide an entry point for attackers to gain unauthorized access and control of the system.
- **Network-based** – Network-based attack vectors focus on exploiting weaknesses in network infrastructure, whether through unsecured wired or wireless networks or vulnerable Bluetooth connections. Attackers may eavesdrop on network traffic, intercept sensitive data, or gain access to connected devices.
- **Supply-chain** – Supply-chain attack vectors target the relationships between organizations and their managed service providers (MSPs), vendors, or suppliers. By compromising

a trusted third party, attackers can infiltrate the target organization's systems or networks, bypassing security measures in place.

Chapter 4, "Securing Your Network," discusses direct access virtual private networks (VPNs) as potential threat vectors. Chapter 5, "Securing Hosts and Data," discusses wireless, removable media, and cloud resources as potential threat vectors. Chapter 8, "Using Risk Management Tools," discusses the supply chain as a potential threat vector.

An organization's **attack surface** consists of all of the threat vectors that it is exposed to – all of the ways that an attacker might come after them. One of the key responsibilities of security professionals is to reduce the attack surface. For example, if an organization has an old, unused web server sitting on their network, that server might provide an attacker with a pathway to enter the organization's network. The server isn't needed for any legitimate purpose, so cybersecurity professionals should remove it, which reduces the organization's attack surface.

> ### ✦ *Remember This!*
>
> Attackers use many different threat vectors to gain access to an organization. So far, we've discussed message-based, image-based, and file-based attack vectors as well as voice calls, removable devices, vulnerable software, unsecure networks, open service ports, default credentials, and the supply chain. Later in this chapter, we'll discuss human vectors and social engineering attacks.

Shadow IT

Shadow information technology (IT) refers to any unauthorized systems or applications within an organization, including cloud services. Most organizations have specific processes in place to approve new systems and applications. However, users sometimes install systems without approval, often to bypass security controls. Shadow IT increases risks because these systems aren't always well-managed.

The IT department will normally manage all systems and applications under its control. This includes things like keeping them up to date and maintaining backups. However, if these systems and applications are hidden from the IT department, they won't be managed and will be susceptible to emerging vulnerabilities.

Determining Malware Types

Malware (malicious software) includes a wide range of software that has malicious intent. Malware is not software that you would knowingly purchase or download and install. Instead, it is installed onto your system through devious means. Infected systems give various symptoms, such as running slower, starting unknown processes, sending out email without user action, rebooting randomly, and more.

You might hear people use the term virus to describe all types of malware, but that isn't accurate. A virus is a specific type of malware, and malware includes many other types of malicious software, including worms, logic bombs, Trojans, ransomware, rootkits, spyware, and more.

Different types of malware have different indicators. By recognizing these indicators, you have a better chance of determining the type of attack.

Viruses

A *virus* is malicious code that attaches itself to a host application. The host application must be executed to run, and the malicious code executes when the host application is executed. The virus tries to replicate by finding other host applications to infect with the malicious code. At some point, the virus activates and delivers its payload.

Typically, the payload of a virus is damaging. It may delete files, cause random reboots, join the computer to a botnet, or enable backdoors that attackers can use to access systems remotely. Most viruses won't cause damage immediately. Instead, they give the virus time to replicate first. A user will often execute the virus (though unknowingly), but other times, an operating system will automatically execute it after user interaction. For example, when a user plugs in an infected USB drive, the system might automatically execute the virus, infecting the system.

Worms

A *worm* refers to self-replicating malware that travels throughout a network without the assistance of a host application or user interaction. A worm resides in memory and can travel over the network using different transport protocols.

One of the significant problems caused by worms is that they consume network bandwidth. Worms can replicate themselves hundreds of times and spread to all the systems in the network. Each infected system tries to locate and infect other systems on the network, and network performance can slow to a crawl.

Logic Bombs

A **logic bomb** is a string of code embedded into an application or script that will execute in response to an event. The event might be a specific date, time, or user action, such as when a user launches a specific program. There's an often-repeated story about a company that decided it had to lay off an engineer due to an economic downturn. His bosses didn't see him doing much, so they thought they could do without him. Within a couple of weeks, after he left, they started having all sorts of computer problems they just couldn't resolve. They called him back, and everything was fine after a couple of weeks. A few months later, they determined they had to lay him off again. You guessed it. Within a couple of weeks, things went haywire again.

The engineer had programmed a logic bomb that was executed when the payroll program ran. It checked for his name on the payroll, and when it was there, things were fine, but when his name wasn't there, kaboom—the logic bomb exploded.

> ★ **Remember This!**
>
> A logic bomb executes in response to an event, such as when a specific application is executed, or a specific time arrives.

Trojans

A **Trojan**, also called a Trojan horse, typically looks like something beneficial, but it's actually something malicious. Trojan horses are named after the infamous horse from the Trojan War. In Greek mythology, the Achaeans tried to sack the city of Troy for several years but simply couldn't penetrate the city's defenses. At some point, Odysseus got the idea of building a huge wooden horse and convincing the people of Troy that it was a gift of peace. Warriors hid inside, and the horse was rolled up to the gates.

The people of Troy partied all day and all night, celebrating their good fortune, but when the city slept, the warriors climbed down from inside the horse and opened the gates. The rest of the warriors flooded in. What the Greek warriors couldn't do for years, the Trojan horse helped them do in a single night.

In computers, a Trojan horse can come as pirated software, a useful utility, a game, or something else that users might be enticed to download and try. Attackers have often used drive-by downloads to deliver Trojans and exploits. In a drive-by download, web servers include malicious code that attempts to download and install itself on user computers after the user visits. Here are the typical steps involved in a drive-by download:

- Attackers compromise a website to gain control of it.
- Attackers install a Trojan or run an exploit embedded in the website's code.
- Attackers attempt to trick users into visiting the site. Sometimes, they simply send the link to thousands of users via email, hoping that some of them click the link.
- When users visit, the website attempts to download the Trojan or exploit onto the users' systems.

Another Trojan method that attackers have used is scareware: software that masquerades as a free antivirus program. When a user visits a site, they see a message on the webpage, or a pop-up appears indicating it detected malware on the user's system. The user is encouraged to download and install free antivirus software.

On the surface, this free antivirus software looks useful. However, it isn't. If a user installs and runs it on a system, it appears to do a system scan. After the scan completes, it reports finding multiple issues, such as infections by dozens of viruses. The report isn't true. The application reports these issues even on a freshly installed operating system with zero infections.

It then encourages the user to resolve these issues immediately. If the user tries to resolve the issues, the program informs the user that this is only the trial version and the trial version won't resolve these issues. However, for a fee, such as $79.95, users can unlock the full version to remove the threats. Some scareware installs additional malicious components. For example, they might install a backdoor allowing the attacker to control the infected system remotely.

Many web browser extensions have also included malicious Trojans. Cisco's Duo Security has released CRXcavator, a free automated tool used to assess risks posed by Chrome, Firefox, and Edge browser extensions.

Jamila Kaya, an independent security researcher, used CRXcavator to identify numerous Chrome extensions that initially appeared legitimate but were exhibiting suspicious behavior, exfiltrating data. Google followed up, searching the entire Chrome Web Store, and eventually removed more than 500 Chrome extensions from the store in early 2020.

Further research showed that a single threat actor created most of these extensions during at least the previous two years. Much of the malicious code was very similar and, in some cases, identical. It's suspected that millions of computers had been infected.

> ### ★ *Remember This!*
>
> A Trojan appears to be something useful but includes a malicious component, such as installing a backdoor on a user's system. Many Trojans are delivered via drive-by downloads. They can also infect systems with fake antivirus software, pirated software, games, and browser extensions.

Remote Access Trojan

A *remote access Trojan (RAT)* is a type of malware that allows attackers to control systems from remote locations. It is often delivered via drive-by downloads or malicious attachments in email. Once installed on a system, attackers can then access the infected computer at any time and install additional malware if desired.

Some RATs automatically collect and log keystrokes, usernames and passwords, incoming and outgoing email, chat sessions, browser history, and take screenshots. The RAT can then automatically send the data to the attackers at predetermined times.

Additionally, attackers can explore the network using the credentials of the user or the user's computer. Attackers often do this to discover, and exploit, additional vulnerabilities within the network. It's common for attackers to exploit this one infected system and quickly infect the entire network with additional malware, including installing RATs on other systems.

Keyloggers

Keyloggers attempt to capture a user's keystrokes. The keystrokes are stored in a file and either sent to an attacker immediately or saved until the attacker retrieves the file. While a keylogger is typically software, it can also be hardware. For example, you can purchase a USB keylogger, plug it into the computer, and plug the keyboard into the USB keylogger. This hardware keylogger will record all keystrokes and store them within memory on the USB device.

One of the ways keyloggers can be thwarted is by using two-factor authentication (2FA), such as a text message sent to a phone, as discussed in Chapter 2, "Understanding Identity and Access Management." Even if the attackers capture a password via a keylogger, they won't have access to the text message sent to the phone.

Figure 6.1: Hardware keylogger

Spyware

Spyware is software installed on users' systems without their awareness or consent. Its purpose is often to monitor the user's computer and the user's activity. Spyware takes some level of control over the user's computer to learn information and sends this information to a third party. If spyware can access a user's private data, it results in a loss of confidentiality.

Some examples of spyware activity are changing a user's home page, redirecting web browsers, and installing additional software within the browser. In some situations, these changes can slow a system down, resulting in poor performance. These examples are rather harmless compared to what more malicious spyware (privacy-invasive software) might do.

Privacy-invasive software tries to separate users from their money using data-harvesting techniques. It attempts to gather information to impersonate users, empty bank accounts, and steal identities. For example, some spyware includes keyloggers. The spyware periodically reads the data stored by the keylogger and sends it to the attacker. In some instances, the spyware allows the attacker to take control of the user's system remotely.

Spyware is often included with other software like a Trojan. The user installs one application but unknowingly gets some extras. Spyware can also infect a system in a drive-by download. The user simply visits a malicious website that includes code to automatically download and install the spyware onto the user's system.

> ### ★ Remember This!
>
> Keyloggers capture a user's keystrokes and store them in a file. This file can be automatically sent to an attacker or manually retrieved depending on the keylogger. Spyware monitors a user's computer and often includes a keylogger

Rootkit

A **rootkit** is a program or group of programs that gains administrative access on a system to provide the attacker with administrative privileges and/or hide the fact that the system has been infected or compromised by malicious code. A user might suspect something is wrong, but antivirus scans and other checks might indicate everything is fine because the rootkit hides its running processes to avoid detection.

In addition to modifying the internal operating system processes, rootkits often modify system files such as the Registry. In some cases, the rootkit modifies system access, such as removing users' administrative access.

Rootkits have system-level access to the operating system. This is sometimes called root-level access, or kernel-level access, indicating that they have the same level of access as the operating system. Some rootkits use hooked processes, or hooking techniques, to intercept calls to the operating system. Hooking refers to intercepting system-level function calls, events, or messages in this context. The rootkit installs the hooks into memory and uses them to control the system's behavior.

Antivirus software often calls the operating system to detect malware, but the rootkit prevents the antivirus software from making these calls. This is why antivirus software will sometimes report that everything is OK, even if the system is infected with a rootkit. However, antivirus software can often detect the hooked processes by examining the system's random-access memory (RAM) contents.

Another method used to detect rootkits is to boot into safe mode or have the system scanned before it boots, but this isn't always successful. It's important to remember that rootkits are very difficult to detect because they can hide so much of their activity. A clean bill of health by a malware scanner may not be valid.

It's important to remember that behind any type of malware, you'll likely find an attacker involved in criminal activity. Attackers who have successfully installed a rootkit on a user's system might log on to the user's computer remotely, using a backdoor installed by the rootkit. Similarly, attackers might direct the computer to connect to computers on the Internet and send data. Data can include anything collected from a keylogger, collected passwords, or specific files or file types stored on the user's computer.

> ### ✦ *Remember This!*
>
> Rootkits have system-level or kernel access and can modify system files and system access. Rootkits hide their running processes to avoid detection with hooking and similar techniques. Tools that can inspect RAM can discover these hidden hooked processes.

Ransomware

Ransomware is a type of malicious code that allows the attacker to take control of a computer and data, locking out users. This often happens through the use of encryption, where the attacker encrypts all of the data stored on a system using an encryption key known only to the attacker.

The attacker then demands that the user or organization pay a ransom to regain access to the data or computers. If the ransom is paid, attackers promise to provide the decryption key. If the ransom isn't paid, attackers typically threaten to destroy the key removing access to the data forever.

Criminals often deliver ransomware via drive-by downloads or embedded in other software delivered via email. Attackers originally focused their attacks on individuals demanding payments of about $300 each. However, they have increasingly been targeting organizations demanding larger and larger payoffs.

> ### 📌 Remember This!
>
> Ransomware is a type of malware that takes control of a user's system or data. Criminals then attempt to extort payment from the victim. Ransomware often includes threats of damaging a user's system or data if the victim does not pay the ransom, and attackers increasingly target hospitals, cities, and other larger organizations.

With the massive amounts of revenue these attacks are bringing to criminals, it's logical to think they will continue. The Federal Bureau of Investigation (FBI) and other legal entities discourage the paying of any ransoms. However, some organizations see paying a ransom as cheaper than suffering an outage while trying to re-create their data.

Unfortunately, some organizations haven't received a usable decryption key even after paying the ransom. Worse, the attackers have sometimes demanded additional money after receiving the first ransom. The attackers are criminals, after all.

> ### 📌 Remember This!
>
> Malware includes a wide variety of malicious code, including viruses, worms, Trojans, ransomware, and more. A virus is malicious code that attaches itself to an application and runs when the application is started. A worm is self-replicating and doesn't need user interaction to run.

Bloatware

Bloatware describes programs a user may not want, even if they consented to downloading them. Some of these unwanted programs are legitimate, but some are malicious, such as Trojans. The extras have often been called spyware, adware, junkware, or crapware.

For example, if you download and install 7-Zip, a popular compression tool, from a site other than 7-zip.org, the installer may include bloatware. Some bloatware objects are browser hijackers. They change the user's browser settings without the user's clear consent. They may change the home page, the default search engine, add additional toolbars, open additional tabs when the browser is opened, and inject advertising. Some browser hijackers gather user data and behavior (such as search terms used in search queries) and use it to display unwanted advertisements and other paid links that generate revenue for the author of the browser hijacker.

Often the fine print in the Terms of Use page, presented in the installation program, will explain this. However, it's buried so deep and obfuscated with legalese that most people miss it. They simply click Agree and continue with the install. Worse, some bloatware presents multiple pages of terms and conditions, requiring users to either read them all, or cancel the installation of everything, including the software they wanted.

Potential Indicators of a Malware Attack

There are many indicators of malware attacks. Some generic indicators are:

- **Extra traffic.** Malware typically adds a lot of extra traffic to a network. Abnormal traffic can be identified by comparing it with a baseline of known regular traffic.
- **Data exfiltration.** Data exfiltration refers to the unauthorized transfer of data out of a network. Malware often attempts to download data, such as databases of credentials, to locations controlled by the attacker. Data loss prevention (DLP) techniques can often detect this data as it is being downloaded.
- **Encrypted traffic.** Some malware will encrypt the data before data exfiltration attempts. This can bypass typical DLP techniques because a DLP system can't read the encrypted data. However, a large amount of encrypted data can indicate data exfiltration, even if the data can't be identified.
- **Traffic to specific IPs.** Bot zombies will often attempt to connect to known command and control servers. However, firewalls can blacklist traffic going to the servers when the IPs are known. Attempts to access blacklisted IPs are a strong indicator that a system is compromised. Security teams should monitor firewall logs for this traffic.
- **Outgoing spam.** Desktop computers don't normally send large amounts of email. When they do, it's often because they have been added to a botnet and are sending phishing emails as zombies.

Recognizing Common Attacks

In addition to malware, it's important to understand some other common attacks. Social engineering includes several techniques attackers use to trick users. Additionally, many attackers use email, instant messaging, and the phone to deliver attacks.

Social Engineering and Human Vectors

Human vectors may also be the source of cybersecurity risks. Chief among these, is **social engineering**: the practice of using social tactics to gain information. Social engineering is often low-tech and encourages individuals to do something they wouldn't normally do or cause them to reveal some piece of information, such as user credentials. Some of the individual methods and techniques include:

- Using flattery and conning
- Assuming a position of authority
- Encouraging someone to perform a risky action
- Encouraging someone to reveal sensitive information
- Impersonating someone, such as an authorized technician
- Tailgating or closely following authorized personnel without providing credentials

In the movie *Catch Me If You Can*, Leonardo DiCaprio played Frank Abagnale Jr., an effective con artist. He learned some deep secrets about different professions by conning and flattering people into telling him. He combined all he learned to impersonate pilots and doctors and perform sophisticated forgery.

Social engineers con people in person, as Frank Abagnale Jr. did, and they also use other methods. They may use the phone, send email with phishing tactics, and even use some trickery on websites, such as fooling someone into installing malware.

> 📌 **Remember This!**
>
> Social engineering uses social tactics to trick users into giving up information or performing actions they wouldn't normally take. Social engineering attacks can occur in person, over the phone, while surfing the Internet, and via email.

Consider this scenario as an example of a social engineer using the phone. Bart is busy working and receives a call from Hacker Herman, who identifies himself as a member of the IT department.

Hacker Herman: "Hi, Bart. I just wanted to remind you that we'll be taking your computer down for the upgrade today, and it'll be down for a few hours."

Bart: "Wait. I didn't hear anything about this. I need my computer to finish a project today."

Hacker Herman: "You should have gotten the email. I'm sorry, but I must update the last few computers today."

Bart: "Isn't there any other way? I really need my computer."

Hacker Herman: "Well...it is possible to upgrade it over the network while you're still working. We don't normally do it that way because we need the user's password to do it."

Bart: "If I can still work on my computer, please do it that way."

Hacker Herman: "OK, Bart. Don't tell anyone I'm doing this for you, but if you give me your username and password, I'll do this over the network."

This is certainly a realistic scenario, and many end users will give out their passwords unless security-related awareness and training programs consistently repeat the mantra: "Never give out your password."

Attackers aren't always so blatant, though. Instead of asking you for your password outright, they often ask questions they can use in a password reset system to reset your password. Skilled con artists can ask these questions as though they are genuinely interested in you. Before you know it, you've revealed the name of your first dog, your childhood best friend, the name of your first boss, and more. When people post this information on social media, attackers don't even need to bother con artistry. The following sections describe many common security issues related to social engineering.

> 📌 *Remember This!*
>
> A social engineer can gain unauthorized information just by looking over someone's shoulder. This might be in person, such as when a user is at a computer or remotely using a camera. Screen filters help prevent shoulder surfing by obscuring people's view unless they are directly in front of the monitor.

Impersonation

Some social engineers often attempt to impersonate others. The goal is to convince an authorized user to provide some information or help the attacker defeat a security control.

As an example, an attacker can impersonate a repair technician to gain access to a server room or telecommunications closet. After gaining access, the attacker can install hardware such as a rogue access point, to capture data and send it wirelessly to an outside collection point. Similarly, attackers impersonate legitimate organizations over the phone and try to gain information. Identity verification methods are useful in preventing the success of impersonation attacks.

Shoulder Surfing

Shoulder surfing is simply looking over the shoulder of someone to gain information. The goal is to gain unauthorized information by casual observation, and it's likely to occur within an office environment. This can be to learn credentials, such as a username and password, or a PIN used for a smart card or debit card. Attackers sometimes use cameras to monitor locations where users enter PINs, such as at automatic teller machines (ATMs). A simple way to prevent shoulder surfing is to position monitors and other types of screens so that unauthorized personnel cannot see them. This includes ensuring people can't view them by looking through a window or from reception areas. Another method to reduce shoulder surfing is using a screen filter placed over the monitor. This restricts the visibility of the screen for anyone who isn't looking directly at the monitor.

Disinformation

Attackers may use *disinformation* to carry out their social engineering attacks. Disinformation occurs when an attacker provides false information to their target in order to influence them to take some action or disclose some information.

Hoaxes are an example of a disinformation attack. A hoax is a message, often circulated through email, which tells of impending doom from a virus or other security threat that simply doesn't exist. Users may be encouraged to delete files or change their system configuration.

Serious virus hoaxes have the potential to be as damaging as a real virus. If users are convinced to delete important files, they may make their systems unusable. Additionally, they waste help-desk personnel's time due to needless calls about the hoax or support calls if users damage their systems in response to the hoax.

I recently received several hoax messages telling me that an attacker had infected my system and taken compromising videos of me with my computer's webcam. The attacker then threatened to release them unless I paid a fee. The most compromising thing I've done in front of my computer is fall asleep. However, my webcam is either disconnected or covered on all my computers, so the attacker didn't have any videos of me catching 40 winks. Still, the emails continued and became increasingly threatening. Someone who hadn't covered their webcam might indeed believe the hoax and pay.

Tailgating and Access Control Vestibules

Tailgating is the practice of one person following closely behind another without showing credentials. For example, if Homer uses a badge to gain access to a secure building and Francesca follows closely behind Homer without using a badge, Francesca is tailgating.

Employees often do this as a matter of convenience and courtesy. Instead of shutting the door on the person following closely behind, they often hold the door open for the person, known as piggybacking. However, this bypasses the access control, and if employees tailgate or piggyback, it's easy for a non-employee to slip in behind someone else.

An access control vestibule (sometimes called a mantrap) prevents tailgating. It is a room, or even a building, with two doors that creates a large buffer between secure and unsecured areas. Access through the entry and exit doors is tightly controlled, either with guards or with an access card such as a proximity card. Security guards can check each person's credentials as a matter of protocol.

A simple turnstile, like those used in subways or bus stations, also prevents tailgating. Imagine two adults trying to go through a turnstile like this together. It's just not likely.

Dumpster Diving

Dumpster diving is the practice of searching through trash or recycling containers to gain information from discarded documents. Many organizations either shred or burn paper instead of throwing it away.

For example, old copies of company directories can be valuable to attackers. They may identify the names, phone numbers, and titles of key people within the organization. Attackers may be able to use this information in a whaling attack against executives or social engineering attacks against anyone in the organization. An attacker can exploit any document containing detailed employee or customer information, often finding value in seemingly useless printouts and notes.

On a personal basis, credit card companies' preapproved credit applications or blank checks can be quite valuable to someone attempting to gain money or steal identities. Documentation with any Personally Identifiable Information (PII) or Protected Health Information (PHI) should be shredded or burned.

> ### ✦ *Remember This!*
>
> Tailgating is a social engineering tactic that occurs when one user follows closely behind another user without using credentials. Access control vestibules (sometimes called mantraps) allow only a single person to pass at a time. Sophisticated mantraps can identify and authenticate individuals before allowing access. Dumpster divers search through trash looking for information. Shredding or burning papers instead of throwing them away mitigates this threat.

Watering Hole Attacks

A **watering hole attack** attempts to discover which websites a group of people are likely to visit and then infects those websites with malware that can infect the visitors. The attacker's goal is to infect a website that users trust already, making them more likely to download infected files.

Think of a lion looking for prey. It is much easier to hide by a watering hole and wait for the prey to come than for the lion to chase the prey. Similarly, attackers can use a variety of techniques to infiltrate a network or lay a trap and wait for the prey to come to them. In this analogy, the websites that users visit are watering holes.

For example, imagine that attackers want to infiltrate the Springfield Nuclear Power Plant. The Power Plant has strong cybersecurity, and the attackers have been unsuccessful so far. However, the attackers learn that employees frequently visit the Capital City Capitals baseball team website, which has limited security. The attackers install malware on the baseball team's website, and when Power Plant employees visit it, the site attempts to download malware on the employees' systems.

Watering hole attacks often infect websites with zero-day vulnerabilities giving them a better chance of infecting the ultimate target. Advanced persistent threats have used this as a method of infiltrating high-profile targets.

Business Email Compromise

Business email compromise (BEC) is a type of targeted attack that seeks to exploit the trust and authority of high-level executives or other key personnel within an organization. Attackers use tactics such as phishing, social engineering, and email spoofing to impersonate an executive or other authority figure, often the CEO or CFO, and request sensitive information or authorize fraudulent financial transactions. These attacks can be highly convincing, as the attackers often research the company and its employees to craft realistic-sounding messages, sometimes even mimicking the writing style of the person they are impersonating.

In a typical BEC scenario, an attacker might send an email to an employee in the finance department, requesting an urgent wire transfer or modification of bank account details for an invoice payment. The unsuspecting employee, believing the request to be legitimate, may comply without verifying the authenticity of the email, resulting in significant financial losses for the organization. In other cases, a BEC attack might involve tricking an employee into divulging confidential information, such as employee tax records or sensitive client data.

To mitigate the risks associated with BEC attacks, organizations should implement strong email security measures, provide employee training on how to recognize and respond to suspicious emails, and establish clear procedures for verifying and authorizing sensitive requests. Additionally, multi-factor authentication and other access controls can help protect against unauthorized access to email accounts, further reducing the likelihood of a successful BEC attack.

Typosquatting

Typosquatting occurs when someone buys a domain name that is similar in name to a legitimate domain name. People often do so for malicious purposes. As an example, CompTIA hosts the comptia.org website. If an attacker purchases the name comptai.org with a slight misspelling at the end of comptia, some users might inadvertently go to the attacker's website instead of the legitimate website. Attackers might buy a similar domain for a variety of reasons, including:

- **Hosting a malicious website**. The malicious website might try to install drive-by malware on users' systems when they visit.
- **Earning ad revenue**. The attacker can host pay-per-click ads. When visitors go to the site and click on the ads, advertisers pay revenue to the attacker.
- **Reselling the domain**. Attackers can buy domain names relatively cheap, but resell them to the original site owner for a hefty profit.

Brand Impersonation

Brand impersonation is a type of cyber attack where attackers pose as a well-known and trusted company or brand to deceive their targets. This can involve using the company's logo, design elements, and even email addresses to create a false sense of legitimacy. The primary goal of brand impersonation is to manipulate the target, typically by tricking them into providing sensitive information, clicking on malicious links, or performing fraudulent transactions. These attacks often exploit the trust that people have in established brands, making it more likely that the target will fall for the deception.

In a typical brand impersonation scenario, an attacker might create a fake website or email that closely resembles a popular online retailer, bank, or technology company. This counterfeit site or email may prompt the user to provide their login credentials, credit card information, or other personal details under the guise of verifying their account or completing a purchase. Once the user submits the information, the attacker can use it to carry out identity theft, financial fraud, or other malicious activities.

One common example of brand impersonation is a phishing email that appears to be from a well-known technology company, like Apple or Microsoft, claiming that the user's account has been compromised or needs to be updated. The email may contain a link to a fake login page, designed to harvest the user's credentials. Another example could be a fake customer support message from a major bank, asking the user to verify their account details or transfer funds to a different account for security purposes.

Eliciting Information

Elicitation is the act of getting information without asking for it directly. Social engineers often use casual conversation to gather information without giving targets any idea that the attacker is trying to gather information. They often start by trying to gain trust and build rapport with a target through flattery or by encouraging the target to brag about their accomplishments. Next, social engineers use a variety of techniques to gather information, such as:

- **Active listening.** People are often busy and preoccupied with mobile devices, and they sometimes don't give their full attention when someone is speaking. However, when an attacker gives his full attention to a target, the target is encouraged to keep talking.
- **Reflective questioning.** Reflective questioning demonstrates active listening and encourages a target to talk more. It simply repeats a statement as a question. For example, a target may state that a security system blocked an outgoing email. The attacker may reply with, "You couldn't even send the email."
- **False statements.** The attacker gives a false statement hoping that the target corrects him. For example, the attacker might say, "I've heard that employees aren't able to visit any non-government websites. They can't go to Amazon or Facebook. They can even get disciplined for certain Google searches."
- **Bracketing.** Attackers often try to get specific information by stating a specific number or a range of numbers. For example, the attacker may say, "I heard they have a dozen cameras in the lobby alone," or "I hear they have between 10 and 20 motion detectors activated in the lobby after hours." If the target knows the specific number, he may reveal it to brag about what he knows or correct the attacker.

It's important to realize that this section provides a few techniques used to elicit information, but there are many more. Salespeople are often trained to use similar techniques to develop rapport and gain the information they can use to close the sale. Spy agencies and legal professionals undergo in-depth training on eliciting information. Penetration testers also use elicitation techniques along with other social engineering techniques.

Pretexting

Pretexting is a form of social engineering in which an attacker makes up a convincing story or scenario to manipulate a target into providing sensitive information or granting access to restricted systems or areas. The key to successful pretexting lies in the attacker's ability to create a believable story, often by impersonating a trusted individual, such as an employee, a vendor, or a customer. By doing this, the attacker exploits the target's trust and willingness to help, ultimately persuading them to disclose information or perform actions they would not typically do.

In a pretexting attack, the attacker usually conducts thorough research on the target organization or individual, gathering information that can be used to support their story. This research may involve studying the target's social media profiles, online presence, or even dumpster diving for discarded documents containing valuable data. The more detailed and accurate the information, the more convincing the pretext, making it more likely that the target will comply with the attacker's requests.

A common example of pretexting is an attacker posing as an IT support technician who contacts an employee claiming that there is an issue with their computer or account that requires immediate attention. The attacker may request the employee's login credentials or other sensitive information to "resolve" the issue. Alternatively, the attacker might impersonate a vendor or contractor and request access to a secure area, such as a data center or server room, to perform "maintenance" or "upgrades."

To defend against pretexting attacks, organizations should have comprehensive security awareness programs that educate employees about the risks and tactics associated with social engineering. Employees should be encouraged to verify the identity of any individual requesting sensitive information or access to restricted areas, using established and secure communication channels. Additionally, implementing strict policies and procedures for handling sensitive information and access requests can help minimize the potential impact of pretexting attacks on an organization.

Message-Based Attacks

Attackers have been using email to launch attacks for years. One of the primary reasons is because they've been so successful. Many people don't understand how dangerous a simple email can be for the entire organization. Without understanding the danger, they often click a link within a malicious email, which gives attackers access to an entire network. Email attacks include spam, phishing, smishing, vishing, spear phishing, and whaling.

Spam

Spam is unwanted or unsolicited email. While a lot of technologies have reduced spam, it still exists. Some spam is harmless advertisements, while much more is malicious and can include malicious links, malicious code, or malicious attachments. Even when it's not malicious, when it's almost half of all the email you receive, it can waste a lot of your time.

In some cases, legitimate companies encourage users to opt in if they want to receive email about their products. When users opt in to a mailing list, they agree to the terms. On the surface, you'd think that this means that you agree to receive email from the company, and that's true. However, terms often include agreeing to allow their partners to send you email, which means the original company can share your email address with others.

Legitimate companies don't send you malicious spam, but they might send you more email than you want. Laws require them to include the ability to opt-out, indicating you don't want to receive any more emails from them. Once you opt-out, you shouldn't receive any more emails from that company.

Criminals use a variety of methods to collect email addresses. They buy lists from other criminals, harvest them from websites, and some malware scans address books of infected computers to collect email. Because they are criminals, they don't care about laws, but they might include opt-out instructions in the spam they send. However, instead of using this to remove you from their email list, attackers use this as confirmation that your email address is valid. The result is more spam.

Spam over Instant Messaging

Spam over instant messaging (SPIM) is unwanted messages sent over instant messaging (IM) channels. IM is a technology that allows people to communicate in real-time or chat with each other by sending and receiving short text messages.

The original Short Message Service (SMS) was limited to only 160 text characters. However, advanced texting apps support attachments that can easily be malware. Some scammers have sent SPIM with malicious links.

Mobile devices such as phones and tablets have default texting apps installed. Other messaging apps include Facebook Messenger, WhatsApp, and Snapchat. While spam is sent to email addresses, SPIM can be sent to you via your username or your telephone number. A challenge is that SPIM bypasses typical antivirus and spam filters. During the COVID-19 pandemic, two scam types were quite popular among criminals. In one, the text informs recipients that they have been in contact with someone who has tested positive for COVID-19 and encourages them to take further action. The text includes a malicious link. It may allow attackers access to the user's mobile device if clicked.

In another scam, recipients receive a message related to the U.S. stimulus payments for U.S. citizens. Scammers claimed they could get the money for a fee, but fees were never required. Some scammers attempted to get personal information such as Social Security and bank account numbers and then used the information for identity theft and fraud.

Phishing

Phishing is the practice of sending email to users with the purpose of tricking them into revealing personal information or clicking on a link. A phishing attack often sends the user to a malicious website that appears to the user as a legitimate site. Other times, it includes a malicious attachment and encourages the user to open it.

The classic example is where a user receives an email that looks like it came from eBay, PayPal, a bank, or some other well-known company. The "phisher" doesn't know if the recipient has an account at the company, just as an angler doesn't always know if any fish are in the water when casting a line. However, if the attacker sends out enough emails, the odds are good that someone who receives the email has an account and will be fooled. The email may look like this:

"We have noticed suspicious activity on your account. We will suspend your account to protect your privacy unless you log in and validate your credentials. Click here to validate your account and prevent it from being locked out."

The email often includes the same graphics that you would find on the vendor's website or an actual email from the vendor. Although it might look genuine, it isn't. Legitimate companies do not ask you to revalidate your credentials via email. If you go directly to the actual site, you might be asked to provide additional information to prove your identity beyond your credentials, but legitimate companies don't send emails asking you to follow a link and input your credentials to validate them.

> 📌 *Remember This!*
>
> Spam is unwanted email. Phishing is malicious spam. Attackers attempt to trick users into revealing sensitive or personal information or clicking on a link. Links within email can also lead unsuspecting users to install malware.

Beware of Email from Friends

Criminals have become adept at impersonating your friends. They scan social media sites and identify your friends and family. They then send emails to you that look like they are from your friends or family members, but they really aren't. This has become a common security issue related to social media.

As an example, imagine you are friends with Lisa Simpson and her email address is lisa@simpsons.com. You might receive an email that includes "Lisa Simpson" in the From block. However, if you look closely at the actual email address, you'd find it is something different, such as homer@hacker.com. The underlying email address might belong to someone, but the forgery doesn't mean that they sent the email. To identify the actual sender, you often need to look at the full header of the email address.

I see emails such as this quite often. They seem to be related to comments or "likes" that I've made on social media. For example, after "liking" a Facebook post on Lisa Simpson's Facebook page, I later receive an email with Lisa Simpson in the From block and a forged email address. These emails typically include a single line such as "I thought you might like this" and a malicious link. Clicking the link often takes the user to a server that attempts a drive-by download. It might include a cat or a baby video, but this is just to distract you while the malicious code is being downloaded.

Another possible scenario is that an attacker has joined your friend's computer to a botnet. A bot herder is now using your friend's computer to send out phishing emails.

Phishing to Install Malware

One phishing email looked like it was from a news organization with headlines of recent news events. If the user clicked anywhere in the email, it showed a dialog box indicating that the user's version of Adobe Flash was too old to view the story. It then asked, "Would you like to upgrade your version of Adobe Flash?" If the user clicked Yes, it downloaded and installed malware. The "upgrade" fake has been used successfully over the years and continues to be used today.

Another email had the subject line "We have hijacked your baby" and the following content:

"You must pay once to us $50,000. The details we will send later. We have attached photo of your family."

The English seems off, and the receiver might not even have a baby, making this look bogus right away. However, the attackers are only trying to pique your curiosity. The attached file isn't a photo. Instead, it's malware. If a user clicks on the photo to look at it, it may show a photo, but it also installs malware on the user's system.

Phishing to Validate Email Addresses

A simple method used to validate email addresses is the use of beacons. A beacon is a link included in the email that links to an image stored on an Internet server. The link includes a unique code that identifies the receiver's email address.

For the email application to display the image, it must retrieve the image from the Internet server. When the server hosting the image receives the request, it marks the user's email address indicating it's valid. This is one of the reasons that most email programs won't display images by default.

Phishing to Get Money

The classic Nigerian scam (also called a 419 scam) continues to thrive. You receive an email from someone claiming a relative or acquaintance has millions of dollars. Unfortunately, the sender can't get the money without your help. The email says that you'll get a substantial portion of the money for your troubles if you help retrieve the money.

This scam often requires the victim to pay a small sum of money with the promise of a large sum of money. However, the large sum never appears. Instead, the attackers come up with reasons why they need just a little more money. In many cases, the scammers request access to your bank account to deposit your share, but instead they use it to empty your bank account.

There are countless variations on this scam. Lottery scams inform email recipients they won. Victims sometimes pay small fees to release the funds or provide bank information to get the money deposited. They soon learn there is no prize, but instead they've lost all their savings.

Spear Phishing

Spear phishing is a targeted form of phishing. Instead of sending the email out to everyone indiscriminately, a spear phishing attack attempts to target specific groups of users or even a single user. Spear phishing attacks may target employees within a company or customers of a company.

For example, an attacker might try to impersonate the CEO of an organization in an email. It's relatively simple to change the header of an email so that the From field includes anything, including the CEO's name and title. Attackers can send an email to all employees requesting that they reply with their password. Because the email looks like it's coming from the CEO, these types of phishing emails fool uneducated users.

One solution that deters the success of these types of spear phishing attacks is to use digital signatures. The CEO and anyone else in the company can sign their emails with a digital signature. This gives personnel a high level of certainty on who sent the email. Chapter 10, "Understanding Cryptography and PKI," covers digital signatures in great depth.

Whaling

Whaling is a form of spear phishing that attempts to target high-level executives. Las Vegas casinos refer to the big spenders as whales, and casino managers are willing to spend extra time and effort to bring them into their casinos. Similarly, attackers consider high-level executives the whales, and attackers are willing to put in some extra effort to catch a whale because the payoff can be so great. When successful, attackers gain confidential company information that they might not be able to get anywhere else.

Some whaling attacks target senior executives of organizations. Other whaling attacks impersonate these senior executives and send malicious emails to high-level employees. One attacker sent an email to the HR department of Seagate, making it look like the email came from the company's CEO. The email asked for W-2 tax forms and other Personally Identifiable Information. The HR department released details of almost 10,000 employees.

A similar attack occurred within Snapchat. The payroll team received an email that looked like it was the Snapchat CEO and requested payroll data. The payroll team complied, and the information was soon leaked on the Internet.

Similar whaling attacks have masqueraded as complaints from the Better Business Bureau or the Justice Department. Executives are sensitive to issues that may affect the company's profit and reputation, and these complaints get their attention. Although not as common, some whaling attacks attempt to reach the executive via phone to get the data. However, many executives have assistants who screen calls to prevent attackers from reaching the executive via phone.

> ### ✦ *Remember This!*
>
> A spear phishing attack targets specific groups of users. It could target employees within a company or customers of a company. Digital signatures provide assurances to recipients about who sent an email and can reduce the success of spear phishing. Whaling targets high-level executives or impersonates high-level executives.

Vishing

Vishing attacks use the phone system to trick users into giving up personal and financial information. Vishing often uses Voice over IP (VoIP) technology allowing the attacker to spoof caller ID, making it appear as though the call came from a real company.

In one form of the attack, a machine leaves a phone message saying that you need to return the call concerning one of your credit cards. In another form, you receive an email with the same information. If you call, you'll hear an automated recording giving some vague excuse about a policy and prompting you to verify your identity. One by one, the recording prompts you for more information, such as your name, birthday, Social Security number, credit card number, expiration date, and so on. Sometimes, the recording asks for usernames and passwords. The recording indicates they have verified your account if you give all the requested information. In reality, you just gave up valuable information about yourself.

Another example of vishing is just a regular phone call from a criminal. A popular ploy is a call from a company claiming to be "Credit Services" and offering to give you lower credit card rates. They play around with caller ID and have it display anything they want. A common ploy is to display a number with the same area code as yours, making them appear local. They often announce, "This is your second and final notice," trying to evoke a sense of urgency.

If you answer, the automated system forwards you to a live person who begins asking a series of "qualifying" questions, such as how much credit card debt you have and your interest rates. They then promise that they can help you lower your debt and get you a better rate. Next, they start asking some personal questions. They might ask for the last four digits of your Social Security number so they can "verify your account is in good standing." They might ask you for the code on your credit card "to verify you still have it."

Eventually, they hope to get your credit card number, expiration date, and code so that they can use it to post fraudulent charges. Some people have reported similar callers trying to get their bank information so that they can transfer money out of their accounts.

They hang up right away if you ask them to take you off their list or stop calling. Similarly, they hang up when they hear words such as criminal, thief, and other words I'll leave out of this book. Some even reply with insults. They've called me so often that I've played along a few times. I love it when they ask for information on my credit card. I respond by saying, "Can you hold on so I can get it?" I then put the phone in a drawer and go back to work. Once, they stayed on the line for more than three hours waiting for me.

Smishing

Smishing (a mashup of SMS and phishing) is a form of phishing that uses text instead of email. Some smishing texts include malicious attachments, and some try to trick the user into giving up personal information.

As an example, one smishing attack sent users a text claiming to be from Google security. It reported suspicious activity on the user's Google account and said that Google would be sending a verification code. It then encouraged the user to reply to the text with the verification code and threatened to permanently lock the user's account if the user didn't reply. Google did not send this. An attacker sent it instead. Shortly after sending the text, the attacker went to the Google login page, entered the user's email address, and clicked the Forgot password link. He then clicked through to send a verification code to the user's phone. If the user sends this code to the attacker, it allows the attacker to change the password for the account and log in as the user.

The same method can be used with any organization where a user has implemented 2FA (two-factor authentication). If the user replies with the verification code, the attacker can hijack the user's account. The attacker can quickly empty the victim's account if it is a financial organization.

> 📌 **Remember This!**
>
> Vishing is a form of phishing that uses the phone system or VoIP. Some vishing attempts are fully automated. Others start as automated calls, but an attacker takes over at some point during the call. Smishing is a form of phishing using text messages.

One Click Lets Them In

It's worth stressing that it only takes one click by an uneducated user to give an attacker almost unlimited access to an organization's network. Consider Figure 6.2. It outlines the process APTs have used to launch attacks. Note that the attacker can be located anywhere in the world and only needs access to the Internet. The attacker controls resources within the Internet, such as servers owned and operated by the attackers. They might be in the same country as the attacker, or they might be in another country. In some cases, attackers use servers owned by others but controlled by the attackers, such as servers in a botnet or compromised servers.

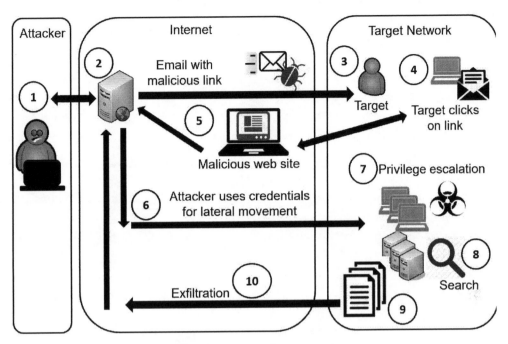

Figure 6.2: Steps in an attack

The target is within an internal network of a targeted organization. Refer to Figure 6.2 as you read the following steps in an attack:

- The attacker uses publicly available intelligence to identify a target. Some typical sources are social media sites and news outlets. Other times, attackers use social engineering tactics via phone calls and emails to get information on the organization or individuals employed by the organization.

- Next, the attacker crafts a spear phishing email with a malicious link. The email might include links to malware hosted on another site and encourage the user to click the link. In many cases, this link can activate a drive-by download that installs itself on the user's computer without the user's knowledge. This download can be any kind of malware, including ransomware. Other attacks use credential harvesting techniques encouraging users to click a link and enter their usernames and passwords on bogus sites that look real. While not shown in the figure, the attacker could include an attachment and encourage the recipient to open it instead of using a malicious link.

- The attacker sends the spear phishing email to the target from an Internet-based system. This email includes a malicious link and uses words designed to trick the user into clicking it.

- If the user clicks on the link, it takes the user to a website that looks legitimate. This website might attempt a drive-by download or mimic a legitimate website and encourage the user to enter a username and password.

- If the malicious link tricked the user into entering credentials, the website sends the information back to the attacker. Suppose the malicious link installed malware on the user's system, such as a RAT. In that case, the attacker uses it to collect information on the user's computer (including the user's credentials, once discovered) and sends it back to the attacker.

- The attacker uses the credentials to access the targeted system. It then uses the targeted system for lateral movement. In other words, it uses the targeted system and the targeted user credentials to access other systems within the network. Windows Management Instrumentation (WMI) and PowerShell are frequently used to scan the network.

- The original target may have limited access within the network. However, attackers use privilege escalation techniques to gain more permissions within the network and access more resources, such as servers holding sensitive data. The attacker uses these elevated permissions to install malware on other systems, along with creating new backdoor accounts within the network.

- Malware searches for data within the network, such as emails and files on computers and servers.

- The malware gathers all data of interest and typically divides it into encrypted chunks.

- These encrypted chunks are exfiltrated from the network and back to the attacker.

The time it takes for an attacker to begin lateral movement within a network after the initial infection is typically less than two hours. At that point, the attacker can begin data exfiltration. In a ransomware attack, the malware can begin encrypting data as soon as it locates it within the network. However, some ransomware attempts to locate important data, such as online backups, before it begins encryption.

Blocking Malware and Other Attacks

The previous sections described several different methods attackers and criminals use to launch new attacks. Malware is a significant threat for any organization. Administrators commonly implement layered security, or a defense-in-depth plan, to protect against malware. The following bullets list some common security controls used to protect against malware:

- **Spam filter on mail gateways**. Phishing attacks are delivered as malicious spam. Spam filters on email servers detect and filter spam before it ever gets to users. Some networks route email through another device first to filter out spam. If users never receive a malicious email, there isn't any chance of them clicking on a malicious link in that email.

- **Anti-malware software on mail gateways**. Malicious email often includes malware as attachments. Anti-malware software on the mail server can detect and block it. The software strips potentially malicious attachments off the email, and typically sends a notification to the user explaining what was removed and why.

- **All systems**. All workstations and servers have anti-malware software installed. Servers may have additional, specialized anti-malware software installed depending on the applications running on the servers.

- **Boundaries or firewalls**. Many networks include detection tools that monitor network traffic through the firewall. For example, unified threat management (UTM) inspects network traffic to reduce the risk of malware entering the network. Chapter 3, "Exploring Network Technologies and Tools," covers UTM systems.

Spam Filters

Organizations often implement a multipronged approach to block spam. For example, many UTM systems include spam filters to detect and block spam. The output of the UTM goes to an email server. Email servers also have methods of detecting and blocking spam. The email server sends all email to the users, except for what it detects as spam. User systems also have anti-spam filters, or junk mail options, as a final check.

The challenge with any *spam filter* is to filter out spam only and never filter out legitimate email. For example, a company wouldn't want a spam filter to filter out an email from a customer trying to buy something. Because of this, most spam filters err on the side of caution, allowing spam through rather than potentially marking valid email as spam. Although the science behind spam filtering continues to improve, criminals have also continued to adapt.

Spam filters typically allow you to identify email addresses as safe or to be blocked. You can add these as individual addresses or entire domains. For example, if you want to ensure you get an email from Homer when he sends an email from springfield.com, you can identify homer@springfield.com as a safe email address. If you want to ensure you get all emails from springfield.com, you can designate springfield.com as a safe domain. Similarly, you can block either the single email address homer@springfield.com or the entire domain springfield.com.

Antivirus and Anti-Malware Software

Anti-malware software protects against many types of malware. You'll often hear the term antivirus software indicating it only protects against viruses. However, the lines have blurred. Viruses aren't the only threats. Attackers have changed their methodologies using different types of malware, and antivirus software vendors have adapted by including methods to detect and block these new threats. Most antivirus software detects, blocks, and removes several types of malware, such as viruses, Trojans, worms, rootkits, spyware, and adware. Antivirus software provides real-time protection and can perform both scheduled and manual scans. The real-time protection continuously monitors the system. For example, when a user visits a website, antivirus software scans the downloaded website files and attempts to block malicious code.

Similarly, when a user downloads or opens a file, antivirus software scans it before opening it. Scheduled scans occur regularly, such as once a week. If users or technicians detect suspicious activity, they can perform manual scans to check the system.

If the antivirus software detects malware, it will typically quarantine it and notify the user. However, the exact way antivirus software does so varies from one vendor to another. The key to analyzing and interpreting the antivirus software's output is to recognize the alert and read it. Some people just click OK without paying attention to alerts and can inadvertently override the antivirus software.

Antivirus software detects viruses using either signature-based detection or heuristic-based detection.

 Remember This!

Antivirus software detects and removes malware, such as viruses, Trojans, and worms. Signature-based antivirus software detects known malware based on signature definitions. Heuristic-based antivirus software detects previously unknown malware based on behavior.

Signature-Based Detection

Viruses and other malware have known patterns. Signature files (also called data definition files) define the patterns, and the antivirus software scans files for matching patterns. When the software identifies a matching pattern, it reports it as an infection and takes action, such as deleting or quarantining the file.

A quarantined virus is not harmful to the system while it is in quarantine, but it's still available for analysis. As an example, a security professional could release a quarantined virus into an unprotected but isolated virtual machine environment for research and study.

Malware developers regularly release new viruses, so it's essential to update signature definition files regularly. Most antivirus software includes the ability to automate the process of checking and downloading updated signature definition files. They typically check for updates several times a day.

It's also possible to download and install signature files manually. Administrators do this when updating systems that do not have Internet access. When doing so, administrators need to ensure the signature file has not lost data integrity by comparing the hash of the signature file posted on the antivirus vendor's website with the hash of the downloaded file.

Heuristic-Based Detection

Some antivirus software includes heuristic-based detection. Heuristic-based detection attempts to detect viruses that were previously unknown and do not have signatures. This includes zero-day exploits mentioned earlier in this chapter.

Heuristic-based analysis runs questionable code in a sandbox or virtualized environment specifically designed to protect the live environment while observing the code's behavior. Most viruses engage in malicious or suspicious activities that you won't see in legitimate programs. The heuristic-based analysis detects these activities. As an example, polymorphic malware adds variations to files when it creates copies. It's highly unusual for any application to add variations in files like this, and heuristic methods are often successful at detecting polymorphic malware.

File Integrity Monitors

Some antivirus scanners use *file integrity monitors* to detect modified system files. A file integrity checker calculates hashes on system files as a baseline. It then periodically recalculates the hashes on these files and compares them with the hashes in the baseline. If the hashes are ever different, it indicates the system files have been modified. When an antivirus scanner detects a modified file, it sends an alert. Many times, these alerts can detect rootkit infections.

Why Social Engineering Works

Social engineers typically use one or more psychology-based principles to increase the effectiveness of their attacks. By teaching users about the different social engineering tactics and these underlying principles, it reduces the chances that they'll be tricked. The following sections introduce these topics.

Authority

Many people were raised to respect authority and are more likely to comply when a person of authority says to do so. As an example, volunteers participating in the Milgram Experiment continued to send shocks to unseen subjects even though they could hear them scream in pain simply because a man in a lab coat told them to continue. They weren't actually sending shocks, and the screams were fake, but everything seemed real to the volunteers. Psychologists have repeated these experiments and have seen similar results. Using authority is most effective with impersonation, whaling, and vishing attacks:

- **Impersonation**. Some social engineers impersonate others to get people to do something. For example, many have called users on the phone claiming they work for Microsoft, the IRS, or some other government agency. Other times, social engineers attempt to impersonate a person of authority, such as an executive within a company or a technician.
- **Whaling**. Executives respect authorities such as legal entities. Many whaling attacks send malicious files as email attachments and identify them as lawsuits or subpoenas, and encourage the executives to open them.
- **Vishing**. Some attackers use the phone to impersonate authority figures.

Intimidation

In some cases, the attacker attempts to intimidate the victim into acting. Intimidation might be through bullying tactics, and it is often combined with impersonating someone else. Using intimidation is most effective with impersonation and vishing attacks.

For example, a social engineer might call an executive's receptionist with this request: "Mr. Simpson is about to give a huge presentation to potential customers, but his files are corrupt. He told me to call you and get you to send the files to me immediately so that I can get him set up for his talk." If the receptionist declines, the social engineer can use intimidation tactics by saying something like: "Look, if you want to be responsible for this million-dollar sale falling through, that's fine. I'll tell him you don't want to help."

Note that this tactic can use multiple principles at the same time. In this example, the attacker is combining intimidation with urgency. The receptionist doesn't have much time to respond.

Consensus

People are often more willing to like something that other people like. Some attackers take advantage of this by creating websites with fake testimonials that promote a product. For example, criminals have set up multiple websites with dozens of testimonials listing all the benefits of their fake antivirus software. If users search the Internet before downloading the fake antivirus software, they will come across these websites and believe that other real people are vouching for the product.

Using consensus, sometimes called social proof, is most effective with Trojans and hoaxes. Victims are more likely to install a Trojan if everyone seems to indicate it's safe. Similarly, if a person suspects a virus notice is just a hoax, but everyone seems to be saying it's real, the victim is more likely to be tricked.

Scarcity

People are often encouraged to act when they think there is a limited quantity of an item. As an example of scarcity, think of Apple iPhones. When Apple first releases a new version, they typically sell out quickly. A phishing email can take advantage of this and encourage users to click a link for exclusive access to a new product. If the users click, they'll end up at a malicious website. Scarcity is often effective with phishing and Trojan attacks. People make quick decisions without thinking them through.

Urgency

Some attacks use urgency as a technique to encourage people to act. As an example, ransomware uses the scarcity principle with a countdown timer and the countdown timer provides a sense of urgency. Victims typically have 72 hours to pay up before they lose all their data. Each time they look at their computer, they'll see the timer counting down.

Using urgency is most effective with ransomware, phishing, vishing, and whaling. For example, phishing emails with malicious links might indicate that there are a limited number of products at a certain price, so the user should "Click Now." Similarly, executives might be tricked into thinking a subpoena requires immediate action.

> ### ★ Remember This!
>
> Many of the reasons that social engineers are effective are because they use psychology-based techniques to overcome users' objections. These techniques include representing themselves as authority figures, using intimidation, faking scarcity, creating a sense of urgency, establishing familiarity, and creating a sense of trust.

Familiarity

If you like someone, you are more likely to do what the person asks. This is why so many big companies hire well-liked celebrities. It's also why they fire them when the celebrity becomes embroiled in a scandal that affects their credibility.

Some social engineers attempt to build rapport with the victim to build a relationship before launching the attack. This principle is most effective with shoulder surfing and tailgating attacks:

- **Shoulder surfing**. People are more likely to accept someone looking over their shoulder when they are familiar with the other person, or they like them. In contrast, if you don't know or don't like someone, you are more likely to recognize a shoulder surfing attack and stop it immediately.
- **Tailgating**. People are much more likely to allow someone to tailgate behind them if they know the person or like the person. Some social engineers use a simple, disarming smile to get the other person to like them.

Trust

In addition to familiarity, some social engineers attempt to build a trusting relationship between them and the victim. This often takes a little time, but the reward for the criminal can be worth it. Vishing attacks often use this method.

As an example, someone identifying himself as a security expert once called me. He said he was working for some company with "Secure" in its name, and they noticed that my computer was sending out errors. He stressed a couple of times that they deploy and support Windows systems. The company name and their experience was an attempt to start building trust.

He then guided me through the process of opening Event Viewer and viewing some errors on my system. He asked me to describe what I saw and eventually said, "Oh my God!" with the voice of a well-seasoned actor. He explained that this indicated my computer was seriously infected. However, I knew that the errors were trivial.

After seriously explaining how much trouble I was in with my computer, he then added a smile to his voice and said, "But this is your lucky day. I'm going to help you." He offered to guide me through the process of fixing my computer before the malware damaged it permanently.

All of this was to build trust. At this point, he went in for the kill. He had me open the Run window and type in a website address, and asked me to click OK. This is where I stopped. I didn't click OK.

I tried to get him to answer some questions, but he was evasive. Eventually, I heard a click. My "lucky day" experience with this social engineering criminal was over.

The link probably would have taken me to a malicious website ready with a drive-by download. Possibly the attacker was going to guide me through the process of installing malware on my system. If my system objected with an error, I'm betting he would have been ready with a soothing voice saying" That's normal. Just click OK. Trust me." He spent a lot of time with me. I suspect that they've been quite successful with this ruse with many other people.

Threat Intelligence Sources

One common method that attackers often use before launching an attack is to gather information from **open-source intelligence (OSINT)**. Penetration testers (discussed in more detail in Chapter 8) also use OSINT methods to gather information on targets. This includes any information that is available to the general public, such as via websites and social media. For example, if attackers want to get the name of the chief executive officer (CEO) of a company, they can probably find it on the company's website. Similarly, many organizations post information on social media sites such as Facebook and Twitter.

In contrast, **closed/proprietary intelligence** refers to trade secrets such as intellectual property. An organization tries to keep these private, but attackers sometimes infiltrate an organization to steal these trade secrets. Some common types of OSINT are:

- **Vulnerability databases**. Vulnerability databases document known vulnerabilities and many public databases help automate vulnerability management. Two examples are the National Vulnerability Database (NVD), maintained by the National Institute of Standards and Technology (NIST) , and the Common Vulnerabilities and Exposures (CVE) list maintained by the MITRE Corporation.

- **Trusted Automated eXchange of Intelligence Information (TAXII).** TAXII is an open standard that defines a set of services and message exchanges used to share information. It provides a standard way for organizations to exchange cyber threat information, but it does not specify what information organizations should exchange.

- **Structured Threat Information eXpression (STIX).** STIX is an open standard that identifies what cyber threat information organizations should share. It provides a common language for addressing a wide range of cyber threat information. STIX data is shared via TAXII.

- **Automated Indicator Sharing (AIS).** The Cybersecurity and Infrastructure Security Agency (CISA) maintains the Automated Indicator Sharing site (https://www.cisa.gov/ais) used for the real-time exchange of threat indicators and defensive measures. AIS uses both TAXII and STIX.

- **Dark web**. The dark web is an area of the Internet that you won't find using a search engine. Criminals and attackers maintain sites on the dark web (sometimes called darknets), but users need specific software or authentication to access them. Criminals often store and sell hacking tools, access to botnets, pirated materials, and more on the dark web. Some dark websites provide up-to-date information on known vulnerabilities. Vulnerabilities are sometimes posted on the dark web before it makes it to vulnerability databases such as the NVD or CVE.

- **Public/private information sharing organizations**. Many public and private organizations are also involved in sharing information on cyber threats. For example, InfraGard is a nonprofit organization that shares information between the Federal Bureau of Investigation (FBI) and members in specific sectors.

- **Indicators of compromise.** Indicators of compromise (IoC) are evidence that a cyberattack is happening or has happened. Obvious IoCs are confirmed alerts from antivirus software or other devices that have detected malware or other potential attacks. Often, an IoC isn't as obvious but alerts indicate what cybersecurity professionals should look for. As an example, CISA released a Malware Analysis Report (AR21-048A) on "AppleJeus: Celas Trade Pro." IoCs included in the report included the URL where users could download the malware, the name of specific files included in the malware, and more. Cybersecurity professionals can use this data to search proxy logs to see if users accessed the URL and then search systems for the specific files.

- **Predictive analysis**. Predictive analysis techniques attempt to predict what attackers will do next and how to thwart their attacks. While cybersecurity professionals are getting better every day at predicting and stopping attacks, it's worth noting that this requires them to predict the future. This may be easy if you have a DeLorean time machine allowing you to travel back to the future at will. Without the DeLorean though, predictive analysis remains challenging.

- **Threat maps**. Threat maps provide a visual representation of active threats. They typically show a replay of recent attacks rather than real-time data. Additionally, the data is anonymized so you don't know who is being attacked, but you can see the location within countries. Redlegg (https://www.redlegg.com/blog/cyber-threat-maps) has a listing and description of many threat maps maintained by other organizations.

- **File/code repositories**. Many repositories include prewritten code that developers can use for a variety of purposes, including gathering intelligence. As an example, GitHub offers distributed version control and source code management for software projects. This allows multiple developers to work together on the same project collaboratively. Some GitHub projects are file repositories. For example, the Awesome Threat Intelligence repository (`https://github.com/hslatman/awesome-threat-intelligence`) provides a curated listing of threat intelligence resources.

Research Sources

There's an almost endless list of additional sources that cybersecurity personnel can reference when researching threats. Chapter 8 discusses some in the context of threat hunting. The following bullets introduce additional resources:

- **Vendor websites.** Vendor websites are a good source for reliable information on a vendor's products. This is especially true related to any vulnerabilities and patches used to fix them.

- **Conferences.** Many organizations host conferences dedicated to sharing cybersecurity information. These typically last three to five days, include several knowledgeable speakers, and include various training tracks allowing attendees to pick what workshops they want to attend.

- **Local industry groups.** A local industry group is any group of people or organizations that work in the same industry and decide to collaborate to share information. This is similar to people joining a networking group to build their contacts.

- **Public/private information sharing centers.** Many public and private organizations are also involved in sharing information on cyber threats. For example, InfraGard is a non-profit organization that shares information between the Federal Bureau of Investigation (FBI) and members in specific sectors.

- **Academic journals.** Cybersecurity professionals often publish scholarly articles in academic journals. These are often used to document research on a technical topic, and it's common for peers to review the articles prior to publication. This gives them added credibility.

- **Request for comments (RFC).** The Internet Engineering Task Force (IETF) publishes documents called RFCs for a variety of purposes. Many are Internet standards, and they are the authoritative source of knowledge for technical specifications. As an example, RFC 6749 describes how authorization tokens are created and exchanged on the Internet. As long as websites follow the specifications in RFC 6749, they can exchange authorization tokens relatively easily.

- **Social media.** Some people exchange data via social media groups, which can be useful. This allows people to communicate with their peers about potential threats. However, it's important to realize that social media groups aren't authoritative, so it's a good idea to verify information shared in social media groups before acting on it.

Chapter 6 Exam Topic Review

When preparing for the exam, make sure you understand these key concepts covered in this chapter.

Understanding Threat Actors

- Nation-state attackers are attackers who are directly employed by or sponsored by a government. Their purpose is to advance that country's interests using hacking tools.
- Unskilled attackers use existing computer scripts or code to launch attacks. They typically have very little expertise or sophistication and very little funding.
- A hacktivist launches attacks as part of an activist movement or to further a cause.
- Insiders (such as employees of a company) have legitimate access to an organization's internal resources. They sometimes become malicious insiders out of greed or revenge. DLP solutions can prevent users from writing data to external media devices.
- Organized crime is an enterprise that employs a group of individuals working together in criminal activities. Their primary motivation is money.
- Shadow IT refers to unauthorized systems or applications used in an organization without authorization or approval.
- Threat actors vary in their attributes. They may be internal or external to the target organization and they have differing levels of resources/funding and level of sophistication/capabilities.
- Threat actors also have very different motivations. Some common attack motivations include data exfiltration, espionage, service disruption, blackmail, financial gain, philosophical or political beliefs, ethical hacking, revenge, disruption or chaos, and war.
- Cybersecurity professionals and attackers use open source intelligence (OSINT) sources to learn about vulnerabilities, how attackers exploit them, and how organizations can protect against the threats.

Determining Malware Types

- Malware includes several different types of malicious code, including ransomware, Trojans, worms, spyware, bloatware, viruses, keyloggers, logic bombs, and rootkits.

- Ransomware is a type of malware that takes control of a user's system or data. Criminals demand a ransom payment before returning control of the computer.

- A Trojan appears to be one thing, such as pirated software or free antivirus software, but is something malicious. A remote access Trojan (RAT) is a type of malware that allows attackers to take control of systems from remote locations.

- A worm is self-replicating malware that travels throughout a network without user intervention.

- Spyware is software installed on user systems without the user's knowledge or consent and it monitors the user's activities. It sometimes includes a keylogger that records user keystrokes.

- Bloatware is software installed when a user installs another program, often without the user's knowledge. Some bloatware changes the default home page of a user's browser or change the default search engine.

- A virus is malicious code that attaches itself to a host application. The code runs and replicates to other systems when the application is launched.

- Hardware or software keyloggers track all of the keyboard activity on a system and report it back to the attacker.

- A logic bomb executes in response to an event, such as a day, time, or condition. Malicious insiders have planted logic bombs into existing systems, and these logic bombs have delivered their payload after the employee left the company.

- Rootkits take root-level or kernel-level control of a system. They hide their processes to avoid detection, and they can remove user privileges and modify system files.

Recognizing Common Attacks

- Social engineering uses social tactics to gain information or trick users into performing actions they wouldn't normally take. Social engineering attacks can occur in person, over the phone, while surfing the Internet, and via email. Many social engineers attempt to impersonate others.

- Shoulder surfing is an attempt to gain unauthorized information through casual observation, such as looking over someone's shoulder, or monitoring screens with a camera. Screen filters can thwart shoulder surfing attempts.

- A hoax is a message, often circulated through email, that tells of impending doom from a virus or other security threat that simply doesn't exist.

- Tailgating is the practice of one person following closely behind another without showing credentials. Access control vestibules (sometimes called mantraps) help prevent tailgating.

- Dumpster divers search through trash looking for information. Shredding or burning documents reduces the risks associated with dumpster diving.
- Watering hole attacks discover sites that a targeted group visits and trusts. Attackers then modify these sites to download malware. When the targeted group visits the modified site, they are more likely to download and install infected files.
- Social engineers use pretexting by presenting a fake scenario before asking for information.
- Spam is unwanted or unsolicited email. Attackers often use spam in different types of attacks.
- Phishing is the practice of sending email to users to trick them into revealing sensitive information, installing malware, or clicking on a link.
- Spear phishing and whaling are types of phishing. Spear phishing targets specific groups of users, and whaling targets high-level executives.
- Vishing is a form of phishing that uses voice over the telephone and often uses Voice over IP (VoIP). Some vishing attacks start with a recorded voice and then switch over to a live person.

Blocking Malware and Other Attacks

- Anti-spam software attempts to block unsolicited email. You can configure a spam filter to block individual email addresses and email domains.
- Antivirus software can detect and block different malware types, such as worms, viruses, and Trojans. Antivirus software uses signatures to detect known malware and heuristics to detect potential malware based on behavior.
- When downloading signatures manually, hashes can verify the integrity of signature files. Antivirus software typically includes a file integrity checker to detect files modified by a rootkit.
- Social engineers and other criminals employ several psychology-based principles to help increase the effectiveness of their attacks. They are authority, intimidation, consensus, scarcity, urgency, familiarity, and trust.

📌 *Online References*

Have you done the online labs? Check out the online content to view some extra materials at **https://getcertifiedgetahead.com/**. They might help you understand some key content

Chapter 6 Practice Questions

1. A tech company recently discovered an attack on its organization, resulting in a significant data breach of customer data. After investigating the attack, they realized it was very sophisticated and likely originated from a foreign country. Which of the following identifies the MOST likely threat actor in this attack?

    A. Hacktivist
    B. Nation-state
    C. Competitors
    D. Insiders

2. An attacker purchased an exploit on the Internet. He then used it to modify an item's price in an online shopping cart during checkout. Which of the following BEST describes this attacker?

    A. Insider
    B. Unskilled attacker
    C. Competitor
    D. Hacktivist
    E. APT

3. Lisa is a database administrator. She received a phone call from someone identifying himself as a representative from a known hardware vendor. He said he's calling customers to inform them of a problem with database servers they've sold, but he said the problem only affects servers running a specific operating system version. He asks Lisa what operating system versions the company is running on their database servers. Which of the following BEST describes the tactic used by the caller in this scenario?

    A. Pretexting
    B. Tailgating
    C. Pharming
    D. Smishing

4. Moe is investigating an attack where the attacker seemed to have information about a computer user who was not available online. After examining the user's computer, he found a small USB device connected between the keyboard and computer. What has he most likely discovered?

    A. Skimmer
    B. Keylogger

   C.   Wiretap

   D.   Buffer overflow

5.   After Bart logged on to his computer, he was unable to access any data. Instead, his screen displayed a message indicating that unless he made a payment, his hard drive would be formatted, and he'd permanently lose access to his data. What does this indicate?

   A.   Keylogger

   B.   Ransomware

   C.   Backdoor

   D.   Trojan

6.   Recently, malware on a computer at the Monty Burns Casino destroyed several important files after it detected that Homer was no longer employed at the casino. Which of the following BEST identifies this malware?

   A.   Logic bomb

   B.   Rootkit

   C.   Backdoor

   D.   Spyware

7.   Maggie is attempting an attack against software developers in a specific company. She knows that those developers frequently visit the same Internet site to share coding tips and posts malware on that site to infect their systems. What term best describes this attack?

   A.   Whaling

   B.   Vishing

   C.   Watering hole

   D.   Pretexting

8.   Homer complained of abnormal activity on his workstation. After investigating, an administrator discovered his workstation connects to systems outside the organization's internal network using uncommon ports. The administrator discovered the workstation is also running several hidden processes. Which of the following choices BEST describes this activity?

    A.   Rootkit

    B.   Backdoor

    C.   Spam

    D.   Trojan

9. Bart downloaded and installed the Nmap security scanner from *https://passsecurityplus. com*. After completing the install, he noticed that his browser's home page and default search engine was changed. What is the MOST likely cause of the activity?

    A.   Bloatware

    B.   Fileless virus

    C.   Worm

    D.   Rootkit

10. You are a security professional for the firm that owns the website **getcertifiedgetahead.com**. You recently learned that someone registered the similar domain names **cetcertifiedgetahead.com**, and **getcertifiedahead.com**. What type of attack should you suspect has taken place?

    A.   Ransomware

    B.   Typosquatting

    C.   Rootkit

    D.   DNS hijacking

11. A man in a maintenance uniform walked up to your organization's receptionist desk. He said he was called by the CIO and asked to fix an issue with the phones and needed access to the wiring closet. The receptionist asked the man to show his building access badge, and then she verified that he was on the list of approved personnel to access this secure area. What type of attack will the checks performed by the receptionist prevent?

    A.   Tailgating

    B.   Phishing

    C.   Impersonation

    D.   Whaling

12. An organization's security policy requires employees to place all discarded paper documents in containers for temporary storage. These papers are later burned in an incinerator. Which of the following attacks are these actions MOST likely trying to prevent?

    A.   Shoulder surfing

    B.   Tailgating

    C.   Smishing

    D.   Dumpster diving

13. Lisa is a database administrator and received a phone call from someone identifying himself as a technician working with a known hardware vendor. He said he's calling customers to inform them of a problem with database servers they've sold, but he said the problem only affects servers running a specific operating system version. He asks Lisa what operating system versions the company is running on their database servers. Which of the following choices is the BEST response from Lisa?

    A.   Let the caller know what operating system and versions are running on the database servers to determine if any further action is needed.

    B.   Thank the caller and end the call, report the call to her supervisor, and independently check the vendor for issues.

    C.   Ask the caller for his phone number so that she can call him back after checking the servers.

    D.   Contact law enforcement personnel because this is a pretexting attack.

14. Homer, the chief financial officer (CFO) of a bank, received an email from Lisa, the company's chief executive officer (CEO). Lisa states she is on vacation and lost her purse, containing all her cash and credit cards. She asks Homer to transfer $5,000 to her account. Which of the following BEST identifies this attack?

    A.   Phishing

    B.   Vishing

    C.   Smishing

    D.   Whaling

15. Homer has been looking for the newest version of a popular smartphone. However, he can't find it in stock anywhere. Today, he received an email advertising the smartphone. After clicking the link, his system was infected with malware. Which of the following principles is the email sender employing?

    A.   Authority

    B.   Intimidation

    C.   Scarcity

    D.   Trust

Chapter 6

Practice Question Answers

1. **B** is correct. This was most likely a nation-state attacker because it was a sophisticated attack and originated from a foreign country. A hacktivist launches attacks to further a cause, but the scenario didn't mention any cause. Competitors might launch attacks, but they would typically focus on proprietary data rather than customer data. An insider would not launch attacks from a foreign country.

2. **B** is correct. An unskilled attacker will typically obtain a ready-made exploit rather than write the code. An insider would cause damage from within the network or use inside knowledge when attacking. A competitor is unlikely to purchase a single item at a lower price but would be more interested in gaining proprietary data. Hacktivists launch attacks as part of an activist movement, not to get a better price on an item. An advanced persistent threat (APT) is typically a state actor sponsored by a nation-state and will use advanced tools to launch sophisticated attacks, rather than just lowering a price for an item.

3. **A** is correct. The caller is using the social engineering tactic of pretexting by setting up a scenario that has a better chance of getting someone to give him information. If he just asked for the operating system versions on the servers without a prepended scenario, his chance of success would be diminished. Tailgating is the practice of one person following closely behind another without showing credentials. A pharming attack attempts to manipulate the DNS name resolution process. Smishing is a form of phishing using text messages.

4. **B** is correct. A keylogger is a hardware device or software program that collects user keyboard activity and reports it back to the attacker. The device that Moe discovered is likely a hardware keylogger. A skimmer plays a similar role but is used to collect credit card information, not keyboard activity. A wiretap is a connection made to a telephone or data line to collect network traffic. A buffer overflow attack sends unexpected data to a system to access system memory or cause it to crash.

5. **B** is correct. Ransomware attempts to take control of users' systems or data and then demands payment (ransom) to return control. A keylogger captures a user's keystrokes and stores them in a file. This file can be automatically sent to an attacker or manually retrieved depending on the keylogger. It's possible that Bart's computer was infected with a Trojan, which created a backdoor. However, not all Trojans or backdoor accounts demand payment as ransom.

6. **A** is correct. A logic bomb executes in response to an event. In this scenario, the logic bomb delivered its payload when it detected that Homer was no longer employed at the company. A rootkit doesn't respond to an event. A backdoor provides another method of accessing a system, but it does not delete files. Spyware is software installed on user systems without their awareness or consent.

7. **C** is correct. A watering hole attack places malware on a site that the attack targets are known to frequently visit. Whaling attacks are social engineering attacks aimed at high-level targets. Vishing is a form of phishing attack that uses voice telephone calls. Pretexting involves making up a story to gain the trust of a target.

8. **A** is correct. A rootkit typically runs hidden processes and it commonly attempts to connect to computers via the Internet. The scenario doesn't address the initial infection. Although an attacker might have used a backdoor to access the user's computer and install the rootkit, backdoors don't run hidden processes. A Trojan is malware that looks like it's beneficial, but it is malicious. Spam is unwanted email and is unrelated to this question.

9. **A** is correct. Bloatware is installed along with a desired program, and bloatware often hijacks browsers by changing the home page and/or changing the default search engine. Because the user downloaded Nmap from a site other than *nmap.org*, it is conceivable that the alternative site added bloatware to the Nmap program. A fileless virus is a type of malicious software that runs in memory, often within a PowerShell script, instead of being a file that is written to disk. A worm is self-replicating malware that travels throughout a network without the assistance of a host application or user interaction. A rootkit is a program or group of programs that provide root-level access to a system.

10. **B** is correct. This describes a typosquatting attack where someone buys a domain name that is close to a legitimate domain name, hoping to attract visitors who mistype the original domain. Ransomware typically encrypts data and the attacker then demands payment as ransom, but there isn't any indication that a ransom is requested in this scenario. A rootkit is a program or group of programs that provide root-level access to a system and

hides itself to evade detection. There is no evidence of a rootkit here. Finally, DNS hijacking steals traffic for a legitimate domain name by redirecting DNS records. That is not the case in this attack, where a different (but similar) domain was used.

11. **C** is correct. These checks are security controls that will help prevent impersonation, a social engineering attack. Tailgating is the practice of one person following closely behind another without showing credentials. Phishing is the practice of sending email to users with the purpose of tricking them into revealing personal information or clicking on a link. Whaling is a form of spear phishing that attempts to target high-level executives.

12. **D** is correct. Dumpster diving is the practice of looking for documents in the trash dumpsters, but shredding or incinerating documents ensures dumpster divers cannot retrieve any paper documents. Shoulder surfers attempt to view something on a monitor or other screen, not papers. Tailgating refers to entering a secure area by following someone else. Smishing is a form of phishing using text messages.

13. **B** is correct. This sounds like a social engineering attack where the caller is attempting to get information on the servers, so it's appropriate to end the call, report the call to a supervisor, and independently check the vendor for potential issues. It is not appropriate to give external personnel information on internal systems from a single phone call. It isn't necessary to ask for a phone number because you wouldn't call back and give information on the servers. While the caller is pretexting the request with a somewhat believable scenario, the caller has not committed a crime by asking questions, so it is not appropriate to contact law enforcement personnel.

14. **D** is correct. This is most likely a whaling attack because an executive (the CFO of the bank) is being targeted. While whaling is a type of phishing, whaling is more specific and a better answer than phishing. Vishing is a form of phishing that uses the phone, but this scenario used email. Smishing is a form of phishing that uses text messages.

15. **C** is correct. The attacker is using scarcity to entice the user to click the link. A user might realize that clicking on links from unknown sources is risky, but the temptation of getting a new smartphone might cause the user to ignore the risk. There isn't any indication that the email is from any specific authority. It isn't trying to intimidate the recipient, and there isn't any indication it is trying to build trust.

Chapter 7

Protecting Against Advanced Attacks

CompTIA Security+ objectives covered in this chapter:

2.3 Explain various types of vulnerabilities.
- Application (Memory injection, Buffer overflow, Race conditions, Time-of-check (TOC), Time-of-use (TOU))
- Web-based (Structured Query Language injection (SQLi), Cross-site scripting (XSS))

2.4 Given a scenario, analyze indicators of malicious activity.
- Network attacks (Distributed denial-of-service (DDoS), Amplified, Reflected, Domain Name System (DNS) attacks, On-path, Credential replay)
- Application attacks (Injection, Buffer overflow, Replay, Forgery, Directory traversal)

4.1 Given a scenario, apply common security techniques to computing resources.
- Application security (Input validation, Secure cookies, Static code analysis, Code signing)
- Sandboxing

4.3 Explain various activities associated with vulnerability management.
- Identification methods (Application security, Static analysis, Dynamic analysis, Package monitoring)

4.5 Given a scenario, modify enterprise capabilities to enhance security.
- DNS filtering

4.7 Explain the importance of automation and orchestration related to secure operations.
- Use cases of automation and scripting (User provisioning, Resource provisioning, Guardrails, Security groups, Ticket creation, Escalation, Enabling/disabling services and access, Continuous integration and testing, Integrations and Application programming interfaces (APIs))
- Benefits (Efficiency/time saving, Enforcing baselines, Standard infrastructure configura-

tions, Scaling in a secure manner, Employee retention, Reaction time, Workforce multiplier)

- Other considerations (Complexity, Cost, Single point of failure, Technical debt, Ongoing supportability)

If there's one thing that's abundant in the IT world, it is attacks and attackers. Attackers lurk almost everywhere. If you have computer systems, you can't escape them. However, you can be proactive in identifying the different types of attacks and take steps to prevent them or at least prevent their effectiveness. This chapter covers a wide assortment of attacks from different sources and how you can use automation and orchestration to better secure your IT operations.

Identifying Network Attacks

This section summarizes many common attacks launched against systems and networks, along with the indicators of these attacks. It's important to realize that effective countermeasures exist for all attacks listed in this book. However, attackers are actively working on beating the countermeasures. As they do, security professionals create additional countermeasures, and the attackers try to beat them. The battle continues daily.

The goal in this section is to become aware of many of the well-known attacks. By understanding these, you'll be better prepared to comprehend the improved attacks as they emerge and the enhanced countermeasures.

Denial of Service Attacks

A **denial-of-service (DoS)** attack is an attack from one attacker against one target. A **distributed denial-of-service (DDoS)** attack is an attack from two or more computers against a single target. The goal of both is **resource exhaustion**, which overloads the system's resources and prevents legitimate users from accessing services on the target computer.

For example, a web server responds to Hypertext Transfer Protocol (HTTP) requests to serve webpages. A DDoS attack can overload the web server by sending thousands of HTTP requests a second from hundreds of different sources. These requests overload the web server leading to resource exhaustion. At some point, the server is no longer able to keep up with the requests. The attacked computer typically slows down significantly, preventing legitimate users from viewing web pages. In extreme cases of resource exhaustion, the attacked computer might crash.

An indicator of a network-based DDoS attack is a sustained, abnormally high amount of network traffic on the network interface card (NIC) of the attacked computer. As the computer is trying to respond to this traffic, it can't respond as quickly to legitimate traffic. Another indicator of a DDoS attack is abnormally high usage of other system resources such as the processor or memory.

There are two major variants of DDoS attacks:

- **Reflected DDoS** attacks involve the attacker sending requests to a third-party server with a spoofed source IP address, which appears to be the target's IP address. When the third-party server responds to the request, it sends the response to the target instead of the attacker, thereby overwhelming the target with unsolicited traffic.
- **Amplified DDoS** attacks use reflection techniques in combination with amplification, where a small request from the attacker generates a significantly larger response from the third-party server. This results in an even greater volume of traffic directed at the target, making it more difficult for the target to withstand the attack.

> ### ★ Remember This!
>
> A distributed denial-of-service (DDoS) attack is an attack from multiple computers against a single target. DDoS attacks typically include sustained, abnormally high network traffic and usage of memory and processor time resulting in resource exhaustion. Major variants of DDoS attacks include reflected attacks, which involve using third-party servers to redirect traffic to the target, and amplified attacks, which combine reflection techniques with amplification to generate an even greater volume of traffic directed at the target.

SYN Flood Attacks

The **SYN flood** attack is a common DoS or DDoS attack used against servers on the Internet. They are easy for attackers to launch and can cause significant problems. The SYN flood attack disrupts the Transmission Control Protocol (TCP) handshake process and can prevent legitimate clients from connecting.

TCP sessions use a three-way handshake when establishing a session. Two systems usually start a TCP session by exchanging three packets in a TCP handshake. For example, when a client establishes a normal session with a server, it takes the following steps:

1. The client sends a SYN (synchronize) packet to the server.
2. The server responds with a SYN/ACK (synchronize/acknowledge) packet.
3. The client completes the handshake by sending an ACK (acknowledge) packet. After establishing the session, the two systems exchange data.

However, in a SYN flood attack, the attacker never completes the handshake by sending the ACK packet. Additionally, the attacker sends a barrage of SYN packets, leaving the server with multiple half-open connections. Figure 7.1 compares a normal TCP handshake with the start of a SYN flood attack. Attackers that control botnets can launch SYN flood attacks from hundreds or thousands of different systems in a DDoS attack.

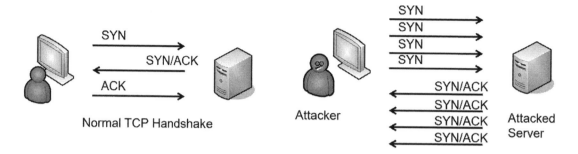

Figure 7.1: TCP handshake and SYN flood attack

In some cases, these half-open connections can consume a server's resources while it is waiting for the third packet, and it can crash. More often, though, the server limits the number of these half-open connections. Once the limit is reached, the device may delete half-open connections to allow new connections or delete half-open connections and block all new connections for a limited time. For example, Linux systems allow administrators to set a threshold for SYN packets, blocking SYN packets after reaching the threshold. Although this prevents the SYN flood attack from crashing the system, it also denies service to legitimate clients.

Forgery

Forgery attacks occur when an attacker creates a fake identity, certificate, file, or other object in an attempt to fool an unsuspecting user or system. *Spoofing* is an example of forgery that occurs when one person or entity impersonates or masquerades as someone or something else. Some common spoofing methods are related to an email address, an Internet Protocol (IP) address, and a media access control (MAC) address.

In email address spoofing, an attacker changes the sender address so it appears the email is coming from someone else. Sometimes they will also change the Reply-to address. Spam and phishing emails commonly forge these email addresses.

With IP spoofing, the attacker changes the source address so that it looks like the IP packet originated from a different source. This can allow an attacker to launch an attack from a single system, while it appears that the attack is coming from different IP addresses.

Host systems on a network have media access control (MAC) addresses assigned to the NIC. These are hard coded into the NIC. However, it's possible to use software methods to associate a different MAC address to the NIC in a MAC spoofing attack.

On-Path Attacks

An **on-path attack** (sometimes referred to as a **man-in-the-middle** attack) is a form of active interception and modification, or active monitoring. It uses a separate computer that accepts traffic from each party in a conversation and forwards the traffic between the two. The two computers are unaware of the attacking computer, but the attacker can interrupt the traffic at will, insert malicious code, or simply eavesdrop.

For example, imagine that Maggie and Bart are exchanging information with their two computers over a network. If Hacker Harry can launch an on-path attack from a third computer, he can intercept all traffic. Maggie and Bart still receive all the information, so they are unaware of the attack. However, Hacker Harry also receives all the information. Because the on-path computer can control the entire conversation, it is easy to insert malicious code and send it to the computers.

A sophisticated on-path attack can create multiple secure connections. Instead of Maggie and Bart having one secure connection between their computers, Maggie would have one secure connection with Hacker Harry, and Hacker Harry would have another secure connection with Bart. Hacker Harry receives the data in an encrypted format. His computer decrypts and stores it, and then encrypts it again before sending it on.

Because traffic goes through the on-path computer, it may cause a delay, especially if it is decrypting and encrypting the data again. This delay can be a strong indicator of an on-path attack. Additionally, the computer certificates used to create the secure sessions may not be issued by a trusted certificate authority. Users will receive certificate warnings and can only continue if they ignore the warnings.

Secure Shell (SSH) sessions are also susceptible to on-path attacks if administrators ignore warnings. When administrators connect to remote systems using SSH, the two systems establish cryptographic keys, and they use these keys in subsequent connections. These keys encrypt the SSH session and provide authentication.

Imagine Lisa established an SSH session with a remote system. SSH creates the two keys (one on her system and one on the remote system) and creates fingerprints to identify them. These fingerprints are expressed in 16 hexadecimal pairs, such as 1A:2B:3C:4E:5F:6A:7B:8C:9D:1E:2F:3 A:4B:5C:6D:7E.

When Lisa connects to the server with SSH, it expects to see the same fingerprint. If it is different, it indicates that the administrator is connecting to a different computer. SSH will issue a warning similar to the following:

```
@@@@@@@@@@@@@@@@@@@@@@@@@@@@@@@@@@@@@@@ WARNING: REMOTE
HOST IDENTIFICATION HAS CHANGED!

@@@@@@@@@@@@@@@@@@@@@@@@@@@@@@@@@@@@@@@ IT IS POSSIBLE
THAT SOMEONE IS DOING SOMETHING NASTY!

Someone could be eavesdropping on you (man-in-the-middle attack)!
The fingerprint for the RSA key sent by the remote host is 1E:2F:3A:
4B:5C:6D:7E:1A:2B:3C:4E:5F:6A:7B:8C:9D:
```

An on-path attack can also be what is known as an attacker-in-the-browser attack. This is a type of proxy Trojan horse that infects vulnerable web browsers with an extension. Successful on-path browser attacks can capture browser session data and modify transactions. This includes keyloggers to capture keystrokes, along with all data sent to and from the web browser. Some of these have included keystroke logging and form grabbing. Once the attackers collect logon information for a user's bank, they use it to log on and transfer money to offshore accounts.

📌 *Remember This!*

An on-path attack is a form of active eavesdropping. It captures data from two other computers in a session. When secure channels are used, the on-path system may use certificates that aren't issued by a CA and will generate certificate warnings. SSH gives a warning if previously established keys have changed.

Secure Sockets Layer Stripping

An **SSL stripping** attack changes an encrypted Hypertext Transfer Protocol Secure (HTTPS) connection to an unencrypted Hypertext Transfer Protocol (HTTP) connection. These days, HTTPS uses Transport Layer Security (TLS) instead of SSL but the name SSL stripping has stuck around.

HTTPS sessions are encrypted, so data sent within a session is unreadable to an outside attacker. However, the session is not encrypted until TLS is set up. If an attacker can intercept the beginning of the TLS negotiation, the attacker can redirect the user to an HTTP page instead of an HTTPS page.

The primary indication of an SSL stripping attack is in the web browser itself. If the area to the left of the URL indicates "Not secure" or the URL includes HTTP instead of HTTPS, an SSL stripping attack may be active.

DNS Attacks

Chapter 3, "Exploring Network Technologies and Tools," covers Domain Name System (DNS) in much more depth, but as a reminder, DNS resolves hostnames to IP addresses. This eliminates the need for you and me to have to remember the IP addresses for websites. Instead, we simply type the hostname into the browser, and it connects. For example, if you type in **getcertifiedgetahead.com** in the address bar of your web browser, your system queries a DNS server for the IP address. DNS responds with the correct IP address and your system connects to the website using the IP address.

DNS Poisoning Attacks

A DNS poisoning attack attempts to modify or corrupt DNS data that is stored on a DNS server. For example, a successful DNS poisoning attack can modify the IP address associated with google.com and replace it with a malicious website's IP address. If successful, and users attempt to go to Google, they will be sent to the malicious website instead. This is the primary indicator of a DNS poisoning attack—users enter the Uniform Resource Locator (URL) of one website but are taken to a different website.

There have been several successful DNS poisoning attacks over the years. Many current DNS servers use Domain Name System Security Extensions (DNSSEC) to protect the DNS records and prevent DNS poisoning attacks. Chapter 3 covers DNSSEC in more depth.

Pharming Attack

A **_pharming attack_** is another type of attack that manipulates the DNS name resolution process. Just as a DNS poisoning attack can redirect users to different websites, a successful pharming attack redirects a user to a different website. The major difference between DNS poisoning and pharming attacks is _where_ they occur. DNS poisoning attacks corrupt DNS records stored on a DNS server. Pharming attacks corrupt DNS information on a user's system.

For example, some pharming attacks modify the **hosts** file used on Windows, Linux, and macOS systems. On Windows systems, this file is in the **C:\Windows\System32\drivers\etc** folder; on macOS the file is in the **/private/etc/** folder; and on Linux the file is in the **/etc/** folder and can include IP addresses along with hostname mappings. If a system contains information in a **hosts** file, that information is used instead of performing a lookup on a DNS server.

By default, the **hosts** file doesn't contain any records for remote systems. However, a mapping might look like this:

```
127.0.0.1       localhost

13.207.21.200   google.com
```

The first entry maps the name localhost to the loopback IP address of 127.0.0.1. The second entry maps the name **google.com** to an IP address that belongs to **bing.com** (13.207.21.200). If a user enters **google.com** into the browser's address bar, the browser will instead go to **bing.com**. Practical jokers might do this to a friend's computer, and it isn't malicious. However, if the IP address points to a malicious server, this might cause the system to download malware.

> ✦ *Remember This!*
>
> A DNS poisoning attack attempts to modify or corrupt DNS data. Pharming is also an attack on DNS, and it manipulates the DNS name resolution process. A primary indicator of both attacks is that a user tries to go to one website but is taken to a different website.

URL Redirection

URL redirection is a common technique used to redirect traffic to a different page within a site (website reorganization), URL shortening, or even a different site completely. For example, I own the **darrilgibson.com** domain, and I sometimes use it to play around with different web technologies such as Python. When I finish, I set up the site to redirect traffic to another one of my sites.

In some cases, attackers use URL redirection for malicious purposes. Imagine an attacker discovers a vulnerability with a website and gains access to the underlying files. He may be able to implement a URL redirection attack and send all traffic to an alternate malicious website. The indicator of a successful URL redirection is simple. You attempt to go to a website, and you're redirected to another website.

Domain Hijacking

In a **domain hijacking attack**, an attacker changes a domain name registration without permission from the owner. Attackers often do so through social engineering techniques to gain unauthorized access to the domain owner's email account.

As an example, imagine that Homer sets up a domain named **homersimpson.com**. He uses his Gmail account as the email address when he registers it, though he rarely checks his Gmail account anymore.

Attackers watch his Facebook page and notice that he often adds simple comments like "Doh!" Later, they try to log on to his Gmail account with a brute force attempt. They try the password of Doh!Doh! and get in. They then go to the domain name registrar and use the Forgot Password feature. It sends a link to Homer's Gmail account to reset the password. After resetting the password at the domain name registrar site, the attackers change the domain ownership. They also delete all the emails tracking what they did. Later, Homer notices his website is completely changed, and he no longer has access to it.

> ★ *Remember This!*
>
> In a domain hijacking attack, an attacker changes a domain name registration without permission from the owner.

DNS Filtering

Administrators may use **DNS filtering** to control the websites that users visit. DNS filtering uses block lists of known malicious domain names and either refuses to provide IP addresses for those malicious sites or provides incorrect results for them.

A **DNS sinkhole** is a DNS server that uses DNS filtering of incorrect results for one or more domain names. If you enter a domain name into your web browser during normal operations, the web browser queries DNS for the website and takes you to the site. However, if the DNS server has a sinkhole for the domain name, your request will be intercepted, and you won't be able to reach the site.

Investigative authorities have used sinkholes to disrupt botnets and malware. Infected computers frequently check in with command-and-control servers, and the malware includes the domain names of these servers. Authorities reverse engineer the malware to discover these domain names, and then they coordinate with DNS owners to redirect traffic destined for these domain names. This effectively prevents infected computers from contacting to the command-and-control servers for instructions.

DNS Log Files

DNS log files record DNS queries, such as each request to resolve a hostname to an IP address. These log entries would include the system that sent the request and the IP address returned for the hostname.

These log entries can be useful in identifying potentially malicious websites. As an example, imagine Bart spends a few hours browsing the Internet using his company computer. One of the websites downloaded malware onto his system, but he doesn't know which one and can't remember all of the sites he visited. By searching the DNS log files, administrators can identify all of the sites he visited based on his DNS queries.

Replay Attacks

A **replay attack** occurs when an attacker replays data that was already part of a communication session. The attacker first captures data sent over a network between two systems. The attacker modifies the data and then tries to impersonate one of the clients in the original session and sends the modified data in session replays. Replay attacks can occur on both wired and wireless networks.

As an example, Maggie and Bart may initiate a session with each other. During the communication, each client authenticates with the other using authentication credentials. Hacker Harry intercepts all the data, including the credentials, and later initiates a conversation with Maggie pretending to be Bart. When Maggie's system challenges Hacker Harry, his system sends Bart's credentials. This is an example of a specific kind of replay attack called **credential replay**.

Many protocols use timestamps and sequence numbers to thwart replay attacks. For example, the Kerberos protocol helps prevent replay attacks with timestamped tickets.

> 📌 **Remember This!**
>
> Replay attacks capture data in a session to impersonate one of the parties in the session. Timestamps, sequence numbers, and multi-factor authentication are effective countermeasures against replay attacks.

Summarizing Secure Coding Concepts

Secure application development and deployment concepts are important for application developers to understand. Additionally, IT security managers who manage development projects should understand these concepts, too, even if they aren't writing the code.

Applications often provide an avenue for attackers to generate attacks unless developers create them using secure coding concepts. This section covers common application security techniques and concepts that developers use to create secure applications.

Input Validation

One of the most important security steps that developers should adopt is to include **_input vali-dation_**. Input validation is the practice of checking data for validity before using it. Input validation prevents an attacker from sending malicious code that an application will use by either sanitizing the input to remove malicious code or rejecting the input.

Improper input handling (or the lack of input validation) is one of the most common security issues with web-based applications. It allows many different types of attacks, such as buffer overflow attacks, Structured Query Language (SQL) injection, dynamic link library (DLL) injection, and cross-site scripting attacks. We'll discuss each of those attacks later in this chapter, but let's first dive into input validation.

Consider a web form that includes a text box for a first name. You can logically expect a valid first name to have only letters and be no more than 25 letters. The developer uses input validation techniques to ensure that the user's name meets this validity check. If a user enters other data, such as numbers, semicolons, or HTML code, it fails the validity check. Instead of using the data, the application rejects it and provides an error to the user.

You've probably seen input validation checks and error-handling routines in use if you've ever filled out a form on a webpage. If you didn't fill out all the required text boxes, or if you entered invalid data into one or more of the boxes, the website didn't crash. Instead, it redisplayed the page and showed an error. Websites often use a red asterisk next to text boxes with missing or invalid data, along with a message about the error. Some common checks performed by input validation include:

- **Verifying proper characters**. Some fields such as a zip code use only numbers, whereas other fields such as state names use only letters. Other fields are a hybrid. For example, a phone number uses only numbers and dashes. Developers can configure input validation code to check for specific character types and even verify that they are entered correctly. For example, a telephone number mask of ###-###-#### accepts only three numbers, a dash, three numbers, a dash, and four numbers.
- **Blocking HTML code**. Some malicious attacks embed HTML code within the input as part of an attack. Input validation code can detect HTML code, such as the < and > characters and not use it.
- **Preventing the use of certain characters**. Some attacks, such as SQL injection attacks, use specific characters such as the dash (-), apostrophe ('), and equal sign (=). Blocking these characters helps to prevent these attacks.
- **Implementing boundary or range checking.** These checks ensure that values are within expected boundaries or ranges. For example, if the maximum purchase for a product is three, a range check verifies the quantity is three or less. The validation check identifies data outside the range as invalid and the application does not use it.

Client-Side and Server-Side Input Validation

It's possible to perform input validation at the client and the server. Client-side execution indicates that the code runs on the client's system, such as a user's web browser. Server-side execution indicates that the code runs on the server, such as on a web server.

Client-side input validation is quicker but is vulnerable to attacks. Server-side input validation takes longer but is secure because it ensures the application doesn't receive invalid data. Many applications use both. Imagine Homer is using a web browser to purchase the newest version of Scrabbleships through the Duff website. Customers cannot purchase more than three at a time.

In client-side input validation, the validation code is included in the HTML page sent to Homer. If he enters a quantity of four or more, the HTML code gives him an error message and doesn't submit the page to the server until Homer enters the correct data.

Unfortunately, it's possible to bypass client-side validation techniques. Many web browsers allow users to disable JavaScript in the web browser, which bypasses client-side validation. It's also possible to use a web proxy to capture the client's data in the Hypertext Transfer Protocol (HTTP) POST command and modify it before forwarding to the server.

Server-side input validation checks the inputted values when it reaches the server. This ensures that the user hasn't bypassed the client-side checks.

Using both client-side and server-side validation provides speed and security. The client-side validation checks prevent roundtrips to the server until the user has entered the correct data. The server-side validation is a final check before the server uses the data.

> ★ *Remember This!*
>
> The lack of input validation is one of the most common security issues on web-based applications. Input validation verifies the validity of inputted data before using it, and server-side validation is more secure than client-side validation. Input validation protects against many attacks, such as buffer overflow, SQL injection, dynamic link library injection, and cross-site scripting attacks.

Other Input Validation Techniques

Other input validation techniques attempt to sanitize HTML code and URLs before sending them to a web browser. These methods are sometimes called HTML escaping or HTML encoding. As a simple example, the greater than symbol (**>**) can be encoded with the ASCII replacement characters (**>**). Doing so and following specific guidelines for not inserting untrusted data into web pages helps prevent many web application attacks such as cross-site scripting, SQL injection, and directory traversal attacks.

Most languages include libraries that developers can use to sanitize the HTML code. For example, the OWASP Enterprise Security API (ESAPI) is a free, open-source library for many programming languages. It includes a rich set of security-based tools, including many used for input validation.

Avoiding Race Conditions

When two or more modules of an application, or two or more applications, attempt to access a resource at the same time, it can cause a conflict known as a **race condition**. Most application developers are aware of race conditions and include methods to avoid them when writing code. However, when new developers aren't aware of race conditions or ignore them, a race condition can cause significant problems.

As a simple example of a potential problem, imagine you are buying a plane ticket online and use a web application to pick your seat. You find a window seat and select it. However, at the same time you're selecting this window seat, someone else is, too. You both make the purchase simultaneously, and you both have tickets with the same seat number. You arrive after the other person, and he's unwilling to move, showing his ticket with the seat number. A flight attendant ultimately helps you find a seat. Unfortunately, it's between two burly gentlemen who have been on an all-cabbage diet for the last week. You probably wouldn't be too happy.

Online ticketing applications for planes, concerts, and other events avoid this type of race condition. In some cases, they lock the selection before offering it to a customer. In other cases, they double-check for a conflict later in the process. Most database applications have internal concurrency control processes to prevent two entities from modifying a value at the same time. However, inexperienced web application developers sometimes overlook race conditions.

Attackers can sometimes exploit a **time of check to time of use (TOCTOU)** race condition. This is sometimes called a state attack. It occurs against a system that we refer to as the target of evaluation (TOE). The attacker tries to race the TOE system to do something malicious with data after the operating system verifies access is allowed (time of check) but before the operating system performs a legitimate action at the time of use.

Think about the plane ticket analogy. Imagine the application first checked to see what seats are available and only offered available seats (time of check). The two people selected the same seats. A secure application would check again before reserving the seat (time of use). The first person to complete the checkout process would reserve the seat, but the second person would learn the seat is no longer available.

As another example, imagine Homer tries to access a file. The operating system checks his permissions to verify he has access. If an attacker can act quickly enough, it is sometimes possible for the attacker to access the original file, modify it, or even replace it with a malicious file. This is sometimes possible when a symbolic link is used instead of a direct path.

Proper Error Handling

Error-handling and exception-handling routines ensure that an application can handle an error gracefully. They catch errors and provide user-friendly feedback to the user. When an application doesn't catch an error, it can cause the application to fail. In the worst-case scenario, improper error-handling techniques within an application can cause the operating system to crash. Using effective error- and exception-handling routines protects the integrity of the underlying operating system.

Improper error handling can often give attackers information about an application. When an application doesn't catch an error, it often provides debugging information that attackers can use against the application. In contrast, when an application catches the error, it can control what information it shows to the user. There are two important points about error reporting:

- **Errors to users should be general**. Detailed errors provide information that attackers can use against the system, so the errors should be general. Attackers can analyze the errors to determine details about the system. For example, if an application is unable to connect with a database, a detailed error can let the attacker know what type of database the system is using. This indirectly lets the attacker know what types of commands the system will accept. Also, detailed errors confuse most users.
- **Detailed information should be logged**. Detailed information on the errors typically includes debugging information. By logging this information, it makes it easier for developers to identify what caused the error and how to resolve it.

> ### ★ Remember This!
>
> Error and exception handling helps protect the operating system's integrity and controls the errors shown to users. Applications should show generic error messages to users but log detailed information.

Code Obfuscation

Developers often spend a lot of time developing code. If it is JavaScript, it is rather easy for other developers to just copy the code and use it. One way to slow this down is with an obfuscation method.

Obfuscation attempts to make something unclear or difficult to understand and code obfuscation attempts to make the code unreadable. It does things like renaming variables, replacing numbers with expressions, replacing strings of characters with hexadecimal codes, and removing whitespace and comments. For example, a meaningful variable of **strFirstName** might be renamed to **94mdiwl**, and the number **11** might be changed to **0xF01B - 0x73 - 0xEF9D** (which still results in the decimal number 11).

It's worth noting that most security experts reject security through obscurity as a reliable method of maintaining security. Similarly, code obfuscation might make the code difficult to understand by most people. However, it's still possible for someone with skills to dissect the code.

Software Diversity

Automated software diversity is sometimes used to mimic the use of multiple different core languages. Normally, a **compiler** converts code written in a programming language into a binary executable file. The compiler checks the program for errors and provides a report of items developers might like to check. Some commonly used compiled programming languages are C++, C#, and Java. Automated software diversity methods use a compiler that mimics the compilers of multiple languages.

In other words, a program written in C# and compiled with this multicompiler would create a binary executable that includes all the functions and modules of the code as if it was written in C# and any number of other languages. Automated software diversity methods also add a level of randomness to the code allowing the same program to behave slightly differently on different systems but still achieving the same result.

The idea is that this automated diversity provides an added layer of protection. An attack that succeeds on one system would fail on another system using the same multicompiled program.

Outsourced Code Development

Not all organizations have developers in-house. They either need to hire developers or outsource code development. When outsourcing code development, organizations should address several specific security concerns. The following list identifies some vulnerabilities to consider:

- **Make sure the code works as expected**. At the top of the list is ensuring that the code works. While potential developers may claim they can write the code, an organization should thoroughly test it before accepting it.
- **Vulnerable code**. If the developers don't follow best practices for secure code, they could easily create code that is vulnerable to attack. Unfortunately, an organization might not discover poor coding practices until it is too late and the application has been exploited.

- **Malicious code**. Developers could insert malicious code such as backdoors or logic bombs. These may be difficult to detect using normal testing procedures.
- **Lack of updates**. Security vulnerabilities are common on code. However, developers are usually able to update the code to fix any vulnerabilities. If the contract for outsourced code development doesn't mention updates, it may be difficult to get updates.

Data Exposure

Most applications work with data, and it's essential to protect the data. Secure coding techniques take steps to protect data at rest, data in transit, and data in processing. If the data isn't protected, it can result in a data breach exposing the data to unauthorized entities. It's common to protect data at rest and in transit with encryption. If an application processes encrypted data, it typically decrypts it first. After processing it in memory, it encrypts it again and stores it. The application should also flush the memory buffers to ensure unauthorized entities can't access unencrypted remnants.

Chapter 10, "Understanding Cryptography and PKI," discusses data at rest, data in transit, and data in processing. It also discusses common encryption methods.

HTTP Headers

Systems send and receive HTTP messages between web servers and web clients. The client sends HTTP requests, and the server sends HTTP responses. These messages have multiple sections including the header. Even the header can have different groups. They are formatted as pairs separated by a colon (:). A general header group applies to the entire message. The request header group typically includes information about the browser, the language (such as English), and any encoding that the client browsers may accept. The entity header group gives information about the body of the message.

The Open Worldwide Application Security Project (OWASP) hosted the Secure Headers Project (https://owasp.org/www-project-secure-headers/), which includes detailed recommendations on what to include in response headers. Some headers that are commonly recommended as a best practice are:

- **HTTP Strict-Transport-Security.** This tells the browser to display the page only if it is sent as HTTP Secure (HTTPS). It includes the max-age=SECONDS and the includeSubDomains values.
- **Content-Security-Policy.** This defines multiple sources of acceptable content. It includes sources allowed for scripts, styles (CSS), images, plug-ins, and more.
- **X-Frame-Options.** This tells the browser if X-frames are allowed. X-Frames are rarely used anymore because they open up the page to vulnerabilities.

Secure Cookie

When a user visits a website, the website often creates a **cookie** and writes it to the user's system. This cookie is a small text file and can include anything that web developers choose to write. When the user returns to the website, the web application reads the cookie and uses it to enhance the user experience. Unfortunately, attackers can sometimes read the cookies and exploit various vulnerabilities.

A **secure cookie** is one that has the secure attribute set. This secure attribute ensures that the cookie is only transmitted over secure, encrypted channels, such as HTTPS. This protects the confidentiality of the cookie's contents and prevents attackers from reading them. Many browsers (such as Chrome and Firefox) will not transfer cookies over HTTP if the cookie has the Secure attribute set.

Code Signing

Chapter 10 describes digital certificates and digital signatures in-depth. They are used for various purposes, such as encryption and authenticating users and computers. They can also be used to authenticate and validate software code. As an example, developers can purchase a certificate and use it to digitally sign an application.

Code signing provides two benefits. First, the certificate identifies the author. Second, the hash verifies the code has not been modified. If malware changes the code, the hash no longer matches, alerting the user that the code has been modified.

Analyzing and Reviewing Code

Many organizations that create applications also employ testers to verify the quality of the code. Testers use a variety of different methods to put the code through its paces. Ideally, they will detect problems with the code before it goes live. Some common methods of testing code include:

- **Static code analysis**. Static code analysis examines the code without executing it. A developer performing a manual code review goes through the code line by line to discover vulnerabilities. It's also possible to use automated tools, which can analyze code and mark potential defects.
- **Manual code review**. Manual code review is static code analysis where someone goes through the code line by line. It is done by someone other than the programmer who wrote the code, and the goal is to identify potential vulnerabilities.
- **Dynamic code analysis**. Dynamic code analysis checks the code as it is running. A common method is to use **fuzzing**. Fuzzing uses a computer program to send random data to an application. In some cases, the random data can crash the program or create

unexpected results, indicating a vulnerability. The goal is to discover problems during a dynamic analysis so that they can be fixed before releasing the application.

- **Sandboxing**. Sandboxing is used to test applications within an isolated area specifically created for testing. The term comes from a sandbox in a playground. Children can play in the sandbox where they are relatively safe (and parents can easily keep their eyes on them). Similarly, application developers can test applications in a sandbox, knowing that any changes they make will not affect anything outside the sandbox. Virtual machines (VMs) are often used for sandboxing. For example, Java virtual machines include a sandbox to restrict untrusted applications.

- **Package monitoring**. Every developer makes use of code written by others in the form of shared libraries and packages. It's important to monitor the use of these shared packages throughout your organization. When vulnerabilities arise in code written by others, you will need the ability to identify all cases where the affected packages were used and patch them.

★ *Remember This!*

Static code analysis examines the code without running it. In a manual review, a developer goes through the code line by line, looking for vulnerabilities. Dynamic code analysis checks the code while it is running. Fuzzing techniques send random strings of data to applications looking for vulnerabilities.

Software Version Control

Software version control tracks the versions of software as it is updated, including who made the update and when. Many advanced software development tools include sophisticated version control systems. Developers check out the code to work on it and check it back into the system when they're done. The version control system can then document every single change made by the developer. Even better, this version control process typically allows developers to roll back changes to a previous version when necessary.

Effective version control processes also help eliminate unauthorized changes. If developers can make changes that aren't tracked, they can easily cause unintended problems.

Secure Development Environment

A secure development environment includes multiple stages and typically includes different systems used for each stage. As an example, imagine a software development team is creating an application that will be used to sell products via the Internet. The different stages used in this process are:

- **Development**. In the development stage, software developers use an isolated development environment to create the application. It's isolated from a production environment to ensure that any bugs don't impact other systems. This typically includes version and change controls to track the application development.
- Test. Testers put the application through its paces and attempt to discover any bugs or errors in the testing stage. The testing environment typically doesn't simulate a full production environment but instead includes enough hardware and software to test software modules.
- **Staging**. The staging environment simulates the production environment and is used for late-stage testing. It provides a complete but independent copy of the production environment. It attempts to discover any bugs that might adversely impact the live environment.
- **Production**. In the production stage, the application goes live as the final product. It includes everything needed to support the application and allow customers to use it. In this example, it would include the live web server, possibly a back-end database server, and Internet access.
- **Quality assurance (QA).** Quality assurance is an ongoing process used throughout the lifetime of the project from the development stage and after it is deployed. It helps ensure that an application maintains a high level of quality and meets the original requirements. Some organizations follow specific standards used for quality assurance, such as those published by the International Organization for Standardization (ISO) and the International Electrotechnical Commission (IEC).

★ *Remember This!*

A secure development environment includes multiple stages. Stages are completed in separate non-production environments. Quality assurance methods are used in each of the stages.

Database Concepts

Several of the secure coding techniques and attacks apply directly to databases, so they're organized in this section. SQL (pronounced as "sequel" or "es-que-el") is a Structured Query Language used to communicate with databases. SQL statements read, insert, update, and delete data to and from a database. Many websites use SQL statements to interact with a database, providing users with dynamic content.

A database is a structured set of data. It typically includes multiple tables, and each table holds multiple columns and rows. As an example, consider Figure 7.2. It shows the database schema for a database intended to hold information about books and their authors.

The Book table (on the left) identifies the column names for the table. Each of these columns has a name and identifies the data type or attribute type allowed in the column. For example, INT represents integer, VARCHAR represents a variable number of alphanumeric characters, TEXT is used for paragraphs, and DECIMAL can store monetary values.

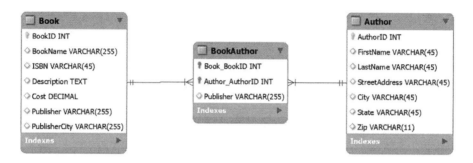

Figure 7.2: Database schema

The Author table holds information on authors, such as their names and addresses. The Book-Author table creates a relationship between the Book table and the Author table. The Publisher column should not be there, but it helps describe normalization in the next section.

Figure 7.3 shows three rows of the Author table. It also shows the difference between columns and rows. Because the column identifies the data type, columns are sometimes referred to as attributes. Also, because each row represents a record, rows are sometimes called records or tuples.

Column
↓

AuthorID	FirstName	LastName	StreetAddress	City	State	
1	Lisa	Simpson	742 Evergreen Terrace	Springfield	IDK	← Row
2	Moe	Szylak	1313 Walnut Street	Springfield	IDK	← Row
3	Ned	Flanders	744 Evergreen Terrace	Springfield	IDK	← Row

Figure 7.3: Database table

Individual elements within a database are called fields. For example, the field in the second row of the FirstName column is a field holding the value of Moe.

SQL Queries

One of the vulnerabilities related to databases is SQL injection attacks. The following sections identify how SQL queries work, how attackers launch a SQL injection attack, and how to protect against SQL injection attacks.

As a simple example of a website that uses SQL queries, think of Amazon.com. When you enter a search term and click Go (as shown in Figure 7.4), the web application creates a SQL query, sends it to a database server, and formats the results into a webpage that it sends back to you.

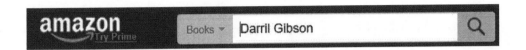

Figure 7.4: Webpage querying a database with SQL

In the example, I selected the Books category and entered Darril Gibson. The result shows a list of books authored by Darril Gibson available for sale on Amazon. The query sent to the database from the Amazon web application might look like this:

```
SELECT * FROM Books WHERE Author ='Darril Gibson'
```

The * is a wildcard and returns all columns in a table. Notice that the query includes the search term entered into the webpage form (Darril Gibson) and encloses the search term in single quotes. If the website simply plugs the search term into the SELECT statement, surrounded by single quotes, it will work, but it's also highly susceptible to SQL injection attacks.

SQL Injection Attacks

In a **SQL injection (SQLi)** attack, the attacker enters additional data into the webpage form to generate different SQL statements. SQL query languages use a semicolon (;) to indicate the SQL line's end and use two dashes (--) as an ignored comment. With this knowledge, the attacker could enter different information into the web form like this:

```
Darril Gibson'; SELECT * FROM Customers;--
```

If the web application plugged this string of data directly into the SELECT statement surrounded by the same single quotes, it would look like this:

```
SELECT * FROM Books WHERE Author ='Darril Gibson'; SELECT * FROM Customers;--'
```

The first line retrieves data from the database, just as before. However, the semicolon signals the end of the line, and the database will accept another command. The next line reads all the data in the Customers table, giving the attacker access to names, credit card data, and more. The last line comments out the second single quote to prevent a SQL error.

Suppose the application doesn't include error-handling routines. In that case, the errors provide details about the type of database the application is using, such as an Oracle, Microsoft SQL Server, or MySQL database. Different databases format SQL statements slightly differently, but once the attacker learns the database brand, it's a simple matter to format the SQL statements required by that brand. The attacker then follows with SQL statements to access the database. This may allow the attacker to read, modify, delete, and/or corrupt data.

This attack won't work against Amazon (please don't try it) because Amazon is using secure coding principles. I don't have access to its code, but I'd bet the developers are using input validation and SQL-based stored procedures (described in the next section).

Many SQL injection attacks use a phrase of **or 1=1** to create a true condition. For example, if an online database allows you to search a Customers table looking for a specific record, it might expect you to enter a name. If you entered Homer Simpson, it would create a query like this:

```
SELECT * FROM Customers WHERE name = 'Homer Simpson'
```

This query will retrieve a single record for Homer Simpson. However, if the attacker enters

' or 1=1;-- instead of Homer Simpson, it will create a query like this:

```
SELECT * FROM Customers WHERE name = '' or 1=1;--
```

Although this is a single SELECT statement, the or clause causes it to behave as two separate SELECT statements:

```
SELECT * FROM Customers WHERE name = ''
```

```
SELECT * FROM Customers WHERE 1=1
```

The first clause will likely not return any records because the table is unlikely to have any records with the name field empty. However, because the number 1 always equals the number 1, the WHERE clause in the second statement always equates to True. The SELECT statement will retrieve all records from the Customers table.

In many cases, a SQL injection attack starts by sending improperly formatted SQL statements to the system to generate errors. Proper error handling prevents the attacker from gaining information from these errors, though. Instead of showing the errors to the user, many websites simply present a generic error webpage that doesn't provide any details.

Protecting Against SQL Injection Attacks

As mentioned previously, input validation provides strong protection against SQL injection attacks. Before using the data entered into a web form, the web application verifies that the data is valid.

Additionally, database developers often use ***stored procedures*** with dynamic webpages. A stored procedure is a group of SQL statements that execute as a whole, similar to a mini-program. A parameterized stored procedure accepts data as an input called a parameter. Instead of copying the user's input directly into a SELECT statement, the input is passed to the stored procedure as a parameter. The stored procedure performs data validation, but it also handles the parameter (the inputted data) differently and prevents a SQL injection attack.

Consider the previous example of searching for a book by an author where an attacker entered the following text: **Darril Gibson'; SELECT * From Customers;--.** The web application passes this search string to a stored procedure. The stored procedure then uses the entire search string in a SELECT statement like this:

> **SELECT * From Books Where Author ='Darril Gibson'; SELECT * From Customers;-- '**

In this case, the user's text is interpreted as harmless text rather than malicious SQL statements. It will look for books with an author name using all of this text: Darril Gibson'; SELECT * From Customers;--. Books don't have author names with SELECT statements embedded in them, so the query comes back empty.

Depending on how well the database server is locked down (or not), SQL injection attacks may allow the attacker to access the structure of the database, all the data, and even modify data. In some cases, attackers have modified the price of products from several hundred dollars to just a few dollars, purchased several of them, and then returned the price to normal.

> ### ★ *Remember This!*
>
> Attackers use SQL injection attacks to pass queries to back-end databases through web servers. Many SQL injection attacks use the code **' or 1=1** to trick the database server into providing information. Input validation techniques and stored procedures help prevent SQL injection attacks.

Web Server Logs

Web server logs typically log activity on the server. These web server logs will show normal activity, such as HTTP requests from users and the server's responses. If your organization owns or controls the server, administrators will have access to the web server logs. However, administrators can't examine logs of servers owned by others. As an example, you can't access logs of Google servers.

These logs will also record abnormal traffic, such as any of the attacks described in this chapter on a web server. As an example, if you suspect that attackers are launching SQL injection attacks, you can search the logs for instances of the phrase `' or 1=1`. Similarly, you can search the logs for indicators of other potential attacks.

Chapter 1, "Mastering Security Basics," introduces centralized logging methods such as security information and event management (SIEM) systems. Instead of analyzing logs manually, it's commonly to send log entries to a centralized logging system and configure it to send alerts after detecting suspicious traffic.

Other Application Attacks

In addition to SQLi attacks, many other attacks target server applications such as those hosted on web servers. Web servers are highly susceptible to several types of attacks because they commonly accept data from users.

Memory Vulnerabilities

Many application attacks take advantage of vulnerabilities in a system's memory or buffers. Because of this, developers need to use secure memory management techniques within their code. For example, poor memory management techniques can result in a memory leak or allow various overflow issues. The following sections describe some common memory issues related to applications.

Memory Leak

A **memory leak** is a bug in a computer application that causes the application to consume more and more memory the longer it runs. In extreme cases, the application can consume so much memory that the operating system crashes.

Memory leaks are typically caused by an application that reserves memory for short-term use but never releases it. For example, imagine a web application that collects user profile data to personalize users' browsing experiences. However, it collects this data every time a user accesses a webpage, and it never releases the memory used to store the data. An initial indicator of a memory leak is a system running slower and slower until it is rebooted. It's possible to detect memory leaks by looking at the memory usage per application in operating system tools, such as the Windows Task Manager.

Buffer Overflows and Buffer Overflow Attacks

A **buffer overflow** occurs when an application receives more input, or different input, than it expects. The result is an error that exposes system memory that would otherwise be protected and inaccessible. Normally, an application will have access only to a specific area of memory, called a buffer. The buffer overflow allows access to memory locations beyond the application's buffer, enabling an attacker to write malicious code into this memory area.

For example, an application may expect to receive a string of 15 characters for a username. If it receives more than 15 characters and tries to store the data in a buffer, it can cause a buffer overflow and expose system memory. The following HTTP GET command shows an example of sending a long string to the system to create a buffer overflow:

```
GET /index.php?username=ZZZZZZZZZZZZZZZZZZZZZZZZZZZZZZZZZZZZZZZZZZ
```

The buffer overflow exposes a vulnerability, but it doesn't necessarily cause damage by itself. However, once attackers discover the vulnerability, they exploit it and overwrite memory locations with their own code. This technique is known as **memory injection**.

More often, the attacker's goal is to insert malicious code in a memory location that the system will execute. It's not easy for an attacker to know the exact memory location where the malicious code is stored, making it difficult to get the computer to execute it. However, an attacker can make educated guesses to get close.

Although error-handling routines and input validation go a long way to preventing buffer overflows, they don't prevent them all. Attackers occasionally discover a bug allowing them to send a specific data string to an application, causing a buffer overflow. When vendors discover buffer overflow vulnerabilities, they usually quickly release a patch or hotfix. From an administrator's perspective, the solution is easy: Keep the systems updated with current patches.

Integer Overflow

An **integer overflow** occurs if an application receives a numeric value that is too big for the application to handle. The result is that the application gives inaccurate results. As an example, if an application reserves 8 bits to store a number, it can store any value between 0 and 255. If the application attempts to multiply two values, such as 95×59, and store the result (5,605) in an 8-bit memory location, it causes an integer overflow.

It's a good practice to double-check the size of memory buffers to ensure they can handle any data generated by applications. It's also possible to use input validation techniques to prevent integer overflow issues. If the application doesn't have adequate error- and exception-handling routines, this might cause an integer overflow condition.

> ★ **Remember This!**
>
> Buffer overflows occur when an application receives more data than it can handle or receives unexpected data that exposes system memory. Buffer overflow attacks often include NOP instructions (such as 0x90) followed by malicious code. When successful, the attack causes the system to execute the malicious code. Input validation helps prevent buffer overflow attacks.

Other Injection Attacks

There are multiple types of injection attacks beyond SQL injection attacks discussed previously in this chapter. They include dynamic link library injection, Lightweight Directory Access Protocol injection, and Extensible Markup Language (XML) injection attacks.

DLL Injection

Applications commonly use a dynamic link library (DLL) or multiple DLLs. A DLL is a compiled set of code that an application can use without re-creating the code. As an example, most programming languages include math-based DLLs. Instead of writing the code to discover a number's square root, a developer can include the appropriate DLL and access the square root function within it.

DLL injection is an attack that injects a DLL into a system's memory and causes it to run. For example, imagine an attacker creates a DLL named malware.dll that includes several malicious functions. In a successful DLL injection attack, the attacker attaches this malicious DLL to a running process, allocates memory within the running process, connects the DLL within the allocated memory, and then executes functions within the DLL.

LDAP Injection

Lightweight Directory Access Protocol (LDAP) specifies the formats and methods used to query databases of objects such as users, computers, and other objects within a network. As an example, Microsoft Active Directory uses LDAP to access objects within a domain.

An **LDAP injection** attack is sometimes possible when a web application is used to query an LDAP-based database. As an example, imagine a help-desk technician needs to access Homer's account to modify it. The technician enters Homer's username into the application, and the application crafts an LDAP query to retrieve Homer's account information.

However, imagine the help-desk technician (or someone else) uses the application to enter more than just Homer's username. In that case, it may be possible to trick the application into crafting a longer LDAP query and accessing much more than just the user's information.

The best way to prevent this is by validating the input before using it, as discussed in the previous "Input Validation" section.

XML Injection

Extensible Markup Language (XML) is a markup language commonly used to transfer data. It is extensible, meaning that it supports the use of any user-defined tags to describe data. Many online applications use XML to transfer data.

As an example, imagine an online web application is used to create and transfer user information. A user would be prompted to enter a username and an email address. The XML data may look like this:

```
<user>

    <username>Homer</username>

    <email>homer@simpson.com</email>

</user>
```

However, imagine the user entered the following data for the email address:

```
homer@simpson.com<user><username>Attacker</username>
<email>attacker@gcgacert.com</email></user>
```

If input validation is not used, this added data will create a second user account. In some instances, the XML application receiving the data will create the second account (Attacker in this example) but ignore the first account.

A primary indicator of XML injection is the creation of unwanted accounts, but it may take detailed logging and auditing to discover this. The best thing to do is to prevent XML injection with strong input validation.

Directory Traversal

Directory traversal is a specific type of injection attack that attempts to access a file by including the full directory path or traversing the directory structure on a computer.

For example, in Linux systems, the **passwd** file includes user logon information, and it is stored in the **/etc** directory with a full directory path of **/etc/passwd**. If a user knows that a web server stores its contents in the **/var/www/** directory, they can use this knowledge to try to access the password file. They know that Linux systems use the **..** operator to refer to the directly one level higher than the current directory. So, to get from **/var/www/** to **/etc/** where the password file is stored, they would need to go up two levels and then down into the **/etc/** directory. They could attempt to access a file called **../../etc/passwd** to traverse the directory structure. If the web server doesn't block the use of directory navigation commands and the file system isn't secured to prevent this access, the server may display the **/etc/passwd** file to the attacker.

Cross-Site Scripting

Cross-site scripting (XSS) is a web application vulnerability that allows attackers to inject scripts into webpages. This generally occurs in one of two ways:

- **Reflected XSS or non-persistent.** This starts by an attacker crafting a malicious email and then encouraging a user to click it. The malicious URL is often placed within a phishing email, but it could also be placed on a public website, such as a link within a comment. When the user clicks the malicious URL, it sends an HTTP request to a server. This request includes malicious code, and the server sends it back to the user in the HTTP response.
- **Stored XSS or persistent.** Instead of the user sending the malicious code to the server, it is stored in a database or other location trusted by the web application. The web application can retrieve the malicious code later, such as when an administrator logs on to the website.

The primary protection against XSS attacks is at the web application with sophisticated input validation techniques. Developers should avoid any methods that allow the webpage to display untrusted data. Additionally, OWASP strongly recommends the use of a security encoding library. When implemented, an encoding library will sanitize HTML code and prevent XSS attacks. OWASP includes more than 10 rules that developers can follow to prevent XSS attacks.

Automation and Orchestration for Secure Operations

It's common to use scripting techniques for automation. SIEM systems include a wide variety of scripts working behind the scenes to collect and analyze log entries. After detecting items of interest, they often trigger a script to respond to the entry based on preconfigured settings. For example, a script may send an email to a group of administrators in response to specific log entries.

Chapter 11, "Implementing Policies to Mitigate Risks," discusses Security Orchestration, Automation, and Response (SOAR) tools. These respond to low-level security events using prewritten scripts. An effective SOAR platform can handle many simple administrative and cybersecurity tasks without taking up the administrator's time.

Automation and Scripting Use Cases

Automation and scripting have become increasingly important in managing secure operations for businesses and organizations. They allow IT and security teams to streamline processes, minimize human error, and ensure a consistent approach to managing various security-related tasks. As you prepare for the Security+ exam, you should be familiar with the following use cases:

- **User provisioning**: Automating the process of creating, updating, and removing user accounts and permissions ensures that access control is maintained efficiently and securely. This can help prevent unauthorized access and maintain the principle of least privilege.
- **Resource provisioning**: Automation can be used to create, configure, and decommission resources such as virtual machines, storage, and networks. This helps maintain a standardized, secure environment while reducing the potential for human error and configuration drift.
- **Guardrails**: Automated guardrails can be put in place to enforce security policies and ensure that security best practices are consistently followed throughout the organization.
- **Security groups**: Automation can be used to manage security groups, ensuring that access controls are consistently applied to network resources and that they are updated as needed to address changes in the threat landscape.
- **Ticket creation**: Automated ticket creation can be used to streamline incident response processes, ensuring that issues are quickly reported and assigned to the appropriate teams for resolution.
- **Escalation**: Automation can be used to escalate security incidents or events to the appropriate personnel or teams based on predetermined criteria, improving response times, and reducing the potential impact of security threats.
- **Enabling/disabling services and access**: Automation can be employed to enable or disable services and access based on various criteria, such as user roles, security policies, or risk assessments. This can help maintain a secure environment by limiting unnecessary access and reducing potential attack surfaces.
- **Continuous integration and testing**: Automation is crucial for continuous integration and testing processes, which help ensure that code is consistently reviewed, tested, and deployed in a secure manner. This can help prevent the introduction of security vulnerabilities and maintain compliance with security standards.
- **Integrations and Application programming interfaces (APIs)**: Automation can be used to integrate various security tools and platforms, allowing them to work together more effectively and share information in real-time. APIs can be employed to enable these integrations, allowing for the secure exchange of data and streamlining security operations.

> **★ Remember This!**
>
> The common use cases for automation and scripting in security operations are user provisioning, resource provisioning, guardrails, security groups, ticket creation, escalation, enabling/disabling services and access, continuous integration and testing, and the use of APIs to create integrations.

Benefits of Automation and Scripting

Automation and scripting offer numerous advantages in managing secure operations, allowing businesses and organizations to improve their security posture while reaping additional benefits. Here are some of the key benefits of automation and scripting:

- **Efficiency/time saving**: Automation and scripting can significantly reduce the time required for various tasks, from provisioning resources to responding to security incidents. This allows IT and security teams to focus on more strategic and high-value activities.

- **Enforcing baselines**: Automation enables the consistent enforcement of security baselines and policies across an organization's infrastructure. This helps ensure that all systems and applications are configured in a secure manner and that any deviations are quickly addressed.

- **Standard infrastructure configurations**: By automating the deployment and management of infrastructure components, organizations can maintain standard configurations that adhere to security best practices. This reduces the risk of misconfigurations and vulnerabilities resulting from manual processes.

- **Scaling in a secure manner**: Automation and scripting allow organizations to scale their operations securely and efficiently. As the number of systems and users grows, automated processes can ensure that security measures are consistently applied and maintained.

- **Employee retention**: Automating repetitive and time-consuming tasks can increase job satisfaction by enabling employees to focus on more engaging and strategic work. This can contribute to higher employee retention rates and a more motivated workforce.

- **Reaction time**: Automation can help improve an organization's reaction time to security incidents and vulnerabilities. Automated processes can quickly detect, report, and address issues, minimizing the potential impact and reducing the time it takes to respond.

- **Workforce multiplier**: Automation and scripting act as a workforce multiplier, allowing IT and security teams to manage more systems and processes without the need for additional personnel. This can result in cost savings and a more efficient allocation of resources.

> 📌 ***Remember This!***
>
> The key benefits of automation and scripting in security operations include improved efficiency and time saving, consistent enforcement of baselines, standardized infrastructure configurations, secure scaling, increased employee retention, faster reaction times, and serving as a workforce multiplier.

Other Considerations

While automation and scripting provide numerous benefits, it is important to consider potential drawbacks and challenges associated with their implementation. Here are some of the key considerations you should keep in mind when implementing automation and scripting in secure operations:

- **Complexity**: Implementing automation and scripting can add complexity to an organization's infrastructure and processes. It is crucial to ensure that the added complexity is manageable and that it does not introduce new vulnerabilities or challenges.
- **Cost**: While automation and scripting can lead to cost savings in the long run, the initial investment in tools, infrastructure, and training may be significant. Organizations should carefully weigh the costs and benefits before embarking on an automation project.
- **Single point of failure**: Over-reliance on automation and scripting can create a single point of failure in some cases. It is important to establish redundancies and fallback mechanisms to minimize the risk of disruptions caused by potential failures in automated processes.
- **Technical debt**: As automation and scripting tools evolve, there may be a need to update or replace existing scripts and integrations. This can result in technical debt, where outdated or poorly maintained scripts cause issues or vulnerabilities. Organizations should plan for regular maintenance and updates to minimize this risk.
- **Ongoing supportability**: Ensuring that automation and scripting solutions are maintainable and supportable is crucial for long-term success. This includes providing training and documentation for team members, as well as monitoring and updating scripts and tools as needed. Organizations should consider the resources required to maintain their automation infrastructure and allocate them accordingly.

> 📌 **Remember This!**
>
> When implementing automation and scripting in security operations, it is essential to consider the potential complexity, cost, single points of failure, technical debt, and ongoing supportability to ensure long-term success and maintainability.

Chapter 7 Exam Topic Review

When preparing for the exam, make sure you understand the key concepts covered in this chapter.

Identifying Network Attacks

- DDoS attacks are DoS attacks from multiple computers. DDoS attacks typically include sustained, abnormally high network traffic, high processor usage, or high memory usage resulting in resource exhaustion.

- Major variants of DDoS attacks include reflected attacks, which involve using third-party servers to redirect traffic to the target, and amplified attacks, which combine reflection techniques with amplification to generate an even greater volume of traffic directed at the target.

- Forgery attacks occur when an attacker creates a fake identity, certificate, file, or other object in an attempt to fool an unsuspecting user or system. Spoofing is an example of forgery that occurs when one person or entity impersonates or masquerades as someone or something else.

- On-path attacks are a form of interception or active eavesdropping. Sophisticated on-path attacks establish secure channels and users may see certificate warnings indicating an on-path attack. SSH will give users a warning if it detects a man-in-the-middle attack.

- Secure Sockets Layer (SSL) stripping is an on-path attack that attempts to convert encrypted HTTPS sessions into unencrypted HTTP sessions.

- DNS poisoning attacks corrupt or modify DNS data stored on a DNS server and can redirect users to malicious sites.

- A pharming attack attempts to manipulate the DNS name resolution process by storing incorrect DNS records on a client system.

- URL redirection causes a web browser to go to a different URL when a user visits a website.

- Domain hijacking attacks allow an attacker to change a domain name registration without permission from the owner. Owners learn of the hijack after they've lost access to the site.

- Replay attacks capture data in a session. After manipulating the capture, they send it back on the network as a session replay. Timestamps and sequence numbers thwart replay attacks.

Summarizing Secure Coding Concepts

- A common coding error in web-based applications is the lack of input validation. Input validation checks the data before passing it to the application and prevents many types of attacks, including buffer overflow, SQL injection, command injection, and cross-site scripting attacks.

- Server-side input validation is the most secure. Attackers can bypass client-side input validation but not server-side input validation. It is common to use both.

- Race conditions allow two processes to access the same data at the same time, causing inconsistent results. Problems can be avoided by locking data before accessing it.

- Error-handling routines within applications can prevent application failures and protect the integrity of the operating systems. Error messages shown to users should be generic, but the application should log detailed information on the error.

- Code signing uses a digital signature within a certificate to authenticate and validate software code.

- Code quality and testing techniques include static code analysis, dynamic analysis (such as fuzzing), stress testing, sandboxing, and model verification.

- SQL injection attacks provide information about a database and can allow an attacker to read, modify, and delete data within a database. They commonly use the phrase ' or 1=1 to trick the database server into providing information. Input validation and stored procedures provide the best protection against SQL injection attacks.

- Secure cookies have an attribute set that instructs web browsers to only send them over encrypted connections, protecting them from eavesdropping attacks.

- A buffer overflow occurs when an application receives more input, or different input, than it expects. The result is an error that exposes system memory that would otherwise be protected and inaccessible.

- Directory traversal is a type of injection attack that attempts to access a file by including the full directory path or traversing the directory structure on a computer.

- Cross-site scripting (XSS) is a web application vulnerability that allows attackers to inject scripts into webpages

Automation and Orchestration for Secure Operations

- Automation and orchestration techniques allow IT and security teams to streamline processes, minimize human error, and ensure a consistent approach to managing various security-related tasks.

- The common use cases for automation and scripting in security operations are user provisioning, resource provisioning, guardrails, security groups, ticket creation, escalation, enabling/disabling services and access, continuous integration and testing, and the use of APIs to create integrations.

- The key benefits of automation and scripting in security operations include improved efficiency and time saving, consistent enforcement of baselines, standardized infrastructure configurations, secure scaling, increased employee retention, faster reaction times, and serving as a workforce multiplier.
- When implementing automation and scripting in security operations, it is essential to consider the potential complexity, cost, single points of failure, technical debt, and ongoing supportability to ensure long-term success and maintainability.

📌 **Online References**

Remember, you have additional resources available online. Check them out at:
`https://getcertifiedgetahead.com.`

Chapter 7 Practice Questions

1. An IDS has sent multiple alerts in response to increased traffic. Upon investigation, you realize it is due to a spike in network traffic from several sources. Assuming this is malicious, which of the following is the MOST likely explanation?

   A. An ARP poisoning attack
   B. A DNS poisoning attack
   C. A domain hijacking attack
   D. A DDoS attack

2. While investigating performance issues on a web server, you verified that the CPU usage was about 10 percent five minutes ago. However, it now shows that CPU usage has been averaging over 98 percent for the last two minutes. Which of the following BEST describes what this web server is experiencing?

   A. Resource exhaustion
   B. DDoS
   C. A buffer overflow attack
   D. A memory leak

3. An administrator regularly connects to a server using SSH without any problems. Today, he sees a message similar to the following graphic when he connects to the server. Which of the following is the MOST likely reason for this message?

```
@@@@@@@@@@@@@@@@@@@@@@@@@@@@@@@@@@@@@@@@@@@@@@@@@@@@@@@@@@@@@@@
@     WARNING: REMOTE HOST IDENTIFICATION HAS CHANGED!      @
@@@@@@@@@@@@@@@@@@@@@@@@@@@@@@@@@@@@@@@@@@@@@@@@@@@@@@@@@@@@@@@
IT IS POSSIBLE THAT SOMEONE IS UP TO NO GOOD!
Someone could be eavesdropping on you right now (man-in-the-middle attack)!
It is also possible that a host key has just been changed.
The fingerprint for the RSA key sent by the remote host is
12:34:56:78:9a:bc:de:f1:23:45:67:89:ab:cd:ef:12.
Please contact your system administrator.
Add correct host key in /home/hostname /.ssh/known_hosts to get rid of this message.
Offending RSA key in /var/lib/sss/pubconf/known_hosts:4
RSA host key for ycda has changed and you have requested strict checking.
Host key verification failed.
```

A. Rogue access point

B. On-path attack

C. Cross-site scripting

D. SQL injection

4. Homer complains that his system started acting erratically today. You discover that malware infected his system, but you learn he didn't open any email during the day. He mentions that he has been browsing the Internet all day. Which of the following could you check to see where the malware MOST likely originated?

A. Web server logs

B. Mail server logs

C. PowerShell logs

D. DNS server logs

5. While reviewing logs for a web application, a security analyst notices that it has crashed several times, reporting a memory error. Shortly after it crashes, the logs show malicious code that isn't part of a known application. Which of the following is MOST likely occurring?

A. Buffer overflow

B. DNS poisoning

C. Privilege escalation

D. Replay

6. Web developers are implementing error handling in a database application accessed by a web server. Which of the following would be the BEST way to implement this?

   A. Display a detailed error message but log generic information on the error
   B. Display a generic error message but log detailed information on the error
   C. Display a generic error message and log generic information on the error
   D. Display a detailed error message and log detailed information on the error

7. A web developer is adding input validation techniques to a website application. Which of the following should the developer implement during this process?

   A. Validation on the server-side
   B. Validation on the client-side
   C. Normalization techniques
   D. Memory management techniques

8. Developers in the YCDA organization have created an application that users can download and install on their computers. Management wants to provide users with a reliable method of verifying that the application has not been modified after YCDA released it. Which of the following methods provides the BEST solution?

   A. Code signing
   B. Input validation
   C. Obfuscation
   D. Stored procedures

9. Your organization is preparing to deploy a web-based application, which will accept user input. Which of the following will BEST test the reliability of this application to maintain availability and data integrity?

   A. Static code analysis
   B. Input validation
   C. Error handling
   D. Dynamic code analysis

10. You are looking for examples of use cases where automation can improve the efficiency of your security operations. Which one of the following is NOT a common automation use case?

   A. Ticket creation
   B. Incident escalation
   C. Continuous integration and testing
   D. Vendor evaluation

11. Homer is trying to convince his manager, Lisa, that automation can improve their security operations. Which one of the following is NOT a common benefit of automation?

    A. Time savings
    B. Increased employee retention
    C. Faster reaction times
    D. Technical debt

12. Looking at logs for an online web application, you see that someone has entered the following phrase into several queries: `' or 1=1;--`. Which of the following provides the BEST protection against this attack?

    A. Normalization
    B. Proper error handling
    C. Removing dead code
    D. Stored procedures

13. You are examining logs generated by an online web application. You notice that the following phrase is appearing in several queries:

    `' or 1=1; --`

    Which of the following is the MOST likely explanation for this?

    A. A buffer overflow attack
    B. A DLL injection attack
    C. A SQL injection attack
    D. A race condition

14. Your organization has created a web application that will go live after testing is complete. An application tester sees the following URL is used on the website:
    `https://getcertifiedgetahead.com/app/info.html`

    The tester resends the following URL to the website:

    `https://getcertifiedgetahead.com/app/../../etc/passwd`

    Which of the following attacks is the tester checking?

    A. Directory traversal
    B. Buffer overflow
    C. Cross-site scripting
    D. Race condition

15. When evaluating a possible automation project, Maggie wants to be certain that she considers all of the potential downsides. Which one of the following is NOT a common downside of security automation?

    A. Cost
    B. Complexity
    C. Workforce multiplier
    D. Single points of failure

Chapter 7

Practice Question Answers

1. **D** is correct. A distributed denial-of-service (DDoS) attack causes spikes in network traffic as multiple systems attempt to connect to a server and deplete the target's resources. An Address Resolution Protocol (ARP) poisoning attack attempts to mislead systems about the source media access control (MAC) address. A Domain Name System (DNS) poisoning attack attempts to redirect web browsers to malicious URLs. In a domain hijacking attack, an attacker changes a domain name registration without permission from the owner.

2. **A** is correct. CPU usage averaging 98 percent indicates resource exhaustion. The scenario doesn't indicate the cause of the increased usage, so resource exhaustion is the best answer. A distributed denial-of-service (DDoS) attack could cause this. However, a surge in traffic from an effective marketing campaign sent via email could also cause a surge in resource usage. A buffer overflow attack is a type of DDoS attack, but the scenario doesn't give enough information to indicate a buffer overflow attack has taken place. The scenario only mentions CPU usage, so there isn't any indication of a memory leak.

3. **B** is correct. The message indicates a potential on-path attack. Specifically, it indicates that the key on the host system has changed, which may be due to the administrator connecting to the attacking system instead of their true target system. None of the other answers are related to incorrect cryptographic keys. A rogue access point is an unauthorized wireless access point. Cross-site scripting and SQL injection attacks are attacks against web applications and there are no web applications in use in this scenario.

4. **D** is correct. Domain Name System (DNS) logs will record DNS queries, such as what hostnames it resolved to IP addresses. The log entries would show all the domains that Homer visited during the day. One of these is most likely the one that downloaded malware onto his system. A web server would show activity on the web server, but you wouldn't have access to web servers controlled by others. Homer didn't open any email, so the mail server

logs wouldn't help. PowerShell logs may show activity, but only if the malware used Power-Shell. However, the PowerShell logs are unlikely to show who ran PowerShell scripts.

5. **A** is correct. Buffer overflow attacks often cause an application to crash and expose system memory. Attackers then write malicious code into the exposed memory and use different techniques to get the system to run this code. None of the other attacks insert malicious code into memory. A DNS poisoning attack attempts to mislead systems about the correct IP address for a domain. Privilege escalation techniques attempt to give an attacker more rights and permissions. In a replay attack, the attacker intercepts data and typically attempts to use the intercepted data to impersonate a user or system.

6. **B** is correct. You should display a generic error message but log detailed information on the error. Detailed error messages to the user are often confusing to them and give attackers information they can use against the system. Logging generic information makes it more difficult to troubleshoot the problem later.

7. **A** is correct. At a minimum, input validation should be performed on the server-side. Client-side validation can be combined with server-side validation, but attackers can bypass client-side input validation if it is used alone. Normalization techniques organize tables and columns in a database to reduce redundant data but have nothing to do with input validation. Memory management is a secure coding technique that helps prevent memory errors.

8. **A** is correct. Code signing provides a digital signature for the code, verifies the publisher of the code, and verifies that it hasn't been modified since the publisher released it. None of the other answers verify the application hasn't been modified. Input validation verifies data is valid before using it. Code obfuscation and code camouflage techniques make the code more difficult to read. Stored procedures are used with SQL databases and can be used for input validation.

9. **D** is correct. Dynamic code analysis techniques test an application during its execution and are the best choice of the available answers to verify the application can maintain availability and data integrity. Static code analysis (such as a manual code review) is done without executing any code, and it won't test its reliability. Input validation is the practice of checking data for validity before using it, but this is done within the application, not as a method to test the application. Error-handling techniques are also done within the application.

10. **D** is correct. The common use cases for automation and scripting in security operations are user provisioning, resource provisioning, guardrails, security groups, ticket creation, incident escalation, enabling/disabling services and access, continuous integration and testing, and the use of APIs to create integrations. Vendor evaluation is typically a manual process performed by human analysts and does not commonly benefit from automation.

11. **D** is correct. The key benefits of automation and scripting in security operations include improved efficiency and time saving, consistent enforcement of baselines, standardized infrastructure configurations, secure scaling, increased employee retention, faster reaction times, and serving as a workforce multiplier. Increasing technical debt is a potential downside to automation, rather than a benefit.

12. **D** is correct. Attackers commonly use the code `' or 1=1;--` in SQL injection attacks, and stored procedures are an effective method of preventing SQL injection attacks. Normalization techniques organize tables and columns in a database to reduce redundant data but don't block SQL injection attacks. This phrase won't cause an error, so proper error-handling techniques won't help. Dead code is code that is never executed, and it should be removed, but dead code is unrelated to a SQL injection attack.

13. **C** is correct. Attackers use the character string `' or 1=1;--` in SQL injection attacks to query or modify databases. A buffer overflow attack sends more data or unexpected data to an application with the goal of accessing system memory. A dynamic link library (DLL) injection attack attempts to inject DLLs into memory, causing DLL commands to run. A race condition is a programming conflict when two or more applications or application models attempt to access a resource at the same time.

14. **A** is correct. This indicates an attempt to launch a directory traversal attack. The key is noticing the directory navigation commands (..) in the URL. A buffer overflow attack sends unexpected data, but the URLs are primarily the same, so it isn't unexpected data. Cross-site scripting attacks include script code and there is none in this URL. A race condition occurs when a system attempts to do two or more operations simultaneously instead of in a specific order.

15. **C** is correct. When implementing automation and scripting in security operations, it is essential to consider the potential complexity, cost, single points of failure, technical debt, and ongoing supportability to ensure long-term success and maintainability. The ability of automation to serve as a workforce multiplier is a benefit, rather than a risk, associated with automation.

Chapter 8

Using Risk Management Tools

CompTIA Security+ objectives covered in this chapter:

1.2 Summarize fundamental security concepts.
- Gap analysis

2.3 Explain various types of vulnerabilities.
- Supply chain (Service provider, Hardware provider, Software provider)

2.4 Given a scenario, analyze indicators of malicious activity.
- Privilege escalation

4.3 Explain various activities associated with vulnerability management.
- Identification methods (Vulnerability scan, Penetration testing, Responsible disclosure program, Bug bounty program, System/process audit)
- Analysis (Confirmation, False positive, False negative, Prioritize, Common Vulnerability Scoring System (CVSS), Common Vulnerabilities and Exposures (CVE), Vulnerability classification, Exposure factor, Environmental variables, Industry/organizational impact, Risk tolerance)
- Vulnerability response and remediation (Patching, Insurance, Segmentation, Compensating controls, Exceptions and exemptions, Validation of remediation, Rescanning, Audit, Verification, Reporting)

4.4 Explain security alerting and monitoring tools and concepts.
- Tools (Security Content Automation Protocol (SCAP), Benchmarks, NetFlow, Vulnerability scanners)

4.9 Given a scenario, use data sources to support an investigation.
- Data sources (Vulnerability scans)

5.2 Explain elements of the risk management process.
- Risk identification

- Risk assessment (Ad hoc, Recurring, One-time, Continuous)
- Risk analysis (Qualitative, Quantitative, Single loss expectancy (SLE), Annualized loss expectancy (ALE), Annualized rate of occurrence (ARO), Probability, Likelihood, Exposure factor, Impact)
- Risk register (Key risk indicators, Risk owners, Risk threshold)
- Risk tolerance
- Risk appetite (Expansionary, Conservative, Neutral)
- Risk management strategies (Transfer, Accept, Exemption, Exception, Avoid, Mitigate)
- Risk reporting

5.5 Explain types and purposes of audits and assessments.

- Attestation
- Internal (Compliance, Audit committee, Self-assessments)
- External (Regulatory, Examinations, Assessment, Independent third-party audit)
- Penetration testing (Physical, Offensive, Defensive, Integrated, Known environment, Partially known environment, Unknown environment, Reconnaissance, Passive, Active)

As a security professional, you need to be aware of the different security issues associated with threats, vulnerabilities, risks, and the tools available to combat them. This chapter digs into risk management concepts, including risk assessment methods. You'll learn about vulnerability scanners and penetration testers, including key differences between them. This chapter also covers some specific tools used to assess networks and manage risks.

Understanding Risk Management

Risk is the likelihood that a threat will exploit a vulnerability. A **vulnerability** is a weakness in a system, application, or process, and a **threat** is a potential danger that might take advantage of a vulnerability. The result of a risk is a negative impact on the organization.

When we evaluate any risk, we use two major criteria. First, we look at the **impact** of the risk. This is the magnitude of harm that can be caused if a threat exploits a vulnerability. Second, we look at the **likelihood** or **probability** of that risk occurring. This tells us how often we expect a risk to occur, if at all.

For example, a system without up-to-date antivirus software is vulnerable to malware. Malware written by malicious attackers is the threat. The likelihood that the malware will reach a vulnerable system represents the risk. Depending on what the malware does, the impact may be an unbootable computer, loss of data, or infection of all computers within a network. However, the likelihood of a risk occurring isn't 100 percent. An isolated system without Internet access, network connectivity, or USB ports has a very low likelihood of malware infection.

The likelihood significantly increases for an Internet-connected system, and it increases even more if a user visits risky websites and downloads and installs unverified files.

It's important to realize that you can't eliminate risk. Sure, you can avoid information technology (IT) risks completely by unplugging your computer and burying it. However, that wouldn't be very useful. Instead, users and organizations practice risk management to reduce the risks.

You practice risk management every day. Driving or walking down roads and streets can be a very dangerous activity. Cars are speeding back and forth, representing significant risks to anyone else on the road. However, you mitigate these risks with caution and vigilance. The same occurs with computers and networks. An organization mitigates risks using different types of security controls.

Threats

A *threat* is a potential danger. Within the context of risk management, a threat is any circumstance or event that can compromise the confidentiality, integrity, or availability of data or systems. Threats come in different forms, including the following:

- **Malicious human threats.** Chapter 6, "Comparing Threats, Vulnerabilities, and Common Attacks," discusses various types of threat actors. They include relatively inexperienced and unskilled attackers, dedicated criminals working within an organized crime group, and sophisticated advanced persistent threats (APTs) sponsored by a government. These are all malicious human threats. Malicious human threats regularly launch different types of attacks, including network attacks, system attacks, and the release of malware.
- **Accidental human threats.** Users can accidentally delete or corrupt data, or accidentally access data that they shouldn't be able to access. Even administrators can unintentionally cause system outages. The common cause is by a well-meaning administrator making a configuration change to fix one problem but inadvertently causing another one.
- **Environmental threats.** This includes long-term power failure, which could lead to chemical spills, pollution, or other possible threats to the environment. It also includes natural threats such as hurricanes, floods, tornadoes, earthquakes, landsides, electrical storms, and other similar events.

A *threat assessment* helps an organization identify and categorize threats. It attempts to predict the threats against an organization's assets, along with the likelihood the threat will occur. Threat assessments also attempt to identify the potential impact from these threats. Once the organization identifies and prioritizes threats, it identifies security controls to protect against the most serious threats.

Risk Identification

As security professionals begin the risk management process, they conduct an exercise known as **risk identification**. This process looks at information arriving from many different sources and tries to list all of the possible risks that might affect the organization. You've already learned about some of the tools used to identify risks, such as application security testing and threat intelligence. Later in this chapter, we'll explore other techniques, such as vulnerability scanning, penetration tests, responsible disclosure programs, and audits of systems and processes. All of this information provides input to the risk management process.

Risk Types

There are several different risk types or risk categories. They include:

- **Internal.** Internal risks are any risks from within an organization. This includes employees and all the hardware and software used within the organization. Internal risks are generally predictable and can be mitigated with standard security controls.

- **External.** External risks are from outside the organization. This includes any threats from external attackers. It also includes any natural threats, such as hurricanes, earthquakes, and tornadoes. While some external risks are predictable, many are not. Attackers are constantly modifying attack methods and trying to circumvent existing security controls.

- **Intellectual property theft.** Intellectual property (IP) includes things like copyrights, patents, trademarks, and trade secrets. Intellectual property is valuable to an organization, and IP theft represents a significant risk.

- **Software compliance/licensing.** Organizations typically put in a lot of time and effort when developing software. They make their money back by selling the licenses to use the software. However, if individuals or organizations use the software without buying a license, the development company loses money. Similarly, an organization can lose money if it purchases licenses, but doesn't protect them. Imagine your organization purchased 10 licenses for a software application, but several people used 5 of the licenses without authorization. Later, your supervisor gives you one of the licenses, but the application gives an error saying the license has already been used when you try to use it. In this scenario, the organization loses the cost of five licenses.

- **Legacy systems and legacy platforms.** The primary risk related to legacy systems and platforms is that the vendor doesn't support them. If vulnerabilities become known, the vendor doesn't release patches, and anyone using the legacy system or software is at risk.

Vulnerabilities

A **_vulnerability_** is a flaw or weakness in software, hardware, or a process that a threat could exploit, resulting in a security breach. Examples of vulnerabilities include:

- **Default configurations**. Hardening a system includes changing systems from their default hardware and software configurations, including changing default usernames and passwords. If systems aren't hardened, they are more susceptible to attacks. Chapter 5, "Securing Hosts and Data," covers hardening systems in more depth.

- **Lack of malware protection or updated definitions**. Antivirus and anti-malware methods protect systems from malware, but if they aren't used and kept up to date, systems are vulnerable to malware attacks. Chapter 6 covers malware types and methods used to protect systems from malware attacks.

- **Improper or weak patch management**. If systems aren't kept up to date with patches, hotfixes, and service packs, they are vulnerable to bugs and flaws in the software, OS, or firmware. Attackers can exploit operating systems, applications, and firmware that have known bugs but aren't patched.

- **Lack of firewalls**. If host-based and network firewalls aren't enabled or configured properly, systems are more vulnerable to network and Internet-based attacks. Chapter 3, "Exploring Network Technologies and Tools," covers firewalls in more depth.

- **Lack of organizational policies**. If job rotation, mandatory vacations, and least privilege policies aren't implemented, an organization may be more susceptible to fraud and collusion from employees. Chapter 11, "Implementing Policies to Mitigate Risks," covers organizational policies.

Not all vulnerabilities are exploited. For example, a user may install a wireless router using the defaults. It is highly vulnerable to an attack, but that doesn't mean that an attacker will discover it and attack. In other words, just because the wireless router has never been attacked, it doesn't mean that it isn't vulnerable. At any moment, a war driving attacker can drive by and exploit the vulnerability.

Risk Management Strategies

Risk management is the practice of identifying, analyzing, monitoring, and limiting risks to a manageable level. It doesn't eliminate risks but instead identifies methods to limit or mitigate them. There are several basic terms that you should understand related to risk management:

- **_Risk awareness_** is the acknowledgment that risks exist and must be addressed to mitigate them. Senior personnel need to acknowledge that risks exist. Before they do, they won't dedicate any resources to manage them.

- **_Inherent risk_** refers to the risk that exists before controls are in place to manage the risk.

- **Residual risk** is the amount of risk that remains after managing or mitigating risk to an acceptable level. Senior management is ultimately responsible for residual risk, and they are responsible for choosing a level of acceptable risk based on the organization's goals. They decide what resources (such as money, hardware, and time) to dedicate to manage the risk.

- **Control risk** refers to the risk that exists if in-place controls do not adequately manage risks. Imagine systems have antivirus software installed, but they don't have a reliable method of keeping it up to date. Additional controls are needed to manage this risk adequately.

- **Risk appetite** refers to the amount of risk an organization is willing to accept. This varies between organizations based on their goals and strategic objectives. The organization uses its risk appetite to determine its risk threshold: the level of risk that a situation must rise to before the organization chooses to take action to manage that risk. There are three main categories of risk appetite:

  - Organizations with **expansionary risk appetites** are willing to take on a high level of risk in pursuit of high rewards. For example, they may invest heavily in cutting-edge security technologies or aggressively pursue new business opportunities, even if they come with additional security risks.

  - Organizations with conservative risk appetites have a preference for low-risk investments and prioritize preserving their current security posture. For example, they may focus on implementing basic security measures or avoiding new technologies that could introduce new security risks.

  - Organizations with neutral risk appetites take a balanced approach to risk-taking. For example, they may adopt new technologies but with a cautious approach to implementation and invest in additional security measures to manage potential risks.

- **Risk tolerance** is closely related to risk appetite. It refers to the organization's ability to withstand risk. While risk appetite describes how much risk the organization is willing to take on, risk tolerance describes their ability to take it on. For example, an organization with more cash in the bank has a greater ability to remain stable when encountering financial risk.

There are multiple risk management strategies available to an organization. They include:

- **Avoidance.** An organization can avoid a risk by not providing a service or not participating in a risky activity. For example, an organization may evaluate an application that requires multiple open ports on the firewall and decide the application is too risky. It can avoid the risk by discontinuing the use of that application.

- **Mitigation.** The organization implements controls to reduce risks. These controls either reduce the vulnerabilities or reduce the impact of the threat. For example, up-to-date antivirus software mitigates the risks of malware. Similarly, a security guard can reduce the risk of an attacker accessing a secure area.

- **Acceptance.** When the cost of a control outweighs the risk, an organization will often accept the risk. For example, spending $100 in hardware locks to secure a $15 mouse doesn't make sense. Instead, the organization accepts the risk of someone stealing a mouse. Similarly, even after implementing controls, residual risk remains, and the organization accepts this residual risk. When an organization decides to accept a risk, it may need to obtain an exemption or an exception to policies, laws, or regulations governing the organization. If the acceptance might cause the organization to violate its own policies and standards, the organization may issue an exemption or exception to those policies or standards.

- **Transference.** When an organization transfers the risk to another entity or at least shares the risk with another entity, that is an example of risk transference. The most common method is purchasing insurance. This moves a portion of the financial risk from the organization itself to an insurance company, which will reimburse the organization for costs or damages relating to the risk.

- **Cybersecurity insurance** helps protect businesses and individuals from some of the losses related to cybersecurity incidents such as data breaches and network damage. Traditional insurance policies often exclude cybersecurity risks such as the loss of data or extortion from criminals using ransomware. Organizations purchase cybersecurity insurance to help cover the gaps left by traditional insurance.

★ Remember This!

It is not possible to eliminate risk, but you can take steps to manage it. An organization can avoid a risk by not providing a service or not participating in a risky activity. Insurance transfers the risk to another entity. You can mitigate risk by implementing controls, but when the cost of the controls exceeds the cost of the risk, an organization accepts the remaining, or residual, risk.

Risk Assessment Types

A **risk assessment**, or risk analysis, is an important task in risk management. It quantifies or qualifies risks based on different values or judgments. Risk assessment may be one-time, or ad hoc, assessments performed to give the organization a point-in-time view of the risk it faces. Organizations may choose to conduct these risk assessments on a recurring basis to reassess risk. For example, the organization might undergo an annual risk assessment exercise. Some organizations are moving toward a **continuous risk assessment** process where risk is constantly re-evaluated and addressed as the business and technical environment changes.

A risk assessment starts by first identifying assets and asset values.

An **asset** includes any product, system, resource, or process that an organization values, and the **asset value (AV)** identifies the value of the asset to the organization. It is normally a specific monetary amount. The asset value helps an organization focus on high-value assets and avoid wasting time on low-value assets.

After identifying asset values, the risk assessment then identifies threats and vulnerabilities and determines the likelihood a threat will attempt to exploit a vulnerability. A risk assessment attempts to identify the impact of potential threats, identify the potential harm, and prioritize risks based on the likelihood of occurrence and impact. Last, a risk assessment includes recommendations on what controls to implement to mitigate risks.

It's common to perform risk assessments on new systems or applications. For example, if an organization is considering adding a new service or application that can increase revenue, it will often perform a risk assessment. This helps it determine if the potential risks may offset the potential gains.

Risk assessments use quantitative measurements or qualitative measurements. Quantitative measurements use numbers, such as a monetary figure representing cost and asset values. Qualitative measurements use judgments. Both methods have the same core goal of helping management make educated decisions based on priorities.

A **risk control assessment** (sometimes called a risk and control assessment) examines an organization's known risks and evaluates the effectiveness of in-place controls. If a risk assessment is available, the risk control assessment will use it to identify the known risks. It then focuses on the in-place controls to determine if they adequately mitigate the known risks.

As a simple example, imagine a risk assessment identified malware as a risk. Further, imagine the organization installed antivirus software on its mail server to block all incoming emails containing malware. The risk control assessment would likely point out that malware comes from multiple sources, so antivirus software on the mail server alone is not adequate to mitigate risks from malware. It may recommend installing antivirus software on all internal hosts and using a network appliance to scan all incoming traffic for malicious traffic.

The **risk control self-assessment** is a risk control assessment, but employees perform it. In contrast, a risk control assessment is performed by a third-party. The danger of doing a self-assessment is that the same employees who installed the controls may be asked to evaluate their effectiveness.

Quantitative Risk Assessment

A **quantitative risk assessment** measures the risk of using a specific monetary amount. This monetary amount makes it easier to prioritize risks. For example, a risk with a potential loss of $30,000 is much more important than a risk with a potential loss of $1,000.

We begin the assessment of an individual risk by identifying two important factors: the **asset value (AV)** and the **exposure factor (EF)**. Many organizations choose to use the replacement cost of an asset as the AV because that is the cost the organization would incur if a risk materializes. The exposure factor is the portion of an asset that we expect would be damaged if a risk materializes.

For example, imagine that we have a rack of equipment in the basement of our office building that would cost us $1,000,000 to replace. We can say that the AV of that equipment is $1,000,000. We might be concerned about the risk of a flood damaging that equipment, so we would then look at how much of the equipment would be damaged by a typical flood. We might assess the situation and decide that a flood would likely destroy half of the equipment. That would give us an EF of 50%.

Next, we calculate the **single loss expectancy (SLE)** of the risk. The SLE is the cost of any single loss of a specific asset. We can calculate it by multiplying the asset value by the exposure factor:

$$SLE = AV \times EF$$

In our example, we know that 50% of our $1,000,000 rack would be damaged by a flood, so the SLE is 50% of $1,000,000, or $500,000. We can expect that each time a flood occurs, it will cause $500,000 in damages.

The SLE is a measure of the impact of a risk. Remember from earlier in the chapter that when we assess a risk, we look at both impact and probability/likelihood. Will a flood occur ten times a year? Or once every ten years? We really need to know that to make an informed decision about this risk.

That brings us to the **annualized rate of occurrence (ARO).** The ARO indicates how many times the loss will occur in a year. If the ARO is less than 1, the ARO is represented as a percentage. For example, if you expect flooding to occur in the basement once every ten years, the ARO is 10% or 0.1. The ARO is a measure of probability/likelihood.

Finally, we need to bring together the measures of impact and probability/likelihood. That's where we use the **annualized loss expectancy (ALE)**. We compute this value using the formula:

$$ALE = SLE \times ARO.$$

In our example, the SLE was $500,000 and the ARO was 0.1. Multiplying them together, we get an ALE of $50,000. We can expect that in any given year, the average cost of flooding will be $50,000. Now that doesn't mean that we will have $50,000 worth of damage every year. We've already discussed that we actually expect to have $500,000 worth of damage once every ten years. The ALE is designed to help us prioritize risks and quantitatively assess their impact on the organization.

Let's try another example. Imagine that employees at your company lose, on average, one laptop a month. Thieves have stolen them when employees left them in conference rooms during lunch, while they were on-site at customer locations, and from training rooms. The laptops are worth $2,000 each and when they are lost, they are completely gone. So, the AV is $2,000 and the EF is 100%.

Someone suggested purchasing hardware locks to secure these laptops for a total of $1,000. These locks work similar to bicycle locks and allow employees to wrap the cable around a piece of furniture and connect into the laptop. A thief needs to either destroy the laptop to remove the lock or take the furniture with him when stealing the laptop. Should your company purchase them? With a little analysis, the decision is easy.

You have identified the AV of these laptops, including the hardware, software, and data, is $2,000 each. This assumes employees do not store entire databases of customer information or other sensitive data on the systems, which can easily result in much higher costs. You can now calculate the SLE, ARO, and ALE as follows:

- **SLE.** The AV is $2,000 and the EF is 100%. Multiplying these together gives us an SLE of $2,000.
- **ARO.** Employees lose about one laptop a month, so the ARO is 12.
- **ALE.** You calculate the ALE as SLE × ARO, so $2,000 × 12 = $24,000.

Security experts estimate that these locks will reduce the number of lost or stolen laptops from 12 a year to only 2 a year. This changes the ALE from $24,000 to only $4,000 (saving $20,000 a year). In other words, the organization can spend $1,000 to save $20,000. It doesn't take a rocket scientist to see that this is a good fiscal decision, saving a net of $19,000. Buy them. Managers use these two simple guidelines for most of these decisions:

- If the cost of the control is less than the savings, purchase it.
- If the cost of the control is greater than the savings, accept the risk.

> ### ★ Remember This!
>
> A quantitative risk assessment uses specific monetary amounts to identify cost and asset values. The SLE identifies each loss's cost, the ARO identifies the number of events in a typical year, and the ALE identifies the expected annual loss from the risk. You calculate the ALE as SLE × ARO. A qualitative risk assessment uses judgment to categorize risks based on the likelihood of occurrence and impact.

Qualitative Risk Assessment

A **qualitative risk assessment** uses judgment to categorize risks based on the **likelihood of occurrence** (or probability) and impact. The likelihood of occurrence is the probability that an event will occur, such as the likelihood that a threat will attempt to exploit a vulnerability. **Impact** is the magnitude of harm resulting from a risk. It includes the negative results of an event, such as the loss of confidentiality, integrity, or availability of a system or data.

Notice that this is much different from the exact numbers provided by a quantitative assessment that uses monetary figures. You can think of quantitative as using a quantity or a number, whereas qualitative is related to quality, which is often a matter of judgment.

Some qualitative risk assessments use surveys or focus groups. They canvass experts to provide their best judgments and then tabulate the results. For example, a survey may ask the experts to rate the probability and impact of risks associated with a web server selling products on the Internet and a library workstation without Internet access. The experts would use words such as low, medium, and high to rate them.

They could rate the probability of a web server being attacked as high, and if the attack takes the web server out of service, the impact is also high. On the other hand, the probability of a library workstation being attacked is low, and, even though a library patron may be inconvenienced, the impact is also low.

It's common to assign numbers to these judgments. For example, you can use low, medium, and high terms and give them values of 1, 5, and 10, respectively. The experts assign a probability and impact of each risk using low, medium, and high, and when tabulating the results, you change the words to numbers. This makes it a little easier to calculate the results.

In the web server and library computer examples, you can calculate the risk by multiplying the probability and the impact:

- **Web server.** High probability and high impact: 10 × 10 = 100
- **Library computer.** Low probability and low impact: 1 × 1 = 1

Management can look at these numbers and easily determine how to allocate resources to protect against the risks. They would allocate more resources to protect the web server than the library computer. One of the challenges with a qualitative risk assessment is gaining consensus on the probability and impact. Unlike monetary values that you can validate with facts, probability and impact are often subject to debate.

Risk Reporting

The final phase of the risk assessment is ***risk reporting***. This identifies the risks discovered during the assessment and the recommended controls. As a simple example, a risk assessment on a database-enabled web application may discover that it's susceptible to SQL injection attacks. The risk assessment will then recommend rewriting the web application with input validation techniques and stored procedures to protect the database.

Management uses this to decide which controls to implement and which controls to accept. In many cases, a final report documents the managerial decisions. Of course, management can decide not to implement a control but instead accept a risk.

Think how valuable this report will be for an attacker. They won't need to dig to identify vulnerabilities or controls. Instead, the report lists all the details. Even when management approves controls to correct the vulnerabilities, it may take some time to implement them. Because of this, it's important to protect the risk assessment report. Normally, only executive management and security professionals will have access to these reports.

Risk Analysis

Risk assessments use a variety of techniques to analyze risks. Generically, a risk analysis identifies potential issues that could negatively impact an organization's goals and objectives. However, different disciplines define it a little differently. As an example, project management professionals would tell you that a risk analysis identifies potential risks that may impact a project's outcomes and objectives instead of the organization's goals and objectives.

Similarly, the following terms might have slightly different definitions within project management circles or with financial management specialists. However, these definitions are valid within cybersecurity:

- **Key risk indicators (KRIs)** are metrics used to measure and monitor the level of risk associated with a particular activity, process, or system. KRIs provide a way for organizations to proactively identify potential risks and take action to mitigate or manage them before they become significant issues. Examples of KRIs may include measures such as the number of security incidents detected per month, the percentage of overdue security patches, or the average time to detect and respond to a security incident. These metrics can help organizations identify trends, detect potential issues early, and take corrective action to minimize the impact of potential risks.
- A **risk register** is a document or tool that organizations use to identify, assess, and manage risks. It typically includes a list of identified risks, along with information about their likelihood, potential impact, and current status. A risk register helps organizations to prioritize risks, allocate resources for risk mitigation, and monitor progress over time. In addition to identifying risks, the risk register assigns risk owners, who are responsible for managing each risk. Risk owners are typically individuals or teams who have the expertise and authority to manage the risk effectively. They are responsible for monitoring the risk, implementing mitigation measures, and reporting on the risk's status.
- **Risk matrix.** A **risk matrix** places risks onto a chart of rows and columns, showing probability and impact. As a simple example, it can plot the likelihood of occurrence data against the impact of a risk, as shown in Figure 8.1.

RISK MATRIX

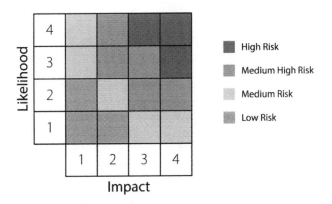

Figure 8.1: Risk Matrix

> ✦ *Remember This!*
>
> A risk register is a comprehensive document listing known information about risks such as the risk owner. It typically includes risk scores along with recommended security controls to reduce the risk scores. A risk matrix plots risks onto a chart.

Supply Chain Risks

A ***supply chain*** includes all the elements required to produce and sell a product. As a simple example, consider the Lard Lad Donuts store. They require a steady supply of flour, sugar, eggs, milk, oil, and other ingredients. They also require refrigerators to store raw materials, space to manufacture the donuts, and fryers to cook them. Last, they need a method to sell the donuts to customers. If any of these items fail, the company won't be able to make and sell donuts.

It's important to realize that the supply chain isn't only the supply of raw materials. It also includes all the processes required to create and distribute a finished product. For an IT organization, conducting a complete review of the supply chain involves looking at every organization that provides some essential component of your technology environment. This should include hardware suppliers, software suppliers, and service providers.

A supply chain can become an attack vector if an attacker can disrupt the supply chain. If an attacker wanted to stop the donut store from producing donuts, it isn't necessary to attack the donut store. Instead, an attacker can attack one of the third-party suppliers in a supply chain attack. A potential indicator of a supply chain attack is a disruption in the supply chain.

Organizations can eliminate the supply chain as a third-party risk simply by ensuring that it has multiple sources for everything that it needs. While this is relatively simple when looking for alternate sources to purchase flour and sugar, it can be difficult when an organization needs complex materials.

Comparing Scanning and Testing Tools

Security administrators use tools to test their networks. Two common categories of tools are vulnerability scanners, which check for weaknesses, and penetration tests, which attempt to exploit the vulnerabilities. This section covers vulnerability scanners and penetration tests in more depth.

Checking for Vulnerabilities

Vulnerabilities are weaknesses, and by reducing vulnerabilities, you can reduce risks. That sounds simple enough. However, how do you identify the vulnerabilities that present the greatest risks? Some common methods are vulnerability assessments and vulnerability scans.

The overall goal of a **vulnerability assessment** is to assess the security posture of systems and networks. They identify vulnerabilities or weaknesses within systems, networks, and organizations and are part of an overall risk management plan.

Vulnerability assessments can include information from a wide variety of sources. This includes reviewing security policies and logs, interviewing personnel, and testing systems. Assessments often use a variety of scans and penetration tests, all discussed in this section. A vulnerability assessment typically includes the following high-level steps:

- Identify assets and capabilities.
- Prioritize assets based on value.
- Identify vulnerabilities and prioritize them.
- Recommend controls to mitigate serious vulnerabilities.

Many organizations perform vulnerability assessments internally. Organizations also hire external security professionals to complete external assessments. The following sections discuss many of the common tools used for vulnerability assessments and vulnerability scans.

Network Scanners

A **network scanner** uses various techniques to gather information about hosts within a network. As an example, Nmap is a popular network scanning tool that can give you a lot of information about hosts within a network. Network scanners typically use the following methods:

- **ARP ping scan**. Chapter 3 discusses the Address Resolution Protocol (ARP) and how systems use it to resolve IP addresses to media access control (MAC) addresses. Any host that receives an ARP packet with its IP address responds with its MAC address. If the host responds, the network scanner knows that a host is operational with that IP address.

■ ***Syn stealth scan***. Chapter 3 discusses the Transmission Control Protocol (TCP) three-way handshake. As a reminder, one host sends out a SYN (synchronize) packet to initiate a TCP session. The other host responds with a SYN/ACK (synchronize/acknowledge) packet. The first host then completes the handshake with an ACK packet to establish the connection. A syn stealth scan sends a single SYN packet to each IP address in the scan range. If a host responds, the scanner knows that a host is operational with that IP address. However, instead of responding with an ACK packet, a scanner typically sends an RST (reset) response to close the connection.

■ ***Port scan***. A port scan checks for open ports on a system. Each open port indicates the underlying protocol is running on the system. For example, if port 443 is open, it indicates the host is running HTTPS, meaning it is probably a web server. A port scan typically uses the ports identified as well-known ports by the Internet Assigned Numbers Authority (IANA) and discussed in Appendix D.

■ ***Service scan***. A service scan is like a port scan, but it goes a step further. A port scan identifies open ports and gives hints about what protocols or services might be running. The service scan verifies the protocol or service. For example, if a port scan identifies port 443 is open, a service scan will send an HTTPS command, such as "Get /." If HTTPS is running on port 443, it will respond to the Get command verifying that it is a web server.

■ ***OS detection***. Operating system (OS) detection techniques analyze packets from an IP address to identify the OS. This is often referred to as TCP/IP fingerprinting. As a simple example, the TCP window size (the size of the receive window in the first packet of a TCP session) is not fixed. Different operating systems use different sizes. Some Linux versions use a size of 5,840 bytes, some Cisco routers use a size of 4,128 bytes, and different Windows versions use sizes of 8,192 and 65,535. OS detection techniques don't rely on a single value but typically evaluate multiple values included in systems responses.

Vulnerability Scanning

Security administrators often use a ***vulnerability scanner*** to identify which systems are susceptible to attacks. Vulnerability scanners identify a wide range of weaknesses and known security issues that attackers can exploit. Most vulnerability scanners combine multiple features into a single package. A vulnerability scan often includes the following actions:

■ Identify vulnerabilities.
■ Identify misconfigurations.
■ Passively test security controls.
■ Identify lack of security controls.
■ Vulnerability Classification Standards

- Vulnerability scanners utilize a database or dictionary of known vulnerabilities and test systems against this database. For example, the MITRE Corporation maintains the **Common Vulnerabilities and Exposures (CVE)** list, which is a dictionary of publicly known security vulnerabilities and exposures. This is similar to how antivirus software detects malware using virus signatures. The difference is that the CVE is one public list funded by the U.S. government, whereas antivirus vendors maintain proprietary signature files.

- The **Common Vulnerability Scoring System (CVSS)** assesses vulnerabilities and assigns severity scores in a range of 0 to 10, with 10 being the most severe. This helps security professionals prioritize their work in mitigating known vulnerabilities.

- Other standards used by vulnerability scanners include the **Security Content Automation Protocol (SCAP)**. SCAP is designed to help facilitate communication between vulnerability scanners and other security and management tools.

Prioritizing Vulnerabilities

After running a vulnerability scan, organizations may find that there are dozens, hundreds, or even thousands of vulnerabilities in their environment. They will need to prioritize those vulnerabilities to address the most important ones first. They do this using many different information sources:

- **Vulnerability classification**. Use an industry-standard classification system to identify the type and severity of a vulnerability. Organizations commonly use the CVSS score for this purpose.

- **Environmental variables**. Every organization is different and operates in a different technical environment. Consider the nature of that environment when prioritizing vulnerabilities.

- **Industry/organizational impact**. Different industries work with different types of data and have different regulations and sensitivities. A vulnerability that is very serious in an online banking environment might be far less worrisome on a system used to monitor water flow.

- **Risk tolerance/threshold**. Organizations need to decide what level of risk a vulnerability must rise to before they will address it. It's unlikely that you will be able to address every vulnerability that exists, so you must use a threshold to determine those that require attention.

Analyzing Vulnerability Scan Output

A vulnerability scan creates a report showing the results of the scan. The output of the scan typically shows the following information:

- A list of hosts that it discovered and scanned
- A detailed list of applications running on each host
- A detailed list of open ports and services found on each host
- A list of vulnerabilities discovered on any of the scanned hosts
- Recommendations to resolve any of the discovered vulnerabilities

Some vulnerability scanners include the ability to run at preconfigured times automatically. Administrators can use predefined vulnerability reports or create customized reports based on their needs. These reports are typically available in logs, and administrators perform log reviews periodically.

When analyzing the scan outputs, it's important to compare them with previous scans. In some cases, you may notice that scans report the same vulnerability. There are two primary reasons for this. It could be that a patch has undesired side effects, so management has decided to accept the risk and not apply the patch. It could also be that the vendor has not created a patch.

Passively Testing Security Controls

An important point about a vulnerability scan is that it does not attempt to exploit any vulnerabilities. Instead, a vulnerability scan is a passive attempt to identify weaknesses. This ensures that the testing does not interfere with normal operations. Security administrators then assess the vulnerabilities to determine which ones to mitigate. In contrast, a penetration test (covered later in this chapter) is an active test that attempts to exploit vulnerabilities.

 Remember This!

A vulnerability scanner can identify vulnerabilities, misconfigured systems, and the lack of security controls such as up-to-date patches. Vulnerability scans may be configured as passive and have little impact on a system during a test. In contrast, a penetration test is intrusive and can potentially compromise a system.

Confirmation of Scan Results

Unfortunately, scanners aren't perfect. Occasionally, they report a vulnerability when it doesn't actually exist. In other words, a scan may indicate a system has a known vulnerability, but the report is false. This is a ***false positive***. As an example, a vulnerability scan on a server might report that the server is missing patches related to a database application, but the server doesn't have a database application installed. One of the major tasks facing security professionals after running a vulnerability scan is confirming whether the vulnerability actually exists and eliminating false positive reports.

This is similar to false positives in an intrusion detection system (IDS), where the IDS alerts on an event, but the event isn't an actual intrusion. Similarly, an antivirus scanner can identify a useful application as malware, even though it does not have any malicious code. False positives can result in higher administrative overhead because administrators have to investigate them.

Scanners can give false negatives also. If a vulnerability exists but the scanner doesn't detect it, this is a **false negative**. As an example, imagine that when patches are applied to an application server, it breaks the application. Management decides to accept the risk of not applying these patches to keep the application running. Even though these patches are missing, the vulnerability scanner doesn't report that the patches are missing. The following list describes the four possibilities when a scanner scans a system looking for vulnerabilities. Refer to Figure 8.2 as you're reading them:

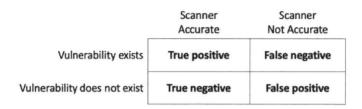

	Scanner Accurate	Scanner Not Accurate
Vulnerability exists	**True positive**	**False negative**
Vulnerability does not exist	**True negative**	**False positive**

Figure 8.2: False positives and false negatives

- **False positive.** A false positive is when a vulnerability scanner incorrectly reports that a vulnerability   exists, but the vulnerability does not exist on the scanned system.
- **False negative.** A false negative is when a vulnerability exists, but the scanner doesn't detect it and doesn't report the vulnerability.
- **True positive.** A true positive indicates that the vulnerability scanner correctly identified a vulnerability.
- **True negative.** A true negative indicates that a system doesn't have a vulnerability, and the vulnerability scanner did not report the vulnerability.

Credentialed vs. Non-Credentialed Scans

Vulnerability scanners can run as a credentialed scan using an account's credentials or as non-credentialed without any user credentials. Attackers typically do not have an internal account's credentials, so when they run scans against systems, they run non-credentialed scans.

Security administrators often run **credentialed scans** with the privileges of an administrator account. This allows the scan to check security issues at a much deeper level than a **non-credentialed scan**. For example, a credentialed scan can list the software versions of installed programs. Additionally, because the credentialed scan can access a system's internal workings, it results in a lower impact on the tested systems, along with more accurate test results and fewer false positives.

It's worth mentioning that attackers typically start without any credentials but use privilege escalation techniques to gain administrative access. This allows them to run a credentialed scan against a network if desired. Similarly, even though a credentialed scan is typically more accurate, administrators often run non-credentialed scans to see what an attacker without credentials would see.

> ### 📌 *Remember This!*
>
> A false positive from a vulnerability scan indicates that a scan detected a vulnerability, but the vulnerability doesn't exist. Credentialed scans run under the context of a valid account and can get more detailed information on targets, such as the software versions of installed applications. They are typically more accurate than non-credentialed scans and result in fewer false positives.

Configuration Review

A configuration compliance scanner performs a configuration review of systems to verify that they are configured correctly. They will often use a file that identifies the proper configuration for systems. When running the scan, the scanner will verify that systems have the same configuration defined in the configuration file. This is also known as configuration validation. Security administrators often configure these tools to use automation or scripting methods so that they automatically run on a set schedule.

Configuration review scans typically need to be run as credentialed scans. This helps ensure they can accurately read the configuration of systems during the scan.

Penetration Testing

Penetration testing actively assesses deployed security controls within a system or network. It starts with reconnaissance to learn about the target but takes it a step further and tries to exploit vulnerabilities by simulating or performing an attack. There are four major categories of penetration test:

1. ***Physical Penetration Testing***: This type of testing focuses on identifying vulnerabilities in the physical security measures of an organization. It involves attempting to gain unauthorized access to physical spaces, such as buildings, data centers, or other secure areas. Physical penetration testing may involve tactics such as social engineering, lock picking, or physical bypassing of security measures. The goal is to identify weaknesses in physical security controls that could be exploited by attackers.
2. ***Offensive Penetration Testing***: This type of testing involves simulating a real-world attack on an organization's network, systems, or applications. It is carried out from the perspective of an attacker and seeks to identify vulnerabilities that could be exploited to gain unauthorized access or cause damage to the organization. Offensive penetration testing often includes techniques such as vulnerability scanning, exploitation of identified vulnerabilities, and lateral movement within the network.

3. **Defensive Penetration Testing**: This type of testing involves evaluating an organization's security controls to identify areas where they may be vulnerable to attack. The goal is to identify weaknesses in security controls before they can be exploited by attackers. Defensive penetration testing may include tactics such as firewall rule analysis, configuration reviews, or penetration testing of web applications.

4. **Integrated Penetration Testing**: This type of testing combines elements of physical, offensive, and defensive testing to provide a comprehensive evaluation of an organization's security posture. It involves simulating a real-world attack on an organization's physical and digital assets to identify vulnerabilities that could be exploited by attackers. Integrated penetration testing is typically conducted by a team of experts who have expertise in physical security, network security, and application security.

Because a penetration test can exploit vulnerabilities, it has the potential to disrupt actual operations and cause system instability. Because of this, it's important to strictly define the boundaries for a test. Ideally, the penetration test will stop right before performing an exploit that can cause damage or result in an outage. However, some tests cause unexpected results.

Testers sometimes perform penetration tests on test systems rather than the live production systems. For example, an organization may be hosting a web application accessible on the Internet. Instead of performing the test on the live server and affecting customers, penetration testers or administrators configure another server with the same web application. If a penetration test cripples the test server, it accurately demonstrates security vulnerabilities, but it doesn't affect customers.

> ★ **Remember This!**
>
> A penetration test is an active test that can assess deployed security controls and determine the impact of a threat. It starts with reconnaissance and then tries to exploit vulnerabilities by attacking or simulating an attack.

Rules of Engagement

It's important to obtain authorization before beginning any vulnerability or penetration testing. This outlines the **rules of engagement** or the boundaries of the tests. If testing results in an outage even though the testers followed the engagement rules, repercussions are less likely.

In most cases, this consent is in writing. If it isn't in writing, many security professionals won't perform any testing. A penetration test without consent is an attack, and an organization may perceive a well-meaning administrator doing an unauthorized penetration test as an attacker. The administrator might be updating his résumé after running an unauthorized scan or penetration test.

Reconnaissance

Penetration testers use a variety of methods for **reconnaissance** (sometimes called **footprinting**). During the reconnaissance phase, the penetration tester (or attacker) attempts to learn as much as possible about a network. Testers use both passive reconnaissance and active network reconnaissance and discovery when gathering information on targets.

Passive and Active Reconnaissance

Passive reconnaissance collects information about a targeted system, network, or organization using open-source intelligence (OSINT). This includes viewing social media sources about the target, news reports, and even the organization's website. If the organization has wireless networks, it could include passively collecting information from the network, such as network SSIDs. Note that because passive reconnaissance doesn't engage a target, it isn't illegal.

As an example, theHarvester is a passive reconnaissance command-line tool used by testers in the early stages of a penetration test. It uses OSINT methods to gather data such as email addresses, employee names, host IP addresses, and URLs. It uses popular (and not so popular) search engines for queries and then correlates the results in a comprehensive report.

Passive reconnaissance does not include using any tools to send information to targets and analyze the responses. However, passive reconnaissance can include using tools to gather information from systems other than the target. For example, you can sometimes gain information about a domain name holder using the Whois lookup site (https://www.whois.com). Other times, you can gain information by querying Domain Name System (DNS) servers.

Active reconnaissance methods use tools to engage targets. The next section describes many tools used to gather information about networks using active reconnaissance methods.

Network Reconnaissance and Discovery

Network reconnaissance and discovery methods use tools to send data to systems and analyze the responses. This phase typically starts by using various scanning tools such as network scanners and vulnerability scanners. It's important to realize that network reconnaissance engages targets and is almost always illegal. It should never be started without first getting explicit authorization to do so.

The "Network Scanners" section earlier in this chapter discussed how tools gather a significant amount of information about networks and individual systems. This includes identifying all IP addresses active on a network, the ports and services active on individual systems, and the operating system running on individual systems. Some tools used during this phase include:

- **IP scanner.** An **IP scanner** (sometimes called a ping scanner) searches a network for active IP addresses. It typically sends an Internet Control Message Protocol (ICMP) ping to a range of IP addresses in a network. If the host responds, the network scanner knows there is a host operational with that IP address. A problem with ping scans is that firewalls often block ICMP, so the scan may give inconsistent results.

- **Nmap. *Nmap*** is a network scanner that you can run from the command prompt. It includes many capabilities, including identifying all the active hosts on a network, their IP addresses, the protocols and services running on each of these hosts, and the host's operating system. When running the command, you include the scan type(s), options, and target specifications.

- **Netcat. *Netcat*** (nc) is a command-line tool that administrators often use for remotely accessing Linux systems. Testers often use it for banner grabbing, a technique used to gain information about remote systems. Banner grabbing will identify the target's operating system along with information about some applications. It can also be used to transfer files and check for open ports.

- **Scanless.** Penetration testers often use **scanless**, a Python-based command-line utility to perform port scans. A benefit is that scanless uses an online website (with or without the website owner's permission) to perform the scans so that the scans don't come from the tester's IP address. Instead, they appear to originate from the website's IP address.

- **Dnsenum.** The **dnsenum** command will enumerate (or list) Domain Name System (DNS) records for domains. It lists the DNS servers holding the records and identifies the mail servers (if they exist) by listing the mx records. Next, it attempts to do an AXFR transfer to download all DNS records from the DNS servers holding the records. However, unauthenticated AXFR transfers are usually blocked on DNS servers so the AXFR requests will normally fail.

- **Nessus.** Nessus is a vulnerability scanner developed by Tenable Network Security. It uses plug-ins to perform various scans against systems and is often used for configuration reviews. AutoNessus is a free tool that can be used to automate Nessus scans.

- **hping.** You can use the hping utility to send pings using TCP, UDP, or ICMP. You can also use it to scan systems for open ports on remote systems.

- **Sn1per.** Sn1per is a robust automated scanner used for vulnerability assessments and to gather information on targets during penetration testing. It combines the features of many common tools into a single application. It comes in two editions: Community and Professional. The Community edition performs vulnerability assessments, listing all discovered vulnerabilities and detailed information on the targets. The Professional edition also includes the ability to exploit the vulnerabilities.

- **cURL.** The Client URL command (cURL) is used to transfer and retrieve data to and from servers, such as web servers. The Uniform Resource Locator (URL) is the address of a webpage. Penetration testers can use scripts to identify all of the URLs of a website and then use cURL to retrieve all of the pages. Most websites prevent unauthorized personnel from posting data to them, but blocking cURL requests isn't as easy.

Footprinting Versus Fingerprinting

Penetration testers often combine footprinting with fingerprinting techniques to identify targets. **Network footprinting** provides a big-picture view of a network, including the Internet Protocol (IP) addresses active on a target network. Fingerprinting then homes in on individual systems to provide details of each. This is similar to how fingerprints identify an individual.

Operating system fingerprinting identifies the operating system. For example, is this a Linux system or a Windows system? A fingerprinting attack sends protocol queries or port scans to a server and analyzes the responses. These responses can verify that a service is running and often include other details about the operating system because different operating systems often respond differently to specific queries. The "Network Scanners" section described how many scanners do this to identify operating systems.

Initial Exploitation

After scanning the target, testers discover vulnerabilities. They then take it further and look for a vulnerability they can exploit. For example, a vulnerability scan may discover that a system doesn't have a patch installed for a known vulnerability. The vulnerability allows attackers (and testers) to remotely access the system and install malware.

With this knowledge, the testers can use known methods to exploit this vulnerability. This gives the testers full access to the system. They can then install additional software on the exploited system.

Persistence

Persistence is an attacker's ability to maintain a presence in a network for weeks, months, or even years without being detected. Penetration testers use similar techniques to maintain persistence within a network.

A common technique used to maintain persistence is to create a backdoor into the network. For example, a tester may create alternate accounts and access them remotely. It's also possible for testers or attackers to install or modify services to connect back into a system in some cases. For example, a tester may enable Secure Shell (SSH) and then create a method used to log on to a system using SSH.

Lateral Movement

When an attacker first exploits a user's computer, the attacker often has the user's credentials. The attacker uses the credentials to access the targeted system and then uses the targeted system for lateral movement. **Lateral movement** refers to the way attackers maneuver throughout a network. As an example, Windows Management Instrumentation (WMI) and PowerShell are frequently used to scan a Windows network.

After discovering other systems, the attacker looks for vulnerabilities and exploits them if possible. By exploiting multiple systems, the attacker has a better chance of maintaining persistence in a network.

Privilege Escalation

In many penetration tests, the tester first gains access to a low-level system or low-level account. For example, a tester might gain access to Homer's computer using Homer's user account. Homer has access to the network, but doesn't have any administrative privileges. However, testers use various techniques to gain more and more privileges on Homer's computer and his network.

Chapter 6 discusses ***privilege escalation*** tactics that attackers often use. The "One Click Lets Them In" section discusses how advanced persistent threats (APTs) often use remote access Trojans (RATs) to gain access to a single system. Attackers trick a user into clicking a malicious link, which gives them access to a single computer. Attackers then use various techniques to scan the network looking for vulnerabilities. By exploiting these vulnerabilities, the attackers gain more and more privileges on the network.

Penetration testers use similar tactics. Depending on how much they are authorized to do, testers can use other methods to gain more and more access to a network.

Pivoting

Pivoting is the process of using various tools to gain access to additional systems on a network after an initial compromise. For example, imagine a tester gains access to Homer's computer within a company's network. The tester can then pivot and use Homer's computer to gather information on other computers. Homer might have access to network shares filled with files on nuclear power plant operations. The tester can use Homer's computer to collect this data and then send it back out of the network from Homer's computer.

Testers (and attackers) can use pivoting techniques to gather a wide variety of information. Many times, the tester must first use privilege escalation techniques to gain more privileges. However, after doing so, the tester can access databases (such as user accounts and password databases), email, and any other type of data stored within a network.

> ### ★ Remember This!
>
> After exploiting a system, penetration testers use privilege escalation techniques to gain more access to target systems. Pivoting is the process of using an exploited system to target other systems.

Known, Unknown, and Partially Known Testing Environments

It's common to identify testing based on the testers' level of knowledge before starting the test. These testers could be internal employees or external security professionals working for a third-party organization hired to perform the test. Testing types are defined based on how much the testers know about the environment. The three types of testing are:

- **Unknown environment testing.** Testers have zero knowledge of the environment prior to starting an ***unknown environment test*** (sometimes called a black box test). Instead, they approach the test with the same knowledge as an attacker. When testing new applications, they wouldn't have any prior experience with the application. When testing networks, they aren't provided any information or documentation on the network before the test. These testers often use fuzzing to check for application vulnerabilities. This has been commonly called a black box test.
- **Known environment testing.** Testers have full knowledge of the environment before starting a ***known environment test*** (sometimes called a white box test). For example, they would have access to product documentation, source code, and possibly even logon details.
- **Partially known environment testing.** Testers have some knowledge of the environment prior to starting a ***partially known environment test*** (sometimes called a gray box test). For example, they might have access to some network documentation but not know the full network layout.

> ### ★ Remember This!
>
> Unknown environment testers have zero prior knowledge of a system prior to a penetration test. Known environment testers have full knowledge of the environment, and partially known environment testers have some knowledge.

Cleanup

Cleanup is one of the last steps of a penetration test. It includes removing all traces of the penetration tester's activities. Of course, this is dependent on what the penetration tester did during the test and the rules of engagement. Cleanup activities include:

- Removing any user accounts created on systems in the network
- Removing any scripts or applications added or installed on systems
- Removing any files, such as logs or temporary files, created on systems
- Reconfiguring all settings modified by testers during the penetration test

This is an extensive list, and testers should not rely on their memory. Instead, it's common for testers to create a log of what they're doing as they're doing it. This makes it easier to reverse all their actions.

Responsible Disclosure Programs

Responsible disclosure (RD) programs for vulnerabilities enable individuals and organizations to report security vulnerabilities or weaknesses they have discovered to the appropriate parties. The goal of responsible disclosure is to allow security issues to be addressed before they are exploited by attackers, ultimately improving overall security for everyone.

RD programs typically involve a coordinated process for reporting vulnerabilities to the appropriate parties, such as vendors, developers, or security teams. This process usually includes guidelines for reporting vulnerabilities, a point of contact for reporting, and expectations for the timeline of the response and resolution. When vulnerabilities are reported, the organization receiving the report is expected to investigate and, if necessary, take appropriate steps to address the issue.

Bug bounty programs are a type of responsible disclosure program that incentivizes individuals or organizations to report vulnerabilities by offering monetary or other rewards for valid submissions. Bug bounty programs can be run by organizations to encourage external researchers or hackers to report vulnerabilities that internal teams may miss. Some bug bounty programs are open to the public, while others are by invitation only. This creates a crowdsourced model of experts looking for vulnerabilities.

System and Process Audits

System and process audits are important tools for assessing an organization's compliance with industry standards, best practices, and internal policies. Audits typically involve a review of an organization's systems, processes, and procedures to identify areas of non-compliance, inefficiencies, or areas of potential risk.

During the audit process, auditors may use a variety of tools and techniques to collect information, including interviews, document reviews, and system scans. As a result, audits can be a source of valuable information on an organization's security posture, including identifying vulnerabilities that may be present.

Intrusive Versus Non-Intrusive Testing

Scans can be either intrusive or non-intrusive. You can also think of these terms as invasive and non-invasive, respectively. Tools using intrusive methods can potentially disrupt the operations of a system. In contrast, tools using non-intrusive methods will not compromise a system. These terms also apply to penetration testing (intrusive) and vulnerability scanning (non-intrusive).

When comparing penetration testing and vulnerability scanning, it's important to remember that penetration tests are intrusive and more invasive than vulnerability scans. They involve probing a system and attempting to exploit any vulnerabilities they discover. If they successfully exploit a vulnerability, a penetration test can potentially disrupt services and even take a system down.

Vulnerability scans are generally non-intrusive and less invasive than penetration tests. Standard scans do not attempt to exploit a vulnerability. Because of this, a vulnerability scan is much safer to run on a system or network because it is significantly less likely that it will affect services.

Responding to Vulnerabilities

Once you've identified the vulnerabilities that exist in your environment and decided that you are going to address them, you have a few options at your disposal.

Remediating Vulnerabilities

The most common method for resolving a vulnerability is **patching** the affected system. Software patches are updates that correct vulnerabilities and other flaws in an application. When software vendors learn of a new vulnerability, they design a patch to correct the problem and release it to their customers. Administrators should apply patches to correct vulnerabilities as promptly as possible.

Sometimes there isn't a patch available. Perhaps the vendor is still working on fixing a vulnerability or a system is beyond its support date and the vendor will not be correcting the issue. In those cases, security professionals may decide to stop operating the system, but that isn't always practical. Business needs may require continuing to operate a vulnerable system. In that scenario, you have a few options available:

- Deploy a **compensating control**. This is a secondary security control that prevents the vulnerability from being exploited. For example, if a web application has a known SQL injection vulnerability, you can protect that application with a web application firewall (WAF) designed to block SQL injection attacks from reaching the application.

- Use **segmentation** to place the system on an isolated network. This reduces the ability of outsiders to reach the system, minimizing the risk of a compromise.

- Grant an **exception** or exemption to security policy that allows the system to continue operating. It's normally only a good idea to do this in conjunction with other measures, such as segmentation or a compensating control. Granting an exception to policy and allowing a vulnerable system to continue to operate without doing anything else to address the problem is very risky!

Validation of Remediation

After remediating a vulnerability, you'll want to confirm that your corrective measures are working properly and that the vulnerability no longer exists. The first thing you should do is rescan the affected system and verify that the vulnerability no longer exists. You may then update your vulnerability reporting to communicate to stakeholders that the vulnerability was addressed. Be sure to maintain records of your work, as they may come in handy if they are questioned during a security audit.

Capturing Network Traffic

Several tools are available for use by security professionals and attackers alike. This chapter covered vulnerability scanners, including their use as ping scanners and port scanners. However, other tools are available. This section discusses tools used to capture network traffic.

Packet Capture and Replay

Packet capture refers to capturing network packets transmitted over a network, and packet replay refers to sending packets back out over the network. You can capture packets using a protocol analyzer, which is sometimes called sniffing or using a sniffer.

Protocol analyzers provide administrators and attackers with the ability to analyze and modify packet headers and their payloads. They typically modify them before sending them back out as a packet replay. Administrators can use a protocol analyzer to troubleshoot communication issues between network systems or identify potential attacks using manipulated or fragmented packets.

Attackers can use a protocol analyzer to capture data sent across a network in cleartext. For example, unencrypted credentials are usernames and passwords sent across a network in cleartext. One of the ways attackers can view this data is by connecting an unauthorized switch within a network to capture traffic and forward it to a system running a protocol analyzer. If cabling isn't protected, they might be able to simply connect a switch above a drop-down ceiling. Wireshark is a free protocol analyzer that you can download from the Wireshark website: **https://www.wireshark.org/**.

Figure 8.3 shows the Wireshark protocol analyzer output after it captured packets transmitted over the network. It includes 155 packets and has packet 121 selected in the top pane. The top pane shows the source and destination IP addresses and the Server Message Block (SMB) protocol. Many networks use SMB to send files over the network, and this packet includes the contents of that file. The middle pane shows details from this packet with the Internet Protocol version 4 header information partially expanded. The bottom pane shows the packet's entire contents (including the unencrypted credentials) displayed in hexadecimal and ASCII characters.

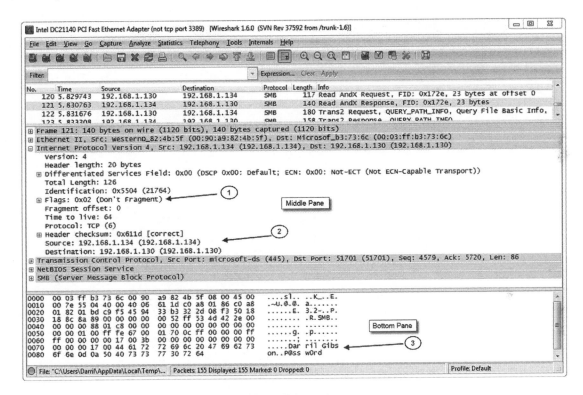

Figure 8.3: Wireshark capture

Although it can be tedious to analyze a packet capture, there is a lot of information in it for anyone willing to take the time to do so. Occasionally, attackers manipulate flags (arrow 1) within the headers for different types of attacks, and the protocol analyzer allows you to verify header manipulation attacks. You can also see the source and destination IP addresses (arrow 2) within the IP header field. You can expand the Ethernet II section to show the media access control (MAC) addresses of the source and destination computers.

Notice that you can view the unencrypted credentials—username (DarrilGibson) and password (P@ssw0rd)— in the bottom pane (arrow 3) because SMB sends usernames and passwords in cleartext. However, if an application encrypted the data before sending it across the network, it would not be readable.

> 📌 **Remember This!**
>
> Administrators use a protocol analyzer to capture, display, and analyze packets sent over a network. It is useful when troubleshooting communication problems between systems. It is also useful to detect attacks that manipulate or fragment packets.

Tcpreplay and Tcpdump

Tcpreplay is a suite of utilities used to edit packet captures and then send the edited packets over the network. It includes tcpreplay, tcpprep, tcprewrite, and more. It is often used for testing network devices.

As an example, administrators can modify packets to mimic known attacks and then send them to an intrusion detection system (IDS). Ideally, an IDS should always detect a known attack and send an alert. Using tcpreplay, security administrators can prove that an IDS can detect specific attacks.

The **tcpdump** command is a command-line protocol analyzer. It allows you to capture packets like you can with Wireshark. The difference is that Wireshark is a Windows-based tool and tcpdump is executed from the command line. Many administrators use tcpdump to capture the packets and later use Wireshark to analyze the packet capture.

Kali Linux includes tcpdump, and as with most Linux command-line tools, tcpdump is case sensitive. You need to enter tcpdump in all lowercase. Additionally, the switches must be entered with the proper case. For example,

-c (lowercase c) represents count and indicates the capture should stop after receiving the specified number of packets. However, -C (uppercase C) represents file size and indicates the maximum size (in millions of bytes) of a packet capture. When the file reaches this size, tcpdump closes it and starts storing packets in a new file. It's not available on Windows systems by default, but there are versions for Windows available for download.

NetFlow

NetFlow is a feature available on many routers and switches that can collect IP traffic statistics and send them to a NetFlow collector. The NetFlow collector receives the data and stores it, and analysis software on the NetFlow collector allows administrators to view and analyze the network activity.

Protocol analyzers like Wireshark allow you to capture and view all data, including headers and payloads of individual packets. In contrast, NetFlow doesn't include payload data and doesn't even include individual packet headers. Instead, a NetFlow record only shows counts, or statistics, related to data a device receives. Cisco created NetFlow, but several other vendors have adopted it.

NetFlow uses templates to identify what data to include in a NetFlow packet, but you'll typically see the following information:

- Timestamps identifying the start and finish time of the flow
- Input interface identifier (on router or switch)
- Output interface identifier (will be zero if a packet is dropped)
- Source information (source IP address and port number, if used)
- Destination information (destination IP address and port, if used)
- Packet count and byte count
- Protocol (such as TCP, UDP, ICMP, or any other Layer 3 protocol)

Understanding Frameworks and Standards

A *framework* is a structure used to provide a foundation. Cybersecurity frameworks typically use a structure of basic concepts, and they provide guidance to professionals on how to implement security in various systems. There are multiple frameworks available that describe best practices and provide instructions on how to secure systems.

ISO Standards

The *International Organization for Standardization (ISO)* is an independent organization that establishes standards. They develop standards for a wide variety of industrial and commercial applications, and some directly address cybersecurity topics. However, these documents are not available for free but must be purchased online. In contrast, documents created by NIST are all free to download and use. The following list shows some standards relevant to cybersecurity.

- **ISO 27001**. ISO 27001, "Information Security Management Systems," provides information on information security management systems (ISMS) requirements. Organizations that implement the ISMS requirements can go through a three-stage certification process, indicating they are ISO 27001 compliant.
- **ISO 27002**. ISO 27002, "Information security, cybersecurity and privacy protection – Information security controls," is a complement to ISO 27001. While ISO 27001 identifies the requirements to become certified, ISO 27002 provides organizations with best practices guidance.
- **ISO 27701**. ISO 27701, "Privacy Information Management System (PIMS)," is an extension to ISO 27001 and ISO 27002, and it outlines a framework for managing and protecting Personally Identifiable Information (PII). It provides organizations with guidance to

comply with global privacy standards, such as the European Union General Data Protection Regulation (EU GDPR).

- **ISO 31000**. ISO 31000, "Risk management," is a family of standards related to risk management. It provides guidelines that organizations can adopt to manage risk.

Industry-Specific Frameworks

Some frameworks and standards only apply to specific industries. As an example, organizations that handle credit cards typically comply with the Payment Card Industry Data Security Standard (PCI DSS). PCI DSS includes 12 principal requirements and additional requirements for different types of entities that organizations follow to protect credit card data. PCI DSS isn't foolproof, but it has helped reduce many of the risks associated with credit card fraud.

The Center for Internet Security (CIS) has a stated mission to "make the connected world a safer place by developing, validating, and promoting timely best practice solutions that help people, businesses, and governments protect themselves against pervasive cyber threats." They provide several free downloads outlining best practices and maintain up-to-date information on cybersecurity threats. Members include corporations, government agencies, and academic institutions and members have access to additional CIS resources.

NIST Frameworks

The National Institute of Standards and Technology (NIST) publishes two important frameworks that are widely used by risk management and cybersecurity professionals. These frameworks are widely respected in the cybersecurity field.

NIST Risk Management Framework

NIST SP 800-37, "Risk Management Framework for Information Systems and Organizations," covers the **Risk Management Framework (RMF)**. While U.S. federal government agencies must adopt the RMF, many private sector organizations adopt it as well. RMF provides organizations with a seven-step process to identify and mitigate risks. The seven steps are:

1. **Prepare.** During this step, an organization identifies key roles for implementing the framework, identifies risk tolerance strategies, updates (or creates) risk assessments, and identifies in-place controls. It also creates a continuous monitoring strategy.
2. **Categorize.** Personnel determine the adverse impact to operations and assets if there is a loss of confidentiality, integrity, and availability to these operations or assets. This allows them to prioritize the systems.
3. **Select.** Personnel select and tailor the controls necessary to protect their operations and assets. They typically start with baselines and then tailor the baselines as needed.

4. **Implement.** In this step, personnel implement the selected controls. If changes are required, personnel document them.

5. **Assess.** Next, personnel assess the controls to see if they are producing the desired outcome. This includes verifying they are implemented correctly and operating as expected.

6. **Authorize.** A senior management official determines if the system is authorized to operate. The official makes this decision based on the output of the previous steps. Government agencies place a higher emphasis on this step than private organizations.

7. **Monitor.** Monitoring is an ongoing step where personnel constantly assess changes in the system and environment. This typically includes performing periodic risk assessments and analyzing risk responses.

NIST Cybersecurity Framework

The **NIST Cybersecurity Framework (CSF)** aligns with the RMF. Many private sector organizations have adopted it to improve their ability to prevent, detect, and respond to cyberattacks. The CSF includes three components:

- **Core.** The core is a set of activities that an organization can select to achieve desired outcomes. It includes five functions: identify, protect, detect, respond, and recover.
- **Tiers.** The tiers help an organization identify how it views risk. The four tiers are Partial (Tier 1), Risk Informed (Tier 2), Repeatable (Tier 3), and Adaptive (Tier 4). Tier 4 is the highest and indicates the organization has (or desires) a mature risk management program.
- **Profile.** The profiles provide a list of outcomes for an organization based on its needs and risk assessments. Current Profiles describe the current state of cybersecurity activities, and Target rPofiles describe the desired outcomes. By comparing Current Profiles with Target Profiles, an organization can identify gaps in its risk management program. Organizations can use different profiles for different systems based on their value.

Reference Architecture

In cybersecurity, **reference architecture** is a document or a set of documents that provides a set of standards. As an example, a software reference architecture documents high-level design decisions. It may stress the need to create reusable modules and follow a specific standard related to interfaces. Some software reference architecture documents list procedures, functions, and methods that a software project should use.

You won't find a single reference architecture that meets the needs of all projects. Instead, the key is that complex projects often use one to standardize everyone's efforts on a project.

Benchmarks and Configuration Guides

In addition to frameworks, you can also use various guides to increase security. This includes benchmarks or secure configuration guides, platform- or vendor-specific guides, and general-purpose guides. On the surface, this is quite simple. When configuring Windows systems, use a Windows guide to identify secure settings. When configuring Linux systems, use a Linux guide.

Additionally, when configuring a specific role system (such as a web server, application server, or network infrastructure device), follow the appropriate guide for that role. As an example, a web server would need ports 80 and 443 open for HTTP and HTTPS, respectively. However, a database application server would not typically need these ports open, so they should be closed on a database application server. The individual guides for each of the roles provide this information.

Audits and Assessments

Business leaders and outside stakeholders often want assurances that their organizations are complying with regulatory requirements and industry standard best practices. Audits and assessments provide them with the ability to achieve this goal.

Audits are a formal evaluation of an organization's policies, procedures, and operations. In the world of cybersecurity, audits confirm that the organization has put security controls in place that are adequate and are effectively protecting critical assets.

Assessments are less formal reviews of an organization's cybersecurity defenses. Assessments may include vulnerability scans, penetration tests, and reviews of cybersecurity controls. Many of the techniques used in an assessment may also play a role in an audit.

Assessments may be performed by many different groups. The organization may hire an outside firm that brings specific expertise, or they may ask the cybersecurity team to perform assessments internally. Audits, on the other hand, are a little more formal and structured, and are performed by a team that is independent from the team responsible for implementing controls.

There are two major categories of audits:

- **External audits** are formal examinations performed by an independent auditing firm. Many organizations undergo an annual financial audit to meet legal requirements and cybersecurity controls are a standard component of those audits. The results of an external audit may be provided to the audit committee of an organization's Board of Directors, to regulators, or other stakeholders.
- **Internal audits** are performed by an auditing team within the organization itself. Most large organizations have an internal audit group that works at the direction of the Board's audit committee. They perform many types of audits to ensure compliance with regulations and perform other self-assessments.

One of the more common tasks assigned to an internal audit group is performing a ***gap analysis***. This is a type of assessment where the reviewers take a standard (such as ISO 27001) and then compare the requirements in that standard to the organization's normal operations. They then note any gaps that may exist where the organization isn't fully living up to the standard and identify them as opportunities for improvement.

The outcome of an audit is an **attestation** made by the auditor. This is a formal statement that specific security controls and processes are in place and operating effectively within an organization. This is a significant statement, as the audit firm is putting their reputation on the line.

Chapter 8 Exam Topic Review

When preparing for the exam, make sure you understand these key concepts covered in this chapter.

Understanding Risk Management

- A risk is the likelihood that a threat will exploit a vulnerability. A threat is a potential danger that can compromise confidentiality, integrity, or availability. A vulnerability is a weakness in software or hardware or a weakness in a process that a threat could exploit, resulting in a security breach.

- Risks are evaluated using the criteria of impact and probability/likelihood. Impact refers to the magnitude of harm that can be caused if a threat exploits a vulnerability. Probability/likelihood tells us how often we expect the risk to occur.

- Risk management attempts to reduce risk to a level that an organization can accept, and the remaining risk is known as residual risk. Senior management is responsible for managing risk and the losses associated from residual risk.

- You can avoid a risk by not providing a service or participating in a risky activity. Purchasing insurance, such as fire insurance, transfers the risk to another entity. Cybersecurity controls mitigate or reduce risks. When the cost of a control outweighs a risk, it is common to accept the risk.

- Risk appetite refers to the amount of risk an organization is willing to accept. This varies between organizations based on their goals and strategic objectives. An organization's risk appetite may be expansionary, conservative, or neutral.

- Risk tolerance refers to the organization's ability to withstand risk.

- A risk assessment quantifies or qualifies risks based on different values or judgments. It starts by identifying asset values and prioritizing high-value items.

- Quantitative risk assessments use numbers, such as costs and asset values. You begin a quantitative analysis by identifying the asset value (AV) of each asset. Next, you determine the percentage of an asset that would be damaged by the risk each time it occurs, which is known as the exposure factor (EF).

- The single loss expectancy (SLE) is the cost of any single loss and it is calculated by multiplying the AV by the EF. The annual rate of occurrence (ARO) indicates how many times the loss will occur annually. You can calculate the annual loss expectancy (ALE) as SLE × ARO.

- Qualitative risk assessments use judgments to prioritize risks based on likelihood of occurrence and impact. These judgments provide a subjective ranking.

- Risk assessment results are sensitive. Only executives and security professionals should be granted access to risk assessment reports.

- A risk register is a detailed document listing information about risks. It typically includes risk scores along with recommended security controls to reduce the risk scores. A risk matrix plots risks on a graph.

- A supply chain assessment evaluates a supply chain needed to produce and sell a product. It includes raw materials and all the processes required to create and distribute a finished product. Supply chain risk analyses should look at hardware providers, software providers, and service providers.

Comparing Scanning and Testing Tools

- A port scanner scans systems for open ports and attempts to discover what services and protocols are running on a system.

- Vulnerability scanners test security controls to identify vulnerabilities, a lack of security controls, and common misconfigurations. They are effective at discovering systems susceptible to an attack without exploiting the systems.

- The Common Vulnerabilities and Exposures (CVE) is a dictionary of publicly known security vulnerabilities and exposures. The Common Vulnerability Scoring System (CVSS) assesses vulnerabilities and assigns severity scores in a range of 0 to 10, with 10 being the most severe.

- A false positive from a vulnerability scan indicates the scan detected a vulnerability, but the vulnerability doesn't exist. A false negative indicates a vulnerability exists, but the scanner did not detect it.

- Vulnerabilities should be prioritized using a number of criteria, including vulnerability classification, environmental variables, industry/organizational impact, and risk tolerance/threshold.

- Credentialed scans run under an account's context and can get more detailed information on targets, such as the software versions of installed applications. They are also more accurate than non-credentialed scans, giving fewer false positives.

- A penetration test is an active test that attempts to exploit discovered vulnerabilities. It starts with a vulnerability scan and then bypasses or actively tests security controls to exploit vulnerabilities. Penetration tests may be focused on physical, offensive, or defensive objectives or they may use integrated approaches that combine these techniques.

- Penetration testers should gain consent prior to starting a penetration test. A rules of engagement document identifies the boundaries of the test.
- Passive reconnaissance gathers information from open-source intelligence. Active network reconnaissance and discovery uses scanning techniques to gather information.
- After initial exploitation, a penetration tester uses privilege escalation techniques to gain more access. Pivoting during a penetration test is the process of using an exploited system to access other systems.
- In unknown environment testing, testers perform a penetration test with zero prior knowledge of the environment. Known environment testing indicates that the testers have full knowledge of the environment, including documentation and source code for tested applications. Partially known environment testing indicates testers have some knowledge of the environment.
- Scans can be either intrusive or non-intrusive. Penetration testing is intrusive (also called invasive) and can potentially disrupt operations. Vulnerability testing is non-intrusive (also called non-invasive).
- Responsible disclosure programs for vulnerabilities enable individuals and organizations to report security vulnerabilities or weaknesses they have discovered to the appropriate parties. Bug bounty programs are a type of responsible disclosure program that incentivizes individuals or organizations to report vulnerabilities by offering monetary or other rewards for valid submissions.
- The most common way to remediate a vulnerability is to apply a patch. In cases where patches are not possible, you may use a compensating control, segmentation, or grant an exception.
- After correcting a vulnerability, you should rescan the affected system to validate that the remediation was effective and that the vulnerability no longer exists.

Capturing Network Traffic

- Protocol analyzers (sniffers) can capture and analyze data sent over a network. Testers (and attackers) use protocol analyzers to capture cleartext data sent across a network.
- Administrators use protocol analyzers for troubleshooting communication issues by inspecting protocol headers to detect manipulated or fragmented packets.
- Captured packets show the type of traffic (protocol), source and destination IP addresses, source and destination MAC addresses, and flags.
- Tcpreplay is a suite of utilities used to edit packet captures and then send the edited packets over the network. Tcpdump is a command-line protocol analyzer. Captured packet files can be analyzed in a graphical protocol analyzer such as Wireshark.
- NetFlow captures IP traffic statistics on routers and switches and sends them to a NetFlow collector.

Understanding Frameworks and Standards

- Frameworks are references that provide a foundation. Cybersecurity frameworks typically use a structure of basic concepts and provide guidance on how to implement security.
- The International Organization for Standardization (ISO) maintains a set of common cybersecurity standards. ISO 27001 covers information security management. ISO 27002 covers information security techniques. ISO 27701 covers privacy information management. ISO 31000 covers risk management.
- Organizations that handle credit cards typically comply with the Payment Card Industry Data Security Standard (PCI DSS).
- The National Institute of Standards and Technology (NIST) publishes very popular frameworks, including their Risk Management Framework (RMF) and Cybersecurity Framework (CSF).
- Vendor-specific guides should be used when configuring specific systems.

Audits and Assessments

- Audits are a formal evaluation of an organization's policies, procedures, and operations. In the world of cybersecurity, audits confirm that the organization has put security controls in place that are adequate and are effectively protecting critical assets.
- Assessments are less formal reviews of an organization's cybersecurity defenses. Assessments may include vulnerability scans, penetration tests, and reviews of cybersecurity controls. Many of the techniques used in an assessment may also play a role in an audit.
- External audits are formal examinations performed by an independent auditing firm. Internal audits are performed by an auditing team within the organization itself.
- The outcome of an audit is an attestation made by the auditor. This is a formal statement that specific security controls and processes are in place and operating effectively within an organization.

★ Online References

Don't forget to check out the online resources. They include additional free practice test questions, labs, and other resources to help you pass the CompTIA Security+ exam. You can access them at:
`https://getcertifiedgetahead.com/`.

Chapter 8 Practice Questions

1. A server within your organization has suffered six hardware failures in the past year. IT management personnel have valued the server at $4,000, and each failure resulted in a 10 percent loss. What is the ALE?

    A. $400
    B. $2,400
    C. $4,000
    D. $6,000

2. Maggie is performing a risk assessment on a database server. While doing so, she created a document showing all the known risks to this server, along with the risk score for each risk. Which of the following BEST identifies the name of this document?

    A. Qualitative risk assessment
    B. Quantitative risk assessment
    C. Risk register
    D. Residual risk

3. Your organization hosts an e-commerce website used to sell digital products. You are tasked with evaluating all the elements used to support this website. What are you performing?

    A. Quantitative assessment
    B. Qualitative assessment
    C. Threat hunting
    D. Supply chain assessment

4. You are conducting a penetration test to review the effectiveness of your organization's security controls. What term best describes your work?

    A. Audit
    B. Attestation
    C. Assessment
    D. Analysis

5. Maggie suspects that a server may be running unnecessary services. Which of the following tools is the BEST choice to identify the services running on the server?

    A. DNSEnum
    B. IP scanner
    C. Passive reconnaissance
    D. Nmap

6. You want to identify all the services running on a server in your network. Which of the following tools is the BEST choice to meet this goal?

    A. Penetration test
    B. Protocol analyzer
    C. Non-credentialed scan
    D. Port scanner

7. You recently completed a vulnerability scan on a database server. The scan didn't report any issues. However, you know that it is missing a patch. The patch wasn't applied because it causes problems with the database application. Which of the following BEST describes this?

    A. False negative
    B. False positive
    C. Credential scan
    D. Non-credentialed scan

8. You suspect that a database server used by a web application is not up to date with current patches. Which of the following is the BEST action to take to verify the server has up-to-date patches?

    A. Network scan
    B. Port scan
    C. Protocol analyzer
    D. Vulnerability scan

9. Lisa periodically runs vulnerability scans on the organization's network. Lately, she has been receiving many false positives. Which of the following actions can help reduce the false positives?

    A. Run the scans credentialed scans.
    B. Run the scans as non-credentialed scans.
    C. Run the scans using passive reconnaissance.
    D. Run the scans using active reconnaissance.

10. Your organization has hired outside penetration testers to identify internal network vulnerabilities. After successfully exploiting vulnerabilities in a single computer, the testers attempt to access other systems within the network. Which of the following BEST describes their current actions?

    A. Partially known environment testing
    B. Persistence
    C. Lateral movement
    D. Privilege escalation

11. Bart, a database administrator in your organization, told you about recent attacks on the network and how they have been disrupting services and network connectivity. In response, he said he has been investigating on his own using Nmap to run vulnerability scans and identify vulnerabilities. Which of the following is wrong with this scenario?

    A. The database administrator was pivoting from his primary job.
    B. A network scan wasn't done first.
    C. Scans weren't done as credentialed scans.
    D. Rules of engagement weren't obtained.

12. Your organization outsourced the development of a software module to modify an existing proprietary application's functionality. The developer completed the module and is now testing it with the entire application. What type of testing is the developer performing?

    A. Known environment
    B. Unknown environment
    C. Partially known environment
    D. Red team

13. You are reviewing the results of a vulnerability scan and are having a hard time determining which vulnerabilities to address first. What standard tool could help you identify the most severe vulnerabilities?

    A. CVSS
    B. CVE
    C. SCAP
    D. MITRE

14. Your organization is setting up an e-commerce site to sell products online. Management wants to ensure the website can accept credit cards for payment. Which of the following standards are they MOST likely to follow?

    A. ISO 27001
    B. PCI DSS
    C. ISO 31000
    D. SSAE SOC 2 Type I

15. You are conducting a supply chain assessment for your organization. Which one of the following groups would not normally be included in this type of assessment?

    A. Catering provider
    B. Hardware provider
    C. Software provider
    D. Service provider

Chapter 8

Practice Question Answers

1. **B** is correct. The annual loss expectancy (ALE) is $2,400. It is calculated as single loss expectancy (SLE) × annual rate of occurrence (ARO). Each failure has resulted in a 10 percent loss (meaning that it cost 10 percent of the asset value to repair it). The SLE is 10 percent of $4,000 ($400), and the ARO is 6. 6 × $400 is $2400.

2. **C** is correct. A risk register lists all known risks for an asset, such as a database server, and it typically includes a risk score (the combination of the likelihood of occurrence and the impact of the risk). Risk assessments (including qualitative and quantitative risk assessments) might use a risk register, but they are not risk registers. Residual risk refers to the remaining risk after applying security controls to mitigate a risk.

3. **D** is correct. A supply chain assessment evaluates all the elements used to create, sell, and distribute a product. The National Institute of Standards and Technology (NIST) Risk Management Framework (RMF) (NIST SP 800-37 r2) provides steps for reducing supply chain risks. Risk assessments (including both quantitative and qualitative risk assessments) evaluate risks, but don't evaluate the supply chain required to support an e-commerce website. Threat hunting is the process of actively looking for threats within a network before an automated tool detects and reports on the threat.

4. **C** is correct. Penetration tests are an assessment technique. They may be used as part of an audit, but they are not audits themselves. Attestation is a formal statement made by an auditor after an audit is complete. Analysis is not a standard auditing/assessment term.

5. **D** is correct. Nmap is a network scanner, and it can detect the protocols and services running on a server. The **dnsenum** command will enumerate (or list) Domain Name System (DNS) records for domains. An IP scanner detects IPs active on a network but not the services running on the individual hosts. Passive reconnaissance uses open-source intelligence (OSINT) instead of active tools.

6. **D** is correct. A port scanner identifies open ports on a system and is commonly used to determine what services are running on the system. Vulnerability scanners often include port-scanning capabilities, and they can help identify potential weak configurations. A penetration test attempts to exploit a vulnerability. A protocol analyzer can analyze traffic and discover protocols in use, but this would be much more difficult than using a port scanner. A non-credentialed scan refers to a vulnerability scan, and while a vulnerability scan may reveal services running on a server, it won't be as specific as a port scan.

7. **A** is correct. A false negative occurs if a vulnerability scanner does not report a known vulnerability. A false positive occurs when a vulnerability scanner reports a vulnerability that doesn't exist. The scenario doesn't indicate if the scan was run under the context of an account (credentialed) or anonymously (non-credentialed), so these answers aren't relevant to the question.

8. **D** is correct. A vulnerability scan determines if the system has current patches. None of the other answers will detect missing patches. A network scan will discover devices on the network. It might look for and detect vulnerabilities on network devices, but it would not be used to scan a single server for patches. A port scan identifies open ports. A protocol analyzer (sniffer) captures traffic for analysis.

9. **A** is correct. Running the scans as credentialed scans (within the context of a valid account) allows the scan to see more information and typically results in fewer false positives. A false positive indicates the scan reported a vulnerability that doesn't exist. Non-credentialed scans run without any user credentials and can be less accurate. Choosing either passive or active scans won't reduce false positives.

10. **C** is correct. Lateral movement refers to actions taken to move through a network after successfully exploiting a single system. While not available as a possible answer, this could also be described as pivoting, which is the process of accessing other systems through a single compromised system. Partially known environment testing (sometimes called gray box testing) indicates the testers have some knowledge of a system or network before starting, but there is no indication in the scenario about their level of knowledge. Persistence

refers to maintaining a presence on the system or network after the initial exploit. Privilege escalation refers to gaining higher privileges after an initial exploit.

11. **D** is correct. Bart should have gotten authorization before doing any scans, and the authorization should outline the rules of engagement. Pivoting refers to an attacker accessing other systems in a network through a single compromised system. While Bart is a database administrator and doing vulnerability scans is outside his normal job functions, his actions wouldn't be described as pivoting. Nmap can do a network scan. The scenario doesn't indicate the scans were credentialed or non-credentialed or what they should have been.

12. **C** is correct. The developer is performing a partially known environment test (sometimes called a gray box test). A partially known environment tester has some knowledge of the application. In this scenario, the tester needs some knowledge of the application (such as input and output data) to develop and test the module. Known environment testers (sometimes called white box testers) have full knowledge about the product or network they are testing, but because this is a proprietary application, it is unlikely the tester has full knowledge. Unknown environment testers (sometimes called black box testers) do not have any knowledge about the product or network they are testing, but this isn't feasible for a developer who needs to develop and test a module to modify an existing application. Red team refers to an exercise type and members on the red team are experts in attacking systems.

13. **A** is correct. The Common Vulnerability Scoring System (CVSS) assesses vulnerabilities and assigns severity scores in a range of 0 to 10, with 10 being the most severe. The MITRE Corporation maintains the Common Vulnerabilities and Exposures (CVE) list, which is a dictionary of publicly known security vulnerabilities and exposures but does not include severity scores. The Security Content Automation Protocol (SCAP) is designed to help facilitate communication between vulnerability scanners and other security and management tools.

14. **B** is correct. When using credit cards, a company would comply with the Payment Card Industry Data Security Standard (PCI DSS). International Organization for Standardization (ISO) 27001 provides information on information security management systems (ISMS) requirements. ISO 31000 is a family of standards related to risk management. A Statement on Standards for Attestation Engagements (SSAE) System and Organization Controls (SOC) 2 Type I report describes an organization's systems and covers the design effectiveness of security controls on a specific date.

15. **A** is correct. Supply chain assessments should include any organization that provides goods or services crucial to delivering your organization's products and services. This includes hardware providers, software providers, and service providers. While getting lunch is important, a catering provider would generally not be included as a critical piece of a supply chain.

Chapter 9

Implementing Controls to Protect Assets

CompTIA Security+ objectives covered in this chapter:

1.2 Summarize fundamental security concepts.

- Physical security (Bollards, Access control vestibule, Fencing, Video surveillance, Security guard, Access badge, Lighting, Sensors, Infrared, Pressure, Microwave, Ultrasonic)

2.4 Given a scenario, analyze indicators of malicious activity.

- Physical attacks (Brute force, Environmental)

3.1 Compare and contrast security implications of different architecture models.

- Architecture and infrastructure concepts (High availability)

3.3 Compare and contrast concepts and strategies to protect data.

- General data considerations (Data sovereignty)

3.4 Explain the importance of resilience and recovery in security architecture.

- High availability (Load balancing vs. clustering)
- Site considerations (Hot, Cold, Warm, Geographic dispersion)
- Platform diversity
- Continuity of operations
- Capacity planning (People, Technology, Infrastructure)
- Testing (Tabletop exercises, Fail over, Simulation, Parallel processing)
- Backups (Onsite/offsite, Frequency, Encryption, Snapshots, Recovery, Replication, Journaling)
- Power (Generators, Uninterruptible power supply (UPS))

4.2 Explain the security implications of proper hardware, software, and data asset management.

- Acquisition/procurement process

- Assignment/accounting (Ownership, Classification)
- Monitoring/asset tracking (Inventory, Enumeration)

5.2 Explain elements of the risk management process.
- Business impact analysis (Recovery time objective (RTO), Recovery point objective (RPO), Mean time to repair (MTTR), Mean time between failures (MTBF))

You can't eliminate risk to an organization's assets. However, you can reduce the impact of many threats by implementing security controls. It's common to implement several controls using a layered strategy with a diverse assortment of controls, vendors, and technologies. Physical security controls help protect access to secure areas. Redundancy and fault tolerance strategies help eliminate single points of failure for critical systems. Backups ensure that data remains available even after data is lost. More in-depth business continuity strategies help ensure mission-critical functions continue to operate even if a disaster destroys a primary business location. This chapter covers these concepts.

Comparing Physical Security Controls

A physical security control is something you can physically touch, such as a hardware lock, a fence, an identification badge, and a security camera. Physical access controls are a subcategory of physical controls that attempt to control entry and exits. Organizations commonly implement different controls at different boundaries, such as the following:

- **Perimeter**. Military bases and many other organizations erect a fence around the entire perimeter of their land. They often post security guards at gates to control access. In some cases, organizations install barricades to block vehicles.
- **Buildings**. Buildings commonly have additional controls for both safety and security. For example, guards and locked doors restrict entry so only authorized personnel enter. Many buildings include lighting and video cameras to monitor the entrances and exits.
- **Secure work areas**. Some companies restrict access to specific work areas when employees perform classified or restricted access tasks. In some cases, an organization restricts access to all internal work areas. In other words, visitors can enter the lobby of a building, but they are not able to enter internal work areas without an escort.
- **Server rooms**. Servers and network devices such as routers and switches are normally stored in areas where only the appropriate IT personnel can access them. These spaces may be designated as server rooms or wiring closets. It's common for an organization to provide additional physical security for these rooms to prevent attackers from accessing the equipment. For example, locking a wiring closet prevents an attacker from installing illicit monitoring hardware, such as a protocol analyzer, to capture network traffic.
- **Hardware**. Additional physical security controls protect individual systems. For example, server rooms often have locking cabinets to protect servers and other equipment installed

in the equipment bays. Cable locks protect laptop computers, and smaller devices can be stored in safes.

Many organizations use camouflage techniques (sometimes called industrial camouflage) to hide buildings, parts of a building, and a wide variety of other items. Generically, camouflage is the use of materials to conceal items or disguise them as something else.

Landscaping can camouflage a building or parts of it. Imagine a strong security fence surrounds an organization. Organizations can conceal it with landscaping such as tall bushes, ornamental grasses, or perennials. This provides aesthetic benefits and obscures the fact that the organization has invested in such a strong security fence.

Access Badges

It's possible to secure access to areas with proximity cards or smart cards that serve as **access badges**. Proximity cards are small credit card-sized cards that activate when they are close to a proximity card reader. Many organizations use these for access points, such as the entry to a building or the entry to a controlled area within a building. The door uses an electronic lock that only unlocks when the user passes the proximity card in front of a card reader.

Similarly, it's possible to use smart cards or physical tokens (described in Chapter 2, "Understanding Identity and Access Management") for door access. In some scenarios, the smart cards include proximity card electronics. In other scenarios, users must insert the smart card into a smart card reader to gain access.

You've probably seen proximity card readers implemented with credit card readers. Many self-serve gasoline stations and fast-food restaurants use them. Instead of swiping your credit card through a magnetic reader, you simply pass it in front of the reader (in close proximity to the reader), and the reader extracts your credit card's information.

These are becoming popular elsewhere, too. For example, if you stay at a Walt Disney World property, they can issue you a bracelet that includes a proximity card's functionality. To enter your hotel room, you wave your bracelet in front of the door. If you want to buy food or souvenirs or pay for almost anything, you can simply wave your bracelet in front of a card reader to complete your purchase.

The card (and bracelet) doesn't require its own power source. Instead, the electronics in the card include a capacitor and a coil that can accept a charge from the proximity card reader. When you pass the card close to the reader, the reader excites the coil and stores a charge in the capacitor. Once charged, the card transmits the information to the reader using a radio frequency. When used with door access systems, the proximity card can send just a simple signal to unlock the door. Some systems include details on the user and record when the user enters or exits the area. When used this way, it's common to combine the proximity card reader with a keypad requiring the user to enter a personal identification number (PIN). This identifies and authenticates the user with multifactor authentication. The user has something (the proximity card) and knows something (a PIN).

Many organizations use proximity cards with turnstiles to provide access for a single person at a time. These are the same type of turnstiles used as entry gates in subways, stadiums, and amusement parks.

📌 *Remember This!*

Proximity cards are typically credit card-sized access cards. Users pass the card near a proximity card reader, and the card reader then reads data on the card. Some access control points use proximity cards with PINs for authentication.

Increasing Security with Personnel

Many organizations use **security guards** to control access to buildings and secure spaces. If employees have access badges, guards can check these badges before granting the employees access. Even if access badges aren't used, guards can still verify people's identities using other identification. Similarly, the security guards can restrict access by checking people's identities against a preapproved access control list.

Security guards can also take a less-active role to deter security incidents. For example, a security guard can deter tailgating incidents by observing personnel when they use their proximity card to gain access to a secure area. Chapter 6, "Comparing Threats, Vulnerabilities, and Common Attacks," discusses tailgating. In some cases, guards record access in visitor logs. This provides a written record of any visitors.

Instead of guards, many organizations use a reception desk or reception area to control access. Visitors need to check in with the receptionist before they're allowed into secure areas. While receptionists aren't guards, they typically have easy access to security personnel with a quick phone call.

Monitoring Areas with Video Surveillance

Organizations are increasingly using security cameras in the workplace and surrounding areas for **video surveillance**. This includes areas outside of a building, such as a parking lot and all building entrances and exits. Additionally, many organizations use cameras to monitor entrances of high-security areas, such as the entrance of a data center or server room.

A closed-circuit television (CCTV) system transmits signals from video cameras to monitors that are similar to TVs. In addition to providing security, a CCTV system can also enhance safety by deterring threats.

Organizations often use video cameras within a work environment to protect employees and enhance security in the workplace. In addition to live monitoring, most systems include a recording element, and they can verify if someone is stealing the company's assets. By recording activity, videos can be played back later for investigation and even prosecution.

Video surveillance provides the strong proof of a person's location and activity. Digital access logs provide a record, but it's possible to circumvent these logs. For example, if Bart used your proximity card to access a secure space, the log will indicate you entered, not Bart. In contrast, if the video shows that Bart entered the room at a certain time of day, it's not easy for Bart to refute the video.

It's also possible to use a CCTV system as a compensating control. Imagine an organization wants to implement a door access system requiring users to use smart cards to enter secure areas. However, this may take months to implement. The organization can implement a CCTV system to record access until the card access system is installed.

Cameras can be connected to motion detection systems so that they only turn on when they detect motion. This can be effective as a burglary detection system.

Object detection uses camera images and software to detect specific objects. Some can detect still images, but it's more common for them to analyze frames to detect common objects' predictable movement. As an example, some cars use this to detect pedestrians walking into the path of a car.

> ### ★ Remember This!
>
> Video surveillance provides reliable proof of a person's location and activity. It can identify who enters and exits secure areas and can record theft of assets. Many cameras include motion detection and object detection capabilities. CCTV systems can be used as a compensating control in some situations.

Sensors

Many physical security controls use sensors to detect changes in an environment. It's common to use sensors with cameras, alarms, fire detection, and more. There are some common types of sensors used in many organizations:

- **Motion detection.** Many organizations use a combination of automation, light dimmers, and motion sensors to save on electricity costs without sacrificing security. The lights automatically turn on at dusk but in a low, dimmed mode. When the motion sensors detect any movement, the lights turn on at full capacity, and they automatically turn off at dawn. Motion detection sensors can also trigger alarms. Of course, they are only enabled when an area is empty.

- **Noise detection.** Noise detection sensors can detect any noise or when noise exceeds a certain level. They work like motion detection sensors and alert on any sound to control lights or set off alarms. Some Airbnb hosts don't want renters throwing parties in their houses. They can use noise sensors to detect when the noise levels exceed a certain level. Some noise sensors can detect specific sounds, such as smoke alarms or the sound of glass breaking.

- **Infrared.** Infrared sensors detect heat signatures in the form of infrared radiation emitted by people, animals, or objects. These sensors are commonly used for security purposes, as they can detect the presence of people or animals even in complete darkness. They are often integrated into security cameras and alarm systems to improve their detection capabilities.

- **Pressure.** Pressure sensors are designed to detect changes in pressure on a surface or in a specific area. These sensors can be used to detect when someone is walking on a floor or stepping on a mat. They can also be used to monitor doors and windows for forced entry attempts. In addition, pressure sensors can be used in access control systems to ensure that only authorized individuals can enter restricted areas.

- **Microwave.** Microwave sensors use microwave technology to detect movement within a specific area. These sensors emit microwave signals and measure the reflected signals to detect any changes in the environment, such as the presence of a person or a moving object. Microwave sensors are often used in combination with other types of sensors to enhance security systems and reduce false alarms.

- **Ultrasonic.** Ultrasonic sensors emit high-frequency sound waves and measure the time it takes for the sound waves to bounce back after hitting an object or surface. These sensors are used to detect the presence of people or objects and can also be used to measure distance. Ultrasonic sensors are commonly used in parking assistance systems, robotic navigation, and intrusion detection systems.

★ *Remember This!*

Sensors monitor the environment and can detect changes. Common sensor types include motion and noise detection as well as sensors designed to monitor infrared temperature, pressure, microwaves, and ultrasonic waves.

Fencing, Lighting, and Alarms

Fences provide a barrier around a property and deter people from entering. When using a fence, it's common to control access to the area via specific gates. Guards often monitor these gates and ensure only authorized individuals can enter. When additional security is required, organizations sometimes configure dual gates, allowing access into one area where credentials are checked before allowing full access. This effectively creates a cage preventing full access but also prevents unauthorized individuals from escaping.

Installing lights at all the entrances to a building can deter attackers from trying to break in. Similarly, lighting at the entrances of any internal restricted areas can deter people from trying to enter. Many organizations use a combination of automation, light dimmers, and motion sensors to save on electricity costs without sacrificing security. The lights automatically turn on at dusk, but in a low, dimmed mode. When the motion sensors detect any movement, the lights turn on at full capacity. They automatically turn off at dawn.

It's important to protect the lights. For example, if an attacker can remove the light bulbs, it defeats the control. Either place the lights high enough so that they can't be reached or protect them with a metal cage.

Alarms provide additional physical security protection. This includes alarms that detect fire and alarms that detect unauthorized access. Fire alarms detect smoke and/or heat and trigger fire suppression systems. Burglary prevention systems monitor entry points such as doors and windows, detecting when someone opens them.

You can also combine motion detection systems with burglary prevention systems. They detect movement within monitored areas and trigger alarms. Obviously, you wouldn't have motion detection systems turned on all the time. Instead, you'd turn them on when people will not be working in the area, such as during nights or weekends.

Securing Access with Barricades

In some situations, fencing isn't enough to deter potential attackers. To augment fences and other physical security measures, organizations erect stronger barricades. As an example, military bases often erect strong, zigzag barricades that require vehicles to slow down to navigate through them. This prevents attackers from trying to ram through the gates.

Businesses and organizations need to present an inviting appearance, so they can't use such drastic barricades. However, they often use **bollards**, which are short vertical posts composed of reinforced concrete and/or steel. They often place the bollards in front of entrances about three or four feet apart and paint them with colors that match their buildings so that they blend in. You've probably walked through a set of bollards multiple times without giving them a second thought. However, thieves who are contemplating driving a car or truck through the entrance see them.

Many thieves have driven vehicles right through the front of buildings and then proceeded to steal everything in sight. Depending on the walls' strength, criminals might even be able to drive through a wall with a truck. Strategically placed bollards will help prevent these types of attacks.

Access Control Vestibules

Access control vestibules are critical components in data center security. As the first line of defense against unauthorized entry, these secure entry points provide a physical barrier between the outside world and the valuable assets housed within the data center. By implementing stringent access control measures, data center operators can mitigate the risks posed by unauthorized individuals, potential intruders, or even insiders with malicious intent.

An access control vestibule consists of two sets of interlocking doors, designed to create a secure compartment that allows only one person to enter at a time. These entry points are usually equipped with advanced security measures, such as biometric scanners, RFID card readers, or even facial recognition systems. These systems verify the identity of the individual seeking access, ensuring that only authorized personnel can gain entry. Access control vestibules prevent tailgating and deter unauthorized entry by trapping an individual between the two sets of doors if they attempt to bypass security.

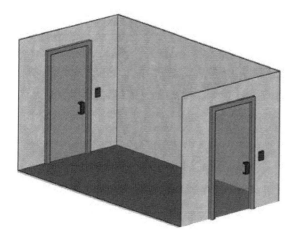

Asset Management

Asset management is the process of tracking valuable assets throughout their life cycles. Asset management programs should include hardware, software, and data assets. From a security perspective, these asset management programs ensure that the organization knows what assets it owns, where those assets are located, and how they are secured. The core activities of any asset management program include:

Figure 9.1: Access Control Vestibule

- An *acquisition/procurement* process that provides consistent procedures for identifying the need for new assets, evaluating the possible options for security, financial, and business requirements, and effectively onboarding and managing new vendors.

- An **assignment/accounting** process that assigns each asset to a named owner who bears responsibility for the asset and a classification system that identifies the sensitivity and criticality of each asset to the organization.
- A **monitoring and asset tracking** process that maintains an inventory of all of the assets owned by the organization and their current location. This process also benefits from periodic enumeration of assets where auditors review the assets owned by the organization and update the inventory.

Hardware Asset Management

Organizations commonly implement **hardware asset management** processes to track servers, desktop computers, laptop computers, routers, switches, and other hardware assets. An effective asset management system can help reduce several vulnerabilities:

- **Architecture and design weaknesses.** Asset management helps reduce architecture and design weaknesses by ensuring that purchases go through an approval process. The approval process does more than just compare costs. It also evaluates the purchase to ensure it fits in the overall network architecture. Unapproved assets often weaken security by adding in additional resources that aren't managed.
- **System sprawl and undocumented assets.** System sprawl occurs when an organization has more systems than it needs, and the systems it owns are underutilized. Asset management begins before the hardware is purchased and helps prevent system sprawl by evaluating the purchase. Additionally, after the purchase is completed, asset management processes ensure the hardware is added to the asset management tracking system. This ensures that the assets are managed and tracked from the cradle to the grave.

Many organizations use automated methods for inventory control. For example, radio-frequency identification (RFID) methods can track the movement of devices. These are the same types of devices used in stores to prevent shoplifting. If someone exits without paying, the RFID device transmits when the shoplifter gets close to the exit door and sounds an alarm. Organizations won't necessarily have an alarm, but they can track device movement by placing RFID tags on the equipment.

Mobile devices are easy to lose track of, so organizations often use asset-tracking methods to reduce losses. For example, when a user receives a mobile device, asset-tracking methods record it. Similarly, if the user leaves the company, asset-tracking methods ensure the user returns the device.

Software Asset Management

Software asset management involves tracking and managing software licenses, installations, and usage within an organization. It helps ensure compliance with licensing agreements, optimizes software usage, and minimizes the risk of security vulnerabilities associated with unpatched or unauthorized software. Effective software asset management includes processes for acquiring, cataloging, and updating software, as well as monitoring usage and ensuring that licenses are maintained and renewed as necessary.

Data Asset Management

Data asset management focuses on the organization's data assets, including databases, files, and other information repositories. It involves defining data ownership, classification, and access controls, as well as ensuring the integrity, availability, and confidentiality of data. Key aspects of data asset management include data governance, data quality management, and data lifecycle management. These processes help organizations maintain accurate, up-to-date, and secure data assets, enabling better decision-making and reducing the risk of data breaches or loss.

Platform Diversity

Defense in depth (also known as **layered security**) refers to the security practice of implementing several layers of protection. You can't simply take a single action, such as installing locks at the entrance of a building and consider yourself protected. You must implement security at several different layers. This way, if one layer fails, you still have additional layers to protect you.

If you drive your car to a local Walmart, put a five-dollar bill on the dash, and leave the keys in the car and the car running, there is a very good chance the car won't be there when you come out of the store. On the other hand, if you ensure nothing of value is visible from the windows, the car is locked, it has an alarm system, and it has stickers on the windows advertising the alarm system, it's less likely that someone will steal it. Not impossible, but less likely.

One of the ways of applying layered security is with diversity. This includes using different vendors, different technologies, and different controls.

Vendor diversity is the practice of implementing security controls from different vendors to increase security. As an example, Chapter 3, "Exploring Network Technologies and Tools," describes a screened subnet (sometimes known as a demilitarized zone). Many screened subnets use two firewalls, and vendor diversity dictates the use of firewalls from different vendors. For example, one firewall could be a Cisco firewall, and the other one could be a Check Point firewall. If a vulnerability is discovered in one of these firewalls, an attacker might be able to exploit it. However, it's unlikely that both firewalls would develop a vulnerability at the same time.

Technology diversity is the practice of using different technologies to protect an environment. For example, an organization may choose a data server room. They may start by limiting the access points, adding biometric locks to open the doors, and monitoring the access points with a CCTV system.

Control diversity is the use of different security control categories, such as technical controls, physical controls, managerial controls, and operational controls. For example, technical security controls such as firewalls, intrusion detection systems (IDSs), and proxy servers help protect a network. Physical security controls can provide extra protection for the server room or other areas where these devices are located. Managerial and operational controls such as vulnerability assessments and penetration tests can help verify that these controls are working as expected.

Physical Attacks

We use physical security controls to protect against physical attacks. Our adversaries have a number of tools at their disposal to try to undermine our physical security.

Card Skimming and Card Cloning

Credit card **skimming** is the practice of capturing credit card data at the point of sale. Attackers often place a skimmer on automated teller machines (ATMs) or gas stations where users swipe their credit cards. The skimmer captures the data on the magnetic strip but also allows the transaction to go through. Some signs of a credit card skimmer are a broken security seal, a loose credit card reader, or a credit card reader that extends past the panel.

Card cloning refers to making a copy of a credit card using data captured from a magnetic strip. Attackers copy the data onto a blank card or overwrite the data on a stolen card. This is relatively easy to do when using the magnetic strip of a credit card. However, the use of chips in credit cards makes it much harder to copy because the chip encrypts the data. The primary indicator of a cloned credit card is unauthorized or fraudulent charges.

Brute Force Attacks

Brute force attacks against physical security attempt to simply crash right through physical security controls. For example, someone might try to drive a vehicle through the front door of a building to gain access to the facility. Or a brute force attack may be less dramatic, such as standing at the keypad used to protect access to a room and trying every possible combination of four-digit passcodes.

Brute force attacks are very simple but they can be effective. They are also usually easily detectable in organizations with good security monitoring programs.

Environmental Attacks

Remember, not every attack tries to gain access to systems or facilities. Some attacks simply want to disrupt the legitimate use of resources. Data centers require carefully controlled power and environmental conditions. If an attacker is able to disrupt these conditions by cutting off power to a facility, raising the temperature to cause equipment overheating, flooding it with water, or causing a similar catastrophe, those **environmental attacks** can be quite damaging.

Adding Redundancy and Fault Tolerance

One of the constants with computers, subsystems, and networks is that they will fail. It's one of the few things you can count on. It's not a matter of if they will fail, but when. However, by adding redundancy into your systems and networks, you can increase the systems' reliability even when they fail. By increasing reliability, you increase a system's resiliency or availability.

Redundancy adds duplication to critical system components and networks and provides **fault tolerance**. If a critical component has a fault, the duplication allows the service to continue as if a fault never occurred. In other words, a system with fault tolerance can suffer a fault, but it can tolerate it and continue to operate. Organizations often add redundancies to eliminate single points of failure:

- Disk redundancies using RAID
- NIC redundancy with NIC teaming
- Server redundancies by adding load balancers
- Power redundancies by adding dual power supplies, generators and/or UPSes
- Site redundancies by adding hot, cold, or warm sites

Single Point of Failure

A **single point of failure** is a component within a system that can cause the entire system to fail if the component fails. When designing redundancies, an organization will examine different components to determine if they are a single point of failure. If so, they take steps to provide redundancy or fault tolerance capabilities. The goal is to increase the reliability and availability of the systems. Some examples of single points of failure include:

- **Disk**. If a server uses a single drive, the system will crash if the single drive fails. A redundant array of inexpensive disks (RAID) provides fault tolerance for hard drives and is a relatively inexpensive method of adding fault tolerance to a system.
- **Server**. If a server provides a critical service and its failure halts the service, it is a single point of failure. Load balancing provides fault tolerance for critical servers.
- **Power**. If an organization only has one source of power for critical systems, the power is a single point of failure. However, elements such as uninterruptible power supplies (UPSes) and power generators provide fault tolerance for power outages.
- **Personnel**. If there are tasks within an organization that only one person can perform, that person becomes a single point of failure. For example, imagine an organization purchased a sophisticated remote-controlled helicopter used to assess damage after storms or disasters. Arnie Pye is the only person who knows how to fly this helicopter. After winning the lottery a week ago, he quit work, and no one can reach him. Because no one knows how to fly the helicopter, the organization cannot assess the damage as planned. Similarly, imagine Nelson

is the only person in the IT department who knows how to run vulnerability scans. If Nelson is no longer available, the organization can no longer run vulnerability scans.

Although IT personnel recognize the risks with single points of failure, they often overlook them until a disaster occurs. However, tools such as business continuity plans (covered later in this chapter) help an organization identify critical services and address single points of failure.

> ### ★ Remember This!
>
> A single point of failure is any component whose failure results in the failure of an entire system. Elements such as RAID, load balancing, UPSes, and generators remove many single points of failure. RAID is an inexpensive method used to add fault tolerance and increase availability. If only one person knows how to perform specific tasks, that person can become a single point of failure.

Disk Redundancies

Any system has four primary resources: processor, memory, disk, and the network interface. Of these, the disk is the slowest and most susceptible to failure. Because of this, administrators often upgrade disk subsystems to improve their performance and redundancy.

A **redundant array of inexpensive disks (RAID)** subsystem provides fault tolerance for disks and increases system availability. Even if a disk fails, most RAID subsystems can tolerate the failure, and the system will continue to operate. RAID systems are becoming much more affordable as the price of drives falls and disk capacity steadily increases. The following sections discuss common RAID levels and how they can contribute to IT resilience.

RAID-0

RAID-0 (striping) is somewhat of a misnomer because it doesn't provide any redundancy or fault tolerance. It includes two or more physical disks. Files stored on a RAID-0 array are spread across each of the disks.

The benefit of a RAID-0 is increased read and write performance. Because a file is spread across multiple physical disks, the different parts of the file can be read from or written to each of the disks simultaneously. If you have three 500-GB drives used in a RAID-0, you have 1,500 GB (1.5 TB) of storage space.

RAID-1

RAID-1 (mirroring) uses two disks. Data written to one disk is also written to a second disk. If one of the disks fails, the other disk still has all the data, so the system can continue to operate without any data loss. With this in mind, if you mirror all the drives in a system, you can actually lose half of the drives and continue to operate.

You can add an additional disk controller to a RAID-1 configuration to remove the disk controller as a single point of failure. In this configuration, each of the disks has its own disk controller. Adding a second disk controller to a mirror is called disk duplexing.

If you have two 500-GB drives used in a RAID-1, you have 500 GB of storage space. The other 500 GB of storage space is dedicated to the fault-tolerant, mirrored volume. RAID-2, RAID-3, and RAID-4 are rarely used.

RAID-5 and RAID-6

A RAID-5 is three or more disks that are striped together, similar to RAID-0. However, the equivalent of one drive includes parity information. This parity information is striped across each of the drives in a RAID-5 and provides fault tolerance. If one of the drives fails, the disk subsystem can read the remaining drives' information and re-create the original data. If two of the drives fail in a RAID-5, the data is lost.

RAID-6 is an extension of RAID-5. The big difference is that it uses an additional parity block and requires an additional disk. A huge benefit is that the RAID-6 disk subsystem will continue to operate even if two disk drives fail. RAID-6 requires a minimum of four disks.

RAID-10

A RAID-10 configuration combines the features of mirroring (RAID-1) and striping (RAID-0). RAID-10 is sometimes called RAID 1+0. A variation of RAID-10 is RAID-01 or RAID 0+1 that also combines mirroring and striping features but implements the drives differently.

The minimum number of drives in a RAID-10 is four. When adding more drives, you add two more (or multiples of two, such as four, six, and so on). If you have four 500-GB drives used in a RAID-10, you have 1 TB of usable storage.

> ★ *Remember This!*
>
> RAID subsystems, such as RAID-1, RAID-5, and RAID-6, provide fault tolerance and increased data availability. RAID-1 and RAID-5 can survive the failure of one disk, and RAID-6 can survive the failure of two disks.

Server Redundancy and High Availability

High availability refers to a system or service that needs to remain operational with almost zero downtime. It's possible to achieve 99.999 percent uptime, commonly called "five nines" by implementing redundancy and fault tolerance methods. This equates to less than 6 minutes of downtime a year: 60 minutes × 24 hours × 365 days × .00001 = 5.256 minutes.

Although five nines is achievable, it's expensive. However, if the potential cost of an outage is high, the high cost of the redundant technologies is justified. For example, some websites generate a significant amount of revenue, and every minute a website is unavailable represents lost money. High-capacity load balancers ensure the service is always available even if a server fails.

Active/Active Load Balancers

An *active/active load balancer* can optimize and distribute data loads across multiple computers or multiple networks. For example, if an organization hosts a popular website, it can use multiple servers hosting the same website in a web farm. Load-balancing software distributes traffic equally among all the servers in the web farm, typically located in a DMZ. Active/active load balancing is one way to implement a concept known as *clustering*, where several different servers work together to appear as one resource to end users.

The term *load balancer* makes it sound like it's a piece of hardware, but a load balancer can be hardware or software. A hardware-based load balancer accepts traffic and directs it to servers based on factors such as processor utilization and the number of current connections to the server. A software-based load balancer uses software running on each of the servers to balance the load. Load balancing primarily provides scalability, but it also contributes to high availability. Scalability refers to the ability of a service to serve more clients without any decrease in performance. Availability ensures that systems are up and operational when needed. By spreading the load among multiple systems, it ensures that individual systems are not overloaded, increasing overall availability.

Consider a web server that can serve 100 clients per minute, but if more than 100 clients connect at a time, performance degrades. You need to either scale up or scale out to serve more clients. You scale the server up by adding additional resources, such as processors and memory, and you scale out by adding additional servers in a load balancer.

Figure 9.2 shows an example of a load balancer with multiple web servers configured in a web farm. Each web server includes the same web application. A load balancer uses a scheduling technique to determine where to send new requests. Some load balancers simply send new requests to the servers in a round-robin fashion. The load balancer sends the first request to Server 1, the second request to Server 2, and so on. Other load balancers automatically detect the load on individual servers and send new clients to the least used server.

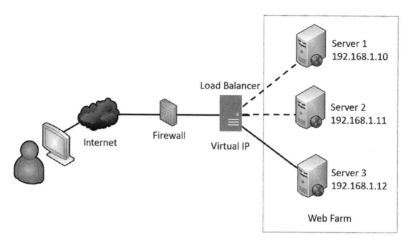

Figure 9.2: Load balancing

Some load balancers use source address affinity to direct the requests. Source address affinity sends requests to the same server based on the requestor's IP address and provides the user with session persistence. As an example, imagine that Homer sends a request to retrieve a webpage. The load balancer records his IP address and sends his request to Server 3. When he interacts with the page and sends another request, the load balancer identifies his IP address and sends his request to Server 3 again. Source address affinity effectively sticks users to a specific server ensuring session persistence.

A software-based load balancer uses a virtual IP address. For example, imagine the IP address of the website is 72.52.206.134. This IP address isn't assigned to a specific server. Instead, clients send requests to this IP address, and the load-balancing software redirects the request to one of the servers in the web farm using their private IP addresses. In this scenario, the IP address is referred to as a virtual IP.

An added benefit of many load balancers is that they can detect when a server fails. If a server stops responding, the load-balancing software no longer sends clients to this server. This contributes to overall high availability.

Active/Passive Load Balancers

Load balancers can also be configured in an active/passive configuration. In an active/passive configuration, one server is active, and the other server is inactive. If the active server fails, the inactive server takes over.

Consider Figure 9.3, which shows a two-node active-passive configuration. (Load balancers can include more than two nodes, but these examples use only two to keep them simple.) Both nodes are individual servers, and they both have access to external data storage used by the active server. Additionally, the two nodes have a monitoring connection to each other used to check each other's health or heartbeat.

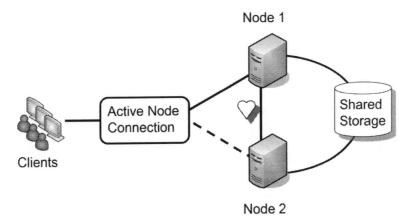

Figure 9.3: Active/Passive Configuration

Imagine that Node 1 is the active node. When any of the clients connect, the load balancer ensures that the clients connect to the active node. If Node 1 fails, Node 2 senses the failure through the heartbeat connection and configures itself as the active node. Because both nodes have access to the shared storage, there is no loss of data for the client. Clients may notice a momentary hiccup or pause, but the service continues.

You might notice that the shared storage in Figure 9.3 represents a single point of failure. It's not uncommon for this to be a robust hardware RAID-10. This ensures that even if a hard drive in the shared storage fails, the service will continue. Additionally, if both nodes are plugged into the same power grid, the power represents a single point of failure. They can each be protected with a separate UPS and use a separate power grid.

★ *Remember This!*

Load balancing increases the overall processing power of a service by sharing the load among multiple servers. Configurations can be active/passive or active/active. Scheduling methods include round-robin and source IP address affinity. Source IP address affinity scheduling ensures clients are redirected to the same server for an entire session.

NIC Teaming

NIC teaming allows you to group two or more physical network adapters into a single software-based virtual network adapter. This provides increased performance because the NIC team handles all the individual NICs' bandwidth as if the NIC team is a single physical network adapter. Additionally, the NIC team uses load-balancing algorithms to distribute outgoing traffic equally among the NICs.

The NIC team also eliminates any physical NIC as a single point of failure. If one NIC in the NIC team fails, the software detects the failure and logically removes the team's failed NIC.

Power Redundancies

Power is a critical utility to consider when reviewing redundancies. For mission-critical systems, you can use uninterruptible power supplies, generators, and managed power distribution units (PDUs) to provide both fault tolerance and high availability:

- **Uninterruptible power supplies.** An uninterruptible power supply (UPS) provides short-term power and can protect against power fluctuations. UPS systems give computing devices enough time to perform a logical shutdown or keep them powered until longer-term power systems come online.
- **Dual supply.** Within the context of power redundancies, a dual power supply (or a redundant power supply) is a second power supply that can power a device if the primary power supply fails. During normal operations, each power supply provides power to the device. Most redundant power supplies are hot-swappable, allowing administrators to replace a failed device without removing power to the system.
- **Generators.** Generators provide long-term power during extended outages. For example, during natural disasters such as hurricanes and floods, communities may experience power outages for days or even weeks. Generators can provide power to critical systems during these outages.
- **Managed power distribution units.** Server racks within a data center house multiple computing devices, and it's common to use power distribution units (PDUs) within the racks to power the devices. Basic PDUs distribute power to devices, similar to how a power strip delivers power via multiple outlets. Managed PDUs (sometimes called switched PDUs) monitor the quality of power such as voltage, current, and power consumption and report these measurements to a central monitoring console. This allows administrators to use a single application to monitor power in all the racks within a data center.

Protecting Data with Backups

Backups are copies of data created to ensure that if the original data is lost or corrupted, it can be restored. The truth is, if you work with computers long enough, you will lose data. The difference between a major catastrophe and a minor inconvenience is the existence of a usable backup.

Ransomware has exploded in recent years. Attackers infect a single system and then move throughout a network looking for data files. As mentioned in Chapter 6, attackers have been launching ransomware attacks against hospitals, cities, and schools, effectively crippling these networks.

The primary protection is to prevent ransomware attacks. However, once they succeed, the best corrective control is up-to-date backups of all critical data.

It's important to realize that redundancy and backups are not the same things. Protecting data with a RAID-1 or RAID-10 does not negate the need for backups. If a fire destroys a server, it also destroys the data on the RAID. Without a backup, all of the data is gone. Forever.

Backup Media

The most common media used for backups is tape. Tapes store more data and are cheaper than other media. Other types of media used to store backups are:

- **Disk.** Backups can also be stored on disks. A benefit is that disk access is much quicker than tape. However, disks are more expensive. The disks can be located on servers or simple USB disk drives.
- **Network-attached storage.** *Network-attached storage (NAS)* is a dedicated computer used for file storage and is accessible on a network. It can have multiple drives and often runs a stripped-down version of Linux for simplicity and to reduce costs. A NAS provides file-level data storage allowing users to access files on NAS devices and copy backup files to NAS devices. A NAS uses a standard Ethernet connection.
- **Storage area network.** A *storage area network (SAN)* provides block-level data storage via a full network. Organizations use SANs to provide high-speed access to disk arrays or tape libraries. SANs can also be used for real-time replication of data. As soon as data changes in its primary location, it is replicated to the SAN. A SAN typically uses a Fibre Channel connection, but can also use Ethernet.
- **Cloud storage.** It's also possible to store backups in the cloud using the services of major cloud providers, such as AWS, Microsoft, and Google. Chapter 5, "Securing Hosts and Data," discusses cloud concepts in more depth.

Online Versus Offline Backups

Offline backups use traditional backup media within a network such as tapes, local disks, drives in a NAS, and even backup targets within a SAN. Offline backups provide an organization with easy access to the backups, better control of the backup media, and relatively fast backup and restore capabilities. Unfortunately, backup media can fail, be destroyed, or even be stolen.

In contrast, online backups are stored within the cloud. Most cloud providers provide data storage that you can access via the Internet from anywhere. Even if a natural disaster destroys all backups, they remain available in the cloud. Additionally, most cloud providers automatically encrypt the data preventing unauthorized access to the backups.

Online and offline backups have a slightly different meaning in the context of databases. An online database backup is a hot backup, meaning that it backs up the database while it is operational. It captures the changes while they're occurring and applies them to the backup when it's done. In contrast, an offline backup is a cold backup or a backup performed while the database is offline. You can also think of an offline backup of a database as a local backup.

Backup utilities support several different types of backups. Even though third-party backup programs can be quite sophisticated in what they do and how they do it, you should have a solid understanding of the basics. As an introduction, many of these utilities commonly use the following backup types:

- **Full backup**. A full (or normal backup) backs up all the selected data.
- **Differential backup**. This backs up all the data that has changed or is different since the last full backup.
- **Incremental backup**. This backs up all the data that has changed since the last full or incremental backup.
- **Snapshot and image backup**. A snapshot backup captures the data at a point in time. It is sometimes referred to as an image backup.

Full Backups

A **full backup** backs up all data specified in the backup. For example, you could have several folders on the D: drive. If you specify these folders in the backup program, the backup program backs up all the data in these folders. Although it's possible to do a full backup on a daily basis, it's rare to do so in most production environments. This is because of two limiting factors:

- **Time.** A full backup can take several hours to complete and can interfere with operations. However, administrators don't always have unlimited time to do backups and other system maintenance. For example, if a system is online 24/7, administrators might need to limit the amount of time for full backups to early Sunday morning to minimize the impact on users.
- **Money.** Backups need to be stored on some type of media, such as tape or hard drives. Performing full backups every day requires more media, and the cost can be prohibitive. Instead, organizations often combine full backups with differential or incremental backups.

Incremental and differential backup strategies must start with a full backup.

Recovering a Full Backup

A full backup is the easiest and quickest to restore. You only need to restore the single full backup, and you're done. If you store backups on tapes, you only need to restore a single tape. However, most organizations need to balance time and money and use either a full/differential or a full/incremental backup strategy.

Differential Backups

A ***differential backup*** strategy starts with a full backup. After the full backup, differential backups back up data that has changed or is different since the last full backup.

For example, a full/differential strategy could start with a full backup on Sunday night. On Monday night, a differential backup would back up all files that changed since the last full backup on Sunday. On Tuesday night, the differential backup would again back up all the files that changed since the last full backup. This repeats until Sunday when another full backup starts the process again. As the week progresses, the differential backup steadily grows in size.

Order of Recovery for a Full/Differential Backup Set

Assume for a moment that administrators store each of the backups on different tapes. If the system crashes on Wednesday morning, how many tapes would they need to recover the data?

The answer is two. They would first recover the full backup from Sunday. Because the differential backup on Tuesday night includes all the files that changed after the last full backup, they would then restore that tape to restore all the changes up to Tuesday night.

Incremental Backups

An ***incremental backup*** strategy also starts with a full backup. After the full backup, incremental backups then back up data that has changed since the last backup. This includes either the last full backup or the last incremental backup.

As an example, a full/incremental strategy could start with a full backup on Sunday night. On Monday night, an incremental backup would back up all the files that changed since the last full backup. On Tuesday night, the incremental backup would back up all the files that changed since the incremental backup on Monday night. Similarly, the Wednesday night backup would back up all the files that changed since the last incremental backup on Tuesday night. This repeats until Sunday, when another full backup starts the process again. As the week progresses, the incremental backups stay about the same size.

Order of Recovery for a Full/Incremental Backup Set

Assume for a moment that administrators store each of the backups on different tapes. If the system crashes on Thursday morning, how many tapes would they need to recover the data?

The answer is four. They would first need to recover the full backup from Sunday. Because the incremental backups would be backing up different data each day of the week, each of the incremental backups must be restored and restored in chronological order.

Sometimes, people mistakenly think the last incremental backup would have all the relevant data. Although it might have some relevant data, it doesn't have everything.

As an example, imagine you worked on a single project file each day of the week, and the system crashed on Thursday morning. In this scenario, the last incremental backup would hold the most recent copy of this file. However, what if you compiled a report every Monday but didn't touch it again until the following Monday? Only the incremental backup from Monday would include the most recent copy. An incremental backup from Wednesday night or another day of the week wouldn't include the report.

> ### 📌 *Remember This!*
>
> If you have unlimited time and money, the full backup alone provides the fastest recovery time. Full/ incremental strategies reduce the amount of time needed to perform backups. Full/differential strategies reduce the amount of time needed to restore backups.

Choosing Full/Incremental or Full/Differential

You may wonder "Why are there so many choices for backups?" The answer is that different organizations have different needs. For example, imagine two organizations perform daily backups to minimize losses. They each do a full backup on Sunday but are now trying to determine if they should use a full/incremental or a full/differential strategy.

The first organization doesn't have much time to perform maintenance throughout the week. In this case, the backup administrator needs to minimize the amount of time required to complete backups during the week. An incremental backup only backs up the data that has changed since the last backup. In other words, it includes changes only from a single day. In contrast, a differential backup contains all the changes since the last full backup. Backing up the changes from a single day takes less time than backing up changes from multiple days, so a full/incremental backup is the best choice.

In the second organization, they want to recover failed systems quickly. If a failure requires restoring data, they want to minimize the amount of time needed to restore the data. A full/differential is the best choice in this situation because it only requires the restoration of two backups, the full and the most recent differential backup. In contrast, a full/incremental can require the restoration of several different backups, depending on when the failure occurs, taking much more time.

Snapshot and Image Backups

A **snapshot backup** captures the data at a moment in time. It is commonly used with virtual machines, but many backup utilities can perform snapshot backups on data. Chapter 5 discusses virtual machines (VMs) in more depth. Administrators often take a snapshot of a VM before a risky operation, such as an update. If the update causes problems, it's relatively easy to revert the VM to the state it was in before the update.

Replication and Journaling

Replication is the process of creating an exact copy of data or a system in real-time or near-real-time. This technique is often used to maintain a secondary site or system that can be quickly brought online in case of a primary site failure or data corruption. Replication can be performed at different levels, such as storage, file, or application level, depending on the organization's requirements.

Journaling is a backup technique that records changes to data or files sequentially in a separate log, also known as a journal. In case of a system failure or data corruption, the journal can be used to recover the data to its most recent state by applying the changes recorded in the journal to a previous backup. Journaling is especially useful when dealing with databases, file systems, or other critical applications where data consistency and integrity are crucial.

Backup Frequency

You want to ensure that you're performing backups often enough that you're capturing data as it changes – the frequency of your backups is very important. When you restore your backups, you will only be able to restore the data as of the time of the last backup. This inevitably means that you will lose some data that changed since the most recent backup. The more frequently you perform backups, the less data you will lose. Of course, the tradeoff is that backups consume space and take time, so there is a cost to performing backups more frequently. Later in this chapter you will learn more about the recovery point objective (RPO), which helps measure the potential data loss.

Testing Backups

I've heard many horror stories in which personnel are regularly performing backups thinking all is well. Ultimately, something happens, and they need to restore some data. Unfortunately, they discover that none of the backups hold valid data. People have been going through the motions, but something in the process is flawed.

The only way to validate a backup is to perform a test restore. Performing a test restore is nothing more than restoring the data from a backup and verifying its integrity. If you want to verify that you can restore the entire backup, you perform a full restore of the backup. If you want to verify that you can restore individual files, you perform a test restore of individual files. It's common to restore data to a different location than the original source location. This still validates the quality of the backup.

As a simple example, an administrator can retrieve a random backup and attempt to restore it. There are two possible outcomes of this test, and both are good:

- The test succeeds. Excellent! You know that the backup process works. You don't necessarily know that every backup tape is valid, but at least you know that the process is sound and at least some of your backups work.
- The test fails. Excellent! You know there's a problem that you can fix before a crisis. If you discovered the problem after you actually lost data, it wouldn't help you restore the data.

An additional benefit of performing regular test restores is that it allows administrators to become familiar with the process. The first time they do a restore shouldn't be in the middle of a crisis with several high-level managers peering over their shoulders.

> 📌 **Remember This!**
>
> Test restores are the best way to test the integrity of a company's backup data. Backup media should be protected with the same level of protection as the data on the backup. Geographic considerations for backups include storing backups off-site, choosing the best location, and considering legal implications and data sovereignty.

Backups and Geographic Considerations

Organizations typically create a backup policy to answer critical questions related to backups. The backup policy is a written document and will often identify what data to back up, how often to back up the data, how to test the backups, and how long to retain the backups. Additionally, it's important to address special geographic considerations, such as the following:

- **Offsite vs onsite storage.** At least one copy of backups should be stored offsite. Storing backups in a separate geographic location protects them against a disaster such as a fire or a flood. Even if a disaster destroys the site, the organization will still have another copy of the critical data. You may also wish to keep a copy of your backups onsite because they will be more readily accessible, speeding up your recovery time if you need to restore the data they contain.
- **Distance.** Many organizations have specific requirements related to geographic dispersal or the distance between the main site and the off-site location. In some scenarios, the goal is to have the off-site location relatively close so that personnel can easily retrieve the backups. However, in other scenarios, the off- site location must be far away, such as 25

miles or farther away. This ensures that a disaster destroying a primary location won't impact the backup's location.

- **Location selection**. The location is often dependent on environmental issues. As an example, consider an organization located in California near the San Andreas fault. The off-site backup location should be far enough away that an earthquake at the primary location doesn't affect the off-site location.

- **Legal implications.** The legal implications related to backups depend on the data stored in the backups. For example, if the backups include Personally Identifiable Information (PII) or Protected Health Information (PHI), the backups need to be protected according to governing laws.

- **Data sovereignty.** Data sovereignty refers to the legal implications when data is stored off-site. If the backups are stored in a different country, they are subject to that country's laws. This can be a concern if the backups are stored in a cloud location and the cloud servers are in a different country. For example, imagine that an organization is located in the United States. It routinely does backups and stores them with a cloud provider. The cloud provider has some servers in the United States, some in Canada, and some in Mexico. If the organization's backups are stored in other countries, the organization can be subject to additional laws and regulations.

- **Encryption.** Protecting sensitive data in backups is crucial to maintain confidentiality and prevent unauthorized access. Encryption plays a vital role in securing the data both in transit and at rest. Organizations should implement strong encryption algorithms and manage encryption keys carefully to ensure that only authorized personnel can access and decrypt the backup data. This adds an extra layer of security to the backup process and mitigates the risk of data breaches, even if the physical backup medium is stolen or compromised.

Comparing Business Continuity Elements

Business continuity planning helps an organization predict and plan for potential outages of critical services or functions. The goal is to ensure that critical business operations continue and the organization can survive the outage. Organizations often create a ***business continuity plan (BCP)***. This plan includes disaster recovery elements that provide the steps used to return critical functions to operation after an outage. Disasters and outages can come from many sources, including:

- **Environmental.** This can include natural disasters, such as hurricanes, floods, tornadoes, and earthquakes. It can also include things like fires caused by lightning strikes rather than by humans. On a larger scale, it can include major environmental disasters such as the Fukushima Daiichi Nuclear Power Plant's nuclear meltdown after an earthquake and tsunami in 2011.

- **Human-made.** Human-made disasters refer to those caused by human activity. This includes fires (caused by people) and train wrecks caused by human error, such as the May

2015 Amtrak derailment. Within an organization, human error can cause hardware and software failures, and data loss. Attacks are also human-made.

■ **Internal versus external.** An internal disaster occurs within an organization. For example, a fire within an organization's data center is an internal disaster that may result in hardware failure and data loss. In contrast, an external disaster is a disaster that occurs outside of an organization but still impacts the organization. As an example, a wildfire near an organization may damage utility lines impacting the stability of power or communication lines.

Addressing all of these possible sources takes a lot of time and effort. The goal is to predict the relevant disasters as well as their impact and then develop recovery strategies to mitigate them. One of the first things an organization completes is a business impact analysis.

Business Impact Analysis Concepts

A *business impact analysis (BIA)* is an important part of a BCP. It helps an organization identify critical systems and components that are essential to the organization's success. These critical systems support *mission-essential functions*. Mission-essential functions are the activities that must continue or be restored quickly after a disaster. The BIA also helps identify vulnerable business processes, which are the processes that support mission-essential functions.

As an example, imagine an organization that has an online e-commerce business. Some basic mission-essential functions might include serving webpages, providing a shopping cart path, accepting purchases, sending email confirmations, and shipping purchases to customers. The shopping cart path alone is a business process. Because it is essential to the mission of e-commerce sales, management will likely consider it a vulnerable business process to protect. The customer needs to view products, select a product, enter customer information, enter credit card data, and complete the purchase. Some critical systems that support the website are web servers and a back-end database application hosted on one or more database servers.

If critical systems and components fail and cannot be restored quickly, it impacts mission-essential functions. If this lasts too long, the organization may not be able to survive the disaster.

For example, if a disaster such as a hurricane hits, which services must the organization restore to stay in business? Imagine a financial institution. It might decide that customers must have uninterrupted access to account data through an online site. If customers can't access their funds online, they might lose faith with the company and leave in droves.

However, the company might decide to implement alternate business practices in other elements of the business. For example, management might decide that accepting and processing loan applications is not important enough to continue during a disaster. Loan processing is still important to the company's bottom line, but a delay will not seriously affect its ability to stay in business. In this scenario, continuous online access is a mission-essential function, but processing loan applications during a disaster is not mission-essential.

The time to make these decisions is not during a crisis. Instead, the organization completes a BIA in advance. The BIA involves collecting information from throughout the organization and documenting the results. This documentation identifies core business or mission requirements. The BIA does not recommend solutions. However, it provides management with valuable information so that they can focus on critical business functions. It helps them address some of the following questions:

- What are the critical systems and functions?
- Are there any dependencies related to these critical systems and functions?
- What is the maximum downtime limit of these critical systems and functions?
- What scenarios are most likely to impact these critical systems and functions?
- What is the potential loss from these scenarios?

As an example, imagine an organization earns an average of $5,000 an hour through online sales. In this scenario, management might consider online sales to be a mission-essential function, and all systems that support online sales are critical systems. This includes web servers and back-end database servers. These servers depend on the network infrastructure connecting them, Internet access, and access to payment gateways for credit card charges.

After analysis, they might determine that the maximum allowable outage for online sales is five hours. Identifying the maximum downtime limit is extremely important. It drives decisions related to recovery objectives and helps an organization identify various contingency plans and policies.

> ★ **Remember This!**
>
> The BIA identifies mission-essential functions and critical systems that are essential to the organization's success. It also identifies maximum downtime limits for these systems and components, various scenarios that can impact these systems and components, and the potential losses from an incident.

Site Risk Assessment

Chapter 8, "Using Risk Management Tools," covers risk assessments such as qualitative and quantitative risk assessments. These are used to assess a wide variety of risks. However, a site risk assessment is a focused assessment of a specific location or site.

For example, the environmental risks for a site in Florida include hurricanes and floods, and these are items an organization should address. However, a San Francisco site doesn't need to worry about hurricanes, but earthquakes are a real risk.

Similarly, if an organization has multiple locations, each site probably has different mission-essential functions. One site may be focused on online sales so a site risk assessment would focus on protecting everything related to online sales. Another location may only focus on warehousing and shipping products after sales are completed. The warehouse site risk assessment will be quite different from that of the online site risk assessment.

Impact

The BIA evaluates various scenarios, such as natural disasters, fires, attacks, power outages, data loss, and hardware and software failures. Additionally, the BIA attempts to identify the impact of these scenarios. When evaluating the impact, a BIA looks at multiple items. For example, it might attempt to answer the following questions related to any of the scenarios:

- Will a disaster result in loss of life?
- Will a disaster result in loss of property?
- Is there a way to minimize the risk to personnel?
- Will a disaster reduce safety for personnel or property?
- What are the potential financial losses to the organization?
- What are the potential losses to the organization's reputation?

For example, a database server might host customer data, including credit card information. If an attacker accesses this customer data, the cost to the organization might exceed millions of dollars. According to IBM, the global average cost of a data breach in 2022 was $4.35 million with the average cost of a data breach in the U.S. being $9.44 million. For the healthcare industry, the average total cost of a breach was $10.10 million. Of course, these are only averages. Many data breaches cost much more.

Recovery Time Objective

The **recovery time objective (RTO)** identifies the maximum amount of time it can take to restore a system after an outage. Many BIAs identify the maximum acceptable outage or maximum tolerable outage time for mission-essential functions and critical systems. If an outage lasts longer than this maximum time, the impact is unacceptable to the organization.

For example, imagine an organization that sells products via a website that generates $10,000 in revenue an hour via online sales. It might decide that the maximum acceptable outage for the web server is five minutes. This results in an RTO of five minutes, indicating any outage must be limited to no more than five minutes.

Imagine that the organization has a database server only used by internal employees, not online sales. Although the database server may be valuable, it is not critical. Management might decide they can accept an outage for as long as 24 hours, resulting in an RTO of 24 hours.

Recovery Point Objective

A **recovery point objective (RPO)** identifies a point in time where data loss is acceptable. Imagine a server hosting archived data that has very few changes weekly. Management might decide that some data loss is acceptable, but they always want to recover data from at least the previous week. In this case, the RPO is one week.

With an RPO of one week, administrators would ensure that they have at least weekly backups. In the event of a failure, they will be able to restore recent backups and meet the RPO.

In some cases, the RPO is up to the minute of the failure. For example, any data loss from an online database recording customer transactions might be unacceptable. In this case, the organization can use various techniques to ensure administrators can restore data up to the moment of failure.

> ### ★ Remember This!
>
> The recovery time objective (RTO) identifies the maximum amount of time it should take to restore a system after an outage. It is derived from the maximum allowable outage time identified in the BIA. The recovery point objective (RPO) refers to the amount of data you can afford to lose.

Comparing MTBF and MTTR

When working with a BIA, experts often attempt to predict the possibility of a failure. For example, what is the likelihood that a hard disk within a RAID configuration will fail? The following two terms are often used to predict potential failures:

- **Mean time between failures (MTBF)**. The MTBF provides a measure of a system's reliability and is usually represented in hours. More specifically, the MTBF identifies the average (the arithmetic mean) time between failures. Higher MTBF numbers indicate higher reliability of a product or system. Administrators and security experts attempt to identify the MTBF for critical systems with the goal of predicting potential outages.
- **Mean time to repair (MTTR)**. The MTTR identifies the average (the arithmetic mean) time it takes to restore a failed system. In some cases, people interpret MTTR as the mean time to recover, and both mean essentially the same thing. Organizations that have maintenance contracts often specify the MTTR as a part of the contract. The supplier

agrees that it will, on average, restore a failed system within the MTTR time. The MTTR does not provide a guarantee that it will restore the system within the MTTR every time. Sometimes, it might take a little longer, and sometimes it might be a little quicker, with the average defined by the MTTR.

> ### 📌 *Remember This!*
>
> The mean time between failures (MTBF) provides a measure of a system's reliability and would provide an estimate of how often the systems will experience outages. The mean time to repair (MTTR) refers to the time it takes to restore a system.

Continuity of Operations Planning

Continuity of operations planning (COOP) focuses on restoring mission-essential functions at a recovery site after a critical outage. For example, suppose a hurricane or other disaster prevents the company from operating in the primary location. In that case, the organization can continue to operate the mission-essential functions at an alternate location that management previously identified as a recovery site. Failover is the process of moving mission-essential functions to the alternate site.

Site Resiliency

A **recovery site** is an alternate processing site that an organization uses for **site resiliency**. If one site suffers a catastrophic failure, an alternate site can take over after the disaster. The three primary types of recovery sites are hot sites, cold sites, and warm sites. These alternate locations could be an office space within a building, an entire building, or even a group of buildings. Other types of recovery sites are mobile sites and mirrored sites.

When planning the location(s) of your recovery site(s), it's important to keep **geographic dispersion** in mind. You definitely don't want your recovery site to be located close to your primary site or the same disaster may affect both locations! Similarly, if you have more than one recovery site, be sure to place them far enough apart that they are unlikely to both go down under the same circumstances.

Hot Site

A **hot site** would be up and operational 24 hours a day, seven days a week, and would be able to take over functionality from the primary site quickly after a primary site failure. It would include all the equipment, software, and communication capabilities of the primary site, and all the data would be up-to-date. In many cases, copies of backup tapes are stored at the hot site as the off-site location.

In many cases, a hot site is another active business location that has the capability to assume operations during a disaster. For example, a financial institution could have locations in two separate cities. The second location provides noncritical support services, but also includes all the resources necessary to assume the functions of the first location.

Some definitions of hot sites indicate they can take over instantaneously, though this isn't consistent. In most cases, it takes a little bit of time to transfer operations to the hot site, and this can take anywhere from a few minutes to an hour.

Clearly, a hot site is the most effective disaster recovery solution for high-availability requirements. If an organization must keep critical systems with high-availability requirements, the hot site is the best choice. However, a hot site is the most expensive to maintain and keep up-to-date.

★ Remember This!

A hot site includes personnel, equipment, software, and communication capabilities of the primary site with all the data up-to-date. A hot site provides the shortest recovery time compared with warm and cold sites. It is the most effective disaster recovery solution, but it is also the most expensive to maintain.

Cold Site

A **cold site** requires power and connectivity but not much else. Generally, if it has a roof, electricity, running water, and an inactive Internet access, you're good to go. The organization brings all the equipment, software, and data to the site when it activates it.

I often take my dogs for a walk at a local army base and occasionally see soldiers activate an extreme example of a cold site. On most weekends, the fields are empty. Other weekends, soldiers have transformed one or more fields into complete operational sites with tents, antennas, cables, generators, and porta-potties.

Because the army has several buildings on the base, they don't need to operate in the middle of fields, but what they're really doing is testing their ability to stand up a cold site wherever they want. If they can do it in the field, they can do it in the middle of a desert, or anywhere else they need to. A cold site is the cheapest to maintain, but it is also the most difficult to test.

Warm Site

You can think of a **warm site** as the Goldilocks solution—not too hot or cold, but just right. Hot sites are generally too expensive for most organizations, and cold sites sometimes take too long to configure for full operation. However, the warm site provides a compromise that an organization can tailor to meet its needs.

For example, an organization can place all the necessary hardware at the warm site location but not include up-to-date data. If a disaster occurs, the organization can copy the data to the warm site and take over operations. This is only one example, but there are many different possibilities of warm site configurations.

Restoration Order

After the disaster has passed, you will want to return all the functions to the primary site. As a best practice, organizations return the least critical functions to the primary site first. Remember, the critical functions are operational at the alternate site and can stay there as long as necessary. If a site has just gone through a disaster, it's very likely that there are still some unknown problems. By moving the least critical functions first, undiscovered problems will appear and can be resolved without significantly affecting mission-essential functions.

> ### ✦ Remember This!
>
> A cold site will have power and connectivity needed for a recovery site, but little else. Cold sites are the least expensive and the hardest to test. A warm site is a compromise between a hot site and a cold site. Mobile sites do not have dedicated locations but can provide temporary support during a disaster.

Disaster Recovery

A ***disaster recovery plan (DRP)*** identifies how to recover critical systems and data after a disaster. Disaster recovery is a part of an overall business continuity plan. Often, the organization will use the business impact analysis to identify the critical systems and components and then develop disaster recovery strategies and DRPs to address the systems hosting these functions.

In some cases, an organization will have multiple DRPs within a BCP, and in other cases, the organization will have a single DRP. For example, it's possible to have individual DRPs that identify the steps to recover individual critical servers and other DRPs that detail the recovery steps after different disasters such as hurricanes or tornadoes. A smaller organization might have a single DRP that simply identifies all the steps used to respond to any disruption.

A DRP or a BCP will include a hierarchical list of critical systems. This list identifies what systems to restore after a disaster and in what order. For example, should a server hosting an online website be restored first, or a server hosting an internal application? The answer is dependent on how the organization values and uses these servers. In some cases, systems have interdependencies requiring administrators to restore systems in a specific order.

If the DRP doesn't prioritize the systems, individuals restoring the systems will use their own judgment, which might not meet the organization's overall needs. For example, Nicky New Guy might not realize that a web server is generating $5,000 an hour in revenue but does know that he's responsible for keeping a generic file server operational. Without an ordered list of critical systems, he might spend his time restoring the file server and not the web server.

This hierarchical list is valuable when using alternate sites such as warm or cold sites, too. When the organization needs to move operations to an alternate site, the organization will want the most important systems and functions restored first.

Similarly, the DRP often prioritizes the services to restore after an outage. As a rule, critical business functions and security services are restored first. Support services are restored last. The different phases of a disaster recovery process typically include the following steps:

- **Activate the disaster recovery plan.** Some disasters, such as earthquakes or tornadoes, occur without much warning, and a DRP is activated after the disaster. Other disasters, such as hurricanes, provide a warning, and the DRP is activated when the disaster is imminent.
- **Implement contingencies.** If the recovery plan requires the implementation of an alternate site, critical functions are moved to these sites. If the disaster destroyed on-site backups, this step retrieves the off-site backups from the off-site location.
- **Recover critical systems.** After the disaster has passed, the organization begins recovering critical systems using the prioritization listed in the DRP. This also includes reviewing change management documentation to ensure that recovered systems include approved changes.
- **Test recovered systems.** Before bringing systems online, administrators test and verify them. This may include comparing the restored system with a performance baseline to verify functionality.
- **After-action report.** The final phase of disaster recovery includes a review of the disaster, sometimes called an after-action review. This often includes a lessons learned review to identify what went right and what went wrong. After reviewing the after-action report, the organization often updates the plan to incorporate any lessons learned.

Some organizations use functional recovery plans to address items that another organization may include in a standard DRP. It may include the hierarchical list of critical systems to ensure that personnel know the systems' priorities and the order of restoration.

📌 *Remember This!*

A disaster recovery plan (DRP) identifies how to recover critical systems after a disaster and often prioritizes services to restore after an outage. Testing validates the plan. The final phase of disaster recovery includes a review to identify any lessons learned and may include an update of the plan.

Testing Plans with Exercises

Business continuity plans and disaster recovery plans include testing. Testing validates that the plan works as desired and will often include testing redundancies and backups. Several types of testing are used with BCPs and DRPs, including tabletop exercises, walk-throughs, simulations, parallel processing, and failover tests.

Tabletop Exercises

A **tabletop exercise** is discussion-based. A coordinator gathers participants in a classroom or conference room and leads them through one or more hypothetical scenarios such as a cyberattack or a natural disaster. As the coordinator introduces each stage of the scenario, the participants identify how they would respond based on an organization's plan. This generates discussion about team members' roles and responsibilities and the decision-making process during an incident.

During a tabletop exercise, the coordinator may inject additional information. As an example, imagine the initial scenario is about a wildfire threatening a remote office. As participants discuss their responses, the coordinator may announce that the winds shifted and the wildfire is now threatening the organization's main location. This additional scenario is planned in advance and mimics potential events that may occur in a real-life situation.

Ideally, the exercise validates that the plan adequately addresses the scenario. However, it sometimes reveals flaws. The BCP coordinator ensures the plans are rewritten, if necessary, after the tabletop exercise.

Simulations

Simulations are functional exercises that allow personnel to test the plans in a simulated operational environment. There is a wide range of functional exercises, from simple simulations to full-blown tests. In a simulation, the participants go through the steps in a controlled manner without affecting the actual system. For example, a simulation can start by indicating that a server failed. Participants then follow the steps to rebuild the server on a test system. A full-blown test goes through all the steps of the plan. In addition to verifying that the test works, this also shows the amount of time it will take to execute the plan.

Parallel Processing

Up until this point, all of the tests we've discussed are theoretical exercises. They involve people *talking* about disaster recovery, but not necessarily taking the actions they would in a real disaster. **Parallel processing** makes sure that the disaster recovery site is actually working by activating it during the test. In a parallel processing test, the recovery site starts operations and runs alongside the main site (in parallel). This allows testers to confirm that everything is working properly.

Fail Over Tests

Fail over tests are the ultimate test of a disaster recovery plan. Also known as full interruption tests, these tests work by actually shutting down the primary site and testing whether the recovery site properly handles the load. Of course, a failed fail over test can be incredibly disruptive to the organization, so they should be planned and scheduled with care. Remember, though, that a self-inflicted wound from a failed fail over test is probably not as bad as discovering that your recovery site doesn't work during an actual disaster!

> 📌 *Remember This!*
>
> You can validate business continuity plans through testing. Tabletop exercises are discussion-based only and are typically performed in a conference setting. Simulations are hands-on exercises using a simulated environment. Parallel processing activates the disaster recovery site and runs it alongside the primary site. Fail over tests shut down the primary site to determine whether the fail over site works properly.

Capacity Planning

Capacity planning is the process of determining the resources required to meet the demands of an organization's operations and growth. It involves analyzing and forecasting the organization's resource needs. By ensuring that adequate resources are in place, capacity planning helps maintain business continuity, optimize performance, and avoid disruptions. Let's look at three main areas where businesses should conduct capacity planning:

People. Assessing the human resources needed to support business operations is a critical aspect of capacity planning. This involves analyzing the current workforce's skills, identifying gaps, and forecasting future requirements based on anticipated growth, new projects, or changes in the business environment. Workforce planning includes hiring, training, and retaining the right talent to ensure that the organization has the necessary expertise and staffing levels to meet its objectives.

Technology. Capacity planning for technology involves determining the hardware, software, and network resources required to support the organization's operations and growth. This includes estimating the computing power, storage, and bandwidth needed to handle current workloads and accommodate future demand. Regularly reviewing and updating technology infrastructure helps to avoid bottlenecks, ensure high availability, and maintain optimal performance levels.

Infrastructure. Infrastructure capacity planning refers to the evaluation and management of the physical facilities, such as data centers, office spaces, and other critical assets, to support the organization's operations. This involves analyzing current infrastructure capacity, identifying potential constraints, and planning for future requirements based on projected growth or changes in the business environment. Effective infrastructure planning ensures that the organization has the necessary space, power, cooling, and other essential resources to maintain business continuity and support growth.

Chapter 9 Exam Topic Review

When preparing for the exam, make sure you understand these key concepts covered in this chapter.

Comparing Physical Security Controls

- Physical security controls are controls you can physically touch. They often control entry and exit points and include various types of locks. Controlled areas such as data centers and server rooms should only have a single entrance and exit point.
- Cable locks secure mobile computers such as laptop computers in a training lab. Small devices can be stored in safes or locking office cabinets to prevent the theft of unused resources.
- Access badges can electronically unlock a door and help prevent unauthorized personnel from entering a secure area. By themselves, proximity cards do not identify and authenticate users. Some systems combine proximity cards with PINs for identification and authentication.
- Security guards are a preventive physical security control, and they can prevent unauthorized personnel from entering a secure area. A benefit of guards is that they can recognize people and compare an individual's picture ID for people they don't recognize.
- Cameras and closed-circuit television (CCTV) systems provide video surveillance and can give reliable proof of a person's identity and activity. Many cameras include motion detection and object detection capabilities. It's also possible to use CCTV systems as a compensating control.
- Sensors can detect changes in the environment, such as motion, noise, and temperature changes. Sensors can also be used to detect changes in pressure, such as when someone is walking on a floor. Motion detection may be accomplished using microwave technology or ultrasonic waves.
- Fencing, lighting, and alarms are commonly implemented with motion detection systems for physical security. Infrared motion detection systems detect human activity based on temperatures.
- Barricades provide stronger physical security than fences and attempt to deter attackers. Bollards are effective barricades that allow people through but block vehicles.
- Access control vestibules consist of two sets of interlocking doors, designed to create a secure compartment that allows only one person to enter at a time.
- Asset management processes track an organization's hardware, software, and data assets.

They should include acquisition/procurement processes, assignment/accounting processes, and monitoring/asset tracking processes.

- Organizations use diversity methods to provide layered security. Vendor diversity is the practice of implementing security controls from different vendors to increase security. Technology diversity uses different technologies to protect an environment, and control diversity uses different security control types, such as technical controls, managerial controls, operational controls, and physical controls.

- Physical security controls may be subjected to brute force attacks where someone simply crashes through the control. Facilities may also be subject to environmental attacks where the attacker alters the temperature, humidity, or other conditions to disable equipment.

Adding Redundancy and Fault Tolerance

- A single point of failure is any component that can cause the entire system to fail if it fails. It normally refers to hardware but can be a person. If one person is the only person who can perform a task, that person can be a single point of failure.

- RAID disk subsystems provide fault tolerance and increase availability. RAID-1 (mirroring) uses two disks. RAID-5 uses three or more disks and can survive the failure of one disk. RAID-6 and RAID-10 use four or more disks and can survive the failure of two disks.

- Load balancers spread the processing load over multiple servers. In an active/active configuration, all servers are actively processing requests. In an active/passive configuration, at least one server is not active but is instead monitoring activity ready to take over for a failed server. Software-based load balancers use a virtual IP.

- Affinity scheduling sends client requests to the same server based on the client's IP address. This is useful when clients need to access the same server for an entire online session. Round-robin scheduling sends requests to servers using a predefined order.

- NIC teaming groups two or more physical network adapters into a single software-based network adapter. It provides load balancing for outgoing traffic and fault tolerance if one of the NICs fails.

- Power redundancies include a UPS, a dual power supply, and generators. Managed PDUs monitor the quality of power delivered to devices within a server rack.

Protecting Data with Backups

- Offline backups use traditional backup media such as tapes, local disks, drives in a NAS, and even backup targets within a SAN. Online backups are stored in the cloud.

- Traditional backup methods include full, full/differential, full/incremental, snapshot, and image strategies. A full backup strategy alone allows the quickest recovery time.

- Full/incremental backup strategies minimize the amount of time needed to perform daily backups. Full/ differential backup strategies minimize the amount of time required to restore backups.

- A copy of backups should be kept off-site and should be kept far enough away so that a disaster impacting the primary site doesn't impact the backups. It's important to consider the distance between the main site and the off-site location.
- The location of the data backups affects data sovereignty. If backups are stored in a different country, the backups' data is now subject to the laws and regulations of that country.
- Backups should be encrypted to protect the sensitive data they contain from compromise should the backup media be lost or stolen.

Comparing Business Continuity Elements

- A business impact analysis (BIA) is part of a business continuity plan (BCP), and it identifies mission- essential functions, critical systems, and vulnerable business processes that are essential to the organization's success.
- The BIA identifies maximum downtimes for these systems and components. It considers various scenarios that can affect these systems and components, and the impact to life, property, safety, finance, and reputation from an incident.
- A recovery time objective (RTO) identifies the maximum amount of time it should take to restore a system after an outage. The recovery point objective (RPO) refers to the amount of data you can afford to lose.
- The mean time between failures (MTBF) identifies the average (the arithmetic mean) time between failures. The mean time to repair (MTTR) identifies the average (the arithmetic mean) time it takes to restore a failed system.
- Continuity of operations planning identifies alternate processing sites (used for site resiliency) and alternate business practices. Recovery sites provide alternate locations for business functions after a major disaster.
- A hot site includes everything needed to be operational within 60 minutes and is the most effective recovery solution but is also the most expensive. A cold site has power and connectivity requirements and little else and is the least expensive to maintain. Warm sites are a compromise between hot sites and cold sites.
- A disaster recovery plan (DRP) identifies how to recover critical systems after a disaster and often prioritizes services to restore after an outage.
- Periodic testing validates continuity of operations plans. Exercises validate the steps to restore individual systems, activate alternate sites, and document other actions within a plan. Tabletop exercises are discussion-based only. *Simulations* are functional exercises that allow personnel to test the plans in a simulated operational environment. Parallel processing makes sure that the disaster recovery site is actually working by activating it during the test. Fail over tests actually shut down the primary site and test whether the recovery site properly handles the load.

Chapter 9 Practice Questions

1. Employees access the data center by entering a cipher code at the door. However, everyone uses the same code, so it does not identify individuals. After a recent security incident, management has decided to implement a key card system that will identify individuals who enter and exit this secure area. However, the installation might take six months or longer. Which of the following choices can the organization install immediately to identify individuals who enter or exit the secure area?

   A. Access control vestibule
   B. Access list
   C. CCTV
   D. Bollards
   E. Compensating control

2. Your local library is planning to purchase new laptops that patrons can use for Internet research. However, management is concerned about possible theft. Which of the following is the BEST choice to prevent theft of these laptops?

   A. Access control vestibule
   B. Anti-malware software
   C. Cable locks
   D. Disk encryption

3. Which one of the following backup types backs up all of the data that has changed since the last full backup, and only the data that has changed since the last full backup?

   A. Full backup
   B. Differential backup
   C. Snapshot backup
   D. Incremental backup

4. You need to secure access to a data center. Which of the following choices provides the BEST physical security to meet this need? (Select THREE.)

   A. Biometrics
   B. Cable locks
   C. Access control vestibule
   D. CCTV
   E. HVAC

5. You need to add disk redundancy for a critical server in your organization's screened subnet. Management wants to ensure it supports a two-drive failure. Which of the following is the BEST solution for this requirement?

   A. RAID-0
   B. RAID-1
   C. RAID-5
   D. RAID-6

6. Your organization performs a series of full and incremental backups. You perform full backups every Sunday evening and then supplement those with incremental backups on every evening other than Sunday. Your system fails on a Thursday morning. What backup should you restore first?

   A. Sunday's full backup
   B. Monday's incremental backup
   C. Tuesday's incremental backup
   D. Wednesday's incremental backup

7. You are concerned about the potential loss of backup tapes while they are in transit to a remote site by a secured courier. What control can help you protect against the unauthorized disclosure of confidential information?

   A. Maintaining a second set of backup tapes
   B. Adding a second courier
   C. Encryption
   D. All of the above

8. Your organization is planning to deploy a new e-commerce website. Management antici-pates heavy processing requirements for a back-end application used by the website. The current design will use one web server and multiple application servers. Additionally, when beginning a session, a user will connect to an application server and remain connected to the same application server for the entire session. Which of the following BEST describes the configuration of the application servers?

   A. Load balancing
   B. Active/active
   C. Active/passive
   D. Persistence

9. Your organization recently implemented two servers in an active/passive load-balancing configuration. What security goal does this support?

   A. Obfuscation
   B. Integrity
   C. Confidentiality
   D. Resilience

10. Your database backup strategy includes full backups performed on Saturdays at 12:01 a.m. and differential backups performed daily at 12:01 a.m. If the database fails on Thursday afternoon, how many backups are required to restore it?

   A. 1
   B. 2
   C. 3
   D. 5

11. After reading about increased ransomware attacks against the health sector, hospital ad-ministrators want to enhance organizational resilience against these attacks. Which of the following could IT personnel implement to improve their ability to recover from a success-ful ransomware attack?

   A. Use email filtering to block malicious emails
   B. Perform regular testing and validation of full backups
   C. Ensure all systems are patched
   D. Increase end-user training related to ransomware and other risks

12. Your organization hired a security consultant to create a BIA. She is trying to identify processes that can potentially cause losses in revenue if they stop functioning. Which of the
following BEST describes what she is identifying?

    A. Single points of failure
    B. Critical systems
    C. Mission-essential functions
    D. MTBF

13. After a recent attack causing a data breach, an executive is analyzing the financial losses.
She determined that the attack is likely to result in losses of at least $1 million. She wants
to ensure that this information is documented for future planning purposes. Which of the
following documents is she MOST likely to use?

    A. DRP
    B. BIA
    C. MTTR
    D. RTO

14. A project manager is reviewing a business impact analysis. It indicates that a key website can tolerate a maximum of three hours of downtime. Administrators have identified
several systems that require redundancy additions to meet this maximum downtime requirement. Of the following choices, what term refers to the maximum of three hours of
downtime?

    A. RPO
    B. MTTR
    C. MTBF
    D. RTO
    E. DRP

15. Lisa has scheduled quarterly meetings with department leaders to discuss how they would
respond to various scenarios such as natural disasters or cyberattacks. During the meetings, she presents a scenario and asks attendees to indicate their responses. Also, during
the meetings, she injects variations on the scenario similar to what may happen during a
live event and encourages attendees to discuss their responses. What does this describe?

    A. Simulation
    B. Tabletop exercise
    C. Incident response
    D. Testing site resiliency

Chapter 9

Practice Question Answers

1. **C** is correct. Closed-circuit television (CCTV) or a similar video surveillance system can monitor the entrance and record who enters and exits the area. An access control vestibule (sometimes called a mantrap) prevents tailgating, but it doesn't necessarily identify individuals and it can't be installed immediately because it requires construction work. An access list is useful if a guard identifies users and allows access based on the access list, but the access list itself does not identify users. Bollards are a type of barricade that protects building entrances. Using a CCTV until the key card system is installed is an example of a compensating control, but all compensating controls do not identify people.

2. **C** is correct. A cable lock attaches to a computer and wraps around a piece of furniture to secure it to deter and prevent theft. This is like a bike lock used to secure a bicycle to a bike rack. An access control vestibule (sometimes called a mantrap) prevents tailgating but is unrelated to this question. Anti-malware software protects the systems from viruses and other malware. Disk encryption is useful if the computers have confidential information, but it wouldn't be appropriate to put confidential information on a public computer.

3. **B** is correct. A differential backup backs up all of the data that has changed since the last full backup. An incremental backup backs up all of the data that has changed since the last full *or incremental* backup. A snapshot backup copies all data on the volume being snapshotted. A full backup backs up all data, regardless of what other backups have been performed.

4. **A**, **C**, and **D** are correct. A biometric reader used for access control, an access control vestibule (sometimes called a mantrap), and a closed-circuit television (CCTV) system all provide strong physical security for accessing a data center. Cable locks are effective theft deterrents for mobile devices such as laptops, but they don't protect data centers. Heating, ventilation, and air conditioning (HVAC) systems can control the data center's environment, but they don't secure access.

5. **D** is correct. A redundant array of inexpensive disks 6 (RAID-6) is the best solution of the available answers. It supports a two-drive failure meaning that two drives can fail in the RAID-6, and the disk subsystem will continue to operate. RAID-0 (disk striping) doesn't have any fault tolerance and will fail completely if a single drive fails. RAID-1 (disk mirroring) uses only two drives. If one drive fails in a RAID-1, the data is preserved, but if two drives fail, all data is lost. RAID-5 (striping with parity) will continue to operate if one drive fails, but all data is lost if two drives fail.

6. **A** is correct. Because you are performing full and incremental backups, you will need to restore all of these backups. When restoring incremental backups, you always begin by restoring the most recent full backup. In this case, that would be Sunday's backup. You then continue by restoring each of the incremental backups that occurred since that backup, in order from oldest to newest. So, you would first restore Sunday's full backup, followed by Monday's incremental backup, Tuesday's incremental backup and, finally, Wednesday's incremental backup.

7. **C** is correct. Encryption is a security control that protects against the loss of sensitive information. Your goal here is to protect against unauthorized disclosure and encryption is the only control that meets that goal. Adding a second set of tapes or a second courier might reduce the risk of permanently losing the data but those options would not protect against the disclosure of the sensitive information lost on the first set of tapes.

8. **D** is correct. This describes a load-balancing configuration using persistence so that a user will connect to the same application server for an entire session. All the answers are related to load balancing, but the scenario describes load balancing with persistence, so persistence is more correct than load balancing. An active/active load-balancing configuration indicates all the servers are handling user requests. An active/passive load-balancing configuration has at least one server that is not actively serving clients but can take over if another server fails. However, the scenario didn't give enough information to determine if the application servers were configured as active/active or active/passive.

9. **D** is correct. An active/passive load-balancing configuration supports resilience and high availability. An active/passive load-balancing configuration uses redundant servers to ensure a service continues to operate even if one of the servers fails. Obfuscation methods attempt to make something unclear or difficult to understand and are not related to load balancing. Integrity methods ensure that data has not been modified. Confidentiality methods such as encryption prevent the unauthorized disclosure of data.

10. **B** is correct. Two backups are required, the full backup performed on Sunday at 12:01 a.m. and the differential backup performed on Thursday at 12:01 a.m. If you perform only one backup, it would be the full backup. You can't restore a differential backup without restoring the full backup first. This wouldn't include all the changes that occurred during the week. If you were using a full/incremental strategy, you would apply five backups: the full backup, and each of the incremental backups performed daily (Monday, Tuesday, Wednesday, and Thursday).

11. **B** is correct. Performing regular testing and validation of full backups will enhance organizational resilience against ransomware attacks. Resiliency techniques help ensure an organization can recover from a security incident and minimize downtime after an outage. The other answers all refer to preventive methods taken before an outage. Email filtering blocks spam and malicious emails and can help prevent ransomware attacks. Keeping systems patched helps ensure they aren't susceptible to known vulnerabilities. Training users decreases the possibility that they may respond inappropriately to malicious emails.

12. **C** is correct. The security consultant is identifying mission-essential functions, which is a key part of a business impact analysis (BIA). A single point of failure is a component within a system that can cause the entire system to fail if the component fails. It's common to eliminate single points of failure of critical systems, but not all single points of failure are supporting mission-essential functions. Critical systems support mission-essential functions. However, if single points of failure have been eliminated, a critical system can fail but the mission-essential function will continue to operate. The mean time between failures (MTBF) identifies the average (the arithmetic mean) time between failures.

13. **B** is correct. A business impact analysis (BIA) includes information on potential losses and is the most likely document of those listed where this loss would be documented. A disaster recovery plan (DRP) includes methods used to recover from an outage. The mean time to repair (MTTR) identifies the average (the arithmetic mean) time it takes to restore a failed system. The recovery time objective (RTO) identifies the maximum amount of time it should take to restore a system after an outage.

14. **D** is correct. The recovery time objective (RTO) identifies the maximum amount of time it can take to restore a system after an outage. Because the business impact analysis states that the website can only tolerate three hours of downtime, this also identifies the RTO. The recovery point objective (RPO) identifies a point in time where data loss is acceptable,

but it doesn't refer to downtime. The mean time to repair (MTTR) metric identifies the average (the arithmetic mean) time it takes to restore a failed system, but not a maximum amount of time a system can be down. The mean time between failures (MTBF) metric provides a measure of a system's reliability and is usually represented in hours. A disaster recovery plan (DRP) details the recovery steps to take after different types of disasters.

15. **B** is correct. This is a tabletop exercise. A tabletop exercise is discussion-based, and participants discuss their responses to various scenarios. A simulation is a hands-on exercise, not a meeting. Incident response refers to the actual steps taken in response to an incident (preparation, detection, analysis, containment, eradication, recovery, lessons learned), not a meeting discussing steps to take. Site resiliency is tested by seeing if an alternate site (such as a hot site, cold site, or warm site) can take over, if necessary, but the scenario doesn't discuss alternate sites.

Chapter 10

Understanding Cryptography and PKI

CompTIA Security+ objectives covered in this chapter:

1.2 Summarize fundamental security concepts.

- Non-repudiation

1.4 Explain the importance of using appropriate cryptographic solutions.

- Public key infrastructure (PKI) (Public key, private key, key escrow)
- Encryption (Transport/communication, Asymmetric, Symmetric, Key exchange, Algorithms, Key length)
- Tools (Key management system)
- Obfuscation (Steganography, Tokenization, Data masking)
- Hashing
- Salting
- Digital signatures
- Key stretching
- Blockchain
- Open public ledger
- Certificates (Certificate authorities, Certificate revocation lists (CRLs), Online Certificate Status Protocol (OCSP), Self-signed, Third-party, Root of trust, Certificate signing request (CSR) generation, Wildcard)

2.3 Explain various types of vulnerabilities.

- Cryptographic

2.4 Given a scenario, analyze indicators of malicious activity.

- Cryptographic attacks (Downgrade, Collision, Birthday)
- Password attacks (Spraying, Brute force)

3.3 Compare and contrast concepts and strategies to protect data.

- General data considerations (Data states, Data at rest, Data in transit, Data in use)
- Methods to secure data (Encryption, Hashing, Masking, Tokenization, Obfuscation)

Cryptography and Public Key Infrastructure (PKI) topics are challenging for many test takers, mostly because they include topics that aren't familiar to many system administrators. When tackling these topics, don't lose sight of the basics. The first section in this chapter, "Introducing Cryptography Concepts," outlines and summarizes these basics. Don't worry if they aren't clear to you right away—they should be once you complete the chapter. Passwords are commonly hashed and password attacks often try to exploit weaknesses in hashes. After hashes are explained, password attacks are explored. Other sections dig into the details of hashing, encryption, and Public Key Infrastructure (PKI) components.

Introducing Cryptography Concepts

Cryptography includes several important concepts that you need to grasp for the CompTIA Security+ exam, but the topics are often new to many information technology (IT) professionals.

As an introduction, the following bullets identify the important core cryptography concepts. Remember, this is only an overview. If these bullets don't make sense to you now, they should after you complete this chapter:

- **Integrity** provides assurance that data has not been modified. A hashing comparison verifies whether data has retained integrity.
- A **hash** is a string of alphanumeric characters derived from performing a mathematical calculation on data, such as a message, software patch, or file.
- Hashing creates a fixed-length string of bits or hexadecimal characters, which cannot be reversed to re-create the original data.
- A common hashing algorithm in use today is the Secure Hash Algorithm 3 (SHA-3).
- **Confidentiality** ensures that data is only viewable by authorized users. Encryption protects the confidentiality of data.
- **Encryption** scrambles data to make it unreadable if intercepted. Encryption normally includes an algorithm and a key.
- **Symmetric encryption** uses the same key to encrypt and decrypt data. Most symmetric algorithms use either a block cipher or a stream cipher.
- **Stream ciphers** encrypt data 1 bit at a time.
- **Block ciphers** encrypt data in blocks.
- **Asymmetric encryption** uses two keys (public and private) created as a matched key pair.
- Asymmetric encryption requires a Public Key Infrastructure (PKI) to issue certificates.
- Anything encrypted with the public key can only be decrypted with the matching private key.

- Anything encrypted with the private key can only be decrypted with the matching public key.
- **Steganography** provides a level of confidentiality by hiding data within other files. For example, it's possible to embed data within the white space of a picture file.
- **Authentication** validates an identity.
- **Non-repudiation** prevents a party from successfully disputing having performed an action.
- A digital signature provides authentication, non-repudiation, and integrity.
- Users sign emails with a digital signature, which is a hash of an email message encrypted with the sender's private key.
- Only the sender's public key can decrypt the digital signature to reveal the hash, providing verification that the hash was encrypted with the sender's private key.

Providing Integrity with Hashing

You can verify integrity with **hashing**. Hashing is a mathematical algorithm performed on data such as a file or message to produce a fixed-length hexadecimal string of characters called a hash. The hash is used to verify that data is not modified, tampered with, or corrupted. In other words, you can verify the data has maintained integrity.

A key point about a hash is that no matter how many times you execute a particular hashing algorithm against the same data, the hash will always be the same if the data is the same.

Hashes are created at least twice so that they can be compared. For example, imagine a software company is releasing a patch for an application that customers can download. They can calculate the hash of the patch and post both a link to the patch file and its hash on the company website. They might list it as:

- **Patch file: `Patch_v2_3.zip`**
- **SHA-3-256 hash: `d4723ac6f72daea2c779…3ac113863c`**

The Secure Hash Algorithm 3 (SHA-3) hash is the calculated number displayed in hexadecimal. A SHA-3-256 hash is typically displayed as 64 hexadecimal characters, but I've shortened it for brevity. Customers can download the patch file and then calculate the hash on the downloaded file. If the calculated hash is the same as the hash posted on the website, it verifies the file has retained integrity. In other words, the file has not changed.

> ★ **Remember This!**
>
> Hashing verifies integrity for data such as email, downloaded files, and files stored on a disk. A hash is a hexadecimal number created with a hashing algorithm.

Hash Versus Checksum

Hashes and checksums are similar, but there are some differences. In general, hashes are much longer numbers and used in strong cryptographic implementations. A **checksum** is typically a small piece of data, sometimes only 1 or 2 bits, and is used to quickly verify the integrity of data.

As an example of a checksum, a RAID-5 disk subsystem, described in Chapter 9, "Implementing Controls to Protect Assets," uses a single parity bit per byte and can identify corrupted data.

Similarly, the initial check for credit cards often uses a checksum. In a 16-digit credit card, the first six digits identify the institution that issued the card, the next nine represent the account number, and the 16th digit is a check digit or checksum. Imagine Homer enters his credit card online but inadvertently enters it incorrectly. One way this is checked is by calculating the checksum twice. First, it is calculated without the check digit, then it is calculated with the check digit. If both calculations are the same, it indicates the card number was entered correctly. If they're different, the application typically displays an error before even trying to submit the charge.

Checksums are not intended to be cryptographically secure. Instead, they give a quick indication when data integrity has been lost. In contrast, strong hashing algorithms such as SHA-3 are cryptographically secure.

MD5

Message Digest 5 (MD5) is a common hashing algorithm that produces a 128-bit hash value. Hashes are commonly shown in hexadecimal format instead of a stream of 1s and 0s. For example, an MD5 hash is displayed as 32 hexadecimal characters instead of 128 bits. Hexadecimal characters are composed of 4 bits and use the numbers 0 through 9 and the characters a through f.

MD5 has been in use since 1992. Experts discovered significant vulnerabilities in MD5 in 2004 and later years. As the processing power of computers increased, it became easier and easier to exploit these vulnerabilities. Security experts now consider MD5 cracked and discourage its use as a cryptographic hash.

However, it is still sometimes used to verify the integrity of files as a quick checksum. This includes email, files stored on disks, files downloaded from the Internet, executable files, and more. The "Hashing Files" section shows how you can manually calculate hashes.

Secure Hash Algorithms

Secure Hash Algorithms (SHA) are a group of hashing algorithms with variations grouped into four standards— SHA-0, SHA-1, SHA-2, and SHA-3:

- SHA-0 is flawed and not used.
- SHA-1 is an updated version that creates 160-bit hashes. It is similar to the MD5 algorithm. Weaknesses were discovered and it is no longer approved for most cryptographic uses.
- SHA-2 improved SHA-1 to overcome potential weaknesses. It includes four versions. SHA-256 creates 256-bit hashes and SHA-512 creates 512-bit hashes. SHA-224 (224-bit hashes) and SHA-384 (384-bit hashes) create truncated versions of SHA-256 and SHA-512, respectively.
- SHA-3 (previously known as Keccak) is an alternative to SHA-2. The U.S. National Security Agency (NSA) created SHA-1 and SHA-2. SHA-3 was created outside of the NSA and was selected in a non-NSA public competition. It can create hashes of the same size as SHA-2 (224 bits, 256 bits, 384 bits, and 512 bits).

Just as MD5 is used to verify the integrity of files, SHA also verifies file integrity. As an example, it's rare for executable files to be modified. However, some malware modifies executable files by adding malicious code into the file.

Some host-based intrusion detection systems (HIDS) and antivirus software capture hashes of files on a system when they first scan it and include valid hashes of system files in signature definition files. When they scan a system again, they can capture hashes of executable and system files and compare them with known good hashes. If the hashes are different for an executable or system file, it indicates the file has been modified, and it may have been modified by malware.

HMAC

Another method used to provide integrity is with a ***Hash-based Message Authentication Code (HMAC)***. An HMAC is a fixed-length string of bits similar to other hashing algorithms such as MD5 and SHA-256 (known as HMAC-MD5 and HMAC-SHA256, respectively). However, HMAC also uses a shared secret integrity key to add some randomness to the result and only the sender and receiver know the secret key.

For example, imagine that one server is sending a message to another server using HMAC-MD5. It starts by first creating a hash of a message with MD5 and then uses a secret key to complete another calculation on the hash. The server then sends the message and the HMAC-MD5 hash to the second server. The second server performs the same calculations and compares the received HMAC-MD5 hash with its result. Just as with any other hash comparison, if the two hashes are the same, the message retained integrity, but if the hashes are different, the message lost integrity.

The HMAC hash provides both integrity and authenticity of messages. The MD5 portion of the hash provides integrity just as MD5 does. However, because only the server and receiver know the secret key, if the receiver can calculate the same HMAC-MD5 hash as the sender, it knows that the sender used the same key. If an attacker were trying to impersonate the sender, the message wouldn't pass this authenticity check because the attacker wouldn't have the secret key. Even though MD5 by itself isn't cryptographically secure, HMAC-MD5 is secure if the secret key is long enough.

Internet Protocol security (IPsec) and Transport Layer Security (TLS) often use a version of HMAC such as HMAC-MD5 and HMAC-SHA256.

📌 *Remember This!*

Hashing is a one-way function that creates an alphanumeric string of characters. You cannot reverse the hash to re-create the original file. Passwords are often stored as hashes instead of storing the actual password. Additionally, applications often salt passwords with extra characters before hashing them.

Hashing Files

Many applications calculate and compare hashes automatically without any user intervention. For example, digital signatures (described later) use hashes within email, and email applications automatically create and compare the hashes.

Additionally, there are several applications you can use to manually calculate hashes. As an example, sha256sum.exe is a free program anyone can use to create hashes of files.

A Kali Linux image that I recently downloaded had the following hash value:

acf455e6f9ab0720df0abed15799223c2445882b44dfcc3f2216f9464db7915

Administrators at kali.org calculated the hash on the image and then posted both the image and the hash.

After I downloaded the image file, I calculated the hash on the downloaded file. Thankfully, it was the same. This provided proof that the file I downloaded was the file that the kali.org administrators posted on their website. If my hash was different, it would have indicated that the image file had lost integrity. Either it had been modified after it was posted, or it lost some bits during the download. Either way, the file should not be trusted and should not be used. Figure 10.1 shows this. By running the **sha256sum** command against the file, I calculated the hash. I first used the **dir** command to list the files in the directory. I then ran **sha256sum** against the Kali Linux file three times. Each time, **sha256sum** calculated the same hash, as shown in Figure 10.1.

```
Command Prompt                                                    —  □  ✕
C:\Users\Darril>cd /kaliiso

C:\KaliISO>dir
 Volume in drive C is Windows
 Volume Serial Number is 260A-97DE

 Directory of C:\KaliISO

03/11/2020  01:18 PM    <DIR>          .
03/11/2020  01:18 PM    <DIR>          ..
03/09/2020  03:30 PM     2,948,083,712 kali-linux-2020.1-live-amd64.iso  ◄──
03/11/2020  01:18 PM            73,216 sha256sum.exe  ◄──
               2 File(s)  2,948,156,928 bytes
               2 Dir(s)   2,406,252,290,048 bytes free

C:\KaliISO>sha256sum kali-linux-2020.1-live-amd64.iso
acf455e6f9ab0720df0abed15799223c2445882b44dfcc3f2216f9464db79152 *kali-linux-2020.1-live-amd64.iso 1

C:\KaliISO>sha256sum kali-linux-2020.1-live-amd64.iso
acf455e6f9ab0720df0abed15799223c2445882b44dfcc3f2216f9464db79152 *kali-linux-2020.1-live-amd64.iso 2

C:\KaliISO>sha256sum kali-linux-2020.1-live-amd64.iso
acf455e6f9ab0720df0abed15799223c2445882b44dfcc3f2216f9464db79152 *kali-linux-2020.1-live-amd64.iso 3

C:\KaliISO>
```

Figure 10.1: Calculating a hash with sha256sum

Figure 10.1 demonstrates two important points:

- **The hash will always be the same no matter how many times you calculate it using the same hashing algorithm**. In the figure, I ran sha256sum three times, but it would give me the same result if I ran it 3,000 times.
- **Hashing verifies the file has retained integrity**. Because the calculated hash is the same as the hash posted on the download website, it verifies the file has not lost integrity.

It's worth stressing that hashes are one-way functions. In other words, you can calculate a hash on a file or a message, but you can't use the hash to reproduce the original data. The hashing algorithms always create a fixed-size bit string regardless of the size of the original data. The hash doesn't give you a clue about the size of the file, the type of the file, or anything else.

As an example, the SHA-1 hash from the message "I will pass the Security+ exam" is:

765591c4611be5e03bea41882ffdaa159352cf49

However, you can't look at the hash and identify the message, or even know that it is a hash of a six-word message. Similarly, you can't look at the hash shown in Figure 10.1 and know that it was calculated from a 2.9-GB executable file.

If you want to work with hashes yourself, check out the labs in the online resources for this book at: **https:// getcertifiedgetahead.com/**.

Hashing Messages

Hashing provides integrity for messages. It provides assurances to someone receiving a message that the message has not been modified. Imagine that Lisa is sending a message to Bart, as shown in Figure 10.2. The message is "The price is $75." This message is not secret, so there is no need to encrypt it. However, we do want to provide integrity, so this explanation is focused only on hashing.

An application on Lisa's computer calculates the MD5 hash as:

D9B93C99B62646ABD06C887039053F56

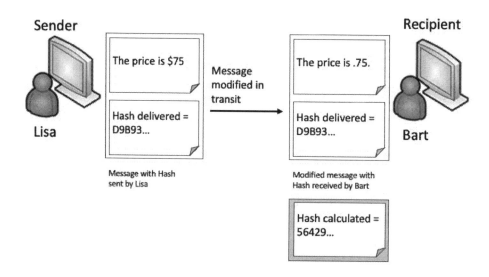

Figure 10.2: Simplified hash process

In the figure, I've shortened the full hash down to just the first five characters of "**D9B93**". Lisa then sends both the message and the hash to Bart.

In this example, something modified the message before it reaches Bart. When Bart receives the message and the original hash, the message is now "The price is .75." Note that the message is modified in transit, but the hash is not modified.

A program on Bart's computer calculates the MD5 hash on the received message as:

564294439E1617F5628A3E3EB75643FE

The program then compares the received hash with the calculated hash:

- The hash created on Lisa's computer, and received by Bart's computer is:
  D9B93C99B62646ABD06C887039053F56
- The hash created on Bart's computer is: **564294439E1617F5628A3E3EB75643FE**

Clearly, the hashes are different, so you know the message lost integrity. The program on Bart's computer would report the discrepancy. Bart doesn't know what caused the problem. It could have been a malicious attacker changing the message, or it could have been a technical problem. However, Bart does know the received message isn't the same as the sent message and he shouldn't trust it.

> ### ★ Remember This!
>
> If you can recognize the hashing algorithms such as MD5, SHA, and HMAC, it will help you answer some exam questions. For example, if a question asks what you would use to encrypt data and it lists three hashing algorithms, you can quickly eliminate them because hashing algorithms don't encrypt data.

Using HMAC

You might have noticed a problem in the explanation of the hashed message. If an attacker can change the message, why can't the attacker change the hash, too? In other words, if Hacker Harry changed the message to "The price is .75," he could also calculate the hash on the modified message and replace the original hash with the modified hash. Here's the result:

- The hash created on Lisa's computer is: **D9B93C99B62646ABD06C887039053F56**
- The modified hash inserted by the attacker after modifying the message is: **564294439E1 617F5628A3E3EB75643FE**
- The hash created for the modified message on Bart's computer is: **564294439E1617F 5628A3E3EB75643FE**

The calculated hash on the modified message would be the same as the received hash. This erroneously indicates that the message has maintained integrity. HMAC helps solve this problem.

With HMAC, both Lisa and Bart's computers would know the same secret integrity key and use it to create an HMAC- MD5 hash instead of just an MD5 hash. Figure 10.3 shows the result.

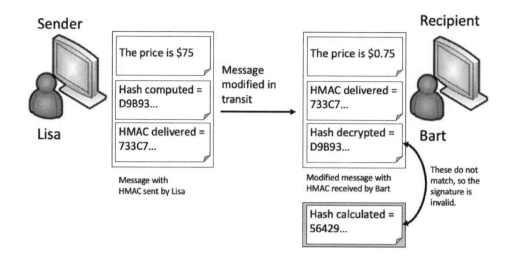

Figure 10.3: Using HMAC

Note that Lisa is still sending the same message. The MD5 hash is **D9B93C99B62646AB-D06C887039053F56**. However, after applying the HMAC secret key, the HMAC-MD5 hash is **733C70A54A13744D5C2C9C4BA3B15034**. For brevity, I shortened this to only the first five characters (**733C7**) in the figure.

An attacker can modify the message in transit just as before. However, the attacker doesn't know the secret key and therefore can't calculate the HMAC hash.

Bart's computer calculates the HMAC-MD5 hash on the received message using the shared secret key. It then compares the calculated hash with the hash received from Lisa:

- The HMAC-MD5 hash created on Lisa's computer is: **733C70A54A13744D5C2C9C4BA3B15034**
- The HMAC-MD5 hash created on Bart's computer is: **1B4FF0F6C04434BF97F1E3DDD4B6C137**

Again, you can see that the hashes are different indicating the message has lost integrity. If the messages weren't modified, the HMAC-MD5 hashes would be the same.

Hashing Passwords

Most systems don't store the actual password for an account. Instead, they store a hash of the password. When a user creates a new password, the system calculates the hash for the password and then stores the hash. Similarly, passwords are rarely sent over the network in cleartext. Instead, the password hash is sent.

Later, when the user authenticates by entering a username and password, the system calculates the hash of the entered password, and then compares it with the stored hash. If the hashes are the same, it indicates that the user entered the correct password.

Unfortunately, tools are available to discover many hashed passwords. For example, MD5 Online (`https://www.md5online.org/md5-decrypt.html`) allows you to enter a hash and it gives you the text of the password. If the password is 12345, the hash is **827ccb0eea8a706c4c34a16891f84e7b**. If you enter that hash into MD5 Online, it returns the password of 12345 in less than a second. MD5 Online uses a database of hashed words from a dictionary. If the hash matches a database entry, the site returns the password.

Because of this, only strong hashing algorithms, such as SHA-3, should be used to store password hashes. However, even this isn't enough, and passwords are commonly salted, as described later in this chapter.

Understanding Hash Collisions

A **hash collision** occurs when the hashing algorithm creates the same hash from different inputs. This is not desirable.

As an example, imagine a simple hashing algorithm creates three-digit hashes. The password "success" might create a hash of 123 and the password "passed" might create the same hash of 123. This is known as a hash collision. In this scenario, an attacker could use either "success" or "passed" as the password and both would work. The attacker doesn't need to guess the correct password, only a password that creates the same hash.

MD5 is highly susceptible to hash collision attacks, which is why it is no longer recommended as a cryptographic hash.

Understanding Password Attacks

Password attacks attempt to discover, or bypass, passwords used for authentication on systems and networks, and for different types of files. Some password attacks are sophisticated cryptographic attacks, while others are rather simple brute force attacks.

An **online password attack** attempts to discover a password from an online system. For example, an attacker can try to log on to an account by repeatedly guessing the username and password. Many tools are available that attackers can use to automate the process. For example, ncrack is a free tool that can be used to run online brute force password attacks.

Offline password attacks attempt to discover passwords from a captured database or captured packet scan. For example, when attackers hack into a system or network causing a data breach, they can download entire databases. They then perform offline attacks to discover the passwords contained within these downloaded databases.

A primary indicator of online password attacks can be found in system logs that record successful and unsuccessful logons. These logs will show repeated attempts to guess passwords. In Windows systems, this is recorded as Event ID 4625 in the Security log available in Event Viewer. If the attacker enters the wrong password too many times, the system will lock the user account. This is recorded as Event ID 4740. The online labs show you how to create a custom filter to view these events.

Dictionary Attacks

A **dictionary attack** is one of the original password attacks. It uses a dictionary of words and attempts every word in the dictionary to see if it works. A dictionary in this context is simply a list of words and character combinations.

Dictionaries used in these attacks have evolved over time to reflect user behavior. Today, they include many of the common passwords that uneducated users configure for their accounts. For example, even though 12345 isn't a dictionary word, many people use it as a password, so character sets such as these have been added to many dictionaries used by dictionary attack tools.

These attacks are thwarted by using complex passwords. A complex password will not include words in a dictionary.

Brute Force Attacks

A **brute force attack** attempts to guess all possible character combinations. One of the first steps to thwart offline brute force attacks is to use complex passwords and to store the passwords in an encrypted or hashed format. Complex passwords include a mix of uppercase letters, lowercase letters, numbers, and special characters. Additionally, longer passwords are much more difficult to crack than shorter passwords.

Password Spraying Attacks

A **password spraying attack** is a special type of brute force or dictionary attack designed to avoid being locked out. An automated program starts with a large list of targeted user accounts. It then picks a password and tries it against every account in the list. It then picks another password and loops through the list again.

Chapter 2, "Understanding Identity and Access Management," discusses account lockout policies used in Windows systems. They are effective against online brute force and dictionary attacks. An account lockout setting locks an account after the user enters the incorrect password a preset number of times in a short period of time. For example, if the user enters the wrong password three times in 30 minutes, the lockout policy locks the account. Because a spraying attack loops through a long list of accounts, it takes a while before it hits the same account twice. This normally exceeds the time limit of account lockout settings, effectively bypassing the account lockout policy. However, you'll still see Event ID 4625 indicating failed logon attempts but there will be a time lapse between each entry.

> ### ★ Remember This!
>
> Online attacks guess the password of an online system. Offline attacks guess the password stored within a downloaded file, such as a database. Logs will show a large volume of failed logon attempts as Event ID 4625 and/or several accounts being locked out as Event ID 4740. Spraying attacks attempt to avoid account lockout policies, but logs will still show a large volume of failed logon attempts, but with a time lapse between each entry.

Pass the Hash Attacks

In a **pass the hash attack**, the attacker discovers the hash of the user's password and then uses it to log on to the system as the user. Any authentication protocol that passes the hash over the network in an unencrypted format is susceptible to this attack. It has been widely associated with Microsoft LAN Manager (LM) and NT LAN Manager (NTLM), two older security protocols used to authenticate Microsoft clients. However, this attack has enjoyed success against other protocols, such as Kerberos.

Attackers first try to gain administrative access to a system, either by gaining access as a member of the local Administrators group or gaining certain equivalent privileges. This is trivial if a user is logged on with an account that has administrator privileges. If the computer is infected with malware, the attacker has the same privileges as the logged-on user.

Once attackers have these privileges, they use them to steal password hashes stored in multiple locations on the computer, such as the Security Accounts Manager (SAM) database, the Local Security Authority Subsystem Service (LSASS) process, the Credential Manager (CredMan) store, and the LSA Secrets stored in the Registry.

A strong indicator of a pass the hash attack is the usage of NTLM as the Authentication Package and/or a Logon Process of NT LAN Manager Security Support Provider (NTLMSSP) shown in Event ID 4624 in the Windows Security log. This can be correlated with Event ID 4672 to determine the privileges used with this connection. Normal users wouldn't use administrative privileges when connecting to other computers. However, an active pass the hash attack would use administrative privileges when moving laterally to similar computers around the network. The online labs show you how to search for and detect these events.

> 📌 **Remember This!**
>
> Passwords are typically stored as hashes. A pass the hash attack attempts to use an intercepted hash to access an account. These attacks can be detected in Event ID 4624 with a Logon Process of NTLMSSP and/or an Authentication Package of NTLM.

Birthday Attacks

A **birthday attack** is named after the birthday paradox in mathematical probability theory. The birthday paradox states that for any random group of 23 people, there is a 50 percent chance that 2 of them have the same birthday. This is not the same year, but instead one of the 366 days in a year, including February 29.

In a birthday attack, an attacker attempts to create a password that produces the same hash as the user's actual password. This is also known as a hash collision, as described earlier. Using the knowledge of the birthday paradox, the attacker doesn't need to guess every possible password before discovering a collision. If the password could only be one of 366 possibilities, the attacker has a 50 percent chance of guessing it after only 23 attempts.

Birthday attacks on hashes are thwarted by increasing the number of bits used in the hash to increase the number of possible hashes. For example, the MD5 algorithm uses 128 bits and is susceptible to birthday attacks. SHA-3 can use as many as 512 bits and is not susceptible to birthday attacks.

> 📌 **Remember This!**
>
> Birthday attacks exploit collisions in hashing algorithms. A hash collision occurs when the hashing algorithm creates the same hash from different passwords. Salting adds random text to passwords before hashing them and thwarts many password attacks, including rainbow table attacks.

Rainbow Table Attacks

Rainbow table attacks are a type of attack that attempts to discover the password from the hash. A rainbow table is a huge database of possible passwords with the precomputed hashes for each. It helps to look at the process of how some password cracker applications discover passwords without a rainbow table. Assume that an attacker has the hash of a password. The application can use the following steps to discover the password that matches the hash:

1. The application guesses a password (or uses a password from a dictionary).
2. The application hashes the guessed password.
3. The application compares the original password hash with the guessed password hash. If they are the same, the application now knows the password.
4. If they aren't the same, the application repeats steps 1 through 3 until finding a match.

From a computing perspective, the most time-consuming part of these steps is hashing the guessed password in step 2. However, by using rainbow tables, applications eliminate this step. Rainbow tables are huge databases of passwords and their calculated hashes. Some rainbow tables are as large as 690 GB in size, and they include hashes for every possible combination of characters up to nine characters in length. Larger rainbow tables are also available using more characters.

Rainbow table attacks are often performed offline on stolen or compromised databases. In a rainbow table attack, the application simply compares the hash of each password in the database against hashes stored in the rainbow table. When the application finds a match, it identifies the password used to create the hash (or at least text that can reproduce the hash of the original password). Admittedly, this is a simplistic explanation of a rainbow table attack, but it is adequate unless you plan on writing an algorithm to create your own rainbow table attack software.

Salting Passwords

Salting passwords is a common method of preventing rainbow table attacks, along with other password attacks such as brute force and dictionary attacks. A salt is a set of random data such as two additional characters. Password salting adds these additional characters to a password before hashing it. These additional characters add complexity to the password, and result in a different hash than the system would create using only the original password. This causes password attacks that compare hashes with a rainbow table to fail.

Key Stretching

Key stretching is an advanced technique used to increase the strength of stored passwords. Instead of just adding a salt to the password before hashing it, key stretching applies a cryptographic stretching algorithm to the salted password. The benefit of key stretching is that it consumes more time and computing resources— frustrating attackers who are trying to guess passwords.

Three common key stretching techniques are bcrypt, Password-Based Key Derivation Function 2 (PBKDF2), and Argon2.

Bcrypt is based on the Blowfish block cipher and is used on many Unix and Linux distributions to protect the passwords stored in the shadow password file. Bcrypt salts the password by adding additional random bits before encrypting it with Blowfish. Bcrypt can go through this process multiple times to further protect against attempts to discover the password. The result is a 60-character string.

As an example, if your password is IL0ve$ecurity, an application can encrypt it with bcrypt and a salt. It might look like this, which the application stores in a database:

`$2b$12$HXIKtJr93DH59BzzKQhehOI9pGjRA/O3ENcFRby1jH7nXwt1TnOkG`

Later, when a user authenticates with a username and password, the application runs bcrypt on the supplied password and compares it with the stored bcrypt-encrypted password. If the bcrypt result of the supplied password is the same as the stored bcrypt result, the user is authenticated. As an added measure, it's possible to add some pepper to the salt to further randomize the bcrypt string. In this context, the pepper is another set of random bits stored elsewhere.

> ### 📌 *Remember This!*
>
> Bcrypt, PBKDF2, and Argon2 are key stretching techniques that help prevent brute force and rainbow table attacks. They salt the password with additional bits and then send the result through a cryptographic algorithm.

PBKDF2 uses salts of at least 64 bits and uses a pseudo-random function such as HMAC to protect passwords. Many algorithms such as Wi-Fi Protected Access 2 (WPA2), Apple's iOS mobile operating system, and Cisco IOS operating system use PBKDF2 to increase the security of passwords. Some applications send the password through the PBKDF2 process as many as 1,000,000 times to create the hash. The size of the resulting hash varies with PBKDF2 depending on how it is implemented. Bit sizes of 128 bits, 256 bits, and 512 bits are most common.

A weakness with PBKDF2 is that it can be configured to use less computing time and less RAM. While this may seem beneficial to users, it also makes it easier for attackers, allowing them to guess many passwords in a short amount of time.

A Password Hashing Competition (PHC) in 2015 selected Argon2 as an alternative key stretching algorithm. Like bcrypt and PBKDF2, Argon2 uses a password and salt that is passed through an algorithm several times. Argon2 has been improved with each new version using a lowercase letter such as Argon2d and Argon2i.

> ### 📌 *Remember This!*
>
> Encryption provides confidentiality and helps ensure that data is viewable only by authorized users. This applies to any data at rest (such as data stored in a database) or data in transit being sent over a network.

Providing Confidentiality with Encryption

Encryption provides confidentiality and prevents unauthorized disclosure of data. Plaintext is human- readable data. An encryption algorithm scrambles the data, creating ciphertext, which is unreadable. Attackers can't read encrypted traffic sent over a network or encrypted data stored on a system. In contrast, if data is sent in cleartext, an attacker can capture and read the data using a protocol analyzer.

Data at rest refers to any data stored on media and it's common to encrypt sensitive data. For example, it's possible to encrypt individual fields in a database (such as the fields holding customer credit card data), individual files, folders, or a full disk.

Data in transit or **data in motion** refers to any data sent over a network and it's common to encrypt sensitive data in transit. For example, e-commerce websites commonly use Hypertext Transfer Protocol Secure (HTTPS) sessions to encrypt transactions that include credit card data. If attackers intercept the transmissions, they only see ciphertext.

Data in use refers to data being used by a computer. Because the computer needs to process the data, it is not encrypted while in use. If the data is encrypted, an application will decrypt it and store it in memory while in use. If the application changes the data, it will encrypt it again before saving it. Additionally, applications usually take extra steps to purge memory of sensitive data after processing it. The two primary encryption methods are symmetric and asymmetric. Symmetric encryption encrypts and decrypts data with the same key. Asymmetric encryption encrypts and decrypts data using a matched key pair of a public key and a private key. These encryption methods include two elements:

- **Algorithm.** The algorithm performs mathematical calculations on data. The algorithm is always the same.
- **Key.** The key is a number that provides variability for the encryption. It is either kept private and/or changed frequently.

Symmetric Encryption

Symmetric encryption uses the same key to encrypt and decrypt data. In other words, if you encrypt data with a key of three, you decrypt it with the same key of three. Symmetric encryption is also called secret-key encryption or session-key encryption. As a simple example, when I was a child, a friend and I used to pass encoded messages back and forth to each other. Our algorithm was:

- **Encryption algorithm.** Move X spaces forward to encrypt.
- **Decryption algorithm.** Move X spaces backward to decrypt.

On the way to school, we would identify the key (X) we would use that day. For example, we may have used the key of three one day. If I wanted to encrypt a message, I would move each character three spaces forward, and he would decrypt the message by moving three spaces backward. Imagine the message "PASS" needs to be sent:

- Three characters past "P" is "S"—Start at P (Q, R, S)
- Three characters past "A" is "D"—Start at A (B, C, D)
- Three characters past "S" is "V"—Start at S (T, U, V)
- Three characters past "S" is "V"—Start at S (T, U, V)

The encrypted message is SDVV. My friend decrypted it by moving backward three spaces and learned that "PASS" was the original message.

We were using a simple letter substitution cipher. A substitution cipher replaces plaintext with ciphertext using a fixed system. In the example, "PASS" is the plaintext, "SDVV" is the ciphertext, and the fixed system is three letters. The ROT13 (short for rotate by 13 places) cipher uses the same substitution algorithm, but always uses a key of 13. To encrypt a message, you would rotate each letter 13 spaces. To decrypt a message, you would rotate each letter 13 spaces. However, because ROT13 uses both the same algorithm and the same key, it doesn't provide true encryption but instead just obfuscates the data.

Obfuscation methods attempt to make something unclear or difficult to understand. This is sometimes referred to as security through obscurity. However, security through obscurity is rarely a reliable method of maintaining security.

Rotating letters with a key shows how symmetric encryption methods fail if the same key isn't used for encryption and decryption. If I encrypted the message with a key of three, and my friend tried to decrypt it with a key of six, he would get a completely different message.

Sophisticated symmetric encryption techniques use the same components of an algorithm and a key. However, the algorithms and keys are much more complex. For example, the Advanced Encryption Standard (AES) symmetric algorithm typically uses 128-bit keys but can use keys with 192 or 256 bits.

★ *Remember This!*

Symmetric encryption uses the same key to encrypt and decrypt data. For example, when transmitting encrypted data, symmetric encryption algorithms use the same key to encrypt and decrypt data at both ends of the transmission media.

Comparing Symmetric Encryption to a Door Key

Occasionally, security professionals compare symmetric keys to a house key and this analogy helps some people understand symmetric encryption a little better. For example, imagine Marge moves into a new home. She'll receive a single key that she can use to lock and unlock her home. Of course, Marge can't use this key to unlock the Flanders' home.

Later, Marge marries Homer, and Homer moves into Marge's home. Marge can create a copy of her house key and give it to Homer. Homer can now use that copy of the key to lock and unlock the house. By sharing copies of the same key, it doesn't matter whether Marge or Homer is the one who locks the door; they can both unlock it.

Similarly, symmetric encryption uses a single key to encrypt and decrypt data. If a copy of the symmetric key is shared, others who have the key can also encrypt and decrypt data.

Imagine two servers sending encrypted traffic back and forth to each other using AES symmetric encryption. They both use the same AES algorithm and the same key for this data. The data is encrypted on one server with AES and a key, sent over the wire or other transmission medium, and the same key is used to decrypt it on the other server. Similarly, if a database includes encrypted data, the key used to encrypt this data is the same key used to decrypt the data.

However, symmetric encryption doesn't use the same key to encrypt and decrypt all data. For example, my friend and I used a different key each day. On the way to school, we decided on a key to use for that day. The next day, we picked a different key. If someone cracked our code yesterday, they couldn't crack our code today using the same key.

Symmetric encryption algorithms change keys much more often than once a day. For example, imagine an algorithm uses a key of 123 to encrypt a project file. It could then use a key of 456 to encrypt a spreadsheet file. The key of 123 can only decrypt the project file and the key of 456 can only decrypt the spreadsheet file.

On the other hand, if symmetric encryption always used the same key of 123, it would add significant vulnerabilities. First, when keys are reused, the encryption is easier to crack. Second, once the key is cracked, all data encrypted with this key is compromised. If attackers discover the key of 123, not only would they have access to the project file, but they would also have access to the spreadsheet file and any other data encrypted with this same key.

Block Versus Stream Ciphers

Most symmetric algorithm cipher suites use either a block cipher or a stream cipher. They are both symmetric, so they both use the same key to encrypt or decrypt data. However, they divide data in different ways.

A **block cipher** encrypts data in specific-sized blocks, such as 64-bit blocks or 128-bit blocks. The block cipher divides large files or messages into these blocks and then encrypts each individual block separately. A **stream cipher** encrypts data as a stream of bits or bytes rather than dividing it into blocks.

In general, stream ciphers are more efficient than block ciphers when the size of the data is unknown or sent in a continuous stream, such as when streaming audio and video over a network. Block ciphers are more efficient when the size of the data is known, such as when encrypting a file or a specific-sized database field.

An important principle when using a stream cipher is that encryption keys should never be reused. If a key is reused, it is easier to crack the encryption.

> ### ✒ *Remember This!*
>
> Stream ciphers encrypt data a single bit, or a single byte, at a time in a stream. Block ciphers encrypt data in a specific-sized block such as 64-bit or 128-bit blocks. Stream ciphers are more efficient than block ciphers when encrypting data in a continuous stream.

Common Symmetric Algorithms

The following sections describe some commonly used symmetric algorithms. This isn't meant to be an exhaustive list of all symmetric algorithms, but instead a short listing of some that are commonly used.

AES

The **_Advanced Encryption Standard (AES)_** is a strong symmetric block cipher that encrypts data in 128-bit blocks. The National Institute of Standards and Technology (NIST) adopted AES from the Rijndael encryption algorithm after a lengthy evaluation of several different algorithms.

AES can use key sizes of 128 bits, 192 bits, or 256 bits, and it's sometimes referred to as AES-128, AES-192, or AES-256 to identify how many bits are used in the key. When more bits are used, it makes it more difficult to discover the key and decrypt the data. AES-128 provides strong protection, but AES-256 provides stronger protection.

In general, the size of the key for any encryption directly corresponds to the key strength. Longer keys for a specific algorithm result in stronger key strength. Because of its strengths, AES has been adopted in a wide assortment of applications. For example, many applications that encrypt data on USB drives use AES. Some of the strengths of AES are:

- **Fast.** AES uses elegant mathematical formulas and only requires one pass to encrypt and decrypt data. In contrast, 3DES (mentioned later in this chapter) requires multiple passes to encrypt and decrypt data.
- **Efficient.** AES is less resource intensive than other encryption algorithms such as 3DES. AES encrypts and decrypts quickly even when ciphering data on small devices, such as USB flash drives.
- **Strong.** AES provides strong encryption of data, providing a high level of confidentiality.

3DES

3DES (pronounced as "Triple DES") is a symmetric block cipher designed as an improvement over the known weaknesses of the legacy Data Encryption Standard (DES). In basic terms, it encrypts data using the DES algorithm in three separate passes and uses multiple keys. 3DES encrypts data in 64-bit blocks.

Although 3DES is a strong algorithm, it isn't used as often as AES today. AES is much less resource intensive. However, if hardware doesn't support AES, 3DES is a suitable alternative. 3DES uses key sizes of 112 bits or 168 bits.

Blowfish and Twofish

Blowfish is a strong symmetric block cipher that is still widely used today. It encrypts data in 64-bit blocks and supports key sizes between 32 and 448 bits. Bruce Schneier (a widely respected voice in IT security) designed Blowfish as a general-purpose algorithm to replace DES.

Interestingly, Blowfish is faster than AES in some instances. This is especially true when comparing Blowfish with AES-256. Part of the reason is that Blowfish encrypts data in smaller 64-bit blocks, whereas AES encrypts data in 128-bit blocks.

Twofish is related to Blowfish, but it encrypts data in 128-bit blocks, and it supports 128-, 192-, or 256-bit keys. It was also one of the finalist algorithms evaluated by NIST.

> ### ✎ *Remember This!*
>
> AES is a strong symmetric block cipher that encrypts data in 128-bit blocks. AES uses 128-bit, 192-bit, or 256-bit keys. 3DES is a block cipher that encrypts data in 64-bit blocks. 3DES was originally designed as a replacement for DES, but NIST selected AES as the current standard. However, 3DES is still used in some applications, such as when legacy hardware doesn't support AES.

Asymmetric Encryption

Asymmetric encryption uses two keys in a matched pair to encrypt and decrypt data—a public key and a private key. There are several important points to remember with these keys:

- If the **public key** encrypts information, only the matching private key can decrypt the same information.
- If the **private key** encrypts information, only the matching public key can decrypt the same information.
- Private keys are always kept private and never shared.
- Public keys are freely shared by embedding them in a shared digital certificate.

Although asymmetric encryption is strong, it is also very resource intensive. It takes a significant amount of processing power to encrypt and decrypt data, especially when compared with symmetric encryption. Most cryptographic protocols that use asymmetric encryption only use it for key exchange.

Key Exchange

Key exchange is a cryptographic method used to share cryptographic keys between two entities. In this context, asymmetric encryption uses key exchange to share a symmetric key. The cryptographic protocol then uses the symmetric encryption to encrypt and decrypt data because symmetric encryption is much more efficient.

The key is that the two entities need to be able to identify a symmetric key that they both know and can use. However, the exchange needs to be encrypted so that no one else knows the symmetric key. The "Encrypting HTTPS Traffic with TLS" section later in this chapter digs deeper into the key exchange method.

Some of the more advanced topics related to asymmetric encryption become harder to understand if you don't understand the relationship of matched public and private key pairs. However, because you can't see these keys, the concepts are hard to grasp for some people. The Rayburn box demonstrates how you can use physical keys for the same purposes as these public and private keys.

The Rayburn Box

I often talk about the Rayburn box in the classroom to help people understand the usage of public and private keys. A Rayburn box is a lockbox that allows people to securely transfer items over long distances. It has two keys. One key can lock the box but can't unlock it. The other key can unlock the box but can't lock it. Both keys are matched to one box and won't work with other boxes:

- Only one copy of one key exists—think of it as the private key.
- Multiple copies of the other key exist, and copies are freely made and distributed—think of these as public keys.

> ### 📌 *Remember This!*
>
> Only a private key can decrypt information encrypted with a matching public key. Only a public key can decrypt information encrypted with a matching private key. A key element of several asymmetric encryption methods is that they require a digital certificate and a PKI.

The box comes in two different versions. In one version, it's used to send secrets in a confidential manner to prevent unauthorized disclosure. In the other version, it's used to send messages with authentication, so you know the sender sent the message and that the message wasn't modified in transit.

The Rayburn Box Used to Send Secrets

Imagine that I wanted you to send some proprietary information and a working model of an invention to me. Obviously, we wouldn't want anyone else to be able to access the information or the working model. I could send you the empty open box with a copy of the key used to lock it. You place everything in the box and then lock it with the public key I've sent with the box.

This key can't unlock the box, so even if other people had copies of the public key that I sent to you, they couldn't use it to unlock the box. When I receive the box from you, I can unlock it with the only key that will unlock it—my private key.

This is similar to how public and private keys are used to send encrypted data over the Internet to ensure confidentiality. The public key encrypts information. Information encrypted with a public key can only be decrypted with the matching private key. Many copies of the public key are available, but only one private key exists, and the private key always stays private. The "Encrypting HTTPS Traffic with TLS" section later in this chapter shows this process in more depth.

The Rayburn Box Used for Authentication

With a little rekeying of the box, I can use it to send messages while giving assurances to recipients that I sent the message. In this context, the message isn't secret and doesn't need to be protected. Instead, it's important that you know I sent the message.

When used this way, the private key will lock the Rayburn box, but it cannot unlock the box. Instead, only a matching public key can unlock it. Multiple copies of the public key exist and anyone with a public key can unlock the box. However, after unlocking the box with a matching public key, it isn't possible to lock it with the public key.

Imagine that you and I are allies in a battle. I want to give you a message of "SY0-701," which is a code telling you to launch a specific attack at a specific time. We don't care if someone reads this message because it's a code. However, we need you to have assurance that I sent the message.

I write the message, place it in the box, and lock it with my private key. When you receive it, you can unlock it with the matching public key. Because the public key opens it, you know this is my box and it was locked with my private key—you know I sent the message.

If an enemy spy intercepted the box and opened it with the public key, the spy wouldn't be able to lock it again using the public key, so you'd receive an open box. The spy could replace the message with something else. However, an open box with a message inside it doesn't prove I sent it. The only way you know that I sent it is if you receive a locked box that you can unlock with the matching public key.

This is similar to how digital signatures use public and private keys. The "Signing Email with Digital Signatures" section later in this chapter explains digital signatures in more depth. In short, I can send you a message digitally signed with my private key. If you can decrypt the digital signature with my matching public key, you know it was encrypted, or signed, with my private key. Because only one copy of the private key exists, and I'm the only person who can access it, you know I sent the message.

The Rayburn Box Demystified

Before you try to find a Rayburn box, let me clear something up. The Rayburn box is just a figment of my imagination. Rayburn is my middle name.

I haven't discovered a real-world example of how public/private keys work, so I've created the Rayburn box as a metaphor to help people visualize how public/private keys work. Feel free to build one if you want.

Certificates

A key element of asymmetric encryption is a ***digital certificate***. A digital certificate is a digital document that typically includes the public key and information on the owner of the certificate. ***Certificate authorities (CAs)*** issue and manage certificates. Digital certificates are used for a variety of purposes beyond just asymmetric encryption, including authentication and digital signatures.

Figure 10.4 shows a sample digital certificate with the public key selected. Users and applications share the digital certificate file to share the public key. They do not share the private key.

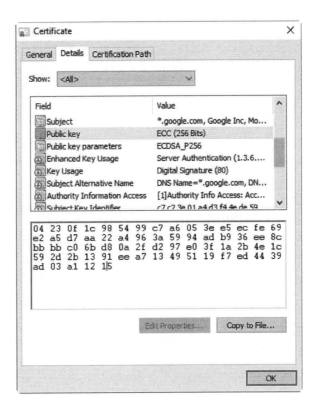

Figure 10.4: Certificate with public key selected

> ★ **Remember This!**
>
> Digital certificates are an important part of asymmetric encryption. Digital certificates include public keys along with details on the owner of the certificate and on the Certificate Authority (CA) that issued the certificate. Certificate owners share their public key by sharing a copy of their digital certificate.

There is much more information in the digital certificate than just the public key, but not all of it is visible in the figure. Common elements within a digital certificate include:

- **Serial number.** The serial number identifies the certificate issued by a CA. It is not globally unique, but rather unique through the issuing CA. The CA uses this serial number to validate a certificate. If the CA revokes the certificate, it publishes this serial number in a certificate revocation list (CRL).
- **Issuer.** This identifies the CA that issued the certificate.
- **Validity dates.** Certificates include "Valid From" and "Valid To" dates. These identify the valid and expiry dates.
- **Subject.** This identifies the owner of the certificate. In the figure, it identifies the subject as Google, Inc and indicates this is a wildcard certificate used for all websites with the google.com root domain name.
- **Public key.** Asymmetric encryption uses the public key in combination with the matching private key.
- **Key usage.** Some certificates are only for encryption or authentication, whereas other certificates support multiple usages.
- **Certificate attributes** identify the issuer using Distinguished Name attributes. Some common attributes are:
- **CN**: Common Name (also known as the Fully Qualified Domain Name such as letsencrypt.org)
- **O**: Organization (such as the Internet Security Research Group)
- **L**: Locality (such as Mountain View)
- **S**: State or Province Name (such as CA)
- **C**: Country Name (such as US)

Ephemeral Keys

Ephemeral refers to something that lasts a short time. In the context of cryptography, an ephemeral key has a short lifetime and is re-created for each session. In contrast, a static key is semipermanent and stays the same over a long period of time.

An ephemeral key pair includes a private ephemeral key and a public ephemeral key. Systems use these key pairs for a single session and then discard them. Some versions of Diffie-Hellman use ephemeral keys.

Certificates are based on static keys. A certificate includes an embedded public key matched to a private key and this key pair is valid for the lifetime of a certificate, such as a year. Certificates have expiration dates and systems continue to use these keys until the certificate expires. A benefit of static keys is that a CA can validate them as discussed in the "Validating a Certificate" section later in this chapter.

Perfect forward secrecy is an important characteristic that ephemeral keys comply with in asymmetric encryption. Perfect forward secrecy indicates that a cryptographic system generates random public keys for each session, and it doesn't use a deterministic algorithm to do so. In other words, given the same input, the algorithm will create a different public key. This helps ensure that systems do not reuse keys. The result is that the compromise of a key does not compromise any past keys.

Elliptic Curve Cryptography

Elliptic curve cryptography (ECC) doesn't take as much processing power as other cryptographic methods. It uses mathematical equations to formulate an elliptical curve. It then graphs points on the curve to create keys. A key benefit is that ECC keys can be much smaller when compared with non-ECC keys.

Digital signatures (described later in this chapter) are commonly used to sign emails. The Digital Signature Algorithm (DSA) uses key pairs managed by a PKI with the public key distributed in a certificate. The Elliptic Curve Digital Signature Algorithm (ECDSA) can also be used for digital signatures. A 256-bit elliptic curve public key is said to provide the same security benefit of a 3072-bit key used with DSA.

Because of this, ECC is often considered with common use cases of low power devices. For example, ECC is sometimes used with small wireless devices because it doesn't take much processing power to achieve the desired security.

Key Length

Because the algorithm always stays the same, the way that any individual algorithm is strengthened is by increasing the length of a key. As an example, consider RSA (Rivest-Shamir-Adleman), the primary public key cryptography algorithm used on the Internet. It supports key sizes of 1024, 2048, and 4096 bits. However, at this time NIST recommends that organizations no longer use 1024-bit keys due to security concerns. The current recommended minimum key length is 2048 bits.

Obfuscation

Sometimes we don't actually need to encrypt data, we just want to hide that data in plain sight or make it impossible for anyone to retrieve sensitive information from data that we've protected. **Obfuscation** is the act of deliberately making something unclear, confusing, or difficult to understand. It is often used to conceal, distort, or obscure information, ideas, or intentions to mislead or deceive.

We'll look at several different obfuscation techniques: steganography, tokenization, and masking.

Steganography

Steganography hides data inside other data, or, as some people have said, it hides data in plain sight. The goal is to hide the data in such a way that no one suspects there is a hidden message. However, if other people know what to look for, they will be able to retrieve the message.

It doesn't encrypt the data, so it can't be classified as either symmetric or asymmetric. However, it can effectively hide information using obfuscation. Obfuscation methods attempt to make something unclear or difficult to understand.

Security professionals use steganalysis techniques to detect steganography, and the most common method is with hashing. If a single bit of a file is modified, the hashing algorithm creates a different hash. By regularly taking the hashes of different files and comparing them with previous hashes, it's easy to detect when a file has been modified.

There are three primary types of files used with steganography. They are audio files, image files, and video files.

Audio Steganography

Audio steganography takes advantage of the limitations of a human ear. Ideally, a human ear can detect sounds in the frequency range of 20 Hz and 20 kHz. Most humans can't detect sounds between 18 kHz and 20 kHz, but these sounds can be detected by most microphones. These sounds, commonly called audio beacons, are used to identify user activity.

SilverPush, an India-based advertising company, used this to track users. Its software development kit (SDK) includes the ability to hear the audio beacons, and once the apps are installed, the app constantly listens for them. Some television advertisements include audio beacons and the Silver-Push apps reported back to SilverPush servers when a user device heard the beacon. This helped them determine what commercials and, ultimately, what shows users were watching.

SilverPush claimed to have stopped doing this in 2016 but other app developers were still using the SilverPush SDK. In 2017, researchers found over 200 Android-based apps that included this SDK were downloaded millions of times from Google Play.

Some audio beacons are used by marketers within stores. They track the location of shoppers as they move through a large store. Apps then send ads or coupons based on the shopper's location.

This technology can also be used to perform cross-device tracking to determine what devices belong to an individual. Apps send audio beacons from one device. When another device repeatedly hears this same beacon, it indicates it is owned by the same user.

Image Steganography

Image steganography is the practice of hiding data within image files such as a .jpeg or .gif file. Two common ways this is done is by manipulating the bits of a file or by hiding data in the white space.

You can embed a message into a file by modifying the least significant bit in some of the individual bytes of a file. Because you are modifying the least significant bit, the changes to the file won't be perceptible to anyone viewing the image. As an example, imagine a pixel of an image is red (having the RGB value of 255, 0, 0). If you change the least significant bit of red from 255 to 254, giving the pixel a value of 254, 0, 0, the change can't be perceived on a monitor. If the image file is large, it's possible to hide a large file within it.

Many files have unused space (called white space) at the end of file clusters. Imagine a small 6-KB file stored in two 4-KB clusters. It has an extra 2 KB of unused space and it's possible to fill this white space with a message. A benefit of using this method is that it is possible to embed a message without altering the size of the file.

Video Steganography

Video steganography is an extension of image steganography and it embeds messages into videos. Videos have become quite popular on the Internet through sites such as Facebook, YouTube, and TikTok.

Because video files are typically large, a common method is to modify the least significant bits of some bytes within the file to embed a message. A drawback of video steganography is that it can cause noise in the audio. To avoid this, many video steganography methods only modify the image portion of video files and they leave the audio portion intact.

Tokenization

Tokenization is an obfuscation technique that involves replacing sensitive data with non-sensitive placeholders or tokens. These tokens retain essential information about the original data without revealing any sensitive information. Tokenization is commonly used in the context of payment processing and securing Personally Identifiable Information (PII). The goal is to reduce the risk of unauthorized access or data breaches while still allowing systems to function with the non-sensitive tokens.

For example, credit card numbers can be tokenized to protect sensitive cardholder information. Instead of storing the actual card number, a random token is generated and stored in its place. The original card number is securely stored in a separate database or token vault, which maps tokens back to their corresponding original data. This way, even if the database containing the tokens is compromised, the attacker cannot access the actual credit card numbers.

Masking

Masking is another obfuscation technique used to protect sensitive data by partially or fully concealing it with characters, symbols, or other data. The primary goal of masking is to prevent unauthorized users from viewing or accessing sensitive information while still allowing authorized users to access and work with the data as needed. Masking is often employed when sharing data with third parties or for development and testing purposes.

For instance, when a user logs into an online banking system, the bank may display the user's account number with a portion of the digits replaced by characters like * or X (e.g., 123*****1208). This way, even if someone glances at the screen, they will not be able to see the full account number.

Another example of masking is in password fields, where the characters entered are replaced by dots or asterisks to prevent anyone from seeing the actual password being typed.

> ### ✪ *Remember This!*
>
> Steganography, tokenization, and masking are examples of obfuscation techniques used to protect sensitive data. Steganography hides messages or data within other files. Tokenization replaces sensitive data with non-sensitive tokens, retaining essential information without revealing sensitive details. Masking partially or fully conceals sensitive data with characters, symbols, or other data.

Using Cryptographic Protocols

With a basic understanding of hashing, symmetric encryption, and asymmetric encryption, it's easier to grasp how cryptography is used. Many applications use a combination of these methods, and it's important to understand how they're intertwined.

When describing public and private keys earlier, it was stressed that one key encrypts and the other key decrypts. A common question is "which one encrypts, and which one decrypts?" The answer depends on what you're trying to accomplish. The following sections describe the details, but as an overview, these are the important points related to these keys:

- Email digital signatures:
- The *sender's private key* encrypts (or signs).
- The sender's public key decrypts.
- Email encryption:
- The recipient's public key encrypts.
- The recipient's private key decrypts.
- Website encryption:
- The website's public key encrypts.
- The website's private key decrypts.
- The symmetric key encrypts data in the website session.

Email and website encryption commonly use a combination of both asymmetric and symmetric encryption. They use asymmetric encryption for key exchange, privately sharing a symmetric key. Symmetric encryption encrypts the data.

> ### ★ *Remember This!*
>
> Knowing which key encrypts and which key decrypts will help you answer some questions on the exam. For example, just by knowing that a private key is encrypting, you know that it is being used for a digital signature.

Protecting Email

Cryptography provides two primary security methods you can use with email: digital signatures and encryption. These are separate processes, but you can digitally sign and encrypt the same email.

Signing Email with Digital Signatures

Digital signatures are similar in concept to handwritten signatures on printed documents that identify individuals, but they provide more security benefits. The Digital Signature Algorithm (DSA) uses an encrypted hash of a message. The hash is encrypted with the sender's private key. If the recipient of a digitally signed email can decrypt the digital signature to reveal the hash, it provides the following three security benefits:

- **Authentication**. This identifies the sender of the email. Email recipients have assurances the email came from who it appears to be coming from. For example, if an executive digitally signs an email, recipients know it came from the executive and not from an attacker impersonating the executive.

- **Non-repudiation**. The sender cannot later deny sending the message. This is sometimes required with online transactions. For example, imagine Homer sends an order to sell stocks using a digitally signed email. If the stocks increase after his sale completes, he can't deny the transaction.
- **Integrity**. This provides assurances that the message has not been modified or corrupted. Recipients know that the message they received is the same as the sent message.

Digital signatures are much easier to grasp if you understand some other cryptography concepts discussed in this chapter. As a short review, these concepts are:

- **Hashing**. Digital signatures start by creating a hash of the message. A hash is simply a hexadecimal number created by executing a hashing algorithm on the message.
- **Certificates**. Digital signatures need certificates, and certificates include the sender's public key.
- **Public/private keys**. In a digital signature, the sender uses the sender's private key to encrypt the hash of the message. The recipient uses the sender's public key to decrypt the digital signature to reveal the hash of the message. The public key is often distributed in an S/MIME.p7s formatted file.

> ### ★ *Remember This!*
>
> A digital signature is an encrypted hash of a message. The sender's private key encrypts the hash of the message to create the digital signature. The recipient decrypts the digital signature to reveal the hash with the sender's public key. If successful, it provides authentication, non-repudiation, and integrity. Authentication identifies the sender. Integrity verifies the message has not been modified. Non-repudiation prevents senders from later denying they sent an email.

Figure 10.5 shows an overview of this process. In the figure, Lisa is sending a message to Bart with a digital signature. Note that the message "I passed" is not secret. If it was, Lisa would encrypt it, which is a separate process. The focus in this explanation is only the digital signature.

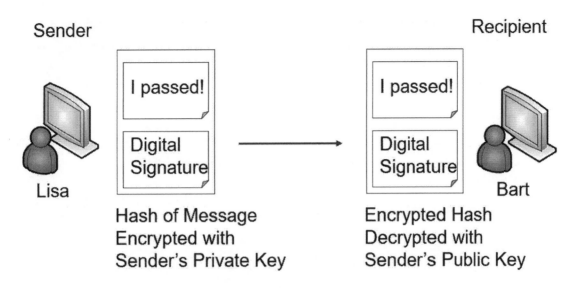

Figure 10.5: Digital signature process

Lisa creates her message in an email program, such as Microsoft Outlook. Once the email program is configured, all she does is click a button to digitally sign the message. Here is what happens when she clicks the button:

1. The application hashes the message.
2. The application retrieves Lisa's private key and encrypts the hash using this private key.
3. The application sends both the encrypted hash (which is the digital signature) and the unencrypted message to Bart.
4. When Bart's system receives the message, it verifies the digital signature using the following steps:
5. Bart's system retrieves Lisa's public key, which is in Lisa's public digital certificate. In some situations, Lisa may have sent Bart a copy of her digital certificate with her public key. In domain environments, Bart's system can automatically retrieve Lisa's digital certificate from a network location.
6. The email application on Bart's system decrypts the digital signature to reveal the hash with Lisa's public key.
7. The application calculates the hash on the received message.
8. The application compares the hash revealed in the decrypted digital signature with the calculated hash.

If the calculated hash of the received message is the same as the hash revealed in the decrypted digital signature, it validates several important checks:

- **Authentication**. Lisa sent the message. The public key can only decrypt something encrypted with the private key, and only Lisa has the private key. If the decryption succeeded,

Lisa's private key must have encrypted the hash. On the other hand, if another key was used to encrypt the hash, Lisa's public key could not decrypt it. In this case, Bart will see an error indicating a problem with the digital signature.

- **Non-repudiation**. Lisa cannot later deny sending the message. Only Lisa has her private key and if her public key revealed the hash, the hash must have been encrypted with her private key. Non-repudiation is valuable in online transactions.
- **Integrity**. Because the hash of the sent message matches the hash of the received message, the message has maintained integrity. It hasn't been modified.

At this point, you might be thinking, if we do all of this, why not just encrypt the message, too? The answer is resources. It doesn't take much processing power to encrypt 256 bits in a SHA-256 hash. In contrast, it would take quite a bit of processing power to encrypt a lengthy email and its attachments. However, if you need to ensure confidentiality of the email, you can encrypt it.

Encrypting Email

There are times when you want to ensure that email messages are only readable by authorized users. You can encrypt email and just as any other time encryption is used, encryption provides confidentiality.

Encrypting Email with Only Asymmetric Encryption

Imagine that Lisa wants to send an encrypted message to Bart. The following steps provide a simplified explanation of the process if only asymmetric encryption is used:

1. Lisa retrieves a copy of Bart's certificate that contains his public key.
2. Lisa encrypts the email with Bart's public key.
3. Lisa sends the encrypted email to Bart.
4. Bart decrypts the email with his private key.

This works because Bart is the only person who has access to his private key. If attackers intercepted the email, they couldn't decrypt it without Bart's private key. It's important to remember that when you're encrypting email contents, the recipient's public key encrypts and the recipient's private key decrypts. The sender's keys are not involved in this process. In contrast, a digital signature only uses the sender's keys but not the recipient's keys.

> ★ *Remember This!*
>
> The recipient's public key encrypts when encrypting an email message and the recipient uses the recipient's private key to decrypt an encrypted email message.

Encrypting Email with Asymmetric and Symmetric Encryption

The previous description provides a simplistic explanation of email encryption used by some email applications. However, most email applications combine both asymmetric and symmetric encryption. You may remember from earlier in this chapter that asymmetric encryption is slow and inefficient, but symmetric encryption is very quick.

Instead of using only symmetric encryption, most email applications use asymmetric encryption to privately share a session key. They then use symmetric encryption to encrypt the data with this session key. For example, imagine that Lisa is sending Bart an encrypted message. Figure 10.6 shows the process of encrypting the message and encrypting the symmetric key. Figure 10.7 shows the process of sending the encrypted message and encrypted session key, and identifies how the recipient can decrypt the data:

1. Lisa's system identifies a symmetric key to encrypt her email. For this example, assume it's a simplistic symmetric key of 53, though a symmetric algorithm like AES would use 128-bit or larger keys.
2. Lisa encrypts the email contents with the symmetric key of 53.
3. Lisa retrieves a copy of Bart's digital certificate that contains his public key.
4. She uses Bart's public key to encrypt the symmetric key of 53.
5. Lisa sends the encrypted email and the encrypted symmetric key to Bart.
6. Bart decrypts the symmetric key with his private key.
7. He then decrypts the email with the decrypted symmetric key.

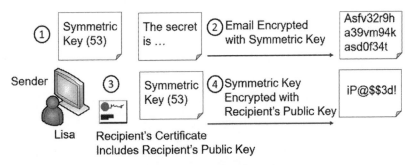

Figure 10.6: Encrypting email

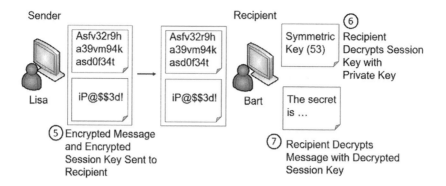

Figure 10.7: Decrypting email

Unauthorized users who intercept the email sent by Lisa won't be able to read it because it's encrypted with the symmetric key. Additionally, they can't read the symmetric key because it's encrypted with Bart's public key, and only Bart's private key can decrypt it.

S/MIME

Secure/Multipurpose Internet Mail Extensions (S/MIME) is one of the most popular standards used to digitally sign and encrypt email. Most email applications that support encryption and digital signatures use S/MIME standards.

S/MIME uses both asymmetric encryption and symmetric encryption. It can encrypt email at rest (stored on a drive) and in transit (data sent over the network). The current version uses the Cryptographic Message Syntax (CMS), which allows it to use a wide variety of different hashing algorithms and encryption algorithms. Many asymmetric algorithms use certificates and require a PKI to distribute and manage certificates. When implementing S/MIME, you typically use the following ports:

- Port 995 for Post Office Protocol 3 (POP3) over Transport Layer Security (TLS), or POP3-over-TLS
- Port 587 for Simple Mail Transfer Protocol (SMTP) over Transport Layer Security (TLS), or SMTP-over-TLS
- Port 993 for Internet Message Access Protocol (IMAP) over Transport Layer Security (TLS), or IMAP-over- TLS

HTTPS Transport Encryption

Transport encryption methods encrypt data in transit to ensure transmitted data remains confidential. This includes data transmitted over the Internet and on internal networks. As an example, Chapter 3, "Exploring Network Technologies and Tools," discusses the use of Secure Shell (SSH) to encrypt traffic, such as Secure File Transfer Protocol (SFTP). This section focuses on transport encryption methods used with HTTPS.

TLS Versus SSL

Transport Layer Security (TLS) and Secure Sockets Layer (SSL) are encryption protocols that have been commonly used to encrypt data sent over the Internet. SSL has significant vulnerabilities and should not be used anymore. However, many people commonly refer to TLS as SSL/TLS as if they are the same. If you see this, you can consider almost all references to SSL as a reference to TLS.

It is common to encrypt HTTPS with TLS to ensure confidentiality of data transmitted over the Internet. It can also be used to encrypt other transmissions such as File Transfer Protocol Secure (FTPS).

TLS provides certificate-based authentication and encrypts data with a combination of both symmetric and asymmetric encryption during a session. It uses asymmetric encryption for the key exchange (to privately share a session key) and symmetric encryption to encrypt data displayed on the webpage and transmitted during the session. The next section shows this process.

It's important to remember that TLS requires certificates. Certificate authorities (CAs) issue and manage certificates, so a CA is required to support TLS. These CAs can be internal or external third-party CAs.

📌 *Remember This!*

TLS is the replacement for SSL. TLS requires certificates issued by certificate authorities (CAs). TLS encrypts HTTPS traffic, but it can also encrypt other traffic.

Encrypting HTTPS Traffic with TLS

HTTP Secure (HTTPS) is commonly used on the Internet to secure web traffic. It commonly uses TLS to encrypt the traffic, with both asymmetric and symmetric encryption. If you're able to grasp the basics of how HTTPS combines both asymmetric and symmetric encryption, you'll have what you need to know for most protocols that use both encryptions.

Because asymmetric encryption isn't efficient to encrypt large amounts of data, symmetric encryption is used to encrypt the session data. However, both the client and the server must know what this symmetric key is before they can use it. They can't whisper it to each other over the Internet. That's like an actor on TV using a loud whisper, or stage whisper, to share a secret. Millions of TV viewers can also hear the secret.

Instead, HTTPS uses asymmetric encryption to transmit a symmetric key using a secure key exchange method. It then uses the symmetric key with symmetric encryption to encrypt all the data in the HTTPS session. Figure 10.8 and the following steps show the overall process of establishing and using an HTTPS session. As you read these steps, try to keep these two important concepts in mind:

- TLS uses asymmetric encryption to securely share the symmetric key.
- TLS uses symmetric encryption to encrypt the session data.

The simplified TLS handshake process is composed of the follow steps:

1. The client begins the process by requesting an HTTPS session. This could be by entering an HTTPS address in the URL or by clicking on an HTTPS link.
2. The server responds by sending the server's certificate. The certificate includes the server's public key. The matching private key is on the server and only accessible by the server.
3. The client creates a symmetric key and encrypts it with the server's public key. As an example, imagine that the symmetric key is 53 (though it would be much more complex in a live session). The client encrypts the symmetric key of 53 using the web server's public key creating ciphertext of UcaNP@$$. This symmetric key will be used to encrypt data in the HTTPS session, so it is sometimes called a session key.
4. The client sends the encrypted session key (UcaNP@$$) to the web server. Only the server's private key can decrypt this. If attackers intercept the encrypted key, they won't be able to decrypt it because they don't have access to the server's private key.
5. The server receives the encrypted session key and decrypts it with the server's private key. At this point, both the client and the server know the session key.
6. All the session data is encrypted with this symmetric session key using symmetric encryption.

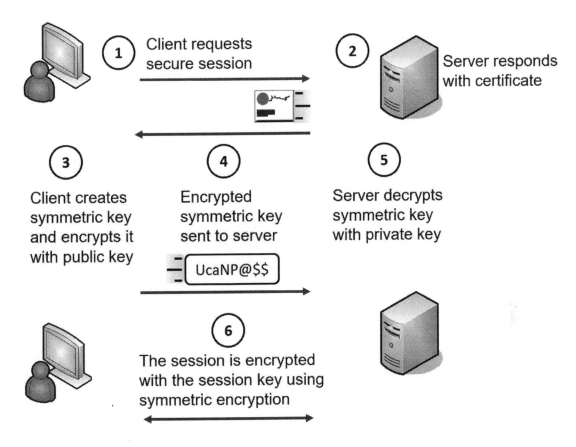

Figure 10.8: Simplified TLS handshake process used with HTTPS

The amazing thing to me is that this happens so quickly. If a web server takes as long as five seconds, many of us wonder why it's taking so long. However, a lot is happening to establish this session.

Downgrade Attacks on Weak Implementations

A **downgrade attack** is a type of attack that forces a system to downgrade its security. The attacker then exploits the lesser security control. It is most often associated with cryptographic attacks due to weak implementations of cipher suites.

An example is with Transport Layer Security (TLS) and Secure Sockets Layer (SSL). Imagine a server has both SSL and TLS installed. If a client is not able to use TLS, the server would downgrade its security and use SSL to accommodate the client.

Attackers exploit this vulnerability by configuring their systems so that they can not use TLS. When they communicate with the server, the server downgrades security to use SSL instead of TLS. This allows attackers to launch SSL-based attacks such as the Padding Oracle On Downgraded Legacy

Encryption (POODLE) attack. After the server downgrades to SSL, the attacker can initiate an on-path (also known as man-in-the-middle) attack.

One way to ensure that SSL isn't used on a website is to ensure that SSL is disabled. Disabling SSL prevents any SSL-based downgrade attacks. Similarly, cipher suites with known vulnerabilities, such as using other deprecated encryption algorithms, should be disabled. If weak cipher suites are enabled on a server, it increases the vulnerabilities.

> ★ **Remember This!**
>
> Administrators should disable weak cipher suites and weak protocols on servers. When a server has both strong and weak cipher suites, attackers can launch downgrade attacks by-passing the strong cipher suite and exploiting the weak cipher suite.

Blockchain

Blockchain is commonly defined as a distributed, decentralized, public ledger. In other words, it is a public record-keeping technology. Banks commonly use ledgers to record transactions such as deposits and withdrawals and blockchain **open public ledgers** are similar. The word block refers to pieces of digital information (the ledger), such as transactions, and chain refers to a public database. Together they create a database of public records. Each block has three parts:

- Information about a transaction, or transactions, such as the date, time, and amount.
- Information on the parties involved with the transaction(s). However, this doesn't include actual names but instead uses a digital signature.
- A unique hash that distinguishes the block from other blocks.

A block is added to the blockchain after four things happen:

1. A transaction occurred.
2. The transaction has been verified by a network of computers.
3. The transaction is accurately recorded in a block.
4. The block is assigned a unique hash.

The block also includes the hash of the most recent block added just before it. This is what creates the chain. Every block has a unique hash, and every block has the hash of the block right before it. These connected hashes create the chain.

Bitcoin is a cryptocurrency that uses blockchain. The network of computers that verify and record transactions are referred to as miners. However, it costs money to maintain all these computers, and miners earn money (in the form of bitcoin) through transaction fees and rewards. Rewards are issued for the blocks and each block includes multiple transactions.

The block reward started at 50 bitcoins per block. The reward is cut in half after 210,000 blocks are mined, which occurs about every four years. In May 2020, it was cut in half again dropping to 6.25 bitcoins per block. Eventually, the rewards will stop, and no more bitcoins will be created. However, miners will still earn money through transaction fees.

Identifying Limitations

When evaluating different algorithms, it is important to consider their possible limitations. When you understand these, it becomes much easier to identify the best algorithm to meet specific requirements. The following sections identify many of the common limitations to consider.

Resource Versus Security Constraints

Organizations frequently need to balance resource availability with security constraints. Consider using encryption to maintain the confidentiality of data. If this is possible, why not just encrypt all the data? The reason is that encryption consumes resources.

As an example, the above paragraph is about 260 characters in cleartext. Encrypted using one algorithm, it is about 360 characters in ciphertext. That's an increase of about 40 percent, which is typical with many encryption methods. If a company decides to encrypt all data, it means that it will need approximately 40 percent more disk space to store the data. Additionally, when processing the data, it consumes more memory. Lastly, it takes additional processing time and processing power to encrypt and decrypt the data.

Security experts might say the cost for additional resources is worth it, but executives looking to increase the value of the company don't. Instead, executives have a responsibility to minimize costs without sacrificing security. They do this by looking for the best balance between resource costs and security needs.

Speed and Time

Speed refers to how long an algorithm takes to compute the result. As an example, encryption algorithms typically perform several rounds, or iterations, on data. How fast the algorithm can perform a round and how many rounds it performs determine its speed. You generally want a quick algorithm when encrypting and decrypting data.

When salting and hashing passwords, a slower algorithm is desirable. The slower speed is not perceptible when validating a single password. However, the slower speed thwarts attackers who are using the algorithm trying to guess the correct password from tens of thousands (or more) of possibilities.

Size and Computational Overhead

Size in cryptography typically relates to the amount of memory space the algorithm needs to execute. On most desktops and servers, the size required is trivial. However, many smaller devices don't have adequate memory and processing power to run the same algorithms. Lightweight cryptography methods are smaller, requiring a smaller overhead.

In some cases, size relates to the size of the output compared with the input. This is relevant when encrypting data. As mentioned previously, encrypted data is larger than unencrypted data and it requires more storage space.

Entropy

Entropy refers to the randomness of a cryptographic algorithm. A higher level of randomness results in a higher level of security when using the algorithm. A lack of entropy results in a weaker algorithm and makes it much easier for the algorithm to be cracked.

Cryptographic algorithms are published so anyone can access them. This results in a significant amount of testing by cryptanalysts. When they discover a weakness or vulnerability, they publish their findings. Other cryptanalysts then peer-review their work attempting to prove or disprove the findings. Weak algorithms are deprecated and eventually fall into disuse.

As an example, cryptographic weaknesses were discovered in SHA-1. It hasn't been approved for most uses since about 2010.

Predictability

In general, predictability refers to knowing what will likely happen based on repeating the same events. When applied to cryptography, it is commonly associated with random number generators used to create encryption keys.

Random number generators are either pseudo-random number generators or true random number generators. A pseudo-random number generator uses a deterministic algorithm. In other words, given the same input, a pseudo-random number generator will produce the same output. If attackers know what is being used as an input to a pseudo-random number generator to create an encryption key, it increases the likelihood that they can predict the key.

True random number generators often use environmental factors such as atmospheric noise as input. When used properly, these sources can add true entropy into random number generators and cryptographic algorithms.

Weak Keys

Even the strongest algorithms can be easily cracked when weak keys are used. A weak key is a short or small key. When weak keys are used, it increases the possibility that an attacker can decrypt the data and read it. As an example, NIST recommends using at least 2048-bit keys with RSA since 2010. At this point, 1024-bit keys are weak and shouldn't be used.

Longevity

Longevity refers to how long you can expect to use an algorithm. This is typically related to the expected improvements in processing power. RSA provides a good example when considering just the keys. By doubling the key size, it increases the longevity of the algorithm.

However, all cryptographic algorithms don't support larger keys. As an example, the Data Encryption Standard (DES) supports key sizes of 56 bits only. The U.S. government approved it as a federal standard in November 1976. AES was chosen as the successor to DES in 2001 and the U.S. government removed its approval of DES in 2005. It is no longer recommended for use.

Reuse

When using symmetric encryption, the same keys shouldn't be reused. This is especially true with stream ciphers. If any key is used twice in the same stream, the algorithm is vulnerable to attacks. This was the problem with the legacy Wired Equivalent Privacy (WEP) algorithm used with early implementations of wireless networks. Because keys were reused in the same stream, it was vulnerable to attacks. Indeed, attackers created apps making it trivial for attackers to discover the passwords used by WEP-based wireless networks. WEP was deprecated in 2004.

Plaintext Attack

A plaintext attack (also called a known-plaintext attack) is possible if an attacker has some known plaintext data and the ciphertext created from this plaintext. As an example, if an attacker captures an encrypted message (the ciphertext) and knows the unencrypted plaintext of the message, he can use both sets of data to discover the encryption and decryption method. If successful, he can use the same decryption method on other ciphertext.

A chosen-plaintext attack is similar, but the attacker doesn't have access to all the plaintext. As an example, imagine a company includes the following sentences at the end of every email:

"The information contained in this email and any accompanying attachments may contain proprietary information about the Pay & Park & Pay parking garage. If you are not the intended recipient of this information, any use of this information is prohibited."

If the entire message is encrypted, the attacker can try various methods to decrypt the chosen plaintext (the last two sentences included in every email). When he's successful, he can use the same method to decrypt the entire message.

In a ciphertext only attack, the attacker doesn't have any information on the plaintext. Known plaintext and chosen plaintext attacks are almost always successful if an attacker has the resources and time. However, ciphertext-only attacks (also called known ciphertext attacks) are typically only successful on weak encryption algorithms. They can be thwarted by not using legacy and deprecated encryption algorithms.

Exploring PKI Components

A **Public Key Infrastructure (PKI)** is a group of technologies used to request, create, manage, store, distribute, and revoke digital certificates. Asymmetric encryption depends on the use of digital certificates for a variety of purposes, such as protecting email and protecting Internet traffic with TLS. For example, HTTPS sessions protect Internet credit card transactions, and these transactions depend on a PKI.

A primary benefit of a PKI is that it allows two people or entities to communicate securely without knowing each other previously. In other words, it allows them to communicate securely through an insecure public medium such as the Internet.

For example, you can establish a secure session with Amazon.com even if you've never done so before. Amazon is using certificates issued by a trusted certificate authority (CA). As shown in the "Encrypting HTTPS Traffic with TLS" section previously, the certificate provides the ability to establish a secure session. A key element in a PKI is a certificate authority.

Certificate Authority

A **certificate authority (CA)** issues, manages, validates, and revokes certificates. CAs can be large, such as Comodo or DigiCert, which are public CAs. A CA can also be small, such as a single service running on a server within a private network.

Public CAs make money by selling certificates. For this to work, the public CA must be trusted. If the CA is trusted, all certificates issued by the CA are trusted. This trust is established through the concept of a **root of trust**, where the CA is a trusted entity that provides a solid foundation for secure systems and processes.

This is similar to how a driver's license is trusted. The Department of Motor Vehicles (DMV) issues driver's licenses after validating a person's identity. If you want to cash a check, you might present your driver's license to prove your identity. Businesses trust the DMV, so they trust the driver's license. On the other hand, if you purchased an ID from Gibson's Instant IDs, businesses might not trust it. Although we might trust the DMV, why would a computer trust a CA? The answer is based on the certificate trust path.

Certificate Trust Models

CAs are trusted by placing a copy of their root certificate in an operating system's trusted root certificate store. Mainstream web browsers also have trusted root certificate stores. The root certificate is the first certificate created by the CA that identifies it, and the store is just a collection of these root certificates. If the CA's root certificate is placed in this store, all certificates issued by this CA are trusted.

Figure 10.9 shows the Trusted Root Certification Authorities store on a Windows computer. You can see that there are many certificates from many different CAs. In the figure, I've selected one of the certificates from COMODO RSA Certification Authority.

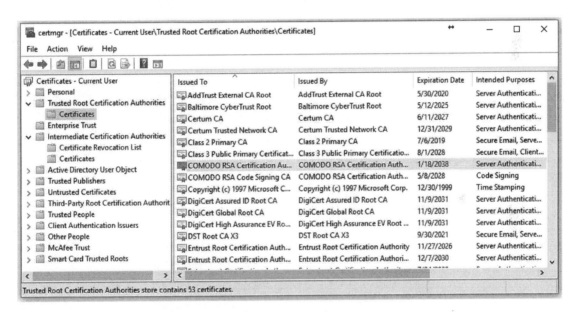

Figure 10.9: Trusted Root Certification Authorities

Public CAs such as DigiCert and Comodo negotiate with web browser developers to have their certificates included with the web browser. This way, any certificates that they sell to businesses are automatically trusted.

The most common trust model is the hierarchical trust model. In this model, the public CA, private CA, or government agency creates the first CA, known as the root CA which serves as the trust anchor. One or more **_intermediate CA_**s are also created since the root CA is kept offline for its own security and safekeeping.. If you look back at Figure 10.9, you can see that it includes a section used to store intermediate CA certificates. A hierarchical trust model works like this:

- The self-signed root CA issues certificates to one or more intermediate CAs and signs their public keys.
- Intermediate CAs issue leaf certificates to end-entities.
- Leaf certificates issued to end-entities such as organizations, governments, or end users can be for application code signing, digital signatures, VPNs, HTTPS for encrypted website sessions, S/MIME for encrypted emails, or the verification of an identity/authentication.

Certificate chaining combines all the certificates from the root CA down to the certificate issued to the end-entities. For example, Figure 10.10 shows the certificate chain for a wildcard certificate issued to google.com. A certificate chain would include all three certificates. In a small organization, the root CA can simply issue certificates to the devices and end users. Although, keeping the root certificate online opens it to the possibility of cybersecurity attacks.

Figure 10.10: Certificate path

Registration Authority and CSRs

Users and systems request digital certificates from a CA using a registration process. In some cases, a user enters information manually into a website form. In other cases, a user sends a specifically formatted file to the CA.

As an example, imagine I wanted to purchase a digital certificate for GetCertifiedGetAhead.com for secure HTTPS sessions. I would first create a public and private key pair. Many programs are available to automate this process. For example, **OpenSSL** is a software library accessible via the command line in many Linux distributions. It creates public/private key pairs in one command and allows you to export the public key to a file in a second command. Technically, OpenSSL and similar applications create the private key first. However, these applications appear to create both keys at the same time.

I would then generate a **certificate signing request (CSR)** for the digital certificate, including the purpose of the certificate and information about the website, the public key, and me. Most CAs require CSRs to be formatted using the Public-Key Cryptography Standards (PKCS) #10 specification. The CSR includes the public key, but not the private key. A CA typically publishes a certificate template showing exactly how to format the CSR.

After receiving the CSR, the CA validates my identity and creates a digital certificate with the public key. The validation process is different based on the usage of the digital certificate. In some cases, it includes extensive checking, and in other cases, verification comes from the credit card I use to purchase it.

I can then register this digital certificate with my website and the private key. Whenever someone initiates an HTTPS connection, the website sends its digital certificate containing its public key. And through negotiations and exchanges between the client and server, a secure session is established.

In large organizations, a **registration authority (RA)** can assist the CA by collecting digital certificate registration information. The RA never issues certificates. Instead, it only assists in the registration process.

> 📌 *Remember This!*
>
> You typically request certificates using a certificate signing request (CSR). The first step is to create the RSA-based private key, which is used to create the public key. You then include the public key in the CSR and the CA will embed the public key in the digital certificate. The private key is not sent to the CA.

Online Versus Offline CAs

If the CA is online, meaning it is accessible over a network, it's possible to submit the CSR using an automated process. However, an organization may keep some CAs offline to protect them from attacks. Offline CAs can only accept CSRs manually.

Large organizations typically keep the root CA offline to reduce the risk of compromise. The root CA issues certificates to the intermediate CAs that are online and accessible. If an intermediate CA becomes compromised, the entire certification path isn't compromised. The root CA can issue new certificates to replace the compromised certificates. However, if the root CA is compromised, the entire certification path is compromised.

Updating and Revoking Certificates

Two common configuration changes related to digital certificates are updating and revoking them. Certificates normally expire based on the Valid From and Valid To dates and can be updated by replacing them with newer certificates. If a certificate is compromised, the CA can revoke it.

Many websites use digital certificates from Let's Encrypt, a nonprofit certificate authority that provides free TLS-based certificates. These certificates are valid for 90 days, but automated processes can be used to automatically update the certificate without additional site administrator interaction.

When desired, the CA can revoke a digital certificate before it expires. As an example, if a private key is somehow leaked to the public, the key pair is compromised. It no longer provides adequate security because the private key is no longer private. Similarly, if the CA itself is compromised through a security breach, certificates issued by the CA may be compromised, so the CA can revoke certificates.

In general, any time a CA does not want anyone to use a certificate, the CA revokes it. Although the most common reasons are due to compromise of a key or compromise of the CA, there are others. A CA can use any of the following reasons when revoking a certificate:

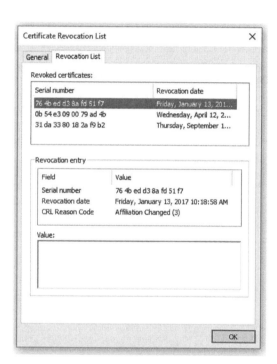

- Private key compromise
- CA compromise
- Change of affiliation
- Superseded by another certificate
- Cease of operation
- Certificate hold
- Certificate holder's request

Certificate Revocation List

CAs use certificate revocation lists (CRLs) to revoke a digital certificate. The CRL is a version 2 certificate that includes a list of revoked certificates identified by their serial numbers. For example, Figure 10.11 shows a copy of a CRL. One of the labs for this chapter shows you how to download and view a CRL.

Figure 10.11: Certificate revocation list

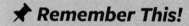 **Remember This!**

CAs revoke certificates for several reasons such as when the private key is compromised or the CA is compromised. The certificate revocation list (CRL) includes a list of revoked certificates and is publicly available. An alternative to using a CRL is the Online Certificate Status Protocol (OCSP), which returns answers such as good, revoked, or unknown.

Validating a Certificate

Before clients use a certificate, they first verify it is valid with some checks. There are many different certificate issues that can result in an invalid certificate. Browsers typically display an error describing the issue and encouraging users not to use the certificate. Applications that detect a certificate issue might display an error using a certificate, but they are typically coded to not use it. Some of the common issues are:

- **Expired.** The first check is to ensure that it isn't expired. If the certificate is expired, the computer system typically gives the user an error indicating the certificate is not valid.
- **Certificate not trusted.** The next check is to see if the certificate was issued by a trusted CA. For example, a Windows system will look in the Trusted Root Certification Authorities store and the Intermediate Certification Authorities store shown previously in Figure 10.9. If the system doesn't have a copy of the CA's digital certificate, it will indicate the certificate is not trusted. Users can override this warning, though there are often warnings encouraging users not to continue.
- **Certificate revoked.** Clients also validate certificates through the CA to ensure they haven't been revoked.

A common method of validating a certificate is by requesting a copy of the CRL, as shown in Figure 10.12. The following steps outline the process:

1. The client initiates a session requiring a certificate, such as an HTTPS session.
2. The server responds with a copy of the certificate that includes the public key.
3. The client queries the CA for a copy of the CRL.
4. The CA responds with a copy of the CRL.

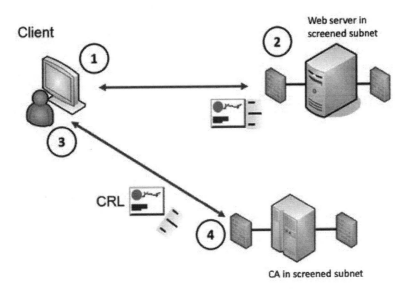

Figure 10.12: Validating a certificate

The client then checks the serial number of the certificate against the list of serial numbers in the CRL. If the certificate is revoked for any reason, the application gives an error message to the user.

CRLs are typically cached after being downloaded the first time. Instead of requesting another copy of the CRL, clients use the cached copy. This reduces the amount of traffic sent between clients and the CA.

Another method of validating a certificate is with the **Online Certificate Status Protocol (OCSP)**. OCSP allows the client to query the CA with the serial number of the certificate. The CA then responds with an answer of "good," "revoked," or "unknown." A response of "unknown" could indicate the certificate is a forgery.

Because OCSP provides a real-time response, it is an excellent example of supporting a common use case of low latency. If a CA revokes a certificate, clients using OCSP will know immediately. In contrast, if clients are using a cached CRL, they will be unaware of the revoked certificate until another copy of the CRL is downloaded.

Over time, authorities realized that OCSP was generating a lot of real-time traffic to the CA because it requires a CA to respond to every request. OCSP **stapling** solves this problem. The certificate presenter obtains a timestamped OCSP response from the CA. Before sending it, the CA signs it with a digital signature. The certificate presenter then appends (or metaphorically staples) a timestamped OCSP response to the certificate during the TLS handshake process. This eliminates the need for clients to query the CA.

> 📌 *Remember This!*
>
> Certificate stapling is an alternative to OCSP. The certificate presenter (such as a web server) appends the certificate with a timestamped digitally signed OCSP response from the CA. This reduces OCSP traffic to and from the CA.

Certificate Pinning

Certificate pinning is a security mechanism designed to prevent attackers from impersonating a website using fraudulent certificates. When configured on a website server, the server responds to client HTTPS requests with an extra header. This extra header includes a list of hashes derived from valid public keys used by the website. It also includes a max-age field specifying how long the client should store and use the data.

When clients connect to the same website again, they recalculate the hashes and then compare the recalculated hashes with the stored hashes. If the hashes match, it verifies that the client is connected to the same website.

Website administrators create hashes of one or more certificates used by the website. This can be the public key used by the website's certificate. It can also include any public keys from certificates in the certificate chain such as the public key from the root CA certificate, and/or the public key from intermediate CA certificates. Last, it must include a backup key that can be used if the current key becomes invalid.

Key Escrow

Key escrow is the process of placing a copy of a private key in a safe environment. This is useful for recovery. If the original key is lost, the organization retrieves the copy of the key to access the data. Key escrow isn't required, but if an organization determines that data loss is unacceptable, it will implement a key escrow process.

In some cases, an organization provides a copy of the key to a third party. Another method is to designate employees within the organization who will be responsible for key escrow. These employees maintain and protect copies of the key, and if the original key is lost, they check out a copy of the key to an administrator or user.

A key recovery agent is a designated individual who can recover or restore cryptographic keys. In the context of a PKI, a recovery agent can recover private keys to access encrypted data. The recovery agent may be a security professional, administrator, or anyone designated by the company.

In some cases, the recovery agent can recover encrypted data using a different key. For example, Microsoft BitLocker supports encryption of entire drives. It's possible to add a data recovery agent field when creating a BitLocker encrypted drive. In this case, BitLocker uses two keys. The user has one key and uses it to unlock the drive during day-to-day use. The second key is only accessible by the recovery agent and is used for recovery purposes if the original key is lost or becomes inaccessible.

Key Management

Key management within a PKI refers to all the steps taken to manage public and private keys used within the PKI. This includes keeping private keys private, distributing public keys in certificates, and revoking certificates when keys are compromised. Proper key management is crucial to the security and integrity of any PKI, as it ensures the authenticity, confidentiality, and integrity of the encrypted data and communications.

A *Key Management System (KMS)* is a centralized system or service responsible for the secure management of cryptographic keys used in various security applications. The primary goal of a KMS is to provide a robust and secure framework for managing the entire lifecycle of cryptographic keys, including key generation, distribution, storage, rotation, revocation, and retirement or destruction. Implementing a KMS helps organizations maintain control over their cryptographic keys and reduces the risks associated with unauthorized access or key misuse.

Some of the tasks handled by a KMS include:

- **Key Generation**. A KMS generates cryptographic keys using strong, industry-standard algorithms to ensure the keys are secure and random. It is essential to use a reliable source of entropy or randomness when generating keys to prevent any patterns or predictability.
- **Key Storage**. The KMS securely stores cryptographic keys, typically in hardware security modules (HSMs) or other tamper-resistant storage devices. This secure storage prevents unauthorized access and protects the keys from being stolen or misused.
- **Key Distribution**. A KMS securely distributes public keys in the form of certificates, while keeping private keys confidential. The certificates, which contain public keys, are signed by a trusted Certificate Authority (CA), ensuring their authenticity and integrity. The KMS may also handle the distribution of symmetric keys, ensuring they are transmitted securely between parties.
- **Key Rotation**. Regular key rotation is an essential practice in key management. A KMS automates the process of key rotation, which involves generating new keys, replacing old keys with new ones, and updating systems and applications to use the new keys. This practice helps reduce the risk of unauthorized access or key compromise over time.
- **Key Retirement/Revocation/Destruction**. When a cryptographic key is no longer needed, or if it has been compromised, the KMS ensures its proper retirement or destruction. This process involves securely removing the key from the system and ensuring it cannot be accessed or used again.

Comparing Certificate Types

Certificates are sometimes identified based on their usage. The following bullets describe some common certificate types:

- **Machine/Computer**. Certificates issued to a device or a computer are commonly called machine certificates or computer certificates. The certificate is typically used to identify the computer within a domain.
- **User**. Certificates can also be issued to users. They can be used for encryption, authentication, smart cards, and more. For example, Microsoft systems can create user certificates allowing the user to encrypt data using Encrypting File System (EFS).
- **Email**. Email certificates are used for encryption of emails and digital signatures, as described earlier in this chapter.
- **Code signing**. Developers often use code signing certificates to validate the authenticity of executable applications or scripts. The code signing certificate verifies the code has not been modified. As an example, a PowerShell script can use a code signing certificate to prove the script hasn't been modified before it is run.
- **Self-signed**. A self-signed certificate is not issued by a trusted CA. Private CAs within an enterprise often create self-signed certificates. They aren't trusted by default. However,

administrators can use automated means to place copies of the self-signed certificate into the trusted root CA store for enterprise computers. Self-signed certificates from private CAs eliminate the cost of purchasing certificates from public CAs.

- **Root**. The root certificate is the highest-level certificate issued by the root CA or a self-signed anchoring certificate.

- **Wildcard**. A wildcard certificate starts with an asterisk (*) and can be used for multiple sub domains if each domain name has the same root domain. For example, Google uses a wildcard certificate issued to *.google.com. This same certificate can be used for other Google domains, such as accounts.google.com and support.google.com. Wildcard certificates can reduce the administrative burden associated with managing multiple certificates.

- **Subject alternative name**. A subject alternative name (SAN) certificate is used for multiple domains that have different names but are owned by the same organization. For example, Google uses SANs of *.google.com, *.android.com, *.cloud.google.com, and more. It is often used for systems with the same base domain names, but different top-level domains. For example, if Google used names such as google. com and google. net, it could use a single SAN certificate for both domain names.

- **Domain validation**. A domain-validated certificate indicates that the certificate requestor has some control over a DNS domain. The CA takes extra steps to contact the requestor such as by email or telephone. The intent is to provide additional evidence to clients that the certificate and the organization are trustworthy.

- **Extended validation**. Extended validation (EV) certificates use additional steps beyond domain validation. Some browsers display the name of the company before the URL when an extended validation certificate is used. Usage of EV certificates is on the decline. Most web browsers stopped including the name in the URL. Part of the reason is that the absence of the company name doesn't mean anything to many users. Think of the user who clicks on a phishing email. He probably doesn't know to look for a company name in the URL, so its absence doesn't alarm him.

Comparing Certificate Formats

Most certificates use one of the X.509 v3 formats. The primary exception is certificates used to distribute certificate revocation lists that use the X.509 v2 format.

Certificates are typically stored as binary files or as BASE64 American Standard Code for Information Interchange (ASCII) encoded files. Binary files are stored as 1s and 0s. BASE64 encoding converts the binary data into an ASCII string format. Additionally, some certificates are also encrypted to provide additional confidentiality.

The base format of certificates **is Canonical Encoding Rules (CER)** or **Distinguished Encoding Rules (DER).** CER and DER formats are defined by the International Telecommunication Union Telecommunication Standardization Sector (ITU-T) in the X.690 standard. They use a variant of the Abstract Syntax Notation One (ASN.1) format, which defines data structures commonly used in cryptography. CER is an ASCII format and DER is a binary format. Some certificates include headers and footers to identify the contents. As an example, the following text shows a header and a footer for a certificate:

```
-----BEGIN CERTIFICATE----- MIIDdTCCAl2gAwIBAgILBAAAAAABFUt
aw5QwDQYJKoZIhvcNAQEFBQAwVzEL

... additional ASCII Characters here... HMUfpIBvFSDJ3gyICh3WZlXi/
EjJKSZp4A==

-----END CERTIFICATE-----
```

Each header starts with five dashes (-----), **BEGIN**, a label, and five more dashes. The footer starts with five dashes, **END**, the same label, and five more dashes. In the previous example, the label is **CERTIFICATE**. Other labels include **PUBLIC KEY, PRIVATE KEY, ENCRYPTED PRIVATE KEY, CERTIFICATE REQUEST**, and **X509 CRL**. DER-based certificates are binary encoded, so they do not have headers and footers.

Certificate files can have many extensions, such as .crt, .cer, .pem, .p7b, .p7c, p7s, pfx, and .p12. However, it's worth stressing that a certificate with the .cer extension doesn't necessarily mean that it is using the CER format.

The Privacy Enhanced Mail (PEM) certificate name implies that PEM-based certificates are used for email only, but that is misleading. PEM-based certificates can be used for just about anything. They can be converted to CER (ASCII files) or DER (binary files). They can also be used to share public keys within a certificate, request certificates from a CA as a CSR, install a private key on a server, publish a CRL, or share the full certificate chain.

Type	Common Extensions	Format	Common Purpose	Can Contain
CER	.cer	ASCII	Used for ASCII certificates	Varies
DER	.der	Binary	Used for binary certificates	Varies
PEM	.pem, .cer, .crt, .key	Binary (DER) or ASCII (CER)	Can be used for almost any certificate purpose	Server certificates, certificate chains, keys, CRL
P7B	.p7b, .p7c	ASCII (CER)	Used to share the public key	Certificates, certificate chains, CRL, but never the private key
P12 PFX	.p12, .pfx	Binary (DER)	Commonly used to store private keys with a certificate	Certificates, certificate chains, and private keys

Table 10.1: Certificate formats

You might see a PEM-encoded certificate with the .pem extension. However, it's more common for the certificate to use other extensions. For example, a PEM-encoded file holding the certificate with the public key typically uses the .cer or .crt extension. A PEM file holding just the private key typically uses the .key extension.

P7B files use the PKCS version 7 (PKCS #7) format and they use base64 ASCII encoding. They are commonly used to share public keys with proof of identity of the certificate holder. Recipients use the public keys to encrypt or decrypt data. For example, a web server might use a P7B file to share its public key. P7B files can also contain a certificate chain or a CRL. However, they never include the private key.

P12 files use the PKCS version 12 (PKCS #12) format and they use binary encoding. They are commonly used to hold certificates with the private key. For example, when installing a certificate on a server to support HTTPS sessions, you might install a P12 file with the private key. Because it holds the private key, it's common to encrypt P12 files. It's also possible to include the full certificate chain in a P12 file.

Personal Information Exchange (PFX) file is a predecessor to the P12 file and it has the same usage. Administrators often use this format on Windows systems to import and export certificates.

When comparing the different formats, it's important to know what they can contain and how to identify them. Table 10.1 provides an overview of the primary formats.

> 📌 *Remember This!*
>
> CER is an ASCII format for certificates and DER is a binary format. PEM is the most used certificate format and can be used for just about any certificate type. P7B files are commonly used to share public keys. P12 and PFX files are commonly used to hold the private key.

Chapter 10 Exam Topic Review

When preparing for the exam, make sure you understand these key concepts covered in this chapter.

Introducing Cryptography Concepts

- Integrity provides assurances that data has not been modified. Hashing ensures that data has retained integrity.
- Confidentiality ensures that data is only viewable by authorized users. Encryption protects the confidentiality of data.

- Symmetric encryption uses the same key to encrypt and decrypt data.
- Asymmetric encryption uses two keys (public and private) created as a matched pair.
- A digital signature provides authentication, non-repudiation, and integrity.
- Authentication validates an identity.
- Non-repudiation prevents a party from denying an action.
- Users sign emails with a digital signature, which is a hash of an email message encrypted with the sender's private key.
- Only the sender's public key can decrypt the digital signature which reveals hash, providing verification the hash was encrypted with the sender's private key.

Providing Integrity with Hashing

- Hashing verifies the integrity of data, such as downloaded files and email messages.
- A hash is a fixed-length string of hexadecimal characters, which cannot be reversed to re-create the original data.
- A checksum is similar to a hash but is typically smaller. It is used to verify the integrity of data but is not intended to be cryptographically secure.
- Hashing algorithms are one-way functions used to create a hash. You cannot reverse the process to re-create the original data.
- A hash collision occurs when a hashing algorithm creates the same hash from different inputs.
- Common hashing algorithms are Message Digest 5 (MD5), Secure Hash Algorithms (SHA), and Hash-based Message Authentication Code (HMAC). HMAC provides both integrity and authenticity of a message.

Understanding Password Attacks

- Password attacks attempt to discover passwords. An online password attack attempts to discover a password from an online system. An offline password attack attempts to discover passwords from a captured database or captured packet scan.
- Passwords are often stored as a hash. Weak hashing algorithms are susceptible to collisions, which allow different passwords to create the same hash.
- A brute force attack attempts to guess all possible character combinations and a dictionary attack uses all the words and character combinations stored in a file. Account lockout policies thwart online brute force attacks and complex passwords thwart offline password attacks.
- A spraying attack attempts to bypass account lockout policies. An automated program starts with a large list of targeted user accounts. It then picks a password and tries it against every account in the list. It then picks another password and loops through the list again.
- In a pass the hash attack, the attacker discovers the hash of the user's password and then uses it to log on to the system as the user.
- In a birthday attack, an attacker attempts to create a password that produces the same hash as the user's actual password.

- Password salting adds additional characters to passwords before hashing them and prevents many types of attacks, including dictionary, brute force, and rainbow table attacks.
- Three commonly used key stretching techniques are bcrypt, Password-Based Key Derivation Function 2 (PBKDF2), and Argon2. They protect passwords against brute force and rainbow table attacks.

Providing Confidentiality with Encryption

- Confidentiality ensures that data is only viewable by authorized users.
- Encryption provides confidentiality of data, including data at rest (any type of data stored on disk) or data in transit (any type of transmitted data).
- Symmetric encryption uses the same key to encrypt and decrypt data.
- Block ciphers encrypt data in fixed-size blocks. Advanced Encryption Standard (AES) encrypts data in 128-bit blocks and 3DES encrypts data in 64-bit blocks.
- Stream ciphers encrypt data 1 bit or 1 byte at a time. They are more efficient than block ciphers when encrypting data of an unknown size or when sent in a continuous stream.
- Asymmetric encryption uses public and private keys as matched pairs.
- If the public key encrypts information, only the matching private key can decrypt it.
- If the private key encrypts information, only the matching public key can decrypt it.
- Private keys are always kept private and never shared.
- Public keys are freely shared by embedding them in a certificate.
- Asymmetric encryption is used to share symmetric keys between two entities. After both parties know the symmetric key, they use it to encrypt data within the session because symmetric encryption is much faster than asymmetric encryption.
- Certificates distribute public keys and the same public key is used for months or years.
- Ephemeral keys last only a short time, such as a few minutes within a session. Perfect forward secrecy ensures that the compromise of a key does not compromise any keys used in the past. It depends on the use of ephemeral keys.
- Elliptic curve cryptography (ECC) is an encryption technology that doesn't take as much processing power as other cryptographic methods. It is commonly used with low power devices.
- Common obfuscation techniques include steganography, tokenization, and masking.
- Steganography is the practice of hiding data within a file. Current steganography methods include audio steganography, image steganography, and video steganography.
- Tokenization replaces sensitive data with non-sensitive tokens, retaining essential information without revealing sensitive details, commonly used in payment processing and securing personally identifiable information.
- Masking partially or fully conceals sensitive data with characters, symbols, or other data, often employed when sharing data with third parties or for development and testing purposes.

Using Cryptographic Protocols

- When using digital signatures with email:
- The sender's private key encrypts (or signs).
- The sender's public key decrypts.
- A digital signature provides authentication (verified identification) of the sender, non-repudiation, and integrity of the message.
- Senders create a digital signature by hashing a message and encrypting the hash with the sender's private key.
- Recipients decrypt the digital signature with the sender's matching public key.
- When encrypting email:
- The recipient's public key encrypts.
- The recipient's private key decrypts.
- Many email applications use the public key to encrypt a symmetric key, and then use the symmetric key to encrypt the email contents.
- S/MIME is used to secure email with encryption and digital signatures. It uses certificates and depends on a PKI. When deploying, use port 587 for SMTP-over-TLS and port 993 for IMAP-over-TLS.
- When encrypting website traffic with TLS:
- The website's public key encrypts a symmetric key.
- The website's private key decrypts the symmetric key.
- The symmetric key encrypts data in the session.

Exploring PKI Components

- A Public Key Infrastructure (PKI) is a group of technologies used to request, create, manage, store, distribute, and revoke digital certificates. A PKI allows two entities to privately share symmetric keys without any prior communication.
- Most public CAs use a hierarchical centralized CA trust model, with a root CA and intermediate CAs. A CA issues, manages, validates, and revokes certificates. Certificate chaining combines all the certificates from the root CA to the certificates issued to the end-entities.
- You request a certificate with a certificate signing request (CSR). You first create a private/public key pair and include the public key in the CSR.
- An online CA is accessible over a network, including the Internet. Many root CAs are taken offline to reduce the risk of compromise.
- Configuration changes related to certificates are updating them and revoking them. Certificates are renewed before their expiration dates to update them. Certificates are revoked if they are compromised.
- A certificate revocation list (CRL) identifies revoked certificates with a list of serial numbers.

- The CA publishes the CRL, making it available to anyone. Web browsers can check certificates they receive from a web server against a copy of the CRL to determine if a certificate is revoked.
- As an alternative to the CRL, the Online Certificate Status Protocol (OCSP) allows clients to query the CA with the serial number of the certificate to determine if it is valid.
- Certificate stapling provides clients with a timestamped, digitally signed OCSP response. This is from the CA and appended to the certificate.
- Certificate pinning provides clients with a list of hashes for each public key it uses.
- A key escrow stores a copy of private keys used within a PKI. If the original private key is lost or inaccessible, the copy is retrieved from escrow, preventing data loss.
- Wildcard certificates use an asterisk (*) for sub domains to reduce the administrative burden of managing certificates. Subject alternative name (SAN) certificates can be used for multiple domains with different domain names.
- CER is an ASCII format and DER is a binary format.
- PEM is the most commonly used certificate format and can be used for just about any certificate type.
- P7B files are commonly used to share public keys. P12 and PFX files are commonly used to hold the private key.

✦ Online References

Remember, there are additional resources at **https://getcertifiedgetahead.com/**.
Resources include labs, sample performance-based questions, and more.

Chapter 10 Practice Questions

1. GCGA, a software development company, occasionally updates its software with major updates and minor patches. Administrators load these updates to the company website along with a hash associated with each update. Which of the following BEST describes the purpose of the hash?

   A. Availability of updates and patches
   B. Integrity of updates and patches
   C. Confidentiality of updates and patches
   D. Integrity of the application

2. Users in your organization sign their emails with digital signatures. Which of the following provides integrity for these digital signatures?

   A. Hashing
   B. Encryption
   C. Non-repudiation
   D. Private key

3. While reviewing logs on a web server hosted by your organization, you notice multiple logon failures to an FTP account, but they're only happening about once every 30 minutes. You also see that the same password is being tried against the SSH account right after the FTP account logon failure. What BEST describes what is happening?

   A. Brute force attack
   B. Dictionary attack
   C. Plaintext attack
   D. Spraying attack

4. An online application requires users to log on with their email address and a password. The application encrypts the passwords in a hashed format. Which of the following can be added to decrease the likelihood that attackers can discover these passwords?

   A. Rainbow tables
   B. Salt
   C. Digital signatures
   D. Input validation

5. What is the primary difference between a block cipher and a stream cipher?

   A. A stream cipher encrypts data 1 bit or 1 byte at a time.
   B. A block cipher encrypts data 1 bit or 1 byte at a time.
   C. Stream ciphers are used for symmetric encryption, but block ciphers are used for asymmetric encryption.
   D. Block ciphers are used for symmetric encryption, but stream ciphers are used for asymmetric encryption.

6. A developer is creating an application that will encrypt and decrypt data on mobile devices. These devices don't have a lot of processing power. Which of the following cryptographic methods has the LEAST overhead and can provide encryption for these mobile devices?

   A. Elliptic curve cryptography
   B. Perfect forward secrecy
   C. Salting
   D. Digital signatures

7. You are configuring a web server that will be used by salespeople via the Internet. Data transferred to and from the server needs to be encrypted, so you are tasked with requesting a certificate for the server. Which of the following would you MOST likely create to request the certificate?

   A. CA
   B. CRL
   C. CSR
   D. OCSP

8. Users within an organization frequently access public web servers using HTTPS. Management wants to ensure that users can verify that certificates are valid even if the public CAs are temporarily unavailable. Which of the following should be implemented to meet this need?

   A. OCSP
   B. CRL
   C. Private CA
   D. CSR

9. Your organization hosts an internal website used only by employees. The website uses a certificate issued by a private CA and the network downloads a CRL from the CA once a week. However, after a recent compromise, security administrators want to use a real-time alternative to the CRL. Which of the following will BEST meet this need?

   A. SAN
   B. CSR
   C. RA
   D. OCSP

10. An organization hosts several web servers in a web farm used for e-commerce. Due to recent attacks, management is concerned that attackers might try to redirect website traffic, allowing the attackers to impersonate their e-commerce site. Which of the following methods will address this issue?

   A. Stapling
   A. Perfect forward secrecy
   A. Pinning
   A. Key stretching

11. Management has mandated the use of digital signatures by all personnel within your organization. Which of the following use cases does this support?

    A. Supporting confidentiality
    B. Supporting availability
    C. Supporting obfuscation
    D. Supporting non-repudiation

12. A DLP system detected confidential data being sent out via email from Bart's account. However, he denied sending the email. Management wants to implement a method that would prevent Bart from denying accountability in the future. Which of the following are they trying to enforce?

    A. Confidentiality
    B. Encryption
    C. Access control
    D. Non-repudiation

13. Your organization recently updated the security policy and mandated that emails sent by all upper-level executives include a digital signature. Which security goal does this policy address?

    A. Confidentiality
    B. Hashing
    C. Obfuscation
    D. Authentication

14. You are tasked with getting prices for certificates. You need to find a source that will provide a certificate that can be used for multiple domains that have different names. Which of the following certificates is the BEST choice?

    A. SAN
    B. Domain validation
    C. Extended validation
    D. Wildcard

15. Your organization recently lost access to some decryption keys, resulting in the loss of some encrypted data. The chief information officer (CIO) mandated the creation of a key escrow. Which of the following cryptographic keys are MOST likely to be stored in key escrow?

    A. Public
    B. Private
    C. Ephemeral
    D. Session

Chapter 10

Practice Question Answers

1. **B** is correct. The hash provides integrity for the updates and patches so that users can verify they have not been modified. Installing updates and patches increases the availability of the application. Confidentiality is provided by encryption. The hashes are for the updates and patches, so they do not provide integrity for the application.

2. **A** is correct. Hashing provides integrity for digital signatures and other data. A digital signature is a hash of the message encrypted with the sender's private key, but the encryption doesn't provide integrity. The digital signature provides non-repudiation, but non-repudiation does not provide integrity. The private key and public key are both needed, but the private key does not provide integrity.

3. **D** is correct. This indicates a password spraying attack. It loops through a list of accounts, guessing a password for one account at a time, and then guessing the same password for a different account. In this scenario, the attacker may be guessing passwords for other servers before returning to the web server. A brute force attack attempts to guess all possible character combinations for a password, and a dictionary attack uses a dictionary of words trying to discover the correct password. A spraying attack could use either a brute force method or a dictionary method when guessing the password; however, these methods do not loop through a list of user accounts. In a plaintext attack (also called a known plaintext attack), an attacker has samples of known plaintext and can use these samples to decrypt ciphertext that includes this plaintext.

4. **B** is correct. A password salt is additional random characters added to a password before hashing the password, and it decreases the success of password attacks. Rainbow tables are used by attackers and contain precomputed hashes, and salting is intended to specifically thwart rainbow table attacks. A digital signature provides authentication, non-repudiation, and integrity, but it doesn't protect passwords. Input validation techniques verify data is valid before using it, and they are unrelated to protecting hashed passwords.

5. **A** is correct. A stream cipher encrypts data a single bit or a single byte at a time and is more efficient when the size of the data is unknown, such as streaming audio or video. A block cipher encrypts data in specific-sized blocks, such as 64-bit blocks or 128-bit blocks. Both are used with symmetric encryption algorithms.

6. **A** is correct. Elliptic curve cryptography (ECC) has minimal overhead and is often used with mobile devices for encryption. Perfect forward secrecy refers to session keys and provides assurances that session keys will not be compromised even if a private key is later compromised. Salting adds random characters to a password before hashing it to thwart rainbow table attacks. Digital signatures provide integrity, authentication, and non-repudiation, but not encryption.

7. **C** is correct. You would request a certificate by creating a certificate signing request (CSR). It uses a specific format to request a certificate. You submit the CSR to a certificate authority (CA), but the request needs to be in the CSR format. A certificate revocation list (CRL) is a list of revoked certificates. The Online Certificate Status Protocol (OCSP) is an alternate method of validating certificates and indicates if a certificate is good, revoked, or unknown.

8. **B** is correct. A certificate revocation list (CRL) can meet this need because CRLs are cached. If the public certificate authority (CA) is not reachable due to any type of connection outage or CA outage, the cached CRL can be used if the cache time has not expired. The Online Certificate Status Protocol (OCSP) works in real-time where the client queries the CA with the serial number of the certificate. If the CA is unreachable, the certificate cannot be validated. A private CA is used within an organization and cannot validate certificates from a public CA. You request a certificate with a certificate signing request (CSR), but the CSR doesn't validate an issued certificate.

9. **D** is correct. The Online Certificate Status Protocol (OCSP) provides real-time responses to validate certificates issued by a certificate authority (CA). A certificate revocation list (CRL) includes a list of revoked certificates, but if it is only downloaded once a week, it can quickly

be out of date. None of the other answers validates certificates. In the context of certificates, a subject alternative name (SAN) certificate is used for multiple domains that have different names but are owned by the same organization. A certificate signing request (CSR) is used to request a certificate. A registration authority (RA) accepts CSRs for a CA.

10. **C** is correct. Certificate pinning provides clients with a list of public key hashes that clients can use to detect website impersonation attempts. Stapling reduces Online Certificate Status Protocol (OCSP) traffic by appending a timestamped, digitally signed OCSP response to a certificate. Perfect forward secrecy ensures that the compromise of one session key does not compromise other session keys used in the past. Key stretching techniques add additional bits (salts) to passwords, making them harder to crack.

11. **D** is correct. Digital signatures will support a use case of supporting non-repudiation. Digital signatures also provide integrity and authentication, but these weren't available answers. Digital signatures don't encrypt data, so they do not support a use case of supporting confidentiality. Redundancy and fault tolerance solutions will increase availability. Steganography is one way of supporting obfuscation.

12. **D** is correct. Non-repudiation methods such as digital signatures prevent users from denying they took an action. In this scenario, if a data loss protection (DLP) system detected the outgoing email and it was signed with Bart's account using a digital signature, he couldn't believably deny sending it. Encryption methods protect confidentiality. Access control methods protect access to data.

13. **D** is correct. A digital signature is an encrypted hash of a message and it can be used to provide authentication, integrity, and non-repudiation. Authentication identifies the sender of the email. Encryption provides confidentiality and prevents unauthorized disclosure. Obfuscation methods attempt to make something harder to read, but a digital signature doesn't provide obfuscation. Hashing is a method used to provide integrity, but hashing by itself isn't a security goal.

14. **A** is correct. A subject alternative name (SAN) certificate is used for multiple domains that have different names but are owned by the same organization. A domain-validated certificate indicates that the certificate requestor has some control over a Domain Name System (DNS) domain. Extended validation certificates use additional steps beyond domain validation. A wildcard certificate starts with an asterisk (*) and can be used for multiple sub domains, but each sub domain name must have the same root domain.

15. **B** is correct. Copies of private keys are typically stored in a key escrow so that data encrypted with a private key can be retrieved if the original private key is no longer accessible. Public keys are available to anyone so there is no need to store them in a key escrow. An ephemeral key has a short lifetime and is re-created for each session. A session key is only used for a single session so wouldn't be stored in a key escrow.

Implementing Policies to Mitigate Risks

CompTIA Security+ objectives covered in this chapter:

1.3 Explain the importance of change management processes and the impact to security.

- Business processes impacting security operation (Approval process, Ownership, Stakeholders, Impact analysis, Test results, Backout plan, Maintenance window, Standard operating procedure)
- Technical implications (Allow lists/deny lists, Restricted activities, Downtime, Service restart, Application restart, Legacy applications, Dependencies)
- Documentation (Updating diagrams, Updating policies/procedures)
- Version control

3.3 Compare and contrast concepts and strategies to protect data.

- Data types (Regulated, Trade secret, Intellectual property, Legal information, Financial information, Human- and non-human-readable)
- Data classifications (Sensitive, Confidential, Public, Restricted, Private, Critical)
- Methods to secure data (Geographic restrictions, Permission restrictions)

4.2 Explain the security implications of proper hardware, software, and data asset management.

- Disposal/decommissioning (Sanitization, Destruction, Certification, Data retention)

4.8 Explain appropriate incident response activities.

- Process (Preparation, Detection, Analysis, Containment, Eradication, Recovery, Lessons learned)
- Training
- Testing (Tabletop exercise, Simulation)
- Root cause analysis

- Threat hunting
- Digital forensics (Legal hold, Chain of custody, Acquisition, Reporting, Preservation, E-discovery)

5.1 Summarize elements of effective security governance.

- Guidelines
- Policies (Acceptable use policy (AUP), Information security policies, Business continuity, Disaster recovery, Incident response, Software development lifecycle (SDLC), Change management)
- Standards (Password, Access control, Physical security, Encryption)
- Procedures (Change management, Onboarding/offboarding, Playbooks)
- External considerations (Regulatory, Legal, Industry, Local/Regional, National, Global)
- Monitoring and revision
- Types of governance structures (Boards, Committees, Government entities, Centralized/decentralized)
- Roles and responsibilities for systems and data (Owners, Controllers, Processors, Custodians/stewards)

5.3 Explain the processes associated with third-party risk assessment and management.

- Vendor assessment (Penetration testing, Right-to-audit clause, Evidence of internal audits, Independent assessments, Supply chain analysis)
- Vendor selection (Due diligence, Conflict of interest)
- Agreement types (Service level agreement (SLA), Memorandum of agreement (MOA), Memorandum of understanding (MOU), Master service agreement (MSA), Work order (WO)/Statement of work (SOW), Non-disclosure agreement (NDA), Business partners agreement (BPA))
- Vendor monitoring
- Questionnaires
- Rules of engagement

5.4 Summarize elements of effective security compliance.

- Compliance reporting (Internal, External)
- Consequences of non-compliance (Fines, Sanctions, Reputational damage, Loss of license, Contractual impacts)
- Compliance monitoring (Due diligence/care, Attestation and acknowledgement, Internal and external, Automation)
- Privacy (Legal implications, Local/regional, National, Global, Data subject, Controller vs. processor, Ownership, Data inventory and retention, Right to be forgotten)

5.6 Given a scenario, implement security awareness practices.

- Phishing (Campaigns, Recognizing a phishing attempt, Responding to reported suspicious messages)
- Anomalous behavior recognition (Risky, Unexpected, Unintentional)
- User guidance and training (Policy/handbooks, Situational awareness, Insider threat, Password management, Removable media and cables, Social engineering, Operational security, Hybrid/remote work environments)
- Reporting and monitoring (Initial, Recurring)
- Development
- Execution

Organizations develop written security policies to help address the various risks that they face. These policies provide guiding principles to the professionals who implement security throughout the organization. In this chapter, we look at many of the issues covered by security policies and related documents. The topics we'll cover include change management, data protection, incident response, security governance, compliance, and awareness.

Change Management

Change happens all the time in the world of technology. Developers update applications to add new features and resolve security issues. Administrators add capacity to systems and perform major upgrades. Application owners modify configuration settings and add and remove new cloud services. All of this change has the potential to bring tremendous business value, but it also may cause disruption if it is not managed properly.

Change management programs try to bring order to the chaos of technology change. They provide a formal process for approving and carrying out changes in a manner that is coordinated with all stakeholders and designed to minimize the risks associated with the change.

Business Processes

As you design a change management program for your organization, you should address several important business process issues:

- A formal **approval process** for changes ensures that every proposed change is properly reviewed and cleared by management before it takes place.
- **Ownership** statements clearly define who is responsible for each change by designating a primary owner who will be the key decisionmaker and sponsor of the change.
- **Stakeholder analysis** identifies all the individuals and groups within the organization and outside the organization that might be affected by the change. This analysis allows

the change team to contact and coordinate with all relevant stakeholders to ensure that nobody is taken by surprise when the change occurs.

- **Impact analysis** reviews the potential effects of the change, including unintended side effects. This is a critical part of the risk management associated with the change because it forces the team to think through the implications of the change on stakeholders and technical systems.

- **Testing** confirms that the change will work as expected by carrying it out in a test environment prior to deploying the change on production systems. The test results should be included in the final change approval request.

- A **backout plan** provides a detailed sequence of steps that the team should follow if the change goes wrong. The backout plan describes how the system will be restored to a previously operational state as quickly as possible.

- **Maintenance windows** offer well-defined and coordinated times where stakeholders are aware that systems may be down due to maintenance. Standard maintenance windows normally take place during off hours (such as Sunday morning) and allow change managers to consolidate changes without making many different announcements.

All of these elements should become part of an organization's standard operating procedure for change management.

Technical Implications

Change management programs must consider the technical implications of any changes and coordinate across teams and technologies to ensure that changes occur smoothly and without unnecessary disruption. Some of the activities that should be included in the technical management of a change include:

- Updating any necessary security controls, such as firewall rules, allow/deny lists, access control lists, and other policies that may need to be adjusted to accommodate the change.

- Identifying restricted activities that may be necessary before or after the change. For example, an organization may decide to freeze new entries in the financial system for a 48-hour period surrounding a major change to that system.

- Communicating downtime expectations to key stakeholders so they may plan for the impact of outages on their business activities.

- Avoiding disruptions as much as possible by putting controls around risky activities, such as application and service restarts and modifications to legacy applications that may not have appropriate support available.

- Tracking dependencies between systems and services to identify downstream effects of current and future changes.

Documentation and Version Control

Documentation is a crucial component of any information technology environment. It provides team members with a repository of information about the way that systems and applications are designed and configured. Documentation serves as a reference for current and future team members, but the reality is that IT staff generally dislike keeping documentation updated because it is dull work.

Change management processes should ensure that changes are not closed out until all documentation and diagrams are updated to reflect the impact of the change. This ensures that future team members will understand the actual state of the operating environment.

Version control is a formal process used to track the current versions of software code and system/application configurations. When making a change, developers modify the code and check it into a version control system that deconflicts their changes with those made by other developers and also tracks the current production and testing versions of code. Most organizations use a formal version control system that is integrated into their software development processes.

Protecting Data

Every company has secrets. Keeping these secrets can often make the difference between success and failure. A company can have valuable research and development data, customer databases, proprietary information on products, and much more. If the company cannot keep private and proprietary data secret, it can directly affect its bottom line.

Data policies assist in the protection of data and help prevent data leakage. This section covers many of the different elements that a data policy may contain.

Understanding Data Types

There are many types of data that an organization must protect. Let's take a look at some of the most common types of sensitive data maintained by organizations:

- *Regulated data* is data that is governed by external laws and regulations with which the organization must comply. For example, the Payment Card Industry Data Security Standard (PCI DSS) governs the use of credit card information and various national, state, and local laws govern the use of personally identifiable information (PII)
- *Financial information* is any data about monetary transactions related to an organization or an individual. This data may also fit under the category of regulated data. For example, financial institutions in the United States are regulated by the Gramm-Leach-Bliley Act (GLBA) which restricts the use of personal financial information.

- **Intellectual property** is information that is crucial to the way that an organization runs its business. Intellectual property may consist of data that is protected by copyright, trademark, and/or patent law. **Trade secrets** are a type of intellectual property that remains sensitive and valuable to an organization because it is kept secret from competitors. For example, the famous secret formulas for Coca-Cola or Kentucky Fried Chicken are considered trade secrets.
- **Legal information** is among the most sensitive information maintained by an organization. Attorney-client privilege protects the confidentiality of that information, as long as it is also properly protected from disclosure. Legal information may include data about current or future lawsuits or other legal strategies. Disclosing this information without authorization may put the organization at risk.

When assessing data types, it is important to remember that not all information comes in human-readable form. Many databases and applications store information in binary format that is non-human-readable. This does not mean that the data is not sensitive, because anyone with the relevant application may be able to access that data if it is not also encrypted.

Classifying Data Types

As a best practice, organizations take the time to identify and classify the data they use. **Data classification systems** provide formal categories for identifying the sensitivity and criticality of data. Classification ensures that users understand the value of data, and the classifications help protect sensitive data. Classifications can apply to data in any form, such as printouts and data files.

As an example, the U.S. government uses classifications such as Top Secret, Secret, Confidential, and Unclassified to identify the sensitivity of government data. Private companies often use terms such as Public, Private, Confidential, and Restricted. The U.S. government identifies classified information using the following three levels:

- **Top secret.** If data in this category is disclosed to unauthorized entities, it could cause exceptionally grave damage to national security.
- **Secret.** If data in this category is disclosed to unauthorized entities, it could cause serious damage to national security.
- **Confidential.** If data in this category is disclosed to unauthorized entities, it could cause damage to national security.

Note that while the U.S. government has published standards for these classifications, there isn't a published standard that all private organizations use. Private organizations can use a wide variety of different terms. The classifications an organization uses are not as important as the fact that they use classifications. Organizations take time to analyze their data, classify it, and provide training to users to ensure the users recognize the value of the data. They also include these classifications within a data policy.

Any organization that has sensitive data needs to take steps to protect it. In this context, **sensitive data** is any data that isn't public and that the organization wants to protect against unauthorized access. It may be critical business information, financial data, trade secrets, customer data, or employee data. An organization may want to protect sensitive data to maintain its reputation for moral reasons, ethical reasons, or regulatory and legal reasons. The following bullets show some identifiers that private companies may use:

- **Public data** is available to anyone. It might be in brochures, press releases, or on websites.
- **Private data** is information about an individual that should remain private. Two classic examples within IT security are Personally Identifiable Information (PII) and protected health information (PHI).
- **Confidential data** is information that an organization intends to keep secret among a certain group of people. For example, most companies consider salary data confidential. Personnel within the Accounting department and some executives have access to salary data, but they keep it secret.
- **Restricted data** is another term for regulated data that is governed by outside obligations. Confidential data may also be restricted data depending upon the circumstances.

Securing Data

Data types and classifications should be used as guiding factors for the ways that an organization secures sensitive data. The more restricted a particular dataset, the more controls should be put in place to protect that information. Throughout this book, you've learned many different ways that organizations can secure data, ranging from the use of strong encryption to the deployment of data loss prevention (DLP) systems.

Organizations should also place **permission restrictions** on data that limit access to authorized users and, in some cases, may also have **geographic restrictions** that prevent users outside a defined geographic area from accessing certain information. For example, a multinational organization may have geographic restrictions in place that prevent users outside the European Union from accessing data belonging to EU residents because that access may violate European law.

Data Retention

A **data retention policy** identifies how long data is retained, and sometimes specifies where it is stored. This reduces the amount of resources, such as hard drive space or backup tapes, required to retain the data. Retention policies also help reduce legal liabilities. For example, imagine if a retention policy states that the company will only keep emails for one year. A court order requiring all emails from the company can only expect to receive email from the last year.

On the other hand, if the organization doesn't have a retention policy, it might need to provide emails from the past 10 years or longer in response to a court order. This can require an extensive amount of work by administrators to recover archives or search for specific emails. Additionally, investigations can uncover other embarrassing evidence from previous years. The retention policy helps avoid these problems.

Some laws mandate the retention of data for specific time frames, such as three years or longer. Proper data governance practices ensure that these time frames are known and followed.

Data Sanitization

Data sanitization methods ensure that data is removed or destroyed from any devices before disposing of the devices. A computing device's life cycle starts when it's put into service and ends when it is disposed of. Information also has a life cycle. It begins when the data is created and should end when the data is no longer needed. However, if computing devices aren't sanitized when they reach the end of their life cycle, unauthorized entities may gain access to the data.

Organizations may donate the hardware devices, recycle them, or sometimes just throw them away. Data sanitization procedures ensure that the devices don't include any data that might be useful to people outside your organization or damaging to your organization if unauthorized people receive it.

It's common for organizations to have a checklist to ensure that personnel sanitizes a system before disposing of it. The goal is to ensure that personnel remove all usable data from the system.

Hard drives represent the greatest risk because they hold the most information, so it's essential to take additional steps when decommissioning old hard drives. Simply deleting a file on a drive doesn't delete it. Instead, it marks the file for deletion and makes the space available for use. Similarly, formatting a disk drive doesn't erase the data. There are many recovery applications available to recover deleted data, file remnants, and data from formatted drives.

Data destruction isn't limited to only hard drives. Organizations often have a policy related to paper containing any type of sensitive data. Shredding or incinerating these papers prevents them from falling into the wrong hands. If personnel just throw this paper away, dumpster divers can sift through the trash and gain valuable information. An organization also needs to take steps to destroy other types of data, such as backup tapes, and other types of devices, such as removable media. Some common methods used to destroy data and sanitize media are:

- **File shredding.** Some applications remove all remnants of a file using a shredding technique. They do so by repeatedly overwriting the space where the file is located with 1s and 0s.
- **Wiping.** Wiping refers to the process of completely removing all remnants of data on a disk. A disk wiping tool might use a bit-level overwrite process that writes different patterns of 1s and 0s multiple times and ensures that the data on the disk is unreadable.

- **Erasing and overwriting.** Solid-state drives (SSDs) require a special process for sanitization. Because they use flash memory instead of magnetic storage platters, traditional drive wiping tools are not effective. Some organizations require personnel to destroy SSDs as the only acceptable method of sanitization, physically.

- **Paper shredding.** You can physically shred papers by passing them through a shredder. When doing so, it's best to use a cross-cut shredder that cuts the paper into fine particles. Large physical shredders can even destroy other hardware, such as disk drive platters removed from a hard disk drive.

- **Burning.** Many organizations burn materials in an incinerator. Obviously, this can be done with printed materials, but isn't as effective with all materials.

- **Pulping.** *Pulping* is an additional step taken after shredding paper. It reduces the shredded paper to mash or puree.

- **Pulverizing.** *Pulverizing* is the process of physically destroying media to sanitize it by grinding it into fine particles. Optical media is often pulverized because it is immune to degaussing methods and many shredders can't handle the size of optical media. It's also possible to remove disk platters from disk drives and physically destroy them.

- **Degaussing.** A degausser is a very powerful electronic magnet. Passing magnetic media through a *degaussing* field renders the data on tape and magnetic disk drives unreadable. Degaussing tape clears the tape and it can be reused. Degaussing magnetic hard drives destroys the drive so that it may not be reused. Degaussing is only effective against magnetic hard drives and does not work against solid state drives (SSD).

- **Third-party solutions.** Many companies provide data destruction services. As an example, you can drop off documents at almost any United Parcel Service (UPS) store and they will shred them for you. Many other companies, such as Shred-it can destroy everything from paper documents to hard drives.

It's also worth mentioning that hard drives and other media can be in devices besides just computers. For example, many copy machines include disk drives, and they can store files of anything that employees recently copied or printed. If personnel don't sanitize the drives before disposing of these devices, it can also result in a loss of confidentiality.

At the conclusion of a data destruction process, the individuals responsible for destroying data may be asked to provide a written **certification** or a Certificate of Destruction (COD) that the destruction was properly carried out. This is especially true when the work is done by third-party contractors and/or takes place off-site.

Incident Response

Many organizations create **incident response** policies to help personnel identify and respond to incidents. A **security incident** is an adverse event or series of events that can negatively affect the confidentiality, integrity, or availability of data or systems within the organization, or that has the potential to do so.

As an example, a **data breach** is a security incident where unauthorized entities access data. Common data breaches occur after an attacker gains access to a network, finds vulnerable systems holding data, and exfiltrates or extracts it.

Other examples of security incidents include cyberattacks, the release of malware, security policy violations, and inappropriate usage of systems. For example, an attack resulting in a data breach is a security incident. Once the organization identifies a security incident, it will respond based on the incident response policy.

Organizations regularly review and update the incident response policy. Reviews might occur on a routine schedule, such as annually, or in response to an incident after performing a lessons-learned review of the incident.

NIST SP 800-61 Revision 2, "Computer Security Incident Handling Guide," provides comprehensive guidance on responding to incidents. It is 79 pages long, so it's obviously more in-depth than this section, but if you want to dig deeper into any of these topics, it's an excellent resource. You'll find a copy at **https://nvlpubs.nist.gov/nistpubs/SpecialPublications/NIST.SP .800-61r2.pdf**.

Incident Response Plan

An **incident response plan** provides more detail than the incident response policy. It provides organizations with a formal, coordinated plan that personnel can use when responding to an incident. Some of the common elements included with an incident response plan include:

- **Definitions of incident types.** This section helps employees identify the difference between an event (that might or might not be a security incident) and an actual incident. Some types of incidents include attacks from botnets, malware delivered via email, data breaches, and a ransom demand after a criminal encrypts an organization's data. The plan may group these incident types using specific category definitions, such as attacks, malware infections, and data breaches.
- **Incident response team.** An incident response team is composed of employees with expertise in different areas. Organizations often refer to the team as an incident response team, a computer incident response team (CIRT), or a security incident response team. Combined, they have the knowledge and skills to respond to an incident. Due to the complex nature of incidents, the team often has extensive training. Training includes concepts such as how to identify and validate an incident, how to triage, communicate, and contain incidents, how to collect and protect evidence, how to recover from an incident, and how to become better prepared by retrospectively analyzing the incident, and reporting on findings.

- **Roles and responsibilities.** Many incident response plans identify specific roles for an incident response team along with their responsibilities. For example, an incident response team might include someone from senior management with enough authority to get things done, a network administrator or engineer with the technical expertise necessary to understand the problems, a security expert who knows how to collect and analyze evidence, and a communications expert to relay information to the public if necessary.

Communication Plan

A communication plan is part of an incident response plan, and it provides direction on how to communicate issues related to an incident. As with all elements of an incident response plan, it's important to create the communication plan before an incident. If a plan isn't in place, the wrong people may talk to the media and give the impression that the incident is causing chaos within the organization. It's common for a communication plan to include the following elements:

- **First responders.** Initial responders, such as a help-desk technician, should know when to inform incident response entities of an incident and who to contact. While a single malware infection may not seem serious, it could easily be the first hint of a significant attack or data breach. If first responders report all incidents, it increases the possibility of catching and thwarting an incident early.

- **Internal communication.** The incident response team should know when to inform senior personnel of an incident. As an example, it's unnecessary to inform the chief executive officer (CEO) of a distributed denial-of-service (DDoS) attack on a web server that is being blocked by automated response systems. Then again, it's appropriate to inform all senior management of a data breach exposing private data of thousands of customers, or serious incidents that have the potential to affect critical operations.

- **Reporting requirements.** Often, a security incident needs to be reported to external entities such as law enforcement. If customer data is exposed, customers need to be notified. Laws and regulations often drive the reporting requirements, and the incident response plan outlines who needs to be notified and when.

- **External communication.** It should be clear who can talk to external entities, such as the media. Just as important, everyone should know they should refer all external queries to the appropriate internal personnel.

- **Law enforcement.** Law enforcement personnel can often provide significant help after an incident. They typically have teams with digital forensics tools and knowledge. However, bringing in law enforcement increases the chance that the incident may get increased public scrutiny. With this mind, a communication plan will typically designate who can authorize bringing law enforcement into the picture.

- **Customer communication.** In some cases, laws dictate when an organization must inform customers of a data breach. In other cases, it becomes a judgment call. Because informing (or not informing) customers of an incident may affect an organization's reputation, a communication plan may designate senior executives as the only people authorized to approve this communication.

 Remember This!

An incident response policy defines a security incident and incident response procedures. Incident response procedures start with preparation to prepare for and prevent incidents. Preparation helps prevent incidents such as malware infections. Personnel review the policy periodically and in response to lessons learned after incidents.

Incident Response Process

Incident response includes multiple phases. It starts with creating an incident response policy and an incident response plan. With the plan in place, personnel are trained and given the tools necessary to handle incidents. Incident response preparation will help an organization prevent or effectively contain and recover from incidents.

The phases of an incident response process are:

- **Preparation.** This phase occurs before an incident and provides guidance to personnel on how to respond to an incident. It includes establishing and maintaining an incident response plan and incident response procedures. It also includes establishing procedures to prevent incidents. For example, preparation includes implementing security controls to prevent malware infections.
- **Detection.** During normal operations, the security team monitors network, system, application, and user behavior, watching for unusual activity. This is normally coordinated by an organization's security operations center (SOC) through the use of tools like security information and event management (SIEM) systems, security orchestration, automation and response (SOAR) systems, extended detection and response (XDR) systems, network detection and response (NDR) systems, intrusion detection and prevention systems (IDS/IPS), data loss prevention (DLP) systems, and related technologies such as user and entity behavior analytics (UEBA) systems.
- **Analysis.** All detected events aren't security incidents, so when a potential incident is reported, personnel take the time to verify it is an actual incident. For example, intrusion detection systems (IDSs) might falsely report an intrusion, but administrators would investigate it and verify if it is a false positive or an incident. After confirming an incident, personnel might try to isolate the system based on established procedures.

- **Containment.** After an incident analysis and verification, security personnel attempt to isolate or contain it. This protects critical systems while maintaining business operations. Containment might include quarantining a device or removing it from the network. This can be as simple as unplugging the system's network interface card to ensure it can't communicate on the network. Similarly, you can isolate a network from the Internet by modifying access control lists on a router or a network firewall. This is similar to how you'd respond to water spilling from an overflowing sink. You wouldn't start cleaning up the water until you first turn off the faucet. The goal of isolation is to prevent the problem from spreading to other areas or other computers in your network or to simply stop the attack.

- **Eradication.** After containing the incident, it's often necessary to remove components from the attack. For example, if attackers installed malware on systems, it's important to remove all remnants of the malware on all hosts within the organization. Similarly, an attack might have been launched from one or more compromised accounts. Eradication would include deleting or disabling these accounts.

- **Recovery.** During the recovery process, administrators return all affected systems to normal operation and verify they are operating normally. This might include rebuilding systems from images, restoring data from backups, and installing updates. Additionally, if administrators have identified the vulnerabilities that caused the incident, they typically take steps to remove the vulnerabilities.

- **Lessons learned.** After handling an incident, security personnel perform a lessons-learned review. The incident may provide some valuable lessons, and the organization might modify procedures or add additional controls to prevent a reoccurrence of the incident. Part of this process normally includes a **_root cause analysis_** that tries to identify what initially went wrong that allowed an incident to occur. The lessons-learned review might indicate a need to provide additional training to users or indicate a need to update the incident response policy. The goal is to learn from the incident and prevent a future reoccurrence of a similar incident.

★ *Remember This!*

The first step in the incident response process is preparation. Next, the organization detects security incidents that occur and analyzes their effects. After identifying an incident, personnel attempt to contain the problem to protect critical systems while maintaining business operations. Eradication attempts to remove all malicious components from an attack, and recovery returns affected systems to normal operation. Reviewing lessons learned allows personnel to analyze the incident and the response to help prevent a future occurrence.

Incident Response Training and Testing

Training and testing play important roles in ensuring the effectiveness of incident response plans. This includes both tabletop exercises and simulations, both of which provide different yet complementary aspects of training.

Tabletop exercises are a type of scenario-based training where participants discuss and analyze a hypothetical incident in a non-threatening environment. This is like a game of chess where you anticipate your opponent's moves and plan your strategy accordingly. In a cybersecurity context, a tabletop exercise could involve a simulated phishing attack or data breach. The incident response team would then discuss the steps they would take to respond to the incident based on the existing incident response plan. The goal is to identify gaps in the plan and refine it based on the insights gained from the exercise.

Simulations, on the other hand, are a more hands-on form of training. Instead of discussing hypothetical situations, simulations involve recreating real-world incidents as closely as possible. This provides the incident response team with practical experience in responding to an incident. Simulations are particularly valuable for training personnel on complex or unusual incidents that can't be easily replicated in a live environment.

Both tabletop exercises and simulations are critical in ensuring an effective incident response. Tabletop exercises allow teams to discuss strategies and refine their plans, while simulations give teams the opportunity to apply their plans in practice. By conducting regular training and testing, organizations can better prepare themselves for the real-world incidents they will inevitably face.

Threat Hunting

Threat hunting is like being a detective in the digital world. It's when skilled computer security experts actively search for sneaky cyber threats that might have slipped past regular security systems. Instead of just waiting for an alarm to go off, these experts go out and look for clues that might suggest a cyber invader is up to no good.

The aim of threat hunting is to catch these cyber invaders as quickly as possible. The quicker you find them, the less damage they can do. This is important because sometimes these cyber invaders can sneak into a network and hide there, causing problems without being noticed for a long time.

To track down these hidden threats, threat hunters use a mix of special tools and techniques. They may use things like threat intelligence feeds which provide regularly updated 'most wanted' lists of cyber threats. They also use smart systems that can spot when users or computers are behaving oddly, which might suggest a cyber invader is at work.

Understanding Digital Forensics

Organizations implement **digital forensics** techniques when collecting information after an incident. These help an organization collect and analyze data as evidence it can use to prosecute a crime. In general, forensic evaluations proceed with the assumption that the data collected will be used as evidence in court. Because of this, forensic practices ensure that evidence is controlled and not modified during the collection or analysis of digital data.

Once an incident has been contained or isolated, the next step is a forensic evaluation. What do you think of when you hear forensics? Many people think about the TV program CSI (short for "crime scene investigation") and all its spin-offs. These shows demonstrate the phenomenal capabilities of science in criminal investigations.

Computer forensics techniques analyze evidence from computers to gather details on computer incidents, similar to how CSI personnel analyze evidence from crime scenes. Forensic experts use a variety of different tools to gather and analyze computer evidence. Although you might not be the computer forensics expert collecting or analyzing evidence, you should know some of the basic concepts related to gathering and preserving the evidence.

Acquisition and Preservation

When performing data acquisition for digital forensics, it's important to follow specific procedures to ensure that the data is not modified. In many cases, this ensures that the evidence is preserved in case it is needed in a legal proceeding. The following sections provide more information on common procedures.

Order of Volatility

Order of volatility refers to the order in which you should collect evidence. Volatile doesn't mean it's explosive, but rather that it is not permanent. In general, you should collect evidence starting with the most volatile and moving to the least volatile.

For example, data in random access memory (RAM) is lost after powering down a computer. Because of this, it is important to realize you shouldn't power a computer down if you suspect it has been involved in a security incident and might hold valuable evidence.

A processor can only work on data in RAM, so all the data in RAM indicates what the system was doing. This includes data that users have been working on, system processes, network processes, application remnants, and much more. All of this can be valuable evidence in an investigation, but if a rookie technician turns the computer off, the evidence is lost.

In contrast, data on a disk drive remains on the drive even after powering a system down. This includes any files and even low-level data such as the Master Boot Record on a drive. The order of volatility from most volatile to least volatile is:

- **Cache.** This is data in the cache memory, including the processor cache and hard drive cache. Data in the cache is removed as new data is used.
- **RAM.** Data in RAM is used by the operating system (OS) and applications.
- **Swap file or pagefile.** A swap file (sometimes called a pagefile) is an extension of RAM and is stored on the system hard drive. However, the pagefile isn't a typical file, and the system rebuilds the pagefile when rebooting. This makes the pagefile more volatile than other files stored on hard drives.
- **Disk.** Data files are stored on local disk drives, and they remain there even after rebooting a system.
- **Attached devices** such as USB drives will also hold data when a system is powered down.
- **Network.** Networks typically have servers and shared folders accessible by users and used to store log files. These remote systems often have more robust backup policies in place, making them the least volatile.

> ### ★ Remember This!
>
> When collecting data for forensic analysis, you should collect it from the most volatile to the least volatile. The order of volatility is cache memory, regular RAM, swap file (or paging file), hard drive data, and data stored on network systems.

Data Acquisition

When performing data acquisition for evidence, it's important to follow specific procedures to ensure that the evidence is not modified. Following the order of volatility, you prevent destroying the data before you collect it. It's also important to know the location of additional forensic data.

Security experts sometimes use **snapshots** to capture data for forensic analysis. Various tools are available to capture snapshots of memory (including cache memory), disk contents, cloud-based storage, and more.

Forensic **artifacts** are pieces of data on a device that regular users are unaware of, but digital forensic experts can identify and extract. In general, logs and data files show direct content, but the artifacts are not so easy to see. Some examples are:

- **Web history.** This includes both pages visited and searches.
- **Recycle bin.** You can view the content of deleted files and the metadata of deleted files.

- **Windows error reporting.** These often give insight into what programs were running when a system crashed.
- **Remote desktop protocol (RDP) cache.** This can provide useful information if an attacker moves laterally through a network, or when an attacker is connecting to a system from an Internet server.

OS forensics refers to the process of collecting data from the OS. This includes things like the cache, RAM, swap files, and artifacts. It can also include much more depending on the operating system. As an example, the Windows Registry includes a wealth of information on installed applications and holds user data to enhance the user experience. Linux doesn't have a registry, but many Linux applications do store data in text-based configuration files.

Firmware forensic methods are useful when a forensic specialist suspects malware has infected firmware. It starts by extracting the firmware code. It then attempts to reverse engineer the code to discover what it is doing. In some cases, the firmware has a backdoor embedded in it that attackers can exploit. In other cases, the firmware has malicious code embedded within it.

Forensic Tools

Forensic specialists have a wide variety of tools available to acquire, preserve, and analyze evidence. These tools use special techniques to ensure the data is not changed while forensic specialists are collecting it.

Capturing Data

A forensic image of captured data will collect the data without modifying it at all. This includes data within the cache, RAM, and entire disk drives. Some tools use bit-by-bit copy methods that can read the data without modifying it. Other methods include hardware devices, such as a write-blocker, connected to the system to write-protect it during the copy process.

These methods capture the entire contents of the disk, including system files, user files, and files marked for deletion but not overwritten. Similarly, many tools, such as FTK Imager, include the ability to capture data within volatile memory and save it as an image.

After capturing an image, experts create a copy and analyze the copy. They do not analyze the original disk and often don't even analyze the original image. They understand that by analyzing the contents of a disk directly, they can modify the contents. By creating and analyzing forensic copies, they never modify the original evidence.

One of the oldest disk imaging tools used for forensics is the **dd** command (short for data duplicator) available in Linux systems, including Kali Linux. It can also be installed on Windows systems.

Kali Linux includes the Volatility Framework, which is a collection of open-source tools used to capture and extract memory contents and digital artifacts.

One of the tools included with Kali is **memdump** (short for memory dumper), which can dump any addressable memory space to the terminal or redirect the output to a dump file.

WinHex is a Windows-based hexadecimal editor used for evidence gathering, data analysis, editing, recovery of data, and data removal. It can work with data on all drives, such as hard drives, CDs, and DVDs. It can also work directly with memory. It is a proprietary tool.

FTK Imager is part of the Forensic Toolkit (FTK) suite of products sold by Exterro. It can capture an image of a disk as a single file or multiple files and save the image in various formats. It also gives you the option of creating images of individual folders or files. After capturing the image, it allows you to view and analyze data within the image.

Autopsy is a graphical user interface (GUI) digital forensics platform. It allows users to add command-line utilities from The Sleuth Kit (TSK). The Sleuth Kit includes forensics tools that can be used to analyze data on Windows, Linux, and macOS operating systems.

Verifying Integrity

Hashes and checksums are important elements of forensic analysis to provide proof that collected data has retained integrity. Chapter 10, "Understanding Cryptography and PKI," covers hashes and checksums. As a reminder, a hash is simply a character string that summarizes a larger data file. You can execute a particular hashing algorithm against data as many times as you want, and if the data is the same, the hash will be the same. The focus in Chapter 10 is on using hashes with files and messages. A captured forensic image (from RAM or a disk) is just a file, and you can use hashing with forensic images to ensure image integrity.

For example, after capturing an image of a disk, with a write-blocker connected, an expert can create a hash or checksum of the image. The expert can then write-protect the image to prevent accidental modifications during the analysis. Later, the expert can take another hash of the image and compare it with the original hash. If both hashes are the same, it proves that the image is the same, and the analysis did not modify it.

Forensic analysts sometimes make a copy of the image to analyze, instead of analyzing the first image they capture. If they ever need to verify the integrity of the copy, they run the same hashing algorithm against it. Again, if the hash is the same, they know the analyzed data is the same as the captured data.

Similarly, some tools allow you to create a hash of an entire drive. These verify that the imaging process has not modified data. For example, you can create a hash of a drive before capturing the image and after capturing the image. If the hashes are the same, it verifies that the imaging process did not modify the drive.

Legal Holds and Electronic Discovery

A **legal hold** refers to a legal obligation to maintain different types of data as evidence. As an example, imagine that ZiffCorp is being sued for fraud and the Securities and Exchange Commission is investigating ZiffCorp. When ZiffCorp believes that a lawsuit is likely, they are then obligated to issue a legal hold to their employees that prevents them from destroying digital or paper records that may be related to the case. ZiffCorp now needs to take steps to preserve the data.

This data may include emails, databases, logs, backup tapes, data stored on servers in file shares and document libraries, and data stored on desktop computers, laptops, tablets, and smartphones owned by the company. The first step management needs to take is to direct the data custodians to preserve this data. On the surface, this might sound easy, but it can be tremendously complex, especially if it is not clear to data custodians what data should be maintained. They might preserve too much data, resulting in a high cost to store it. They might preserve too little data, subjecting the company to more litigation in a suspected cover-up.

Electronic discovery, or **eDiscovery**, is the identification and collection of electronically stored information. This includes files of any kind, including email and voicemail messages, social media entries, and website data.

When collecting this data, it's vital to preserve the metadata related to all the files. Metadata is data about data instead of the data itself. It's common to use digital forensic processes to collect the data. This ensures that the files and the associated metadata aren't modified during the collection. The following list identifies some metadata that can be useful during an investigation:

- **File.** File metadata includes items such as when a file was created, who created it, when it was modified, and when it was last accessed.
- **Email.** Email metadata includes items such as the header, who sent it, who they sent it to, and when they sent it.
- **Web.** Web metadata includes items in the header (or head) of a webpage, such as the title, the character set, and any other information developers add in the meta tag.
- **Mobile.** Mobile device metadata is often a treasure trove of evidence for investigators. It includes users' location (tracked through apps), who they called, who called them, who they messaged, and who messaged them, website history, and more.

Admissibility of Documentation and Evidence

When collecting documentation and evidence, it's essential to follow specific procedures to ensure that the evidence is admissible in a court of law. If personnel don't follow proper procedures, the evidence won't be admissible. Following proper procedures also ensures that personnel control the evidence after collecting it, maintaining an unaltered original.

This evidence often supports non-repudiation. It includes proof that individuals were involved in an incident, preventing them from believably denying they were involved.

Admittedly, every security incident won't end up in court. However, at the beginning of an investigation, it's almost impossible to know if it will go to court. Because of this, it's important to treat every incident as if it will go to court, and personnel follow all relevant procedures.

The **chain of custody** is a process that provides assurances that evidence has been controlled and appropriately handled after collection. Forensic experts establish a chain of custody when they first collect evidence.

Security professionals use a chain of custody form to document this control. The chain of custody form provides a record of every person who was in possession of a physical asset collected as evidence. It shows who had custody of the evidence and where it was stored the entire time since collection. Additionally, personnel often tag the evidence as part of a chain of custody process. A proper chain of custody process ensures that evidence presented in a court of law is the same evidence that security professionals collected.

As an example, imagine that Homer collected a hard drive as part of an investigation. However, instead of establishing a chain of custody, he stores the drive on his desk, intending to analyze it the next day. Is it possible that someone could modify the contents of the drive overnight? Absolutely. Instead, he should immediately establish a chain of custody and lock the drive in a secure storage location.

If evidence is not controlled, someone can modify, tamper with, or corrupt it. Courts will rule the evidence inadmissible if there is a lack of adequate control, or even a lack of documentation showing that personnel maintained adequate control. However, the chain of custody provides proof that personnel handled the evidence properly.

Reporting

After analyzing all the relevant evidence, digital forensic experts create a report documenting their findings.

These often document the tactics, techniques, and procedures (TTP) used in an attack. There aren't any specific requirements for the report, but there are some common things you may see, such as:

- An executive summary listing the findings and recommendations
- A list of the forensic tools used in the investigation
- A list of evidence collected and analyzed
- The findings derived from analyzing each piece of the evidence
- Recommendations based on the findings

A digital forensic analysis report isn't meant to be a legal document. However, if the case goes to court, legal personnel are sure to review every line. The report needs to be technically accurate and focus on the findings that justify the recommendations. If other experts identify any errors in the reported findings, it can result in the entire report being viewed as tainted.

Understanding SOAR

A trend in incident response is the use of **Security Orchestration, Automation, and Response (SOAR)** tools to respond to low-level security events automatically. The key is that SOAR tools respond automatically, which frees up administrators to focus on other administrative and cybersecurity tasks. A SOAR platform is typically a combination of tools that can work together to detect and respond to suspicious activity.

As a simple example, SOAR tools can examine and respond to phishing emails, reducing the amount of time needed by personnel to investigate them. By looking at email elements, such as the header, embedded URLs, and attachments, it's possible to detect suspicious emails. These can be forwarded to other tools to investigate further. For example, a SOAR tool can open attachments within a sandbox and observe the activity. Another SOAR tool may dissect the header looking for discrepancies common in phishing emails such as spoofed email addresses.

When the SOAR platform verifies an email is malicious, it can automatically respond. The response is dependent on the organization's available tools and internal guidelines. It may include quarantining or deleting the email and blocking access to the embedded URLs.

Similarly, it's common for a network with Internet traffic to experience a lot of potentially malicious traffic. When a tool raises an alarm, administrators often must go through the same steps to verify if the threat is real or not. If it is, they usually repeat the same steps to mitigate the threat. In contrast, a SOAR platform can do these same steps automatically to verify if the threat is real or not, and if it is real, implement the appropriate steps to mitigate it.

SOAR platforms use **playbooks** and **runbooks**. In general terms, a playbook provides general guidelines, and a runbook provides the technical details to implement the playbook guidelines.

Playbooks

As an example, a playbook for phishing may include a checklist of what to check within a suspected phishing email. It may look for discrepancies between the Reply to and the From addresses, indicating a spoofed email. If it has an attachment, it may dictate that the email needs to be forwarded to another system, which opens the attachment within a sandbox.

These steps document formal procedures to follow for well-known incidents. They typically identify the same steps that human administrators should take for each suspected incident. Of course, humans can make mistakes even when there is a checklist, but automating the playbook reduces potential human error. Appendix A of NIST SP 800-184 provides a checklist of items to include in a playbook.

Although some playbooks can trigger automated actions, they typically document the steps to take in response to the action, and let the runbook automate the response.

Runbooks

Runbooks implement the guidelines documented in the playbooks using the available tools within the organization. As an example, if a phishing email has discrepancies in the header indicating it is a phishing email, it can implement a rule to quarantine or delete the email. If it has an attachment, it can forward the email to a system that can automatically open the attachment within a sandbox.

Ideally, a runbook can automatically respond to all potential incidents. However, there are times when a runbook may instead assign the task to an administrator to investigate.

> ★ *Remember This!*
>
> Security Orchestration, Automation, and Response (SOAR) platforms use internal tools to respond to low-level security events automatically, reducing administrator workload. A SOAR playbook provides a checklist of things to check for suspected incidents. A SOAR runbook implements the playbook checklist using available tools within the organization.

Security Governance

Security governance is the set of responsibilities and processes established by an organization's top-level management to direct, evaluate, and control the organization's security efforts. It provides the framework and structure for making decisions about the organization's security. Security governance involves setting the strategic direction for security, aligning security goals with the organization's broader goals, and ensuring that security risks are appropriately managed.

Governance Structures

The governance structure of an organization may include various boards, committees, and government entities, each playing a unique role in shaping security practices. This structure can be centralized or decentralized, depending on the organization's size and complexity.

Boards often consist of executives and high-ranking individuals within the organization who make critical decisions about security policy and strategy. **Committees** are usually specialized groups focusing on specific aspects of security, such as risk management or compliance. **Government entities** might have a role if the organization operates in a heavily regulated industry or if it deals with sensitive data like protected health information or national security matters.

Centralized governance structures concentrate decision-making authority at the top of the organization. This approach can lead to consistent security policies and practices across the entire organization. In contrast, **decentralized structures** allow different parts of the organization to make their own security decisions. While this can enable quicker responses to local challenges, it can also lead to inconsistencies in security practices.

External Considerations

In setting up and managing security governance, organizations need to take into account a range of external considerations. These may include regulatory requirements, legal obligations, industry standards, and the security environment at local, regional, national, and global levels.

Regulatory requirements may be imposed by government bodies and may dictate specific security measures or standards that organizations need to follow. Legal considerations can involve matters like data privacy laws, which can have significant implications for how an organization handles personal data.

Industry standards are often developed by professional associations and can provide benchmarks for best practices in security. Local, regional, national, and global security environments can impact an organization's security strategy. For example, the prevalence of cyber threats in a certain region or country might influence the kinds of security measures an organization decides to implement.

Security Policies

Security policies are written documents that lay out a security plan within a company. They are one of many administrative controls used to reduce and manage risk. When created early enough, they help ensure that personnel implement security throughout the life cycle of various systems in the company. When employees follow the policies and procedures, they help prevent incidents, data loss, and theft.

Policies include brief, high-level statements that identify goals based on an organization's overall beliefs and principles. After creating the policy, personnel within the organization create procedures to support the policies. Although the policies are often high-level statements, the procedures provide details on policy implementation.

A security policy can be a single large document or be divided into several smaller documents, depending on the needs of the company. The following sections identify many of the common elements of a security policy.

Let's look at some of the common security policies found in most organizations:

- **Acceptable Use Policies (AUP)** describe the purpose of computer systems and networks, how users can access them, and the responsibilities of users when they access the systems. It's common for organizations to require users to read and sign a document indicating they understand the acceptable use policy when they're hired and in conjunction with annual security training. Other methods, such as logon banners or periodic emails, help reinforce an AUP.

- **Information Security Policies** protect an organization's data and information systems. They define the rules for how to manage, protect, and distribute information. They might include rules about password complexity, rules about handling sensitive data, and guidelines for safe internet usage.

- **Business Continuity and Disaster Recovery Policies** outline the steps an organization should take to continue operations in the event of a major disruption or disaster. They include plans for data backup, data recovery, and the restoration of IT infrastructure. They also outline roles and responsibilities for personnel during and after a disaster.

- **Incident Response Policies** provide rules for how the organization will respond to a security incident, such as a data breach or cyberattack. They outline the steps to take when an incident occurs, who is responsible for each step, and how to communicate during and after the incident. They also outline procedures for analyzing the incident to prevent similar ones in the future.

- **Software Development Lifecycle (SDLC) Policies** provide structure for how software should be developed within the organization. They outline the phases of software development and detail the security measures that should be taken at each phase. They may also provide standards for code quality and testing procedures.

- **Change Management Policies** outline how changes to IT systems, applications, and networks should be managed within the organization. They specify how to request a change, who needs to approve it, how to test and implement the change, and how to document the entire process. These policies help ensure that changes don't unintentionally introduce security vulnerabilities or disrupt operations.

Security Standards

Security policies are typically high-level documents that set forth general requirements without getting into specific details. This allows them to remain fairly constant even when technology and the business changes. **Security standards**, on the other hand, are where the details surface. Security standards outline technical and business requirements for security.

Some common security standards include:

- **Password standards** specify the requirements for creating secure passwords in the organization. They might include rules about the minimum and maximum length of passwords, complexity requirements (like the use of uppercase and lowercase letters, numbers, and special characters), password expiration intervals, and restrictions against using easily guessed or common passwords.
- **Access control standards** set rules for who can access the organization's information systems and resources and to what extent. They might specify user roles, mandatory access controls, discretionary access controls, and least privilege principles. They may also detail the procedures for granting, modifying, and revoking access rights.
- **Physical security standards** lay out the requirements for protecting physical assets like buildings, server rooms, data centers, and equipment. They can include standards for door locks, alarm systems, security cameras, visitor management, and protection against environmental hazards like fire and flooding.
- **Encryption standards** outline the methods and protocols to be used for encrypting sensitive data in the organization. They may specify approved encryption algorithms, key lengths, key management practices, and procedures for encrypting data at rest, in transit, and in use.

Security Procedures

As mentioned earlier, security policies are high-level statements, while security standards get into the technical details of requirements. Security procedures go to the next level of detail, providing very specific step-by-step instructions for carrying out security-related tasks.

Some examples of security procedures include:

- **Change management procedures** describe how requests, approvals, and change implementations are to be carried out under the organization's change management program.
- **Onboarding procedures** describe how a new hire is granted access to an organization's computing resources. This includes providing the employee with a user account and granting access to appropriate resources. One of the key considerations during the onboarding process is to follow the principle of least privilege. In other words, it's appropriate to grant the new employees access to what they need for their job, but no more.
- **Offboarding procedures** describe how to remove an employee's access when they leave the company. This includes disabling the user's account or deleting it depending on company policy. It also includes collecting equipment (such as corporate-owned smartphones, tablets, or laptops), and security badge or proximity card the organization issued to the employee. This is more than just a cost issue. Equipment often has proprietary data, and the company needs to take steps to protect the data. Additionally, smart cards and proximity cards can allow individuals access to protected areas.

Security Guidelines

While security policies, standards, and procedures are all mandatory for employees to follow, *security guidelines* are optional sets of best practices that may help employees carry out their work. You can think of policies, standards, and procedures as the "rules of the road" for cybersecurity within an organization. Guidelines, on the other hand, are just friendly advice.

For example, a security guideline might give employees advice on how to best implement encryption on a laptop device. There might be several different ways to meet the requirements of the organization's encryption policy and standards, but the guideline shares wisdom on the most effective way to get the job done.

Data Governance

Data governance refers to the processes an organization uses to manage, process, and protect data. At a basic level, organizations attempt to ensure that data is stored consistently, even in different databases. This improves the data quality and allows an organization to integrate data from multiple databases and efficiently perform in-depth analysis. However, data governance encompasses much more than just data consistency. It also includes methods used to manage the availability, usability, integrity, and security of data used by an organization.

Critical data is data that is critical to the success of a mission within an organization. This can be the primary mission of the entire organization or any specific function within the organization. Proper data governance practices ensure that critical data elements within an organization are identified. Once they are identified, additional data governance processes can be implemented to manage the availability, usability, integrity, and security of the critical data.

> ★ *Remember This!*
>
> Data governance refers to the processes an organization uses to manage, process, and protect data. Some data governance methods help ensure or improve the quality of data. Other methods are driven by regulations and laws. Proper data governance practices ensure that critical data elements are identified.

Data Roles

In the world of data governance, it's crucial to understand the various roles that are involved in the handling and protection of data. Each role has its unique responsibilities and functions, contributing to the overall security and integrity of the data. Let's explore these roles and their specific duties and impacts on data governance and security:

- **Data owner.** Data owners have primary responsibility for a specific type of data within the organization. The data owner is typically a senior executive responsible for the area with oversight of the data. Data owners ensure that data is classified correctly and ensuring that it is labeled to match the classification. They are also responsible for ensuring adequate security controls protect the data. While they often delegate day-to-day tasks to data stewards and custodians, they cannot delegate their high-level responsibility.

- **Data steward.** Data owners typically have senior-level positions and can't do the day-to-day work of data governance. For this reason, they typically delegate authority to data stewards on their teams who are responsible for carrying out the intent of the data owner's requirements.

- **Data custodian.** Data custodians are responsible for routine daily tasks such as backing up data, storage of the data, and implementation of business rules. As an example, a database administrator (DBA) would be the data custodian for all data contained within databases the DBA oversees. The data custodian is typically an IT professional, while the data steward is typically a business manager.

- **Data controller.** If your organization collects information from your employees to carry out payroll operations, that makes your organization the data controller for that employee information.

- **Data processor.** Data processors are third-party organizations that use and manipulate the data on behalf of the data controller. A payroll company would accept the personal data from the data controller and use it to process payroll functions.

Monitoring and Revision

Effective security governance is not a one-time task. Instead, it involves regular monitoring and revision to ensure that the organization's security efforts continue to align with its goals and keep up with evolving threats and regulatory changes. Monitoring involves continuously checking the effectiveness of the organization's security measures, while revision involves adjusting policies, standards, and procedures as needed based on the results of monitoring.

Monitoring could involve a variety of activities, including routine security audits, regular reviews of access logs, ongoing vulnerability scanning, and analysis of incident response metrics. The insights gained from these activities can highlight areas where the organization's security measures are working well and identify areas where improvements are needed.

Revision is the process of updating security governance documents and practices based on the insights gained from monitoring. Revisions might be needed for several reasons. For example, if monitoring reveals that a particular security measure isn't effectively mitigating a risk, the relevant policy or standard may need to be updated. Or if a new regulatory requirement comes into play, the organization may need to revise its policies, standards, or procedures to ensure compliance.

Additionally, if the organization's strategic goals or operating environment change, its security governance may need to be revised to stay aligned.

Through regular monitoring and revision, an organization can ensure that its security governance remains relevant, effective, and compliant, and that it continues to support the organization's overall goals and strategy.

Third-Party Risk Management

Organizations interact with entities outside the organization (commonly called third parties) for various reasons, such as purchasing supplies, creating partnerships, and more. These relationships can often introduce risks that need to be managed, and security policies sometimes address these risks.

Supply Chain and Vendors

A **supply chain** includes all the elements required to produce and sell products and services. In some cases, the supply chain becomes an attack vector. By exploiting vulnerabilities in the supply chain, attackers can impact the primary organization. Organizations should regularly conduct a **supply chain analysis** that identifies all of the vendors that make up their supply chain and assesses any risks associated with those relationships.

Supply chain policies vary depending on the vendors. A vendor is an entity in the supply chain that provides goods or services to an organization. In general, it's best to limit the amount of access that vendors have to internal networks or data to only what they need, and vendor management systems provide vendors with limited access. Vendors often need to provide feedback to an organization, such as order status, and vendor management systems provide vendors with limited system integration. As an example, some organizations use web-based applications, allowing vendors to enter data. These web-based applications limit access with credentials. Additionally, these web applications have limited integration with internal systems.

Organizations sometimes implement policies requiring **vendor diversity** to provide cybersecurity resilience. Using more than one vendor for the same supply reduces the organization's risk if that vendor can no longer provide the product or service.

Supply chain policies will also provide guidelines on limiting vendor access to an organization's network and data. The goal is to limit damage to the organization if an attacker exploits a vendor. Vendor management policies include limiting system integration and understanding when vendor support stops.

When working with vendors, it's also important to be aware of **end of life (EOL)** and **end of service life (EOSL)** policies. EOL generally refers to the date when a product will no longer be offered for sale. You can think of this as the shelf life of the product. EOSL indicates the date when you expect a lack of vendor support because vendors no longer create patches or upgrades to resolve vulnerabilities for the product.

Attack on Vendor Exposes Customer Data

M. J. Brunner, Inc., is a software development and marketing agency and is a vendor for multiple companies. They developed and maintained the online enrollment portal of SEI Investments Co., a vendor for other clients such as Pacific Investment Management Co. (PIMCO), Fortress Investment Group LLC, and more. In May 2020, attackers launched a successful ransomware attack against M. J. Brunner, Inc. Before encrypting the data, attackers exfiltrated it and gained access to customer data from SEI Investments Co. and their clients.

In this case, attackers accessed PIMCO investor data, but not due to a vulnerability at PIMCO. It wasn't even due to a vulnerability of their vendor, SEI Investments Co. Instead, this ransomware attack on M. J. Brunner, Inc., caused this data breach.

Attackers reportedly collected information such as names, usernames, emails, physical addresses, and phone numbers. While attackers may not have collected passwords in this data breach, they could still use the other information to target individuals in smishing, vishing, or phishing attacks.

Vendor Assessment

Cloud providers are expected to implement rigorous safeguards to protect the data they maintain and ensure the security of the services they provide. However, this isn't always readily visible, prompting customers to increasingly demand that contracts include a **right-to-audit clause**. This clause permits the customer to hire an auditor to review the cloud provider's records and systems.

Auditing can assist the customer in ensuring that the cloud provider is executing sufficient security measures. In addition to audits, customers can also request evidence of internal audits, where the provider assesses their own security measures and practices, demonstrating their commitment to maintaining security integrity.

Penetration testing can also be included in the vendor assessment process. Penetration testing is a simulated cyberattack on the system to check for vulnerabilities. This allows the cloud provider to identify and address potential security weaknesses before they can be exploited by malicious actors.

Customers may also demand independent assessments to provide an unbiased evaluation of the cloud provider's security measures. Independent assessments can provide an extra layer of assurance that the cloud provider is adhering to industry-standard security practices.

In addition to these evaluations, the use of security questionnaires can be beneficial. These are comprehensive questionnaires that the cloud provider must complete, detailing their security practices and measures in place. It gives the customer a clear view of the provider's security infrastructure and helps in making informed decisions.

Customers should also engage in ongoing monitoring of the cloud provider's services. This ongoing vigilance helps ensure that the provider maintains a consistent security posture, promptly addresses any emerging threats, and continually meets the customer's security expectations.

Incorporating these elements in the vendor assessment can offer a comprehensive understanding of the cloud provider's security landscape. It also helps the customer verify that the cloud provider is implementing the advertised security controls and maintaining high standards of data protection and service security.

Vendor Selection

When selecting a new vendor, **due diligence** is a critical step to ensure that you're partnering with a trustworthy and competent provider. Conducting due diligence involves a thorough evaluation of potential vendors' capabilities, credentials, reputation, and financial stability.

Start with assessing the vendor's history and reputation in the marketplace. Consider factors such as their years of experience, the range of their clientele, and any case studies or testimonials they can provide. Additionally, consider their financial health as a sign of their ability to provide stable, long-term service.

As part of due diligence, review potential vendors' security and compliance practices. Check their compliance with necessary standards and regulations, and evaluate their response to security breaches, if any. It's also essential to review their data handling and privacy policies to ensure they align with your organization's requirements and values.

Penetration testing and independent assessments, as discussed in the previous section, also form an integral part of due diligence. These assessments provide a realistic view of a vendor's security posture and readiness to tackle cyber threats.

In parallel to due diligence, it's crucial to assess potential **conflicts of interest**. A conflict of interest might arise if the vendor has business relationships that could influence their decision-making or compromise their ability to prioritize your organization's needs. For instance, a vendor may have an affiliation with a competitor or may be offering services to entities that could conflict with your organizational goals or principles.

Ensure that the vendor discloses all such relationships and assess whether they pose a risk to your organization. It's important to have contractual clauses that address these potential conflicts and provide solutions or exit strategies in case a conflict does occur.

Vendor Agreements

Organizations often utilize different types of agreements to help identify various responsibilities. Organizations use them when working with other organizations, but they can also use them when working with different departments within the same organization. These include:

- **Service level agreement (SLA).** An SLA is an agreement between a company and a vendor that stipulates performance expectations, such as minimum uptime and maximum downtime levels. Organizations use SLAs when contracting services from service providers, such as Internet Service Providers (ISPs). Many SLAs include a monetary penalty if the vendor is unable to meet the agreed-upon expectations.

- **Memorandum of understanding (MOU).** An MOU, sometimes called a **memorandum of agreement (MOA)**, expresses an understanding between two or more parties indicating their intention to work together toward a common goal. You can also compare an MOU with an SLA because it defines the responsibilities of each of the parties. However, it is less formal than an SLA and does not include monetary penalties.

- **Business partners agreement (BPA).** A BPA is a written agreement that details the relationship between business partners, including their obligations toward the partnership. It typically identifies the shares of profits or losses each partner will take, their responsibilities to each other, and what to do if a partner chooses to leave the partnership. One of the primary benefits of a BPA is that it can help settle conflicts when they arise.

- A **non-disclosure agreement (NDA)** is used between two entities to ensure that proprietary data is not disclosed to unauthorized entities. For example, imagine BizzFad wants to collaborate with Costington's on a project. BizzFad management realizes they need to share proprietary data with Costington's personnel, but they want to ensure that the distribution of the data is limited. The NDA is a legal document that BizzFad can use to hold Costington's legally responsible if the proprietary data is shared. Similarly, many organizations use an NDA to prohibit employees from sharing proprietary data either while they are employed or after leaving the organization. It's common to remind employees of an existing NDA during offboarding or an exit interview.

- **Master Services Agreements (MSA)** provide structure to the agreements for vendors that you will work with repeatedly. Instead of writing separate full contracts for each project, you write a single MSA that contains all of the general terms. Then, when you have a new project for the vendor, you write a simple **work order (WO)** or a **statement of work (SOW)** that contains the details of that specific project and references the general terms in the MSA.

- **Rules of engagement** are particularly important when a vendor will be conducting security testing activities on your behalf. The rules of engagement specify what the vendor is, and is not, allowed to do during their testing.

Security Compliance

Security professionals often find themselves responsible for ensuring that their organizations comply with a variety of laws and external regulations affecting the security of systems and data. These laws are often written to protect individual privacy and include detailed requirements on protecting data and notifying **data subjects** (the individuals about whom data is collected) when there is a potential compromise of their information.

You don't need to know the details of the various security laws and regulations when you take the Security+ exam, so let's just take a quick high-level look at four of the most important:

- **Health Insurance Portability and Accountability Act (HIPAA).** HIPAA mandates that organizations protect health information. This includes any information related to the health of an individual that might be held by doctors, hospitals, or any health facility. It also applies to any information held by an organization related to health plans offered to employees. Fines for not complying with the law have been as high as $4.3 million.

- **Gramm-Leach Bliley Act (GLBA).** This is also known as the Financial Services Modernization Act and includes a Financial Privacy Rule. This rule requires financial institutions to provide consumers with a privacy notice explaining what information they collect and how it is used.

- **General Data Protection Regulation (GDPR).** This European Union (EU) directive mandates the protection of privacy data for individuals who live in the EU. It applies to any organization that collects and maintains this data, regardless of the location of the organization.

- **Payment Card Industry Data Security Standard (PCI DSS)** is not actually a law but is a private contractual relationship between the banks that issue credit cards and the merchants who accept them. PCI DSS outlines a set of strict security requirements for handling cardholder data.

While this section outlined four specific regulations related to data, there are others. The key is that organizations must know which laws apply to them and implement data governance methods to comply with the laws. This includes any national, territory, or state laws.

The consequences for failing to comply with regulations vary depending upon the nature of the regulation and the jurisdiction. They may include fines and other sanctions and the loss of business or professional licenses. Businesses known to violate security laws may suffer reputational damage and may incur penalties based upon the contracts they have with customers and suppliers.

Compliance Monitoring and Reporting

Implementing compliance programs within an organization is vital, but the task does not stop there. An equally essential facet of a successful compliance program involves ongoing monitoring and reporting. This process is crucial in maintaining a steady state of compliance, identifying potential issues, and ensuring accountability and transparency.

Internal and external monitoring and reporting are two primary components of an effective compliance monitoring system. Internal monitoring includes regular audits and reviews by internal teams or committees, ensuring that the company's operations adhere to the established policies and standards. External monitoring, on the other hand, is conducted by third-party organizations or industry regulators who can provide an unbiased perspective on the organization's compliance status. It is beneficial to employ both approaches as they complement each other in achieving a comprehensive review of the company's compliance status.

Due diligence and due care are critical aspects of this process. **Due diligence** refers to the actions taken to ensure the organization is aware of all legal requirements applicable to its operations. It involves understanding the risks, regulations, and standards relevant to the business and taking the necessary steps to align with them. **Due care**, meanwhile, is the continuous effort of ensuring the organization adheres to these requirements and addresses any identified non-compliance in a timely manner.

Attestation and acknowledgement form another crucial part of the compliance monitoring and reporting process. **Attestation** refers to the verification by individuals within the organization or third parties that the organization is compliant with the relevant rules and regulations. **Acknowledgement**, on the other hand, is the recognition and acceptance of these compliance standards by employees and other stakeholders. These processes help establish a culture of compliance within the organization, emphasizing everyone's responsibility in maintaining the organization's compliance status.

Finally, the role of automation cannot be overstated in modern compliance monitoring and reporting. Automation tools can help streamline and standardize the compliance process, reducing the likelihood of errors that can result from manual processes. They can facilitate real-time reporting, making it easier to identify and address non-compliance issues quickly. Moreover, automation can also aid in maintaining accurate records of compliance efforts, which is essential for demonstrating due diligence in the event of a compliance audit.

Privacy

Privacy is an important concern in today's digital world. Massive amounts of data are generated, collected, and stored each day. An organization's approach to privacy must account for a complex set of local, regional, national, and global regulations. Each jurisdiction can have its unique privacy laws, and the challenge for businesses is in interpreting and adhering to all relevant regulations.

Local and regional privacy laws tend to reflect the specific concerns and cultural attitudes of a particular area. For instance, some states in the U.S., like California with its **California Consumer Privacy Act (CCPA)**, have established their privacy regulations that go beyond the federal level. Similarly, regions like the European Union have enacted comprehensive privacy laws, such as the General Data Protection Regulation (GDPR), which apply across multiple countries within that region.

At the national level, countries have diverse privacy regulations reflecting their societal and governmental structures. For instance, the U.S. primarily has a sector-specific approach to privacy regulation, focusing on industries like health care (HIPAA) and financial services (GLBA). In contrast, countries like Canada and Australia have more comprehensive, across-the-board privacy laws.

Global privacy regulations are less concrete, given the differing views on privacy worldwide. However, there are international principles and guidelines that many countries adhere to, such as those provided by the Organisation for Economic Co-operation and Development (OECD). Businesses operating internationally need to be mindful of these diverse privacy landscapes and design their privacy policies accordingly.

A significant aspect of many modern privacy regulations is the concept of the **right to be forgotten**. Included in laws such as the GDPR, this right empowers individuals to request that their personal data be erased from a company's records under specific circumstances. The implementation of this right can be complex, involving technical challenges in data removal and balancing against other rights, such as freedom of expression and the public's right to know. However, it reflects the increasing emphasis on individual control over personal data, a theme likely to shape future privacy regulations globally.

Data Inventory and Retention

Knowing where your data is in your organization is important for keeping it safe and making sure privacy rules are followed. This is why having a good system to keep track of data, known as a **data inventory**, is a must. A data inventory is a detailed list of where important data is kept, who can get to it, and why it's used. It's like a map of all the data in a company and is the starting point for both privacy and security programs.

Without a clear picture of where important data is kept, it's almost impossible to make sure it's safe. The first step in protecting data is knowing where it is. Also, data inventory helps companies follow privacy rules like GDPR or CCPA that require that companies know what personal data they have and where it's kept.

Data inventories also help find data that is old, not needed, or taking up space that could be used for something else. This kind of data can be managed better and, if needed, removed from the system in a safe way.

Once a good data inventory is set up, the next important thing is to have rules about how long to keep data. These are called **data retention** policies. Retention policies say how long data should be kept and how to dispose of it safely when it's not needed anymore. These rules are important for both privacy and security because they limit the amount of data that could be exposed if there's a data breach. Plus, many privacy rules require data to be deleted when it's not needed anymore, so data retention policies help companies follow the law.

Security Awareness

Security awareness is an essential part of organizational security. This includes training personnel on security policies and training to help ensure personnel remain up to date with current technologies and threats.

When users understand risks related to their actions, they're less likely to take risky actions. As a simple example, attackers are constantly sending out phishing emails with malicious links. If users engage in risky behaviors, such as clicking these links, they can give attackers a path into an organization's network. However, providing regular training to users on common threats and emerging threats helps them avoid these attacks.

People learn differently. Knowing this, it's important to use a diversity of training techniques to ensure all employees within an organization understand cybersecurity threats. The following sections describe some commonly used training methods.

Computer-Based Training

Computer-based training (CBT) refers to any training where an individual interacts with an application on a computer. It can be courseware installed on a single computer or web-based training available over the Internet or an intranet.

One benefit of CBT is that students can learn at their own pace. One person may enjoy a topic and absorb it quickly, while another person may need to take more time with it. Some CBT courseware includes videos, allowing students to pause and rewind the video, and watch videos repeatedly if desired. Similarly, students can typically review any text pages as often as they desire.

CBT courseware often includes quizzes or tests so that students can gauge their understanding of the material. When an organization purchases CBT courseware, they often require students to pass these quizzes or tests to show that they went through the courseware and understand the topic.

The Industrial Control Systems Cyber Emergency Response Team (ICS-CERT) provides a lot of free training via their website. Their focus is on preventing attacks on industrial control systems (ICSs). However, attacks on many organizations start the same way. As an example, spear-phishing attacks are a risk for any organization, whether it has an ICS or not. You can access the training here: `https://ics-training.inl.gov/learn/`.

Phishing Campaigns

Attackers are constantly launching phishing campaigns trying to trick users into clicking malicious links or opening malicious attachments. They are continually trying new approaches and improving their tactics. When cybersecurity personnel learn of new phishing campaigns, they often inform users of these new campaigns and methods. An important part of any security awareness program is training users on how they can recognize phishing attempts and respond to suspicious messages.

If a single employee within an organization clicks on a malicious link within an email or responds with private information, it may be enough for an attacker to take over an entire network. Some organizations want to know if any of their employees will be tricked by phishing emails. A phishing simulation sends out fake phishing emails to employees to see if anyone will click a link or respond to it.

Organizations often hire an outside security company to help with phishing simulations. Some security companies provide access to an online app that an organization's representative can use. The representative can choose who to send the phishing emails to (such as everyone or specific groups), how often to send the emails (such as one time or monthly), when to start the simulation, and more. These online apps often have multiple templates that the representatives can choose from, such as emails with attachments, emails with URLs, and emails asking them to respond with information.

This culminates with a report documenting any inappropriate responses. It gives management insight into the effectiveness, or ineffectiveness, of current training.

Recognizing Anomalous Behavior

Sometimes, risky or unusual behavior can indicate a security problem. This could be a person doing something they don't normally do, like accessing data they don't usually need for their job, or it could be a computer or network acting strangely. This is why it's so important to understand what normal behavior looks like in your organization, so you can spot anything that's out of the ordinary. Unintentional actions can also be a problem. For example, someone might accidentally click on a dangerous link or share sensitive data without realizing it. Training people to recognize and report this kind of behavior is a key part of security awareness.

User Guidance and Training

Users are generally not security experts, and they need guidance and training to assist them as they navigate the digital world. This information helps them maintain situational awareness regarding their digital activities. That just means that they are aware of what is going on around them. Training should reinforce security messages and help users understand the information that might be found in policies and handbooks.

Some specific issues that should be covered in user training include:

- **Insider threat**. This is a potential threat of harm to the organization by someone within the organization. It could be a disgruntled employee, a careless employee, or even an uninformed employee who unwittingly becomes a pawn for attackers. Training should include the signs of potential insider threats and the steps to report such activities.
- **Password management**. One of the simplest yet most essential security practices involves strong password management. Users need to understand the importance of creating strong, unique passwords and updating them regularly. Training should also cover the use of password managers, which can help users securely manage multiple passwords.
- **Removable media and cables**. These can be a significant security risk as they can be used to introduce malware or export sensitive data. Users should be trained to handle such devices carefully, avoid using untrusted ones, and understand the procedure to report lost or found devices.
- **Social engineering**. Training should explain common types of social engineering attacks, such as phishing and impersonation, and how to recognize and respond to them.
- **Operational security**. Training should cover the importance of limiting information shared on social media, discussing sensitive matters in public, and disposing of sensitive information properly.
- **Hybrid/remote work environments**. With many employees working from home or other remote locations, new security challenges have arisen. Training should cover how to secure home networks, the use of VPNs, the importance of securing physical devices when not in use, and other security best practices specific to remote work.

Awareness Program Development and Execution

Managing a security awareness program means regularly checking how well the program is working and making updates as needed. This can involve reporting and monitoring activities to see what's working and what's not, and then making changes based on what you find. This might mean starting new initiatives, or improving existing ones. For example, you might find that more training is needed on a particular topic, or that a certain type of attack is becoming more common and needs to be addressed. You also need to make sure that the program is being carried out as planned. This can involve things like making sure training sessions are happening on schedule, that people are attending them, and that they're learning what they need to. Automation can also play a role in managing a security awareness program, such as by helping to track progress and flagging areas that need attention.

Chapter 11 Exam Topic Review

When preparing for the exam, make sure you understand these key concepts covered in this chapter.

Change Management

- Change management programs provide a formal process for approving and carrying out changes in a manner that is coordinated with all stakeholders and designed to minimize the risks associated with the change.

- The business process issues covered by change management programs include an approval process, ownership, stakeholder analysis, impact analysis, testing, a backout plan, and the use of maintenance windows and standard operating procedures.

- The technical implications of change management plans include updating security controls, identifying restricted activities, communicating downtime expectations, tracking dependencies, and avoiding disruptions by managing application and service restarts.

- Change management processes should ensure that changes are not closed out until all documentation and diagrams are updated to reflect the impact of the change.

- **Version control** is a formal process used to track the current versions of software code and system/application configurations.

Protecting Data

- **Regulated data** is data that is governed by external laws and regulations with which the organization must comply.

- **Financial information** is any data about monetary transactions related to an organization or an individual.

- **Intellectual property** is information that is crucial to the way that an organization runs its business. Intellectual property may consist of data that is protected by copyright, trademark, and/or patent law. Trade secrets are a type of intellectual property that remains sensitive and valuable to an organization because it is kept secret from competitors.

- **Data classification systems** provide formal categories for identifying the sensitivity and criticality of data. Classification ensures that users understand the value of data, and the classifications help protect sensitive data.

- **Public data** is available to anyone. It might be in brochures, press releases, or on websites. **Private data** is information about an individual that should remain private.

- **Confidential data** is information that an organization intends to keep secret among a certain group of people. **Restricted data** is another term for regulated data that is governed by outside obligations. Confidential data may also be restricted data depending upon the circumstances.
- A data retention policy identifies how long data is retained, and sometimes specifies where it is stored.
- **Data sanitization** methods ensure that data is removed or destroyed from devices before disposing of the devices.

Incident Response

- An incident response policy defines incident and response procedures. Organizations review and update incidents periodically and after reviewing lessons learned after actual incidents.
- A communication plan identifies who to inform when an incident occurs. It also outlines the roles and responsibilities of various personnel, including a communication expert that would communicate with the media.
- The first step in incident response is preparation. It includes creating and maintaining an incident response policy and includes prevention steps such as implementing security controls to prevent malware infections.
- After detecting a potential incident, personnel perform an analysis to confirm that a security incident is underway. Next, they attempt to contain or isolate the problem. Disconnecting a computer from a network will isolate it.
- Eradication attempts to remove all malicious components left after an incident. Recovery restores a system to its original state. Depending on the scope of the incident, administrators might completely rebuild the system, including applying all updates and patches.
- A review of lessons learned helps an organization prevent a reoccurrence of an incident.
- **Tabletop exercises** are a type of scenario-based training where participants discuss and analyze a hypothetical incident in a non-threatening environment. **Simulations** involve recreating real-world incidents as closely as possible.

Understanding Digital Forensics

- When collecting documentation and evidence, it's important to follow specific procedures to ensure that the evidence is admissible in a court of law.
- A chain of custody provides assurances that personnel controlled and handled evidence properly after collecting it. It may start with a tag attached to the physical item, followed by a chain of custody form that documents everyone who handled it and when they handled it.
- A **legal hold** refers to a legal obligation to maintain different types of data as evidence. Electronic discovery, or **eDiscovery**, is the identification and collection of electronically stored information. A legal hold requires an organization to protect existing data as evidence.
- Event logs often help investigators reconstruct the timeline of an event by looking at the

timestamps of entries. However, investigators need to consider any time offsets based on the time zone used by the logs.

- Investigators provide a report on their findings. They typically include tactics, techniques, and procedures (TTPs) used by attackers and recommendations based on the results.

- The order of volatility for data from most volatile to least volatile on a system is cache memory, regular RAM, a swap or paging file, and hard drive data.

- Snapshots can capture data from almost any location, and the snapshot can be used for forensic analysis.

- Forensic artifacts are pieces of data that most users are unaware of, but digital forensic experts can extract and analyze the artifacts.

- Hard drive imaging creates a forensic copy and prevents the forensic capture and analysis from modifying the original evidence. A forensic image is a bit-by-bit copy of the data and does not modify the data during the capture.

- Hashes or checksums are used to verify the integrity of captured data. They provide proof the capturing process did not modify data.

- Security Orchestration, Automation, and Response (SOAR) platforms use internal tools to respond to low-level security events automatically, reducing administrator workload.

- A SOAR playbook provides a checklist of things to check for suspected incidents.

- A SOAR runbook implements the playbook checklist using available tools within the organization.

Security Governance

- Security governance is the set of responsibilities and processes established by an organization's top-level management to direct, evaluate, and control the organization's security efforts.

- Boards often consist of executives and high-ranking individuals within the organization who make critical decisions about security policy and strategy. Committees are usually specialized groups focusing on specific aspects of security, such as risk management or compliance. Government entities might have a role if the organization operates in a heavily regulated industry or if it deals with sensitive data like protected health information or national security matters.

- ***Centralized governance structures*** concentrate decision-making authority at the top of the organization. **Decentralized structures** allow different parts of the organization to make their own security decisions.

- In setting up and managing security governance, organizations need to take into account a range of external considerations. These may include regulatory requirements, legal obligations, industry standards, and the security environment at local, regional, national, and global levels.

- Written security policies are administrative controls that identify an overall security plan for an organization and reduce overall risk. Procedures identify security controls used to enforce security policies.

- Common security policies include acceptable use policies (AUP), information security policies, business continuity and disaster recovery policies, incident response policies, software development lifecycle (SDLC) policies, and change management policies.
- Security standards outline technical and business requirements for security. Common security standards include password standards, access control standards, physical security standards, and encryption standards.
- Security procedures provide very specific step-by-step instructions for carrying out security-related tasks.
- Security guidelines offer advice on achieving security objectives. Common security procedures include change management procedures and employee onboarding/offboarding procedures.
- Security guidelines are optional advice, while compliance with policies, procedures, and standards is mandatory.
- Data owners have primary responsibility for a specific type of data within the organization. The data owner is typically a senior executive responsible for the area with oversight of the data.
- Data owners typically have senior-level positions and can't do the day-to-day work of data governance. For this reason, they typically delegate authority to data stewards on their teams who are responsible for carrying out the intent of the data owner's requirements.
- A data custodian is responsible for routine daily tasks such as backing up data, storage of the data, and implementation of business rules.
- A data controller is the organization that is responsible for a dataset. A data processor handles information on behalf of a data controller.

Third-Party Risk Management

- A supply chain includes all the elements required to produce and sell products and services. Organizations should regularly conduct a supply chain analysis that identifies all of the vendors that make up their supply chain and assesses any risks associated with those relationships.
- Security controls used to assess and manage vendor relationships include right-to-audit clauses, penetration testing, collecting evidence of internal audits, and conducting independent assessments.
- Conducting due diligence involves a thorough evaluation of potential vendors' capabilities, credentials, reputation, and financial stability.
- A conflict of interest might arise if the vendor has business relationships that could influence their decision-making or compromise their ability to prioritize your organization's needs.
- A service level agreement (SLA) is an agreement between a company and a vendor that stipulates performance expectations, such as minimum uptime and maximum downtime levels.

- Memorandum of understandings (MOUs) expresses an understanding between two or more parties, indicating their intention to work together toward a common goal.
- A business partners agreement (BPA) is a written agreement that details the relationship between business partners, including their obligations toward the partnership.
- A **non-disclosure agreement (NDA)** is used between two entities to ensure that proprietary data is not disclosed to unauthorized entities.
- **Master Services Agreements (MSA)** provide structure to the agreements for vendors that you will work with repeatedly. Then, when you have a new project for the vendor, you write a simple **work order (WO)** or a **statement of work (SOW)** that contains the details of that specific project and references the general terms in the MSA.

Security Compliance

- **Compliance programs** ensure that an organization complies with all of its legal and contractual obligations.
- **Due diligence** refers to the actions taken to ensure the organization is aware of all legal requirements applicable to its operations. It involves understanding the risks, regulations, and standards relevant to the business and taking the necessary steps to align with them. **Due care**, meanwhile, is the continuous effort to ensure the organization adheres to these requirements and addresses any identified non-compliance in a timely manner.
- Attestation refers to the verification by individuals within the organization or third parties that the organization is compliant with the relevant rules and regulations. Acknowledgement is the recognition and acceptance of these compliance standards by employees and other stakeholders.
- The right to be forgotten empowers individuals to request that their personal data be erased from a company's records under specific circumstances.
- A data inventory is a detailed list of where important data is kept, who can get to it, and why it's used. Data retention policies say how long data should be kept and how to get rid of it safely when it's not needed anymore.

Security Awareness

- User training includes training personnel on security policies and reducing risks by training users on current technologies and threats.
- Computer-based training (CBT) allows students to learn at their own pace.
- Training programs should help users recognize and properly respond to phishing attacks. Phishing simulations mimic the type of phishing campaigns used by attackers and allow an organization to safely check to see if employees will respond to phishing emails.

- Users should be trained to recognize anomalous behavior, such as risky, unexpected, or unintentional activity.
- Security awareness training should cover a variety of relevant issues, including the insider threat, password management, removable media and cables, social engineering, operational security, and remote/hybrid work environments.

📌 *Online References*

Have you used the extra materials that are free with this book? Check out the online extras at **https://getcertifiedgetahead.com/**.

Chapter 11 Practice Questions

1. Management within your organization wants to ensure that users understand the rules of behavior when they access the organization's computer systems and networks. Which of the following BEST describes what they would implement to meet this requirement?

   A. AUP
   B. NDA
   C. SLA
   D. MSA

2. Which one of the following statements about change management is incorrect?

   A. Change management is primarily focused on preventing security issues.
   B. Change management should conduct stakeholder analyses.
   C. Change management should conduct impact analyses.
   D. Change management should require the use of testing and backout plans.

3. Lisa is coordinating a minor change to an IT system that is a moderate priority and will take only a short amount of time to complete. When would be the best time to complete this change?

   A. During a maintenance window
   B. Immediately
   C. At the first available time when systems are not busy
   D. This change should be scheduled for the next weekend

4. Nelson is reviewing the types of information maintained by his organization. He discovers that a server contains sensitive product plans that have not been shared widely. What term best describes this information?

   A. Intellectual property
   B. Financial information
   C. Trade secrets
   D. Legal information

5. Your organization recently suffered a costly malware attack. Management wants to take steps to prevent damage from malware in the future. Which of the following phases of common incident response procedures is the BEST phase to address this?

   A. Preparation
   B. Detection
   C. Containment
   D. Eradication

6. An incident response team is following typical incident response procedures. Which of the following phases is the BEST choice for analyzing an incident to identify steps to prevent a reoccurrence of the incident?

   A. Preparation
   B. Detection
   C. Eradication
   D. Lessons learned

7. After a recent cybersecurity incident resulting in a significant loss, your organization decided to create a security policy for incident response. Which of the following choices is the BEST choice to include in the policy when an incident requires confiscation of a physical asset?

   A. Ensure hashes are taken first.
   B. Maintain the order of volatility.
   C. Keep a record of everyone who took possession of the physical asset.
   D. Require interviews of all witnesses present when the asset is confiscated.

8. Moe is unsure whether he can delete an old dataset that he no longer uses in his work. What document should he consult for the best guidance on this issue?

   A. Data retention policy
   B. Acceptable use policy
   C. Information security policy
   D. Disaster recovery policy

9. Homer called the help desk complaining his computer is giving random errors. Cybersecurity professionals suspect his system is infected with malware and decide to use digital forensic methods to acquire data on his system. Which of the following should be collected before turning the system off? (Choose TWO.)

    A. Image of disk
    B. RAM
    C. OS
    D. ROM
    E. Cache

10. After a recent incident, a forensic analyst was given several hard drives to analyze. Which of the following actions should she take FIRST?

    A. Capture drive images for integrity.
    B. Take hashes for provenance.
    C. Review the logs on the disks.
    D. Create a chain of custody document.

11. Which one of the following methods would not be appropriate for destroying paper records?

    A. Burning
    B. Shredding
    C. Pulping
    D. Degaussing

12. Shirley is combing through information systems looking for signs that an intruder has compromised the system. What term best describes this activity?

    A. Threat hunting
    B. Simulations
    C. Tabletop exercises
    D. Eradication

13. When is the earliest time that an organization is required to issue a legal hold?

    A. When it receives a lawsuit
    B. When it is ordered to do so by a court
    C. When it believes a lawsuit is likely
    D. When it engages in any business activity

14. Your organization is updating the data policy, and management wants to ensure that employees get training on their responsibilities based on their role. Which of the following BEST describes the responsibilities of data owners and indicates what training they need?

    A. Backing up data in accordance with the data policy
    B. Ensuring data is classified and labeled correctly
    C. Creating the organization's security policy
    D. Training end users on common threats, such as malware and phishing attacks

15. Maggie is reviewing all of the security documents that exist in her organization and would like to know which she is required to comply with. Which of the following documents require compliance? (Select three)

    A. Policies
    B. Standards
    C. Guidelines
    D. Procedures

Chapter 11

Practice Question Answers

1. **A** is correct. An acceptable use policy (AUP) informs users of company expectations when they use computer systems and networks, and it defines acceptable rules of behavior. A non-disclosure agreement (NDA) ensures that individuals do not share proprietary data with others. A service level agreement (SLA) is an agreement between a company and a vendor that stipulates performance expectations, such as minimum uptime and maximum downtime levels. A master services agreement (MSA) provides general terms and conditions for a vendor relationship.

2. **A** is correct. Change management is broadly focused on managing the impact of change on an organization. This includes, but is not limited to, security issues. Change management should conduct stakeholder and impact analyses and should require the use of testing and backout plans.

3. **A** is correct. Routine changes should take place during maintenance windows. There is no indication that this is an urgent change requiring immediate attention or a specially scheduled timeslot.

4. **C** is correct. This question is a little bit tricky because there are two possible correct answers. The information is definitely intellectual property, but it is also a trade secret, which is a specific type of intellectual property. Since trade secret is a more specific answer, it is the better choice. There is no indication that this information would fit into the categories of legal or financial information.

5. **A** is correct. The preparation phase is the first phase of common incident response procedures and attempts to prevent security incidents. Incident identification occurs after a potential incident occurs and the team verifies it is an incident. Containment attempts to limit the damage by preventing an incident from spreading, but it doesn't prevent the original incident. Eradication attempts to remove all malicious elements of an incident after it has been contained. All six steps in order are preparation, detection, analysis, containment, eradication, recovery, and lessons learned.

6. **D** is correct. You should analyze an incident during the lessons learned phase of incident response to identify steps to prevent reoccurrence. Preparation is a planning step done before an incident, to prevent incidents and identify methods to respond to incidents. Detection is the first step after hearing about a potential incident to verify it is an incident. Eradication attempts to remove all malicious elements of an incident after containing it.

7. **C** is correct. It's important to keep a chain of custody for any confiscated physical items, and the chain of custody is a record of everyone who took possession of the asset after it was first confiscated. Hashes should be taken before capturing an image of a disk, but hashes are not required before confiscating equipment. Security personnel should be aware of the order of volatility and protect volatile data, but there isn't any way to maintain the order of volatility. It's important to perform interviews of anyone who observed the incident, but it isn't necessary to interview people who were present when the asset is confiscated.

8. **A** is correct. The purpose of a data retention policy is to document requirements for preserving and destroying information and it would be the most likely document to contain the information Moe needs. An acceptable use policy describes that ways that Moe may use computer systems. The information security policy contains information on managing the organization's information security program and the disaster recovery policy contains similar information for the disaster recovery program.

9. **B** and **E** are correct. Random access memory (RAM) and cache are the most volatile of the items listed and should be collected before the system is turned off. You can collect an image of the disk and the operating system (OS) after it is powered off. Read-only memory (ROM) will be retained even when the power is removed. While the swap/pagefile is not listed, it should also be collected. If the system is turned back on after it is turned off, the swap/pagefile will be overwritten.

10. **B** is correct. Forensic analysts take hashes to prove provenance of the copy. The hash (or checksum) provides proof that the copy is the same as the original and has not lost integrity. A drive image shouldn't be captured before creating a hash, and just having a drive image doesn't provide integrity or prove that it is the same as the original. Reviewing any data on an original disk will potentially modify the data so it shouldn't be done. A chain of custody document is created when evidence is collected, so it should already exist.

11. **D** is correct. Degaussing uses strong magnetic fields to destroy electronic information and would not be effective against paper records. Burning, pulping, and shredding are all effective tools for destroying paper records.

12. **A** is correct. This is an example of threat hunting: searching through systems for clues that they have already been compromised. Simulations and tabletop exercises are tests used to evaluate an organization's incident response process and are not used to identify signs of compromise. Eradication is used to remove traces of a past security incident, rather than hunt for evidence of an incident.

13. **C** is correct. Organizations must issue a legal hold and preserve evidence when they believe that a lawsuit is likely. They are not permitted to wait until they actually are served with a lawsuit or receive a court order. There is no obligation to issue a legal hold simply because they are engaging in business activity.

14. **B** is correct. Owners are responsible for identifying the proper classification of data, ensuring it is labeled correctly, and ensuring security controls are implemented to protect the data. A data custodian is responsible for routine daily tasks such as backing up data. A data owner would be required to comply with organizational policy but would not have the authority to create a policy themselves because it would also affect other data owners. End users need to be trained on common threats, such as malware and phishing attacks, but this is normally the responsibility of a cybersecurity team, not a data owner.

15. **A**, **B**, and **D** are correct. Policies, standards, and procedures are all mandatory documents that organizations must comply with. Guidelines offer optional advice and do not require compliance.

Post-Assessment Questions

1. Your organization hosts an e-commerce web server. The server randomly experiences a high volume of sales and usage from mid-November to the end of December, causing spikes in resource usage. These spikes have resulted in outages during the past year. Which of the following should be implemented to prevent these outages?

   A. Stored procedures
   B. Scalability
   C. Version control
   D. Memory management

2. Employees currently log in with their usernames and passwords but management wants to increase login security by implementing smart cards. However, the IT department anticipates it will take a long time to purchase the necessary equipment and issue smart cards for everyone. You need to identify a solution that will provide comparable security until the smart cards are implemented. Which of the following is a compensating control that will meet these needs?

   A. Implement an account lockout policy.
   B. Increase password policy requirements.
   C. Implement a TOTP solution.
   D. Require users to change their password more often.

3. Your organization is a document destruction company, and you have a variety of clients who hire you to handle the disposal of documents containing sensitive personal information. Which one of the following terms best describes your organization's role?

   A. Data processor
   B. Data controller
   C. Data owner
   D. Data subject

4. Maggie is preparing to conduct a penetration test for a new client. She has obtained proper permission and has documented the rules of engagement. At the beginning of the test, the client provided her with full access to the documentation for the environment she is testing. What type of test is she performing?

   A. Unknown environment
   B. Partially known environment
   C. Semifamiliar environment
   D. Known environment

5. You are working with a team to develop a security awareness program and you are developing content that will educate managers about the importance of monitoring their own employees for unusual behavior. What type of threat are you trying to protect against?

   A. Nation-state
   B. Insider threat
   C. Unskilled attacker
   D. Social engineer

6. Marge is developing a new change management program for her organization. She wants to ensure that everyone who may be impacted by a change is informed of upcoming changes in advance. What change management activity should she conduct?

   A. Approval
   B. Impact analysis
   C. Stakeholder analysis
   D. Backout plan

7. Homer is working to onboard a new vendor that will be providing IaaS cloud services to his organization. He would like to document the expectations for infrastructure uptime and include penalties for failure to meet those expectations. What type of document should he use for this task?

   A. SLA
   B. MOU
   C. NDA
   D. MSA

8. Management wants to increase security for any users accessing the network with a VPN. They plan to implement a method that will require users to install an application on their smartphones. This application will generate a key that they'll have to enter in addition to their username and password. What is the BEST description of this added authentication method?

   A. Something you know
   B. Something you have
   C. Something you are
   D. Somewhere you are

9. Users normally log on using a smart card, a username, and a password. Management wants administrators to use a third factor of authentication. Which of the following will meet this need?

   A. PIN
   B. Token
   C. Fingerprints
   D. Push notification

10. Developers are planning to develop an application using role-based access control. Which of the following would they MOST likely include in their planning?

    A. A listing of labels reflecting classification levels
    B. A listing of rules that the application must be able to trigger
    C. A listing of owners
    D. A matrix of functions matched with required privileges

11. Your organization has implemented a system that stores user credentials in a central database. Users log on once with their credentials. They can then access other systems in the organization without logging on again. Which of the following does this describe?

    A. Federation
    B. SAML
    C. SSO
    D. OAuth

12. The Mapple organization is creating a help-desk team to assist employees with account issues. Members of this team need to create and modify user accounts and occasionally reset user passwords. Which of the following is the BEST way to accomplish this goal?

    A. Give each help-desk employee appropriate privileges individually.
    B. Add each member of the help-desk team to the administrator group within the domain.
    C. Add members of the help-desk team to a security group that has the appropriate privileges.
    D. Assign attributes to members of the help-desk team and give these attributes appropriate privileges.

13. Your organization's security policy states that administrators should follow the principle of least privilege. Which of the following tools can ensure that administrators are following the policy?

    A. Account audits
    B. Risk assessment
    C. Vulnerability assessment
    D. Threat assessment

14. Lisa is responsible for managing and monitoring network devices, such as routers and switches, in your network. Which of the following protocols is she MOST likely to use?

    A. NAT
    B. SRTP
    C. SNMPv3
    D. DNSSEC

15. Your organization's network looks like the following graphic and you've been asked to verify that Firewall 2 has the correct settings.

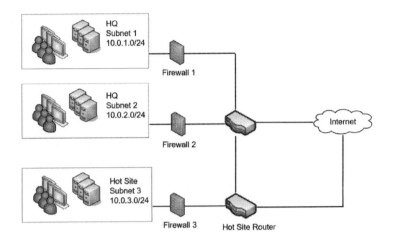

All firewalls should enforce the following requirements:

■ Use only secure protocols for remote management.
■ Block cleartext web traffic.

The following table shows the current rules configured in Firewall 2.

Rule	Destination	Source	Protocol	Action
HTTPS Outbound	Any	10.0.3.0/24	HTTPS	Allow
HTTP Outbound	Any	10.0.3.0/24	HTTP	Block
DNS	Any	10.0.1.0/24	DNS	Allow
HTTPS Inbound	10.0.3.0/24	Any	HTTPS	Allow
HTTP Inbound	10.0.3.0/24	Any	HTTP	Block
Telnet	10.0.3.0/24	Any	Telnet	Block
SSH	10.0.3.0/24	Any	SSH	Allow

Which rule, if any, should be changed in Firewall 2?

A. HTTPS Outbound
B. HTTP Outbound
C. DNS
D. Telnet
E. SSH
F. None. All rules are correct.

16. Your organization recently landed a contract with the federal government. Developers are fine-tuning an application that will process sensitive data. The contract mandates that all computers using this application must be isolated. Which of the following would BEST meet this need?

    A. Create a bastion host in a screened subnet.
    B. Implement a boundary firewall.
    C. Create an air-gapped network.
    D. Implement an IPS.

17. Your organization handles the personal information of residents of the European Union. You recently received a request from an EU citizen asking you to delete all of the personal information you maintain about them. What right is the data subject invoking?

    A. Right of correction
    B. Right of consent
    C. Right of notice
    D. Right to be forgotten

18. Your organization hosts a web server accessed by employees within the network, and via the Internet. Management wants to increase its security. You are tasked with separating all web-facing traffic from internal network traffic. Which of the following provides the BEST solution?

    A. Screened subnet
    B. VLAN
    C. Firewall
    D. WAF

19. Developers recently configured a new service on a server called GCGA1. GCGA1 is in a screened subnet and accessed by employees in the internal network, and by others via the Internet. Network administrators modified firewall rules to access the service. Testing shows the service works when accessed from internal systems. However, it does not work when accessed from the Internet. Which of the following is MOST likely configured incorrectly?

    A. The new service
    B. An ACL
    C. The GCGA1 server
    D. A VLAN

20. Bart recently hooked up a switch incorrectly causing a switching loop problem, which took down part of an organization's network. Management wants to implement a solution that will prevent this from occurring in the future. Which of the following is the BEST choice to meet this need?

    A. Flood guard
    B. SNMPv3
    C. SRTP
    D. RSTP

21. Your organization is undergoing a formal examination of security controls that was requested by the Board of Directors and is being conducted by an independent auditing firm. What term best describes this review?

    A. Assessment
    B. External audit
    C. Internal audit
    D. Regulatory audit

22. Which of the following is an example of a detective control?

    A. An IPS reconfigured to monitor traffic instead of blocking it
    B. A backup solution that includes off-site backups
    C. Security guards
    D. A cable lock

23. Your organization is planning to implement a wireless network using WPA2 Enterprise. Of the following choices, what is required?

    A. An authentication server with a digital certificate installed on the authentication server
    B. An authentication server with DHCP installed on the authentication server
    C. An authentication server with DNS installed on the authentication server
    D. An authentication server with WPS running on the access point

24. Bart was in a coffee shop going through emails and messages on his smartphone. He then started receiving several text messages promoting a political party and encouraging him to visit websites. After he left the coffee shop, he didn't receive any more messages. What does this describe?

    A. Bluesnarfing
    B. Bluejacking
    C. Malware
    D. WPS attack

25. Management within your organization wants employees to be able to access internal network resources from remote locations, including from their homes. Which of the following is the BEST choice to meet this need?

    A. NAC
    B. VPN
    C. IDS
    D. IPS

26. Security experts want to reduce risks associated with updating critical operating systems. Which of the following will BEST meet this goal?

    A. Implement patches when they are released.
    B. Implement a change management policy.
    C. Use only trusted operating systems.
    D. Implement operating systems with secure configurations.

27. Your organization has a segmented network used to process highly classified material. Management wants to prevent users from copying documents to USB flash drives from any computer in this network. Which of the following can be used to meet this goal?

    A. DLP
    B. HSM
    C. COPE
    D. SED

28. Your organization hosts an e-commerce website using a back-end database. The database stores product data and customer data, including credit card numbers. Which of the following is the BEST way to protect the credit card data?

    A. Full database encryption
    B. Full disk encryption
    C. Database column encryption
    D. File-level encryption

29. The Springfield Nuclear Power Plant has created and maintains an online application used to teach the basics of nuclear physics. Only students and teachers in Springfield Elementary School can access this application via the cloud. What type of cloud service model is this?

    A. IaaS
    B. PaaS
    C. SaaS
    D. XaaS

30. Your organization has implemented a CYOD security policy. The policy mandates the use of security controls to protect the devices, and any data on them if they are lost or stolen. Which of the following would BEST meet this goal?

    A. Screen locks and GPS tagging
    B. Patch management and change management
    C. Screen locks and device encryption
    D. Full device encryption and XaaS

31. Management within your company wants to implement a method that will authorize employee access to the network based on several elements. These elements include the employee's identity, location, the time of day, and the type of device used by the employee. Which of the following will BEST meet this need?

    A. Geofencing
    B. Containerization
    C. Tethering
    D. Attribute-based access control

32. Personnel should be able to run the BizzFadd app from their mobile devices. However, certain features should only be operational when employees are within the company's property. When an employee leaves the property, access to these features should be blocked. Which of the following answers provides the BEST solution to meet this goal?

    A. Geofencing
    B. Geolocation
    C. GPS tagging
    D. Containerization

33. A large city is using a SCADA system to manage a water treatment plant. City managers have asked IT personnel to implement security controls to reduce the risk of cybersecurity attacks against ICSs controlled by the SCADA system. Which of the following security controls would be MOST relevant to protect this system?

    A. DLP
    B. TPM
    C. FPGA
    D. NIPS

34. IT auditors have found several unmanaged VMs in a network. They discovered that these were created by administrators for testing but weren't removed after testing was completed. Which of the following should be implemented to prevent this in the future?

    A. A policy related to VM sprawl
    B. A policy related to VM escape protection
    C. A policy related to XaaS
    D. A policy related to SDNs

35. Bart recently launched an attack on a company website using scripts he found on the Internet. Which of the following BEST describes Bart as a threat actor?

    A. Insider threat
    B. Hacktivist
    C. Unskilled attacker
    D. Shadow IT

36. The Marvin Monroe Memorial Hospital recently suffered a serious attack preventing employees from accessing any computer data. The attackers scattered ReadMe files throughout the network that appeared on user screens. They indicated that the attackers encrypted all the data, and it would remain encrypted until the attackers received a hefty sum as payment. Which of the following identifies the MOST likely threat actor in this attack?

    A. Organized crime
    B. Ransomware
    C. Competitors
    D. Hacktivist

37. Gil Gunderson, a salesperson in your organization, received an email on his work computer that included a malicious link. After clicking the link, his computer was infected with malware. The malware was not detected by antivirus software installed on his computer, the organization's email server, or the organization's UTM appliance. After infecting his computer, the malware then searched the network and encrypted data in all the network shares that Gil could access. Which of the following BEST describes how this occurred?

    A. The malware represents a zero-day exploit.
    B. The antivirus software indicated false positives.
    C. The malware infection was the result of a backdoor.
    D. The principle of least privilege was not implemented.

38. Logs on a web server show that it is receiving a significant number of SYN packets from multiple sources on the Internet, but it isn't receiving the corresponding ACK packets. Of the following choices, what is the MOST likely source of these packets?

    A. DDoS
    B. Ransomware
    C. Worm
    D. Bots

39. Management recently mandated that computer monitors be repositioned to ensure they cannot be viewed from outside any windows. Additionally, users are directed to place screen filters over their monitors. What is the purpose of this policy?

    A. Reduce success of phishing
    B. Reduce success of shoulder surfing
    C. Reduce success of dumpster diving
    D. Reduce success of prepending

40. Bart's supervisor told him to clean his desk to comply with the organization's clean desk space policy. While doing so, he threw several papers containing PII into the recycle bin. Which type of attack can exploit this action?

    A. SPIM
    B. Dumpster diving
    C. Shoulder surfing
    D. Tailgating

41. Your organization's CFO recently received an email indicating the organization is being sued. More, the email names her specifically as a defendant in the lawsuit. It includes an attachment described as a subpoena and encourages her to open it for more information. Which of the following BEST describes the social engineering principle used by the sender in this scenario?

    A. Whaling
    B. Phishing
    C. Authority
    D. Consensus

42. Users are complaining about intermittent connectivity with a web server. After examining the logs, you identify a large volume of connection attempts from public IP addresses. You realize these connection attempts are overloading the server, preventing it from responding to other connections. Which of the following is MOST likely occurring?

    A. DDoS attack
    B. DNS poisoning attack
    C. Replay attack
    D. ARP poisoning attack

43. An application on one of your database servers has crashed several times recently. Examining detailed debugging logs, you discover that just prior to crashing, the database application is receiving a long series of unusual characters. What is MOST likely occurring?

    A. SQL injection
    B. Buffer overflow
    C. XML injection
    D. Zero-day

44. Your organization recently experienced a significant data breach. After an investigation, cybersecurity professionals found that the initial attack originated from an internally developed application. Normally users can only access the application by logging on. However, the application allowed the attacker access to the application without requiring the attacker to log on. Which of the following would have the BEST chance of preventing this attack?

    A. Static code analysis
    B. Backdoor
    C. DDoS protection
    D. Keylogger

45. A software development process merges code changes from developers working on a project several times a day. It uses automation to validate the code and tracks changes using version control processes. Which of the following BEST describes this process?

    A. Continuous integration
    B. Continuous validation
    C. Continuous delivery
    D. Continuous monitoring

46. Martin is performing a risk assessment. He is trying to identify the number of times a specific type of incident occurred in the previous year. Which of the following BEST identifies this?

    A. ALE
    B. ARO
    C. SLE
    D. RPO

47. Lisa recently received a security advisory. She's using it to review logs and looking for activity mentioned in the security advisory. Which of the following BEST describes what she is doing?

    A. Creating OSINT
    B. Threat hunting
    C. Penetration testing
    D. Performing reconnaissance

48. You recently completed a vulnerability scan on your network. It reported that several servers are missing key operating system patches. However, after checking the servers, you've verified that the servers have these patches installed. Which of the following BEST describes this?

    A. False negative
    B. Misconfiguration on servers
    C. False positive
    D. Non-credentialed scan

49. An external security auditor recently completed a security assessment. He discovered that a system has a vulnerability that two previous security assessments detected. Which of the following BEST explains this?

    A. The scanner is reporting a false negative.
    B. The vendor has not created a security patch.
    C. The scans ran as credentialed scans.
    D. The system is misconfigured.

50. IT administrators created a VPN for employees to use while working from home. The VPN is configured to provide AAA services. Which of the following would be presented to the AAA system for identification?

    A. Password
    B. Permissions
    C. Username
    D. Tunneling certificate
    E. Hardware token

51. You are running a vulnerability scanner with an access level that gives it the best chance of detecting vulnerabilities. Which of the following BEST describes the type of scan you are running?

    A. Non-credentialed scan
    B. A port scan
    C. A non-intrusive scan
    D. Credentialed scan

52. You suspect that an attacker has been sending specially crafted TCP packets to a server trying to exploit a vulnerability. You decide to capture TCP packets being sent to this server for later analysis and you want to use a command-line tool to do so. Which of the following tools will BEST meet your need?

    A. Tcpreplay
    B. Tcpdump
    C. Netcat
    D. Wiredump

53. Your company wants to control access to a restricted area of the building by adding an additional physical security control that includes facial recognition. Which of the following provides the BEST solution?

    A. Bollards
    B. Guards
    C. Retina scanners
    D. Cameras

54. Thieves recently rammed a truck through the entrance of one of your organization's buildings in the middle of the night. They then proceeded to steal a significant amount of IT equipment. Which of the following choices can prevent this from happening again?

    A. Bollards
    B. Guards
    C. CCTV
    D. Alarms

55. Fileserver1 hosts several files accessed by users in your organization, and it's important that they can always access these files. Management wants to implement a solution to increase cybersecurity resilience. Which of the following is the LOWEST cost solution to meet this requirement?

    A. Active/active load balancing
    B. Active/passive load balancing
    C. RAID
    D. Warm site

56. A coffee shop recently stopped broadcasting the SSID (coffeewifi) for its wireless network. Instead, paying customers can view it on their receipt and use it to connect to the coffee shop's wireless network. Today, Lisa turned on her laptop computer, saw the SSID coffeewifi, and connected to it. Which of the following attacks is MOST likely occurring?

    A. Rogue AP
    B. Evil twin
    C. Jamming
    D. Bluejacking

57. Compu-Global-Hyper-Mega-Net hosts a website selling digital products. Marketing personnel have launched several successful sales. The server has been overwhelmed, resulting in slow responses from the server, and lost sales. Management wants to implement a solution that will provide cybersecurity resilience. Which of the following is the BEST choice?

    A. Managed PDUs
    B. Certificates
    C. Web application firewall
    D. Load balancing

58. The backup policy for a database server states that the amount of time needed to perform backups should be minimized. Which of the following backup plans would BEST meet this need?

    A. Full backups on Sunday and full backups on the other six days of the week
    B. Full backups on Sunday and differential backups on the other six days of the week
    C. Full backups on Sunday and incremental backups on the other six days of the week
    D. Differential backups on Sunday and incremental backups on the other six days of the week

59. A security analyst is creating a document that includes the expected monetary loss from a major outage. She is calculating the potential impact on life, property, finances, and the organization's reputation. Which of the following documents is she MOST likely creating?

    A. BCP
    B. BIA
    C. MTBF
    D. RPO

60. You are helping a risk management team update the business impact analysis for your organization. For one system, the plan requires an RTO of five hours and an RPO of one day. Which of the following would meet this requirement?

    A. Ensure the system can be restored within five hours and ensure it does not lose more than one day of data.
    B. Ensure the system can be restored within one day and ensure it does not lose more than five hours of data.
    C. Ensure the system can be restored between five hours and one day after an outage.
    D. Ensure critical systems can be restored within five hours and noncritical systems can be restored within one day.

61. Marge is updating the business impact analysis (BIA) for your organization. She needs to document the time needed to return a database server to an operational state after a failure. Which of the following terms would she use?

    A. MTTR
    B. MTBF
    C. SLE
    D. ARO

62. Lisa needs to transmit PII via email and she wants to maintain its confidentiality. Which of the following choices is the BEST solution?

    A. Use hashes.
    B. Encrypt it before sending.
    C. Protect it with a digital signature.
    D. Use RAID.

63. Employees in your organization recently received an email that appeared to come from your organization's CEO. The email mentioned that IT personnel were troubleshooting an authentication issue and needed employees to reply to the email with their credentials. Several employees responded with their credentials. This was a phishing campaign created for user training, and it spoofed the CEO's email. Executives want to ensure that employees have proof that any emails that appear to be coming from the executives, did come from them. Which of the following should be implemented?

    A. Digital signatures
    B. Spam filter
    C. Role-based training
    D. Heuristic-based detection

64. As an administrator, you receive an antivirus alert from a server in your network indicating one of the files has a hash of known malware. The file was pushed to the server from the organization's patch management system and is scheduled to be applied to the server early the next morning. The antivirus software indicates that the file and hash of the malware on the server are:

    - File: gcga_upgrade.exe
    - Hash: bd64571e26035d95e5e9232b4aff b915

    Checking the logs of the patch management system, you see the following information:

Status	Update Name	Hash
Pushed	gcga_upgrade.exe	b815571e26035d95e5e9232b4aff48db

    Which of the following indicates what MOST likely occurred?

    A. The file was infected after it was pushed out to the server.
    B. The file was embedded with crypto-malware before it was pushed to the server.
    C. The file was listed in the patch management system's blocklist.
    D. The file was infected when the patch management system downloaded it.

65. Tony hid several plaintext documents within an image file. He then sent the image file to Louie. Which of the following BEST describes the purpose of his actions?

    A. To support steganography
    B. To support integrity
    C. To support resilience
    D. To support obfuscation

66. Lisa and Bart need to exchange emails over the Internet using a nonsecure channel. These emails need to provide non-repudiation. They decide to use certificates on each of their computers. What would they use to sign their emails?

    A. CRL
    B. OCSP
    C. CSR
    D. CA
    E. DSA

67. Administrators have noticed a significant amount of OCSP traffic sent to an intermediate CA. They want to reduce this traffic. Which of the following is the BEST choice to meet this need?

    A. Pinning
    B. Digital signatures
    C. Stapling
    D. Hashing

68. A company is hosting an e-commerce site that uses certificates for HTTPS. Management wants to ensure that users can verify the validity of these certificates even if elements of the Internet suffer an extended outage. Which of the following provides the BEST solution?

    A. OCSP
    B. PEM
    C. SAN
    D. CRL

69. A security auditor discovered that several employees in the Accounting department can print and sign checks. In her final report, she recommended restricting the number of people who can print checks and the number of people who can sign them. She also recommended that no one should be authorized to both print and sign checks. Which security control type does this describe?

    A. Preventive
    B. Detective
    C. Corrective
    D. Compensating

70. Bart recently resigned and left your organization. Later, IT personnel determined that he deleted several files and folders on a server share after he left the organization. Further, they determined that he did so during the weekend while the organization was closed. Which of the following account management practices would have BEST prevented his actions?

    A. Onboarding
    B. Time-of-day restrictions
    C. Account audit
    D. Offboarding

71. Your organization hired a third-party security professional to assess vulnerabilities. The security professional discovered a server was running an application that hasn't been updated for eight years. Management decided to keep the application online because there isn't a newer version from the vendor. Which of the following BEST describes why the application doesn't have a newer version?

    A. MSA
    B. AUP
    C. MSSP
    D. EOL

72. A help-desk professional has begun to receive several calls from employees related to malware. Using common incident response procedures, which of the following should be her FIRST response to these calls?

    A. Preparation
    B. Detection
    C. Eradication
    D. Recovery

73. Homer reported suspicious activity on his computer. After investigating, you verify that his computer is infected with malware. Which of the following steps should you take NEXT?

    A. Detection
    B. Preparation
    C. Containment
    D. Eradication

74. Security personnel confiscated Bart's workstation after a security incident. Administrators removed the hard drive for forensic analysis but were called away to troubleshoot an outage before capturing an image of the drive. They left it unattended for several hours before returning to begin their analysis. Later, legal personnel stated that the analysis results would not be admissible in a court of law. What is the MOST likely reason for the lack of admissibility?

    A. Witnesses were not identified.
    B. A chain of custody was not maintained.
    C. An order of volatility was not maintained.
    D. A hard drive analysis was not complete.

75. Your organization is involved in a lawsuit, and a judge issued a court order requiring your organization to keep all emails from the last three years. Your data retention policy states that email should only be maintained from the previous 12 months. After investigating, administrators realize that backups contain emails from the last three years. What should they do with these backups?

    A. Backups older than 12 months should be deleted to comply with the data retention policy.
    B. Backups for the last 12 months should be protected to comply with the legal hold.
    C. Backups for the last two years should be protected to comply with the legal hold.
    D. Backups for the last three years should be protected to comply with the legal hold.

76. Management at the Goody New Shoes retail chain decided to allow employees to connect to the internal network using their personal mobile devices. However, the organization is having problems with these devices, including the following:

    - Employees do not keep their devices updated.
    - There is no standardization among the devices.
    - The organization doesn't have adequate control over the devices.

Management wants to implement a mobile device deployment model to overcome these problems while still allowing employees to use their own devices. Which of the following is the BEST choice?

A. BYOD
B. COPE
C. CYOD
D. IaaS

77. Homer received an email letting him know he won the lottery. To claim the prize, he needs to confirm his identity by providing his name, phone number, address, and birth date. The email states he'll receive the prize after providing this information. What does this describe?

A. Spear phishing
B. Phishing
C. Smishing
D. Whaling

78. Your organization hosts a web application selling digital products. Customers can also post comments related to their purchases. Management suspects that attackers are looking for vulnerabilities that they can exploit. Which of the following will BEST test the cybersecurity resilience of this application?

A. Fuzzing
B. Input validation
C. Error handling
D. Anti-malware

79. Your SIEM system sent an alert related to multiple failed logins. Reviewing the logs, you notice login failures for about 100 different accounts. The logs then show the same accounts indicate login failures starting about three hours after the first login failure. Which of the following BEST describes this activity?

A. A brute force attack
B. A dictionary attack
C. A spraying attack
D. An account lockout attack

80. Your organization recently developed an incident response policy and is beginning to implement an incident response plan. Which of the following items is the FIRST step in an incident response process?

    A. Preparation
    B. Detection
    C. Containment
    D. Eradication

81. Your organization has hired an outside service provider to respond to security incidents and provide forensic analysis services. You want to write into the contract specific terms about their response, including the time required to arrive on site. Which of the following documents is BEST suited to achieving this goal?

    A. AUP
    B. NDA
    C. SLA
    D. MSA

82. A forensic expert is preparing to analyze a hard drive. Which of the following should the expert do FIRST?

    A. Capture an image of the disk.
    B. Identify the order of volatility.
    C. Copy the contents of memory.
    D. Create a chain of custody document.

83. Ned runs a small business selling products designed for left-handed individuals. He would like to purchase a security device for his business that combines the functions of several security technologies into a single cost-effective package. Which one of the following would BEST meet his needs?

    A. UTM
    B. NGFW
    C. SIEM
    D. IPS

84. Your organization hires an outside vendor to destroy electronic media containing sensitive information and you want to be able to demonstrate the confirmed deletion of data to others. What activity can you request from the vendor to meet this goal?

    A. Sanitization
    B. Pulverization
    C. Certification
    D. Retention

85. What standard allows vulnerability scanners to more easily communicate with other security tools to facilitate automation?

    A. SCAP
    B. CVE
    C. CVSS
    D. OSI

86. Waylon is searching through his organization's networks and systems for signs that intruders have successfully compromised devices. What term best describes his activity?

    A. Threat intelligence
    B. Reconnaissance
    C. Penetration testing
    D. Threat hunting

87. Willie recently joined a new organization. In getting to know the organization's risk appetite, he is learning that the organization is willing to take on significant risks when the potential for reward is high. What term best describes this risk appetite?

    A. Unjustified
    B. Expansionary
    C. Conservative
    D. Neutral

88. Which one of the following controls is designed to provide power to electronic equipment during a period of momentary power failure?

    A. Dual power supplies
    B. UPS
    C. Generator
    D. Solar power

89. Which one of the following types of disaster recovery tests has the greatest potential to disrupt normal business operations?

    A. Fail over
    B. Simulation
    C. Parallel processing
    D. Walkthrough

90. Edna would like to restrict the devices that can connect to her wired network by requiring that they authenticate. What technology can BEST help her achieve this goal?

    A. TLS
    B. WEP
    C. 802.1X
    D. WPA3

Post-Assessment Answers

1. **B** is correct. Scalability is the best choice because it allows administrators to manually scale the server up or out as needed in response to this predictable high resource usage. Stored procedures are a group of SQL statements that execute as a whole and help prevent SQL injection attacks. Version control tracks software versions as it is updated and is unrelated to this question. Memory management techniques help ensure that applications don't cause memory problems such as memory leaks or integer overflows. This question comes from exam objective 3.1, "Compare and contrast security implications of different architecture models" and is covered in Chapter 5.

2. **C** is correct. A Time-based One-Time Password (TOTP) solution can be implemented as a compensating control. It can be implemented with hardware tokens or with an app on a smartphone. The smart cards provide two-factor authentication, so the compensating control should provide two-factor control, and TOTP fills that need. None of the other answer choices provide an additional factor of authentication. An account lockout policy locks out users after entering an incorrect password too many times. The password policy can be used to increase password security. Requiring users to change their password more often is in the password policy as password expiration. This question comes from exam objective 4.6, "Given a scenario, implement and maintain identity and access management" and is covered in Chapter 1.

3. **A** is correct. In this scenario, you are best described as a data processor because you are handling data on behalf of another organization that is the actual data controller. The data controller is the person or organization that bears primary responsibility for the data. The data owner is the individual within the data controller organization that is responsible for a specific type of data. The data subject is the individual about whom personally identifiable information is collected. This question comes from exam objective 5.4, "Summarize elements of effective security compliance" and is covered in Chapter 11.

4. **D** is correct. Maggie has full access to the documentation for this environment, so this is a known environment test. In an unknown environment test, the tester does not have access to any information about the test environment. In a partially known environment test, the tester has access to limited information. Semifamiliar environment testing is a made-up term and is not a type of penetration test. This question comes from exam objective 5.5, "Explain types and purposes of audits and assessments" and is covered in Chapter 8.

5. **B** is correct. Managers should monitor employee behavior to watch for cases of the insider threat, where a rogue employee takes malicious actions that undermine security. This type of awareness campaign is not specifically targeted at sophisticated nation-state attackers, un-skilled attackers, or social engineering attempts. This question comes from exam objective 5.6, "Given a scenario, implement security awareness practices" and is covered in Chapter 11.

6. **C** is correct. All of these activities are an important part of the change management process, but the stakeholder analysis is the activity that identifies all of the individuals and groups within the organization and outside the organization that might be affected by the change. Approval comes only after other steps have been satisfied and the change is ready to be deployed. The impact analysis reviews the effects of the change and comes after the stakeholder analysis. The backout plan provides a detailed sequence of steps that the team should follow if the change goes wrong. This question comes from exam objective 1.3, "Explain the importance of change management processes and the impact to security" and is covered in Chapter 11.

7. **A** is correct. A service-level agreement (SLA) is an agreement between a company and a vendor that stipulates performance expectations, such as minimum uptime and maximum downtime levels. A memorandum of understanding (MOU) expresses an understanding between two or more parties indicating their intention to work together toward a common goal. A non-disclosure agreement (NDA) is used between two entities to ensure that proprietary data is not disclosed to unauthorized entities. Master Services Agreements (MSA) provide structure to the agreements for vendors that you will work with repeatedly. This question comes from exam objective 5.3, "Explain the processes associated with third-party risk assessment and management" and is covered in Chapter 11.

8. **B** is correct. This is in the something you have factor of authentication. Users are required to have a smartphone with the authentication application installed. The application generates a key of numbers, but users don't know this key until the application generates it. Biometrics are in the something you are factor, but biometric methods aren't mentioned. Somewhere you are factors require a user to be in a specific geographic location, such

as a corporate office. The password is an example of a something you know factor but that is not what this question is asking about. This question comes from exam objective 4.6, "Given a scenario, implement and maintain identity and access management" and is covered in Chapter 2.

9. **C** is correct. Fingerprints are in the something you are factor of authentication and will meet this need. All the other answers are in either the something you have factor (already used by the smart card) or the something you know factor (already used by the password). A personal identification number (PIN) is in the something you know factor. Tokens and push notifications are in the something you have factor. This question comes from exam objective 4.6, "Given a scenario, implement and maintain identity and access management" and is covered in Chapter 2.

10. **D** is correct. A matrix of functions, roles, or job titles matched with the required access privileges for each of the functions, roles, or job titles is a common planning document for a role-based access control model. The mandatory access control (MAC) model uses sensitivity labels and classification levels. Rule-based access control models use rules, but role-based access control models don't use rules. The discretionary access control (DAC) model specifies that every object has an owner and it might identify owners in a list. This question comes from exam objective 4.6, "Given a scenario, implement and maintain identity and access management" and is covered in Chapter 2.

11. **C** is correct. This describes a single sign-on (SSO) solution in which users only log on once. Although a federation supports SSO, not all SSO systems use a federation. Security Assertions Markup Language (SAML) is an SSO solution used for web-based applications, but not all SSO solutions use SAML. OAuth (Open Authorization) is an authorization protocol used with HTTP-based apps, not internal organizations. This question comes from exam objective 4.6, "Given a scenario, implement and maintain identity and access management" and is covered in Chapter 2.

12. **C** is correct. The best solution of the available choices is to add members of the help-desk team to a security group that has the appropriate privileges. Assigning permissions to users individually adds to the administrative workload. Giving members administrator privileges violates the principle of least privilege by giving them too many privileges. An attribute-based access control model can use attributes to grant access but would add to the administrative workload if done individually. This question comes from exam objective 4.6, "Given a scenario, implement and maintain identity and access management" and is covered in Chapter 2.

13. **A** is correct. Account audits verify users have the permissions they need for their job, and no more, which verifies the principle of least privilege is being followed. Risk, vulnerability, and threat assessments assess current risks. While they might verify the principle of least privilege is being followed, they do much more. This question comes from exam objective 2.5, "Explain the purpose of mitigation techniques used to secure the enterprise" and is covered in Chapter 1.

14. **C** is correct. Simple Network Management Protocol version 3 (SNMPv3) is used to securely manage and monitor network devices. None of the other choices is related to managing and monitoring network devices. Network Address Translation (NAT) translates public IP addresses to private IP addresses and private addresses back to public. The Secure Real-time Transport Protocol (SRTP) secures voice and other streaming media transmissions. Domain Name System Security Extensions (DNSSEC) helps prevent DNS cache poisoning attacks. This question comes from exam objective 4.4, "Explain security alerting and monitoring concepts and tools" and is covered in Chapter 3.

15. **D** is correct. The Telnet rule should be changed to block Telnet traffic. Telnet sends credentialed and other data in cleartext and should not be used. Secure Shell (SSH) encrypts traffic and should be used instead of Telnet. All other rules are correct. This question comes from exam objective 4.5, "Given a scenario, modify enterprise capabilities to enhance security" and is covered in Chapter 3.

16. **C** is correct. An air-gapped network would best meet this need. An air gap indicates that the network is isolated from other networks with space or air. The application would be developed and compiled in this isolated network. All the other answers have a level of connectivity with the Internet and don't provide the best protection. A bastion host is a hardened server that can be accessed via the Internet and it may be directly on the Internet or within a screened subnet (sometimes called a demilitarized zone or DMZ). A boundary firewall (sometimes called a perimeter firewall) is placed at the edge of the network between the Internet and the internal network or within the screened subnet. An intrusion prevention system (IPS) is typically placed inline with traffic between the Internet and the internal network and attempts to detect and block attacks. This question comes from exam objective 3.1, "Compare and contrast security implications of different architecture models" and is covered in Chapter 3.

17. **D** is correct. The European Union (EU) General Data Protection Regulation (GDPR) provides EU residents with a broad right to request that data controllers delete any personally identifiable information (PII) that they maintain about the data subject. This right is known as the right to be forgotten. The right of notice says that data controllers must inform data

subjects about data processing activities. The right of correction says that data controllers must correct any errors in personally identifiable information. The right of consent says that data subjects must consent to data collection and processing. This question comes from exam objective 5.4, "Summarize elements of effective security compliance" and is covered in Chapter 11.

18. **A** is correct. A screened subnet (sometimes called a demilitarized zone, DMZ) is a buffered zone between a private network and the Internet, and it will separate the web server's web-facing traffic from the internal network. You can use a virtual local area network (VLAN) to group computers together based on job function or some other administrative need, but it is created in the internal network. A firewall does provide protection for the web server but doesn't necessarily separate the web-facing traffic from the internal network. A web application firewall (WAF) protects a web server from incoming attacks, but it does not necessarily separate Internet and internal network traffic. This question comes from exam objective 4.5, "Given a scenario, modify enterprise capabilities to enhance security" and is covered in Chapter 3.

19. **B** is correct. The most likely problem of the available choices is that an access control list (ACL) is configured incorrectly. The server is in a screened subnet (sometimes called a demilitarized zone or DMZ) and the most likely problem is an incorrectly configured ACL on the border firewall (between the Internet and the screened subnet). The service is working when accessed by internal systems, so it isn't likely that it is the problem. Also, the GCGA1 server works for internal systems indicating it is working correctly. There isn't any indication a virtual local area network (VLAN) is in use. This question comes from exam objective 2.5, "Explain the purpose of mitigation techniques used to secure the enterprise" and is covered in Chapter 3.

20. **D** is correct. Rapid Spanning Tree Protocol (RSTP) prevents switching loop problems and should be enabled on the switches to meet this need. While not available as a possible answer, the older Spanning Tree Protocol (STP) also provides loop protection. A flood guard on a switch helps prevent a media access control (MAC) flood attack. Simple Network Management Protocol version 3 (SNMPv3) is used to manage and monitor network devices. The Secure Real-time Transport Protocol (SRTP) provides encryption, message authentication, and integrity for video and voice data. This question comes from exam objective 4.1, "Given a scenario, apply common security techniques to computing resources" and is covered in Chapter 3.

21. **B** is correct. This review is being conducted by an independent, outside audit firm, so it is an example of an external audit. Assessments are informal reviews, not formal examinations. Internal audits are conducted by an auditing team within the organization itself. Regulatory audits are performed in response to specific legal or contractual requirements and no such requirements are described in the question. This question comes from exam objective 5.5, "Explain types and purposes of audits and assessments" and is covered in Chapter 8.

22. **A** is correct. An intrusion prevention system (IPS) is normally placed in line with traffic to block malicious traffic. However, it can be reconfigured to monitor traffic, effectively operating as an intrusion detection system (IDS). A backup solution is a corrective or recovery control. Security guards are preventive and deterrent controls. Cable locks are physical controls that prevent the theft of devices such as laptops. This question comes from exam objective 1.1, "Compare and contrast various types of security controls" and is covered in Chapter 1.

23. **A** is correct. WPA2 Enterprise requires an 802.1x authentication server and most implementations require a digital certificate installed on the server. The network will likely have Dynamic Host Configuration Protocol (DHCP) and Domain Name System (DNS) services, but it isn't necessary to install them on the authentication server. Wi-Fi Protected Setup (WPS) makes it easier to set up wireless devices, but it isn't related to WPA2 Enterprise. This question comes from exam objective 4.1, "Given a scenario, apply common security techniques to computing resources" and is covered in Chapter 4.

24. **B** is correct. Bluejacking is the practice of sending unsolicited messages to other Bluetooth devices. It has a limited range of about 30 feet when sent from one mobile phone to another so the attacker couldn't send additional messages after he left. Bluesnarfing allows attackers to access data (including email contact lists) on a smartphone but the scenario only indicates the user is receiving unwanted messages. Malware would not stop after a person leaves a coffee shop. A Wi-Fi Protected Setup (WPS) attack attempts to discover an access point WPS PIN by guessing PIN numbers, but this is not related to smartphone messages. This question comes from exam objective 2.2, "Explain common threat vectors and attack surfaces" and is covered in Chapter 4.

25. **B** is correct. A virtual private network (VPN) provides access to a private network over a public network such as the Internet via remote locations and is the best choice to meet this requirement. Network access control (NAC) methods can check VPN clients for health before allowing them access to the network, but it doesn't directly provide the access. Intrusion detection systems (IDSs) and intrusion prevention systems (IPSs) protect

networks but do not provide remote access. This question comes from exam objective 3.2, "Given a scenario, apply security principles to secure enterprise infrastructure" and is covered in Chapter 4.

26. **B** is correct. A change management policy helps reduce risk associated with making any changes to systems, including updating them. Patches should be tested and evaluated before implementing them and implementing them when they are released sometimes causes unintended consequences. The use of a trusted operating system or operating systems with secure configurations doesn't address how they are updated. This question comes from exam objective 1.3, "Explain the importance of change management processes and the impact to security" and is covered in Chapter 5.

27. **A** is correct. A data loss prevention (DLP) solution can prevent users from copying documents to a USB drive. None of the other answers control USB drives. A hardware security module (HSM) is an external security device used to manage, generate, and securely store cryptographic keys. COPE (corporate-owned, personally enabled) is a mobile device deployment model. A self-encrypting drive (SED) includes the hardware and software to encrypt all data on the drive and securely store the encryption keys. This question comes from exam objective 4.5, "Given a scenario, modify enterprise capabilities to enhance security" and is covered in Chapter 5.

28. **C** is correct. Database column (or field) encryption is the best choice because it can be used to encrypt the fields holding credit card data, but not fields that don't need to be encrypted. Full database encryption and full disk encryption aren't appropriate because of the resources needed to encrypt everything compared with the security desire of protecting only the credit card data. File-level encryption isn't appropriate on a database and will often make it inaccessible to the database application. This question comes from exam objective 1.4, "Explain the importance of using appropriate cryptographic solutions" and is covered in Chapter 5.

29. **C** is correct. This is a Software as a Service (SaaS) model. The software is the online application and the cloud provider (the Springfield Nuclear Power Plant in this example) maintains it. Infrastructure as a Service (IaaS) provides customers with the hardware via the cloud. Customers are responsible for installing the operating system and any applications. Platform as a Service (PaaS) is a computing platform. Anything as a Service (XaaS) refers to cloud services beyond IaaS, PaaS, and SaaS but this scenario clearly describes a SaaS model. This question comes from exam objective 3.1, "Compare and contrast security implications of different architecture models" and is covered in Chapter 5.

30. **C** is correct. Screen locks provide protection for lost devices by making it more difficult for someone to access the device. Device encryption protects the confidentiality of the data. Global Positioning System (GPS) tagging includes location information on pictures and other files but won't help protect a lost or stolen device. Patch management keeps devices up to date, and change management helps prevent outages from unauthorized changes. Anything as a Service (XaaS) refers to cloud services beyond IaaS, PaaS, and SaaS. This question comes from exam objective 4.1, "Given a scenario, apply common security techniques to computing resources" and is covered in Chapter 5.

31. **D** is correct. Attribute-based access control (ABAC) can authenticate a user and a mobile device using multiple elements, including identity, geolocation, time of day, and type of device. None of the other answers meets all the requirements of the question. A geofence creates a virtual fence, or geographic boundary, and can be used with attribute-based access control. Containerization isolates an application, protecting it and its data. Tethering allows one device to share its Internet connection with other devices. This question comes from exam objective 4.6, "Given a scenario, implement and maintain identity and access management" and is covered in Chapter 2.

32. **A** is correct. Geofencing can be used to create a virtual fence or geographic boundary, outlining the company's property. Geolocation is used to identify the location of an object, such as a mobile device. Geofencing will use geolocation to determine when a mobile device is within a geographic boundary, but geolocation without geofencing won't detect if a user is on the company's property. Global Positioning System (GPS) tagging adds geographic data (such as latitude and longitude data) to files indicating where the file was created and is unrelated to this question. Containerization runs applications in a container to isolate them. This question comes from exam objective 3.3, "Compare and contrast concepts and strategies to protect data" and is covered in Chapter 5.

33. **D** is correct. A network intrusion prevention system (NIPS) is the most relevant security control of those listed to reduce risks related to cybersecurity attacks of the supervisory control and data acquisition (SCADA) system, or industrial control systems (ICSs) controlled by the SCADA system. The SCADA system should be within an isolated network, and the NIPS helps provide that isolation. A data loss prevention (DLP) system helps prevent loss of data but wouldn't protect a SCADA system from potential attacks. A Trusted Platform Module (TPM) is a hardware chip on a computer's motherboard that stores cryptographic keys used for encryption. A field programmable gate array (FPGA) is an integrated circuit that can be configured after it is sold and is unrelated to this question. This question comes from exam objective 3.2, "Given a scenario, apply security principles to secure enterprise infrastructure" and is covered in Chapter 5.

34. **A** is correct. Virtual machine (VM) sprawl occurs when an organization has many VMs that aren't managed properly, and a policy addressing VM sprawl can reduce or eliminate them. Unmonitored VMs often aren't updated and can be vulnerable to attacks. A policy related to VM escape protection addresses problems that allow successful VM escape protection attacks, such as not keeping VMs updated. Anything as a Service (XaaS) refers to cloud services beyond IaaS, PaaS, and SaaS and is unrelated to VMs. A software-defined network (SDN) creates an infrastructure with code instead of hardware routers and switches and is unrelated to VMs. This question comes from exam objective 3.1, "Compare and contrast security implications of different architecture models" and is covered in Chapter 5.

35. **C** is correct. In this scenario, Bart is acting as a unskilled attacker because he is using existing scripts without applying any real personal knowledge. An insider works for an organization, but there isn't any indication that Bart is an employee of the company he attacked. A hacktivist launches attacks as part of an activist movement, but this scenario doesn't indicate Bart's actions are trying to increase awareness about a cause. Shadow information technology (IT) refers to IT systems deployed by non-IT departments to get around shortcomings with IT systems deployed by a central IT department in a large organization. This question comes from exam objective 2.1, "Compare and contrast common threat actors and motivations" and is covered in Chapter 6.

36. **A** is correct. An organized crime group most likely launched this attack because their motivation is primarily money. While the scenario describes ransomware, ransomware is the malware, not the threat actor. Competitors often want to obtain proprietary information, but it would be rare for a hospital competitor to put lives at risk by taking down a hospital's network and trying to extort money from another hospital. A hacktivist typically launches attacks to further a cause, not to extort money. This question comes from exam objective 2.1, "Compare and contrast common threat actors and motivations" and is covered in Chapter 6.

37. **A** is correct. The malware is likely a zero-day attack because the malware was not detected by antivirus software, the email server, or the unified threat management (UTM) appliance. A zero-day exploit wouldn't be known by antivirus software, so it wouldn't detect it. A false positive occurs when antivirus software raises an alert indicating a file is malicious when it isn't. However, there isn't any indication that the antivirus software raised an alert. Malware often installs backdoors that allow attackers access to infected systems without user intervention, but the scenario indicates that Gil clicked the malicious link causing the infection. If the malware encrypted all network shares, it would indicate that Gil had too many permissions, and the principle of least privilege wasn't implemented. However, the scenario indicates that the malware only encrypted shares that Gil could access. This question comes from exam objective 2.3, "Explain various types of vulnerabilities" and is covered in Chapter 4.

38. **D** is correct. These packets are most likely coming from bots within a botnet that are launching a distributed denial-of-service (DDoS) attack using a SYN flood attack. The attacker sends the SYN packet, the web server responds with the SYN/ACK packet, but the attacker never finished the TCP handshake with the ACK packet. While this is a DDoS attack, the question is asking for the likely source of the packets, not what type of attack is taking place. Ransomware would encrypt data on the system, not send packets to it. A worm is self-replicating malware that spreads throughout a network. This question comes from exam objective 2.4, "Given a scenario, analyze indicators of malicious activity" and is covered in Chapter 7.

39. **B** is correct. Shoulder surfing is the practice of viewing data by looking over someone's shoulder and it includes looking at computer monitors. Positioning monitors so that they cannot be viewed through a window and/or placing screen filters over the monitors reduces this threat. Phishing is an email attack. Dumpster diving is the practice of looking through dumpsters. Prepending simply means to add something to the beginning of something else, and social engineers often prepend queries with valid information to make their query seem valid. This question comes from exam objective 2.2, "Explain common threat vectors and attack surfaces" and is covered in Chapter 6.

40. **B** is correct. Dumpster divers look through trash or recycling containers for valuable paperwork, such as documents that include Personally Identifiable Information (PII). Instead, paperwork should be shredded or incinerated. Spam over instant messaging (SPIM) refers to unwanted text messages sent to mobile devices. Shoulder surfers attempt to view monitors or screens, not papers thrown into the trash or recycling containers. Tailgating is the practice of following closely behind someone else without using proper credentials. This question comes from exam objective 2.2, "Explain common threat vectors and attack surfaces" and is covered in Chapter 6.

41. **C** is correct. The sender is using the social engineering principle of authority in this scenario. A chief financial officer (CFO) would respect legal authorities and might be more inclined to open an attachment from such an authority. The scenario describes whaling, which is a specific type of phishing attack. However, whaling and phishing are attacks, not social engineering principles. The social engineering principle of consensus attempts to show that other people like a product, but this is unrelated to this scenario. This question comes from exam objective 2.2, "Explain common threat vectors and attack surfaces" and is covered in Chapter 6.

42. **A** is correct. A distributed denial-of-service (DDoS) attack includes attacks from multiple systems with the goal of depleting the target's resources, and this scenario indicates multiple connection attempts from different IP addresses. A Domain Name System (DNS) poisoning attack attempts to redirect web browsers to malicious URLs. A replay attack doesn't overload a system but instead allows the attacker to intercept data and use it to impersonate a user or system. An Address Resolution Protocol (ARP) poisoning attack gives clients false hardware address updates, and attackers use it to redirect or intercept network traffic. This question comes from exam objective 2.4, "Given a scenario, analyze indicators of malicious activity" and is covered in Chapter 7.

43. **B** is correct. Buffer overflow attacks include a long series of unusual characters designed to fill the allocated area of memory. When successful, they can crash applications and expose memory, allowing attackers to run malicious code on the system. SQL injection attacks and Extensible Markup Language (XML) injection attacks do not use this approach. Zero-day attacks are unknown or undocumented, but attacks using NOP commands are known. This question comes from exam objective 2.4, "Given a scenario, analyze indicators of malicious activity" and is covered in Chapter 7.

44. **A** is correct. Static code analysis would have the best chance of preventing this attack. The scenario describes a backdoor in the internally developed application, but the backdoor is a vulnerability that allowed the attack and won't prevent the attack. Distributed denial-of-service (DDoS) protection can help thwart DDoS attacks, but there's no indication that this is a DDoS attack. A keylogger logs keystrokes of users so would not prevent an attack. This question comes from exam objective 4.1, "Given a scenario, apply common security techniques to computing resources" and is covered in Chapter 7.

45. **A** is correct. This describes continuous integration, which merges changes from multiple developers and uses version control processes to track the changes. Continuous validation revalidates code after every change and is frequently part of CI, but continuous validation by itself doesn't include version control. Continuous delivery comes after CI and provides an automated process that delivers changes to a testing or staging environment. Continuous monitoring monitors code changes to detect compliance issues and security threats. This question comes from exam objective 4.7, "Explain the importance of automation and orchestration related to secure operations" and is covered in Chapter 7.

46. **B** is correct. The annual rate of occurrence (ARO) is the best choice to identify how many times a specific type of incident occurs in a year. Annual loss expectancy (ALE) identifies the expected monetary loss for a year and single loss expectancy (SLE) identifies the ex-

pected monetary loss for a single incident. ALE = SLE × ARO and if you know any two of these values, you can identify the third value. For example, ARO = ALE / SLE. The recovery point objective (RPO) identifies a point in time where data loss is acceptable, but it doesn't refer to the number of times an incident occurred. This question comes from exam objective 5.2, "Explain elements of the risk management process" and is covered in Chapter 8.

47. **B** is correct. Threat hunting is the process of actively looking for threats within a network, and security advisories provide information on threats, including their tactics, techniques, and procedures (TTPs). Security advisories are one type of open source intelligence (OSINT) used in threat hunting, but she is reading the OSINT, not creating it. Penetration testing actively assesses deployed security controls within a system or network. It is much more than reviewing logs. Reconnaissance methods attempt to learn as much as possible about a target, but Lisa is examining her own network. This question comes from exam objective 4.8, "Explain appropriate incident response activities" and is covered in Chapter 11.

48. **C** is correct. In this scenario, the vulnerability scanner reported a false positive indicating that the servers had a vulnerability, but the servers did not have the vulnerability. A false negative occurs if a vulnerability scanner does not report a known vulnerability. There isn't any indication that the servers are misconfigured. The scenario doesn't indicate if the scan was run under an account's context (credentialed or non-credentialed), so this answer isn't relevant to the question. This question comes from exam objective 4.3, "Explain various activities associated with vulnerability management" and is covered in Chapter 8.

49. **B** is correct. If a vendor has not created a patch for a known vulnerability, vulnerability scanners will report the vulnerability (assuming they know about the vulnerability). False negatives are not reported so they will not appear in a vulnerability scanner's output. If scans are reporting the same vulnerability, it may be because a non-credentialed scan is reporting incorrect results, but a credentialed scan is more accurate than a non-credentialed scan. There isn't any indication that the system is misconfigured. This question comes from exam objective 4.3, "Explain various activities associated with vulnerability management" and is covered in Chapter 8.

50. **C** is correct. Users would typically enter a username as identification for an authentication, authorization, and accounting (AAA) system. Users would provide a password as proof that the claimed identity (the username) is theirs. The password provides authentication. Users are assigned permissions based on their proven identity, but the permissions do not provide identification. The virtual private network (VPN) would encrypt traffic sent via the VPN

tunnel, and this traffic may be encrypted with the use of a certificate. However, this is not called a tunneling certificate, and the certificate used for encryption does not provide identification. A hardware token is often used as an additional method of authentication, but it does not provide identification. This question comes from exam objective 1.2 "Summarize fundamental security concepts" and is covered in Chapter 2.

51. **D** is correct. A credentialed scan runs with a high level of access and is better at detecting vulnerabilities than a non-credential scan. A non-credentialed scan runs without any account privileges. A port scan detects open ports on a server. Vulnerability scanners are generally non-intrusive, but this doesn't give a scanner any specific access level. This question comes from exam objective 4.3, "Explain various activities associated with vulnerability management" and is covered in Chapter 8.

52. **B** is correct. The **tcpdump** command-line tool is the best choice of the given answers. It is a command-line packet analyzer (or protocol analyzer) and its primary purpose is to capture packets. Tcpreplay is a suite of utilities used to edit packet captures and resend them, not capture packets. Netcat is useful for remotely accessing systems and can be used for banner grabbing, but it doesn't capture packets. Wiredump isn't a valid tool name. Wireshark (not included as an answer choice) is a graphic-based packet analyzer that can be started from the command line, but **tcpdump** includes more command-line options than Wireshark. This question comes from exam objective 4.9, "Given a scenario, use data sources to support an investigation" and is covered in Chapter 8.

53. **B** is correct. Security guards can protect access to restricted areas with facial recognition and by checking the identities of personnel before letting them in. In some cases, the guards might recognize people, and in other situations, they might compare people's faces with their security badge. None of the other answers use facial recognition. Bollards are effective barricades to block vehicles, but they do not block personnel. Retina scanners are effective biometric access devices, but they only scan part of the eye, not the whole face. Cameras can monitor who goes in and out of an area, but they do not control the access. This question comes from exam objective 1.2, "Summarize fundamental security concepts" and is covered in Chapter 9.

54. **A** is correct. Bollards are effective barricades that can block vehicles. Guards can restrict access for personnel, but they cannot stop trucks from ramming through a building. Closed-circuit television (CCTV) or a similar video surveillance system can monitor the entrance, but it won't stop the attack. Alarms can go off after the truck rams through the

entrance, but they won't stop the attack. This question comes from exam objective 1.2, "Summarize fundamental security concepts" and is covered in Chapter 9.

55. **C** is correct. A redundant array of inexpensive disks (RAID) subsystem is a relatively low-cost solution for disks' fault tolerance. By providing fault tolerance, it increases availability and resilience. Load balancing (active/active and active/passive) requires additional servers, which are significantly more expensive than RAID. A warm site is a separate location, which can also be expensive. This question comes from exam objective 3.1, "Compare and contrast security implications of different architecture models" and is covered in Chapter 1.

56. **B** is correct. An evil twin is a rogue access point (AP) with the same or similar service set identifier (SSID) as a legitimate access point. The actual SSID coffeewifi has broadcasting turned off, but the evil twin SSID of coffewifi is broadcasting, allowing users to see it. While it is also a rogue AP, evil twin is a more accurate answer since it is similar to the actual SSID. Jamming typically prevents anyone from connecting to a wireless network. Bluejacking is related to Bluetooth, not wireless networks. This question comes from exam objective 2.2 "Explain common threat vectors and attack surfaces" and is covered in Chapter 4.

57. **D** is correct. Load balancing shifts the load among multiple servers and provides cybersecurity resilience by increasing the site's availability by adding additional nodes when necessary. Managed power distribution units (PDUs) are used to remotely monitor energy consumption in a data center. Certificates can be used for identity, authentication, confidentiality, and integrity but won't provide resilience due to overloading resources on a server. A web application firewall helps protect a web server against attacks, but it does not increase availability from normal client requests. This question comes from exam objective 3.4, "Explain the importance of resilience and recovery in security architecture" and is covered in Chapter 9.

58. **C** is correct. A full/incremental backup strategy is the best option with one full backup on one day and incremental backups on the other days. The incremental backups will take a relatively short time compared with the other methods. A full backup every day would require the most time every day. Differential backups become steadily larger as the week progresses and take more time to back up than incremental backups. Backups must start with a full backup, so a differential/incremental backup strategy is not possible. This question comes from exam objective 3.4, "Explain the importance of resilience and recovery in security architecture" and is covered in Chapter 9.

59. **B** is correct. A business impact analysis (BIA) includes information on potential monetary losses along with information on essential and critical functions, recovery plans, and more. It is the most likely document of those listed that would include this information. A business continuity plan (BCP) includes a BIA, but the BIA is more likely to include this information than the BCP. The mean time between failures (MTBF) provides a measure of a system's reliability. The recovery point objective (RPO) refers to the amount of data you can afford to lose, but it does not include monetary losses. This question comes from exam objective 5.2, "Explain elements of the risk management process" and is covered in Chapter 9.

60. **A** is correct. The recovery time objective (RTO) identifies the maximum amount of time it should take to restore a system after an outage. The recovery point objective (RPO) refers to the amount of data you can afford to lose. RTO only refers to time, not data. RPO refers to data recovery points, not time to restore a system. This question comes from exam objective 5.2, "Explain elements of the risk management process" and is covered in Chapter 9.

61. **A** is correct. The mean time to repair (MTTR) identifies the average time (the arithmetic mean) it takes to restore a failed system and is commonly used when preparing a business impact analysis (BIA). The mean time between failures (MTBF) identifies the average (the arithmetic mean) time between failures. The single loss expectancy (SLE) identifies the cost of any single loss. The annual rate of occurrence (ARO) identifies how many times a loss is expected to occur in a year. Multiplying SLE * ARO identifies the annual loss expectancy (ALE). This question comes from exam objective 5.2, "Explain elements of the risk management process" and is covered in Chapter 9.

62. **B** is correct. Encryption is used to maintain confidentiality of any data, including Personally Identifiable Information (PII). Hashes provide integrity, not confidentiality. A digital signature provides authentication, non-repudiation, and integrity, but not confidentiality. A redundant array of inexpensive disks (RAID) provides higher availability for a disk subsystem. This question comes from exam objective 1.4, "Explain the importance of using appropriate cryptographic solutions" and is covered in Chapter 10.

63. **A** is correct. A digital signature provides assurances of who sent an email and meets the goal of this scenario. Although a spam filter might filter a spear phishing attack, it does not provide assurances about who sent   an email. Role-based training provides targeted training for employees based on their roles, but any type of training wouldn't provide assurances about who sent an email. Some antivirus software includes heuristic-based detection. Heuristic-based detection attempts to detect viruses that were previously unknown and

do not have virus signatures. This question comes from exam objective 1.4, "Explain the importance of using appropriate cryptographic solutions" and is covered in Chapter 10.

64. **A** is correct. Of the given choices, the file was most likely infected after it was pushed out to the server. This is because the hash of the file is different on the server than it is on the patch management system. The scenario doesn't indicate what type of infection the malware has, so it isn't possible to tell if it is crypto-malware or another type of malware. A blocklist blocks files so if the file were listed in the patch management system's blocklist, the patch management system wouldn't push it out to systems. If it were infected before it was pushed out to the server, it would have the same hash. This question comes from exam objective 1.4, "Explain the importance of using appropriate cryptographic solutions" and is covered in Chapter 10.

65. **D** is correct. Hiding data within data is one way to support a use case of supporting obfuscation and Tony is attempting to send the text files within the image file to obscure his intent. In this scenario, Tony is using steganography to hide the files within the image, but that is the method, not the purpose. Hashing methods and digital signatures support integrity. Redundancy and fault tolerance methods increase availability supporting resiliency. This question comes from exam objective 1.4, "Explain the importance of using appropriate cryptographic solutions" and is covered in Chapter 10.

66. **E** is correct. A Digital Signature Algorithm (DSA) is used to create a digital signature and they would sign their emails with a digital signature. A certificate revocation list (CRL) is a list of revoked certificates. Online Certificate Status Protocol (OCSP) is an alternative to a CRL and provides a real-time response indicating the validity of a certificate. The certificate signing request (CSR) is used to request a certificate. A certificate authority (CA) manages certificates and would sign certificates issued to users. A certificate is needed to create a digital signature, but the certificate itself can't sign an email. This question comes from exam objective 1.4, "Explain the importance of using appropriate cryptographic solutions" and is covered in Chapter 10.

67. **C** is correct. Online Certificate Status Protocol (OCSP) stapling reduces OCSP traffic sent to a certificate authority (CA). Certificate presenters append a timestamped, digitally signed OCSP response to a certificate. Public key pinning includes a list of public key hashes in HTTPS responses from the web server. While pinning helps validate certificates, it is unrelated to OCSP. Neither digital signatures (used for non-repudiation) nor hashing (used for integrity) will reduce OCSP traffic. This question comes from exam objective 1.4, "Explain the importance of using appropriate cryptographic solutions" and is covered in Chapter 10.

68. **D** is correct. A certificate revocation list (CRL) provides the best solution in this scenario. After a CRL is retrieved, systems hold a copy of it in cache. Instead of downloading the same CRL every time a system needs to validate a certificate, they just look at the cached copy of the CRL. Online Certificate Status Protocol (OCSP) is an alternative to a CRL and provides a real-time response to validate certificates. Because OCSP responds in real time, it is susceptible to Internet outages. Privacy enhanced mail (PEM) certificates are not used to validate other certificates. A subject alternative name (SAN) certificate is used for multiple domains that have different names but are owned by the same organization. This question comes from exam objective 1.4, "Explain the importance of using appropriate cryptographic solutions" and is covered in Chapter 10.

69. **A** is correct. This is an example of a preventive control because it prevents any individual person from performing multiple job functions that might allow the person to commit fraud. Detective controls are used to identify incidents that do occur, while corrective controls are designed to resolve incidents. Compensating controls are used when it is not possible to meet a control objective using the standard technique. This question comes from exam objective 1.1, "Compare and contrast various types of security controls" and is covered in Chapter 1.

70. **D** is correct. Offboarding is the process of removing an employee's access when he leaves the organization, and this is typically done during the exit interview. Because the employee deleted the files and shares after he left the organization, it indicates offboarding processes were not performed. Onboarding is the process of granting appropriate access to employees when they are first hired. Time-of-day restrictions might have prevented the employee from accessing resources during the weekend while the organization was closed. However, there isn't any indication that the organization wanted to restrict employees from accessing resources during off- hours. An account audit might have identified the account but not as quickly as offboarding processes done during an exit interview. Additionally, audits are typically done periodically, such as monthly. This question comes from exam objective 5.1, "Summarize elements of effective security governance" and is covered in Chapter 11.

71. **D** is correct. When a system reaches its end of life (EOL), a vendor no longer offers it for sale, and the vendor stops releasing updates for it. This scenario indicates management has weighed the risks and decided to keep the application. While not available as a possible answer, end of service life (EOSL) would be more specific. EOSL is the date when a vendor no longer supports a product and would no longer create patches or upgrades. The other answers are unrelated to the question. Measurement systems analysis (MSA) evaluates processes and tools used to make measurements. An acceptable use policy (AUP) defines proper system usage for employees when using IT systems. A managed security service

provider (MSSP) is a third-party vendor that provides security services for smaller companies. This question comes from exam objective 2.3, "Explain various types of vulnerabilities" and is covered in Chapter 11.

72. **B** is correct. At this stage, the first response is incident detection. The preparation phase is performed before an incident and includes steps to prevent incidents. After detecting this as a valid incident (malware infection), the next steps are analysis, containment, eradication, recovery, and lessons learned. This question comes from exam objective 4.8, "Explain appropriate incident response activities" and is covered in Chapter 11.

73. **C** is correct. After detecting an incident and analyzing it, the next step is containment. The scenario indicates you have identified the incident as a malware infection. Preparation is the first step in an incident response process. Eradication attempts to remove all elements of the incident after first containing it. The last two steps in the incident response process are recovery and lessons learned. This question comes from exam objective 4.8, "Explain appropriate incident response activities" and is covered in Chapter 11.

74. **B** is correct. A chain of custody was not maintained because the hard drive was left unattended for several hours before capturing an image. Witnesses were not mentioned but are not needed for the hard drive if the chain of custody was maintained. The order of volatility is not relevant to this scenario, and the hard drive is also not volatile storage. Analysis would occur after capturing an image, but there isn't any indication it wasn't done or wasn't complete. This question comes from exam objective 4.8, "Explain appropriate incident response activities" and is covered in Chapter 11.

75. **D** is correct. The court order specified a legal hold on email from the last three years, so all the backups for the last three years should be kept. If the backups had been destroyed before the court order, they wouldn't be available, so the legal hold wouldn't apply to them. Deleting them after the court order is illegal. Protecting only the backups from the last 12 months or the last two years doesn't comply with the court order. This question comes from exam objective 4.8, "Explain appropriate incident response activities" and is covered in Chapter 11.

76. **C** is correct. A choose your own device (CYOD) mobile device deployment model includes a list of acceptable devices that employees can purchase and connect to the network. IT management can then implement a mobile device management (MDM) system to provide standardized management for these devices. The current policy is a bring your own device (BYOD) policy, but because of the lack of standardization, it's difficult for IT departments

to adequately manage the devices and ensure they don't introduce vulnerabilities to the network. A corporate-owned personally enabled (COPE) policy indicates the organization owns the devices, not the employees. Infrastructure as a Service (IaaS) is a cloud computing option where the vendor provides access to a computer, but customers must install the operating system and maintain the system. This question comes from exam objective 4.1 "Given a scenario, apply common security techniques to computing resources" and is covered in Chapter 5.

77. **B** is correct. This describes a phishing email that is trying to trick the user into revealing personal information. Spear phishing targets a group of people with a common connection, such as employees of a company. Smishing is a form of phishing that uses text messages. Whaling is a form of spear phishing that targets high- level executives in an organization. This question comes from exam objective 2.2 "Explain common threat vectors and attack surfaces" and is covered in Chapter 6.

78. **A** is correct. Fuzzing is a type of dynamic code analysis, and it can test the application's cybersecurity resilience. Fuzzing sends random data to an application to verify the random data doesn't crash the application or expose the system to a data breach. Input validation and error-handling techniques protect applications but do not test them. Anti-malware protects systems from malware attacks, but it doesn't test a system. This question comes from exam objective 4.3 "Explain various activities associated with vulnerability" and is covered in Chapter 7.

79. **C** is correct. This describes a spraying attack. The security information and event management (SIEM) logs would show that the attack loops through a long list of accounts, guessing one password for one account   at a time. A brute force attack attempts to guess all possible character combinations for a password, and a dictionary attack uses a dictionary of words trying to discover the correct password. However, neither a brute force attack nor a dictionary attack loops through a list of user accounts. A spraying attack attempts to bypass an account lockout policy. An account lockout attack isn't relevant in this scenario. This question comes from exam objective 2.4 "Given a scenario, analyze indicators of malicious activity" and is covered in Chapter 10.

80. **A** is correct. The first step in an incident response process is preparation. When a potential incident occurs, the next step is detection followed by analysis. If the event is a security incident, the fourth step is containment to isolate the incident and limit the damage. Next, personnel take steps to eradicate all elements that caused the incident, such as malware or compromised accounts. The last two steps in the incident response process are recovery

and lessons learned. This question comes from exam objective 4.8 "Explain appropriate incident response activities" and is covered in Chapter 11.

81. **C** is correct. A service level agreement (SLA) is an agreement between a company and a vendor that stipulates performance expectations, such as response time. A master services agreement (MSA) may be used to specify general terms, but the SLA would contain specific performance details. An acceptable use policy (AUP) informs users of company expectations when they use computer systems and networks, and it defines acceptable rules of behavior. A non-disclosure agreement (NDA) ensures that individuals do not share proprietary data with others. This question comes from exam objective 5.3 "Explain the processes associated with third-party risk assessment and management" and is covered in Chapter 11.

82. **A** is correct. Before analyzing a hard drive, a forensic expert should capture an image of the hard drive and then analyze the image. This protects the original disk from accidental modifications and preserves it as usable evidence. While not available as a possible answer, a hash of the original drive should be created before capturing an image. The order of volatility identifies which data is most volatile (such as cache) and which is least volatile (such as hard drives). Although forensic investigators may copy the contents of memory early in an investigation, this scenario is focused on a hard drive. A chain of custody document should be created when evidence is first collected. This question comes from exam objective 4.8 "Explain appropriate incident response activities" and is covered in Chapter 11.

83. **A** is correct. Unified threat management (UTM) devices combine the functions of several different security technologies into a single, cost-effective product commonly used by small businesses. Next-generation firewalls (NGFW), security information and event management (SIEM) platforms, and intrusion prevention systems (IPS) are all part of a strong enterprise security infrastructure, but they are purpose-specific devices. The functionality of all three of those products may be found in a UTM. This question comes from exam objective 3.2, "Given a scenario, apply security principles to secure enterprise infrastructure" and is covered in Chapter 3.

84. **C** is correct. Certification provides the customer of a data destruction service with written assurance that appropriate destruction procedures were carried out. Pulverization and sanitization are specific destruction techniques but they do not, by themselves, provide evidence that data was destroyed. Retention is the process of keeping data for a specified period of time and does not destroy data. This question comes from exam objective 4.2, "Explain the security implications of proper hardware, software, and data asset management" and is covered in Chapter 11.

85. **A** is correct. The Security Content Automation Protocol (SCAP) is designed to help facilitate communication between vulnerability scanners and other security and management tools. The Common Vulnerabilities and Exposures (CVE) list is a dictionary of publicly known security vulnerabilities and exposures. The Common Vulnerability Scoring System (CVSS) assesses vulnerabilities and assigns severity scores in a range of 0 to 10, with 10 being the most severe. The Open Systems Interconnection (OSI) model is a theoretical model for network communications. This question comes from objective 4.4, "Explain security alerting and monitoring concepts and tools" and is covered in Chapter 8.

86. **D** is correct. This is an example of threat hunting: searching an environment for signs of existing compromises. Threat intelligence gathers information about known threats but does not actively search for their presence. Reconnaissance is an activity undertaken by attackers seeking to gain information about their target. Penetration testing actively tests security controls to identify weaknesses. This question comes from exam objective 4.8, "Explain appropriate incident response activities" and is covered in Chapter 11.

87. **B** is correct. Organizations with expansionary risk appetites are willing to take on a high level of risk in pursuit of high rewards. Organizations with conservative risk appetites have a preference for low-risk investments and prioritize preserving their current security posture. Organizations with neutral risk appetites take a balanced approach to risk-taking. Willie should not make judgements about whether the organization's risk appetite is justified or not until he gets to know the organization and its leadership better. This question comes from exam objective 5.2, "Explain elements of the risk management process" and is covered in Chapter 8.

88. **B** is correct. Uninterruptible power supplies (UPS) contain large batteries designed to cover brief power outages. Generators may be used for extended outages, but they take some time to start up and are not ready to immediately cover a brief outage. Dual power supplies protect against the failure of a single power supply but do not protect against disruptions of power to the device. Solar power is a power generation technique rather than a security control. This question comes from objective 3.4, "Explain the importance of resilience and recovery in security architecture" and is covered in Chapter 9.

89. **A** is correct. A fail over test stops operations at the primary facility and shifts them to the alternate processing facility. If the test fails, normal operations may be disrupted. Parallel processing tests also activate the alternate processing facility but only as a test while all normal processing continues at the primary facility. Neither simulations nor walkthroughs activate any alternate sites and will not disrupt normal processing. This question comes

from objective 3.4, "Explain the importance of resilience and recovery in security architecture" and is covered in Chapter 9.

90. **C** is correct. 802.1X authentication can restrict access to both wired and wireless networks. While Wi-Fi Protected Access v3 (WPA3) and Wired Equivalent Privacy (WEP) technology can limit access to a network, those technologies only work on wireless networks and are not used on wired networks. Additionally, the WEP protocol is outdated and insecure. Transport Layer Security (TLS) is used to protect network traffic while in transit over a network and does not authenticate network clients. This question comes from exam objective 3.2, "Given a scenario, apply security principles to secure enterprise infrastructure" and is covered in Chapter 4.

Index

Made in the USA
Monee, IL
31 December 2023

50852905R10369